한국의 토익 수험자 여러분께,

토익 시험은 세계적인 직무 영어능력 평가 시험으로, 지난 40여 년간 비즈니스 현장에서 필요한 영어능력 평가의 기준을 제시해 왔습니다. 토익 시험 및 토익스피킹, 토익라이팅 시험은 세계에서 가장 널리 통용되는 영어능력 검증 시험으로, 160여 개국 14,000여 기관이 토익 성적을 의사결정에 활용하고 있습니다.

YBM은 한국의 토익 시험을 주관하는 ETS 독점 계약사입니다.

ETS는 한국 수험자들의 효과적인 토익 학습을 돕고자 YBM을 통하여 'ETS 토익 공식 교재'를 독점 출간하고 있습니다. 또한 'ETS 토익 공식 교재' 시리즈에 기출문항을 제공해 한국의 다른 교재들에 수록된 기출을 복제하거나 변형한 문항으로 인하여 발생할 수 있는 수험자들의 혼동을 방지하고 있습니다.

복제 및 변형 문항들은 토익 시험의 출제의도를 벗어날 수 있기 때문에 기출문항을 수록한 'ETS 토익 공식 교재'만큼 시험에 잘 대비할 수 없습니다.

'ETS 토익 공식 교재'를 통하여 수험자 여러분의 영어 소통을 위한 노력에 큰 성취가 있기를 바랍니다.

감사합니다.

Dear TOEIC Test Takers in Korea,

The TOEIC program is the global leader in English-language assessment for the workplace. It has set the standard for assessing English-language skills needed in the workplace for more than 40 years. The TOEIC tests are the most widely used English language assessments around the world, with 14,000+ organizations across more than 160 countries trusting TOEIC scores to make decisions.

YBM is the ETS Country Master Distributor for the TOEIC program in Korea and so is the exclusive distributor for TOEIC Korea.

To support effective learning for TOEIC test-takers in Korea, ETS has authorized YBM to publish the only Official TOEIC prep books in Korea. These books contain actual TOEIC items to help prevent confusion among Korean test-takers that might be caused by other prep book publishers' use of reproduced or paraphrased items.

Reproduced or paraphrased items may fail to reflect the intent of actual TOEIC items and so will not prepare test-takers as well as the actual items contained in the ETS TOEIC Official prep books published by YBM.

We hope that these ETS TOEIC Official prep books enable you, as test-takers, to achieve great success in your efforts to communicate effectively in English.

Thank you.

입문부터 실전까지 수준별 학습을 통해 최단기 목표점수 달성!

ETS TOEIC® 공식수험서
스마트 학습 지원

구글플레이, 앱스토어에서
ETS 토익기출 수험서 다운로드

구글플레이   앱스토어

ETS 토익 모바일 학습 플랫폼!

ETS® 토익기출 수험서 어플

교재 학습 지원
1. 교재 해설 강의
2. LC 음원 MP3
3. 교재/부록 모의고사 채점 및 분석
4. 단어 암기장

부가 서비스
1. 데일리 학습(토익 기출문제 풀이)
2. 토익 최신 경향 무료 특강
3. 토익 타이머

모의고사 결과 분석
1. 파트별/문항별 정답률
2. 파트별/유형별 취약점 리포트
3. 전체 응시자 점수 분포도

ETS TOEIC 공식카페 ▾

etstoeicbook.co.kr

ETS 토익 학습 전용 온라인 커뮤니티!

ETS TOEIC® Book 공식카페

강사진의 학습 지원   토익 대표강사들의 학습 지원과 멘토링

교재 학습관 운영   교재별 학습게시판을 통해 무료 동영상 강의 등 학습 지원

학습 콘텐츠 제공   토익 학습 콘텐츠와 정기시험 예비특강 업데이트

---

www.ybmbooks.com에서도 무료 MP3를 다운로드 받을 수 있습니다.

ETS. TOEIC.

토익® 정기시험 기출문제집 3

1000

LISTENING

YBM

토익 정기시험
기출문제집 3
1000
LISTENING

발행인	허문호
발행처	YBM

편집	이혜진
디자인	이현숙
마케팅	정연철, 박천산, 고영노, 박찬경, 김동진, 김윤하

초판발행	2021년 11월 22일
10쇄발행	2024년 4월 15일

신고일자	1964년 3월 28일
신고번호	제 300-1964-3호
주소	서울시 종로구 종로 104
전화	(02) 2000-0515 [구입문의] / (02) 2000-0436 [내용문의]
팩스	(02) 2285-1523
홈페이지	www.ybmbooks.com

ISBN	978-89-17-23853-2

토익®정기시험 기출문제집 3

1000
LISTENING

Preface

Dear test taker,

English-language proficiency has become a vital tool for success. It can help you excel in business, travel the world, and communicate effectively with friends and colleagues. The TOEIC® test measures your ability to function effectively in English in these types of situations. Because TOEIC scores are recognized around the world as evidence of your English-language proficiency, you will be able to confidently demonstrate your English skills to employers and begin your journey to success.

The test developers at ETS are excited to help you achieve your personal and professional goals through the use of the ETS® TOEIC® 정기시험 기출문제집 1000 Vol. 3. This book contains test questions taken from actual, official TOEIC tests. It also contains three tests that were developed by ETS to help prepare you for actual TOEIC tests. All these materials will help you become familiar with the TOEIC test's format and content. This book also contains detailed explanations of the question types and language points contained in the TOEIC test. These test questions and explanations have all been prepared by the same test specialists who develop the actual TOEIC test, so you can be confident that you will receive an authentic test-preparation experience.

Features of the ETS® TOEIC® 정기시험 기출문제집 1000 Vol. 3 include the following.

- Seven full-length actual tests plus three full-length tests of equal quality created by ETS for test preparation use, all accompanied by answer keys and official scripts
- Specific and easy to understand explanations for learners
- The very same ETS voice actors that you will hear in an official TOEIC test administration

---

By using the ETS® TOEIC® 정기시험 기출문제집 1000 Vol. 3. to prepare for the TOEIC test, you can be assured that you have a professionally prepared resource that will provide you with accurate guidance so that you are more familiar with the tasks, content, and format of the test and that will help you maximize your TOEIC test score. With your official TOEIC score certificate, you will be ready to show the world what you know!

We are delighted to assist you on your TOEIC journey with the ETS® TOEIC® 정기시험 기출문제집 1000 Vol. 3. and wish you the best of success.

최신 기출문제 전격 공개!

유일무이

'출제기관이 독점 제공한' 기출문제가 담긴 유일한 교재!

이 책에는 정기시험 기출문제 7세트와 토익 예상문제 3세트가 수록되어 있다. 시험에 나온 토익 문제로
실전 감각을 키우고, 동일한 난이도의 예상문제로 시험에 확실하게 대비하자!

국내최고

'정기시험 성우 음성'으로 실전 대비!

이 책에 수록된 10세트의 LC 음원은 모두 실제 시험에서 나온 정기 시험 성우의 음원이다.
시험장에서 듣게 될 음성으로 공부하면 까다로운 영국·호주식 발음도 걱정 없다.

독점제공

'ETS가 제공하는' 표준점수 환산표!

출제기관 ETS가 독점 제공하는 표준점수 환산표를 수록했다. 채점 후 환산표를 통해 자신의 실력이
어느 정도인지 가늠해 보자!

What is the TOEIC?

TOEIC은 어떤 시험인가요?

Test of English for International Communication(국제적 의사소통을 위한 영어 시험)의 약자로서, 영어가 모국어가 아닌 사람들이 일상생활 또는 비즈니스 현장에서 꼭 필요한 실용적 영어 구사 능력을 갖추었는가를 평가하는 시험이다.

시험 구성

구성	Part	내용		문항수	시간	배점
듣기(L/C)	1	사진 묘사		6	45분	495점
	2	질의 응답		25		
	3	짧은 대화		39		
	4	짧은 담화		30		
읽기(R/C)	5	단문 빈칸 채우기(문법/어휘)		30	75분	495점
	6	장문 빈칸 채우기		16		
	7	독해	단일 지문	29		
			이중 지문	10		
			삼중 지문	15		
Total	**7 Parts**			**200문항**	**120분**	**990점**

TOEIC 접수는 어떻게 하나요?

TOEIC 접수는 한국 토익 위원회 사이트(www.toeic.co.kr)에서 온라인 상으로만 접수가 가능하다. 사이트에서 매월 자세한 접수 일정과 시험 일정 등의 구체적 정보 확인이 가능하니, 미리 일정을 확인하여 접수하도록 한다.

시험장에 반드시 가져가야 할 준비물은요?

신분증 규정 신분증만 가능

(주민등록증, 운전면허증, 기간 만료 전의 여권, 공무원증 등)

필기구 연필, 지우개 (볼펜이나 사인펜은 사용 금지)

시험은 어떻게 진행되나요?

09:20	입실 (09:50 이후는 입실 불가)
09:30 – 09:45	답안지 작성에 관한 오리엔테이션
09:45 – 09:50	휴식
09:50 – 10:05	신분증 확인
10:05 – 10:10	문제지 배부 및 파본 확인
10:10 – 10:55	듣기 평가 (Listening Test)
10:55 – 12:10	독해 평가 (Reading Test)

TOEIC 성적 확인은 어떻게 하죠?

시험일로부터 약 10-11일 후 인터넷과 ARS(060-800-0515)로 성적을 확인할 수 있다. TOEIC 성적표는 우편이나 온라인으로 발급 받을 수 있다(시험 접수시, 양자 택일). 우편으로 발급 받을 경우는 성적 발표 후 대략 일주일이 소요되며, 온라인 발급을 선택하면 유효기간 내에 홈페이지에서 본인이 직접 1회에 한해 무료 출력할 수 있다. TOEIC 성적은 시험일로부터 2년간 유효하다.

TOEIC은 몇 점 만점인가요?

TOEIC 점수는 듣기 영역(LC) 점수, 읽기 영역(RC) 점수, 그리고 이 두 영역을 합계한 전체 점수 세 부분으로 구성된다. 각 부분의 점수는 5점 단위이며, 5점에서 495점에 걸쳐 주어지고, 전체 점수는 10점에서 990점까지이며, 만점은 990점이다. TOEIC 성적은 각 문제 유형의 난이도에 따른 점수 환산표에 의해 결정된다.

토익 경향 분석

1인 등장 사진
주어는 He/She, A man/woman 등이며 주로 앞부분에 나온다.

2인 이상 등장 사진
주어는 They, Some men/women/people, One of the men/women 등이며 주로 중간 부분에 나온다.

사물/배경 사진
주어는 A car, Some chairs 등이며 주로 뒷부분에 나온다.

사람 또는 사물 중심 사진
주어가 일부는 사람, 일부는 사물이며 주로 뒷부분에 나온다.

사람 또는 사물 중심 사진 **33**%

1인 등장 사진 **33**%

사물/배경 사진 **17**%

2인 이상 등장 사진 **17**%

PART 1 최신 출제 경향

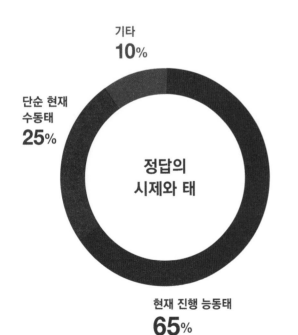

기타 **10**%

단순 현재 수동태 **25**%

정답의 시제와 태

현재 진행 능동태 **65**%

현재 진행 능동태
〈is/are + 현재분사〉 형태이며 주로 사람이 주어이다.

단순 현재 수동태
〈is/are + 과거분사〉 형태이며 주로 사물이 주어이다.

기타
〈is/are + being + 과거분사〉 형태의 현재 진행 수동태, 〈has/have + been + 과거 분사〉 형태의 현재 완료 수동태, '타동사 + 목적어' 형태의 단순 현재 능동태, There is/are와 같은 단순 현재도 나온다.

평서문
질문이 아니라 객관적인 사실이나 화자의 의견 등을 나타내는 문장이다.

명령문
동사원형이나 Please 등으로 시작한다.

의문사 의문문
각 의문사마다 1~2개씩 나온다. 의문사가 단독으로 나오기도 하지만 What time ~?, How long ~?, Which room ~? 등에서처럼 다른 명사나 형용사와 같이 나오기도 한다.

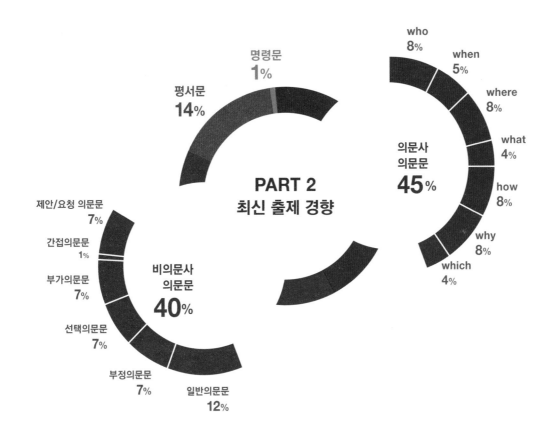

비의문사 의문문

일반(Yes/No) 의문문 적게 나올 때는 한두 개, 많이 나올 때는 서너 개씩 나오는 편이다.

부정의문문 Don't you ~?, Isn't he ~? 등으로 시작하는 문장이며 일반 긍정의문문보다는 약간 더 적게 나온다.

선택의문문 A or B 형태로 나오며 A와 B의 형태가 단어, 구, 절일 수 있다. 구나 절일 경우 문장이 길어져서 어려워진다.

부가의문문 ~ don't you?, ~ isn't he? 등으로 끝나는 문장이며, 일반 부정의문문과 비슷하다고 볼 수 있다.

간접의문문 의문사가 문장 처음 부분이 아니라 문장 중간에 들어 있다.

제안/요청 의문문 정보를 얻기보다는 상대방의 도움이나 동의 등을 얻기 위한 목적이 일반적이다.

토익 경향 분석

- 3인 대화의 경우 남자 화자 두 명과 여자 화자 한 명 또는 남자 화자 한 명과 여자 화자 두 명이 나온다. 따라서 문제에서는 2인 대화에서와 달리 the man이나 the woman이 아니라 the men이나 the women 또는 특정한 이름이 언급될 수 있다.

- 대화 & 시각 정보는 항상 파트의 뒷부분에 나온다.

- 시각 정보의 유형으로 chart, map, floor plan, schedule, table, weather forecast, directory, list, invoice, receipt, sign, packing slip 등 다양한 자료가 골고루 나온다.

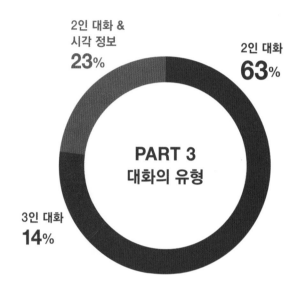

- 주제, 목적, 이유, 대화의 장소, 화자의 직업/직장 등과 관련된 문제는 주로 대화의 첫 번째 문제로 나오며 다음 행동/일어날 일 등과 관련된 문제는 주로 대화의 세 번째 문제로 나온다.

- 화자의 의도 파악 문제는 주로 2인 대화에 나오지만, 가끔 3인 대화에 나오기도 한다. 시각 정보 연계 대화에는 나오지 않고 있다.

- Part 3 안에서 화자의 의도 파악 문제는 2개가 나오고 시각 정보 연계 문제는 3개가 나온다.

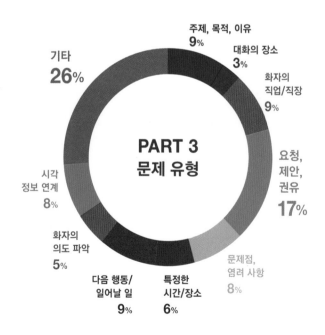

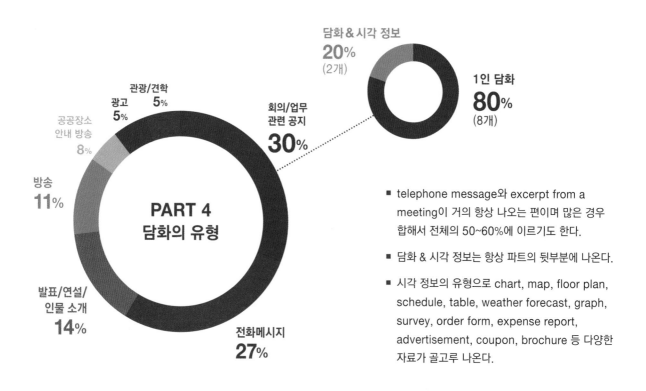

- telephone message와 excerpt from a meeting이 거의 항상 나오는 편이며 많은 경우 합해서 전체의 50~60%에 이르기도 한다.

- 담화 & 시각 정보는 항상 파트의 뒷부분에 나온다.

- 시각 정보의 유형으로 chart, map, floor plan, schedule, table, weather forecast, graph, survey, order form, expense report, advertisement, coupon, brochure 등 다양한 자료가 골고루 나온다.

- 문제 유형은 기본적으로 Part 3과 거의 비슷하다.

- 주제, 목적, 이유, 담화의 장소, 화자의 직업/직장 등과 관련된 문제는 주로 담화의 첫 번째 문제로 나오며 다음 행동/일어날 일 등과 관련된 문제는 주로 담화의 세 번째 문제로 나온다.

- Part 4 안에서 화자의 의도 파악 문제는 3개가 나오고 시각 정보 연계 문제는 2개가 나온다.

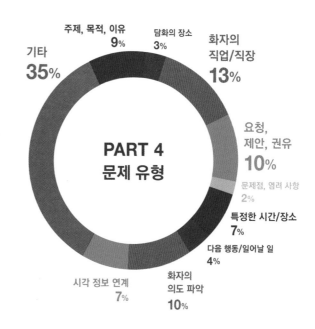

토익 경향 분석

문법 문제

시제와 대명사와 관련된 문법 문제가 2개씩, 한정사와 분사와 관련된 문법 문제가 1개씩 나온다. 시제 문제의 경우 능동태/수동태나 수의 일치와 연계되기도 한다. 그 밖에 한정사, 능동태/수동태, 부정사, 동명사 등과 관련된 문법 문제가 나온다.

어휘 문제

동사, 명사, 형용사, 부사와 관련된 어휘 문제가 각각 2~3개씩 골고루 나온다. 전치사 어휘 문제는 3개씩 꾸준히 나오지만, 접속사나 어구와 관련된 어휘 문제는 나오지 않을 때도 있고 3개가 나올 때도 있다.

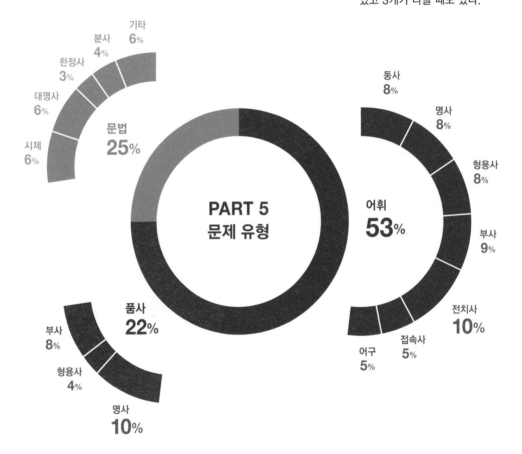

품사 문제

명사와 부사와 관련된 품사 문제가 2~3개씩 나오며, 형용사와 관련된 품사 문제가 상대적으로 적은 편이다.

한 지문에 4문제가 나오며 평균적으로 어휘 문제가 2개, 품사나 문법 문제가 1개, 문맥에 맞는 문장 고르기 문제가 1개 들어간다. 문맥에 맞는 문장 고르기 문제를 제외하면 문제 유형은 기본적으로 파트 5와 거의 비슷하다.

어휘 문제

동사, 명사, 부사, 어구와 관련된 어휘 문제는 매번 1~2개씩 나온다. 부사 어휘 문제의 경우 therefore(그러므로)나 however(하지만)처럼 문맥의 흐름을 자연스럽게 연결해 주는 부사가 자주 나온다.

문맥에 맞는 문장 고르기

문맥에 맞는 문장 고르기 문제는 지문당 한 문제씩 나오는데, 나오는 위치의 확률은 4문제 중 두 번째 문제, 세 번째 문제, 네 번째 문제, 첫 번째 문제 순으로 높다.

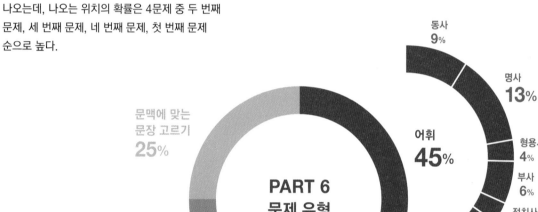

문법 문제

문맥의 흐름과 밀접하게 관련이 있는 시제 문제가 2개 정도 나오며, 능동태/수동태나 수의 일치와 연계되기도 한다. 그 밖에 대명사, 능동태/수동태, 부정사, 접속사/전치사 등과 관련된 문법 문제가 나온다.

품사 문제

명사나 형용사 문제가 부사 문제보다 좀 더 자주 나온다.

PART 7	독해 Reading Comprehension

지문 유형	지문당 문제 수	지문 개수	비중 %
단일 지문	2문항	4개	약 15%
	3문항	3개	약 16%
	4문항	3개	약 22%
이중 지문	5문항	2개	약 19%
삼중 지문	5문항	3개	약 28%

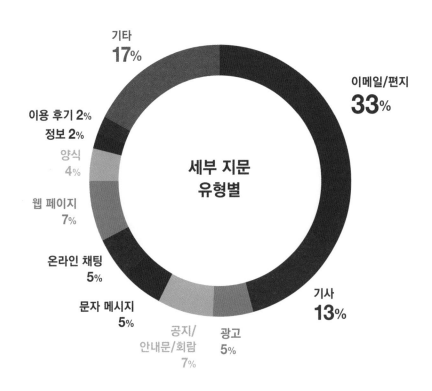

세부 지문
유형별

기타 17%
이용 후기 2%
정보 2%
양식 4%
웹 페이지 7%
온라인 채팅 5%
문자 메시지 5%
공지/안내문/회람 7%
광고 5%
기사 13%
이메일/편지 33%

■ 이메일/편지, 기사 유형 지문은 거의 항상 나오는 편이며 많은 경우 합해서 전체의 50~60%에 이르기도 한다.

■ 기타 지문 유형으로 agenda, brochure, comment card, coupon, flyer, instructions, invitation, invoice, list, menu, page from a catalog, policy statement, report, schedule, survey, voucher 등 다양한 자료가 골고루 나온다.

(이중 지문과 삼중 지문 속의 지문들을 모두 낱개로 계산함 – 총 23지문)

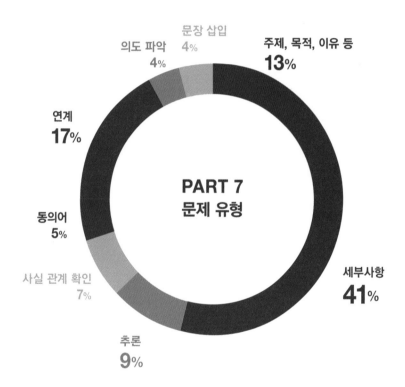

의도 파악
4%

문장 삽입
4%

주제, 목적, 이유 등
13%

연계
17%

**PART 7
문제 유형**

세부사항
41%

동의어
5%

사실 관계 확인
7%

추론
9%

- 동의어 문제는 주로 이중 지문이나 삼중 지문에 나온다.

- 연계 문제는 일반적으로 이중 지문에서 한 문제, 삼중 지문에서 두 문제가 나온다.

- 의도 파악 문제는 문자 메시지(text-message chain)나 온라인 채팅(online chat discussion) 지문에서 출제되며 두 문제가 나온다.

- 문장 삽입 문제는 주로 기사, 이메일, 편지, 회람 지문에서 출제되며 두 문제가 나온다.

점수 환산표 및 산출법

점수 환산표 이 책에 수록된 각 Test를 풀고 난 후, 맞은 개수를 세어 점수를 환산해 보세요.

LISTENING Raw Score (맞은 개수)	LISTENING Scaled Score (환산 점수)	READING Raw Score (맞은 개수)	READING Scaled Score (환산 점수)
96-100	475-495	96-100	460-495
91-95	435-495	91-95	425-490
86-90	405-470	86-90	400-465
81-85	370-450	81-85	375-440
76-80	345-420	76-80	340-415
71-75	320-390	71-75	310-390
66-70	290-360	66-70	285-370
61-65	265-335	61-65	255-340
56-60	240-310	56-60	230-310
51-55	215-280	51-55	200-275
46-50	190-255	46-50	170-245
41-45	160-230	41-45	140-215
36-40	130-205	36-40	115-180
31-35	105-175	31-35	95-150
26-30	85-145	26-30	75-120
21-25	60-115	21-25	60-95
16-20	30-90	16-20	45-75
11-15	5-70	11-15	30-55
6-10	5-60	6-10	10-40
1-5	5-50	1-5	5-30
0	5-35	0	5-15

점수 산출 방법   아래의 방식으로 점수를 산출할 수 있다.

STEP 1

자신의 답안을 수록된 정답과 대조하여 채점한다. 각 Section의 맞은 개수가 본인의 Section별 '실제 점수 (통계 처리하기 전의 점수, raw score)'이다. Listening Test와 Reading Test의 정답 수를 세어, 자신의 실제 점수를 아래의 해당란에 기록한다.

	맞은 개수	환산 점수대
LISTENING		
READING		
총점		

Section별 실제 점수가 그대로 Section별 TOEIC 점수가 되는 것은 아니다. TOEIC은 시행할 때마다 별도로 특정한 통계 처리 방법을 사용하며 이러한 실제 점수를 환산 점수(converted[scaled] score)로 전환하게 된다. 이렇게 전환함으로써, 매번 시행될 때마다 문제는 달라지지만 그 점수가 갖는 의미는 같아지게 된다. 예를 들어 어느 한 시험에서 총점 550점의 성적으로 받는 실력이라면 다른 시험에서도 거의 550점대의 성적을 받게 되는 것이다.

▼

STEP 2

실제 점수를 위 표에 기록한 후 왼쪽 페이지의 점수 환산표를 보도록 한다. TOEIC이 시행될 때마다 대개 이와 비슷한 형태의 표가 작성되는데, 여기 제시된 환산표는 본 교재에 수록된 Test용으로 개발된 것이다. 이 표를 사용하여 자신의 실제 점수를 환산 점수로 전환하도록 한다. 즉, 예를 들어 Listening Test의 실제 정답 수가 61~65개이면 환산 점수는 265점에서 335점 사이가 된다. 여기서 실제 정답 수가 61개이면 환산 점수가 265점이고, 65개이면 환산 점수가 335점 임을 의미하는 것은 아니다. 본 책의 Test를 위해 작성된 이 점수 환산표가 자신의 영어 실력이 어느 정도인지 대략적으로 파악하는 데 도움이 되긴 하지만, 이 표가 실제 TOEIC 성적 산출에 그대로 사용된 적은 없다는 사실을 밝혀 둔다.

토익° 정기시험
기출문제집

LC

기출 TEST

01

LISTENING TEST

In the Listening test, you will be asked to demonstrate how well you understand spoken English. The entire Listening test will last approximately 45 minutes. There are four parts, and directions are given for each part. You must mark your answers on the separate answer sheet. Do not write your answers in your test book.

PART 1

Directions: For each question in this part, you will hear four statements about a picture in your test book. When you hear the statements, you must select the one statement that best describes what you see in the picture. Then find the number of the question on your answer sheet and mark your answer. The statements will not be printed in your test book and will be spoken only one time.

Statement (C), "They're sitting at a table," is the best description of the picture, so you should select answer (C) and mark it on your answer sheet.

1.

2.

GO ON TO THE NEXT PAGE ➤

3.

4.

5.

6.

GO ON TO THE NEXT PAGE ➡

PART 2

Directions: You will hear a question or statement and three responses spoken in English. They will not be printed in your test book and will be spoken only one time. Select the best response to the question or statement and mark the letter (A), (B), or (C) on your answer sheet.

7. Mark your answer on your answer sheet.

8. Mark your answer on your answer sheet.

9. Mark your answer on your answer sheet.

10. Mark your answer on your answer sheet.

11. Mark your answer on your answer sheet.

12. Mark your answer on your answer sheet.

13. Mark your answer on your answer sheet.

14. Mark your answer on your answer sheet.

15. Mark your answer on your answer sheet.

16. Mark your answer on your answer sheet.

17. Mark your answer on your answer sheet.

18. Mark your answer on your answer sheet.

19. Mark your answer on your answer sheet.

20. Mark your answer on your answer sheet.

21. Mark your answer on your answer sheet.

22. Mark your answer on your answer sheet.

23. Mark your answer on your answer sheet.

24. Mark your answer on your answer sheet.

25. Mark your answer on your answer sheet.

26. Mark your answer on your answer sheet.

27. Mark your answer on your answer sheet.

28. Mark your answer on your answer sheet.

29. Mark your answer on your answer sheet.

30. Mark your answer on your answer sheet.

31. Mark your answer on your answer sheet.

PART 3

Directions: You will hear some conversations between two or more people. You will be asked to answer three questions about what the speakers say in each conversation. Select the best response to each question and mark the letter (A), (B), (C), or (D) on your answer sheet. The conversations will not be printed in your test book and will be spoken only one time.

32. What is the woman preparing for?

    (A) A move to a new city
    (B) A business trip
    (C) A building tour
    (D) A meeting with visiting colleagues

33. Who most likely is the man?

    (A) An accountant
    (B) An administrative assistant
    (C) A marketing director
    (D) A company president

34. What does the woman want to pick up on Friday morning?

    (A) A building map
    (B) A room key
    (C) An ID card
    (D) A parking pass

35. What task is the man responsible for?

    (A) Writing a budget
    (B) Reviewing job applications
    (C) Organizing a company newsletter
    (D) Updating an employee handbook

36. What does the woman want to do next year?

    (A) Organize a trade show
    (B) Open a new store
    (C) Redesign a product catalog
    (D) Hire some team members

37. What does the man ask the woman to do?

    (A) Order some business cards
    (B) Write a press release
    (C) Provide some additional details
    (D) Set up a meeting time

38. What does the woman need a suit for?

    (A) A job interview
    (B) A fashion show
    (C) A family celebration
    (D) A television appearance

39. What does the woman dislike about a suit on display?

    (A) The fabric
    (B) The price
    (C) The style
    (D) The color

40. What does the man say that the price includes?

    (A) Some accessories
    (B) Alterations
    (C) Sales tax
    (D) Delivery

41. What kind of a business does the man most likely work for?

    (A) A legal consulting firm
    (B) An architecture firm
    (C) A film production company
    (D) A book publishing company

42. What does the woman say she is concerned about?

    (A) The length of a project
    (B) The cost of an order
    (C) The opinion of the public
    (D) The skills of some workers

43. What does the woman agree to let the man do?

    (A) Submit an application
    (B) Speak at a meeting
    (C) Review some books
    (D) Measure a space

GO ON TO THE NEXT PAGE

44. Who most likely is Axel Schmidt?

   (A) A store manager
   (B) A construction worker
   (C) A journalist
   (D) An artist

45. What renovation does the woman mention?

   (A) Some walls are being painted.
   (B) Some floors are being replaced.
   (C) Some windows are being installed.
   (D) Some light fixtures are being repaired.

46. What does the woman encourage the man to do?

   (A) Visit a gift shop
   (B) Send a package
   (C) Wait for a bus
   (D) Take a photograph

47. What does the speakers' company most likely sell?

   (A) Electronics
   (B) Clothing
   (C) Food
   (D) Automobiles

48. Why is the woman surprised?

   (A) Some software is expensive.
   (B) A color is very bright.
   (C) The man has completed a report.
   (D) The man bought a new car.

49. Why does the woman say, "The slides are available on our company intranet"?

   (A) To request assistance reviewing a document
   (B) To recommend using a document as a reference
   (C) To report that a task has been completed
   (D) To indicate that a file is in the wrong location

50. According to the woman, what will happen at the end of November?

   (A) An executive will visit.
   (B) An employee will retire.
   (C) A product will be released.
   (D) A study will be completed.

51. What does the man want to know?

   (A) Where he would be working
   (B) When he would be starting a job
   (C) How to get to an office building
   (D) Why an event time has changed

52. What does the woman say the company will pay for?

   (A) A work vehicle
   (B) A private office
   (C) Moving expenses
   (D) Visitors' meals

53. What industry do the speakers work in?

   (A) Manufacturing
   (B) Agriculture
   (C) Transportation
   (D) Construction

54. What does the woman say a project will do for a city?

   (A) Increase tourism
   (B) Generate electricity
   (C) Preserve natural resources
   (D) Improve property values

55. What does Gerhard say needs to be done?

   (A) Permits need to be approved.
   (B) Employees need to be trained.
   (C) Materials need to be ordered.
   (D) Inspections need to be made.

56. What does the woman imply when she says, "I don't have much to do"?

(A) She has time to help.
(B) She plans to leave work early.
(C) Her computer is not working.
(D) She has not received an assignment.

57. What does the man notice about some medication?

(A) It needs to be refrigerated.
(B) It has expired.
(C) The dosage has changed.
(D) The supply is limited.

58. What does the man suggest doing in the future?

(A) Installing some shelves
(B) Confirming with a doctor
(C) Increasing an order amount
(D) Recommending a different medication

59. Who most likely is the woman?

(A) A travel agent
(B) A bank teller
(C) A lawyer
(D) A mail-room worker

60. What kind of document are the speakers discussing?

(A) A user agreement
(B) An employment contract
(C) A list of travel expenses
(D) An insurance certificate

61. Why must the document be revised by the end of the month?

(A) To be included in a personnel file
(B) To use in a merger negotiation
(C) To meet a production deadline
(D) To avoid paying a fine

Giordano Wedding

Service	Cost
Flowers	$4,456
Photography	$1,300
Catering	$10,200
Shuttle bus	$400
Total:	$16,356

62. Look at the graphic. How much did the man's company charge for its service?

(A) $4,456
(B) $1,300
(C) $10,200
(D) $400

63. Why does the man apologize?

(A) Business hours have changed.
(B) A price was wrong.
(C) Some staff arrived late.
(D) A request could not be fulfilled.

64. What does the woman like about a venue?

(A) It has a nice view.
(B) It is conveniently located.
(C) It is tastefully decorated.
(D) It can host large events.

GO ON TO THE NEXT PAGE

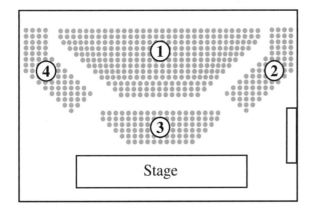

Stage

65. Why is the man surprised?

(A) A popular band is coming to town.
(B) The woman plays a musical instrument.
(C) The woman was able to get concert tickets.
(D) Some musicians scheduled a second concert.

66. Look at the graphic. In which section does the woman have seats?

(A) Section 1
(B) Section 2
(C) Section 3
(D) Section 4

67. What is the woman doing this weekend?

(A) Practicing with her band
(B) Entering a radio contest
(C) Moving to Boston
(D) Attending a party

Bellevue Apartments	
1A	Tanaka
1B	Zhao
2A	Mukherjee
2B	Tremblay

68. Who most likely is the man?

(A) A maintenance worker
(B) A property manager
(C) A real estate agent
(D) A bank employee

69. Look at the graphic. Which name needs to be changed?

(A) Tanaka
(B) Zhao
(C) Mukherjee
(D) Tremblay

70. What does the woman say she is going to do tomorrow?

(A) Fill out a registration form
(B) Meet with some neighbors
(C) Order some furniture
(D) Make a payment

PART 4

Directions: You will hear some talks given by a single speaker. You will be asked to answer three questions about what the speaker says in each talk. Select the best response to each question and mark the letter (A), (B), (C), or (D) on your answer sheet. The talks will not be printed in your test book and will be spoken only one time.

71. What kind of business is the speaker most likely calling?

   (A) A hair salon
   (B) An insurance company
   (C) A car dealership
   (D) An eye doctor's office

72. What does the speaker say about her appointment?

   (A) It is too far away.
   (B) It needs to be rescheduled.
   (C) It is too expensive.
   (D) It should be with a different person.

73. What is the speaker interested in learning more about?

   (A) Payment methods
   (B) Delivery options
   (C) A warranty
   (D) A job opening

74. What is being advertised?

   (A) A factory tour
   (B) A baking competition
   (C) A grand opening
   (D) An art show

75. What will participants receive?

   (A) A poster
   (B) A promotional mug
   (C) A company T-shirt
   (D) A photograph

76. What can the listeners do on a Web site?

   (A) Find a recipe
   (B) Fill out an entry form
   (C) View a product list
   (D) Download a coupon

77. Where does the announcement take place?

   (A) At a sports arena
   (B) At a concert hall
   (C) At an art museum
   (D) At a movie theater

78. Why does the speaker apologize?

   (A) A presenter has been delayed.
   (B) Some lights have gone out.
   (C) A sound system is broken.
   (D) A construction project is noisy.

79. What does the speaker offer the listeners?

   (A) A promotional item
   (B) A parking voucher
   (C) Discounted snacks
   (D) Free tickets

80. What event is taking place?

   (A) A technology conference
   (B) A product demonstration
   (C) A company fund-raiser
   (D) A training workshop

81. Why does the speaker say, "And over 300 people are here"?

   (A) To propose moving to a larger venue
   (B) To indicate that some advertising was successful
   (C) To emphasize the importance of working quickly
   (D) To suggest more volunteers are needed

82. What does the speaker ask the listeners to do?

   (A) Provide feedback
   (B) Silence mobile phones
   (C) Review an event program
   (D) Enjoy some refreshments

GO ON TO THE NEXT PAGE

83. What is the purpose of the plan?

    (A) To support local businesses
    (B) To promote tourism
    (C) To decrease traffic
    (D) To reduce government spending

84. Who does the speaker say will receive a discount?

    (A) Commuters
    (B) Senior citizens
    (C) Students
    (D) City officials

85. What will happen after three months?

    (A) A survey will be distributed.
    (B) A new director will take over.
    (C) A bus line will be added.
    (D) A program evaluation will take place.

86. What event is the speaker discussing?

    (A) A sports competition
    (B) A music festival
    (C) A cooking demonstration
    (D) A historical play

87. Why does the speaker say, "tickets are almost sold out"?

    (A) To encourage the listeners to enter a contest
    (B) To suggest that the listeners arrive early
    (C) To complain that an event space is too small
    (D) To praise the results of a marketing plan

88. What will happen tomorrow morning?

    (A) A new venue will open.
    (B) A prize winner will be announced.
    (C) An interview will take place.
    (D) A video will be filmed.

89. What type of business does the speaker work for?

    (A) A computer company
    (B) A construction firm
    (C) A furniture manufacturer
    (D) An office-supply distributor

90. What does the speaker say is an advantage of the new material?

    (A) It is inexpensive.
    (B) It is durable.
    (C) It is lightweight.
    (D) It comes in many colors.

91. What will the listeners do next?

    (A) Sign up for a mailing list
    (B) Watch an instructional video
    (C) Enter a contest
    (D) Look at a sample

92. Which department does the speaker work in?

    (A) Product Development
    (B) Human Resources
    (C) Legal
    (D) Accounting

93. Why does the speaker say, "there is a need for a skilled software engineer"?

    (A) To recommend an employee sign up for more training
    (B) To indicate that a project deadline will be extended
    (C) To approve a request to transfer
    (D) To suggest consulting with an expert

94. What does the speaker want to discuss with the listener?

    (A) Some sales results
    (B) Some client feedback
    (C) An office renovation
    (D) A work schedule

This Week's Guests	
Monday	Ling Yu—Part 1
Tuesday	Ling Yu—Part 2
Wednesday	Hilda Orman
Thursday	Haru Nakamura
Friday	Joseph Samir

95. Why are guests invited on the speaker's radio show?

(A) To discuss their businesses
(B) To talk about local history
(C) To teach communication skills
(D) To offer travel tips

96. What can the listeners do on a Web site?

(A) View photos of famous guests
(B) Sign up for a special service
(C) Read about upcoming programs
(D) Listen to previous episodes

97. Look at the graphic. Which day is this episode being aired?

(A) Tuesday
(B) Wednesday
(C) Thursday
(D) Friday

Shelf 1
Shelf 2
Shelf 3
Shelf 4

98. Look at the graphic. Where will the scarves and ties be displayed?

(A) On Shelf 1
(B) On Shelf 2
(C) On Shelf 3
(D) On Shelf 4

99. What should be displayed near the cash registers?

(A) Coupons
(B) Hats
(C) Gloves
(D) Socks

100. What should the listener expect to receive in an e-mail?

(A) A payment schedule
(B) Photographs
(C) Shipping information
(D) Display measurements

This is the end of the Listening test.

토익® 정기시험
기출문제집

LC

기출 TEST

02

LISTENING TEST

In the Listening test, you will be asked to demonstrate how well you understand spoken English. The entire Listening test will last approximately 45 minutes. There are four parts, and directions are given for each part. You must mark your answers on the separate answer sheet. Do not write your answers in your test book.

PART 1

Directions: For each question in this part, you will hear four statements about a picture in your test book. When you hear the statements, you must select the one statement that best describes what you see in the picture. Then find the number of the question on your answer sheet and mark your answer. The statements will not be printed in your test book and will be spoken only one time.

Statement (C), "They're sitting at a table," is the best description of the picture, so you should select answer (C) and mark it on your answer sheet.

1.

2.

GO ON TO THE NEXT PAGE →

3.

4.

5.

6.

GO ON TO THE NEXT PAGE

PART 2

Directions: You will hear a question or statement and three responses spoken in English. They will not be printed in your test book and will be spoken only one time. Select the best response to the question or statement and mark the letter (A), (B), or (C) on your answer sheet.

7. Mark your answer on your answer sheet.

8. Mark your answer on your answer sheet.

9. Mark your answer on your answer sheet.

10. Mark your answer on your answer sheet.

11. Mark your answer on your answer sheet.

12. Mark your answer on your answer sheet.

13. Mark your answer on your answer sheet.

14. Mark your answer on your answer sheet.

15. Mark your answer on your answer sheet.

16. Mark your answer on your answer sheet.

17. Mark your answer on your answer sheet.

18. Mark your answer on your answer sheet.

19. Mark your answer on your answer sheet.

20. Mark your answer on your answer sheet.

21. Mark your answer on your answer sheet.

22. Mark your answer on your answer sheet.

23. Mark your answer on your answer sheet.

24. Mark your answer on your answer sheet.

25. Mark your answer on your answer sheet.

26. Mark your answer on your answer sheet.

27. Mark your answer on your answer sheet.

28. Mark your answer on your answer sheet.

29. Mark your answer on your answer sheet.

30. Mark your answer on your answer sheet.

31. Mark your answer on your answer sheet.

PART 3

Directions: You will hear some conversations between two or more people. You will be asked to answer three questions about what the speakers say in each conversation. Select the best response to each question and mark the letter (A), (B), (C), or (D) on your answer sheet. The conversations will not be printed in your test book and will be spoken only one time.

32. Why does the man want to buy Ms. Jefferson some flowers?

    (A) She was promoted.
    (B) She won an award.
    (C) She is moving.
    (D) She is retiring.

33. According to the woman, where is Greenwood Flower Shop?

    (A) In a shopping mall
    (B) In a train station
    (C) Next to a café
    (D) Across from the library

34. What does the man say he will do before he leaves the office?

    (A) Fill out a time sheet
    (B) Send an e-mail
    (C) Finish a budget proposal
    (D) Arrange a meeting

35. What did the man just do?

    (A) He upgraded a flight.
    (B) He arranged for a rental car.
    (C) He prepared some presentation slides.
    (D) He made a hotel reservation.

36. What does the man remind the woman to do?

    (A) Save her receipts
    (B) Bring her ID badge
    (C) Sign a form
    (D) Arrive early

37. What does the woman ask the man about?

    (A) A bank
    (B) A post office
    (C) A restaurant
    (D) A conference center

38. What industry do the speakers most likely work in?

    (A) Television
    (B) Fashion
    (C) Home furnishings
    (D) Advertising

39. What does the man suggest doing?

    (A) Providing tours of a facility
    (B) Opening a branch office
    (C) Designing special fabric
    (D) Installing brighter lights

40. What is the woman concerned about?

    (A) A plan would be time-consuming.
    (B) A color is too bright.
    (C) Some sales figures have declined.
    (D) Some supplies will be expensive.

41. What problem is being discussed?

    (A) A company manual contains some errors.
    (B) A shipment was not delivered on time.
    (C) Some materials are missing from a cabinet.
    (D) An e-mail system is not functioning properly.

42. Who most likely is the man?

    (A) A computer technician
    (B) A security guard
    (C) A warehouse manager
    (D) A sales representative

43. What are the women most likely planning to do next?

    (A) Sign a contract
    (B) Attend a training
    (C) Go to the airport
    (D) Revise a presentation

GO ON TO THE NEXT PAGE

44. Where does the woman work?

    (A) At an amusement park
    (B) At a fitness center
    (C) At a bicycle-tour company
    (D) At an automobile dealership

45. Why is the man unable to make a reservation for next Thursday?

    (A) A calendar is fully booked.
    (B) An employee is on vacation.
    (C) Some roads will be closed.
    (D) Some equipment will be replaced.

46. What will the man most likely do next?

    (A) Pick up a brochure
    (B) Make a down payment
    (C) Provide a membership number
    (D) Write a customer review

47. Who is the man?

    (A) A news reporter
    (B) A photographer
    (C) A fashion designer
    (D) A translator

48. Why does the woman say, "The issue is already being printed"?

    (A) To apologize for an error
    (B) To provide reassurance
    (C) To indicate a schedule change
    (D) To decline an offer

49. What does the woman ask the man to do?

    (A) Come in for an interview
    (B) Appear in a feature story
    (C) Travel for an assignment
    (D) Post some information online

50. What kind of business do the speakers most likely work for?

    (A) An automobile manufacturer
    (B) An insurance company
    (C) A county hospital
    (D) A construction firm

51. What problem do the women mention?

    (A) A building site did not pass an inspection.
    (B) A vehicle needs to be repaired.
    (C) Potential clients have not made a decision.
    (D) Some vendors are making late deliveries.

52. What does the man recommend?

    (A) Offering a discount
    (B) Changing suppliers
    (C) Forming a committee
    (D) Closing a branch

53. What has the woman volunteered to do?

    (A) Try out some new products
    (B) Purchase beverages for a luncheon
    (C) Lead a workshop session
    (D) Organize a hiring event

54. What does the man ask the woman to sign?

    (A) An employee contract
    (B) An attendance sheet
    (C) A participant agreement
    (D) A service estimate

55. What will the woman most likely do next?

    (A) Set up her computer
    (B) Go to another room
    (C) Have some lunch
    (D) Make a phone call

56. Where most likely are the speakers?

(A) At a hair salon
(B) At a catering hall
(C) At a laundry service
(D) At an energy company

57. Why does the woman say, "they don't have as many clients, though"?

(A) To express pride in her company's growth
(B) To explain why an expense is so high
(C) To suggest that a strategy should continue
(D) To question the accuracy of a client list

58. What will happen later today?

(A) Some supplies will be delivered.
(B) An inspection will be conducted.
(C) An employee meeting will be held.
(D) An expense report will be submitted.

59. Which industry do the speakers most likely work in?

(A) Tourism
(B) Agriculture
(C) Education
(D) Engineering

60. What does the man say he is concerned about?

(A) Expenses
(B) Safety
(C) Competition
(D) Space

61. What does the man agree to do?

(A) Apply for some funding
(B) Do some research
(C) Organize a business trip
(D) Assemble a work crew

HARTSVILLE EXITS

Maple Road	Exit 5
Carter Lane	Exit 7
Berk Street	Exit 8
High Road	Exit 10

62. What does the woman remind the man about?

(A) She used to live in the area.
(B) She needs to stop at a store.
(C) She attended a seminar last year.
(D) She has just bought a new car.

63. Look at the graphic. Which exit will the speakers take?

(A) Maple Road
(B) Carter Lane
(C) Berk Street
(D) High Road

64. What will the man ask his coworkers to do?

(A) Cancel a reservation
(B) Save some seats
(C) Sign in at an event
(D) Print some materials

GO ON TO THE NEXT PAGE

65. Where does the conversation most likely take place?

(A) At a hotel
(B) At an accounting firm
(C) At a doctor's office
(D) At a school

66. Look at the graphic. Which bin will the man use?

(A) Bin 1
(B) Bin 2
(C) Bin 3
(D) Bin 4

67. What does the woman suggest?

(A) Using a cart
(B) Waiting for a confirmation
(C) Giving an assignment to a colleague
(D) Rescheduling an appointment with a client

68. What type of event are the speakers organizing?

(A) An award ceremony
(B) A grand-opening celebration
(C) A foreign official's reception
(D) A fund-raiser

69. Look at the graphic. What time does the man think the music should begin?

(A) At 5:00 P.M.
(B) At 6:00 P.M.
(C) At 7:00 P.M.
(D) At 8:00 P.M.

70. What information does the man suggest adding to the invitation?

(A) The name of a sponsor
(B) The location of a concert hall
(C) A Web site address
(D) A list of performers

PART 4

Directions: You will hear some talks given by a single speaker. You will be asked to answer three questions about what the speaker says in each talk. Select the best response to each question and mark the letter (A), (B), (C), or (D) on your answer sheet. The talks will not be printed in your test book and will be spoken only one time.

71. What did Starbright Corporation recently do?
    - (A) It changed its company logo.
    - (B) It opened a new factory.
    - (C) It conducted a financial audit.
    - (D) It upgraded a product line.

72. What type of product does Starbright Corporation make?
    - (A) Footwear
    - (B) Cosmetics
    - (C) Housewares
    - (D) Electronics

73. What is available online?
    - (A) An application
    - (B) A schedule
    - (C) A video interview
    - (D) A virtual tour

74. What event is taking place?
    - (A) An orientation session
    - (B) A gallery opening
    - (C) An awards ceremony
    - (D) A retirement party

75. What type of business does Mustafa Perez work for?
    - (A) An advertising agency
    - (B) An art gallery
    - (C) A newspaper publisher
    - (D) A camera shop

76. What has the speaker created for the event?
    - (A) A slideshow
    - (B) A T-shirt design
    - (C) A Web site
    - (D) A brochure

77. What does the speaker's company produce?
    - (A) Medications
    - (B) Textbooks
    - (C) Exercise clothing
    - (D) Construction materials

78. What are the listeners reminded to do?
    - (A) Recruit some staff
    - (B) Enter some data
    - (C) Attend some training sessions
    - (D) Turn on a fan

79. What can be found online?
    - (A) A product database
    - (B) An employee directory
    - (C) A handbook
    - (D) A contract

80. What will the speaker do at a park?
    - (A) Watch a performance
    - (B) Sell fruit
    - (C) Plant trees
    - (D) Take photographs

81. Why does the speaker say, "but it's supposed to be cloudy all day"?
    - (A) To ask for help
    - (B) To express frustration
    - (C) To reject the listener's suggestion
    - (D) To reassure the listener

82. What does the speaker remind the listener to do?
    - (A) Register for a competition
    - (B) Purchase some supplies
    - (C) Prepare a shipment
    - (D) Speak to a customer

GO ON TO THE NEXT PAGE

83. Where is the announcement being made?

(A) At a technology firm
(B) At a repair shop
(C) At a factory
(D) At a law office

84. Where should the listeners go at the end of their shifts?

(A) To the company cafeteria
(B) To the receptionist's desk
(C) To the locker room
(D) To the parking area

85. What will happen tomorrow?

(A) Some office furniture will be delivered.
(B) New board members will be elected.
(C) A city official will conduct an inspection.
(D) Some time-reporting software will be fixed.

86. Where do the listeners work?

(A) At an employment agency
(B) At a sports arena
(C) At a conference center
(D) At a medical clinic

87. What does the speaker imply when she says, "Ms. Jenkins has retired"?

(A) A role needs to be filled.
(B) An e-mail will not be answered.
(C) A marketing strategy should be revised.
(D) A process will be less efficient.

88. What will the listeners most likely do next?

(A) Check a schedule
(B) Complete a registration form
(C) Eat a meal
(D) Brainstorm some ideas

89. What is scheduled for Friday?

(A) A job fair
(B) A wellness workshop
(C) A client meeting
(D) An employee luncheon

90. Why does the speaker say, "the advertising business is very competitive"?

(A) To explain a decision to retire
(B) To justify an employee's promotion
(C) To question the listener's abilities
(D) To express confidence in an approach

91. What does the speaker say about Isabel?

(A) She has recently joined the company.
(B) She can recommend some activities.
(C) She will approve expense reports.
(D) She used to work on the NVC Industries account.

92. What type of business does the speaker most likely work for?

(A) A television studio
(B) A hardware store
(C) A publishing company
(D) A grocery store

93. What is the speaker concerned about?

(A) A business has lost customers.
(B) An advertising plan has not been effective.
(C) A stockroom is overcrowded.
(D) A Web site is not working.

94. What does the speaker plan to do?

(A) Transfer to another location
(B) Offer discounts online
(C) Hire more employees
(D) Add videos to a Web site

List of Fees		Paid	Not paid
Filing:	$50.00	✓	
Contract processing:	$250.00		✓
Vehicle title:	$125.00		✓
Vehicle registration:	$100.00		✓

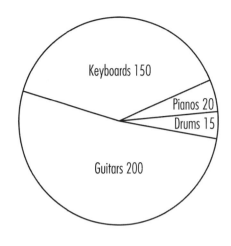

95. Who most likely is the speaker?

(A) A car salesperson
(B) An auto mechanic
(C) A car rental agent
(D) A vehicle inspector

96. Look at the graphic. Which fee must be paid in cash?

(A) Filing
(B) Contract processing
(C) Vehicle title
(D) Vehicle registration

97. What service does the speaker remind the listener about?

(A) Shuttle service
(B) Maintenance reminders
(C) Free car washes
(D) Replacement keys

98. Who most likely is the speaker?

(A) A jazz singer
(B) A music teacher
(C) A shop manager
(D) A radio host

99. What event will take place in September?

(A) A music festival
(B) A press conference
(C) A charity dinner
(D) A talent contest

100. Look at the graphic. Which type of instrument does the speaker focus on?

(A) Keyboards
(B) Pianos
(C) Drums
(D) Guitars

This is the end of the Listening test.

토익® 정기시험
기출문제집

LC

기출 TEST

03

LISTENING TEST

In the Listening test, you will be asked to demonstrate how well you understand spoken English. The entire Listening test will last approximately 45 minutes. There are four parts, and directions are given for each part. You must mark your answers on the separate answer sheet. Do not write your answers in your test book.

PART 1

Directions: For each question in this part, you will hear four statements about a picture in your test book. When you hear the statements, you must select the one statement that best describes what you see in the picture. Then find the number of the question on your answer sheet and mark your answer. The statements will not be printed in your test book and will be spoken only one time.

Statement (C), "They're sitting at a table," is the best description of the picture, so you should select answer (C) and mark it on your answer sheet.

1.

2.

GO ON TO THE NEXT PAGE

3.

4.

5.

6.

GO ON TO THE NEXT PAGE

PART 2

Directions: You will hear a question or statement and three responses spoken in English. They will not be printed in your test book and will be spoken only one time. Select the best response to the question or statement and mark the letter (A), (B), or (C) on your answer sheet.

7. Mark your answer on your answer sheet.

8. Mark your answer on your answer sheet.

9. Mark your answer on your answer sheet.

10. Mark your answer on your answer sheet.

11. Mark your answer on your answer sheet.

12. Mark your answer on your answer sheet.

13. Mark your answer on your answer sheet.

14. Mark your answer on your answer sheet.

15. Mark your answer on your answer sheet.

16. Mark your answer on your answer sheet.

17. Mark your answer on your answer sheet.

18. Mark your answer on your answer sheet.

19. Mark your answer on your answer sheet.

20. Mark your answer on your answer sheet.

21. Mark your answer on your answer sheet.

22. Mark your answer on your answer sheet.

23. Mark your answer on your answer sheet.

24. Mark your answer on your answer sheet.

25. Mark your answer on your answer sheet.

26. Mark your answer on your answer sheet.

27. Mark your answer on your answer sheet.

28. Mark your answer on your answer sheet.

29. Mark your answer on your answer sheet.

30. Mark your answer on your answer sheet.

31. Mark your answer on your answer sheet.

PART 3

Directions: You will hear some conversations between two or more people. You will be asked to answer three questions about what the speakers say in each conversation. Select the best response to each question and mark the letter (A), (B), (C), or (D) on your answer sheet. The conversations will not be printed in your test book and will be spoken only one time.

32. Why is the woman seeking a temporary position?
    (A) To become familiar with local opportunities
    (B) To gain experience in a new field
    (C) To have more scheduling flexibility
    (D) To focus on a specific project

33. What skill does the woman have?
    (A) Accounting
    (B) Event organizing
    (C) Team management
    (D) Computer programming

34. Why does the man tell the woman to come in on Wednesday?
    (A) To complete some paperwork
    (B) To visit a job site
    (C) To fill out a survey
    (D) To present a certificate

35. Why does the man ask Rosa to go to Montreal?
    (A) To meet with a client
    (B) To attend a trade show
    (C) To train for a position
    (D) To oversee a construction project

36. What does the woman ask permission to do?
    (A) Take a coworker
    (B) Change a flight
    (C) Postpone a deadline
    (D) Increase an advertising budget

37. What will the man most likely do next?
    (A) Prepare some sales data
    (B) Order some business cards
    (C) Make a phone call
    (D) Go to lunch

38. Who is the man?
    (A) A lawyer
    (B) An electrician
    (C) A dentist
    (D) A banker

39. Why does the man apologize?
    (A) Some documents are missing.
    (B) Some equipment is not working.
    (C) An assistant is late.
    (D) A policy was not explained.

40. Why is Ms. Yamamoto asked to fill out a form?
    (A) To update her contact information
    (B) To set up a payment plan
    (C) To request some records
    (D) To opt for paperless statements

41. Who will the woman give a presentation to?
    (A) New employees
    (B) Government officials
    (C) Potential investors
    (D) Board members

42. What does the woman ask the man about?
    (A) Adjusting a microphone
    (B) Turning on a monitor
    (C) Connecting a speaker
    (D) Using a camera

43. What will the man do next?
    (A) Check a manual
    (B) Give a demonstration
    (C) Ask a colleague for help
    (D) Look for a tool

GO ON TO THE NEXT PAGE

44. What is the man concerned about?

   (A) Venue availability
   (B) Product efficiency
   (C) A project budget
   (D) A guest list

45. Who is Stefan Vogel?

   (A) A furniture designer
   (B) A photographer
   (C) An accountant
   (D) An event planner

46. What will the speakers do this afternoon?

   (A) Review some plans
   (B) Consult with a graphic designer
   (C) Choose some colors
   (D) Survey other team members

47. Where do the speakers work?

   (A) At a hardware store
   (B) At a construction site
   (C) At a factory
   (D) At a hotel

48. What does the man mean when he says, "And the rooms are so close together"?

   (A) Some renovations will be finished quickly.
   (B) A work schedule will be revised.
   (C) Noise levels will be a problem.
   (D) An architect should be consulted.

49. What does the woman hope to do before June?

   (A) Take inventory
   (B) Order new uniforms
   (C) Test out some technology
   (D) Prepare for an inspection

50. What type of product are the speakers discussing?

   (A) Pencils
   (B) Backpacks
   (C) Sneakers
   (D) Folders

51. What is the woman frustrated by?

   (A) Some customers wrote a negative review.
   (B) Some equipment is malfunctioning.
   (C) Some team members are unavailable.
   (D) Some packages have not arrived.

52. Why does the man say, "The school year is starting in three months"?

   (A) To request some time off from work
   (B) To correct an error in a schedule
   (C) To express interest in an assignment
   (D) To emphasize the need for urgency

53. What does the women's company sell?

   (A) Construction vehicles
   (B) Power tools
   (C) Wood products
   (D) Home appliances

54. Why is the man visiting the company?

   (A) To interview for a job
   (B) To revise a contract
   (C) To investigate a problem
   (D) To make a complaint

55. What does the man ask the women to do?

   (A) Lead him to a specific location
   (B) Provide him a discounted service
   (C) Demonstrate a technical procedure
   (D) Explain a company policy

56. What is the woman renovating?

(A) A kitchen
(B) A swimming pool
(C) A bathroom
(D) A garden

57. What service does the man's company provide?

(A) Landscaping
(B) Waste removal
(C) Safety inspections
(D) Concrete mixing

58. According to the man, how is a cost determined?

(A) By number of workers
(B) By project duration
(C) By weight
(D) By area

59. Where does the woman work?

(A) At a museum
(B) At a movie theater
(C) At a newspaper office
(D) At a photography studio

60. Who does the woman say she has hired?

(A) An engineer
(B) A musician
(C) An interpreter
(D) A scientist

61. What problem does the man mention?

(A) Traffic noise
(B) Late deliveries
(C) Uncomfortable seating
(D) Inadequate lighting

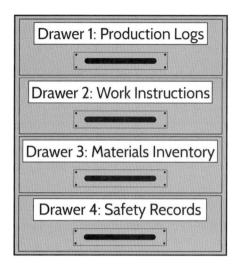

62. Why is the woman calling?

(A) To compliment a staff member
(B) To schedule an appointment
(C) To criticize a policy
(D) To check on an assignment

63. Look at the graphic. Which drawer will the man probably check next?

(A) Drawer 1
(B) Drawer 2
(C) Drawer 3
(D) Drawer 4

64. What does the man say about some processes?

(A) They are described in a training program.
(B) They take too long to complete.
(C) They meet regulations.
(D) They are easy to learn.

GO ON TO THE NEXT PAGE

Bonus per Surveys Collected	
$400	70+
$300	60-69
$200	50-59
$100	40-49

65. Where do the speakers work?

   (A) At a restaurant
   (B) At a hotel
   (C) At a travel agency
   (D) At a marketing firm

66. Look at the graphic. How much extra money will the man receive in his next paycheck?

   (A) $400
   (B) $300
   (C) $200
   (D) $100

67. What does the man say he will do with the extra money?

   (A) Fix his car
   (B) Give it to his parents
   (C) Put it in the bank
   (D) Buy a new phone

♪ *Sunville Music Festival*
Sunville City Park

Thursday, March 21, 7 P.M.–10 P.M.
Friday, March 22, 7 P.M.–11 P.M.
Saturday, March 23, noon–11 P.M.
Sunday, March 24, noon–10 P.M.

68. What is the woman planning a celebration for?

   (A) A business merger
   (B) A colleague's promotion
   (C) A product launch
   (D) A company anniversary

69. Look at the graphic. Which day is the man attending a music festival?

   (A) On Thursday
   (B) On Friday
   (C) On Saturday
   (D) On Sunday

70. What does the woman say she will do next?

   (A) Purchase a gift
   (B) Decorate a room
   (C) Make a reservation
   (D) Send an invitation

PART 4

Directions: You will hear some talks given by a single speaker. You will be asked to answer three questions about what the speaker says in each talk. Select the best response to each question and mark the letter (A), (B), (C), or (D) on your answer sheet. The talks will not be printed in your test book and will be spoken only one time.

71. Where is the announcement most likely being made?

(A) At a train station
(B) At a bus station
(C) At an airport
(D) At a ferry terminal

72. Why is a change being made?

(A) It will improve traffic flow.
(B) It will keep prices low.
(C) It will increase energy efficiency.
(D) It will save staff time.

73. What does the speaker recommend?

(A) Filling out a survey
(B) Printing some tickets
(C) Checking online for updates
(D) Allowing extra time

74. What event is taking place?

(A) A grand opening
(B) A focus group
(C) A food festival
(D) A sales workshop

75. What does the speaker say is distinct about a coffee blend?

(A) It is locally sourced.
(B) It is available in glass bottles.
(C) It comes in several different flavors.
(D) It contains a lot of caffeine.

76. What is the speaker offering customers?

(A) Free delivery
(B) Two-day shipping
(C) A full refund
(D) A discount

77. How does each tour begin?

(A) Refreshments are served.
(B) Safety equipment is explained.
(C) A video is shown.
(D) Maps are distributed.

78. What kind of gift do participants receive?

(A) A discount coupon
(B) A bag of snacks
(C) A T-shirt
(D) A postcard

79. What does the speaker warn the listeners about?

(A) How to pay for food
(B) What clothes to wear
(C) Where to park
(D) Which days to visit

80. Where does the speaker work?

(A) At an architecture firm
(B) At an accounting firm
(C) At a roofing company
(D) At an auto repair shop

81. Why does the speaker say, "an official estimate includes parts and labor"?

(A) To compare her company to another one
(B) To correct a colleague's mistake
(C) To complain about an expense
(D) To ask for help with a project

82. What does the speaker offer to do this afternoon?

(A) Visit the listener's home
(B) Update the listener's contact information
(C) Consult a financial advisor
(D) Post a job announcement

GO ON TO THE NEXT PAGE

83. What is the broadcast about?

(A) Financing your company
(B) Using social media
(C) Recruiting staff
(D) Getting a business license

84. What will the speaker help the listeners with today?

(A) Choosing a service
(B) Lowering costs
(C) Analyzing feedback
(D) Setting goals

85. What will most likely happen next?

(A) The speaker will conduct an interview.
(B) The speaker will give a weather update.
(C) An advertisement will play.
(D) A contest winner will be announced.

---

86. Who most likely are the listeners?

(A) Potential investors
(B) Marketing specialists
(C) Quality control inspectors
(D) Product designers

87. According to the speaker, what is the company going to change?

(A) The material it uses
(B) The financing it makes available
(C) The maintenance schedule for its equipment
(D) The publisher for its catalog

88. Why does the speaker say, "but I use these products"?

(A) To reject an offer
(B) To correct an advertisement
(C) To provide reassurance
(D) To explain a decision

---

89. Where is the talk taking place?

(A) At an awards ceremony
(B) At an exhibit opening
(C) At a club meeting
(D) At a national park tour

90. What did Kentaro Nakamura recently do?

(A) He published a book.
(B) He started a conservation society.
(C) He won a photography contest.
(D) He conducted a research project.

91. What are the listeners invited to do after the event?

(A) Enjoy some refreshments
(B) Sign up to volunteer
(C) Purchase some souvenirs
(D) Take some maps

---

92. What type of work do the listeners most likely do?

(A) Architectural planning
(B) Software design
(C) Therapy
(D) Sales

93. What does the speaker thank the listeners for?

(A) Finalizing a business contract
(B) Preparing a presentation
(C) Sharing some ideas
(D) Meeting with some clients

94. Why does the speaker say, "we have a limited number of computers available"?

(A) To warn the listeners about a maintenance issue
(B) To encourage the listeners to sign up quickly
(C) To suggest that the listeners buy a device
(D) To remind the listeners about budget cuts

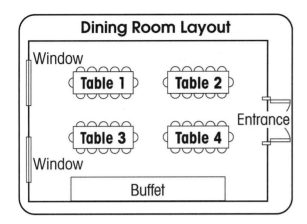

Dining Room Layout

Window

Table 1   Table 2

Entrance

Table 3   Table 4

Window

Buffet

AGENDA TOPICS

1. Interviewing

2. Training

3. Displaying merchandise

4. Tracking inventory

95. What will take place this Friday?

(A) An industry award ceremony
(B) A fund-raising dinner
(C) A company anniversary event
(D) A holiday celebration

96. Look at the graphic. Where does the speaker want some audio equipment?

(A) Next to table 1
(B) Next to table 2
(C) Next to table 3
(D) Next to table 4

97. What has the speaker shipped to the hotel?

(A) Some tablecloths
(B) Some vases
(C) Some aprons
(D) Some glasses

98. Who most likely are the listeners?

(A) Event planners
(B) Fashion designers
(C) Sales analysts
(D) Store managers

99. Look at the graphic. Which topic does the speaker start the workshop with?

(A) Topic 1
(B) Topic 2
(C) Topic 3
(D) Topic 4

100. What does the speaker say the listeners will do next?

(A) Introduce themselves
(B) Discuss some pictures
(C) Practice doing interviews
(D) Try out some software

This is the end of the Listening test.

토익® 정기시험
기출문제집

LC

기출 TEST

04

LISTENING TEST

In the Listening test, you will be asked to demonstrate how well you understand spoken English. The entire Listening test will last approximately 45 minutes. There are four parts, and directions are given for each part. You must mark your answers on the separate answer sheet. Do not write your answers in your test book.

PART 1

Directions: For each question in this part, you will hear four statements about a picture in your test book. When you hear the statements, you must select the one statement that best describes what you see in the picture. Then find the number of the question on your answer sheet and mark your answer. The statements will not be printed in your test book and will be spoken only one time.

Statement (C), "They're sitting at a table," is the best description of the picture, so you should select answer (C) and mark it on your answer sheet.

1.

2.

GO ON TO THE NEXT PAGE

3.

4.

5.

6.

GO ON TO THE NEXT PAGE ➤

PART 2

Directions: You will hear a question or statement and three responses spoken in English. They will not be printed in your test book and will be spoken only one time. Select the best response to the question or statement and mark the letter (A), (B), or (C) on your answer sheet.

7. Mark your answer on your answer sheet.

8. Mark your answer on your answer sheet.

9. Mark your answer on your answer sheet.

10. Mark your answer on your answer sheet.

11. Mark your answer on your answer sheet.

12. Mark your answer on your answer sheet.

13. Mark your answer on your answer sheet.

14. Mark your answer on your answer sheet.

15. Mark your answer on your answer sheet.

16. Mark your answer on your answer sheet.

17. Mark your answer on your answer sheet.

18. Mark your answer on your answer sheet.

19. Mark your answer on your answer sheet.

20. Mark your answer on your answer sheet.

21. Mark your answer on your answer sheet.

22. Mark your answer on your answer sheet.

23. Mark your answer on your answer sheet.

24. Mark your answer on your answer sheet.

25. Mark your answer on your answer sheet.

26. Mark your answer on your answer sheet.

27. Mark your answer on your answer sheet.

28. Mark your answer on your answer sheet.

29. Mark your answer on your answer sheet.

30. Mark your answer on your answer sheet.

31. Mark your answer on your answer sheet.

PART 3

Directions: You will hear some conversations between two or more people. You will be asked to answer three questions about what the speakers say in each conversation. Select the best response to each question and mark the letter (A), (B), (C), or (D) on your answer sheet. The conversations will not be printed in your test book and will be spoken only one time.

32. What is the woman preparing for?

(A) A holiday raffle
(B) A grand opening
(C) A retirement party
(D) A charity event

33. What does the man say he can do?

(A) Rush an order
(B) Apply a discount
(C) Include some free samples
(D) Set up a product display

34. What does the woman ask about?

(A) Payment methods
(B) Store hours
(C) Return policies
(D) Color options

35. What most likely is the woman's profession?

(A) Sound engineer
(B) Travel agent
(C) Actor
(D) Musician

36. Why is the man calling?

(A) To ask the woman for a favor
(B) To offer the woman a job
(C) To purchase some tickets
(D) To recommend a colleague

37. According to the woman, what might cause a problem?

(A) A billing error
(B) A schedule conflict
(C) A visa requirement
(D) A mechanical failure

38. What kind of event is taking place?

(A) A trade show
(B) A job fair
(C) A fund-raiser
(D) A grand opening

39. According to the man, what did a client request?

(A) Projection equipment
(B) Vegetarian meals
(C) Additional parking
(D) An earlier start time

40. What will Fatima do next?

(A) Locate some keys
(B) Process a payment
(C) Make a phone call
(D) Check some seating arrangements

41. Where is the conversation most likely taking place?

(A) At a vegetable farm
(B) At an electronics store
(C) At a motorcycle repair shop
(D) At a grocery store

42. What does the woman ask the man to do?

(A) Describe a phone
(B) Show a receipt
(C) Contact a manufacturer
(D) Speak to a mechanic

43. What information does the woman give the man?

(A) The price of an item
(B) The name of a supervisor
(C) The location of a product
(D) The size of an order

GO ON TO THE NEXT PAGE

44. What field do the speakers most likely work in?

(A) Accounting
(B) Engineering
(C) Education
(D) Agriculture

45. Why does the man say, "It won't take that long"?

(A) To request the woman's permission
(B) To convince the woman to meet
(C) To decline an invitation
(D) To express surprise about a decision

46. What does the woman say she will do after work?

(A) Pack for a business trip
(B) Go to a dental appointment
(C) Pick up a food order
(D) Attend a retirement party

47. According to the woman, what do the results of a survey indicate about a company?

(A) It should create an employee award.
(B) It should provide free transportation.
(C) Its employees are happy with a training program.
(D) Its employees are concerned about the environment.

48. What does the man say he did recently?

(A) He accepted a job offer.
(B) He read an article.
(C) He downloaded a schedule.
(D) He met a sales goal.

49. What does the woman suggest?

(A) Hiring a consultant
(B) Changing a venue
(C) Modifying a production process
(D) Recruiting volunteers

50. What type of event did the woman attend?

(A) A theater performance
(B) A grand opening
(C) A professional conference
(D) A retirement party

51. What does the woman imply when she says, "That'll be quite challenging"?

(A) She wants to apply for a new position.
(B) She does not think she can meet a deadline.
(C) She will need additional funding for a project.
(D) She admires a colleague's plan.

52. What does the woman say she will do now?

(A) Speak with her assistant
(B) Print out her résumé
(C) Order some food
(D) Make travel arrangements

53. Why is the man calling the Springfield Community Center?

(A) He is looking for a backpack.
(B) He is researching a historical place.
(C) He is asking about a meeting space.
(D) He is interested in joining a club.

54. What does the woman warn the man about?

(A) A busy time of the month
(B) An early store closing
(C) The cost of an event
(D) A missing document

55. What does the man ask about using?

(A) A library
(B) A message board
(C) A mobile phone
(D) A projector

56. Who most likely is the woman?

   (A) A cafeteria manager
   (B) A hotel receptionist
   (C) A laboratory technician
   (D) An interior designer

57. Why will the woman visit the man's business this afternoon?

   (A) To perform an inspection
   (B) To select a product
   (C) To learn a new skill
   (D) To interview for a job

58. What does the man recommend that the woman bring?

   (A) Some measurements
   (B) Some photographs
   (C) A handbook
   (D) A business card

59. Who most likely are the program participants?

   (A) Sales recruiters
   (B) Prospective clients
   (C) Building inspectors
   (D) Management trainees

60. What does the man ask about?

   (A) An office location
   (B) A budget amount
   (C) A length of time
   (D) A list of attendees

61. How should the participants communicate a request?

   (A) By making a phone call
   (B) By speaking with Ms. Park
   (C) By sending an e-mail
   (D) By filling out a form

Model	Capacity
Country	1
Classic	1-2
Premier	3-4
Deluxe	5

62. What kind of products does the woman's store sell?

   (A) Kitchen appliances
   (B) Sporting goods
   (C) Luggage
   (D) Bathroom furnishings

63. Look at the graphic. Which model will the man buy?

   (A) Country
   (B) Classic
   (C) Premier
   (D) Deluxe

64. What is the man concerned about?

   (A) A price
   (B) A warranty
   (C) The installation
   (D) The quality

GO ON TO THE NEXT PAGE

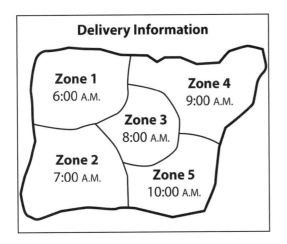

Delivery Information

Zone 1
6:00 A.M.

Zone 4
9:00 A.M.

Zone 3
8:00 A.M.

Zone 2
7:00 A.M.

Zone 5
10:00 A.M.

Doctor	Work Hours (Monday-Friday)
Dr. Fontana	8:00 A.M.–5:00 P.M.
Dr. Miller	10:00 A.M.–4:00 P.M.
Dr. Smith	10:00 A.M.–6:00 P.M.
Dr. Yang	8:00 A.M.–3:00 P.M.

65. What type of business is the woman calling?

(A) A catering company
(B) A laundry service
(C) A flower shop
(D) A furniture store

66. What does the man say his company is known for?

(A) Its prices
(B) Its locations
(C) Its reliability
(D) Its products

67. Look at the graphic. What time will the delivery be made?

(A) 6:00 A.M.
(B) 7:00 A.M.
(C) 8:00 A.M.
(D) 9:00 A.M.

68. Why does the man want to change an appointment?

(A) His car broke down.
(B) He has to attend a meeting.
(C) He has a family event.
(D) He has to wait for a delivery.

69. Look at the graphic. Who will the man see on Friday?

(A) Dr. Fontana
(B) Dr. Miller
(C) Dr. Smith
(D) Dr. Yang

70. What will the man most likely do next?

(A) Answer some questions
(B) Visit a Web site
(C) Make a payment
(D) Drive to an office

PART 4

Directions: You will hear some talks given by a single speaker. You will be asked to answer three questions about what the speaker says in each talk. Select the best response to each question and mark the letter (A), (B), (C), or (D) on your answer sheet. The talks will not be printed in your test book and will be spoken only one time.

71. Who are the listeners?

    (A) Residents in an apartment building
    (B) Employees in an office building
    (C) Visitors to a historical site
    (D) Guests in a hotel

72. What service does the speaker say will be unavailable?

    (A) Telephone
    (B) Electric
    (C) Water
    (D) Natural gas

73. According to the speaker, why should the listeners go online?

    (A) To download software
    (B) To check for status updates
    (C) To register a complaint
    (D) To view a price list

74. Where does the announcement most likely take place?

    (A) At a train station
    (B) At a convention center
    (C) At a restaurant
    (D) At an outdoor market

75. According to the speaker, what should customers be told?

    (A) The Wi-Fi is not working.
    (B) A room is closed for renovations.
    (C) A schedule has been changed.
    (D) An item is unavailable.

76. What does the speaker encourage the listeners to do?

    (A) Work together
    (B) Arrive early
    (C) Take extra shifts
    (D) Greet customers

77. Who most likely are the listeners?

    (A) Building contractors
    (B) Potential investors
    (C) Fashion models
    (D) News reporters

78. What type of clothing does the company sell?

    (A) Swimwear
    (B) Hats
    (C) Business suits
    (D) Athletic shoes

79. What does the speaker's company hope to purchase?

    (A) A new software program
    (B) A larger storage facility
    (C) Some delivery trucks
    (D) Some manufacturing equipment

80. What industry do the listeners most likely work in?

    (A) Construction
    (B) Retail
    (C) Energy
    (D) Broadcast

81. What does the speaker imply when he says, "But there is a lot of paperwork to fill out"?

    (A) The listeners may have to work overtime.
    (B) The listeners will not begin work immediately.
    (C) A permit will be difficult to obtain.
    (D) Additional help is needed for a project.

82. What will the speaker do next?

    (A) Take some photographs
    (B) Look at a model home
    (C) Collect some viewer feedback
    (D) Go to the cafeteria

GO ON TO THE NEXT PAGE

83. According to the speaker, what event will be held tonight?

(A) An anniversary party
(B) A press conference
(C) A board meeting
(D) A product launch

84. Why does the speaker say, "I'll be driving to Holtsville from the office"?

(A) To correct a mistake
(B) To provide an excuse
(C) To make an offer
(D) To request directions

85. What does the speaker say he needs to pick up?

(A) Some promotional materials
(B) Some refreshments
(C) Customer surveys
(D) Event programs

86. Which department does the speaker most likely work for?

(A) Product Development
(B) Research
(C) Engineering
(D) Information Technology

87. What does the speaker say recently happened?

(A) Some certification classes began.
(B) Name badges were handed out.
(C) A virus infected some computers.
(D) A manager retired.

88. What does the speaker ask the listeners to do?

(A) Sign an attendance sheet
(B) Open a software program
(C) Submit some photos
(D) View a slideshow

89. Where do the listeners most likely work?

(A) At a software development company
(B) At a book publishing company
(C) At a graphic design firm
(D) At a news Web site

90. What is the speaker concerned about?

(A) Addressing a customer complaint
(B) Keeping up with competitors
(C) Exceeding an annual budget
(D) Improving employee productivity

91. What does the speaker imply when he says, "we have technology interns starting next week"?

(A) A task must be finished soon.
(B) An assignment should be delayed.
(C) Volunteers are needed to greet interns.
(D) Interns can assist with a new project.

92. Where is the speaker?

(A) At a public library
(B) At a history museum
(C) At a community center
(D) At a sports arena

93. What will happen next week?

(A) A new exhibit will be set up.
(B) A fund-raiser will take place.
(C) A local election will be held.
(D) A construction project will begin.

94. What are visitors encouraged to do?

(A) Park on a side street
(B) Wear ear protection
(C) Donate money
(D) Take photographs

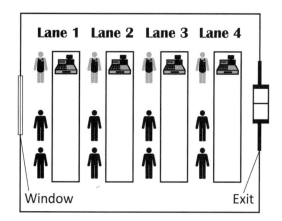

95. Where is the announcement being made?

(A) At a supermarket
(B) At a clothing store
(C) At an office supply store
(D) At a home garden center

96. Look at the graphic. Which lane is the express lane?

(A) Lane 1
(B) Lane 2
(C) Lane 3
(D) Lane 4

97. According to the speaker, what can the listeners receive assistance with?

(A) Checking a price
(B) Moving large items
(C) Getting a refund
(D) Locating some merchandise

98. Who most likely is the speaker?

(A) A musician
(B) An actor
(C) A writing instructor
(D) An art teacher

99. What are the listeners asked to do?

(A) Arrive early
(B) Help clean an area
(C) Silence mobile phones
(D) Provide feedback

100. Look at the graphic. On which date will there be a special guest?

(A) June 7
(B) June 9
(C) June 13
(D) June 15

This is the end of the Listening test.

토익® 정기시험
기출문제집

LC

기출 TEST

05

LISTENING TEST

In the Listening test, you will be asked to demonstrate how well you understand spoken English. The entire Listening test will last approximately 45 minutes. There are four parts, and directions are given for each part. You must mark your answers on the separate answer sheet. Do not write your answers in your test book.

PART 1

Directions: For each question in this part, you will hear four statements about a picture in your test book. When you hear the statements, you must select the one statement that best describes what you see in the picture. Then find the number of the question on your answer sheet and mark your answer. The statements will not be printed in your test book and will be spoken only one time.

Statement (C), "They're sitting at a table," is the best description of the picture, so you should select answer (C) and mark it on your answer sheet.

1.

2.

GO ON TO THE NEXT PAGE

3.

4.

5.

6.

GO ON TO THE NEXT PAGE ➤

PART 2

Directions: You will hear a question or statement and three responses spoken in English. They will not be printed in your test book and will be spoken only one time. Select the best response to the question or statement and mark the letter (A), (B), or (C) on your answer sheet.

7. Mark your answer on your answer sheet.

8. Mark your answer on your answer sheet.

9. Mark your answer on your answer sheet.

10. Mark your answer on your answer sheet.

11. Mark your answer on your answer sheet.

12. Mark your answer on your answer sheet.

13. Mark your answer on your answer sheet.

14. Mark your answer on your answer sheet.

15. Mark your answer on your answer sheet.

16. Mark your answer on your answer sheet.

17. Mark your answer on your answer sheet.

18. Mark your answer on your answer sheet.

19. Mark your answer on your answer sheet.

20. Mark your answer on your answer sheet.

21. Mark your answer on your answer sheet.

22. Mark your answer on your answer sheet.

23. Mark your answer on your answer sheet.

24. Mark your answer on your answer sheet.

25. Mark your answer on your answer sheet.

26. Mark your answer on your answer sheet.

27. Mark your answer on your answer sheet.

28. Mark your answer on your answer sheet.

29. Mark your answer on your answer sheet.

30. Mark your answer on your answer sheet.

31. Mark your answer on your answer sheet.

PART 3

Directions: You will hear some conversations between two or more people. You will be asked to answer three questions about what the speakers say in each conversation. Select the best response to each question and mark the letter (A), (B), (C), or (D) on your answer sheet. The conversations will not be printed in your test book and will be spoken only one time.

32. Who most likely is the man?
(A) A photographer
(B) A journalist
(C) A florist
(D) A caterer

33. What is the man concerned about?
(A) Contacting his assistant
(B) Locating a conference room
(C) Moving some equipment
(D) Printing a document

34. What does the woman give the man?
(A) Some keys
(B) A parking pass
(C) A mobile phone charger
(D) A cart

35. What will be constructed at an airport?
(A) A runway
(B) A parking area
(C) A storage facility
(D) A fueling station

36. What is the residents' biggest concern?
(A) Money
(B) Safety
(C) Noise
(D) Traffic

37. Why has a new meeting location been chosen?
(A) It is available on the weekend.
(B) It is closer to public transportation.
(C) It provides more space.
(D) It costs less to rent.

38. Who most likely is the woman?
(A) An event organizer
(B) A marketing consultant
(C) A department manager
(D) A travel agent

39. What did the man order for the woman?
(A) A computer tablet
(B) A credit card
(C) Some furniture
(D) Some office supplies

40. What does the man suggest the woman do?
(A) Save receipts
(B) Return a handbook
(C) E-mail a client
(D) Consult with a supervisor

41. What will the man do next week?
(A) Meet with some customers
(B) Attend a conference
(C) Go on vacation
(D) Move to another city

42. What does the man want the woman to recommend?
(A) City tours
(B) Transportation services
(C) Hotels
(D) Restaurants

43. What does the man say he will do next?
(A) Look up an address
(B) Check a bus route
(C) Pack some equipment
(D) Activate a credit card

GO ON TO THE NEXT PAGE

44. What does the woman want to discuss?

    (A) Job candidates
    (B) Vendor selections
    (C) Customer survey results
    (D) Computer system updates

45. Why does the man say, "The report's only half a page long"?

    (A) To confirm some details
    (B) To express disappointment
    (C) To ask for another assignment
    (D) To refuse an offer

46. What does the woman remind the man about?

    (A) Checking a social media account
    (B) Unpacking some equipment
    (C) Making a reservation
    (D) Going to a print shop

47. What city department does the man work in?

    (A) Parks and Recreation
    (B) Water Management
    (C) Transportation
    (D) Education

48. Why is the woman calling?

    (A) To report a fallen tree
    (B) To ask about city-job openings
    (C) To find out the cost of a project
    (D) To inquire about a tree planting program

49. What does the man tell the woman to do?

    (A) Review a policy
    (B) Make an appointment
    (C) Complete an online form
    (D) Contact a different office

50. What did the woman recently review?

    (A) A sales report
    (B) An assembly line
    (C) Some online brochures
    (D) Some assembly directions

51. What does the woman ask the man about?

    (A) Packaging additional shipments
    (B) Hiring temporary employees
    (C) Changing a deadline
    (D) Sending a press release

52. What information will the man provide this afternoon?

    (A) Overtime schedules
    (B) Design improvements
    (C) Production costs
    (D) Inventory status

53. What project are the speakers working on?

    (A) A news article
    (B) A training session
    (C) An advertising campaign
    (D) A research experiment

54. What problem does the man mention?

    (A) He has a scheduling conflict.
    (B) He missed a presentation.
    (C) Some data is unavailable.
    (D) There are errors in a report.

55. What will the man do next?

    (A) Make a phone call
    (B) Share some images
    (C) Change a password
    (D) Edit a document

56. Where does the conversation most likely take place?

(A) At a hotel
(B) At a flower farm
(C) At a clothing factory
(D) At a ferry station

57. What did the man have a problem with this morning?

(A) An identification badge
(B) A parking pass
(C) A time card
(D) A uniform

58. What will the speakers most likely do next?

(A) Fill out some forms
(B) Tour a facility
(C) Watch a video
(D) Practice a skill

59. What field do the speakers most likely work in?

(A) Education
(B) Finance
(C) Law
(D) Medicine

60. What does the woman mean when she says, "I've presented at that conference before"?

(A) She has a lot of professional experience.
(B) She dislikes giving presentations.
(C) She understands the man's situation.
(D) She has completed a requirement.

61. What do the speakers agree to do?

(A) Temporarily close an office
(B) Postpone hiring an employee
(C) Work on a presentation together
(D) Contact some clients

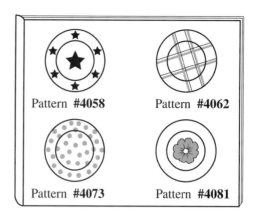

Pattern #4058   Pattern #4062

Pattern #4073   Pattern #4081

62. Look at the graphic. Which dish pattern is the man interested in?

(A) #4058
(B) #4062
(C) #4073
(D) #4081

63. According to the man, what will happen in May?

(A) A store will take inventory.
(B) A new restaurant will open.
(C) A product line will launch.
(D) A factory will move to a new location.

64. What problem does the woman mention?

(A) Some shipping fees will increase.
(B) Some items will become unavailable.
(C) Some items were damaged during shipping.
(D) Some catalogs contain inaccurate information.

GO ON TO THE NEXT PAGE

Ticket Confirmation Code: 0146H	
Number of Passengers	3
Date	June 22
Departure Time	11 A.M.
Price per Ticket	$14
Total Price	$42

Electronic Trackers	
Brand	**Battery Life**
Beep It	6 months
Filez	4 months
Loc Pro	2 years
XMarks	1 year

65. What type of business is the woman calling?

(A) A railway company
(B) A bus company
(C) An airline
(D) A ferry service

66. Look at the graphic. What number will be updated?

(A) 3
(B) 22
(C) 11
(D) 14

67. What will the man most likely do next?

(A) Collect some money
(B) Check a seat assignment
(C) Make an announcement
(D) Send an e-mail

68. What does the man ask the woman for?

(A) Some plastic ties
(B) Some computer cables
(C) An Internet password
(D) A storage room key

69. What is the man doing tomorrow?

(A) Inspecting a factory
(B) Upgrading a company database
(C) Leading a tour
(D) Going on a business trip

70. Look at the graphic. Which brand did the man buy?

(A) Beep It
(B) Filez
(C) Loc Pro
(D) XMarks

Directions: You will hear some talks given by a single speaker. You will be asked to answer three questions about what the speaker says in each talk. Select the best response to each question and mark the letter (A), (B), (C), or (D) on your answer sheet. The talks will not be printed in your test book and will be spoken only one time.

71. What is most likely being advertised?

(A) A convention center
(B) A restaurant
(C) A supermarket
(D) A shipping company

72. What is the business famous for?

(A) Its prices
(B) Its location
(C) Its history
(D) Its staff

73. What does the speaker say is on a Web site?

(A) Some catering options
(B) Some driving directions
(C) Current discounts
(D) Business hours

74. Who most likely are the listeners?

(A) Product developers
(B) Investment bankers
(C) Book publishers
(D) Building contractors

75. What does the speaker say is favorable about a contract?

(A) There is 24-hour service call availability.
(B) There is an extended warranty.
(C) There is an immediate payment.
(D) There is a low interest rate.

76. What does the speaker imply when he says, "I'll send you the document later"?

(A) He is having computer problems.
(B) He wants the listeners' opinions.
(C) He has missed a deadline.
(D) He is almost finished with some work.

77. Where is the tour taking place?

(A) At an art gallery
(B) At a construction site
(C) At a solar-panel factory
(D) At a car-part warehouse

78. What does the speaker remind the listeners to do?

(A) Wear protective hats
(B) Follow posted signs
(C) Stay together as a group
(D) Store personal belongings

79. What will the listeners see first on the tour?

(A) A map of the grounds
(B) An informational video
(C) Some product models
(D) Some historic photographs

80. What is the focus of the episode?

(A) Improving training programs
(B) Changing careers
(C) Designing Web sites
(D) Increasing sales

81. What does the speaker say is important?

(A) Complying with industry regulations
(B) Emphasizing transferable skills
(C) Offering promotional discounts
(D) Attending networking events

82. Who is So-Hee Chung?

(A) A company executive
(B) A government official
(C) A news reporter
(D) A financial analyst

GO ON TO THE NEXT PAGE

83. What is the message mainly about?

   (A) Scheduling auditions
   (B) Purchasing tickets
   (C) Designing a set
   (D) Revising a script

84. Why does the speaker say, "we have a large team"?

   (A) To make a complaint
   (B) To provide reassurance
   (C) To express surprise
   (D) To refuse an offer

85. Why is the speaker unable to meet tomorrow?

   (A) Her car needs repairs.
   (B) She is moving to a new apartment.
   (C) She is going hiking.
   (D) She is visiting family.

86. Who most likely are the listeners?

   (A) Board members
   (B) Government officials
   (C) Clients
   (D) Interns

87. What did the listeners receive?

   (A) An event ticket
   (B) An information packet
   (C) A project invoice
   (D) An annual report

88. According to the speaker, what will the listeners do in an hour?

   (A) Have lunch
   (B) Join a conference call
   (C) Get security badges
   (D) Take a building tour

89. What did the speaker do last month?

   (A) She relocated to another building.
   (B) She hired additional employees.
   (C) She organized a luncheon.
   (D) She attended a conference.

90. What do some customers have trouble locating?

   (A) Delivery schedules
   (B) Password requirements
   (C) Contact information
   (D) Account archives

91. What will the speaker do next?

   (A) Give a demonstration
   (B) Introduce a guest
   (C) Distribute some documents
   (D) Hand out some awards

92. Who is the speaker?

   (A) A real-estate developer
   (B) A city official
   (C) A history professor
   (D) A television reporter

93. What happened last year in Madison?

   (A) An international hotel convention was held.
   (B) A national sports event was hosted.
   (C) A documentary movie was filmed.
   (D) A historic landmark was named.

94. Why does the speaker say, "Those roads weren't designed for traffic"?

   (A) To make a complaint
   (B) To show surprise
   (C) To express concern
   (D) To offer an apology

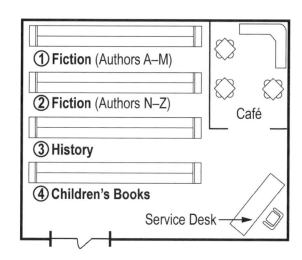

95. According to the speaker, what will happen this Friday?

(A) A delivery will arrive.
(B) A holiday sale will begin.
(C) An employee will retire.
(D) An author will visit.

96. Look at the graphic. Which aisle does the speaker direct the listeners to?

(A) Aisle 1
(B) Aisle 2
(C) Aisle 3
(D) Aisle 4

97. What can the listeners win?

(A) A gift card
(B) A book
(C) A free membership
(D) A calendar

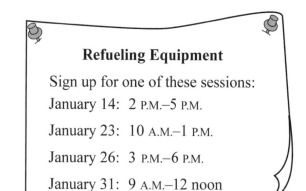

Refueling Equipment

Sign up for one of these sessions:

January 14: 2 P.M.–5 P.M.

January 23: 10 A.M.–1 P.M.

January 26: 3 P.M.–6 P.M.

January 31: 9 A.M.–12 noon

98. Where does the speaker most likely work?

(A) At a boat dock
(B) At an auto repair shop
(C) At a warehouse
(D) At a job training school

99. What will the speaker's department be doing at the end of the month?

(A) Fixing some equipment
(B) Attending a trade show
(C) Interviewing job candidates
(D) Preparing a large order

100. Look at the graphic. Which session does the man request to attend?

(A) January 14
(B) January 23
(C) January 26
(D) January 31

This is the end of the Listening test.

토익® 정기시험
기출문제집

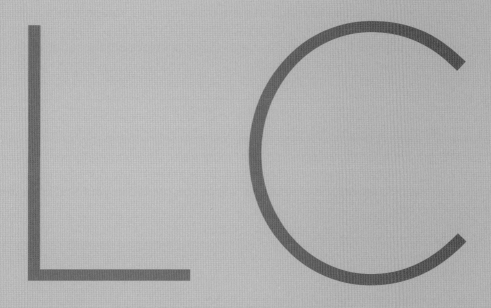

LC

기출 TEST

06

LISTENING TEST

In the Listening test, you will be asked to demonstrate how well you understand spoken English. The entire Listening test will last approximately 45 minutes. There are four parts, and directions are given for each part. You must mark your answers on the separate answer sheet. Do not write your answers in your test book.

PART 1

Directions: For each question in this part, you will hear four statements about a picture in your test book. When you hear the statements, you must select the one statement that best describes what you see in the picture. Then find the number of the question on your answer sheet and mark your answer. The statements will not be printed in your test book and will be spoken only one time.

Statement (C), "They're sitting at a table," is the best description of the picture, so you should select answer (C) and mark it on your answer sheet.

1.

2.

GO ON TO THE NEXT PAGE

3.

4.

5.

6.

Directions: You will hear a question or statement and three responses spoken in English. They will not be printed in your test book and will be spoken only one time. Select the best response to the question or statement and mark the letter (A), (B), or (C) on your answer sheet.

7. Mark your answer on your answer sheet.

8. Mark your answer on your answer sheet.

9. Mark your answer on your answer sheet.

10. Mark your answer on your answer sheet.

11. Mark your answer on your answer sheet.

12. Mark your answer on your answer sheet.

13. Mark your answer on your answer sheet.

14. Mark your answer on your answer sheet.

15. Mark your answer on your answer sheet.

16. Mark your answer on your answer sheet.

17. Mark your answer on your answer sheet.

18. Mark your answer on your answer sheet.

19. Mark your answer on your answer sheet.

20. Mark your answer on your answer sheet.

21. Mark your answer on your answer sheet.

22. Mark your answer on your answer sheet.

23. Mark your answer on your answer sheet.

24. Mark your answer on your answer sheet.

25. Mark your answer on your answer sheet.

26. Mark your answer on your answer sheet.

27. Mark your answer on your answer sheet.

28. Mark your answer on your answer sheet.

29. Mark your answer on your answer sheet.

30. Mark your answer on your answer sheet.

31. Mark your answer on your answer sheet.

PART 3

Directions: You will hear some conversations between two or more people. You will be asked to answer three questions about what the speakers say in each conversation. Select the best response to each question and mark the letter (A), (B), (C), or (D) on your answer sheet. The conversations will not be printed in your test book and will be spoken only one time.

32. What kind of business does the man own?

(A) A laundry service
(B) A cosmetics company
(C) A public relations firm
(D) A beverage manufacturer

33. What does the man want to know?

(A) Who to contact about a purchase
(B) Where to send some documents
(C) When a delivery will arrive
(D) How to use a product

34. What does the woman ask the man to provide?

(A) An order number
(B) A return mailing address
(C) A signed contract
(D) An online payment

35. Where most likely are the speakers?

(A) On a bus
(B) On a train
(C) On an airplane
(D) On a boat

36. What type of entertainment are the speakers discussing?

(A) Music
(B) Games
(C) Movies
(D) Books

37. What does the woman say is convenient?

(A) Being able to download an item
(B) Taking a direct route
(C) Having reclining seats
(D) Selecting meal options online

38. What industry does the woman most likely work in?

(A) Landscaping
(B) Health care
(C) Event planning
(D) Agriculture

39. What does the man say he is concerned about?

(A) Cost
(B) Variety
(C) Service dates
(D) Location

40. What will the speakers do next?

(A) Look at a slideshow
(B) Have a meal
(C) Discuss an estimate
(D) Go on a tour

41. What product are the speakers discussing?

(A) Cameras
(B) Fitness trackers
(C) Wireless speakers
(D) Mobile phones

42. What complaint did customers have about the product?

(A) It was unavailable in stores.
(B) The price was too high.
(C) The battery life was short.
(D) Some features were difficult to use.

43. What does the man suggest doing?

(A) Revising a budget
(B) Postponing a product launch
(C) Visiting a manufacturing plant
(D) Creating a good marketing campaign

GO ON TO THE NEXT PAGE

44. What is the topic of the conversation?

   (A) Recruiting staff
   (B) Marketing a product
   (C) Repairing a vehicle
   (D) Booking a tour

45. Where does the man say he used to work?

   (A) At a driving school
   (B) At an automobile factory
   (C) At a hotel
   (D) At an airport

46. Who will the speakers meet with next?

   (A) A real estate agent
   (B) A delivery person
   (C) Lawyers
   (D) Insurance agents

47. What problem does the woman have?

   (A) She lost her keys.
   (B) Her phone screen has cracked.
   (C) She injured her finger.
   (D) Her phone is malfunctioning.

48. What did the woman pay extra for?

   (A) An extended warranty
   (B) Twenty-four-hour assistance
   (C) Express service
   (D) A personalized design

49. What does the man suggest the woman do?

   (A) Fill out a refund request
   (B) Call another store
   (C) Look at some accessories
   (D) Change a pass code

50. Who is the man?

   (A) A software designer
   (B) A landscape architect
   (C) A factory supervisor
   (D) A furniture store clerk

51. What reason does the woman give for making a change?

   (A) The business hours would be more convenient.
   (B) The quality of materials would be better.
   (C) A discount is being offered.
   (D) Fewer workers would be needed.

52. What does the man ask the woman to do?

   (A) Visit a work site
   (B) Send a contract
   (C) Make a counteroffer
   (D) Request some samples

53. What are the speakers preparing for?

   (A) A client visit
   (B) An employee orientation
   (C) A trade show
   (D) A fund-raising event

54. What does the woman say she needs to do?

   (A) Send some instructions
   (B) Make a reservation
   (C) Order some badges
   (D) Write a speech

55. Why does the woman say, "The office supply store has a sale"?

   (A) To extend an invitation
   (B) To make a correction
   (C) To express satisfaction
   (D) To explain a decision

56. Which department do the speakers most likely work in?

(A) Human Resources
(B) Shipping
(C) Information Technology
(D) Sales

57. Why are the women surprised?

(A) An event was canceled.
(B) A coworker retired on short notice.
(C) Some business hours were changed.
(D) Some equipment arrived early.

58. What complaint does the man have about a previous training?

(A) It was not offered to all workers.
(B) It was not detailed enough.
(C) It did not include lunch.
(D) It was not held during work hours.

59. Why does the woman want to move out of her current apartment?

(A) It is far from her workplace.
(B) It is too small.
(C) It is in a noisy area.
(D) It is too expensive.

60. What does the man mean when he says, "I should be able to lease that unit pretty quickly"?

(A) A rental payment will likely be reduced.
(B) Investing in a property would be profitable.
(C) Some renovations will not take long.
(D) An apartment has a modern layout.

61. What will the woman most likely do next?

(A) Post an advertisement
(B) Complete a form
(C) Order some supplies
(D) Provide a reference

Book Title	Copies In Stock
Cooking with Kids	6
Delicious Dinners	9
Easy Meals at Home	7
Extraordinary Desserts	5

62. Why does the man ask the woman to work an extra shift?

(A) The store needs cleaning.
(B) A sale will happen soon.
(C) A shipment is arriving.
(D) A coworker has an injury.

63. Look at the graphic. Which book is needed for an upcoming event?

(A) *Cooking with Kids*
(B) *Delicious Dinners*
(C) *Easy Meals at Home*
(D) *Extraordinary Desserts*

64. Why does the man expect an event to be crowded?

(A) It is on a holiday weekend.
(B) It was advertised on television.
(C) An author is well-known.
(D) Free food will be served.

GO ON TO THE NEXT PAGE

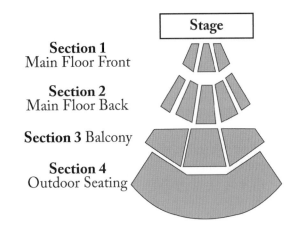

Section 1
Main Floor Front

Section 2
Main Floor Back

Section 3 Balcony

Section 4
Outdoor Seating

Stage

Natalia's Schedule			
	Monday	Tuesday	Wednesday
9–11 A.M.	Budget Meeting Room B	Team Meeting Room A	Contract Meeting Lawyer's office
1–3 P.M.	Training Meeting Room C	Client Meeting Video call	
3–5 P.M.			

65. What did the East Lake Band recently do?

(A) They won a music award.
(B) They went on a national tour.
(C) They released a new recording.
(D) They added a new member to the group.

66. Look at the graphic. Where do the speakers plan to sit?

(A) In Section 1
(B) In Section 2
(C) In Section 3
(D) In Section 4

67. What does the man offer to do?

(A) Pick up some tickets
(B) Provide transportation
(C) Bring some umbrellas
(D) Make a dinner reservation

68. What does the man plan to do during his meeting?

(A) Resolve a security issue
(B) Review a travel policy
(C) Conduct some job interviews
(D) Compare some software packages

69. Look at the graphic. Which one of the woman's meetings will be changed?

(A) Budget Meeting
(B) Training Meeting
(C) Team Meeting
(D) Contract Meeting

70. What does the woman say she would like to improve?

(A) Her technical knowledge
(B) Her organizational skills
(C) A training manual
(D) A presentation

PART 4

Directions: You will hear some talks given by a single speaker. You will be asked to answer three questions about what the speaker says in each talk. Select the best response to each question and mark the letter (A), (B), (C), or (D) on your answer sheet. The talks will not be printed in your test book and will be spoken only one time.

71. Why has the Movie Night event been rescheduled?

    (A) A projector is not available.
    (B) A nearby road is being repaired.
    (C) The space is double booked.
    (D) The event organizer is ill.

72. When will the event be held?

    (A) Tomorrow
    (B) This weekend
    (C) In two weeks
    (D) In one month

73. How can the listener request a refund?

    (A) By mailing a ticket
    (B) By visiting an office
    (C) By completing an online form
    (D) By making a phone call

74. Who most likely is the speaker?

    (A) A park ranger
    (B) A travel agent
    (C) A landscaper
    (D) A building inspector

75. What are the listeners asked to check for?

    (A) Expired identification cards
    (B) Local construction regulations
    (C) Hazardous outdoor conditions
    (D) Sudden price increases

76. What does the speaker distribute?

    (A) Maps
    (B) Uniforms
    (C) Visitor passes
    (D) Employee handbooks

77. Who is the speaker addressing?

    (A) Potential investors
    (B) Tourists
    (C) Staff members
    (D) Job applicants

78. Why does the speaker say, "This is only a trial period"?

    (A) To correct a colleague's statement
    (B) To apologize for a meeting conflict
    (C) To express surprise about a policy
    (D) To encourage the listeners to remain productive

79. What will the speaker do later?

    (A) Send a document
    (B) Make a phone call
    (C) Leave for a business trip
    (D) Introduce some managers

80. According to the speaker, what is causing traffic?

    (A) Some bad weather
    (B) Some construction projects
    (C) A sporting event
    (D) A city festival

81. Why should the listeners call the radio station?

    (A) To ask a question
    (B) To request a song
    (C) To win some tickets
    (D) To sign up as a volunteer

82. What does the speaker say will be broadcast later?

    (A) An interview
    (B) A political debate
    (C) A comedy show
    (D) A concert

GO ON TO THE NEXT PAGE

83. What is the talk mainly about?

(A) A business opening
(B) A company anniversary
(C) A new advertising service
(D) A renovation project

84. What does the speaker mean when she says, "several local business leaders will be here tonight"?

(A) Extra staff is needed.
(B) An event will be televised.
(C) A larger venue should be reserved.
(D) Employees should provide good service.

85. What does the speaker ask some of the listeners to do?

(A) Arrive early
(B) Check a schedule
(C) Hand out some surveys
(D) Consult a manager about problems

---

86. Why does the speaker say, "I couldn't find a later flight"?

(A) To refuse an invitation
(B) To apologize for an inconvenience
(C) To suggest canceling a trip
(D) To ask for help

87. Who most likely is Adriana Lopez?

(A) A repair technician
(B) An airline pilot
(C) An administrative assistant
(D) A city official

88. What does the speaker say the listener will receive?

(A) A client file
(B) A list of restaurants
(C) Some log-in credentials
(D) Some promotional materials

---

89. What is the topic of the seminar?

(A) Choosing an advertising strategy
(B) Finding investors
(C) Leading focus groups
(D) Creating a budget

90. What does the speaker recommend the listeners do first?

(A) Get employee input
(B) Hire a consultant
(C) Revise a plan
(D) Make a list

91. What will most likely happen next?

(A) A video will be shown.
(B) Information packets will be distributed.
(C) Some questions will be answered.
(D) There will be a lunch break.

---

92. What is the purpose of the meeting?

(A) To celebrate a recent contract
(B) To explain a new sales strategy
(C) To introduce a new employee
(D) To address employee concerns

93. What is causing a delay?

(A) A computer is being set up.
(B) A microphone stopped working.
(C) Some additional chairs are needed.
(D) The speaker misplaced some notes.

94. What are the listeners encouraged to sign up for?

(A) A staff feedback session
(B) A conference presentation
(C) A health initiative
(D) A mentoring program

Southern Barbecue Restaurant
Coupon

Groups 3–5	10% off
Groups 5–9	15% off
Groups 10–15	20% off
Groups 16–20	25% off

95. What type of event will take place on Friday?

(A) A retirement party
(B) A graduation celebration
(C) A cooking competition
(D) An award ceremony

96. Look at the graphic. Which discount will be applied?

(A) 10%
(B) 15%
(C) 20%
(D) 25%

97. What does the speaker ask the listener?

(A) Who will decorate a space
(B) What type of gift will be purchased
(C) If an event should be rescheduled
(D) If an order has been placed

Agenda	
Speaker	**Topic**
William Schmidt	Staff performance review
Paul Cohen	Corporate giving campaign
Jung-Soo Park	Public relations program
Santiago Reyes	IT transformation initiative

98. Look at the graphic. Who most likely is the speaker?

(A) William Schmidt
(B) Paul Cohen
(C) Jung-Soo Park
(D) Santiago Reyes

99. According to the speaker, what is different about a program this year?

(A) A list of organizations is longer.
(B) A deadline has been extended.
(C) More employees are assigned to help.
(D) An operating budget has been increased.

100. What will the speaker make available to the listeners?

(A) A research report
(B) A training video
(C) A magazine article
(D) A corporate calendar

TEST 6

This is the end of the Listening test.

토익® 정기시험
기출문제집

LC

기출 TEST

07

LISTENING TEST

In the Listening test, you will be asked to demonstrate how well you understand spoken English. The entire Listening test will last approximately 45 minutes. There are four parts, and directions are given for each part. You must mark your answers on the separate answer sheet. Do not write your answers in your test book.

PART 1

Directions: For each question in this part, you will hear four statements about a picture in your test book. When you hear the statements, you must select the one statement that best describes what you see in the picture. Then find the number of the question on your answer sheet and mark your answer. The statements will not be printed in your test book and will be spoken only one time.

Statement (C), "They're sitting at a table," is the best description of the picture, so you should select answer (C) and mark it on your answer sheet.

1.

2.

GO ON TO THE NEXT PAGE

TEST 7

3.

4.

5.

6.

GO ON TO THE NEXT PAGE

PART 2

Directions: You will hear a question or statement and three responses spoken in English. They will not be printed in your test book and will be spoken only one time. Select the best response to the question or statement and mark the letter (A), (B), or (C) on your answer sheet.

7. Mark your answer on your answer sheet.

8. Mark your answer on your answer sheet.

9. Mark your answer on your answer sheet.

10. Mark your answer on your answer sheet.

11. Mark your answer on your answer sheet.

12. Mark your answer on your answer sheet.

13. Mark your answer on your answer sheet.

14. Mark your answer on your answer sheet.

15. Mark your answer on your answer sheet.

16. Mark your answer on your answer sheet.

17. Mark your answer on your answer sheet.

18. Mark your answer on your answer sheet.

19. Mark your answer on your answer sheet.

20. Mark your answer on your answer sheet.

21. Mark your answer on your answer sheet.

22. Mark your answer on your answer sheet.

23. Mark your answer on your answer sheet.

24. Mark your answer on your answer sheet.

25. Mark your answer on your answer sheet.

26. Mark your answer on your answer sheet.

27. Mark your answer on your answer sheet.

28. Mark your answer on your answer sheet.

29. Mark your answer on your answer sheet.

30. Mark your answer on your answer sheet.

31. Mark your answer on your answer sheet.

PART 3

Directions: You will hear some conversations between two or more people. You will be asked to answer three questions about what the speakers say in each conversation. Select the best response to each question and mark the letter (A), (B), (C), or (D) on your answer sheet. The conversations will not be printed in your test book and will be spoken only one time.

32. Where most likely are the speakers?

(A) At a fitness center
(B) At a doctor's office
(C) At a pharmacy
(D) At a bank

33. What did the woman do in advance?

(A) She checked some business hours.
(B) She made a list of questions.
(C) She paid for a service online.
(D) She completed some forms.

34. What does the woman say she will do?

(A) Get her coat
(B) Return to a parking garage
(C) Look through a magazine
(D) Connect to the Internet

35. Where most likely are the speakers?

(A) At a farm
(B) At a restaurant
(C) At a grocery store
(D) At a catering company

36. What does the woman say will happen soon?

(A) Some friends will join her.
(B) She will apply for a job.
(C) She will pay her bill.
(D) An anniversary will be celebrated.

37. What does the man imply when he says, "They're selling quickly"?

(A) An item may be unavailable soon.
(B) An item is not expensive.
(C) A delivery should be made immediately.
(D) Some help will be needed.

38. Where does the man most likely work?

(A) At a ferry terminal
(B) At a bus depot
(C) At an airport
(D) At a train station

39. What problem does the woman have?

(A) Her colleague is late.
(B) Her suitcase is broken.
(C) A security line is long.
(D) She lost her ticket.

40. What will the man borrow from one of his coworkers?

(A) A pen
(B) A key
(C) A jacket
(D) A mobile phone

41. Where do the women work?

(A) At a construction company
(B) At an automotive factory
(C) At a chemical plant
(D) At an interior design firm

42. What is the man's job?

(A) Warehouse manager
(B) Computer engineer
(C) Sales representative
(D) Building inspector

43. What does Insook plan to do in the afternoon?

(A) Finalize a contract
(B) Watch a demonstration
(C) Visit a property
(D) Meet with potential investors

GO ON TO THE NEXT PAGE

44. Why is the man calling?

   (A) To hire a moving truck
   (B) To schedule a job interview
   (C) To make a payment
   (D) To ask about renting an apartment

45. What does the woman suggest the man do soon?

   (A) Create an online account
   (B) Schedule an appointment
   (C) Take some measurements
   (D) Review a contract

46. What does the man say he will do?

   (A) Call back next week
   (B) Write a report
   (C) Use another agency
   (D) Contact some references

47. Why was the man late to work?

   (A) He was stuck in traffic.
   (B) He missed a train.
   (C) He had a doctor's appointment.
   (D) He woke up late.

48. What is scheduled to be delivered today?

   (A) Company uniforms
   (B) Desktop computers
   (C) Cleaning supplies
   (D) Informational brochures

49. What business will the man call?

   (A) A plumbing service
   (B) A catering company
   (C) An automotive repair company
   (D) An electronics recycling center

50. Who most likely is the woman?

   (A) A client
   (B) A supervisor
   (C) An intern
   (D) A vendor

51. What is a benefit of a new material?

   (A) It is strong.
   (B) It is lightweight.
   (C) It is warm.
   (D) It is soft.

52. What will the speakers do next?

   (A) Contact a colleague
   (B) Plan a celebration
   (C) Look at some samples
   (D) Review a document

53. What type of event are the speakers discussing?

   (A) A holiday party
   (B) A conference
   (C) A grand opening
   (D) A job fair

54. What does the woman say attendees will receive?

   (A) A discounted rate
   (B) A raffle ticket
   (C) Free transportation
   (D) A city map

55. What do the speakers need to do soon?

   (A) Write a short speech
   (B) Submit a budget report
   (C) Notify some employees
   (D) Sign a contract

56. Who most likely is the man?

(A) An advertising executive
(B) A factory manager
(C) A customer service representative
(D) A product designer

57. What does the woman imply when she says, "Our clients are interested in environmentally friendly products"?

(A) She is frustrated with her clients.
(B) She is surprised by some feedback.
(C) She approves of the man's idea.
(D) She thinks the man is unfamiliar with a topic.

58. What does the man say will take place on Friday?

(A) An awards ceremony
(B) A managers' meeting
(C) A safety inspection
(D) A training class

---

59. Who is the man?

(A) An art gallery owner
(B) A store manager
(C) A hair stylist
(D) A real estate agent

60. What does the woman say happened last week?

(A) She visited some relatives.
(B) She received a raise.
(C) She gave a presentation.
(D) She purchased a building.

61. What does the man recommend doing?

(A) Postponing a project
(B) Using a mobile phone application
(C) Creating some promotional flyers
(D) Ordering some name tags

Inbox: ✉ 📄 ! 📎		
From	**Subject**	**Received**
Claudine Li	Nature documentary	12:45 P.M.
Elise Choi	Riverton promotional video	1:10 P.M.
Anya Lundly	Training schedule	2:25 P.M.
Madoka Ito	Location suggestions	3:50 P.M.

62. What problem are the speakers mainly discussing?

(A) An event venue is unavailable.
(B) A project deadline has passed.
(C) A document contains spelling errors.
(D) A video file is not working.

63. Look at the graphic. Whose e-mail does the woman mention?

(A) Claudine Li's
(B) Elise Choi's
(C) Anya Lundly's
(D) Madoka Ito's

64. What event will happen this weekend?

(A) A local election
(B) A corporate fund-raiser
(C) A city festival
(D) A sports competition

GO ON TO THE NEXT PAGE

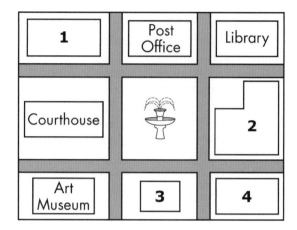

65. What does the man say the store has recently done?

(A) Replaced some equipment
(B) Updated a company logo
(C) Installed a security system
(D) Painted some shelving units

66. Look at the graphic. Which item will the store order?

(A) Item 231
(B) Item 498
(C) Item 540
(D) Item 762

67. What does the man say he will do next?

(A) Print a receipt
(B) Stock some shelves
(C) Finalize a schedule
(D) Find a credit card

68. Who most likely are the speakers?

(A) Lawyers
(B) Bakers
(C) Accountants
(D) Doctors

69. Look at the graphic. Which building does the man say he likes?

(A) Building 1
(B) Building 2
(C) Building 3
(D) Building 4

70. What does the woman ask the man to do?

(A) E-mail a real estate agent
(B) Make a lunch reservation
(C) Contact some colleagues
(D) Upload some photographs

PART 4

Directions: You will hear some talks given by a single speaker. You will be asked to answer three questions about what the speaker says in each talk. Select the best response to each question and mark the letter (A), (B), (C), or (D) on your answer sheet. The talks will not be printed in your test book and will be spoken only one time.

71. Why is the speaker calling?
    (A) To explain a schedule change
    (B) To discuss an upcoming conference
    (C) To request approval for an expense
    (D) To confirm an e-mail address

72. What does the speaker say about a job candidate?
    (A) He requires additional training.
    (B) He has good references.
    (C) He speaks several languages.
    (D) He does not live in the area.

73. What did the speaker send in an e-mail?
    (A) A résumé
    (B) A cost estimate
    (C) A meeting agenda
    (D) A tour itinerary

74. Where are the listeners?
    (A) In an airport
    (B) On a train
    (C) At a theater
    (D) On a ferry

75. What are the listeners with e-tickets asked to do?
    (A) Check their seat numbers
    (B) Increase their screen's brightness
    (C) Come to the front of the line
    (D) Download a mobile application

76. Why does the speaker say, "you shouldn't leave any belongings on the seat next to you"?
    (A) To ask the listeners to clear space
    (B) To remind the listeners about forgotten items
    (C) To explain safety regulations
    (D) To clarify the checked baggage policy

77. Why is the speaker calling?
    (A) To reschedule an inspection
    (B) To request a demonstration
    (C) To book a vacation package
    (D) To change an order

78. What has the speaker's company recently done?
    (A) It changed its hours of operation.
    (B) It hired additional staff.
    (C) It moved to a new location.
    (D) It started a health program.

79. What does the speaker encourage the listener to do?
    (A) Display some products
    (B) Offer some coupons
    (C) Create a handbook
    (D) Expedite a delivery

80. Where do the listeners most likely work?
    (A) At a health food store
    (B) At a restaurant
    (C) At a spice factory
    (D) At a vegetable farm

81. What are the listeners preparing for today?
    (A) A seasonal sale
    (B) A cooking class
    (C) A baking contest
    (D) A grand opening

82. Who is Ingrid Vogel?
    (A) A newspaper journalist
    (B) A health inspector
    (C) A famous chef
    (D) An interior decorator

GO ON TO THE NEXT PAGE

83. Where is the tour taking place?

    (A) At an art museum
    (B) At a pottery workshop
    (C) At a clothing design studio
    (D) At a glass factory

84. Why does the speaker say, "we ship to customers all over the world"?

    (A) To reassure the listeners about a service
    (B) To explain why a storage area is large
    (C) To emphasize the popularity of some products
    (D) To make a suggestion for a gift

85. What does the speaker say is available to the listeners?

    (A) An event calendar
    (B) A discount on a purchase
    (C) A subscription to a newsletter
    (D) Entry in a prize drawing

86. What is the purpose of the speaker's organization?

    (A) To advise businesses about mergers
    (B) To arrange travel for executives
    (C) To share resources with new business owners
    (D) To recruit volunteers for a research study

87. What did the listeners do on March 15 ?

    (A) They signed some documents.
    (B) They purchased some materials.
    (C) They downloaded some software.
    (D) They wrote some proposals.

88. What will the listeners do in a few minutes?

    (A) Congratulate a colleague
    (B) Vote on a policy change
    (C) Create an advertisement
    (D) Meet with mentors

89. What does the speaker say is a top priority?

    (A) Increasing product sales
    (B) Keeping quality employees
    (C) Improving worker efficiency
    (D) Lowering manufacturing costs

90. Who is Helen Liu?

    (A) A company spokesperson
    (B) A human resources consultant
    (C) A digital marketing expert
    (D) A course instructor

91. Why does the speaker say, "this affects all of us"?

    (A) To encourage participation
    (B) To congratulate a team
    (C) To discourage future errors
    (D) To apologize for a delay

92. What is the purpose of the talk?

    (A) To demonstrate a work process
    (B) To choose a job applicant
    (C) To present a marketing plan
    (D) To review some sales reports

93. What does the speaker say about the company's current customers?

    (A) They are unhappy with a service.
    (B) They live mainly in cities.
    (C) Many of them work in technology.
    (D) Many of them are young.

94. What feature of Soft-Palm 51 does the speaker emphasize?

    (A) It is easy to carry.
    (B) It is less expensive than expected.
    (C) It is energy efficient.
    (D) It is faster than previous models.

Monday	Tuesday	Wednesday	Thursday

Fall Lecture Series	
Date	**Name**
September 19	Jung-Hoon Kim
October 17	Mei Na Zhang
November 14	Maryam Alaoui
December 15	Isamu Nakamura

95. What is causing a delay?

   (A) A holiday parade
   (B) A broken traffic light
   (C) An icy road
   (D) A fallen tree

96. What does the speaker advise the listeners to do?

   (A) Take an alternate route home
   (B) Take public transportation
   (C) Drive carefully
   (D) Postpone travel

97. Look at the graphic. When will a sporting event take place?

   (A) On Monday
   (B) On Tuesday
   (C) On Wednesday
   (D) On Thursday

98. Who most likely are the listeners?

   (A) Librarians
   (B) Engineers
   (C) Politicians
   (D) Biologists

99. Look at the graphic. Which lecturer is the speaker excited to hear?

   (A) Jung-Hoon Kim
   (B) Mei Na Zhang
   (C) Maryam Alaoui
   (D) Isamu Nakamura

100. What will the listeners most likely do next?

   (A) Vote for a board member
   (B) Share a meal
   (C) Participate in a workshop
   (D) Pay membership fees

This is the end of the Listening test.

토익®정기시험
기출문제집

LC

ETS TEST

08

LISTENING TEST

In the Listening test, you will be asked to demonstrate how well you understand spoken English. The entire Listening test will last approximately 45 minutes. There are four parts, and directions are given for each part. You must mark your answers on the separate answer sheet. Do not write your answers in your test book.

PART 1

Directions: For each question in this part, you will hear four statements about a picture in your test book. When you hear the statements, you must select the one statement that best describes what you see in the picture. Then find the number of the question on your answer sheet and mark your answer. The statements will not be printed in your test book and will be spoken only one time.

Statement (C), "They're sitting at a table," is the best description of the picture, so you should select answer (C) and mark it on your answer sheet.

1.

2.

GO ON TO THE NEXT PAGE

TEST 8

3.

4.

5.

6.

GO ON TO THE NEXT PAGE

PART 2

Directions: You will hear a question or statement and three responses spoken in English. They will not be printed in your test book and will be spoken only one time. Select the best response to the question or statement and mark the letter (A), (B), or (C) on your answer sheet.

7. Mark your answer on your answer sheet.

8. Mark your answer on your answer sheet.

9. Mark your answer on your answer sheet.

10. Mark your answer on your answer sheet.

11. Mark your answer on your answer sheet.

12. Mark your answer on your answer sheet.

13. Mark your answer on your answer sheet.

14. Mark your answer on your answer sheet.

15. Mark your answer on your answer sheet.

16. Mark your answer on your answer sheet.

17. Mark your answer on your answer sheet.

18. Mark your answer on your answer sheet.

19. Mark your answer on your answer sheet.

20. Mark your answer on your answer sheet.

21. Mark your answer on your answer sheet.

22. Mark your answer on your answer sheet.

23. Mark your answer on your answer sheet.

24. Mark your answer on your answer sheet.

25. Mark your answer on your answer sheet.

26. Mark your answer on your answer sheet.

27. Mark your answer on your answer sheet.

28. Mark your answer on your answer sheet.

29. Mark your answer on your answer sheet.

30. Mark your answer on your answer sheet.

31. Mark your answer on your answer sheet.

PART 3

Directions: You will hear some conversations between two or more people. You will be asked to answer three questions about what the speakers say in each conversation. Select the best response to each question and mark the letter (A), (B), (C), or (D) on your answer sheet. The conversations will not be printed in your test book and will be spoken only one time.

32. Where are the speakers?
    (A) At a museum
    (B) At a public library
    (C) At an art supply shop
    (D) At a botanical garden

33. What type of pass does the woman qualify for?
    (A) Student
    (B) Local resident
    (C) Senior citizen
    (D) Tour group

34. What will the man check?
    (A) A ticket
    (B) A receipt
    (C) An event schedule
    (D) An identification card

35. What type of business does the woman work for?
    (A) A construction company
    (B) A real estate agency
    (C) A law firm
    (D) A medical office

36. What does the man ask the woman to do?
    (A) Reschedule an appointment
    (B) Forward a telephone call
    (C) Send an invoice
    (D) Provide a refund

37. What does the woman say a business has recently done?
    (A) It has updated a payment system.
    (B) It has purchased new equipment.
    (C) It has renovated a room.
    (D) It has hired temporary staff.

38. Why is a street blocked off?
    (A) A tree is being removed.
    (B) A car is being towed.
    (C) Some charging stations are being installed.
    (D) Some holes are being filled.

39. What most likely is the woman's profession?
    (A) Auto mechanic
    (B) Musician
    (C) Park ranger
    (D) Teacher

40. What does the man suggest the woman do?
    (A) Purchase an electric car
    (B) File a complaint
    (C) Postpone a meeting
    (D) Drive to another location

41. Where do the speakers work?
    (A) At a grocery store
    (B) At a cooking school
    (C) At a restaurant
    (D) At a food-processing plant

42. What does the woman ask the man to do?
    (A) Make some deliveries
    (B) Open a cash register
    (C) Label some products
    (D) Clean some machinery

43. What does the woman imply when she says, "we open at seven"?
    (A) The man must work quickly.
    (B) The man should take a break.
    (C) The man unlocked the doors too early.
    (D) The man is mistaken about a schedule.

GO ON TO THE NEXT PAGE

44. Who most likely is the woman?

(A) A graphic designer
(B) A sales person
(C) An auto mechanic
(D) A human resources executive

45. Why is the woman worried she might not be offered a job?

(A) She missed an application deadline.
(B) She has limited experience.
(C) She is competing with other qualified candidates.
(D) She did not perform well in a telephone interview.

46. What does the woman say she will do on Thursday?

(A) Call a recruiter
(B) Tour a factory
(C) Sign a contract
(D) Update a résumé

47. Where does the conversation take place?

(A) At a bookshop
(B) At a supermarket
(C) At a furniture store
(D) At a craft store

48. What is the purpose of the man's visit?

(A) To have an item appraised
(B) To film a commercial
(C) To deliver some supplies
(D) To conduct some repairs

49. According to Margaret, what can be found by the entrance?

(A) A shopping basket
(B) A brochure
(C) A light switch
(D) A plastic cover

50. Where does the man most likely work?

(A) At a hotel
(B) At a post office
(C) At a travel agency
(D) At an office supply store

51. Why was the woman unavailable for two weeks?

(A) She was on vacation.
(B) She was moving to a new location.
(C) She was traveling for business.
(D) She was without phone service.

52. What does the man recommend doing?

(A) Filing a complaint
(B) Visiting another location
(C) Making reservations online
(D) Downloading a mobile application

53. According to the speakers, what has recently been completed?

(A) A map
(B) A brochure
(C) A hiking trail
(D) A memorial statue

54. What do the women suggest doing?

(A) Expanding parking areas
(B) Organizing an art festival
(C) Changing a bus route
(D) Offering walking tours

55. Why will Priyanka post a public notice?

(A) To identify ticket sale locations
(B) To encourage people to vote
(C) To request volunteers
(D) To announce some winners

56. Where do the speakers most likely work?

(A) At a cosmetics company
(B) At a home appliance outlet
(C) At an art supply store
(D) At a textile factory

57. What does the man say about some new machinery?

(A) It requires very little maintenance.
(B) It is easy to learn how to use.
(C) It has made a process faster.
(D) It has not been installed yet.

58. What does the woman ask the man to prepare?

(A) A price list
(B) A meeting invitation
(C) A handbook
(D) A report

59. Why did the man miss a conference?

(A) His plane was delayed.
(B) He was busy with a project.
(C) He was not feeling well.
(D) He missed a registration deadline.

60. What does the man recommend the woman do?

(A) Edit a press release
(B) Consult with a coworker
(C) Hire a marketing expert
(D) Review a departmental budget

61. What does the woman mean when she says, "I ran out of handouts"?

(A) She was unprepared for a presentation.
(B) A coworker made an error.
(C) A presentation was well attended.
(D) Some information can only be found online.

Destination	Platform	Departure time
Shanghai	3	8:28
Hong Kong	9	8:47
Beijing	12	9:15
Guangzhou	17	9:24

62. What will the speakers ask about?

(A) A refund
(B) A seat change
(C) Food options
(D) Internet access

63. What do the speakers want to prepare for?

(A) An employee interview
(B) A meeting with potential clients
(C) An annual safety inspection
(D) A product-testing session

64. Look at the graphic. What platform will speakers go to?

(A) Platform 3
(B) Platform 9
(C) Platform 12
(D) Platform 17

GO ON TO THE NEXT PAGE

Property Map

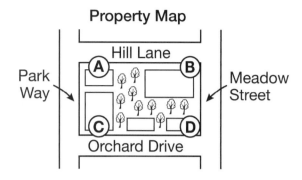

Hill Lane

Park Way

Meadow Street

Orchard Drive

Subscription Options and Monthly Rates

Option 1: Print and online access	$14
Option 2: Online access only	$9
Option 3: Weekend delivery (print only)	$8
Option 4: Student rate (online only)	$5

65. Who most likely are the speakers?

(A) Landscapers
(B) Photographers
(C) Architects
(D) Real estate agents

66. What will the man do after he leaves?

(A) Have a vehicle repaired
(B) E-mail a contract
(C) Return some equipment
(D) Go to a bank

67. Look at the graphic. Where will the woman put up a sign?

(A) At location A
(B) At location B
(C) At location C
(D) At location D

68. Who recommended that the woman subscribe to the *Portsville Times*?

(A) A professor
(B) A friend
(C) A colleague
(D) A relative

69. Look at the graphic. Which subscription option does the man recommend?

(A) Option 1
(B) Option 2
(C) Option 3
(D) Option 4

70. What will the man most likely do next?

(A) Confirm an address
(B) Choose a password
(C) Provide a discount code
(D) Process a payment

PART 4

Directions: You will hear some talks given by a single speaker. You will be asked to answer three questions about what the speaker says in each talk. Select the best response to each question and mark the letter (A), (B), (C), or (D) on your answer sheet. The talks will not be printed in your test book and will be spoken only one time.

71. Where does the speaker work?

    (A) At a roofing company
    (B) At a catering company
    (C) At a community park headquarters
    (D) At an interior-design firm

72. What information was incorrect?

    (A) An order number
    (B) A file name
    (C) An address
    (D) A price

73. Why does the speaker recommend placing an order soon?

    (A) A material is in high demand.
    (B) The rainy season is coming.
    (C) Some new fees will be introduced.
    (D) A permit is about to expire.

74. Who are the listeners?

    (A) Artists
    (B) Journalists
    (C) Real estate agents
    (D) Sales representatives

75. What does the speaker say the listeners should learn to do?

    (A) Manage their time
    (B) Negotiate prices
    (C) Give memorable presentations
    (D) Create effective advertisements

76. What does the speaker mention about Insook Lee?

    (A) She has won an award.
    (B) She is on a lecture tour.
    (C) She hosts a popular podcast.
    (D) She recently started a company.

77. What happened last January?

    (A) There was an election.
    (B) There was a snowstorm.
    (C) A shopping mall opened.
    (D) A bridge was closed.

78. Why have some citizens complained?

    (A) A toll has increased.
    (B) Traffic lights are badly timed.
    (C) There is not enough parking.
    (D) The roads are in poor condition.

79. Who has been invited to attend a city council meeting?

    (A) Engineers
    (B) Educators
    (C) Finance experts
    (D) Business owners

80. What is the purpose of an equipment update?

    (A) To promote healthy lifestyles
    (B) To protect consumer privacy
    (C) To comply with safety standards
    (D) To increase energy efficiency

81. What are the listeners warned about?

    (A) Price increases
    (B) Service interruptions
    (C) Loud noises
    (D) Increased traffic

82. What are some listeners encouraged to do?

    (A) Sign up early for a service
    (B) Use a community space
    (C) Attend an information session
    (D) Take public transportation

GO ON TO THE NEXT PAGE

83. Who is the speaker?

(A) A sports coach
(B) A computer programmer
(C) A company executive
(D) A sales representative

84. What is the speaker mainly discussing?

(A) An upcoming retirement
(B) A corporate fund-raiser
(C) An innovative product
(D) An annual dinner

85. Why does the speaker say, "There are a lot of talented people in this group"?

(A) To question a management policy
(B) To suggest a group size be decreased
(C) To reassure the listeners about a decision
(D) To express appreciation for an award

86. Who is the man most likely calling?

(A) A police officer
(B) A customer
(C) A mechanic
(D) A supervisor

87. What will take place tomorrow?

(A) A store sale
(B) A road closure
(C) A farmers market
(D) A musical performance

88. What does the speaker mean when he says, "there are three cars parked there now"?

(A) An event is not popular.
(B) A task cannot be completed.
(C) A parking fee has been paid.
(D) A delivery will be delayed.

89. What change does the speaker announce?

(A) Departments will be reorganized.
(B) New technicians will be hired.
(C) An additional warehouse will open.
(D) An automated system will be used.

90. Who most likely are the listeners?

(A) Accountants
(B) Warehouse stockers
(C) Human resources managers
(D) Customer service representatives

91. What does the speaker ask the listeners to do?

(A) Update service numbers
(B) Submit salary requirements
(C) Keep a record of complaints
(D) Post some shipping schedules

92. What is the speaker promoting?

(A) Audio equipment
(B) Cleaning tools
(C) A security device
(D) A software program

93. What industry do the listeners most likely work in?

(A) Transportation
(B) Manufacturing
(C) Banking
(D) Health care

94. What does the speaker mean when he says, "the manual's just fifteen pages long"?

(A) The listeners should read the manual now.
(B) A manual would be inexpensive to print.
(C) A product is not ready to be released.
(D) A product is easy to use.

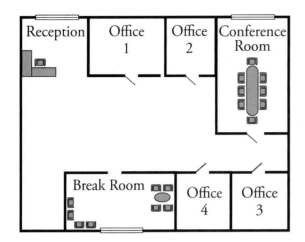

Item	Quantity
Safety Goggles	20 pairs
Cloth Rags	12 boxes
Adjustable Stools	8
Hard Hats	15

95. What is the speaker's company planning to purchase?

(A) A 3-D printer
(B) A large-screen television
(C) Some new laptops
(D) Some adjustable desks

96. Why has the company decided to make the purchase?

(A) More employees were hired.
(B) A vendor increased its prices.
(C) A store went out of business.
(D) Some software was out-of-date.

97. Look at the graphic. Where will Jerome move to?

(A) Office 1
(B) Office 2
(C) Office 3
(D) Office 4

98. Where does the speaker most likely work?

(A) At a factory
(B) At an architecture firm
(C) At a landscaping service
(D) At a government inspection office

99. Look at the graphic. Which number does the speaker want to change?

(A) 20
(B) 12
(C) 8
(D) 15

100. What information would the speaker like added to a list?

(A) His home address
(B) His office location
(C) His telephone number
(D) His e-mail address

This is the end of the Listening test.

토익® 정기시험
기출문제집

LC

ETS TEST

09

LISTENING TEST

In the Listening test, you will be asked to demonstrate how well you understand spoken English. The entire Listening test will last approximately 45 minutes. There are four parts, and directions are given for each part. You must mark your answers on the separate answer sheet. Do not write your answers in your test book.

PART 1

Directions: For each question in this part, you will hear four statements about a picture in your test book. When you hear the statements, you must select the one statement that best describes what you see in the picture. Then find the number of the question on your answer sheet and mark your answer. The statements will not be printed in your test book and will be spoken only one time.

Statement (C), "They're sitting at a table," is the best description of the picture, so you should select answer (C) and mark it on your answer sheet.

1.

2.

GO ON TO THE NEXT PAGE

3.

4.

5.

6.

GO ON TO THE NEXT PAGE ➡

TEST 9

PART 2

Directions: You will hear a question or statement and three responses spoken in English. They will not be printed in your test book and will be spoken only one time. Select the best response to the question or statement and mark the letter (A), (B), or (C) on your answer sheet.

7. Mark your answer on your answer sheet.

8. Mark your answer on your answer sheet.

9. Mark your answer on your answer sheet.

10. Mark your answer on your answer sheet.

11. Mark your answer on your answer sheet.

12. Mark your answer on your answer sheet.

13. Mark your answer on your answer sheet.

14. Mark your answer on your answer sheet.

15. Mark your answer on your answer sheet.

16. Mark your answer on your answer sheet.

17. Mark your answer on your answer sheet.

18. Mark your answer on your answer sheet.

19. Mark your answer on your answer sheet.

20. Mark your answer on your answer sheet.

21. Mark your answer on your answer sheet.

22. Mark your answer on your answer sheet.

23. Mark your answer on your answer sheet.

24. Mark your answer on your answer sheet.

25. Mark your answer on your answer sheet.

26. Mark your answer on your answer sheet.

27. Mark your answer on your answer sheet.

28. Mark your answer on your answer sheet.

29. Mark your answer on your answer sheet.

30. Mark your answer on your answer sheet.

31. Mark your answer on your answer sheet.

Directions: You will hear some conversations between two or more people. You will be asked to answer three questions about what the speakers say in each conversation. Select the best response to each question and mark the letter (A), (B), (C), or (D) on your answer sheet. The conversations will not be printed in your test book and will be spoken only one time.

32. Where does the man work?

(A) At a department store
(B) At a bank
(C) At an electronics store
(D) At an apartment complex

33. Why is the woman calling?

(A) To confirm a payment amount
(B) To schedule an appointment
(C) To ask for a replacement item
(D) To check on a delayed shipment

34. What does the man ask for?

(A) A confirmation number
(B) A location
(C) An event date
(D) A completed form

35. Where does the conversation most likely take place?

(A) At a museum
(B) At a library
(C) At a theater
(D) At an art school

36. Why is the man visiting?

(A) To meet a friend
(B) To take some photographs
(C) To do research for a book
(D) To deliver a shipment

37. Why does the woman suggest that the man hurry?

(A) An event will begin shortly.
(B) Closing time is approaching.
(C) A wait time is long.
(D) Seating is limited.

38. Who is Chris Suzuki?

(A) A shift manager
(B) An inspector
(C) An apprentice
(D) A new client

39. Where is the conversation most likely taking place?

(A) In a hardware store
(B) In a factory
(C) In a storage facility
(D) In a product showroom

40. What will the woman probably do next?

(A) Negotiate a contract with Chris
(B) Review scheduling procedures with Chris
(C) Introduce Chris to some colleagues
(D) Show Chris the cafeteria

41. What will most likely be celebrated on Friday?

(A) A promotion
(B) A retirement
(C) A graduation
(D) A business deal

42. What does the man offer to do?

(A) Look for a receipt
(B) Send invitations
(C) Reserve a room
(D) Prepare a dessert

43. What does the woman say she is looking forward to?

(A) Visiting her family
(B) Moving to a different city
(C) Traveling internationally
(D) Organizing a team

TEST 9

GO ON TO THE NEXT PAGE

44. What was the problem with the man's previous floor mat?

(A) It was not durable.
(B) It had a strong odor.
(C) It damaged the floor.
(D) It was too small.

45. What does the woman invite the man to do?

(A) View images in a catalog
(B) Read about special features
(C) Watch a demonstration
(D) Open a package

46. According to the woman, why is a manufacturer proud of its floor mats?

(A) They are easy to clean.
(B) They can be used on a variety of surfaces.
(C) They allow for free movement.
(D) They can be rolled or folded.

47. What industry do the speakers most likely work in?

(A) Music
(B) Restaurant
(C) Film production
(D) Book publishing

48. What does the man mean when he says, "we just switched to a new software program"?

(A) He needs to consult a user's manual.
(B) The quality of his work will improve.
(C) A task may take longer than expected.
(D) A training session should be organized.

49. Why does the woman congratulate the man?

(A) He won an award.
(B) He received a promotion.
(C) He will be leading a team.
(D) He developed some new software.

50. What do the women want to do?

(A) Rent a car
(B) Buy ferry tickets
(C) Take a city tour
(D) Book a hotel

51. What does the man say was recently introduced?

(A) A customer loyalty program
(B) An online feedback form
(C) A cashless payment system
(D) A renovated waiting area

52. What does the man suggest the women do?

(A) Purchase some postcards
(B) Visit a historic site
(C) Call a taxi service
(D) Download a mobile application

53. Where are the speakers?

(A) At a fund-raiser
(B) At a trade show
(C) At a job fair
(D) At a store opening

54. What kind of products does the man's company make?

(A) Jewelry
(B) Handbags
(C) Floor rugs
(D) Picture frames

55. What does the man suggest doing?

(A) Leaving a business card
(B) Registering online
(C) Placing an order
(D) Taking a catalog

56. Who most likely are the speakers?

(A) News reporters
(B) Travel agents
(C) Bus drivers
(D) City officials

57. Why is the man concerned?

(A) He forgot to make a phone call.
(B) He might miss a deadline.
(C) A contract requires a signature.
(D) A colleague is late for work.

58. Why does the woman say, "they're hosting a big press conference at noon"?

(A) To suggest attending an event
(B) To inform the man about a schedule change
(C) To complain about a decision
(D) To ask the man for a ride

59. Where do the speakers most likely work?

(A) At a real estate agency
(B) At a florist shop
(C) At a construction company
(D) At an interior design firm

60. What do the speakers agree to do?

(A) Promote some products on a Web site
(B) Send e-mails to previous customers
(C) Leave brochures in a building lobby
(D) Put up signs near a highway

61. Who does the man say he will contact?

(A) An administrative assistant
(B) An Internet provider
(C) A photographer
(D) An accountant

Vega Event Center	
Arroyo Room	100–200 people
Salinas Room	200–300 people
Reyes Room	300–400 people
Miramar Room	400–500 people

62. What is the woman planning?

(A) A product launch
(B) A charity event
(C) A retirement party
(D) A factory inspection

63. Look at the graphic. Which room will the woman most likely reserve?

(A) The Arroyo Room
(B) The Salinas Room
(C) The Reyes Room
(D) The Miramar Room

64. What does the man say he will provide?

(A) Some measurements
(B) Some menu options
(C) Proof of insurance
(D) A list of musicians

TEST 9

GO ON TO THE NEXT PAGE

Flight Delays by Airport, in Minutes

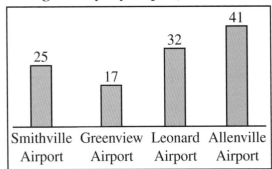

$5.00 $6.00

$7.00 $8.00

65. Who most likely is the woman?

(A) A commercial pilot
(B) A regional manager
(C) A travel agent
(D) A news reporter

66. Look at the graphic. Which airport does the man point out?

(A) Smithville Airport
(B) Greenview Airport
(C) Leonard Airport
(D) Allenville Airport

67. What does the man recommend?

(A) Adjusting travel plans
(B) Changing a delivery time
(C) Finding discounted tickets
(D) Hiring additional agents

68. What event is taking place next month?

(A) A concert
(B) A fund-raiser
(C) An anniversary celebration
(D) A community festival

69. Look at the graphic. How much will the selected item cost?

(A) $5.00
(B) $6.00
(C) $7.00
(D) $8.00

70. What will the man do next?

(A) Revise a design
(B) Search a Web site
(C) Book a venue
(D) Place an order

PART 4

Directions: You will hear some talks given by a single speaker. You will be asked to answer three questions about what the speaker says in each talk. Select the best response to each question and mark the letter (A), (B), (C), or (D) on your answer sheet. The talks will not be printed in your test book and will be spoken only one time.

71. What does the company sell?

   (A) Racing bicycles
   (B) Motorcycle parts
   (C) Camping equipment
   (D) Electric cars

72. What does the speaker emphasize about the products?

   (A) They are safe for the environment.
   (B) They come with an extended warranty.
   (C) They can be used with a mobile application.
   (D) They are designed for all weather conditions.

73. What ends on Sunday?

   (A) A contest
   (B) A festival
   (C) A factory tour
   (D) A special offer

74. What does the business make?

   (A) Ice cream
   (B) Beverages
   (C) Candy
   (D) Pretzels

75. What does the speaker say the business is known for?

   (A) Its high-quality ingredients
   (B) Its clever packaging
   (C) Its unique flavors
   (D) Its handmade products

76. What does the speaker ask the listeners to do?

   (A) Leave their personal items in a locker
   (B) Turn in their tickets
   (C) Divide into smaller groups
   (D) Put on some protective clothing

77. What is the speaker mainly discussing?

   (A) An upcoming conference
   (B) A vacation policy
   (C) Some new software
   (D) Some new equipment

78. What does the speaker tell the listeners to take note of?

   (A) Some travel arrangements will be made online.
   (B) Some log-on information will remain the same.
   (C) A training session will be rescheduled.
   (D) A security policy will be enforced.

79. What should the listeners do tomorrow?

   (A) Confirm their work schedules
   (B) Prepare a presentation
   (C) Park in a different location
   (D) Dress professionally

80. Where does Ms. Thompson work?

   (A) At an art supply store
   (B) At a museum
   (C) At a photography studio
   (D) At a library

81. According to the speaker, what special talent does Ms. Thompson have?

   (A) Raising money
   (B) Painting landscapes
   (C) Negotiating contracts
   (D) Taking photographs

82. What does Ms. Thompson plan to do after she retires?

   (A) Restore paintings
   (B) Volunteer as a consultant
   (C) Relocate to France
   (D) Become an author

GO ON TO THE NEXT PAGE

83. Who most likely are the listeners?

(A) Journalists
(B) Editors
(C) Photographers
(D) Salespeople

84. According to the speaker, what will the listeners receive in an e-mail?

(A) A book title
(B) A concert ticket
(C) A restaurant name
(D) An account number

85. Why does the speaker say, "thousands of people will buy this issue"?

(A) To reassure the listeners
(B) To correct a misunderstanding
(C) To express surprise about a decision
(D) To emphasize the importance of a task

86. Where are the listeners?

(A) In a community center
(B) In a medical clinic
(C) In a university classroom
(D) In a government office

87. Why does the speaker say, "many eye problems are easily treated"?

(A) To indicate that a health fair is unnecessary
(B) To suggest hiring additional staff
(C) To encourage the listeners to get tested
(D) To correct a statistical error

88. What will the listeners do next?

(A) Pick up some nutritional information
(B) Sign up for an appointment
(C) Listen to a presentation
(D) Watch a product demonstration

89. What is the talk mainly about?

(A) Cleaning a carpet
(B) Installing a carpet
(C) Designing a carpet
(D) Choosing a carpet

90. What does the speaker say about wool carpets?

(A) They are difficult to find.
(B) They are expensive.
(C) They are hard to clean.
(D) They are durable.

91. What does the speaker say his company provides?

(A) A free in-store consultation
(B) A children's play area
(C) Flooring design samples
(D) One-year warranties

92. Why does the speaker thank the listener?

(A) For renewing a magazine subscription
(B) For inspecting a medical facility
(C) For writing an article
(D) For giving a demonstration

93. What does the speaker imply when she says, "this is just one of our many products"?

(A) A company is prepared for more competition.
(B) A company also sells less expensive products.
(C) A team will need to work more quickly.
(D) A supervisor will be impressed by some work.

94. Why does the speaker ask the listener to call back?

(A) To provide an address
(B) To confirm a deadline
(C) To place an order
(D) To arrange a meeting

Oakfield Public Park

Elm Fountain	🪑 Picnic Area 1	Community Garden
🪑 Picnic Area 4		🪑 Picnic Area 2
Dogwood Pond	🪑 Picnic Area 3	Children's Playground

Please check the box to indicate your availability:

☐ Mondays @ 2:30 P.M.

☐ Wednesdays @ 8:30 A.M.

☐ Thursdays @ 11:00 A.M.

☐ Saturdays @ 12:00 P.M.

95. Who most likely is the speaker?
    (A) A tour guide
    (B) A city official
    (C) A photographer
    (D) A landscape artist

96. Look at the graphic. Which picnic area does the speaker recommend?
    (A) Picnic Area 1
    (B) Picnic Area 2
    (C) Picnic Area 3
    (D) Picnic Area 4

97. Why are some volunteers needed?
    (A) To maintain a garden
    (B) To hand out water bottles
    (C) To organize park events
    (D) To provide free tours

98. Where do the listeners most likely work?
    (A) At a supermarket
    (B) At a hospital
    (C) At a community center
    (D) At a fitness club

99. What does the speaker say is his goal?
    (A) To attract qualified job candidates
    (B) To reduce costs
    (C) To boost membership sales
    (D) To encourage healthy eating habits

100. Look at the graphic. On which days can the speaker change his schedule?
    (A) Mondays
    (B) Wednesdays
    (C) Thursdays
    (D) Saturdays

This is the end of the Listening test.

토익® 정기시험
기출문제집

LC

ETS TEST

10

LISTENING TEST

In the Listening test, you will be asked to demonstrate how well you understand spoken English. The entire Listening test will last approximately 45 minutes. There are four parts, and directions are given for each part. You must mark your answers on the separate answer sheet. Do not write your answers in your test book.

PART 1

Directions: For each question in this part, you will hear four statements about a picture in your test book. When you hear the statements, you must select the one statement that best describes what you see in the picture. Then find the number of the question on your answer sheet and mark your answer. The statements will not be printed in your test book and will be spoken only one time.

Statement (C), "They're sitting at a table," is the best description of the picture, so you should select answer (C) and mark it on your answer sheet.

1.

2.

GO ON TO THE NEXT PAGE

TEST 10

3.

4.

5.

6.

GO ON TO THE NEXT PAGE →

TEST 10

PART 2

Directions: You will hear a question or statement and three responses spoken in English. They will not be printed in your test book and will be spoken only one time. Select the best response to the question or statement and mark the letter (A), (B), or (C) on your answer sheet.

7. Mark your answer on your answer sheet.

8. Mark your answer on your answer sheet.

9. Mark your answer on your answer sheet.

10. Mark your answer on your answer sheet.

11. Mark your answer on your answer sheet.

12. Mark your answer on your answer sheet.

13. Mark your answer on your answer sheet.

14. Mark your answer on your answer sheet.

15. Mark your answer on your answer sheet.

16. Mark your answer on your answer sheet.

17. Mark your answer on your answer sheet.

18. Mark your answer on your answer sheet.

19. Mark your answer on your answer sheet.

20. Mark your answer on your answer sheet.

21. Mark your answer on your answer sheet.

22. Mark your answer on your answer sheet.

23. Mark your answer on your answer sheet.

24. Mark your answer on your answer sheet.

25. Mark your answer on your answer sheet.

26. Mark your answer on your answer sheet.

27. Mark your answer on your answer sheet.

28. Mark your answer on your answer sheet.

29. Mark your answer on your answer sheet.

30. Mark your answer on your answer sheet.

31. Mark your answer on your answer sheet.

Directions: You will hear some conversations between two or more people. You will be asked to answer three questions about what the speakers say in each conversation. Select the best response to each question and mark the letter (A), (B), (C), or (D) on your answer sheet. The conversations will not be printed in your test book and will be spoken only one time.

32. What is the conversation mainly about?

    (A) A product launch
    (B) A grand opening
    (C) Some investment options
    (D) Some travel plans

33. Why has the man been busy?

    (A) He has been working on a presentation.
    (B) He has just returned from a family vacation.
    (C) He is organizing a conference.
    (D) He has been assigned a new client account.

34. What does the woman suggest that the man do soon?

    (A) Make a reservation
    (B) Review some sales data
    (C) Use a voucher before it expires
    (D) Speak with an adviser

35. Where is the conversation taking place?

    (A) At a bakery
    (B) At an employment agency
    (C) At a farmers market
    (D) At a restaurant

36. What does the woman ask about?

    (A) An upcoming event
    (B) A project deadline
    (C) A delivery service
    (D) A job opening

37. What does the man remind the woman to do?

    (A) Register on a Web site
    (B) Send a document
    (C) Update a budget
    (D) Change an address

38. Where do the women work?

    (A) At a bookstore
    (B) At a computer store
    (C) At a food market
    (D) At a publishing company

39. What are the women worried about?

    (A) Opening a branch office
    (B) Competing with online stores
    (C) Finding a new supplier
    (D) Hiring enough delivery drivers

40. What does the man recommend?

    (A) Advertising online
    (B) Attending a trade show
    (C) Adding food service
    (D) Offering a home repair service

41. What kind of products do the speakers sell?

    (A) Cleaning products
    (B) Car accessories
    (C) Kitchen tools
    (D) Garden supplies

42. What does the woman mean when she says, "He's probably waiting outside"?

    (A) A customer needs help immediately.
    (B) A manager wants to discuss a complaint.
    (C) A store is unusually crowded.
    (D) Some instructions were confusing.

43. What do the staff sometimes forget to do?

    (A) Restock inventory
    (B) Sign receipts
    (C) Hand out flyers
    (D) Mention an upcoming sale

TEST 10

GO ON TO THE NEXT PAGE

44. Who most likely are the men?

　(A) Teachers
　(B) Bakers
　(C) Electricians
　(D) Doctors

45. Why are the men frustrated?

　(A) Some work will have to be redone.
　(B) Some tools have been misplaced.
　(C) Some staff members are unavailable.
　(D) Some supplies have run out.

46. What does the woman want the men to review?

　(A) A revised budget
　(B) A meeting agenda
　(C) Some design plans
　(D) Some contract terms

47. What does the man want to do?

　(A) Renovate a building
　(B) Create a community garden
　(C) Install some new road signs
　(D) Move a business to a new location

48. What problem does the woman mention about a project?

　(A) It will be noisy.
　(B) It will be expensive.
　(C) Finding available space may be difficult.
　(D) The approval process may take a long time.

49. What does the woman suggest the man do?

　(A) Apply for a loan
　(B) Check a city map
　(C) Collect some signatures
　(D) Post an announcement online

50. What industry does the woman work in?

　(A) Finance
　(B) Farming
　(C) Advertising
　(D) Hospitality

51. What did the woman do recently?

　(A) She received an award.
　(B) She opened a new business.
　(C) She invented a new product.
　(D) She published a book.

52. What will the woman most likely discuss next?

　(A) Choosing an appropriate software program
　(B) Preparing for a job interview
　(C) Deciding on a program of study
　(D) Improving networking skills

53. What kind of business do the speakers most likely own?

　(A) An architecture studio
　(B) A restaurant
　(C) A real estate agency
　(D) An accounting firm

54. What does the man want to order?

　(A) Furniture
　(B) Office supplies
　(C) Food
　(D) Lighting fixtures

55. Why does the woman say, "I just checked the account balance an hour ago"?

　(A) To offer an excuse
　(B) To make a complaint
　(C) To provide reassurance
　(D) To express surprise

56. Who most likely is the man?

   (A) The woman's former landlord
   (B) The woman's professor
   (C) The woman's relative
   (D) The woman's previous employer

57. What does the woman say she will do soon?

   (A) Return to her parents' house
   (B) Apply for a job
   (C) Pick up her belongings
   (D) Begin coursework at school

58. What does the woman ask for?

   (A) A house key
   (B) A copy of a certificate
   (C) A reference letter
   (D) A colleague's e-mail address

59. Where most likely are the speakers?

   (A) In a government office
   (B) In a television studio
   (C) At a bus terminal
   (D) At a construction site

60. What does the man mention about the Lansing Bridge?

   (A) There is a lot of traffic on it today.
   (B) There is a beautiful view from it.
   (C) It now has a walkway.
   (D) It is temporarily closed.

61. How can the listeners find out more information?

   (A) By visiting an information desk
   (B) By requesting a brochure
   (C) By checking a Web site
   (D) By calling a help line

Community Center Class Schedule				
Monday	**Tuesday**	**Wednesday**	**Thursday**	**Friday**
Ceramics	Knitting	Painting	Sculpture	Drawing

62. Why is the man calling?

   (A) To confirm he will teach a class
   (B) To complain about a recent class
   (C) To inquire about class supplies
   (D) To request directions to a community center

63. Look at the graphic. Which class are the speakers discussing?

   (A) Knitting
   (B) Painting
   (C) Sculpture
   (D) Drawing

64. What does the man plan to do in Chicago?

   (A) Go to a graduation ceremony
   (B) Attend a wedding
   (C) Complete a certification
   (D) See an art exhibit

GO ON TO THE NEXT PAGE

TEST 10

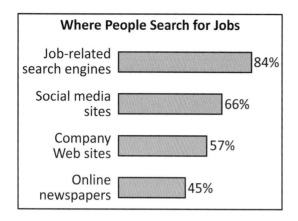

Where People Search for Jobs

Job-related search engines	84%
Social media sites	66%
Company Web sites	57%
Online newspapers	45%

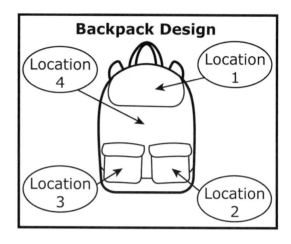

Backpack Design

Location 4

Location 1

Location 3

Location 2

65. Where do the speakers most likely work?

(A) At a car rental service
(B) At a market research firm
(C) At an electronics store
(D) At a trucking company

66. Look at the graphic. Where do the speakers plan to start advertising job openings?

(A) On job-related search engines
(B) On social media sites
(C) On company Web sites
(D) In online newspapers

67. What does the man say he will do later today?

(A) Propose a budget adjustment
(B) Attend a training session
(C) Write a letter of recommendation
(D) Approve a timeline

68. What is the woman having difficulty deciding on?

(A) A color
(B) A fabric
(C) Storage capacity
(D) Strap placement

69. Why was the company's logo redesigned?

(A) To reflect design trends
(B) To celebrate an anniversary
(C) To appeal to a wider audience
(D) To avoid a copyright problem

70. Look at the graphic. Where will the company's logo be placed?

(A) Location 1
(B) Location 2
(C) Location 3
(D) Location 4

Directions: You will hear some talks given by a single speaker. You will be asked to answer three questions about what the speaker says in each talk. Select the best response to each question and mark the letter (A), (B), (C), or (D) on your answer sheet. The talks will not be printed in your test book and will be spoken only one time.

71. What kind of product did the speaker order?

(A) Printer ink
(B) Eyeglasses
(C) Picture frames
(D) Furniture

72. What problem does the speaker mention?

(A) A package was not received.
(B) An invoice is missing.
(C) A product is the wrong color.
(D) A Web site is down.

73. What does the speaker ask about?

(A) A refund policy
(B) A delivery fee
(C) A shipping time
(D) A mailing address

74. What award is being announced?

(A) Best design
(B) Top salesperson
(C) Employee of the month
(D) Excellence in research

75. According to the speaker, what will the winner receive?

(A) A commemorative plaque
(B) A parking space
(C) A gift certificate
(D) A recognition dinner

76. What does the speaker say will be published on a Web site?

(A) A photograph
(B) A biography
(C) Professional accomplishments
(D) Company event details

77. What kind of product does the speaker's company sell?

(A) Bicycles
(B) Tools
(C) Cars
(D) Toys

78. What will the listeners do next?

(A) Watch a video
(B) Vote on a policy
(C) Inspect a brochure
(D) Tour a facility

79. What does the speaker mean when he says, "I come in at eight"?

(A) He is very busy this week.
(B) A store usually opens early.
(C) The listeners should arrive at that time.
(D) The listeners should prepare a shipment.

80. What does the speaker mainly discuss?

(A) Offering training opportunities
(B) Changing product packaging
(C) Updating safety regulations
(D) Revising an advertising strategy

81. What did the company do last month?

(A) It expanded its social media presence.
(B) It agreed to organize a conference.
(C) It published a training manual.
(D) It hired an outside consultant.

82. What should interested listeners do?

(A) Contact their managers
(B) Recruit some volunteers
(C) Answer a survey
(D) Watch a video

TEST 10

GO ON TO THE NEXT PAGE

83. Who most likely are the listeners?

(A) Engineers
(B) Dentists
(C) Educators
(D) Architects

84. Why does the speaker say, "I'll be at the booth in the lobby until noon"?

(A) To request volunteers for the afternoon
(B) To explain that a booth location has changed
(C) To apologize for a scheduling conflict
(D) To indicate availability to answer questions

85. What does the speaker say will happen tonight?

(A) A book signing
(B) A photo shoot
(C) A dinner reception
(D) An award ceremony

86. What is Geeta Prasad's profession?

(A) Research scientist
(B) Medical doctor
(C) University professor
(D) Government official

87. According to the speaker, what are some data used for?

(A) To evaluate a budget
(B) To design new products
(C) To make hiring decisions
(D) To develop an exercise program

88. Why should the listeners visit a Web site?

(A) To download a manual
(B) To read a report
(C) To register for a study
(D) To provide some feedback

89. Where do the listeners most likely work?

(A) At a home appliance store
(B) At a hardware store
(C) At a shipping company
(D) At a furniture store

90. According to the speaker, what has caused a problem?

(A) Low-quality merchandise
(B) Competition from other businesses
(C) Increased rental costs
(D) Poor customer service

91. What will happen next month?

(A) A focus group will be assembled.
(B) A customer loyalty program will be introduced.
(C) Some employees will receive training.
(D) New advertisements will be designed.

92. Where is the speech being given?

(A) At a training session
(B) At a press conference
(C) At a job fair
(D) At a store grand opening

93. Why does the speaker apologize?

(A) Some repair work has caused delays.
(B) Some employees have been transferred.
(C) Some materials have not arrived.
(D) Some businesses have been temporarily closed.

94. What does the speaker mean when she says, "the tracks and trains are not city property"?

(A) She did not follow a recommendation.
(B) She is not responsible for a problem.
(C) Some directions were misleading.
(D) A contract contained errors.

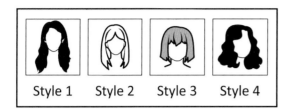

Style 1   Style 2   Style 3   Style 4

95. Look at the graphic. Which hairstyle does the speaker recommend?

(A) Style 1
(B) Style 2
(C) Style 3
(D) Style 4

96. What does the speaker say is included in the price?

(A) A comb
(B) A beverage
(C) Blow-drying
(D) Hair care instructions

97. What does the speaker say happened yesterday?

(A) A photo shoot was held.
(B) A popular product arrived.
(C) A new hairstylist was hired.
(D) A product demonstration was conducted.

Plastic Molding Output

Machine Number	Cycle Duration
1	5:30
2	6:22
3	4:15
4	5:02

98. According to the speaker, what did the company do last week?

(A) It installed software to monitor machines.
(B) It added a new machine to an assembly line.
(C) It hired some expert technicians.
(D) It reorganized a production team.

99. Look at the graphic. Which machine will a technician look at?

(A) Machine 1
(B) Machine 2
(C) Machine 3
(D) Machine 4

100. What does the company hope to do next quarter?

(A) Update their logo
(B) Meet their production targets
(C) Purchase similar technologies
(D) Begin replacing outdated computers

This is the end of the Listening test.

ANSWER SHEET

ETS® TOEIC® 토익 정기시험 기출문제집

성명	한글
	한자
	영자

수험번호

응시일자 : 20 년 월 일

Test 01 (Part 1~4)

#					#					#					#					#				
1	ⓐ ⓑ ⓒ ⓓ				21	ⓐ ⓑ ⓒ ⓓ				41	ⓐ ⓑ ⓒ ⓓ				61	ⓐ ⓑ ⓒ ⓓ				81	ⓐ ⓑ ⓒ ⓓ			
2	ⓐ ⓑ ⓒ ⓓ				22	ⓐ ⓑ ⓒ ⓓ				42	ⓐ ⓑ ⓒ ⓓ				62	ⓐ ⓑ ⓒ ⓓ				82	ⓐ ⓑ ⓒ ⓓ			
3	ⓐ ⓑ ⓒ ⓓ				23	ⓐ ⓑ ⓒ ⓓ				43	ⓐ ⓑ ⓒ ⓓ				63	ⓐ ⓑ ⓒ ⓓ				83	ⓐ ⓑ ⓒ ⓓ			
4	ⓐ ⓑ ⓒ ⓓ				24	ⓐ ⓑ ⓒ ⓓ				44	ⓐ ⓑ ⓒ ⓓ				64	ⓐ ⓑ ⓒ ⓓ				84	ⓐ ⓑ ⓒ ⓓ			
5	ⓐ ⓑ ⓒ ⓓ				25	ⓐ ⓑ ⓒ ⓓ				45	ⓐ ⓑ ⓒ ⓓ				65	ⓐ ⓑ ⓒ ⓓ				85	ⓐ ⓑ ⓒ ⓓ			
6	ⓐ ⓑ ⓒ ⓓ				26	ⓐ ⓑ ⓒ ⓓ				46	ⓐ ⓑ ⓒ ⓓ				66	ⓐ ⓑ ⓒ ⓓ				86	ⓐ ⓑ ⓒ ⓓ			
7	ⓐ ⓑ ⓒ				27	ⓐ ⓑ ⓒ ⓓ				47	ⓐ ⓑ ⓒ ⓓ				67	ⓐ ⓑ ⓒ ⓓ				87	ⓐ ⓑ ⓒ ⓓ			
8	ⓐ ⓑ ⓒ				28	ⓐ ⓑ ⓒ ⓓ				48	ⓐ ⓑ ⓒ ⓓ				68	ⓐ ⓑ ⓒ ⓓ				88	ⓐ ⓑ ⓒ ⓓ			
9	ⓐ ⓑ ⓒ				29	ⓐ ⓑ ⓒ ⓓ				49	ⓐ ⓑ ⓒ ⓓ				69	ⓐ ⓑ ⓒ ⓓ				89	ⓐ ⓑ ⓒ ⓓ			
10	ⓐ ⓑ ⓒ				30	ⓐ ⓑ ⓒ ⓓ				50	ⓐ ⓑ ⓒ ⓓ				70	ⓐ ⓑ ⓒ ⓓ				90	ⓐ ⓑ ⓒ ⓓ			
11	ⓐ ⓑ ⓒ				31	ⓐ ⓑ ⓒ ⓓ				51	ⓐ ⓑ ⓒ ⓓ				71	ⓐ ⓑ ⓒ ⓓ				91	ⓐ ⓑ ⓒ ⓓ			
12	ⓐ ⓑ ⓒ				32	ⓐ ⓑ ⓒ ⓓ				52	ⓐ ⓑ ⓒ ⓓ				72	ⓐ ⓑ ⓒ ⓓ				92	ⓐ ⓑ ⓒ ⓓ			
13	ⓐ ⓑ ⓒ				33	ⓐ ⓑ ⓒ ⓓ				53	ⓐ ⓑ ⓒ ⓓ				73	ⓐ ⓑ ⓒ ⓓ				93	ⓐ ⓑ ⓒ ⓓ			
14	ⓐ ⓑ ⓒ				34	ⓐ ⓑ ⓒ ⓓ				54	ⓐ ⓑ ⓒ ⓓ				74	ⓐ ⓑ ⓒ ⓓ				94	ⓐ ⓑ ⓒ ⓓ			
15	ⓐ ⓑ ⓒ				35	ⓐ ⓑ ⓒ ⓓ				55	ⓐ ⓑ ⓒ ⓓ				75	ⓐ ⓑ ⓒ ⓓ				95	ⓐ ⓑ ⓒ ⓓ			
16	ⓐ ⓑ ⓒ				36	ⓐ ⓑ ⓒ ⓓ				56	ⓐ ⓑ ⓒ ⓓ				76	ⓐ ⓑ ⓒ ⓓ				96	ⓐ ⓑ ⓒ ⓓ			
17	ⓐ ⓑ ⓒ				37	ⓐ ⓑ ⓒ ⓓ				57	ⓐ ⓑ ⓒ ⓓ				77	ⓐ ⓑ ⓒ ⓓ				97	ⓐ ⓑ ⓒ ⓓ			
18	ⓐ ⓑ ⓒ				38	ⓐ ⓑ ⓒ ⓓ				58	ⓐ ⓑ ⓒ ⓓ				78	ⓐ ⓑ ⓒ ⓓ				98	ⓐ ⓑ ⓒ ⓓ			
19	ⓐ ⓑ ⓒ				39	ⓐ ⓑ ⓒ ⓓ				59	ⓐ ⓑ ⓒ ⓓ				79	ⓐ ⓑ ⓒ ⓓ				99	ⓐ ⓑ ⓒ ⓓ			
20	ⓐ ⓑ ⓒ				40	ⓐ ⓑ ⓒ ⓓ				60	ⓐ ⓑ ⓒ ⓓ				80	ⓐ ⓑ ⓒ ⓓ				100	ⓐ ⓑ ⓒ ⓓ			

Test 02 (Part 1~4)

#					#					#					#					#				
1	ⓐ ⓑ ⓒ ⓓ				21	ⓐ ⓑ ⓒ ⓓ				41	ⓐ ⓑ ⓒ ⓓ				61	ⓐ ⓑ ⓒ ⓓ				81	ⓐ ⓑ ⓒ ⓓ			
2	ⓐ ⓑ ⓒ ⓓ				22	ⓐ ⓑ ⓒ ⓓ				42	ⓐ ⓑ ⓒ ⓓ				62	ⓐ ⓑ ⓒ ⓓ				82	ⓐ ⓑ ⓒ ⓓ			
3	ⓐ ⓑ ⓒ ⓓ				23	ⓐ ⓑ ⓒ ⓓ				43	ⓐ ⓑ ⓒ ⓓ				63	ⓐ ⓑ ⓒ ⓓ				83	ⓐ ⓑ ⓒ ⓓ			
4	ⓐ ⓑ ⓒ ⓓ				24	ⓐ ⓑ ⓒ ⓓ				44	ⓐ ⓑ ⓒ ⓓ				64	ⓐ ⓑ ⓒ ⓓ				84	ⓐ ⓑ ⓒ ⓓ			
5	ⓐ ⓑ ⓒ ⓓ				25	ⓐ ⓑ ⓒ ⓓ				45	ⓐ ⓑ ⓒ ⓓ				65	ⓐ ⓑ ⓒ ⓓ				85	ⓐ ⓑ ⓒ ⓓ			
6	ⓐ ⓑ ⓒ ⓓ				26	ⓐ ⓑ ⓒ ⓓ				46	ⓐ ⓑ ⓒ ⓓ				66	ⓐ ⓑ ⓒ ⓓ				86	ⓐ ⓑ ⓒ ⓓ			
7	ⓐ ⓑ ⓒ				27	ⓐ ⓑ ⓒ ⓓ				47	ⓐ ⓑ ⓒ ⓓ				67	ⓐ ⓑ ⓒ ⓓ				87	ⓐ ⓑ ⓒ ⓓ			
8	ⓐ ⓑ ⓒ				28	ⓐ ⓑ ⓒ ⓓ				48	ⓐ ⓑ ⓒ ⓓ				68	ⓐ ⓑ ⓒ ⓓ				88	ⓐ ⓑ ⓒ ⓓ			
9	ⓐ ⓑ ⓒ				29	ⓐ ⓑ ⓒ ⓓ				49	ⓐ ⓑ ⓒ ⓓ				69	ⓐ ⓑ ⓒ ⓓ				89	ⓐ ⓑ ⓒ ⓓ			
10	ⓐ ⓑ ⓒ				30	ⓐ ⓑ ⓒ ⓓ				50	ⓐ ⓑ ⓒ ⓓ				70	ⓐ ⓑ ⓒ ⓓ				90	ⓐ ⓑ ⓒ ⓓ			
11	ⓐ ⓑ ⓒ				31	ⓐ ⓑ ⓒ ⓓ				51	ⓐ ⓑ ⓒ ⓓ				71	ⓐ ⓑ ⓒ ⓓ				91	ⓐ ⓑ ⓒ ⓓ			
12	ⓐ ⓑ ⓒ				32	ⓐ ⓑ ⓒ ⓓ				52	ⓐ ⓑ ⓒ ⓓ				72	ⓐ ⓑ ⓒ ⓓ				92	ⓐ ⓑ ⓒ ⓓ			
13	ⓐ ⓑ ⓒ				33	ⓐ ⓑ ⓒ ⓓ				53	ⓐ ⓑ ⓒ ⓓ				73	ⓐ ⓑ ⓒ ⓓ				93	ⓐ ⓑ ⓒ ⓓ			
14	ⓐ ⓑ ⓒ				34	ⓐ ⓑ ⓒ ⓓ				54	ⓐ ⓑ ⓒ ⓓ				74	ⓐ ⓑ ⓒ ⓓ				94	ⓐ ⓑ ⓒ ⓓ			
15	ⓐ ⓑ ⓒ				35	ⓐ ⓑ ⓒ ⓓ				55	ⓐ ⓑ ⓒ ⓓ				75	ⓐ ⓑ ⓒ ⓓ				95	ⓐ ⓑ ⓒ ⓓ			
16	ⓐ ⓑ ⓒ				36	ⓐ ⓑ ⓒ ⓓ				56	ⓐ ⓑ ⓒ ⓓ				76	ⓐ ⓑ ⓒ ⓓ				96	ⓐ ⓑ ⓒ ⓓ			
17	ⓐ ⓑ ⓒ				37	ⓐ ⓑ ⓒ ⓓ				57	ⓐ ⓑ ⓒ ⓓ				77	ⓐ ⓑ ⓒ ⓓ				97	ⓐ ⓑ ⓒ ⓓ			
18	ⓐ ⓑ ⓒ				38	ⓐ ⓑ ⓒ ⓓ				58	ⓐ ⓑ ⓒ ⓓ				78	ⓐ ⓑ ⓒ ⓓ				98	ⓐ ⓑ ⓒ ⓓ			
19	ⓐ ⓑ ⓒ				39	ⓐ ⓑ ⓒ ⓓ				59	ⓐ ⓑ ⓒ ⓓ				79	ⓐ ⓑ ⓒ ⓓ				99	ⓐ ⓑ ⓒ ⓓ			
20	ⓐ ⓑ ⓒ				40	ⓐ ⓑ ⓒ ⓓ				60	ⓐ ⓑ ⓒ ⓓ				80	ⓐ ⓑ ⓒ ⓓ				100	ⓐ ⓑ ⓒ ⓓ			

ANSWER SHEET

ETS® TOEIC® 토익 정기시험 기출문제집

수험번호

응시일자 : 20 년 월 일

성명	한글
	한자
	영자

Test 03 (Part 1~4)

Test 04 (Part 1~4)

ANSWER SHEET

ETS® TOEIC® 토익 정기시험 기출문제집

성명 한글
한자
영자

수험번호

응시일자 : 20   년   월   일

Test 05 (Part 1~4)

1	ⓐⓑⓒⓓ	21	ⓐⓑⓒⓓ	41	ⓐⓑⓒⓓ	61	ⓐⓑⓒⓓ	81	ⓐⓑⓒⓓ
2	ⓐⓑⓒⓓ	22	ⓐⓑⓒⓓ	42	ⓐⓑⓒⓓ	62	ⓐⓑⓒⓓ	82	ⓐⓑⓒⓓ
3	ⓐⓑⓒⓓ	23	ⓐⓑⓒ	43	ⓐⓑⓒⓓ	63	ⓐⓑⓒⓓ	83	ⓐⓑⓒⓓ
4	ⓐⓑⓒⓓ	24	ⓐⓑⓒ	44	ⓐⓑⓒⓓ	64	ⓐⓑⓒⓓ	84	ⓐⓑⓒⓓ
5	ⓐⓑⓒⓓ	25	ⓐⓑⓒ	45	ⓐⓑⓒⓓ	65	ⓐⓑⓒⓓ	85	ⓐⓑⓒⓓ
6	ⓐⓑⓒ	26	ⓐⓑⓒ	46	ⓐⓑⓒⓓ	66	ⓐⓑⓒⓓ	86	ⓐⓑⓒⓓ
7	ⓐⓑⓒ	27	ⓐⓑⓒ	47	ⓐⓑⓒⓓ	67	ⓐⓑⓒⓓ	87	ⓐⓑⓒⓓ
8	ⓐⓑⓒ	28	ⓐⓑⓒ	48	ⓐⓑⓒⓓ	68	ⓐⓑⓒⓓ	88	ⓐⓑⓒⓓ
9	ⓐⓑⓒ	29	ⓐⓑⓒ	49	ⓐⓑⓒⓓ	69	ⓐⓑⓒⓓ	89	ⓐⓑⓒⓓ
10	ⓐⓑⓒ	30	ⓐⓑⓒ	50	ⓐⓑⓒⓓ	70	ⓐⓑⓒⓓ	90	ⓐⓑⓒⓓ
11	ⓐⓑⓒ	31	ⓐⓑⓒ	51	ⓐⓑⓒⓓ	71	ⓐⓑⓒⓓ	91	ⓐⓑⓒⓓ
12	ⓐⓑⓒ	32	ⓐⓑⓒ	52	ⓐⓑⓒⓓ	72	ⓐⓑⓒⓓ	92	ⓐⓑⓒⓓ
13	ⓐⓑⓒ	33	ⓐⓑⓒ	53	ⓐⓑⓒⓓ	73	ⓐⓑⓒⓓ	93	ⓐⓑⓒⓓ
14	ⓐⓑⓒ	34	ⓐⓑⓒ	54	ⓐⓑⓒⓓ	74	ⓐⓑⓒⓓ	94	ⓐⓑⓒⓓ
15	ⓐⓑⓒ	35	ⓐⓑⓒ	55	ⓐⓑⓒⓓ	75	ⓐⓑⓒⓓ	95	ⓐⓑⓒⓓ
16	ⓐⓑⓒ	36	ⓐⓑⓒ	56	ⓐⓑⓒⓓ	76	ⓐⓑⓒⓓ	96	ⓐⓑⓒⓓ
17	ⓐⓑⓒ	37	ⓐⓑⓒ	57	ⓐⓑⓒⓓ	77	ⓐⓑⓒⓓ	97	ⓐⓑⓒⓓ
18	ⓐⓑⓒ	38	ⓐⓑⓒ	58	ⓐⓑⓒⓓ	78	ⓐⓑⓒⓓ	98	ⓐⓑⓒⓓ
19	ⓐⓑⓒ	39	ⓐⓑⓒ	59	ⓐⓑⓒⓓ	79	ⓐⓑⓒⓓ	99	ⓐⓑⓒⓓ
20	ⓐⓑⓒ	40	ⓐⓑⓒ	60	ⓐⓑⓒⓓ	80	ⓐⓑⓒⓓ	100	ⓐⓑⓒⓓ

Test 06 (Part 1~4)

1	ⓐⓑⓒⓓ	21	ⓐⓑⓒⓓ	41	ⓐⓑⓒⓓ	61	ⓐⓑⓒⓓ	81	ⓐⓑⓒⓓ
2	ⓐⓑⓒⓓ	22	ⓐⓑⓒⓓ	42	ⓐⓑⓒⓓ	62	ⓐⓑⓒⓓ	82	ⓐⓑⓒⓓ
3	ⓐⓑⓒⓓ	23	ⓐⓑⓒ	43	ⓐⓑⓒⓓ	63	ⓐⓑⓒⓓ	83	ⓐⓑⓒⓓ
4	ⓐⓑⓒⓓ	24	ⓐⓑⓒ	44	ⓐⓑⓒⓓ	64	ⓐⓑⓒⓓ	84	ⓐⓑⓒⓓ
5	ⓐⓑⓒⓓ	25	ⓐⓑⓒ	45	ⓐⓑⓒⓓ	65	ⓐⓑⓒⓓ	85	ⓐⓑⓒⓓ
6	ⓐⓑⓒ	26	ⓐⓑⓒ	46	ⓐⓑⓒⓓ	66	ⓐⓑⓒⓓ	86	ⓐⓑⓒⓓ
7	ⓐⓑⓒ	27	ⓐⓑⓒ	47	ⓐⓑⓒⓓ	67	ⓐⓑⓒⓓ	87	ⓐⓑⓒⓓ
8	ⓐⓑⓒ	28	ⓐⓑⓒ	48	ⓐⓑⓒⓓ	68	ⓐⓑⓒⓓ	88	ⓐⓑⓒⓓ
9	ⓐⓑⓒ	29	ⓐⓑⓒ	49	ⓐⓑⓒⓓ	69	ⓐⓑⓒⓓ	89	ⓐⓑⓒⓓ
10	ⓐⓑⓒ	30	ⓐⓑⓒ	50	ⓐⓑⓒⓓ	70	ⓐⓑⓒⓓ	90	ⓐⓑⓒⓓ
11	ⓐⓑⓒ	31	ⓐⓑⓒ	51	ⓐⓑⓒⓓ	71	ⓐⓑⓒⓓ	91	ⓐⓑⓒⓓ
12	ⓐⓑⓒ	32	ⓐⓑⓒ	52	ⓐⓑⓒⓓ	72	ⓐⓑⓒⓓ	92	ⓐⓑⓒⓓ
13	ⓐⓑⓒ	33	ⓐⓑⓒ	53	ⓐⓑⓒⓓ	73	ⓐⓑⓒⓓ	93	ⓐⓑⓒⓓ
14	ⓐⓑⓒ	34	ⓐⓑⓒ	54	ⓐⓑⓒⓓ	74	ⓐⓑⓒⓓ	94	ⓐⓑⓒⓓ
15	ⓐⓑⓒ	35	ⓐⓑⓒ	55	ⓐⓑⓒⓓ	75	ⓐⓑⓒⓓ	95	ⓐⓑⓒⓓ
16	ⓐⓑⓒ	36	ⓐⓑⓒ	56	ⓐⓑⓒⓓ	76	ⓐⓑⓒⓓ	96	ⓐⓑⓒⓓ
17	ⓐⓑⓒ	37	ⓐⓑⓒ	57	ⓐⓑⓒⓓ	77	ⓐⓑⓒⓓ	97	ⓐⓑⓒⓓ
18	ⓐⓑⓒ	38	ⓐⓑⓒ	58	ⓐⓑⓒⓓ	78	ⓐⓑⓒⓓ	98	ⓐⓑⓒⓓ
19	ⓐⓑⓒ	39	ⓐⓑⓒ	59	ⓐⓑⓒⓓ	79	ⓐⓑⓒⓓ	99	ⓐⓑⓒⓓ
20	ⓐⓑⓒ	40	ⓐⓑⓒ	60	ⓐⓑⓒⓓ	80	ⓐⓑⓒⓓ	100	ⓐⓑⓒⓓ

ANSWER SHEET

ETS® TOEIC® 토익® 정기시험 기출문제집

수험번호						

응시일자 : 20 년 월 일

성명		
	한 글	
	한 자	
	영 자	

Test 07 (Part 1~4)

1	ⓐ ⓑ ⓒ ⓓ	21	ⓐ ⓑ ⓒ	41	ⓐ ⓑ ⓒ ⓓ	61	ⓐ ⓑ ⓒ ⓓ	81	ⓐ ⓑ ⓒ ⓓ
2	ⓐ ⓑ ⓒ ⓓ	22	ⓐ ⓑ ⓒ	42	ⓐ ⓑ ⓒ ⓓ	62	ⓐ ⓑ ⓒ ⓓ	82	ⓐ ⓑ ⓒ ⓓ
3	ⓐ ⓑ ⓒ ⓓ	23	ⓐ ⓑ ⓒ	43	ⓐ ⓑ ⓒ ⓓ	63	ⓐ ⓑ ⓒ ⓓ	83	ⓐ ⓑ ⓒ ⓓ
4	ⓐ ⓑ ⓒ ⓓ	24	ⓐ ⓑ ⓒ	44	ⓐ ⓑ ⓒ ⓓ	64	ⓐ ⓑ ⓒ ⓓ	84	ⓐ ⓑ ⓒ ⓓ
5	ⓐ ⓑ ⓒ ⓓ	25	ⓐ ⓑ ⓒ	45	ⓐ ⓑ ⓒ ⓓ	65	ⓐ ⓑ ⓒ ⓓ	85	ⓐ ⓑ ⓒ ⓓ
6	ⓐ ⓑ ⓒ ⓓ	26	ⓐ ⓑ ⓒ	46	ⓐ ⓑ ⓒ ⓓ	66	ⓐ ⓑ ⓒ ⓓ	86	ⓐ ⓑ ⓒ ⓓ
7	ⓐ ⓑ ⓒ	27	ⓐ ⓑ ⓒ	47	ⓐ ⓑ ⓒ ⓓ	67	ⓐ ⓑ ⓒ ⓓ	87	ⓐ ⓑ ⓒ ⓓ
8	ⓐ ⓑ ⓒ	28	ⓐ ⓑ ⓒ	48	ⓐ ⓑ ⓒ ⓓ	68	ⓐ ⓑ ⓒ ⓓ	88	ⓐ ⓑ ⓒ ⓓ
9	ⓐ ⓑ ⓒ	29	ⓐ ⓑ ⓒ	49	ⓐ ⓑ ⓒ ⓓ	69	ⓐ ⓑ ⓒ ⓓ	89	ⓐ ⓑ ⓒ ⓓ
10	ⓐ ⓑ ⓒ	30	ⓐ ⓑ ⓒ	50	ⓐ ⓑ ⓒ ⓓ	70	ⓐ ⓑ ⓒ ⓓ	90	ⓐ ⓑ ⓒ ⓓ
11	ⓐ ⓑ ⓒ	31	ⓐ ⓑ ⓒ	51	ⓐ ⓑ ⓒ ⓓ	71	ⓐ ⓑ ⓒ ⓓ	91	ⓐ ⓑ ⓒ ⓓ
12	ⓐ ⓑ ⓒ	32	ⓐ ⓑ ⓒ ⓓ	52	ⓐ ⓑ ⓒ ⓓ	72	ⓐ ⓑ ⓒ ⓓ	92	ⓐ ⓑ ⓒ ⓓ
13	ⓐ ⓑ ⓒ	33	ⓐ ⓑ ⓒ ⓓ	53	ⓐ ⓑ ⓒ ⓓ	73	ⓐ ⓑ ⓒ ⓓ	93	ⓐ ⓑ ⓒ ⓓ
14	ⓐ ⓑ ⓒ	34	ⓐ ⓑ ⓒ ⓓ	54	ⓐ ⓑ ⓒ ⓓ	74	ⓐ ⓑ ⓒ ⓓ	94	ⓐ ⓑ ⓒ ⓓ
15	ⓐ ⓑ ⓒ	35	ⓐ ⓑ ⓒ ⓓ	55	ⓐ ⓑ ⓒ ⓓ	75	ⓐ ⓑ ⓒ ⓓ	95	ⓐ ⓑ ⓒ ⓓ
16	ⓐ ⓑ ⓒ	36	ⓐ ⓑ ⓒ ⓓ	56	ⓐ ⓑ ⓒ ⓓ	76	ⓐ ⓑ ⓒ ⓓ	96	ⓐ ⓑ ⓒ ⓓ
17	ⓐ ⓑ ⓒ	37	ⓐ ⓑ ⓒ ⓓ	57	ⓐ ⓑ ⓒ ⓓ	77	ⓐ ⓑ ⓒ ⓓ	97	ⓐ ⓑ ⓒ ⓓ
18	ⓐ ⓑ ⓒ	38	ⓐ ⓑ ⓒ ⓓ	58	ⓐ ⓑ ⓒ ⓓ	78	ⓐ ⓑ ⓒ ⓓ	98	ⓐ ⓑ ⓒ ⓓ
19	ⓐ ⓑ ⓒ	39	ⓐ ⓑ ⓒ ⓓ	59	ⓐ ⓑ ⓒ ⓓ	79	ⓐ ⓑ ⓒ ⓓ	99	ⓐ ⓑ ⓒ ⓓ
20	ⓐ ⓑ ⓒ	40	ⓐ ⓑ ⓒ ⓓ	60	ⓐ ⓑ ⓒ ⓓ	80	ⓐ ⓑ ⓒ ⓓ	100	ⓐ ⓑ ⓒ ⓓ

Test 08 (Part 1~4)

1	ⓐ ⓑ ⓒ ⓓ	21	ⓐ ⓑ ⓒ	41	ⓐ ⓑ ⓒ ⓓ	61	ⓐ ⓑ ⓒ ⓓ	81	ⓐ ⓑ ⓒ ⓓ
2	ⓐ ⓑ ⓒ ⓓ	22	ⓐ ⓑ ⓒ	42	ⓐ ⓑ ⓒ ⓓ	62	ⓐ ⓑ ⓒ ⓓ	82	ⓐ ⓑ ⓒ ⓓ
3	ⓐ ⓑ ⓒ ⓓ	23	ⓐ ⓑ ⓒ	43	ⓐ ⓑ ⓒ ⓓ	63	ⓐ ⓑ ⓒ ⓓ	83	ⓐ ⓑ ⓒ ⓓ
4	ⓐ ⓑ ⓒ ⓓ	24	ⓐ ⓑ ⓒ	44	ⓐ ⓑ ⓒ ⓓ	64	ⓐ ⓑ ⓒ ⓓ	84	ⓐ ⓑ ⓒ ⓓ
5	ⓐ ⓑ ⓒ ⓓ	25	ⓐ ⓑ ⓒ	45	ⓐ ⓑ ⓒ ⓓ	65	ⓐ ⓑ ⓒ ⓓ	85	ⓐ ⓑ ⓒ ⓓ
6	ⓐ ⓑ ⓒ ⓓ	26	ⓐ ⓑ ⓒ	46	ⓐ ⓑ ⓒ ⓓ	66	ⓐ ⓑ ⓒ ⓓ	86	ⓐ ⓑ ⓒ ⓓ
7	ⓐ ⓑ ⓒ	27	ⓐ ⓑ ⓒ	47	ⓐ ⓑ ⓒ ⓓ	67	ⓐ ⓑ ⓒ ⓓ	87	ⓐ ⓑ ⓒ ⓓ
8	ⓐ ⓑ ⓒ	28	ⓐ ⓑ ⓒ	48	ⓐ ⓑ ⓒ ⓓ	68	ⓐ ⓑ ⓒ ⓓ	88	ⓐ ⓑ ⓒ ⓓ
9	ⓐ ⓑ ⓒ	29	ⓐ ⓑ ⓒ	49	ⓐ ⓑ ⓒ ⓓ	69	ⓐ ⓑ ⓒ ⓓ	89	ⓐ ⓑ ⓒ ⓓ
10	ⓐ ⓑ ⓒ	30	ⓐ ⓑ ⓒ	50	ⓐ ⓑ ⓒ ⓓ	70	ⓐ ⓑ ⓒ ⓓ	90	ⓐ ⓑ ⓒ ⓓ
11	ⓐ ⓑ ⓒ	31	ⓐ ⓑ ⓒ	51	ⓐ ⓑ ⓒ ⓓ	71	ⓐ ⓑ ⓒ ⓓ	91	ⓐ ⓑ ⓒ ⓓ
12	ⓐ ⓑ ⓒ	32	ⓐ ⓑ ⓒ ⓓ	52	ⓐ ⓑ ⓒ ⓓ	72	ⓐ ⓑ ⓒ ⓓ	92	ⓐ ⓑ ⓒ ⓓ
13	ⓐ ⓑ ⓒ	33	ⓐ ⓑ ⓒ ⓓ	53	ⓐ ⓑ ⓒ ⓓ	73	ⓐ ⓑ ⓒ ⓓ	93	ⓐ ⓑ ⓒ ⓓ
14	ⓐ ⓑ ⓒ	34	ⓐ ⓑ ⓒ ⓓ	54	ⓐ ⓑ ⓒ ⓓ	74	ⓐ ⓑ ⓒ ⓓ	94	ⓐ ⓑ ⓒ ⓓ
15	ⓐ ⓑ ⓒ	35	ⓐ ⓑ ⓒ ⓓ	55	ⓐ ⓑ ⓒ ⓓ	75	ⓐ ⓑ ⓒ ⓓ	95	ⓐ ⓑ ⓒ ⓓ
16	ⓐ ⓑ ⓒ	36	ⓐ ⓑ ⓒ ⓓ	56	ⓐ ⓑ ⓒ ⓓ	76	ⓐ ⓑ ⓒ ⓓ	96	ⓐ ⓑ ⓒ ⓓ
17	ⓐ ⓑ ⓒ	37	ⓐ ⓑ ⓒ ⓓ	57	ⓐ ⓑ ⓒ ⓓ	77	ⓐ ⓑ ⓒ ⓓ	97	ⓐ ⓑ ⓒ ⓓ
18	ⓐ ⓑ ⓒ	38	ⓐ ⓑ ⓒ ⓓ	58	ⓐ ⓑ ⓒ ⓓ	78	ⓐ ⓑ ⓒ ⓓ	98	ⓐ ⓑ ⓒ ⓓ
19	ⓐ ⓑ ⓒ	39	ⓐ ⓑ ⓒ ⓓ	59	ⓐ ⓑ ⓒ ⓓ	79	ⓐ ⓑ ⓒ ⓓ	99	ⓐ ⓑ ⓒ ⓓ
20	ⓐ ⓑ ⓒ	40	ⓐ ⓑ ⓒ ⓓ	60	ⓐ ⓑ ⓒ ⓓ	80	ⓐ ⓑ ⓒ ⓓ	100	ⓐ ⓑ ⓒ ⓓ

ANSWER SHEET

ETS TOEIC® 토익 정기시험 기출문제집

수험번호

응시일자 : 20 년 월 일

성	한글
	한자
명	영자

Test 09 (Part 1~4)

1	ⓐⓑⓒⓓ	21	ⓐⓑⓒⓓ	41	ⓐⓑⓒⓓ	61	ⓐⓑⓒⓓ	81	ⓐⓑⓒⓓ
2	ⓐⓑⓒⓓ	22	ⓐⓑⓒⓓ	42	ⓐⓑⓒⓓ	62	ⓐⓑⓒⓓ	82	ⓐⓑⓒⓓ
3	ⓐⓑⓒⓓ	23	ⓐⓑⓒⓓ	43	ⓐⓑⓒⓓ	63	ⓐⓑⓒⓓ	83	ⓐⓑⓒⓓ
4	ⓐⓑⓒⓓ	24	ⓐⓑⓒⓓ	44	ⓐⓑⓒⓓ	64	ⓐⓑⓒⓓ	84	ⓐⓑⓒⓓ
5	ⓐⓑⓒⓓ	25	ⓐⓑⓒⓓ	45	ⓐⓑⓒⓓ	65	ⓐⓑⓒⓓ	85	ⓐⓑⓒⓓ
6	ⓐⓑⓒⓓ	26	ⓐⓑⓒⓓ	46	ⓐⓑⓒⓓ	66	ⓐⓑⓒⓓ	86	ⓐⓑⓒⓓ
7	ⓐⓑⓒⓓ	27	ⓐⓑⓒ	47	ⓐⓑⓒⓓ	67	ⓐⓑⓒⓓ	87	ⓐⓑⓒⓓ
8	ⓐⓑⓒⓓ	28	ⓐⓑⓒ	48	ⓐⓑⓒⓓ	68	ⓐⓑⓒⓓ	88	ⓐⓑⓒⓓ
9	ⓐⓑⓒⓓ	29	ⓐⓑⓒ	49	ⓐⓑⓒⓓ	69	ⓐⓑⓒⓓ	89	ⓐⓑⓒⓓ
10	ⓐⓑⓒⓓ	30	ⓐⓑⓒ	50	ⓐⓑⓒⓓ	70	ⓐⓑⓒⓓ	90	ⓐⓑⓒⓓ
11	ⓐⓑⓒⓓ	31	ⓐⓑⓒ	51	ⓐⓑⓒⓓ	71	ⓐⓑⓒⓓ	91	ⓐⓑⓒⓓ
12	ⓐⓑⓒ	32	ⓐⓑⓒ	52	ⓐⓑⓒⓓ	72	ⓐⓑⓒⓓ	92	ⓐⓑⓒⓓ
13	ⓐⓑⓒ	33	ⓐⓑⓒ	53	ⓐⓑⓒⓓ	73	ⓐⓑⓒⓓ	93	ⓐⓑⓒⓓ
14	ⓐⓑⓒ	34	ⓐⓑⓒ	54	ⓐⓑⓒⓓ	74	ⓐⓑⓒⓓ	94	ⓐⓑⓒⓓ
15	ⓐⓑⓒ	35	ⓐⓑⓒ	55	ⓐⓑⓒⓓ	75	ⓐⓑⓒⓓ	95	ⓐⓑⓒⓓ
16	ⓐⓑⓒ	36	ⓐⓑⓒ	56	ⓐⓑⓒⓓ	76	ⓐⓑⓒⓓ	96	ⓐⓑⓒⓓ
17	ⓐⓑⓒ	37	ⓐⓑⓒ	57	ⓐⓑⓒⓓ	77	ⓐⓑⓒⓓ	97	ⓐⓑⓒⓓ
18	ⓐⓑⓒ	38	ⓐⓑⓒ	58	ⓐⓑⓒⓓ	78	ⓐⓑⓒⓓ	98	ⓐⓑⓒⓓ
19	ⓐⓑⓒ	39	ⓐⓑⓒ	59	ⓐⓑⓒⓓ	79	ⓐⓑⓒⓓ	99	ⓐⓑⓒⓓ
20	ⓐⓑⓒ	40	ⓐⓑⓒ	60	ⓐⓑⓒⓓ	80	ⓐⓑⓒⓓ	100	ⓐⓑⓒⓓ

Test 10 (Part 1~4)

1	ⓐⓑⓒⓓ	21	ⓐⓑⓒⓓ	41	ⓐⓑⓒⓓ	61	ⓐⓑⓒⓓ	81	ⓐⓑⓒⓓ
2	ⓐⓑⓒⓓ	22	ⓐⓑⓒⓓ	42	ⓐⓑⓒⓓ	62	ⓐⓑⓒⓓ	82	ⓐⓑⓒⓓ
3	ⓐⓑⓒⓓ	23	ⓐⓑⓒⓓ	43	ⓐⓑⓒⓓ	63	ⓐⓑⓒⓓ	83	ⓐⓑⓒⓓ
4	ⓐⓑⓒⓓ	24	ⓐⓑⓒⓓ	44	ⓐⓑⓒⓓ	64	ⓐⓑⓒⓓ	84	ⓐⓑⓒⓓ
5	ⓐⓑⓒⓓ	25	ⓐⓑⓒⓓ	45	ⓐⓑⓒⓓ	65	ⓐⓑⓒⓓ	85	ⓐⓑⓒⓓ
6	ⓐⓑⓒⓓ	26	ⓐⓑⓒⓓ	46	ⓐⓑⓒⓓ	66	ⓐⓑⓒⓓ	86	ⓐⓑⓒⓓ
7	ⓐⓑⓒⓓ	27	ⓐⓑⓒ	47	ⓐⓑⓒⓓ	67	ⓐⓑⓒⓓ	87	ⓐⓑⓒⓓ
8	ⓐⓑⓒⓓ	28	ⓐⓑⓒ	48	ⓐⓑⓒⓓ	68	ⓐⓑⓒⓓ	88	ⓐⓑⓒⓓ
9	ⓐⓑⓒⓓ	29	ⓐⓑⓒ	49	ⓐⓑⓒⓓ	69	ⓐⓑⓒⓓ	89	ⓐⓑⓒⓓ
10	ⓐⓑⓒⓓ	30	ⓐⓑⓒ	50	ⓐⓑⓒⓓ	70	ⓐⓑⓒⓓ	90	ⓐⓑⓒⓓ
11	ⓐⓑⓒⓓ	31	ⓐⓑⓒ	51	ⓐⓑⓒⓓ	71	ⓐⓑⓒⓓ	91	ⓐⓑⓒⓓ
12	ⓐⓑⓒ	32	ⓐⓑⓒ	52	ⓐⓑⓒⓓ	72	ⓐⓑⓒⓓ	92	ⓐⓑⓒⓓ
13	ⓐⓑⓒ	33	ⓐⓑⓒ	53	ⓐⓑⓒⓓ	73	ⓐⓑⓒⓓ	93	ⓐⓑⓒⓓ
14	ⓐⓑⓒ	34	ⓐⓑⓒ	54	ⓐⓑⓒⓓ	74	ⓐⓑⓒⓓ	94	ⓐⓑⓒⓓ
15	ⓐⓑⓒ	35	ⓐⓑⓒ	55	ⓐⓑⓒⓓ	75	ⓐⓑⓒⓓ	95	ⓐⓑⓒⓓ
16	ⓐⓑⓒ	36	ⓐⓑⓒ	56	ⓐⓑⓒⓓ	76	ⓐⓑⓒⓓ	96	ⓐⓑⓒⓓ
17	ⓐⓑⓒ	37	ⓐⓑⓒ	57	ⓐⓑⓒⓓ	77	ⓐⓑⓒⓓ	97	ⓐⓑⓒⓓ
18	ⓐⓑⓒ	38	ⓐⓑⓒ	58	ⓐⓑⓒⓓ	78	ⓐⓑⓒⓓ	98	ⓐⓑⓒⓓ
19	ⓐⓑⓒ	39	ⓐⓑⓒ	59	ⓐⓑⓒⓓ	79	ⓐⓑⓒⓓ	99	ⓐⓑⓒⓓ
20	ⓐⓑⓒ	40	ⓐⓑⓒ	60	ⓐⓑⓒⓓ	80	ⓐⓑⓒⓓ	100	ⓐⓑⓒⓓ

ETS® TOEIC® 기출문제 한국 독점출간

토익® 정기시험
기출문제집 3

정답 및 해설

1000
LISTENING

YBM

토익® 정기시험
기출문제집 3
1000
LISTENING

정답 및 해설

기출 TEST 1

1 (B)	**2** (C)	**3** (B)	**4** (A)	**5** (D)
6 (C)	**7** (B)	**8** (A)	**9** (C)	**10** (C)
11 (A)	**12** (B)	**13** (C)	**14** (A)	**15** (B)
16 (A)	**17** (C)	**18** (B)	**19** (C)	**20** (A)
21 (C)	**22** (B)	**23** (A)	**24** (B)	**25** (C)
26 (C)	**27** (A)	**28** (A)	**29** (A)	**30** (B)
31 (C)	**32** (D)	**33** (B)	**34** (B)	**35** (A)
36 (D)	**37** (C)	**38** (A)	**39** (D)	**40** (B)
41 (C)	**42** (A)	**43** (B)	**44** (D)	**45** (B)
46 (A)	**47** (D)	**48** (C)	**49** (B)	**50** (B)
51 (B)	**52** (C)	**53** (D)	**54** (B)	**55** (A)
56 (A)	**57** (D)	**58** (C)	**59** (C)	**60** (A)
61 (D)	**62** (C)	**63** (C)	**64** (A)	**65** (C)
66 (C)	**67** (D)	**68** (B)	**69** (C)	**70** (D)
71 (D)	**72** (B)	**73** (C)	**74** (A)	**75** (D)
76 (D)	**77** (D)	**78** (C)	**79** (D)	**80** (A)
81 (B)	**82** (C)	**83** (C)	**84** (A)	**85** (D)
86 (B)	**87** (A)	**88** (C)	**89** (C)	**90** (B)
91 (D)	**92** (B)	**93** (C)	**94** (D)	**95** (A)
96 (D)	**97** (C)	**98** (A)	**99** (D)	**100** (C)

PART 1

1 M-Au

(A) He's parking a truck.
(B) He's lifting some furniture.
(C) He's starting an engine.
(D) He's driving a car.

(A) 남자가 트럭을 주차하고 있다.
(B) 남자가 가구를 들어올리고 있다.
(C) 남자가 시동을 걸고 있다.
(D) 남자가 차를 몰고 있다.

어휘 lift 들어올리다   start an engine 시동을 걸다

해설 1인 등장 사진 – 사람의 동작/상태 묘사
(A) 동사 오답. 남자가 트럭을 주차하고 있는(is parking a truck) 모습이 아니므로 오답.
(B) 정답. 남자가 가구를 들어올리고 있는(is lifting some furniture) 모습이므로 정답.
(C) 동사 오답. 남자가 시동을 걸고 있는(is starting an engine) 모습이 아니므로 오답.

(D) 동사 오답. 남자가 차를 몰고 있는(is driving a car) 모습이 아니므로 오답.

2 W-Br

(A) Some curtains have been closed.
(B) Some jackets have been laid on a chair.
(C) Some people are gathered around a desk.
(D) Someone is turning on a lamp.

(A) 커튼이 닫혀 있다.
(B) 재킷들이 의자 위에 놓여 있다.
(C) 사람들이 책상 주위에 모여 있다.
(D) 누군가가 램프를 켜고 있다.

어휘 gather 모이다

해설 혼합 사진 – 사람/사물/풍경 혼합 묘사
(A) 동사 오답. 커튼(some curtains)이 닫혀 있는(have been closed) 모습이 아니므로 오답.
(B) 동사 오답. 재킷들(some jackets)이 의자 위에 놓여 있는(have been laid on a chair) 모습이 아니므로 오답.
(C) 정답. 사람들이 책상 주위에 모여 있는(are gathered around a desk) 모습이므로 정답.
(D) 동사 오답. 누군가(someone)가 램프를 켜고 있는(is turning on a lamp) 모습이 아니므로 오답.

3 M-Cn

(A) One of the women is reaching into her bag.
(B) The women are waiting in a line.
(C) The man is leading a tour group.
(D) The man is opening a cash register.

(A) 여자들 중 한 명이 가방 안에 손을 넣고 있다.
(B) 여자들이 줄을 서서 기다리고 있다.
(C) 남자가 관광단을 이끌고 있다.
(D) 남자가 금전 등록기를 열고 있다.

어휘 reach into ~ 안에 손을 넣다   cash register 금전 등록기

해설 2인 이상 등장 사진 – 사람의 동작/상태 묘사
(A) 동사 오답. 가방 안에 손을 넣고 있는(is reaching into her bag) 여자의 모습이 보이지 않으므로 오답.
(B) 정답. 여자들이 줄을 서서 기다리고 있는(are waiting in a line) 모습이므로 정답.

(C) 동사 오답. 남자가 관광단을 이끌고 있는(is leading a tour group) 모습이 아니므로 오답.

(D) 사진에 없는 명사를 이용한 오답. 사진에 금전 등록기(a cash register)의 모습이 보이지 않으므로 오답.

4 W-Am

(A) The man is bending over a bicycle.
(B) A wheel has been propped against a stack of bricks.
(C) The man is collecting some pieces of wood.
(D) A handrail is being installed.

(A) 남자가 자전거 위로 몸을 굽히고 있다.
(B) 바퀴를 벽돌 더미에 기대 놓았다.
(C) 남자가 나무 조각들을 모으고 있다.
(D) 난간이 설치되고 있다.

어휘 bend 굽히다 prop against ~에 기대 놓다 a stack of ~ 더미 handrail 난간 install 설치하다

해설 혼합 사진 – 사람/사물/풍경 혼합 묘사

(A) 정답. 남자가 자전거 위로 몸을 굽히고 있는(is bending over a bicycle) 모습이므로 정답.

(B) 사진에 없는 명사를 이용한 오답. 사진에 벽돌 더미(a stack of bricks)의 모습이 보이지 않으므로 오답.

(C) 동사 오답. 남자가 나무 조각들을 모으고 있는(is collecting some pieces of wood) 모습이 아니므로 오답.

(D) 동사 오답. 난간(a handrail)이 설치되고 있는(is being installed) 모습이 아니므로 오답.

5 M-Au

(A) An armchair has been placed under a window.
(B) Some reading materials have fallen on the floor.
(C) Some flowers are being watered.
(D) Some picture frames are hanging on a wall.

(A) 안락의자가 창문 아래에 놓여 있다.
(B) 읽을거리들이 바닥에 떨어져 있다.
(C) 꽃에 물을 주고 있다.
(D) 액자들이 벽에 걸려 있다.

어휘 armchair 안락의자

해설 사물/풍경 사진 – 사물 묘사

(A) 사진에 없는 명사를 이용한 오답. 사진에 창문(a window)의 모습이 보이지 않으므로 오답.

(B) 사진에 없는 명사를 이용한 오답. 사진에 읽을거리들(some reading materials)의 모습이 보이지 않으므로 오답.

(C) 동사 오답. 꽃(some flowers)에 물을 주고 있는(are being watered) 모습이 아니므로 오답.

(D) 정답. 액자들(some picture frames)이 벽에 걸려 있는(are hanging on a wall) 모습이므로 정답.

6 W-Br

(A) She's adjusting the height of an umbrella.
(B) She's inspecting the tires on a vending cart.
(C) There's a mobile food stand on a walkway.
(D) There are some cooking utensils on the ground.

(A) 여자가 파라솔 높이를 조절하고 있다.
(B) 여자가 가판 수레의 타이어를 점검하고 있다.
(C) 이동식 식품 판매대가 보도 위에 있다.
(D) 조리 기구들이 바닥에 있다.

어휘 adjust 조절하다 inspect 점검하다 cooking utensil 조리 기구

해설 혼합 사진 – 사람/사물/풍경 혼합 묘사

(A) 동사 오답. 여자가 파라솔 높이를 조절하고 있는(is adjusting the height of an umbrella) 모습이 아니므로 오답.

(B) 동사 오답. 여자가 가판 수레의 타이어를 점검하고 있는(is inspecting the tires on a vending cart) 모습이 아니므로 오답.

(C) 정답. 이동식 식품 판매대(a mobile food stand)가 보도 위에(on a walkway) 있는 모습이므로 정답.

(D) 위치 오답. 조리 기구들(some cooking utensils)이 바닥에(on the ground) 있는 모습이 아니므로 오답.

PART 2

7
M-Au Why was this afternoon's meeting canceled?
W-Br (A) Room 206, I think.
　　　(B) Because the manager is out of the office.
　　　(C) Let's review the itinerary for our trip.

오늘 오후 회의는 왜 취소됐나요?
(A) 206호실 같아요.
(B) 매니저가 자리를 비워서요.
(C) 여행 일정을 검토해 봅시다.

어휘 cancel 취소하다 itinerary (여행) 일정

해설 회의가 취소된 이유를 묻는 Why 의문문

(A) 질문과 상관없는 오답. Where 의문문에 대한 응답이므로 오답.

(B) 정답. 오늘 오후 회의가 취소된 이유를 묻는 질문에 매니저가 자리를
비웠기 때문이라고 이유를 제시하고 있으므로 정답.

(C) 질문과 상관없는 오답.

8

W-Br You use the company fitness center, don't
you?

M-Cn (A) Yes, every now and then.
(B) Please center the text on the page.
(C) I think it fits you well.

회사 피트니스 센터를 이용하시죠?

(A) 네, 가끔이요.
(B) 본문을 페이지 중앙에 오도록 맞추세요.
(C) 잘 어울리시네요.

어휘 every now and then 가끔 center 중심에 두다 fit 어울리다

해설 회사 피트니스 센터 이용 여부를 확인하는 부가 의문문

(A) 정답. 회사 피트니스 센터를 이용하는지 여부를 확인하는 질문에 네
(Yes)라고 대답한 뒤, 가끔 한다며 긍정 답변과 일관된 내용을 덧붙이
고 있으므로 정답.

(B) 단어 반복 오답. 질문의 center를 반복 이용한 오답.

(C) 유사 발음 오답. 질문의 fitness와 부분적으로 발음이 유사한 fits를
이용한 오답.

9

W-Am Do you have the images from the graphics
department?

M-Au (A) OK, that won't be a problem.
(B) A high-definition camera.
(C) No, they're not ready yet.

그래픽부에서 보낸 이미지 있나요?

(A) 좋아요, 문제없어요.
(B) 고화질 카메라예요.
(C) 아니요, 아직 준비가 안 됐어요.

어휘 high-definition 고화질

해설 그래픽부에서 보낸 이미지가 있는지 여부를 확인하는 조동사(Do)
의문문

(A) 질문과 상관없는 오답.

(B) 연상 단어 오답. 질문의 graphics에서 연상 가능한 high-definition
을 이용한 오답.

(C) 정답. 그래픽부에서 보낸 이미지가 있는지를 묻는 질문에 아니요(No)
라고 대답한 뒤, 아직 준비가 되지 않았다며 부정 답변과 일관된 내용
을 덧붙이고 있으므로 정답.

10

M-Cn When are you moving to your new office?

W-Am (A) The office printer over there.
(B) The water bill is high this month.
(C) The schedule is being revised.

언제 새 사무실로 옮기시나요?

(A) 저쪽에 있는 사무실 프린터요.
(B) 이번 달은 수도 요금이 많이 나왔어요.
(C) 일정이 수정되고 있어요.

어휘 revise 수정하다

해설 새 사무실로의 이전 시기를 묻는 When 의문문

(A) 단어 반복 오답. 질문의 office를 반복 이용한 오답.

(B) 질문과 상관없는 오답.

(C) 정답. 새 사무실로 옮기는 시기를 묻는 질문에 일정이 수정되고 있다
며 정확한 시기를 알지 못한다는 것을 우회적으로 응답하고 있으므로
정답.

11

W-Am Would you like to sign up for the company
retreat?

M-Au (A) Sure, I'll write my name down.
(B) Twenty people, maximum.
(C) Can I replace the sign?

회사 수련회 신청하실래요?

(A) 네, 이름을 적을게요.
(B) 최대 20명이요.
(C) 표지판을 교체해도 될까요?

어휘 company retreat 회사 수련회 replace 교체하다

해설 제안/권유의 의문문

(A) 정답. 회사 수련회에 신청할 것을 제안하는 질문에 네(Sure)라고 수락
한 뒤, 이름을 적겠다며 긍정 답변과 일관된 내용을 덧붙이고 있으므
로 정답.

(B) 질문과 상관없는 오답. How many 의문문에 대한 응답이므로 오답.

(C) 단어 반복 오답. 질문의 sign을 반복 이용한 오답.

12

M-Cn How often do I have to submit my time
sheet?

W-Br (A) Five sheets of paper.
(B) You need to do it once a week.
(C) No, I don't usually wear a watch.

근무 시간 기록부를 얼마나 자주 제출해야 하나요?

(A) 다섯 장이요.
(B) 일주일에 한 번 해야 합니다.
(C) 아니요, 저는 시계를 잘 안 차요.

어휘 time sheet 근무 시간 기록부

해설 근무 시간 기록부의 제출 빈도를 묻는 How often 의문문

(A) 단어 반복 오답. 질문의 sheet를 반복 이용한 오답.

(B) 정답. 근무 시간 기록부를 얼마나 자주 제출해야 하는지 묻는 질문에 일주일에 한 번씩 해야 한다고 구체적인 빈도를 제시하고 있으므로 정답.

(C) Yes/No 불가 오답. How often 의문문에는 Yes/No 응답이 불가능하므로 오답.

13

W-Br I can buy a monthly gym membership, right?

M-Cn (A) A very popular exercise routine.

(B) The exercise room is on your right.

(C) Yes, at the front desk.

헬스클럽 월 회원권을 살 수 있죠?

(A) 아주 일반적인 운동 과정이에요.

(B) 운동실은 오른쪽에 있습니다.

(C) 네, 접수처에서요.

해설 헬스클럽 월 회원권의 구입 가능 여부를 확인하는 부가 의문문

(A) 연상 단어 오답. 질문의 gym에서 연상 가능한 exercise를 이용한 오답.

(B) 연상 단어 오답. 질문의 gym에서 연상 가능한 exercise를 이용한 오답.

(C) 정답. 헬스클럽 월 회원권을 살 수 있는지 여부를 확인하는 질문에 네(Yes)라고 대답한 뒤, 접수처에서 살 수 있다고 구입 장소를 알려 주며 긍정 답변과 일관된 내용을 덧붙이고 있으므로 정답.

14

M-Au Have you put price tags on all the clearance items?

W-Am (A) Yes, everything's been labeled.

(B) It is a little cloudy.

(C) Where is your name tag?

재고 정리 품목에 가격표를 전부 붙였나요?

(A) 네, 전부 라벨이 붙어 있어요.

(B) 구름이 좀 꼈네요.

(C) 명찰은 어디 있나요?

어휘 clearance 재고 정리

해설 재고 정리 품목에 가격표를 부착했는지 여부를 묻는 조동사 (Have) 의문문

(A) 정답. 재고 정리 품목에 가격표를 모두 붙였는지 여부를 묻는 질문에 네(Yes)라고 대답한 뒤, 전부 라벨이 붙어 있다며 긍정 답변과 일관된 내용을 덧붙이고 있으므로 정답.

(B) 질문과 상관없는 오답.

(C) 파생어 오답. 질문의 tags와 파생어 관계인 tag를 이용한 오답.

15

W-Br Don't we still need to change the newspaper layout?

M-Cn (A) Down the hall on your right.

(B) No, it's already been changed.

(C) A new computer program.

그래도 신문 배치는 바꿔야 하지 않나요?

(A) 복도를 따라 가다 오른쪽이에요.

(B) 아니요, 이미 바뀌었어요.

(C) 새로운 컴퓨터 프로그램이에요.

해설 신문 배치 변경의 필요성 여부를 확인하는 부정 의문문

(A) 질문과 상관없는 오답. Where 의문문에 대한 응답이므로 오답.

(B) 정답. 신문 배치를 바꿔야 할지 여부를 확인하는 질문에 아니요(No)라고 대답한 뒤, 이미 바뀌었다며 더 이상 변경할 필요가 없음을 설명하고 있고 이는 부정 답변과 일관된 내용이므로 정답.

(C) 연상 단어 오답. 질문의 change에서 연상 가능한 new를 이용한 오답.

16

W-Br What's the total cost of the repair work?

W-Am (A) It's free because of the warranty.

(B) I have some boxes you can use.

(C) In a couple of hours.

총 수리비가 얼마죠?

(A) 보증 때문에 무료입니다.

(B) 쓰실 수 있는 상자가 제게 몇 개 있어요.

(C) 두 시간 후에요.

어휘 warranty 보증

해설 총 수리 비용을 묻는 What 의문문

(A) 정답. 총 수리비가 얼마인지 묻는 질문에 보증 때문에 무료라고 응답하고 있으므로 정답.

(B) 질문과 상관없는 오답.

(C) 질문과 상관없는 오답. When 의문문에 대한 응답이므로 오답.

17

W-Am Where can I get a new filing cabinet?

M-Au (A) All of the cabins have been rented.

(B) I'll put the tiles in the corner.

(C) All furniture requests must be approved first.

새 서류 캐비닛은 어디서 구할 수 있나요?

(A) 객실은 전부 임대됐어요.

(B) 타일을 구석에 놓을게요.

(C) 가구 요청은 모두 승인부터 받아야 해요.

어휘 cabin (여객선) 객실 approve 승인하다

해설 새 캐비닛을 구할 수 있는 장소를 묻는 Where 의문문

(A) 유사 발음 오답. 질문의 cabinet과 부분적으로 발음이 유사한 cabins를 이용한 오답.

(B) 유사 발음 오답. 질문의 filing과 부분적으로 발음이 유사한 tiles를 이용한 오답.

(C) 정답. 새 서류 캐비닛을 구할 수 있는 장소를 묻는 질문에 가구 요청은 모두 승인부터 받아야 한다며 새 캐비닛을 구하기 위해 밟아야 할 절차를 알려 주고 있으므로 정답.

18

M-Cn　How do I reset my password?

W-Am　(A) By the end of the month.

　　　(B) You should call the help desk.

　　　(C) Thanks for setting the table.

비밀번호는 어떻게 재설정하나요?

(A) 월말까지요.

(B) 컴퓨터 상담 접수 부서에 전화하세요.

(C) 식탁을 차려 줘서 고마워요.

어휘 help desk 컴퓨터 상담 접수 부서

해설 비밀번호 재설정 방법을 묻는 How 의문문

(A) 질문과 상관없는 오답. When 의문문에 대한 응답이므로 오답.

(B) 정답. 비밀번호를 재설정하는 방법을 묻는 질문에 컴퓨터 상담 접수 부서에 전화하라고 대신 문의할 곳을 알려 주며 자신은 답변해 줄 수 없다는 것을 우회적으로 표현하고 있으므로 정답.

(C) 유사 발음 오답. 질문의 reset과 부분적으로 발음이 유사한 setting을 이용한 오답.

19

M-Au　Could you check to see if that monitor is plugged in?

M-Cn　(A) I didn't send them yet.

　　　(B) A longer power cord.

　　　(C) Do you want me to check them all?

저 모니터 전원이 연결돼 있는지 확인해 주시겠어요?

(A) 아직 안 보냈어요.

(B) 더 긴 전선이요.

(C) 전부 확인해 드릴까요?

해설 부탁/요청의 의문문

(A) 질문과 상관없는 오답.

(B) 연상 단어 오답. 질문의 plugged in에서 연상 가능한 power cord를 이용한 오답.

(C) 정답. 모니터 전원이 연결되어 있는지 확인해 달라는 요청에 전부 확인해 주기를 원하는지 되물으며 요청대로 해 주겠다는 것을 간접적으로 표현하고 있으므로 정답.

20

M-Cn　Is the new inventory process more efficient?

W-Br　(A) It only took me an hour.

　　　(B) Yes, she's new here.

　　　(C) I'll have the fish.

새로운 재고 조사 절차가 더 효율적인가요?

(A) 한 시간밖에 안 걸렸어요.

(B) 네, 그녀는 새로 왔어요.

(C) 저는 생선으로 할게요.

어휘 inventory 재고 조사　efficient 효율적인

해설 새로운 절차가 더 효율적인지 여부를 묻는 Be동사 의문문

(A) 정답. 새로운 재고 조사 절차가 더 효율적인지 묻는 질문에 한 시간밖에 안 걸렸다며 긍정하는 대답을 우회적으로 표현하고 있으므로 정답.

(B) 단어 반복 오답. 질문의 new를 반복 이용한 오답.

(C) 유사 발음 오답. 질문의 efficient와 부분적으로 발음이 유사한 fish를 이용한 오답.

21

M-Au　Would you like some ice cream or cake for dessert?

W-Am　(A) Because I'm hungry.

　　　(B) Yes, I liked it.

　　　(C) I'm trying to avoid sugar.

디저트는 아이스크림으로 하시겠어요, 아니면 케이크로 하시겠어요?

(A) 배가 고파서요.

(B) 네, 좋았어요.

(C) 설탕은 피하려고 하고 있어요.

어휘 avoid 피하다

해설 원하는 디저트를 묻는 선택 의문문

(A) 연상 단어 오답. 질문의 ice cream과 cake에서 연상 가능한 hungry를 이용한 오답.

(B) 파생어 오답. 질문의 like와 파생어 관계인 liked를 이용한 오답.

(C) 정답. 아이스크림과 케이크 중 원하는 디저트를 묻는 질문에 설탕은 피하려고 하고 있다며 둘 다 원하지 않는다는 것을 우회적으로 응답하고 있으므로 정답.

22

W-Br　Who's doing the product demonstration this afternoon?

M-Au　(A) That bus station is closed, sorry.

　　　(B) I'm leaving for New York at lunchtime.

　　　(C) Let me show you a few more.

오늘 오후에 제품 시연은 누가 하나요?

(A) 저 버스 정류장은 폐쇄됐어요, 죄송해요.

(B) 제가 점심시간에 뉴욕으로 떠나요.

(C) 몇 개 더 보여 드릴게요.

어휘 demonstration 시연

해설 제품 시연자를 묻는 Who 의문문

(A) 유사 발음 오답. 질문의 demonstration과 부분적으로 발음이 유사한 bus station을 이용한 오답.

(B) 정답. 오늘 오후에 제품 시연을 할 사람이 누구인지 묻는 질문에 제가 점심시간에 뉴욕으로 떠난다며 자신이 제품 시연자임을 간접적으로 알려 주고 있으므로 정답.

(C) 연상 단어 오답. 질문의 demonstration에서 연상 가능한 show를 이용한 오답.

23

M-Cn Your presentation's being reviewed at today's managers' meeting.

W-Br (A) I didn't have much time to complete it.
(B) Next slide, please.
(C) That movie had great reviews.

오늘 관리자 회의에서 당신의 발표를 검토할 거예요.

(A) 마무리할 시간이 별로 없었어요.
(B) 다음 슬라이드 주세요.
(C) 그 영화는 평이 아주 좋았어요.

해설 정보 전달의 평서문

(A) 정답. 오늘 관리자 회의에서 당신의 발표를 검토할 것이라는 평서문에 마무리할 시간이 별로 없었다며 발표 준비를 다 하지 못했음을 간접적으로 응답하고 있으므로 정답.

(B) 연상 단어 오답. 평서문의 presentation에서 연상 가능한 slide를 이용한 오답.

(C) 파생어 오답. 평서문의 reviewed와 파생어 관계인 reviews를 이용한 오답.

24

W-Br Don't you carry these shoes in red?

M-Au (A) I'll lift from this end.
(B) There's a new shipment coming tomorrow.
(C) I have time to read it now.

이 신발 빨간색은 없나요?

(A) 제가 이쪽 끝에서 들게요.
(B) 내일 새로 배송품이 와요.
(C) 지금 읽을 시간 있어요.

어휘 carry (매장에서 상품을) 취급하다

해설 빨간 신발이 있는지 여부를 확인하는 부정 의문문

(A) 연상 단어 오답. 질문의 carry에서 연상 가능한 lift를 이용한 오답.

(B) 정답. 원하는 신발이 빨간색으로도 있는지 여부를 묻는 질문에 내일 새로 배송품이 온다며 현재는 재고가 없음을 우회적으로 응답하고 있으므로 정답.

(C) 질문과 상관없는 오답.

25

W-Am Would you like to have lunch with the clients?

M-Cn (A) About a three-hour flight.
(B) The first stage of the project.
(C) Sure, we can go to the café downstairs.

고객들과 같이 점심 드실래요?

(A) 약 3시간 비행이에요.
(B) 프로젝트의 첫 단계예요.
(C) 네, 아래층 카페로 가면 돼요.

해설 제안/권유의 의문문

(A) 유사 발음 오답. 질문의 clients와 부분적으로 발음이 유사한 flight을 이용한 오답.

(B) 질문과 상관없는 오답.

(C) 정답. 고객들과 같이 점심을 먹겠는지 제안하는 질문에 네(Sure)라고 받아들인 뒤, 아래층 카페로 가면 된다며 긍정 답변과 일관된 내용을 덧붙이고 있으므로 정답.

26

M-Au How about hiring an event planner to organize the holiday party?

W-Br (A) I think it's on the lower shelf.
(B) Sure, I'd love to attend.
(C) There's not much money in the budget.

명절 파티를 준비하기 위해 행사 기획자를 고용하는 건 어때요?

(A) 아마 아래쪽 선반에 있을 거예요.
(B) 네, 참석하고 싶어요.
(C) 예산이 많지 않아요.

어휘 organize 준비하다 budget 예산

해설 제안/권유의 의문문

(A) 질문과 상관없는 오답. Where 의문문에 대한 응답이므로 오답.

(B) 연상 단어 오답. 질문의 party에서 연상 가능한 attend를 이용한 오답.

(C) 정답. 명절 파티를 준비하기 위해 행사 기획자를 고용하자는 제안에 예산이 많지 않다는 이유를 들어 우회적으로 거절하고 있으므로 정답.

27

M-Cn Isn't that carmaker planning to start exporting electric cars?

W-Am (A) Yes, I've heard that's the plan.
(B) A ticket to next year's car show.
(C) Congratulations on your promotion!

저 자동차 회사는 전기 자동차 수출을 시작할 계획 아닌가요?

(A) 네, 그럴 계획이라고 들었어요.
(B) 내년 자동차 쇼 티켓이에요.
(C) 승진 축하해요!

어휘 export 수출하다 promotion 승진

해설 자동차 회사가 전기 자동차 수출을 시작할 계획인지 확인하는 부정 의문문

(A) 정답. 자동차 회사가 전기 자동차 수출을 시작할 계획인지 여부를 묻는 질문에 네(Yes)라고 대답한 뒤, 그럴 계획이라고 들었다며 긍정 답변과 일관된 내용을 덧붙이고 있으므로 정답.

(B) 파생어 오답. 질문의 cars와 파생어 관계인 car를 이용한 오답.

(C) 질문과 상관없는 오답.

28

W-Am David trained the interns to use the company database, didn't he?

M-Cn (A) Actually, it was Hillary.
(B) An internal audit.
(C) He's good company.

데이비드가 인턴들에게 회사 데이터베이스를 활용하도록 교육했죠?
(A) 실은 힐러리였어요.
(B) 내부 감사예요.
(C) 그는 좋은 동료예요.

어휘 internal 내부의 audit 감사 company 동료, 일행

해설 데이비드의 인턴 교육 여부를 확인하는 부가 의문문

(A) 정답. 데이비드가 인턴들에게 회사 데이터베이스를 활용하도록 교육했는지 여부를 확인하는 질문에 실은 힐러리가 했다며 데이비드가 인턴들을 교육하지 않았음을 우회적으로 알려 주고 있으므로 정답.

(B) 유사 발음 오답. 질문의 interns와 발음이 유사한 internal을 이용한 오답.

(C) 단어 반복 오답. 질문의 company를 반복 이용한 오답.

29

M-Au Who's responsible for researching the housing market in India?

W-Br (A) The senior director is heading up that team.
(B) Every morning at ten o'clock.
(C) Yes, it's on Main Street.

인도 주택 시장 조사는 누가 담당하나요?
(A) 상무님이 그 팀을 이끌고 있어요.
(B) 매일 아침 10시예요.
(C) 네, 메인 가에 있어요.

어휘 responsible for ~을 담당하는 head up (부서 등을) 이끌다

해설 인도 주택 시장 조사 담당자를 묻는 Who 의문문

(A) 정답. 인도 주택 시장 조사를 담당하는 사람을 묻는 질문에 상무님이 그 팀을 이끌고 있다고 알려 주고 있으므로 정답.

(B) 질문과 상관없는 오답. When 의문문에 대한 응답이므로 오답.

(C) Yes/No 불가 오답. Who 의문문에는 Yes/No 응답이 불가능하므로 오답.

30

W-Am Have you arranged a ride to take us to the convention center, or should I?

M-Au (A) Unfortunately, there isn't an extra bag.
(B) I don't have the phone number for the taxi service.
(C) We've accepted credit cards before.

우리가 컨벤션 센터까지 가는 교통편을 마련하셨나요, 아니면 제가 해야 하나요?
(A) 아쉽지만 여분의 가방이 없네요.
(B) 택시 회사 전화번호가 없어요.
(C) 전에는 신용카드를 받았어요.

어휘 arrange 마련하다 unfortunately 아쉽지만 accept 받다

해설 교통편을 마련했는지 여부를 묻는 선택 의문문

(A) 질문과 상관없는 오답.

(B) 정답. 컨벤션 센터까지 가는 교통편을 마련했는지 묻는 질문에 택시 회사 전화번호가 없다며, 자신은 교통편을 준비하지 않았으므로 질문자(I)가 그 일을 해야 할 것임을 우회적으로 응답하고 있으므로 정답.

(C) 질문과 상관없는 오답.

31

M-Cn These purchases should have been entered on your expense report.

W-Br (A) No thanks, I don't need anything from the store.
(B) The entrance is on Thirty-First Street.
(C) I thought I had until Friday to do that.

이 구매품들은 지출 보고서에 입력됐어야 해요.
(A) 아니요, 괜찮아요. 가게에서 아무것도 필요 없어요.
(B) 입구는 31번 가에 있어요.
(C) 금요일까지 하면 된다고 생각했어요.

해설 정보 전달의 평서문

(A) 연상 단어 오답. 평서문의 purchases에서 연상 가능한 store를 이용한 오답.

(B) 파생어 오답. 평서문의 entered와 파생어 관계인 entrance를 이용한 오답.

(C) 정답. 구매품들이 지출 보고서에 입력되었어야 한다는 평서문에 금요일까지 하면 된다고 생각했다며 정보가 누락되어 있는 이유를 설명하고 있으므로 정답.

PART 3

32-34

W-Br	Hi, it's Martina from Accounting. ^{32, 33} **I'd like to reserve the main conference room for a meeting I'll be leading on Friday with colleagues from our New York office.**
M-Cn	Sure, that shouldn't be a problem. ³³ **What time is the meeting?**
W-Br	It's from nine to eleven A.M.
M-Cn	OK—³³ **I'll block off that time slot for you. Do you need any special equipment besides a laptop and projector?**
W-Br	No, but ³⁴ **I'll need the key so I can go in a little early and set up. Can I pick that up on Friday morning?**
M-Cn	Absolutely.

여	안녕하세요, 회계부 마르티나예요. **주 회의실을 예약하려고요.** 제가 금요일에 뉴욕 사무소 동료들과 회의를 진행하거든요.
남	그럼요, 문제없어요. **회의가 몇 시죠?**
여	오전 9시부터 11시까지예요.
남	알겠습니다. **그 시간대는 막아 둘게요. 노트북과 프로젝터 외에 특별한 장비가 필요한가요?**
여	아니요, 하지만 좀 일찍 들어가서 설치할 수 있도록 열쇠가 필요해요. 금요일 아침에 열쇠를 찾으러 가도 될까요?
남	물론이죠.

어휘	reserve 예약하다 colleague 동료 block off 막다 time slot 시간대 equipment 장비

32

What is the woman preparing for?

(A) A move to a new city
(B) A business trip
(C) A building tour
(D) **A meeting with visiting colleagues**

여자는 무엇을 준비하고 있는가?
(A) 새로운 도시로 이사
(B) 출장
(C) 건물 시찰
(D) **방문하는 동료들과 회의**

해설 세부 사항 관련 - 여자가 준비하고 있는 것

여자가 첫 대사에서 금요일에 뉴욕 사무소 동료들과 회의를 진행하기 위해 주 회의실을 예약하려 한다(I'd like to reserve ~ colleagues from our New York office)고 말하고 있으므로 여자는 뉴욕에서 방문하는 동료들과의 회의를 준비 중임을 알 수 있다. 따라서 정답은 (D)이다.

33

Who most likely is the man?

(A) An accountant
(B) **An administrative assistant**
(C) A marketing director
(D) A company president

남자는 누구이겠는가?
(A) 회계사
(B) **사무 보조**
(C) 마케팅 책임자
(D) 사장

해설 전체 내용 관련 - 남자의 직업

여자가 첫 대사에서 회의를 위해 주 회의실을 예약하려 한다(I'd like to reserve the main conference room for a meeting)고 하자, 남자가 회의가 몇 시인지(What time is the meeting?) 확인하고 있고 뒤이어 두 번째 대사에서 그 시간대는 막아 두겠다(I'll block off that time slot for you)며 노트북과 프로젝터 외에 특별한 장비가 필요한지(Do you need any special equipment besides a laptop and projector?)를 묻는 것으로 보아 남자는 업무를 보조하는 일을 하고 있음을 알 수 있다. 따라서 정답은 (B)이다.

34

What does the woman want to pick up on Friday morning?

(A) A building map
(B) **A room key**
(C) An ID card
(D) A parking pass

여자는 금요일 아침에 무엇을 찾아가려고 하는가?
(A) 건물 지도
(B) **방 열쇠**
(C) 신분증
(D) 주차권

해설 세부 사항 관련 - 여자가 금요일 아침에 찾아가려고 하는 것

여자가 세 번째 대사에서 좀 일찍 들어가서 설치할 수 있도록 열쇠가 필요하다(I'll need the key so I can go in a little early and set up)며 금요일 아침에 열쇠를 찾으러 가도 되는지(Can I pick that up on Friday morning?) 묻고 있으므로 정답은 (B)이다.

35-37

W-Am	Satoshi, ³⁵ **have you already started working on the budget for next year?**
M-Au	Not yet... but I do plan to start it in the next day or so.
W-Am	OK, perfect. ³⁶ **I'd like to add some new engineers to my team next year if we can afford it.** I thought one might be enough,

but I realized we'll probably need three to handle our company's new contracts.

M-Au No problem. I can include that in the budget. [37]**I'll just need the details about the positions, including the job titles and expected salaries. Could you send that to me?**

여 사토시, **내년 예산안 짜는 일** 벌써 시작했어요?

남 아직이요… 그래도 내일쯤에는 시작할 계획이에요.

여 그렇군요, 완벽해요. **형편이 되면 내년에 새 엔지니어 몇 명을 제 팀에 추가하고 싶어요.** 한 명이면 충분할 거라 생각했는데, 회사에서 새로 따낸 계약들을 처리하려면 세 명이 필요하겠어요.

남 문제없어요. 제가 예산안에 포함시키면 되니까요. **직책과 예상 연봉 같은 세부 정보만 있으면 돼요. 저한테 보내 주실래요?**

어휘 budget 예산 afford 형편이 되다 expected 예상되는

35

What task is the man responsible for?

(A) Writing a budget
(B) Reviewing job applications
(C) Organizing a company newsletter
(D) Updating an employee handbook

남자는 어떤 업무를 맡고 있는가?

(A) 예산안 작성
(B) 입사 지원서 검토
(C) 사보 준비
(D) 직원 편람 개정

어휘 application 지원(서) organize 준비하다 employee handbook 직원 편람

해설 세부 사항 관련 – 남자가 맡고 있는 업무

여자가 첫 대사에서 남자에게 내년 예산안 짜는 일을 시작했는지(have you already started working on the budget for next year?) 묻고 있는 것으로 보아 정답은 (A)이다.

▶▶ Paraphrasing 대화의 working on the budget → 정답의 Writing a budget

36

What does the woman want to do next year?

(A) Organize a trade show
(B) Open a new store
(C) Redesign a product catalog
(D) Hire some team members

여자는 내년에 무엇을 하고 싶어 하는가?

(A) 무역 박람회 준비하기
(B) 신규 매장 열기
(C) 제품 카탈로그 디자인 고치기
(D) 팀원 채용하기

해설 세부 사항 관련 – 여자가 내년에 하고 싶어 하는 일

여자가 두 번째 대사에서 형편이 되면 내년에 새 엔지니어 몇 명을 내 팀에 추가하고 싶다(I'd like to add some new engineers to my team next year if we can afford it)고 말하고 있으므로 정답은 (D)이다.

▶▶ Paraphrasing 대화의 add some new engineers to my team → 정답의 Hire some team members

37

What does the man ask the woman to do?

(A) Order some business cards
(B) Write a press release
(C) Provide some additional details
(D) Set up a meeting time

남자는 여자에게 무엇을 해 달라고 요청하는가?

(A) 명함 주문하기
(B) 보도 자료 작성하기
(C) 추가 세부 정보 제공하기
(D) 회의 시간 정하기

어휘 press release 보도 자료

해설 세부 사항 관련 – 남자의 요청 사항

남자가 마지막 대사에서 직책과 예상 연봉 같은 세부 정보가 필요하다(I'll just need the details about the positions, including the job titles and expected salaries)며 보내 줄 수 있는지(Could you send that to me?) 묻고 있으므로 정답은 (C)이다.

38-40

M-Cn Welcome to Business Suit Outlet. How can I help you?

W-Br Hello. [38]**I'm interviewing for a job next week, and I wanted to buy a new suit.**

M-Cn Congratulations! Do you have anything particular in mind?

W-Br Well, [39]**there's one in your display window that looks nice. But I don't really like the color...**

M-Cn That one only comes in black. But we do have suits in other colors that are fashionable and appropriate for business.

W-Br OK. I can only spend 150 dollars, and I'd like a style similar to the one in the window.

M-Cn Let me show you some suits in that price range. By the way, **⁴⁰any alterations needed for the suit are included in the price.**

남	정장 아울렛에 오신 것을 환영합니다. 어떻게 도와 드릴까요?
여	안녕하세요. **다음 주에 취업 면접이 있어서 새 정장을 사려고요.**
남	축하합니다! 특별히 마음에 두고 있는 게 있나요?
여	저, **진열창에 근사해 보이는 정장이 있네요. 그런데 색상이 별로 마음에 안 들어요…**
남	저건 검정밖에 안 나와요. 하지만 멋있고 업무용으로 적합한 다른 색상 정장들도 있어요.
여	그렇군요. 쓸 수 있는 돈이 150달러밖에 없는데, 진열창에 있는 것과 비슷한 스타일로 주세요.
남	그 가격대 정장을 보여 드리겠습니다. 아 참, **정장에 필요한 수선은 모두 가격에 포함돼 있습니다.**

어휘	have in mind ~을 마음에 두다 appropriate 적합한 similar to ~와 비슷한 alteration 수선

38

What does the woman need a suit for?

(A) A job interview
(B) A fashion show
(C) A family celebration
(D) A television appearance

여자는 무엇 때문에 정장이 필요한가?

(A) 취업 면접
(B) 패션쇼
(C) 가족 축하 행사
(D) 텔레비전 출연

어휘 appearance 출연

해설 세부 사항 관련 - 여자에게 정장이 필요한 이유

여자가 첫 대사에서 다음 주에 취업 면접이 있어서 새 정장을 사려 한다(I'm interviewing for a job next week, and I wanted to buy a new suit)고 말하고 있으므로 정답은 (A)이다.

39

What does the woman dislike about a suit on display?

(A) The fabric
(B) The price
(C) The style
(D) The color

여자는 진열된 정장의 어떤 점을 싫어하는가?

(A) 소재
(B) 가격
(C) 스타일
(D) 색상

해설 세부 사항 관련 - 여자가 진열된 정장에서 싫어하는 점

여자가 두 번째 대사에서 진열창에 근사해 보이는 정장이 있다(there's one in your display window that looks nice)면서 그런데 색상이 별로 마음에 안 든다(But I don't really like the color)고 지적하고 있으므로 정답은 (D)이다.

40

What does the man say that the price includes?

(A) Some accessories
(B) Alterations
(C) Sales tax
(D) Delivery

남자는 가격에 무엇이 포함된다고 말하는가?

(A) 액세서리
(B) 수선
(C) 판매세
(D) 배송

해설 세부 사항 관련 - 남자가 가격에 포함되어 있다고 말하는 것

남자가 마지막 대사에서 정장에 필요한 수선은 모두 가격에 포함돼 있다(any alterations needed for the suit are included in the price)고 말하고 있으므로 정답은 (B)이다.

41-43

W-Br Ellenville Public Library. How can I help you?

M-Cn Hi, I'm calling from the company Grover and James. **⁴¹We're interested in filming a scene for a movie in the lobby of the library.** Its historic architecture is just what we're looking for.

W-Br Well… **⁴²we actually had a film shoot in our library last year. And the thing is… they said it would take one day and it ended up taking three. I'm concerned that will happen again.**

M-Cn I understand, but this is a very short scene.

W-Br Well, **⁴³we have a board meeting here next week. I could give you ten minutes at the beginning to give us the details.**

여	엘렌빌 공공 도서관입니다. 어떻게 도와 드릴까요?
남	안녕하세요, 그로버 앤 제임스 사에서 전화드렸습니다. **도서관 로비에서 영화 장면을 촬영하고 싶어요.** 도서관의 역사적인 건축 양식이 딱 저희가 찾는 거예요.
여	저… **실은 지난해에 도서관에서 영화 촬영이 있었어요. 그런데 문제는… 하루가 걸린다고 했는데 결국 사흘이 걸렸어요. 또 그런 일이 있을까 봐 걱정되네요.**
남	이해해요. 하지만 아주 짧은 장면이에요.

여	음, 다음 주에 여기서 이사회가 있어요. 처음에 10분 정도 시간을 드릴 테니 자세히 설명해 주세요.
어휘	architecture 건축 양식　shoot 촬영　end up 결국 ~으로 끝나다　concerned 걱정하는　board meeting 이사회

41

What kind of a business does the man most likely work for?

(A) A legal consulting firm
(B) An architecture firm
(C) A film production company
(D) A book publishing company

남자는 어떤 업종에서 일하겠는가?

(A) 법률 자문 회사
(B) 건축 사무소
(C) 영화 제작사
(D) 도서 출판사

해설　전체 내용 관련 - 남자의 근무 업종

남자가 첫 대사에서 도서관 로비에서 영화 장면을 촬영하고 싶다(We're interested in filming a scene for a movie in the lobby of the library)고 말하는 것으로 보아 영화를 제작하는 일을 하고 있음을 알 수 있다. 따라서 정답은 (C)이다.

42

What does the woman say she is concerned about?

(A) The length of a project
(B) The cost of an order
(C) The opinion of the public
(D) The skills of some workers

여자는 무엇이 걱정된다고 말하는가?

(A) 프로젝트 기간
(B) 주문품의 가격
(C) 여론
(D) 일부 작업자의 기술

해설　세부 사항 관련 - 여자가 걱정된다고 말하는 것

여자가 두 번째 대사에서 실은 지난해에 도서관에서 영화 촬영이 있었다 (we actually had a film shoot in our library last year)고 했고 그런 데 문제는 하루가 걸린다고 했는데 결국 사흘이 걸렸다(And the thing is ~ it ended up taking three)며 또 그런 일이 있을까 봐 걱정된다(I'm concerned that will happen again)고 말하고 있으므로 약속된 영화 촬영 기간이 제대로 지켜지지 않을 것을 우려하고 있음을 알 수 있다. 따라서 정답은 (A)이다.

43

What does the woman agree to let the man do?

(A) Submit an application
(B) Speak at a meeting
(C) Review some books
(D) Measure a space

여자는 남자가 무엇을 하는 데 동의하는가?

(A) 신청서 제출
(B) 회의에서 발언
(C) 책 비평
(D) 공간 측량

어휘　measure 측량하다

해설　세부 사항 관련 - 여자가 남자가 하는 데 동의하는 일

여자가 마지막 대사에서 다음 주에 여기서 이사회가 있다(we have a board meeting here next week)며 처음에 10분 정도 설명할 시간을 주겠다(I could give you ten minutes ~ give us the details)고 말하고 있으므로 정답은 (B)이다.

> ▸▸ Paraphrasing　대화의 **give us the details**
> → 정답의 **Speak**

44-46

M-Au	Excuse me, ⁴⁴**I'm looking for Axel Schmidt's painting titled** *The Tulips*.
W-Am	Unfortunately, his paintings aren't on display. But it's just temporary—⁴⁵**we're putting new flooring in that gallery.** If you come back in a couple of weeks, the floors will be done, and you can see all of Schmidt's artwork.
M-Au	Oh, that's too bad. I really wanted to see that painting.
W-Am	I'm sorry about that. But ⁴⁶**we sell items featuring that painting in the gift shop. You could buy a souvenir so you could enjoy** *The Tulips* **every day!**

남	실례합니다. 악셀 슈미트의 〈튤립〉이라는 제목의 그림을 찾고 있는데요.
여	아쉽게도 그의 그림은 전시되어 있지 않아요. 하지만 잠시뿐이에요. 화랑 바닥을 새로 깔고 있거든요. 2주 후에 다시 오시면 바닥이 완성돼 슈미트 씨의 작품을 전부 보실 수 있어요.
남	저런, 아쉽네요. 그 그림을 정말 보고 싶었거든요.
여	죄송합니다. 하지만 선물 가게에서 그 그림이 그려진 상품을 판매해요. 기념품을 사면 매일 〈튤립〉을 즐기실 수 있어요!

어휘	unfortunately 아쉽게도　temporary 일시적인 feature 특별히 포함하다　souvenir 기념품

44

Who most likely is Axel Schmidt?

(A) A store manager
(B) A construction worker
(C) A journalist
(D) An artist

12

악셀 슈미트는 누구이겠는가?
(A) 점장
(B) 공사장 작업자
(C) 기자
(D) 화가

해설 세부 사항 관련 - 악셀 슈미트의 직업

남자가 첫 대사에서 악셀 슈미트의 〈튤립〉이라는 제목의 그림을 찾고 있다 (I'm looking for Axel Schmidt's painting titled *The Tulips*)고 말하고 있으므로 정답은 (D)이다.

45

What renovation does the woman mention?
(A) Some walls are being painted.
(B) Some floors are being replaced.
(C) Some windows are being installed.
(D) Some light fixtures are being repaired.

여자는 어떤 개조 공사를 언급하는가?
(A) 벽을 페인트칠하고 있다.
(B) 바닥을 교체하고 있다.
(C) 창문을 설치하고 있다.
(D) 조명 기구를 수리하고 있다.

어휘 light fixture 조명 기구   repair 수리하다

해설 세부 사항 관련 - 여자가 언급하는 개조 공사

여자가 첫 대사에서 화랑 바닥을 새로 깔고 있다(we're putting new flooring in that gallery)고 말하고 있으므로 정답은 (B)이다.

▸▸ Paraphrasing 대화의 we're putting new flooring
→ 정답의 Some floors are being replaced

46

What does the woman encourage the man to do?
(A) Visit a gift shop
(B) Send a package
(C) Wait for a bus
(D) Take a photograph

여자는 남자에게 무엇을 하라고 권하는가?
(A) 선물 가게 방문하기
(B) 소포 보내기
(C) 버스 기다리기
(D) 사진 찍기

해설 세부 사항 관련 - 여자의 권고 사항

여자가 마지막 대사에서 선물 가게에서 그 그림이 그려진 상품을 판매한다 (we sell items featuring that painting in the gift shop)고 했고 기념품을 사면 매일 〈튤립〉을 즐길 수 있다(You could buy a souvenir ~ *The Tulips* every day!)며 선물 가게에 가서 기념품을 살 것을 권유하고 있으므로 정답은 (A)이다.

47-49

W-Br Hey, Dmitry. ⁴⁷Are you still working on your sales report? Collecting all the data from the car dealerships in my region is taking me such a long time. Especially because this year management wants additional information on vehicle purchases, like model and color...

M-Au ⁴⁸Are you using the sales computation software? That's what I used for my report, and it worked really well.

W-Br Oh—⁴⁸you already finished it?

M-Au Well—I'm done collecting and analyzing the data, but ⁴⁹I'm having trouble with the presentation. We didn't get any guidelines for that.

W-Br ⁴⁹Remember Julie's presentation last year? It was very impressive. The slides are available on our company intranet.

여 안녕, 드미트리. 아직 판매 보고서를 작성하고 있어요? 제 담당 지역의 자동차 대리점들에서 데이터를 전부 수집하는 데 시간이 너무 걸리네요. 특히 올해는 경영진이 모델과 색상 같은 차량 구매에 관한 추가 정보를 원하거든요…

남 판매 계산 소프트웨어 쓰고 있어요? 제가 보고서에 그걸 썼는데, 정말 효과가 좋았어요.

여 아, 벌써 끝냈어요?

남 그게, 데이터 수집과 분석은 마쳤는데 발표 때문에 애를 먹고 있어요. 어떤 지침도 받지 못했거든요.

여 지난해 줄리 발표 기억나요? 대단했죠. 회사 내부 전산망에서 슬라이드를 볼 수 있어요.

어휘 especially 특히   purchase 구매   computation 계산   analyze 분석하다

47

What does the speakers' company most likely sell?
(A) Electronics
(B) Clothing
(C) Food
(D) Automobiles

화자들의 회사는 무엇을 판매하겠는가?
(A) 전자 제품
(B) 의류
(C) 식품
(D) 자동차

해설 세부 사항 관련 - 화자들의 회사가 판매하는 것

여자가 첫 대사에서 아직 판매 보고서를 작성하고 있는지(Are you still working on your sales report?)를 물으며 담당 지역의 자동차 대리점들에서 데이터를 전부 수집하는 데 시간이 너무 걸린다(Collecting all the data from ~ such a long time)고 말하는 것으로 보아 화자들은 자동차를 판매하는 회사에 근무하고 있음을 알 수 있다. 따라서 정답은 (D)이다.

48

Why is the woman surprised?

(A) Some software is expensive.

(B) A color is very bright.

(C) The man has completed a report.

(D) The man bought a new car.

여자는 왜 놀라는가?
(A) 소프트웨어가 비싸다.
(B) 색상이 매우 밝다.
(C) 남자가 보고서를 끝냈다.
(D) 남자가 새 차를 샀다.

해설 세부 사항 관련 – 여자가 놀라는 이유

남자가 첫 대사에서 판매 계산 소프트웨어를 쓰고 있는지(Are you using the sales computation software?)를 물으며 보고서에 그것을 썼는데 정말 효과가 좋았다(That's what I used for my report, and it worked really well)며 자신은 소프트웨어를 활용해 보고서 작성을 끝냈음을 내비치자 여자가 벌써 끝냈느냐(you already finished it?)며 놀라서 묻고 있는 것으로 보아 정답은 (C)이다.

49

Why does the woman say, "The slides are available on our company intranet"?

(A) To request assistance reviewing a document

(B) To recommend using a document as a reference

(C) To report that a task has been completed

(D) To indicate that a file is in the wrong location

여자가 "회사 내부 전산망에서 슬라이드를 볼 수 있어요"라고 말하는 이유는 무엇인가?
(A) 문서를 검토하는 데 도움을 요청하려고
(B) 문서를 참고로 활용하도록 권하려고
(C) 작업이 완료되었다고 보고하려고
(D) 파일이 엉뚱한 곳에 있다고 지적하려고

해설 화자의 의도 파악 – 회사 내부 전산망에서 슬라이드를 볼 수 있다는 말의 의도

앞에서 남자가 발표 때문에 애를 먹고 있다(I'm having trouble with the presentation)며 어떤 지침도 받지 못했다(We didn't get any guidelines for that)고 말하자 여자가 지난해 줄리의 발표를 기억하는지(Remember Julie's presentation last year?) 물으며 정말 대단했다(It was very impressive)고 말한 뒤 인용문을 언급하고 있으므로, 남자에게 회사 내부 전산망에 있는 줄리의 발표 자료를 참고하면 발표 준비에 도움이 된다고 권유하려는 의도로 한 말임을 알 수 있다. 따라서 정답은 (B)이다.

50-52

W-Am	Thanks for coming in, Omar. **⁵⁰You might've heard that Rosa Garcia is retiring at the end of November. This means her position as director of information security in Singapore will be vacant.** I'd like to know if you'd be interested.
M-Cn	Oh! That would be a promotion for me. Well, hmm. I'll need a little time to think about it and talk it over with my family. **⁵¹I do have a question. When would I start the position?**
W-Am	The first week of December ideally. **⁵²We'd pay for all your moving expenses, of course.** If you decide to accept the offer.

여	와 줘서 고마워요, 오마르. **로사 가르시아가 11월 말에 퇴직한다는 소식 들으셨을 거예요. 그러니까 싱가포르 정보보안국장 자리가 공석이 되죠.** 관심 있는지 궁금해서요.
남	아! 그렇게 되면 저에게는 승진이네요. 저, 음. 생각해 보고 가족과 상의할 시간이 좀 필요할 것 같아요. **질문이 있어요. 언제부터 그 직책을 맡게 되나요?**
여	12월 첫째 주면 딱 좋아요. **이사 비용은 물론 우리가 전부 지불하고요.** 제안을 수락하기로 결정하신다면요.

어휘	retire 퇴직하다 vacant 비어 있는 promotion 승진 expense 비용 accept 수락하다

50

According to the woman, what will happen at the end of November?

(A) An executive will visit.

(B) An employee will retire.

(C) A product will be released.

(D) A study will be completed.

여자의 말에 따르면, 11월 말에 무슨 일이 일어날 것인가?
(A) 임원이 방문한다.
(B) 직원이 퇴직한다.
(C) 제품이 출시된다.
(D) 연구가 완료된다.

어휘 executive 임원

해설 세부 사항 관련 – 여자가 11월 말에 있을 것이라고 말하는 일

여자가 첫 대사에서 로사 가르시아가 11월 말에 퇴직한다는 소식을 들었을 것(You might've heard that Rosa Garcia is retiring at the end of November)이라고 했고 그러면 싱가포르 정보보안국장 자리가 공석이 될 것(This means her position ~ will be vacant)이라고 말하고 있으므로 11월 말에 로사 가르시아라는 직원이 퇴직할 것임을 알 수 있다. 따라서 정답은 (B)이다.

51

What does the man want to know?

(A) Where he would be working

(B) When he would be starting a job

(C) How to get to an office building

(D) Why an event time has changed

남자는 무엇을 알고 싶어 하는가?

(A) 자신이 일할 곳

(B) **자신이 일을 시작하는 시기**

(C) 사무실 건물로 가는 방법

(D) 행사 시간이 변경된 이유

해설 세부 사항 관련 – 남자가 알고 싶어 하는 것

남자가 첫 대사에서 질문이 있다(I do have a question)며 언제부터 그 직책을 맡게 되는지(When would I start the position?) 묻고 있으므로 정답은 (B)이다.

▸▸ **Paraphrasing** 대화의 the position → 정답의 a job

52

What does the woman say the company will pay for?

(A) A work vehicle

(B) A private office

(C) Moving expenses

(D) Visitors' meals

여자는 회사에서 어떤 비용을 지불할 것이라고 말하는가?

(A) 업무용 차량

(B) 개인 사무실

(C) **이사 비용**

(D) 방문자 식사

해설 세부 사항 관련 – 여자가 회사에서 지불할 비용이라고 말한 것

여자가 마지막 대사에서 이사 비용은 물론 우리가 전부 지불할 것(We'd pay for all your moving expenses, of course)이라고 말하고 있으므로 정답은 (C)이다.

53-55 3인 대화

M-Cn	Maryam, ⁵³**did you hear that our construction company won the bid to build the river dam next to Burton City?**
W-Br	I did! This is such a major project for us... ⁵⁴**the dam's expected to produce enough electricity to power all of Burton.**
M-Cn	Right. Say, do you know when construction will begin?
W-Br	I don't, but here comes the project manager now. He may have a better idea... ⁵⁵**Gerhard, are there any updates on the dam construction?**

M-Au Well, ⁵⁵**we're going to have to wait until all the permits are approved.** It'll be a while before anything else can happen.

남1	마리암, 우리 건설사가 버튼 시티 옆에 강 댐을 건설하는 입찰을 따냈다는 소식 들었어요?
여	들었어요! 우리한테 아주 중요한 프로젝트죠… 그 댐이 버튼 시 전체에 전력을 공급할 만큼 충분한 전기를 생산하리라 기대하고 있거든요.
남1	맞아요. 저기, 공사가 언제 시작되는지 아세요?
여	몰라요, 그런데 지금 프로젝트 매니저가 오네요. 매니저는 알지도 몰라요… 게르하르트, 댐 건설 관련해서 새로운 소식이 있나요?
남2	글쎄요, 허가가 전부 승인될 때까지 기다려야 해요. 다른 일이 생기려면 시간이 좀 걸릴 거에요.

어휘	win the bid 입찰을 따내다 be expected to ~하리라 예상되다 permit 허가(증) approve 승인하다

53

What industry do the speakers work in?

(A) Manufacturing

(B) Agriculture

(C) Transportation

(D) Construction

화자들은 어떤 업종에서 일하는가?

(A) 제조

(B) 농업

(C) 운송

(D) **건설**

해설 전체 내용 관련 – 화자들의 근무 업종

남자가 첫 대사에서 우리 건설사가 버튼 시티 옆에 강 댐을 건설하는 입찰을 따냈다는 소식을 들었는지(did you hear that our construction company won the bid to build the river dam next to Burton City?) 물으며 '우리 건설사'라고 언급하고 있으므로 정답은 (D)이다.

54

What does the woman say a project will do for a city?

(A) Increase tourism

(B) Generate electricity

(C) Preserve natural resources

(D) Improve property values

여자는 프로젝트가 도시를 위해 무엇을 할 것이라고 말하는가?

(A) 관광업 증대

(B) **전기 생산**

(C) 천연자원 보존

(D) 자산 가치 향상

어휘 generate 생산하다 preserve 보존하다 property 자산

해설 세부 사항 관련 - 여자가 프로젝트가 도시를 위해 할 것이라고 말하는 일

여자가 첫 대사에서 그 댐이 버튼 시 전체에 전력을 공급할 만큼 충분한 전기를 생산하리라 기대하고 있다(the dam's expected to produce enough electricity to power all of Burton)고 말하고 있으므로 정답은 (B)이다.

> ▸ Paraphrasing 대화의 produce → 정답의 Generate

55

What does Gerhard say needs to be done?

(A) Permits need to be approved.
(B) Employees need to be trained.
(C) Materials need to be ordered.
(D) Inspections need to be made.

게르하르트는 무엇이 처리되어야 한다고 말하는가?
(A) 허가를 받아야 한다.
(B) 직원들이 교육을 받아야 한다.
(C) 자재를 주문해야 한다.
(D) 점검이 필요하다.

어휘 inspection 점검

해설 세부 사항 관련 - 게르하르트가 처리되어야 한다고 말하는 것

여자가 두 번째 대사에서 게르하르트(Gerhard)를 부르면서 댐 건설 관련해서 새로운 소식이 있는지(are there any updates on the dam construction?)를 묻자 두 번째 남자가 답변을 하는 것으로 보아 이 사람이 게르하르트이며 허가가 전부 승인될 때까지 기다려야 한다(we're going to have to wait until all the permits are approved)고 말하고 있으므로 정답은 (A)이다.

56-58

M-Au	⁵⁶I have a question about a customer's prescription—he's... oh, I'm sorry. I see you're busy.
W-Am	I don't have much to do.
M-Au	⁵⁷His doctor prescribed a 30-day supply of this allergy medication, but I noticed we only have enough on the shelf for fifteen days.
W-Am	Our weekly delivery arrives early tomorrow morning. Go ahead and give him the fifteen, and ask him to please come back for the rest. It's allergy season, so we're selling a lot of that medicine.
M-Au	Then ⁵⁸maybe we should increase the number of bottles in our next order from the distributor.

| 남 | 고객 처방전에 관해 물어볼 게 있어요. 그는… 아, 죄송해요. 바쁘시네요. |

여	별로 할 일이 없어요.
남	고객의 주치의가 이 알레르기 약을 30일치 처방했는데, 보니까 선반에 15일치 분량밖에 없어요.
여	매주 오는 배송품이 내일 아침 일찍 도착해요. 가서 고객에게 15일치를 주고 나머지는 다시 와서 받으라고 부탁하세요. 알레르기가 심한 계절이라 그 약이 많이 팔리고 있어요.
남	그럼 다음에 유통업체에 주문할 때는 병 개수를 늘려야겠네요.

| 어휘 | prescription 처방전 medication 약 medicine 약 increase 늘리다 distributor 유통업체 |

56

What does the woman imply when she says, "I don't have much to do"?

(A) She has time to help.
(B) She plans to leave work early.
(C) Her computer is not working.
(D) She has not received an assignment.

여자가 "별로 할 일이 없어요"라고 말하는 의도는 무엇인가?
(A) 도울 시간이 있다.
(B) 일찍 퇴근할 계획이다.
(C) 컴퓨터가 작동하지 않는다.
(D) 아직 업무를 받지 못했다.

어휘 assignment 업무

해설 화자의 의도 파악 - 별로 할 일이 없다는 말의 의도

앞에서 남자가 고객 처방전에 관해 물어볼 게 있다(I have a question about a customer's prescription)고 말한 뒤 죄송하다(I'm sorry)며 바쁘신 것 같다(I see you're busy)고 말하자 여자가 인용문을 언급한 것으로 보아, 남자의 질문에 응답할 시간이 있다고 말하려는 의도로 볼 수 있다. 따라서 정답은 (A)이다.

57

What does the man notice about some medication?

(A) It needs to be refrigerated.
(B) It has expired.
(C) The dosage has changed.
(D) The supply is limited.

남자는 약에 대해 무엇을 알아차렸는가?
(A) 냉장 보관해야 한다.
(B) 유통 기한이 지났다.
(C) 복용량이 바뀌었다.
(D) 비축량이 부족하다.

어휘 expire 유통 기한이 지나다 dosage 복용량 supply 비축량

해설 세부 사항 관련 - 남자가 약에 대해 알아차린 것

남자가 두 번째 대사에서 고객의 주치의가 알레르기 약을 30일치 처방했는데 보니까 선반에 15일치 분량밖에 없다(His doctor prescribed a 30-day supply ~ only have enough on the shelf for fifteen days)고 말하고 있으므로 정답은 (D)이다.

58

What does the man suggest doing in the future?

(A) Installing some shelves

(B) Confirming with a doctor

(C) Increasing an order amount

(D) Recommending a different medication

남자는 앞으로 무엇을 하자고 제안하는가?

(A) 선반 설치하기

(B) 의사에게 확인하기

(C) 주문량 늘리기

(D) 다른 약 권하기

해설 세부 사항 관련 - 남자가 앞으로 하자고 제안하는 일

남자가 마지막 대사에서 다음에 유통업체에 주문할 때는 병 개수를 늘려야겠다(maybe we should increase the number of bottles in our next order from the distributor)고 말하고 있으므로 정답은 (C)이다.

▸▸ Paraphrasing 　대화의 the number of bottles in our next order → 정답의 an order amount

59-61 3인 대화

M-Cn 　**59 Good morning, Ms. Davis. 60 We've received comments from your legal team on the terms and agreements for the travel rewards credit card that we issued.**

M-Au 　Could you explain the revisions we need to make to be in compliance with the law?

W-Am 　Sure. **60 The problem with the agreement is this: it doesn't disclose to users that if a card isn't used for a year, the account will be suspended.**

M-Cn 　Oh, that's an oversight on our part. We're glad you caught that.

W-Am 　**61 We don't want to be fined by banking regulators, so all cardholders will need to be notified by the end of the month.**

남1 　안녕하세요, 데이비스 씨. 우리가 발행한 여행 보상 신용카드 약관에 대한 그쪽 법무팀의 의견을 받았습니다.

남2 　법을 준수하려면 우리가 뭘 개정해야 하는지 설명해 주시겠어요?

여 　그러죠. 약관의 문제는 이거예요. 1년 동안 카드를 쓰지 않으면 계정이 정지된다는 것을 사용자에게 공개하지 않았어요.

남1 　아, 그건 우리 쪽 실수예요. 발견하셔서 다행이에요.

여 　은행 규제 당국에서 과태료를 부과받고 싶진 않으니까 모든 카드 소지자에게 월말까지 통보해야겠어요.

어휘　terms and agreements 약관　revision 개정　disclose 공개하다　suspend 정지하다　oversight 실수　fine 과태료를 부과하다　regulator 규제 당국

59

Who most likely is the woman?

(A) A travel agent

(B) A bank teller

(C) A lawyer

(D) A mail-room worker

여자는 누구이겠는가?

(A) 여행사 직원

(B) 은행원

(C) 변호사

(D) 우편실 근무자

해설 전체 내용 관련 - 여자의 직업

첫 번째 남자가 첫 대사에서 여자에게 인사(Good morning, Ms. Davis)하며 우리가 발행한 여행 보상 신용카드 약관에 대한 그쪽 법무팀의 의견을 받았다(We've received comments from your legal team ~ that we issued)고 말하는 것으로 보아 여자는 법무팀에 소속되어 있으므로 정답은 (C)이다.

60

What kind of document are the speakers discussing?

(A) A user agreement

(B) An employment contract

(C) A list of travel expenses

(D) An insurance certificate

화자들은 어떤 종류의 문서를 의논하는가?

(A) 사용자 약관

(B) 고용 계약

(C) 여행 경비 목록

(D) 보험 증서

어휘 insurance 보험　certificate 증서

해설 세부 사항 관련 - 화자들이 논의하고 있는 문서

첫 번째 남자가 첫 대사에서 우리가 발행한 여행 보상 신용카드 약관에 대한 법무팀의 의견을 받았다(We've received ~ agreements for the travel rewards credit card that we issued)고 했고, 여자가 첫 대사에서 약관의 문제는 1년 동안 카드를 쓰지 않으면 계정이 정지된다는 것을 사용자에게 공개하지 않았다는 점(The problem with the agreement is ~ the account will be suspended)이라며 약관에 대해 반복적으로 언급하고 있으므로 정답은 (A)이다.

61

Why must the document be revised by the end of the month?

(A) To be included in a personnel file
(B) To use in a merger negotiation
(C) To meet a production deadline
(D) To avoid paying a fine

문서는 왜 월말까지 수정되어야 하는가?

(A) 인사 파일에 포함되려고
(B) 합병 협상에 활용하려고
(C) 생산 기한을 맞추려고
(D) 과태료 납부를 피하려고

어휘 personnel 인사 merger 합병 negotiation 협상 avoid 피하다

해설 세부 사항 관련 - 월말까지 문서가 수정되어야 하는 이유

여자가 마지막 대사에서 은행 규제 당국에서 과태료를 부과받고 싶지는 않으니까 모든 카드 소지자에게 월말까지 통보해야겠다(We don't want to be fined ~ by the end of the month)고 말하고 있으므로 정답은 (D)이다.

▶▶ Paraphrasing 대화의 don't want to be fined
→ 정답의 avoid paying a fine

62-64 대화 + 비용 목록

M-Au	Ms. Giordano, it looks like the last of the wedding guests have left. ⁶²**My staff's going to start packing up our dishes and loading the van**.
W-Br	That's fine, thank you. ⁶²**The food was delicious. My son and his new wife were very happy with your service**.
M-Au	I'm glad you enjoyed it. And, again, ⁶³**I'm sorry that some of our waitstaff were late arriving**. They said they drove right past the turnoff.
W-Br	I understand. The venue is difficult to see from the road. ⁶⁴**I really like this location, though, with its view of the mountains from the gardens in the back**.

남	조르다노 씨, 마지막 결혼식 하객들이 떠난 것 같군요. **저희 직원이 접시를 챙겨서 승합차에 실을 겁니다.**
여	좋아요, 감사합니다. **음식이 맛있었어요. 아들과 며느리가 서비스에 아주 만족했어요.**
남	즐거우셨다니 다행이네요. 그리고 다시 말씀드리지만 **종업원 몇 명이 늦게 도착해서 죄송합니다.** 차를 몰다가 갈림길을 지나쳤다고 하네요.
여	이해해요. 도로에선 이 장소가 잘 보이지 않죠. **하지만 뒤뜰에서 산 경치가 보여서 저는 이곳이 정말 마음에 들어요.**

어휘 waitstaff 종업원들 turnoff 갈림길 venue 장소

Giordano Wedding	
Service	**Cost**
Flowers	$4,456
Photography	$1,300
⁶²Catering	$10,200
Shuttle bus	$400
Total:	**$16,356**

조르다노 웨딩	
서비스	**비용**
꽃	4,456달러
사진	1,300달러
⁶²음식	10,200달러
셔틀버스	400달러
총계:	**16,356달러**

62

Look at the graphic. How much did the man's company charge for its service?

(A) $4,456
(B) $1,300
(C) $10,200
(D) $400

시각 정보에 의하면 남자의 회사는 서비스 비용을 얼마나 청구했는가?

(A) 4,456달러
(B) 1,300달러
(C) 10,200달러
(D) 400달러

해설 시각 정보 연계 - 남자의 회사가 청구한 서비스 비용

남자가 첫 대사에서 저희 직원이 접시를 챙겨 승합차에 실을 것(My staff's going to start packing up our dishes and loading the van)이라고 했고 뒤이어 여자가 음식이 맛있었다(The food was delicious)며 아들과 며느리가 귀사의 서비스에 아주 만족했다(My son and his new wife were very happy with your service)고 말하고 있으므로, 남자의 회사는 음식 서비스를 제공했음을 알 수 있다. 목록에 따르면 음식 비용은 10,200달러이므로 정답은 (C)이다.

63

Why does the man apologize?

(A) Business hours have changed.
(B) A price was wrong.
(C) Some staff arrived late.
(D) A request could not be fulfilled.

남자는 왜 사과하는가?

(A) 영업 시간이 바뀌었다.
(B) 가격이 틀렸다.
(C) 직원 몇 명이 늦게 도착했다.
(D) 요구 사항을 이행할 수 없었다.

어휘 fulfill 이행하다

해설 세부 사항 관련 - 남자가 사과하는 이유

남자가 두 번째 대사에서 종업원 몇 명이 늦게 도착해서 죄송하다(I'm sorry that some of our waitstaff were late arriving)고 사과하고 있으므로 정답은 (C)이다.

64

What does the woman like about a venue?

(A) It has a nice view.
(B) It is conveniently located.
(C) It is tastefully decorated.
(D) It can host large events.

여자는 장소의 어떤 점을 마음에 들어 하는가?

(A) 경치가 좋다.
(B) 위치가 편리하다.
(C) 장식이 품위 있다.
(D) 큰 행사를 개최할 수 있다.

어휘 tastefully 품위 있는

해설 세부 사항 관련 - 여자가 장소에 대해 마음에 들어 하는 점

여자가 마지막 대사에서 뒤뜰에서 산 경치가 보여서 이곳이 정말 마음에 든다(I really like this location, ~ from the gardens in the back)고 말하고 있으므로 정답은 (A)이다.

65-67 대화 + 좌석 배치도

W-Am Hey, Thomas? You like concerts. **65Any chance you're interested in the local band showcase this weekend? I have two tickets that I don't need.**

M-Au **65You got tickets to that? That's surprising! I heard that they sold out in just a few days.**

W-Am They did, but I actually won these in a radio contest. That's why I'm giving them away instead of selling them. **66Good seats, too. Right in the middle, close to the stage.**

M-Au Sure, I'll take them. Thanks! Why can't you go?

W-Am **67This weekend is my parents' anniversary. My sisters and I are planning a party for them at their home in Boston.**

여 안녕, 토마스? 콘서트 좋아하죠. **이번 주말에 지역 밴드 공개 행사가 있는데 혹시 관심 있어요? 내게 필요 없는 표가 두 장 있어서요.**

남 **그 표가 있어요? 놀랍네요! 며칠 만에 다 팔렸다고 들었는데.**

여 그랬죠. 그런데 실은 라디오 경연 대회에서 표를 상품으로 받았어요. 그래서 팔지 않고 그냥 드리려고요. **자리도 좋아요. 한가운데, 무대 가까이예요.**

남 네, 제가 받을게요. 고마워요! 왜 못 가요?

여 **이번 주말이 부모님 기념일이에요. 여동생들과 함께 보스턴에 있는 부모님 댁에서 파티를 열 계획이에요.**

어휘 anniversary 기념일

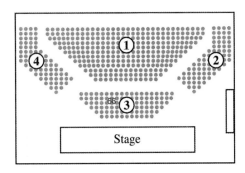

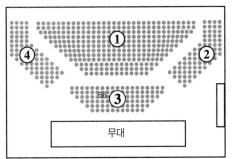

65

Why is the man surprised?

(A) A popular band is coming to town.
(B) The woman plays a musical instrument.
(C) The woman was able to get concert tickets.
(D) Some musicians scheduled a second concert.

남자는 왜 놀라는가?

(A) 인기 있는 밴드가 시내에 온다.
(B) 여자가 악기를 연주한다.
(C) 여자가 콘서트 티켓을 구할 수 있었다.
(D) 음악가들이 두 번째 콘서트를 계획했다.

해설 세부 사항 관련 - 남자가 놀라는 이유

여자가 첫 대사에서 이번 주말에 지역 밴드 공개 행사가 있는데 혹시 관심이 있는지(Any chance you're interested in the local band showcase this weekend?) 물으며 내게는 필요 없는 표가 두 장 있다 (I have two tickets that I don't need)고 말하자 남자가 그 표가 있는지(You got tickets to that?)를 되묻고는 놀란다(That's surprising!) 면서 며칠 만에 다 팔렸다고 들었다(I heard that they sold out in just a few days)고 말하는 것으로 보아, 여자가 인기 많은 콘서트의 입장권을 구했다는 점에 놀라고 있음을 알 수 있다. 따라서 정답은 (C)이다.

66

Look at the graphic. In which section does the woman have seats?

(A) Section 1
(B) Section 2
(C) Section 3
(D) Section 4

시각 정보에 의하면 여자의 좌석은 어느 구역에 있는가?

(A) 1구역
(B) 2구역
(C) 3구역
(D) 4구역

해설 시각 정보 연계 - 여자의 좌석이 있는 구역

여자가 두 번째 대사에서 자리가 좋다(Good seats)며 한가운데 무대 가까이(Right in the middle, close to the stage)라고 말하고 있고, 좌석 배치도에 따르면 무대가 가까우면서 가운데인 구역은 3구역이므로 정답은 (C)이다.

67

What is the woman doing this weekend?

(A) Practicing with her band
(B) Entering a radio contest
(C) Moving to Boston
(D) Attending a party

여자는 이번 주말에 무엇을 하는가?

(A) 밴드와 함께 연습
(B) 라디오 경연 대회 참가
(C) 보스턴으로 이사
(D) 파티 참석

해설 세부 사항 관련 - 여자가 이번 주말에 할 일

여자가 마지막 대사에서 이번 주말이 부모님 기념일(This weekend is my parents' anniversary)이라며, 여동생들과 함께 보스턴에 있는 부모님 댁에서 파티를 열 계획(My sisters and I are planning a party for them at their home in Boston)이라고 말하고 있으므로 여자는 주말에 부모님의 기념일 파티에 참석할 것임을 알 수 있다. 따라서 정답은 (D)이다.

68-70 대화 + 명부

M-Cn Hello. 68**Bellevue Apartments Management Office. Can I help you?**

W-Am Hi. I'm Azusa Suzuki. 69**I'm a new tenant here, and I live in 2A.**

M-Cn How's everything in your apartment so far?

W-Am Very good. One thing, though... 69**When can you put my name on the building**

directory? It still says the previous tenant's name.

M-Cn No problem. I can send someone over now. Unit 2A, you said?

W-Am Yes. And, 70**I'll be stopping by your office tomorrow with my February rent check.**

M-Cn OK. See you then.

남 안녕하세요. **벨뷰 아파트 관리소입니다. 도와 드릴까요?**

여 안녕하세요. 저는 아즈사 스즈키예요. **여기 새로 입주한 세입자로, 2A에 살고 있어요.**

남 지금까지 아파트는 별 문제 없으시죠?

여 아주 좋아요. 하지만 한 가지··· **건물 명부에 제 이름을 언제 올려 주실 수 있나요? 아직도 이전 세입자의 이름이 적혀 있어요.**

남 문제없어요. 지금 그리로 사람을 보내 드릴 수 있습니다. 2A호라고 하셨죠?

여 네. 그리고 내일 2월 임대료를 가지고 관리소에 들를게요.

남 네. 그럼 그때 뵙겠습니다.

어휘 tenant 세입자 previous 이전의

Bellevue Apartments	
1A	Tanaka
1B	Zhao
69 2A	Mukherjee
2B	Tremblay

벨뷰 아파트	
1A	타나카
1B	자오
69 2A	무커지
2B	트렘블레이

68

Who most likely is the man?

(A) A maintenance worker
(B) A property manager
(C) A real estate agent
(D) A bank employee

남자는 누구이겠는가?

(A) 정비 담당자
(B) 아파트 관리소 직원
(C) 부동산 중개업자
(D) 은행 직원

해설 전체 내용 관련 - 남자의 직업

남자가 첫 대사에서 벨뷰 아파트 관리소(Bellevue Apartments Management Office)라고 전화를 받으며 도와 드릴까요(Can I help you?)라고 묻고 있는 것으로 보아 아파트 관리소 직원임을 알 수 있다. 따라서 정답은 (B)이다.

69

Look at the graphic. Which name needs to be changed?

(A) Tanaka

(B) Zhao

(C) Mukherjee

(D) Tremblay

시각 정보에 의하면 어떤 이름을 변경해야 하는가?

(A) 타나카

(B) 자오

(C) **무커지**

(D) 트렘블레이

해설 시각 정보 연계 - 변경해야 하는 이름

여자가 첫 대사에서 여기 새로 입주한 세입자로 2A에 살고 있다(I'm a new tenant here, and I live in 2A)고 했고 건물 명부에 이름을 언제 올려 줄 수 있는지(When can you put my name on the building directory?) 물으며 아직도 이전 세입자의 이름이 적혀 있다(It still says the previous tenant's name)고 말하고 있으므로 2A의 세입자 이름이 변경되어야 함을 알 수 있다. 건물 명부에 따르면 2A에 표기된 이름은 무커지이므로 정답은 (C)이다.

70

What does the woman say she is going to do tomorrow?

(A) Fill out a registration form

(B) Meet with some neighbors

(C) Order some furniture

(D) Make a payment

여자는 내일 무엇을 하겠다고 말하는가?

(A) 신청서 작성하기

(B) 이웃 만나기

(C) 가구 주문하기

(D) **납부하기**

해설 세부 사항 관련 - 여자가 내일 하겠다고 말하는 일

여자가 세 번째 대사에서 내일 2월 임대료를 가지고 관리소에 들르겠다 (I'll be stopping by your office tomorrow with my February rent check)고 말하고 있으므로 여자는 내일 임대료를 지불할 것임을 알 수 있다. 따라서 정답은 (D)이다.

PART 4

71-73 전화 메시지

W-Am Hello, this is Karen Smith. **71I have an appointment with Dr. Miller for my annual eye exam on Tuesday. 72Unfortunately, I won't be able to make it. If possible, I'd like to reschedule for later in the week.** If Dr. Miller is available in the afternoon, that would work better for me. **73I also wanted to ask about your warranty for eyeglasses. What exactly does the warranty cover?** Thank you, and please call me back at 555-0110.

여보세요, 캐런 스미스예요. 해마다 받는 시력 검사 때문에 화요일에 밀러 박사님께 예약했는데요. 아쉽게도 못 가게 됐어요. 가능하면 이번 주 후반으로 일정을 바꾸고 싶어요. 밀러 박사님이 오후에 시간이 되면 저한테는 그게 더 좋을 것 같아요. 안경 보증에 대해서도 문의하고 싶어요. 정확히 어떤 사항이 보증되나요? 감사드리고 555-0110으로 전화 부탁드려요.

어휘 appointment 예약 warranty 보증 cover (보험 등으로) 보장하다

71

What kind of business is the speaker most likely calling?

(A) A hair salon

(B) An insurance company

(C) A car dealership

(D) **An eye doctor's office**

화자는 어떤 업체에 전화를 걸고 있겠는가?

(A) 미용실

(B) 보험 회사

(C) 자동차 대리점

(D) **안과**

해설 세부 사항 관련 - 화자가 전화를 건 업체

화자가 초반부에 해마다 받는 시력 검사 때문에 화요일에 밀러 박사님께 예약했다(I have an appointment with Dr. Miller for my annual eye exam on Tuesday)고 말하고 있으므로 정답은 (D)이다.

72

What does the speaker say about her appointment?

(A) It is too far away.

(B) **It needs to be rescheduled.**

(C) It is too expensive.

(D) It should be with a different person.

화자는 예약에 대해 무엇을 언급하는가?

(A) 너무 멀다.

(B) 일정을 바꿔야 한다.

(C) 너무 비싸다.

(D) 다른 사람과 해야 한다.

해설 세부 사항 관련 – 화자가 예약에 대해 언급하는 것

화자가 중반부에 아쉽게도 못 가게 됐다(Unfortunately, I won't be able to make it)며 가능하면 이번 주 후반으로 일정을 바꾸고 싶다(If possible, I'd like to reschedule for later in the week)고 말하고 있으므로 정답은 (B)이다.

73

What is the speaker interested in learning more about?

(A) Payment methods

(B) Delivery options

(C) A warranty

(D) A job opening

화자는 무엇을 더 알고 싶어 하는가?

(A) 결제 방식

(B) 배송 선택 사항

(C) 보증

(D) 일자리

해설 세부 사항 관련 – 화자가 더 알고 싶어 하는 것

화자가 후반부에 안경 보증에 대해서도 문의하고 싶다(I also wanted to ask about your warranty for eyeglasses)며 정확히 어떤 사항이 보증되는지(What exactly does the warranty cover?)를 묻고 있으므로 정답은 (C)이다.

74-76 광고

M-Cn **74Curious about how chocolate is made? Then come visit us at Bodin's Chocolate Factory!** You'll have a great time. **74We offer guided tours every Saturday and Sunday at our factory, located directly across from Appleton Shopping Center.** During your two-hour visit, you'll observe the creation and packaging of Bodin's products. And **75each visitor will get their picture taken with Cheery, our adorable chocolate mascot, to take home as a souvenir.** Right now, **76with the coupon available on our Web site, you can bring in a group of twelve or more people for half the price.** Download yours today!

초콜릿이 어떻게 만들어지는지 궁금하신가요? 그렇다면 보딘 초콜릿 공장으로 오세요! 아주 재미있으실 겁니다. **매주 토요일과 일요일, 애플턴 쇼핑센터 바로 맞은편에 있는 공장에서 가이드 견학을 제공합니다.** 두 시간의 방문 동안 보딘 제품을 만들고 포장하는 과정을 지켜보시게 됩니다. 그리고 **모든 방문객은 당사의 귀여운 초콜릿 마스코트인 치어리와**

함께 사진을 찍고 기념품으로 가져가실 수 있습니다. 현재 **웹사이트에서 받을 수 있는 쿠폰이 있으면 반값에 12인 이상 단체로 오실 수 있습니다.** 지금 내려받으세요!

어휘 adorable 귀여운 souvenir 기념품

74

What is being advertised?

(A) A factory tour

(B) A baking competition

(C) A grand opening

(D) An art show

무엇이 광고되고 있는가?

(A) 공장 견학

(B) 제빵 대회

(C) 개업식

(D) 미술 전시회

해설 전체 내용 관련 – 광고되고 있는 것

화자가 도입부에 초콜릿이 어떻게 만들어지는지 궁금한지(Curious about how chocolate is made?) 물으며 그렇다면 보딘 초콜릿 공장으로 오라(Then come visit us at Bodin's Chocolate Factory!)고 했고 매주 토요일과 일요일에 애플턴 쇼핑센터 바로 맞은편에 있는 공장에서 가이드 견학을 제공한다(We offer guided tours ~ Appleton Shopping Center)며 공장 견학을 홍보하고 있으므로 정답은 (A)이다.

75

What will participants receive?

(A) A poster

(B) A promotional mug

(C) A company T-shirt

(D) A photograph

참가자들은 무엇을 받을 것인가?

(A) 포스터

(B) 판촉용 머그

(C) 회사 티셔츠

(D) 사진

해설 세부 사항 관련 – 참가자들이 받을 것

화자가 중반부에 모든 방문객은 당사의 귀여운 초콜릿 마스코트인 치어리와 함께 사진을 찍고 기념품으로 가져갈 수 있다(each visitor will get their picture taken with Cheery, our adorable chocolate mascot, to take home as a souvenir)고 말하고 있으므로 정답은 (D)이다.

76

What can the listeners do on a Web site?

(A) Find a recipe

(B) Fill out an entry form

(C) View a product list

(D) Download a coupon

청자들은 웹사이트에서 무엇을 할 수 있는가?

(A) 조리법 찾기
(B) 참가 신청서 작성하기
(C) 제품 목록 보기
(D) 쿠폰 내려받기

해설 세부 사항 관련 – 청자들이 웹사이트에서 할 수 있는 것

화자가 후반부에 현재 웹사이트에서 받을 수 있는 쿠폰이 있으면 반값에 12인 이상 단체로 올 수 있다(with the coupon available on our Web site, you can bring in a group of twelve or more people for half the price)며 지금 내려받으라(Download yours today!)고 말하고 있으므로 정답은 (D)이다.

77-79 안내 방송

> W-Br Attention, everyone. **77 Unfortunately, we've had to stop the movie.** As you've probably noticed, **78 we're having technical difficulties with the audio. I'm very sorry about this**—we take our sound quality seriously and want you to know we'll have technicians here as soon as possible to resolve this issue. As you exit, **79 please stop by the customer service desk in the lobby to pick up two free tickets for your next movie.** Again, my apologies for the inconvenience.
>
> 여러분께 알립니다. **안타깝게도 영화를 중단해야 했습니다.** 아마 아시겠지만, **오디오에 기술적인 문제가 있습니다. 정말 죄송합니다.** 저희는 음질을 중대하게 여기고 있으며, 가능한 한 빨리 기술자를 불러 이 문제를 해결하겠습니다. 나가실 때 **로비에 있는 고객 상담 창구에 들러 다음에 보실 수 있는 영화 무료 입장권 두 장을 받으세요.** 다시 한번 불편을 끼쳐 죄송합니다.
>
> 어휘 resolve 해결하다 inconvenience 불편

77

Where does the announcement take place?

(A) At a sports arena
(B) At a concert hall
(C) At an art museum
(D) At a movie theater

어디에서 나오는 안내 방송인가?

(A) 스포츠 경기장
(B) 공연장
(C) 미술관
(D) 영화관

해설 전체 내용 관련 – 안내 방송의 장소

화자가 초반부에 안타깝게도 영화를 중단해야 했다(Unfortunately, we've had to stop the movie)고 말하는 것으로 보아 안내 방송이 나오고 있는 장소는 영화를 상영하는 곳이므로 정답은 (D)이다.

78

Why does the speaker apologize?

(A) A presenter has been delayed.
(B) Some lights have gone out.
(C) A sound system is broken.
(D) A construction project is noisy.

화자는 왜 사과하는가?

(A) 발표자가 늦었다.
(B) 조명이 꺼졌다.
(C) 음향 설비가 고장났다.
(D) 건설 공사로 시끄럽다.

해설 세부 사항 관련 – 화자가 사과하는 이유

화자가 초반부에 오디오에 기술적인 문제가 있다(we're having technical difficulties with the audio)며 정말 죄송하다(I'm very sorry about this)고 사과하고 있으므로 정답은 (C)이다.

> ▸▸ Paraphrasing 담화의 we're having technical difficulties with the audio
> → 정답의 A sound system is broken

79

What does the speaker offer the listeners?

(A) A promotional item
(B) A parking voucher
(C) Discounted snacks
(D) Free tickets

화자는 청자들에게 무엇을 제공하는가?

(A) 판촉물
(B) 주차권
(C) 할인 간식
(D) 무료 티켓

해설 세부 사항 관련 – 화자가 청자들에게 제공하는 것

화자가 후반부에 로비에 있는 고객 상담 창구에 들러 다음 영화 무료 입장권 두 장을 받으라(please stop by the customer service desk in the lobby to pick up two free tickets for your next movie)고 말하고 있으므로 정답은 (D)이다.

80-82 담화

> W-Am **80 Welcome to Branson Tech's second annual conference on computer security. 81 We decided to try something different to publicize the event this year. We advertised primarily through social media rather than by e-mail newsletters or on company Web sites.** And over 300 people are here! The first presentations will begin in fifteen minutes. The talks will take place in different rooms throughout

the building, so ⁸²**please be sure to check your programs for the list of topics, speakers, and locations.**

브랜슨 테크 사의 컴퓨터 보안 2차 연례 회의에 오신 것을 환영합니다. 올해는 이 행사를 홍보하는 데 색다른 방법을 시도하기로 결정했죠. 이메일 소식지나 회사 웹사이트 대신 주로 소셜 미디어를 통해 광고했습니다. 그런데 300명 넘게 오셨네요! 15분 뒤 첫 번째 발표가 시작됩니다. 강연은 건물 곳곳에 있는 여러 방들에서 진행되므로 프로그램에서 주제, 강연자, 장소 목록을 꼭 확인하세요.

어휘 publicize 홍보하다   primarily 주로

80

What event is taking place?

(A) A technology conference
(B) A product demonstration
(C) A company fund-raiser
(D) A training workshop

어떤 행사가 열리고 있는가?
(A) 기술 회의
(B) 제품 시연
(C) 기업 모금 행사
(D) 교육 워크숍

어휘 demonstration 시연

해설 세부 사항 관련 - 열리고 있는 행사
화자가 도입부에 브랜슨 테크 사의 컴퓨터 보안 2차 연례 회의에 온 것을 환영한다(Welcome to Branson Tech's second annual conference on computer security)고 말하고 있으므로 정답은 (A)이다.

▸▸ Paraphrasing   담화의 computer security
              → 정답의 technology

81

Why does the speaker say, "And over 300 people are here"?

(A) To propose moving to a larger venue
(B) To indicate that some advertising was successful
(C) To emphasize the importance of working quickly
(D) To suggest more volunteers are needed

화자가 "그런데 300명 넘게 오셨네요"라고 말하는 이유는 무엇인가?
(A) 더 넓은 장소로 옮기자고 제안하려고
(B) 광고가 성공했음을 알리려고
(C) 신속한 작업의 중요성을 강조하려고
(D) 더 많은 자원봉사자가 필요함을 암시하려고

어휘 emphasize 강조하다   volunteer 자원봉사자

해설 화자의 의도 파악 - 그런데 300명 넘게 오셨다는 말의 의도
앞에서 올해는 이 행사를 홍보하는 데 색다른 방법을 시도하기로 결정했다(We decided to try something different ~ this year)며 이메일 소식지나 회사 웹사이트 대신 주로 소셜 미디어를 통해 광고했다(We

advertised primarily through social media ~ on company Web sites)고 말한 뒤 인용문을 언급하고 있으므로, 새롭게 시도한 소셜 미디어를 통한 홍보 방식이 효과가 좋았음을 알리려는 의도로 한 말임을 알 수 있다. 따라서 정답은 (B)이다.

82

What does the speaker ask the listeners to do?

(A) Provide feedback
(B) Silence mobile phones
(C) Review an event program
(D) Enjoy some refreshments

화자는 청자들에게 무엇을 해 달라고 요청하는가?
(A) 의견 제공하기
(B) 핸드폰 무음으로 설정하기
(C) 행사 프로그램 확인하기
(D) 다과 즐기기

해설 세부 사항 관련 - 화자의 요청 사항
화자가 마지막에 프로그램에서 주제, 강연자, 장소 목록을 꼭 확인하라(please be sure to check your programs for the list of topics, speakers, and locations)고 말하고 있으므로 정답은 (C)이다.

▸▸ Paraphrasing   담화의 check your programs
              → 정답의 Review an event program

83-85 담화

M-Au Welcome, everyone. ⁸³**On behalf of the Department of Transportation, I'd like to announce a new experimental program to reduce traffic in Greenville.** Beginning in January, there will be a ten-dollar fee for each car that enters the city. ⁸⁴**There will, however, be a lower fee for people who commute to Greenville for work.** They will be asked to pay five dollars rather than ten dollars. These charges are aimed at deterring drivers from coming into this very crowded area. ⁸⁵**The program will be in effect for three months. After that, we will determine if the program has decreased traffic congestion enough to continue it permanently.**

어서 오세요, 여러분. 교통부를 대표해서 그린빌의 교통량을 줄이기 위한 새롭고 실험적인 프로그램을 발표하려고 합니다. 1월부터는 시내로 진입하는 차 한 대당 10달러 요금이 부과됩니다. 하지만 일하기 위해 그린빌로 통근하는 사람들에게는 더 낮은 요금이 부과됩니다. 이들은 10달러가 아니라 5달러 지불을 요구받습니다. 이 요금은 운전자들이 매우 붐비는 이 지역에 들어오는 것을 막으려는 것입니다. 이 프로그램은 석 달 동안 시행됩니다. 이후에 영구히 계속할 수 있을 만큼 이 프로그램으로 교통 체증이 충분히 줄었는지 판단하겠습니다.

어휘 on behalf of ~을 대표하여   experimental 실험적인
reduce 줄이다   commute 통근하다   aim 목표로 삼다   deter
(못하게) 막다   in effect 시행 중인   decrease 줄이다   traffic
congestion 교통 체증   permanently 영구히

83

What is the purpose of the plan?

(A) To support local businesses
(B) To promote tourism
(C) To decrease traffic
(D) To reduce government spending

계획의 목적은 무엇인가?
(A) 지역 기업을 지원하려고
(B) 관광업을 촉진하려고
(C) 교통량을 줄이려고
(D) 정부 지출을 감소하려고

해설 세부 사항 관련 - 계획의 목적

화자가 초반부에 교통부를 대표해서 그린빌의 교통량을 줄이기 위
한 새롭고 실험적인 프로그램을 발표하려고 한다(On behalf of the
Department of Transportation, ~ to reduce traffic in Greenville)
고 말하고 있으므로 정답은 (C)이다.

▸▸ Paraphrasing 담화의 reduce traffic
→ 정답의 decrease traffic

84

Who does the speaker say will receive a discount?

(A) Commuters
(B) Senior citizens
(C) Students
(D) City officials

화자는 누가 할인을 받는다고 말하는가?
(A) 통근자
(B) 고령자
(C) 학생
(D) 시 공무원

해설 세부 사항 관련 - 화자가 할인을 받는다고 말하는 사람

화자가 중반부에 일하기 위해 그린빌로 통근하는 사람들에게는 더 낮은 요
금이 부과된다(There will, however, be a lower fee for people who
commute to Greenville for work)고 말하고 있으므로 통근자들은 할
인을 받게 될 것임을 알 수 있다. 따라서 정답은 (A)이다.

▸▸ Paraphrasing 담화의 people who commute
→ 정답의 Commuters

85

What will happen after three months?

(A) A survey will be distributed.
(B) A new director will take over.
(C) A bus line will be added.
(D) A program evaluation will take place.

석 달 뒤에 무슨 일이 일어날 것인가?
(A) 설문지를 배포할 것이다.
(B) 신임 이사가 인계할 것이다.
(C) 버스 노선이 추가될 것이다.
(D) 프로그램 평가를 실시할 것이다.

어휘 distribute 배포하다   evaluation 평가

해설 세부 사항 관련 - 석 달 뒤에 일어날 일

화자가 마지막에 이 프로그램은 석 달 동안 시행된다(The program will
be in effect for three months)고 했고 이후에 영구히 계속할 수 있
을 만큼 이 프로그램으로 교통 체증이 충분히 줄었는지 판단하겠다(After
that, we will determine ~ enough to continue it permanently)고
말하고 있으므로 석 달 후에 프로그램의 효율성을 평가할 것임을 알 수 있
다. 따라서 정답은 (D)이다.

86-88 방송

W-Br Thanks for tuning in to *Music Today* on
Radio 49. First, **86 a reminder that the Classical
Music Festival is this weekend.** **87 Radio 49 is
giving listeners a chance to win a pair of tickets
by entering a contest.** And tickets are almost sold
out. Just go to our Web site and tell us what you
enjoy most on our station, and we'll pick a winner
at random. This year is the tenth anniversary
of the event, which was founded by a famous
classical musician, Umesh Gupta. **88 On tomorrow
morning's program, Mr. Gupta will be here for an
interview about the history of the festival.** Be sure
to join us for that.

라디오 49 〈뮤직 투데이〉를 들어 주셔서 감사합니다. 먼저, **클래식 음
악 축제가 이번 주말이라는 점을 알려 드립니다. 라디오 49는 청취자 여
러분께 대회에 참가해 티켓 두 장을 얻을 수 있는 기회를 드리고 있는데
요.** 티켓은 거의 매진되었습니다. 웹사이트에 가서 저희 방송국에서 가
장 즐겨 듣는 것을 알려 주시면 무작위로 당첨자를 선정합니다. 올해는
유명한 클래식 음악가 우메쉬 굽타 씨가 설립한 이 행사가 10주년을 맞
습니다. **내일 아침 프로그램에서 굽타 씨가 이곳에 오셔서 축제의 역사
에 대해 인터뷰하십니다.** 꼭 저희와 함께해 주세요.

어휘 tune in to (채널을) 맞추다, 열심히 듣다   at random
무작위로

86

What event is the speaker discussing?

(A) A sports competition

(B) A music festival

(C) A cooking demonstration

(D) A historical play

화자는 어떤 행사를 이야기하는가?

(A) 스포츠 경기

(B) 음악 축제

(C) 요리 시연

(D) 역사극

해설 세부 사항 관련 - 화자가 이야기하는 행사

화자가 초반부에 클래식 음악 축제가 이번 주말이라는 점을 알려 드린다(a reminder that the Classical Music Festival is this weekend)고 말하고 있으므로 정답은 (B)이다.

87

Why does the speaker say, "tickets are almost sold out"?

(A) To encourage the listeners to enter a contest

(B) To suggest that the listeners arrive early

(C) To complain that an event space is too small

(D) To praise the results of a marketing plan

화자가 "티켓은 거의 매진되었습니다"라고 말하는 이유는 무엇인가?

(A) 청취자들에게 대회 참가를 권하려고

(B) 청취자들에게 일찍 도착하라고 제안하려고

(C) 행사 공간이 너무 좁다고 불평하려고

(D) 마케팅 계획의 성과를 칭찬하려고

어휘 praise 칭찬하다

해설 화자의 의도 파악 - 티켓은 거의 매진되었다는 말의 의도

앞에서 라디오 49는 청취자 여러분께 대회에 참가해 티켓 두 장을 얻을 수 있는 기회를 드리고 있다(Radio 49 is giving listeners a chance to win a pair of tickets by entering a contest)고 말한 뒤 인용문을 언급하고 있으므로, 티켓이 얼마 남지 않아 티켓을 받으려면 서둘러 대회에 참여해야 한다고 권하려는 의도로 한 말임을 알 수 있다. 따라서 정답은 (A)이다.

88

What will happen tomorrow morning?

(A) A new venue will open.

(B) A prize winner will be announced.

(C) An interview will take place.

(D) A video will be filmed.

내일 아침에 무슨 일이 일어날 것인가?

(A) 새로운 장소가 문을 열 것이다.

(B) 수상자가 발표될 것이다.

(C) 인터뷰가 있을 것이다.

(D) 동영상이 촬영될 것이다.

해설 세부 사항 관련 - 내일 아침에 일어날 일

화자가 후반부에 내일 아침 프로그램에서 굽타 씨가 이곳에 와서 축제의 역사에 대해 인터뷰를 한다(On tomorrow morning's program, ~ about the history of the festival)고 말하고 있으므로 정답은 (C)이다.

89-91 담화

W-Am Thank you for visiting our booth here at the trade fair. [89]**We're so excited to show you our new patio furniture.** You're probably familiar with our wooden outdoor tables and chairs, and [90]**we want you to know that we've expanded that line to include plastic furniture. This furniture is very durable.** It can withstand any kind of weather—and it needs no maintenance. [91]**I'm going to hand out a sample of the plastic material we use. Please pass it around after you've had a chance to look at it.**

이곳 무역 박람회에서 저희 부스를 방문해 주셔서 감사합니다. **신상품 파티오 가구를 보여 드리게 되어 벅차네요.** 아마 당사의 야외 나무 테이블과 의자는 익히 아실 테니 **저희가 플라스틱 가구로 제품군을 확장했다는 점을 아셨으면 합니다. 이 가구는 내구성이 아주 뛰어납니다.** 어떤 날씨에도 견딜 수 있으므로 유지 관리가 필요 없습니다. **당사가 사용하는 플라스틱 자재 샘플을 나눠 드릴게요. 보실 기회를 가지셨다면 옆으로 돌려 주세요.**

어휘 familiar with ~을 익히 아는 expand 확장하다 durable 내구성이 좋은 withstand 견디다

89

What type of business does the speaker work for?

(A) A computer company

(B) A construction firm

(C) A furniture manufacturer

(D) An office-supply distributor

화자는 어떤 업종에서 일하는가?

(A) 컴퓨터 회사

(B) 건설 회사

(C) 가구 제조업체

(D) 사무용품 유통업체

어휘 manufacturer 제조업체 distributor 유통업체

해설 전체 내용 관련 - 화자의 근무 업종

화자가 초반부에 신상품 파티오 가구를 보여 드리게 되어 벅차다(We're so excited to show you our new patio furniture)고 말하고 있으므로 화자는 가구업체에서 근무하고 있다는 것을 알 수 있다. 따라서 정답은 (C)이다.

90

What does the speaker say is an advantage of the new material?

(A) It is inexpensive.

(B) It is durable.

(C) It is lightweight.

(D) It comes in many colors.

화자는 새로운 소재의 장점이 무엇이라고 말하는가?

(A) 비싸지 않다.

(B) 내구성이 좋다.

(C) 가볍다.

(D) 여러 가지 색상이 있다.

해설 세부 사항 관련 - 화자가 새로운 소재의 장점이라고 말하는 것

화자가 중반부에 우리가 플라스틱 가구로 제품군을 확장했다(we've expanded that line to include plastic furniture)면서 이 가구는 내구성이 아주 뛰어나다(This furniture is very durable)고 말하고 있으므로 정답은 (B)이다.

91

What will the listeners do next?

(A) Sign up for a mailing list

(B) Watch an instructional video

(C) Enter a contest

(D) Look at a sample

청자들은 다음에 무엇을 할 것인가?

(A) 우편물 수신자 명단에 등록하기

(B) 설명 영상 보기

(C) 대회에 참가하기

(D) 샘플 보기

해설 세부 사항 관련 - 청자들이 다음에 할 일

화자가 마지막에 당사가 사용하는 플라스틱 자재 샘플을 나눠주겠다(I'm going to hand out a sample of the plastic material we use)며 볼 기회를 가지고 나면 옆으로 돌려 달라(Please pass it around after you've had a chance to look at it)고 말하고 있으므로 정답은 (D)이다.

92-94 전화 메시지

W-Br **92This is Noriko, the human resources supervisor here in Albany. 93I'm calling about your request to transfer to our branch in Havertown... I know your commute is difficult, and it takes you over an hour to drive to this office. So I've contacted the manager at that location**, and there is a need for a skilled software engineer. There are a few forms that you'll need to fill out, though, to complete the request. **94Now we need to talk about your work schedule to decide when you'll start at the new location**. Please call me back.

올버니 인사팀장 노리코입니다. 하버타운 지점으로 가시려는 전근 요청 때문에 전화드렸어요… 통근이 어렵다는 거 알아요, 이 사무실까지 차로 한 시간 넘게 걸리죠. 그래서 그곳 지점 매니저에게 연락했더니 숙련된 소프트웨어 엔지니어가 필요하더군요. 그런데 요청을 마무리하려면 몇 가지 양식을 작성하셔야 해서요. 이제 근무 일정을 논의해서 새 지점에서 언제 근무를 시작하실지 결정해야 합니다. 다시 전화해 주세요.

어휘 commute 통근 fill out ~을 작성하다

92

Which department does the speaker work in?

(A) Product Development

(B) Human Resources

(C) Legal

(D) Accounting

화자는 어느 부서에서 일하는가?

(A) 제품 개발

(B) 인사

(C) 법무

(D) 회계

해설 전체 내용 관련 - 화자의 근무 부서

화자가 도입부에 올버니 인사팀장 노리코(This is Noriko, the human resources supervisor here in Albany)라고 자신을 소개하고 있으므로 정답은 (B)이다.

93

Why does the speaker say, "there is a need for a skilled software engineer"?

(A) To recommend an employee sign up for more training

(B) To indicate that a project deadline will be extended

(C) To approve a request to transfer

(D) To suggest consulting with an expert

화자가 "숙련된 소프트웨어 엔지니어가 필요하더군요"라고 말하는 이유는 무엇인가?

(A) 직원에게 추가 교육 신청을 권하려고

(B) 프로젝트 기한이 연장된다고 말하려고

(C) 전근 요청을 승인하려고

(D) 전문가와 상담을 제안하려고

어휘 extend 연장하다

해설 화자의 의도 파악 - 숙련된 소프트웨어 엔지니어가 필요하다는 말의 의도

앞에서 하버타운 지점으로 가려는 전근 요청 때문에 전화했다(I'm calling about your request to transfer to our branch in Havertown)고 했고 이 사무실까지 차로 한 시간이 넘게 걸리고 통근이 어렵다는 점을 알고 있다(I know your commute is difficult, ~ an hour to drive to this office)며 그래서 그곳 지점 매니저에게 연락했다(So I've contacted the manager at that location)고 말한 뒤 인용문을 언급하고 있으므로, 청

자가 전근을·요청한 하버타운 지점에 알아본 결과 근무할 수 있는 자리가 있으므로 전근 요청을 인가하겠다는 의도로 한 말임을 알 수 있다. 따라서 정답은 (C)이다.

94

What does the speaker want to discuss with the listener?

(A) Some sales results
(B) Some client feedback
(C) An office renovation
(D) A work schedule

화자는 청자와 무엇을 의논하고 싶어 하는가?

(A) 판매 결과
(B) 고객 의견
(C) 사무실 개조
(D) 근무 일정

해설 세부 사항 관련 - 화자가 청자와 의논하고 싶어 하는 것

화자가 후반부에 이제 근무 일정을 논의해서 새 지점에서 언제 근무를 시작할지 결정해야 한다(Now we need to talk about your work schedule ~ the new location)고 말하고 있으므로 정답은 (D)이다.

95-97 방송 + 일정표

M-Cn You're listening to *Making My Company* with Mark Sullivan. **95In each episode I invite entrepreneurs from around the world to talk about how they built their successful businesses.** In celebration of our radio show's ten-year anniversary, **96our Web site now has all of our previously aired episodes. You can access them with the click of a button.** You can even download them onto mobile devices to listen to on the go! OK, now, I welcome Haru Nakamura to the show. **97Ms. Nakamura is excited to be here today.**

여러분은 지금 마크 설리번과 함께하는 〈내 회사 세우기〉를 듣고 계십니다. 매 회마다 저는 전 세계 기업가들을 초청해 그들이 성공 기업을 구축한 방법을 이야기하고 있습니다. 라디오 쇼 10주년을 기념해 이제 웹사이트에 과거 방송된 회차들이 전부 있습니다. 버튼만 클릭하면 들으실 수 있죠. 모바일 장치에 내려받아 이동하면서 들을 수도 있고요! 자, 이제 하루 나카무라 씨를 쇼에 모시겠습니다. 나카무라 씨는 오늘 여기 와서 설레어 보이네요.

어휘 entrepreneur 기업가 previously 과거에 on the go 이동하면서

This Week's Guests	
Monday	Ling Yu—Part 1
Tuesday	Ling Yu—Part 2
Wednesday	Hilda Orman
97Thursday	Haru Nakamura
Friday	Joseph Samir

이번 주 게스트	
월요일	링 유—1부
화요일	링 유—2부
수요일	힐다 오먼
97목요일	하루 나카무라
금요일	조셉 사미르

95

Why are guests invited on the speaker's radio show?

(A) To discuss their businesses
(B) To talk about local history
(C) To teach communication skills
(D) To offer travel tips

게스트들은 왜 화자의 라디오 쇼에 초대받는가?

(A) 사업에 대해 논의하려고
(B) 지역 역사를 이야기하려고
(C) 소통 기술을 가르치려고
(D) 여행 정보를 제공하려고

해설 세부 사항 관련 - 게스트들이 화자의 라디오 쇼에 초대받는 이유

화자가 초반부에 매 회마다 전 세계 기업가들을 초청해 그들이 성공 기업을 구축한 방법을 이야기하고 있다(In each episode I invite entrepreneurs ~ how they built their successful businesses)고 말하고 있으므로 정답은 (A)이다.

96

What can the listeners do on a Web site?

(A) View photos of famous guests
(B) Sign up for a special service
(C) Read about upcoming programs
(D) Listen to previous episodes

청자들은 웹사이트에서 무엇을 할 수 있는가?

(A) 유명 게스트 사진 보기
(B) 특별 서비스 가입하기
(C) 곧 있을 프로그램에 대해 읽기
(D) 이전 회차 듣기

해설 세부 사항 관련 - 청자들이 웹사이트에서 할 수 있는 것

화자가 중반부에 이제 웹사이트에 과거 방송된 회차들이 전부 있다(our Web site now has all of our previously aired episodes)며 버튼만 클릭하면 들을 수 있다(You can access them with the click of a button)고 말하고 있으므로 정답은 (D)이다.

97

Look at the graphic. Which day is this episode being aired?

(A) Tuesday
(B) Wednesday
(C) Thursday
(D) Friday

시각 정보에 의하면 이 회차는 어떤 요일에 방송되고 있는가?
(A) 화요일
(B) 수요일
(C) 목요일
(D) 금요일

해설 시각 정보 연계 - 해당 회차가 방송되고 있는 요일

화자가 마지막에 나카무라 씨가 오늘 여기 와서 설레어 보인다(Ms. Nakamura is excited to be here today)고 말하고 있고, 일정표에 따르면 나카무라 씨가 게스트로 오는 날은 목요일이므로 정답은 (C)이다.

98-100 전화 메시지 + 매장 진열대

M-Au It's Akira, calling from the district manager's office. The visual merchandising team wants to make a slight change to the fall display standards that we sent you yesterday. [98]**They want to move the shirts with the vertical stripes—hang them instead of having them displayed on the shelf. We'll display some colorful accessories there instead, like scarves and ties.** Also, [99]**hang all the socks on gridwall panels by the cash registers.** Those sell best when people can grab them when they walk up to pay. [100]**The thicker, cold-weather socks will be shipped to you soon. You'll get an e-mail confirmation with the details when they're sent.**

아키라예요. 지역장 사무실에서 전화드려요. 시각 판촉팀에서 어제 보내 드린 가을철 진열 기준을 조금 변경하려고 합니다. **세로 줄무늬 셔츠를 옮기고 싶어 하네요. 셔츠들을 선반에 진열하지 말고 걸어 놓으세요. 거기에는 대신 스카프와 넥타이 같은 화려한 액세서리를 진열할 겁니다.** 또 **양말은 전부 금전 등록기 옆에 있는 격자형 판에 거세요.** 사람들이 계산하려고 걸어가면서 양말을 집을 수 있을 때 가장 잘 팔리니까요. **더 두꺼운 겨울철 양말은 곧 배송됩니다. 배송될 때 자세한 내용을 담은 이메일 확인서를 받을 거예요.**

어휘 visual merchandising 시각 판촉(진열·디자인 등 시각적 효과로 판매를 촉진하는 일) vertical 세로의

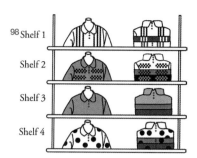

[98] Shelf 1
Shelf 2
Shelf 3
Shelf 4

[98] 선반 1
선반 2
선반 3
선반 4

98

Look at the graphic. Where will the scarves and ties be displayed?

(A) On Shelf 1
(B) On Shelf 2
(C) On Shelf 3
(D) On Shelf 4

시각 정보에 의하면 스카프와 넥타이는 어디에 진열될 것인가?
(A) 선반 1
(B) 선반 2
(C) 선반 3
(D) 선반 4

해설 시각 정보 연계 - 스카프와 넥타이가 진열될 위치

화자가 초반부에 판촉팀이 세로 줄무늬 셔츠를 옮기고 싶어 하는데 선반에 진열하지 말고 걸어 놓으라(They want to move the shirts ~ instead of having them displayed on the shelf)고 했고 거기에는 대신 스카프와 넥타이 같은 화려한 액세서리를 진열할 것(We'll display some ~ like scarves and ties)이라고 말하고 있으므로 스카프와 넥타이는 세로 줄무늬 셔츠가 있던 자리에 진열될 예정임을 알 수 있다. 매장 진열대에 따르면, 세로 줄무늬 셔츠는 선반 1에 있으므로 정답은 (A)이다.

99

What should be displayed near the cash registers?

(A) Coupons
(B) Hats
(C) Gloves
(D) Socks

금전 등록기 근처에 진열되어야 하는 것은 무엇인가?
(A) 쿠폰
(B) 모자
(C) 장갑
(D) 양말

해설 세부 사항 관련 – 금전 등록기 근처에 진열되어야 하는 것

화자가 중반부에 양말은 전부 금전 등록기 옆에 있는 격자형 판에 걸라 (hang all the socks on gridwall panels by the cash registers)고 말하고 있으므로 정답은 (D)이다.

100

What should the listener expect to receive in an e-mail?

(A) A payment schedule
(B) Photographs
(C) Shipping information
(D) Display measurements

청자는 이메일로 무엇을 받을 예정인가?

(A) 지급 일정
(B) 사진
(C) 배송 정보
(D) 진열 평가

해설 세부 사항 관련 – 청자가 이메일로 받을 것

화자가 마지막에 더 두꺼운 겨울철 양말이 곧 배송될 것(The thicker, cold-weather socks will be shipped to you soon)이라며 배송될 때 자세한 내용을 담은 이메일 확인서를 받을 것(You'll get an e-mail confirmation with the details when they're sent)이라고 말하고 있으므로 양말 배송에 관련된 정보를 받아볼 것임을 알 수 있다. 따라서 정답은 (C)이다.

기출 TEST 2

1 (B)	**2** (D)	**3** (C)	**4** (C)	**5** (B)
6 (A)	**7** (A)	**8** (C)	**9** (B)	**10** (A)
11 (C)	**12** (B)	**13** (A)	**14** (C)	**15** (B)
16 (A)	**17** (B)	**18** (A)	**19** (B)	**20** (B)
21 (A)	**22** (C)	**23** (C)	**24** (B)	**25** (C)
26 (A)	**27** (A)	**28** (B)	**29** (B)	**30** (B)
31 (A)	**32** (D)	**33** (B)	**34** (C)	**35** (D)
36 (A)	**37** (C)	**38** (B)	**39** (C)	**40** (A)
41 (D)	**42** (A)	**43** (C)	**44** (C)	**45** (D)
46 (C)	**47** (B)	**48** (D)	**49** (A)	**50** (B)
51 (C)	**52** (A)	**53** (A)	**54** (C)	**55** (B)
56 (A)	**57** (B)	**58** (C)	**59** (D)	**60** (D)
61 (B)	**62** (A)	**63** (C)	**64** (B)	**65** (D)
66 (C)	**67** (A)	**68** (D)	**69** (B)	**70** (A)
71 (B)	**72** (A)	**73** (C)	**74** (D)	**75** (C)
76 (A)	**77** (A)	**78** (D)	**79** (C)	**80** (B)
81 (D)	**82** (A)	**83** (C)	**84** (B)	**85** (D)
86 (D)	**87** (A)	**88** (C)	**89** (C)	**90** (D)
91 (B)	**92** (D)	**93** (B)	**94** (D)	**95** (A)
96 (D)	**97** (C)	**98** (C)	**99** (D)	**100** (B)

PART 1

1　W-Am

(A) He's folding some clothes.
(B) He's looking into a laundry cart.
(C) He's removing some clothes from hangers.
(D) He's standing in front of a washing machine.

(A) 남자가 옷을 개고 있다.
(B) 남자가 세탁물 운반차를 들여다보고 있다.
(C) 남자가 옷걸이에서 옷을 꺼내고 있다.
(D) 남자가 세탁기 앞에 서 있다.

어휘　fold 개다　laundry 세탁(물)　remove 꺼내다　in front of ~의 앞에

해설　1인 등장 사진 - 사람의 동작/상태 묘사

(A) 동사 오답. 남자가 옷을 개고 있는(is folding some clothes) 모습이 아니므로 오답.
(B) 정답. 남자가 세탁물 운반차를 들여다보고 있는(is looking into a laundry cart) 모습이므로 정답.

(C) 동사 오답. 남자가 옷걸이에서 옷을 꺼내고 있는(is removing some clothes from hangers) 모습이 아니므로 오답.
(D) 사진에 없는 명사를 이용한 오답. 사진에 세탁기(a washing machine)의 모습이 보이지 않으므로 오답.

2　M-Cn

(A) The man is leaning against a doorway.
(B) The man is opening up a package.
(C) One of the women is plugging in a printer.
(D) One of the women is wearing glasses.

(A) 남자가 출입구에 기대어 있다.
(B) 남자가 꾸러미를 열고 있다.
(C) 여자들 중 한 명이 프린터 플러그를 꽂고 있다.
(D) 여자들 중 한 명이 안경을 쓰고 있다.

어휘　lean against ~에 기대다

해설　2인 이상 등장 사진 - 사람의 동작/상태 묘사

(A) 동사 오답. 남자가 출입구에 기대어 있는(is leaning against a doorway) 모습이 아니므로 오답.
(B) 사진에 없는 명사를 이용한 오답. 사진에 꾸러미(a package)의 모습이 보이지 않으므로 오답.
(C) 동사 오답. 프린터 플러그를 꽂고 있는(is plugging in a printer) 여자의 모습이 보이지 않으므로 오답.
(D) 정답. 여자들 중 한 명(one of the women)이 안경을 쓰고 있는(is wearing glasses) 모습이므로 정답.

3　W-Br

(A) She is attaching price tags to some merchandise.
(B) She is piling up some boxes.
(C) She is holding up some fruit.
(D) She is throwing away a plastic bag.

(A) 여자가 상품에 가격표를 붙이고 있다.
(B) 여자가 상자를 쌓고 있다.
(C) 여자가 과일을 들고 있다.
(D) 여자가 비닐봉지를 버리고 있다.

어휘　attach 붙이다　merchandise 상품　pile up ~을 쌓다　throw away 버리다

해설 1인 등장 사진 – 사람의 동작/상태 묘사

(A) 동사 오답. 여자가 상품에 가격표를 붙이고 있는(is attaching price tags to some merchandise) 모습이 아니므로 오답.

(B) 동사 오답. 여자가 상자를 쌓고 있는(is piling up some boxes) 모습이 아니므로 오답.

(C) 정답. 여자가 과일을 들고 있는(is holding up some fruit) 모습이므로 정답.

(D) 동사 오답. 여자가 비닐봉지를 버리고 있는(is throwing away a plastic bag) 모습이 아니므로 오답.

---

4   M-Au

(A) A jacket has been placed on the ground.
(B) A man is watering some flowers.
(C) A garden has been planted outside of a building.
(D) A man is putting some tools in a toolbox.

(A) 재킷이 땅에 놓여 있다.
(B) 남자가 꽃에 물을 주고 있다.
(C) 건물 밖 정원에 식물이 심겨져 있다.
(D) 남자가 공구 상자에 공구를 넣고 있다.

어휘 plant 식물을 심다   tool 공구

해설 혼합 사진 – 사람/사물/풍경 혼합 묘사

(A) 동사 오답. 재킷(a jacket)이 땅에 놓여 있는(has been placed on the ground) 모습이 아니므로 오답.

(B) 동사 오답. 남자가 꽃에 물을 주고 있는(is watering some flowers) 모습이 아니므로 오답.

(C) 정답. 정원(a garden)이 건물 밖에 식물들로 가꿔져 있는(has been planted outside of a building) 모습이므로 정답.

(D) 사진에 없는 명사를 이용한 오답. 사진에 공구 상자(a toolbox)의 모습이 보이지 않으므로 오답.

---

5   W-Am

(A) Some chairs are stacked in the corner.
(B) Some light fixtures are mounted on the walls.
(C) Some tables are covered with tablecloths.
(D) Some furniture is on display in a window.

(A) 의자들이 구석에 쌓여 있다.
(B) 조명 기구들이 벽면에 설치되어 있다.
(C) 탁자들이 식탁보로 덮여 있다.
(D) 가구들이 진열창에 진열되어 있다.

어휘 stack 쌓다   light fixture 조명 기구   mount 설치하다

해설 사물/풍경 사진 – 사물 묘사

(A) 동사 오답. 의자들(some chairs)이 구석에 쌓여 있는(are stacked in the corner) 모습이 아니므로 오답.

(B) 정답. 조명 기구들(some light fixtures)이 벽면에 설치되어 있는(are mounted on the walls) 모습이므로 정답.

(C) 사진에 없는 명사를 이용한 오답. 사진에 식탁보(tablecloths)의 모습이 보이지 않으므로 오답.

(D) 동사 오답. 가구들(some furniture)이 진열창에 진열되어 있는(is on display in a window) 모습이 아니므로 오답.

---

6   M-Au

(A) One of the employees is walking with an empty tray.
(B) One of the employees is taping signs to a board.
(C) One of the employees is carrying a pair of scissors.
(D) One of the employees is hanging an apron on a hook.

(A) 직원들 중 한 명이 빈 쟁반을 들고 걸어가고 있다.
(B) 직원들 중 한 명이 게시판에 표지판을 테이프로 붙이고 있다.
(C) 직원들 중 한 명이 가위를 들고 있다.
(D) 직원들 중 한 명이 앞치마를 고리에 걸고 있다.

어휘 tray 쟁반   tape 테이프로 붙이다

해설 2인 이상 등장 사진 – 사람의 동작/상태 묘사

(A) 정답. 직원들 중 한 명(one of the employees)이 빈 쟁반을 들고 걸어가고 있는(is walking with an empty tray) 모습이므로 정답.

(B) 동사 오답. 게시판에 표지판을 테이프로 붙이고 있는(is taping signs to a board) 사람의 모습이 보이지 않으므로 오답.

(C) 사진에 없는 명사를 이용한 오답. 사진에 가위(a pair of scissors)의 모습이 보이지 않으므로 오답.

(D) 사진에 없는 명사를 이용한 오답. 사진에 앞치마(an apron)의 모습이 보이지 않으므로 오답.

PART 2

7

M-Cn Who should write the press release?

W-Br (A) George can take care of that.

　　　(B) Press the red button.

　　　(C) At the corner newsstand.

보도 자료를 누가 작성해야 하나요?

(A) 조지가 처리할 수 있어요.

(B) 빨간 버튼을 누르세요.

(C) 모퉁이 신문 가판대에서요.

어휘　press release 보도 자료　take care of ~을 처리하다

해설　보도 자료를 작성할 사람을 묻는 Who 의문문

(A) 정답. 보도 자료를 작성할 사람이 누구인지 묻는 질문에 조지가 처리할 수 있다고 알려 주고 있으므로 정답.

(B) 단어 반복 오답. 질문의 press를 반복 이용한 오답.

(C) 연상 단어 오답. 질문의 press release에서 연상 가능한 newsstand를 이용한 오답.

8

M-Au Where is the company's headquarters?

W-Am (A) Before we went to work.

　　　(B) His name is Mr. Lee.

　　　(C) In Berlin, Germany.

회사 본사는 어디예요?

(A) 우리가 출근하기 전에요.

(B) 그의 이름은 리 씨예요.

(C) 독일 베를린에요.

어휘　headquarters 본사

해설　회사 본사의 위치를 묻는 Where 의문문

(A) 연상 단어 오답. 질문의 company에서 연상 가능한 work를 이용한 오답.

(B) 질문과 상관없는 오답.

(C) 정답. 회사 본사의 위치를 묻는 질문에 독일 베를린이라고 응답하고 있으므로 정답.

9

W-Br Why are you visiting the clients tomorrow?

M-Cn (A) After two o'clock.

　　　(B) I need to renew their contract.

　　　(C) The Dubai airport.

내일 거래처에 왜 가세요?

(A) 2시 이후에요.

(B) 계약을 갱신해야 해요.

(C) 두바이 공항이에요.

어휘　renew 갱신하다　contract 계약(서)

해설　거래처를 방문하는 이유를 묻는 Why 의문문

(A) 질문과 상관없는 오답. When 의문문에 대한 응답이므로 오답.

(B) 정답. 내일 거래처를 방문하는 이유를 묻는 질문에 계약을 갱신해야 한다고 이유를 제시하고 있으므로 정답.

(C) 질문과 상관없는 오답. Where 의문문에 대한 응답이므로 오답.

10

W-Am Does Dr. Allen work at the hospital or at a private practice?

M-Cn (A) At the hospital, I think.

　　　(B) We'll need to practice that.

　　　(C) An annual exam.

앨런 박사님은 일반 병원에서 일하시나요, 아니면 개인 병원에서 일하시나요?

(A) 일반 병원일 거예요.

(B) 우리 연습 좀 해야겠어요.

(C) 연례 검진이에요.

어휘　private practice (의사 한 명이 개업해서 운영하는) 개인 병원　annual 해마다 일어나는

해설　앨런 박사의 근무지를 묻는 선택 의문문

(A) 정답. 앨런 박사가 근무하는 병원의 종류를 묻는 질문에 일반 병원일 것이라며 둘 중 하나를 선택해 응답하고 있으므로 정답.

(B) 단어 반복 오답. 질문의 practice를 반복 이용한 오답.

(C) 연상 단어 오답. 질문의 hospital에서 연상 가능한 annul exam을 이용한 오답.

11

M-Au What's the best way for us to get to the conference center?

W-Am (A) I haven't heard from her, either.

　　　(B) It was a great presentation.

　　　(C) Let's take a look at the train schedule.

회의장으로 가는 가장 좋은 방법이 뭐죠?

(A) 나도 그녀에게 소식을 듣지 못했어요.

(B) 훌륭한 발표였어요.

(C) 기차 시간표를 봅시다.

어휘　hear from ~에게서 소식을 듣다

해설　회의장에 가는 방법을 묻는 What 의문문

(A) 질문과 상관없는 오답.

(B) 연상 단어 오답. 질문의 conference에서 연상 가능한 presentation을 이용한 오답.

(C) 정답. 회의장으로 가는 가장 좋은 방법을 묻는 질문에 기차 시간표를 보자며 기차 시간에 따라 회의장에 가는 방법이 달라질 수 있음을 우회적으로 표현하고 있으므로 정답.

12

W-Br When will the forklift be repaired?
M-Cn (A) A fork and a knife, please.
(B) Probably next week.
(C) Several pairs.

지게차는 언제 수리되나요?
(A) 포크와 나이프 주세요.
(B) 아마 다음 주에요.
(C) 여러 쌍이요.

어휘 forklift 지게차 repair 수리하다

해설 지게차가 수리되는 시기를 묻는 When 의문문
(A) 유사 발음 오답. 질문의 forklift와 부분적으로 발음이 유사한 fork를 이용한 오답.
(B) 정답. 지게차가 수리되는 시기를 묻는 질문에 아마 다음 주일 거라고 알려 주고 있으므로 정답.
(C) 유사 발음 오답. 질문의 repaired와 부분적으로 발음이 유사한 pairs를 이용한 오답.

13

M-Au Would you like me to send you an appointment reminder?
M-Cn (A) Yes, I'd appreciate that.
(B) The apartment downstairs.
(C) Do you accept credit cards?

예약 알림을 보내 드릴까요?
(A) 네, 그렇게 해 주시면 감사하죠.
(B) 아래층 아파트요.
(C) 신용카드 받습니까?

어휘 appointment 예약 reminder (일깨워 주는) 안내문 appreciate 감사하다 accept 받다

해설 제안/권유의 의문문
(A) 정답. 예약 알림을 보내 주겠다고 제안하는 질문에 네(Yes)라고 대답한 뒤, 그렇게 해 주면 감사하겠다며 긍정 답변과 일관된 내용을 덧붙이고 있으므로 정답.
(B) 유사 발음 오답. 질문의 appointment와 부분적으로 발음이 유사한 apartment를 이용한 오답.
(C) 질문과 상관없는 오답.

14

W-Br Did you remember to book a photographer for today's museum opening?
M-Au (A) Oh, have you read it too?
(B) I'd like to have it framed.
(C) She should have been here by now.

오늘 박물관 개관식에 사진사 예약하는 거 잊지 않으셨죠?
(A) 아, 당신도 읽어 보셨어요?
(B) 액자에 넣어 주세요.
(C) 지금쯤이면 여기 도착해야 하는데요.

해설 사진사 예약 여부를 확인하는 조동사(Did) 의문문
(A) 연상 단어 오답. 질문의 book을 '책'으로 잘못 이해했을 경우 연상 가능한 read를 이용한 오답.
(B) 연상 단어 오답. 질문의 photographer에서 연상 가능한 framed를 이용한 오답.
(C) 정답. 오늘 박물관 개관식에 사진사 예약하는 것을 잊지 않았는지 묻는 질문에 지금쯤이면 여기 도착해야 한다며 잊지 않고 사진사를 예약했음을 간접적으로 알려 주고 있으므로 정답.

15

M-Cn Why is my computer so slow today?
W-Br (A) The printer is down that hall.
(B) Because some updates are being installed.
(C) Next year's computer seminar.

오늘 제 컴퓨터가 왜 이렇게 느리죠?
(A) 프린터는 복도를 따라가면 있습니다.
(B) 업데이트가 설치되고 있기 때문이에요.
(C) 내년 컴퓨터 세미나요.

어휘 install 설치하다

해설 컴퓨터가 느린 이유를 묻는 Why 의문문
(A) 연상 단어 오답. 질문의 computer에서 연상 가능한 printer를 이용한 오답.
(B) 정답. 오늘 자신의 컴퓨터가 느린 이유를 묻는 질문에 업데이트가 설치되고 있기 때문이라며 이유를 알려 주고 있으므로 정답.
(C) 단어 반복 오답. 질문의 computer를 반복 이용한 오답.

16

W-Br Who's going to stock these shelves?
W-Am (A) The overnight workers will do it.
(B) No, I haven't gone yet.
(C) To make room for more items.

누가 이 선반들을 채울 건가요?
(A) 야간 근무자들이 할 거예요.
(B) 아니요, 저는 아직 안 갔어요.
(C) 물건을 더 많이 넣을 공간을 만들려고요.

어휘 stock 채우다 room 공간

해설 선반을 채울 사람을 묻는 Who 의문문
(A) 정답. 선반을 채울 사람이 누구인지 묻는 질문에 야간 근무자들이 할 것이라고 알려 주고 있으므로 정답.
(B) Yes/No 불가 오답. Who 의문문에는 Yes/No 응답이 불가능하므로 오답.
(C) 질문과 상관없는 오답. Why 의문문에 대한 응답이므로 오답.

17

M-Cn How many bottles can these machines produce each hour?

W-Br (A) Mainly soft drinks and juices.

(B) I just started working here.

(C) It stays fresh for a long time.

이 기계는 시간당 몇 개의 병을 생산할 수 있나요?

(A) 주로 청량음료와 주스요.

(B) 저는 이곳에서 최근에 일을 시작했어요.

(C) 그것은 오랫동안 신선하게 유지됩니다.

어휘 bottle 병 produce 생산하다 stay 유지되다 fresh 신선한

해설 기계의 시간당 생산량을 확인하는 How many 의문문

(A) 연상 단어 오답. 질문의 bottles에서 연상 가능한 soft drinks와 juices를 이용한 오답.

(B) 정답. 기계의 생산량을 묻는 질문에 최근에 일을 시작해서 알지 못함을 우회적으로 알려 주고 있으므로 정답.

(C) 연상 단어 오답. 질문의 hour에서 연상 가능한 a long time을 이용한 오답.

18

W-Am Aren't these hiking boots supposed to be discounted?

M-Au (A) Oh yes, sorry about that.

(B) Let's pose for a picture.

(C) No, we haven't met yet.

이 등산화는 할인되는 거 아닌가요?

(A) 아 맞아요, 죄송합니다.

(B) 포즈 취하고 사진 찍어요.

(C) 아니요, 우리는 아직 만나지 않았어요.

어휘 be supposed to ~하기로 되어 있다

해설 등산화가 할인되는지 여부를 확인하는 부정 의문문

(A) 정답. 등산화가 할인되는 것이 아닌지 확인하는 질문에 맞다(yes)라고 대답한 뒤, 죄송하다고 착오에 대해 사과하며 긍정 답변과 일관된 내용을 덧붙이고 있으므로 정답.

(B) 유사 발음 오답. 질문의 supposed와 부분적으로 발음이 유사한 pose를 이용한 오답.

(C) 질문과 상관없는 오답.

19

W-Br Do we have enough time to finish this report?

M-Au (A) She borrowed your newspaper.

(B) I'll reschedule my next appointment.

(C) It's a beautiful trail.

이 보고서를 끝낼 시간이 충분한가요?

(A) 그녀가 당신 신문을 빌렸어요.

(B) 제 다음 약속 시간을 변경할게요.

(C) 아름다운 오솔길이에요.

어휘 borrow 빌리다 reschedule 일정을 다시 잡다 appointment 약속 trail 오솔길

해설 보고서 작성 시간이 충분한지 여부를 묻는 조동사(Do) 의문문

(A) 질문과 상관없는 오답. 질문에 3인칭 대명사 She로 지칭할 인물이 언급된 적이 없으므로 오답.

(B) 정답. 보고서를 끝낼 시간이 충분한지 여부를 묻는 질문에 자신의 다음 약속 시간을 변경하겠다며 시간이 충분하지 않아 일정을 조정해야 한다는 것을 우회적으로 알려 주고 있으므로 정답.

(C) 질문과 상관없는 오답.

20

M-Cn When do you usually start packing for a trip?

W-Br (A) A round-trip ticket.

(B) About two days in advance.

(C) They delivered the package.

여행할 때 짐은 보통 언제 꾸리기 시작하나요?

(A) 왕복 표예요.

(B) 이틀 정도 전에요.

(C) 그들은 소포를 배달했어요.

어휘 in advance 미리, 사전에

해설 여행용 짐을 꾸리기 시작하는 시점을 묻는 When 의문문

(A) 단어 반복 오답. 질문의 trip을 반복 이용한 오답.

(B) 정답. 여행할 때 짐을 보통 꾸리기 시작하는 시점을 묻는 질문에 이틀 정도 전이라고 응답하고 있으므로 정답.

(C) 파생어 오답. 질문의 packing과 파생어 관계인 package를 이용한 오답.

21

W-Am I'm going to take a walk at lunchtime.

W-Br (A) Oh, I'll be visiting clients then.

(B) He took the survey.

(C) A copy of the lunch menu.

점심시간에 산책할 거예요.

(A) 아, 그럼 제가 거래처를 방문할게요.

(B) 그는 설문 조사에 참여했어요.

(C) 점심 메뉴판이요.

어휘 take a survey 설문 조사에 참여하다

해설 의사 전달의 평서문

(A) 정답. 점심시간에 산책할 것이라는 평서문에 그럼 자신은 거래처를 방문하겠다고 따로 할 일을 언급하며 산책을 하겠다는 상대방의 의사를 존중하는 응답을 하고 있으므로 정답.

(B) 파생어 오답. 평서문의 take와 파생어 관계인 took을 이용한 오답.

(C) 연상 단어 오답. 평서문의 lunchtime에서 연상 가능한 lunch menu를 이용한 오답.

22

W-Am Can you make sure we have a sign-up sheet available?

M-Au (A) I just turned up the heat.
(B) Sign here, please.
(C) **Sure, no problem.**

저희가 이용할 가입 신청서가 있는지 확인해 주시겠어요?
(A) 방금 온도를 높였어요.
(B) 여기에 서명해 주세요.
(C) **그럼요, 그렇게 할게요.**

어휘 available 이용할 수 있는

해설 부탁/요청의 의문문
(A) 유사 발음 오답. 질문의 sheet와 부분적으로 발음이 유사한 heat를 이용한 오답.
(B) 단어 반복 오답. 질문의 sign을 반복 이용한 오답.
(C) 정답. 이용할 수 있는 가입 신청서가 있는지 확인해 달라는 요청에 그럼요(Sure)라고 수락한 뒤, 그렇게 하겠다며 긍정 답변과 일관된 내용을 덧붙이고 있으므로 정답.

23

M-Cn They're going to give each of us copies of the press release, aren't they?

W-Am (A) No, I don't drink coffee.
(B) I can unlock that for you later.
(C) **I'd better remind them about that.**

그들이 보도 자료 사본을 우리 각자에게 나눠주겠죠?
(A) 아니요, 저는 커피 안 마셔요.
(B) 나중에 제가 열어 드릴게요.
(C) **그 점을 그들에게 알려 주는 게 좋겠어요.**

어휘 press release 보도 자료   unlock (열쇠로) 열다

해설 보도 자료를 각자에게 배포하는지 여부를 확인하는 부가 의문문
(A) 유사 발음 오답. 질문의 copies와 부분적으로 발음이 유사한 coffee를 이용한 오답.
(B) 연상 단어 오답. 질문의 release을 '풀어 주다'로 잘못 이해했을 때 연상 가능한 unlock을 이용한 오답.
(C) 정답. 보도 자료를 각자에게 나눠줄지 여부를 확인하는 질문에 그 점을 그들에게 상기시키는 게 좋겠다며 모두에게 보도 자료를 나눠주도록 할 것임을 우회적으로 표현하고 있으므로 정답.

24

M-Au What do most people do for a living around here?

W-Am (A) About 40 kilometers away.
(B) **They work at the car manufacturing plant.**
(C) Yes, the living room furniture's new.

여기는 대다수가 생업으로 어떤 일을 하나요?
(A) 약 40킬로미터 떨어져 있어요.
(B) **그들은 자동차 제조 공장에서 일해요.**
(C) 네, 거실 가구가 새것이에요.

어휘 do for a living 생업으로 하다   manufacturing 제조

해설 지역민들의 주요 생업을 묻는 What 의문문
(A) 질문과 상관없는 오답. How far 의문문에 대한 응답이므로 오답.
(B) 정답. 지역 주민 대다수가 생업으로 하는 일을 묻는 질문에 자동차 제조 공장에서 일한다고 구체적으로 응답하고 있으므로 정답.
(C) Yes/No 불가 오답. What 의문문에는 Yes/No 응답이 불가능하므로 오답.

25

W-Br How do you add toner to the printer?

M-Cn (A) No, it's not made of stone.
(B) Because we ran out.
(C) **The instructions are on the box.**

프린터에 토너를 어떻게 추가하나요?
(A) 아니요, 그건 돌로 만든 게 아니에요.
(B) 다 떨어져요.
(C) **사용 설명서가 상자 위에 있어요.**

어휘 run out ~이 다 떨어지다   instructions (제품의) 사용 설명서

해설 프린터에 토너를 추가하는 방법을 묻는 How 의문문
(A) Yes/No 불가 오답. How 의문문에는 Yes/No 응답이 불가능하므로 오답.
(B) 질문과 상관없는 오답. Why 의문문에 대한 응답이므로 오답.
(C) 정답. 프린터에 토너를 추가하는 방법을 묻는 질문에 사용 설명서가 상자 위에 있다고 원하는 정보가 나와 있는 자료의 위치를 알려 주며 우회적으로 응답하고 있으므로 정답.

26

W-Am Can you send me a link to that company's Web site?

M-Au (A) **Our e-mail's not working right now.**
(B) Express delivery, please.
(C) Sure, I'll drive you to the job site.

그 회사 웹사이트 링크를 보내 주실래요?
(A) **우리 이메일이 지금 작동하지 않네요.**
(B) 속달로 해 주세요.
(C) 물론이죠, 제가 작업 현장까지 태워다 드릴게요.

어휘 express delivery 속달

해설 부탁/요청의 의문문
(A) 정답. 회사 웹사이트의 링크를 보내 달라는 요청에 우리 이메일이 지금 작동하지 않는다며 우회적으로 거절하고 있으므로 정답.
(B) 연상 단어 오답. 질문의 send에서 연상 가능한 delivery를 이용한 오답.
(C) 단어 반복 오답. 질문의 site를 반복 이용한 오답.

27

M-Au Isn't the air conditioner set to turn off at night?

W-Br (A) No, we always keep it on.
(B) He's going to be late today.
(C) Hair products are in aisle four.

에어컨이 밤에 꺼지도록 설정되어 있지 않나요?

(A) 아니요, 우리는 항상 켜 놓습니다.
(B) 그는 오늘 늦을 거예요.
(C) 헤어 제품은 4번 통로에 있습니다.

어휘 turn off (전기, 기계 등을) 끄다   aisle 통로

해설 에어컨이 밤에 꺼지도록 설정되어 있는지 확인하는 부정 의문문

(A) 정답. 밤에 에어컨이 꺼지도록 설정되어 있는지 확인하는 질문에 아니요(No)라고 대답한 뒤, 항상 켜 놓는다며 부정 답변과 일관된 내용을 덧붙이고 있으므로 정답.
(B) 연상 단어 오답. 질문의 night에서 연상 가능한 late를 이용한 오답.
(C) 질문과 상관없는 오답. Where 의문문에 대한 응답이므로 오답.

28

W-Am Oh, there's no clock in this room.

M-Cn (A) A six-week training program.
(B) It's about two-thirty.
(C) They took an early flight.

어, 이 방에는 시계가 없네요.
(A) 6주짜리 교육 프로그램이에요.
(B) 2시 30분쯤 됐어요.
(C) 그들은 아침 비행기를 탔어요.

해설 정보 전달의 평서문

(A) 질문과 상관없는 오답.
(B) 정답. 이 방에 시계가 없다는 평서문에 2시 30분쯤 되었다며 시간을 알려 주고 있으므로 정답.
(C) 질문과 상관없는 오답.

29

W-Br Where can I go to have my car engine checked?

M-Au (A) No, I don't need one—thanks, though.
(B) The mechanic around the corner.
(C) In April of every year.

제 자동차 엔진을 점검받으려면 어디로 가면 되나요?
(A) 아니요, 저는 필요 없어요. 그래도 고마워요.
(B) 근처에 정비사가 있어요.
(C) 매년 4월이요.

어휘 mechanic 정비사   around the corner 근처에

해설 자동차 엔진을 점검받을 수 있는 장소를 묻는 Where 의문문

(A) Yes/No 불가 오답. Where 의문문에는 Yes/No 응답이 불가능하므로 오답.
(B) 정답. 자동차 엔진을 점검받을 수 있는 장소를 묻는 질문에 근처에 정비사가 있다고 알려 주고 있으므로 정답.
(C) 질문과 상관없는 오답. When 의문문에 대한 응답이므로 오답.

30

M-Au To get into the building, do I use an ID badge or a passcode?

W-Am (A) A building next door.
(B) Enter three-four-three on the keypad.
(C) The exit is down the hall.

건물에 들어가려면 신분증을 사용하나요, 아니면 비밀번호를 사용하나요?
(A) 옆 건물이에요.
(B) 키패드에 3-4-3을 입력하세요.
(C) 출구는 복도를 따라가면 있습니다.

어휘 passcode 비밀번호   exit 출구

해설 건물에 들어가기 위한 방법을 묻는 선택 의문문

(A) 단어 반복 오답. 질문의 building을 반복 이용한 오답.
(B) 정답. 건물에 들어가기 위한 방법을 묻는 질문에 키패드에 3-4-3을 입력하라고 알려 주며 비밀번호를 사용해야 한다고 간접적으로 응답하고 있으므로 정답.
(C) 연상 단어 오답. 질문의 building에서 연상 가능한 exit를 이용한 오답.

31

W-Br The order can still be changed, right?

W-Am (A) That process is very complicated.
(B) I still remember that day, too.
(C) Yes, he does.

아직 주문을 변경할 수 있죠?
(A) 절차가 아주 복잡해요.
(B) 저도 아직 그날을 기억해요.
(C) 네, 그는 그렇습니다.

어휘 process 절차   complicated 복잡한

해설 주문 변경 가능 여부를 확인하는 부가 의문문

(A) 정답. 아직 주문을 변경할 수 있는지 묻는 질문에 절차가 아주 복잡하다며 힘들지만 아직 가능하다는 점을 간접적으로 알려 주고 있으므로 정답.
(B) 단어 반복 오답. 질문의 still을 반복 이용한 오답.
(C) 질문과 상관없는 오답. 질문에 3인칭 대명사 he로 지칭할 인물이 언급된 적이 없으므로 오답.

PART 3

32-34

M-Au	Hi, Anusha. ³² **This afternoon I'll be meeting with our financial consultant, Ms. Jefferson, for the last time. Since she's retiring next week, I wanted to get her some flowers.** Do you know a good florist?
W-Br	³³ **The place I like best is called Greenwood Flower Shop. It's located just inside the train station, on the right-hand side.**
M-Au	Thanks. ³⁴ **I just need to finalize this budget proposal, and then I'll head over to the station.**

남	안녕, 아누샤. 오늘 오후 금융 컨설턴트인 제퍼슨 씨를 마지막으로 만나기로 했어요. 그녀가 다음 주에 은퇴하기 때문에 꽃을 주고 싶었거든요. 좋은 꽃집 아는 데 있어요?
여	제가 가장 좋아하는 곳은 그린우드 꽃집이에요. 기차역 안에 들어가면 바로 오른쪽에 있어요.
남	고마워요. 저는 이 예산안만 마무리하면 돼요. 그러고 나서 기차역으로 갈 거예요.

어휘	located 위치한 budget 예산 head 향하다

32

Why does the man want to buy Ms. Jefferson some flowers?

(A) She was promoted.
(B) She won an award.
(C) She is moving.
(D) She is retiring.

남자는 왜 제퍼슨 씨에게 꽃을 사 주려고 하는가?
(A) 그녀가 승진했다.
(B) 그녀가 상을 받았다.
(C) 그녀가 이사할 것이다.
(D) 그녀가 은퇴할 것이다.

어휘 promote 승진시키다 retire 은퇴하다

해설 세부 사항 관련 - 남자가 제퍼슨 씨에게 꽃을 사 주려는 이유
남자가 첫 대사에서 오늘 오후 금융 컨설턴트인 제퍼슨 씨를 마지막으로 만나기로 했다(This afternoon I'll be meeting with our financial consultant, Ms. Jefferson, for the last time)면서 그녀가 다음 주에 은퇴하기 때문에 꽃을 주고 싶다(Since she's retiring next week, I wanted to get her some flowers)고 말하고 있으므로 정답은 (D)이다.

33

According to the woman, where is Greenwood Flower Shop?

(A) In a shopping mall
(B) In a train station
(C) Next to a café
(D) Across from the library

여자의 말에 따르면, 그린우드 꽃집은 어디에 있는가?
(A) 쇼핑몰 안
(B) 기차역 안
(C) 카페 옆
(D) 도서관 건너편

해설 세부 사항 관련 - 여자가 말하는 그린우드 꽃집의 위치
여자가 첫 대사에서 자신이 가장 좋아하는 곳은 그린우드 꽃집(The place I like best is called Greenwood Flower Shop)이라면서, 기차역 안에 들어가면 바로 오른쪽에 있다(It's located just inside the train station, on the right-hand side)고 말하고 있으므로 정답은 (B)이다.

34

What does the man say he will do before he leaves the office?

(A) Fill out a time sheet
(B) Send an e-mail
(C) Finish a budget proposal
(D) Arrange a meeting

남자는 자신이 퇴근하기 전에 무엇을 할 것이라고 말하는가?
(A) 출퇴근 기록표 작성
(B) 이메일 발송
(C) 예산안 마무리
(D) 회의 준비

어휘 fill out ~을 작성하다 arrange 준비하다

해설 세부 사항 관련 - 남자가 퇴근하기 전에 할 것이라고 말하는 일
남자가 마지막 대사에서 이 예산안만 마무리하고 나서 역으로 가겠다(I just need to finalize this budget proposal, and then I'll head over to the station)고 말하고 있으므로 정답은 (C)이다.

35-37

M-Au	Ms. Weber, ³⁵ **I've just booked the accommodations for your trip to Melbourne next week.** I found you a hotel within a mile of the conference center.
W-Am	That's great! Thank you for arranging that.
M-Au	No problem. And ³⁶ **remember to keep your receipts**—you'll need them to get reimbursed.
W-Am	OK, I'll do that. Oh, and ³⁷ **does the hotel have a restaurant on-site?** I'll be working

in the hotel a lot, so it'd be convenient if I could eat there.

남	웨버 씨, **다음 주 당신의 멜버른 여행을 위한 숙소를 방금 예약했어요.** 회의장에서 1마일 이내에 있는 호텔을 찾아 드렸어요.
여	잘됐네요! 준비해 줘서 고마워요.
남	뭘요. 그리고 **잊지 말고 영수증을 보관하세요.** 환급받으려면 영수증이 필요할 거예요.
여	알았어요, 그렇게 할게요. 아, 그리고 **호텔 건물 안에 식당이 있나요?** 호텔에서 일을 많이 할 거라서 거기서 식사하면 편할 것 같아요.

어휘	accommodation 숙소 arrange 준비하다 receipt 영수증 reimburse 환급하다 on-site 건물 안에 convenient 편리한

35

What did the man just do?

(A) He upgraded a flight.
(B) He arranged for a rental car.
(C) He prepared some presentation slides.
(D) He made a hotel reservation.

남자는 방금 무엇을 했는가?
(A) 비행기 좌석을 업그레이드했다.
(B) 렌터카를 예약했다.
(C) 발표용 슬라이드를 준비했다.
(D) 호텔을 예약했다.

어휘 reservation 예약

해설 세부 사항 관련 – 남자가 방금 한 일
남자가 첫 대사에서 다음 주 당신의 멜버른 여행을 위한 숙소를 방금 예약했다(I've just booked the accommodations for your trip to Melbourne next week)고 말하고 있으므로 정답은 (D)이다.

> ▸▸ Paraphrasing 대화의 **booked the accommodations**
> → 정답의 **made a hotel reservation**

36

What does the man remind the woman to do?

(A) Save her receipts
(B) Bring her ID badge
(C) Sign a form
(D) Arrive early

남자는 여자에게 무엇을 하라고 일러 주는가?
(A) 영수증 보관
(B) 신분증 지참
(C) 양식에 서명
(D) 일찍 도착

해설 세부 사항 관련 – 남자가 여자에게 하라고 말하는 일
남자가 두 번째 대사에서 잊지 말고 영수증을 보관하라(remember to keep your receipts)고 말하고 있으므로 정답은 (A)이다.

> ▸▸ Paraphrasing 대화의 **keep** → 정답의 **Save**

37

What does the woman ask the man about?

(A) A bank
(B) A post office
(C) A restaurant
(D) A conference center

여자는 남자에게 무엇을 문의하는가?
(A) 은행
(B) 우체국
(C) 식당
(D) 회의장

해설 세부 사항 관련 – 여자의 문의 사항
여자가 마지막 대사에서 호텔 건물 안에 식당이 있는지(does the hotel have a restaurant on-site?) 묻고 있으므로 정답은 (C)이다.

38-40

W-Br	Antonio, [38] **I'd like your input about how we can make our spring athletic clothing line more original.**
M-Cn	[39] **How about designing some geometric patterns that we can have printed onto our fabric?** That would set our clothing apart from other brands that use muted, solid colors.
W-Br	I like that idea, but [40] **I'm worried it would add a step or two to our production schedule. We have several hard deadlines coming up soon.** Let's try designing one patterned fabric for this season's line. If everything goes smoothly, we can do more next season.

여	안토니오, 봄 운동복 라인을 어떻게 하면 좀 더 독창적으로 만들지 의견을 듣고 싶어요.
남	**직물에 인쇄할 수 있는 기하학 패턴을 디자인하는 건 어떨까요?** 그렇게 하면 우리 의류가 채도가 낮고 단색인 다른 브랜드와 차별화돼요.
여	그 아이디어가 마음에 들긴 한데, **생산 일정에 한두 단계 더 추가될까 봐 걱정이에요. 곧 있으면 연장이 불가능한 마감 기한이 여러 건 돌아와요.** 이번 시즌 라인에서 패턴 있는 원단을 하나 디자인해 봐요. 만사 순조롭게 진행되면 다음 시즌에는 더 많이 할 수 있겠죠.

어휘	athletic 운동의 geometric 기하학의 muted 채도가 낮은 solid color 단색 hard deadline 연장이 불가능한 마감 기한

38

What industry do the speakers most likely work in?

(A) Television

(B) Fashion

(C) Home furnishings

(D) Advertising

화자들은 어떤 업종에서 일하겠는가?

(A) 텔레비전

(B) 패션

(C) 가재도구

(D) 광고

해설 전체 내용 관련 - 화자들의 근무 업종

여자가 첫 대사에서 봄 운동복 라인을 어떻게 하면 좀 더 독창적으로 만들지 의견을 듣고 싶다(I'd like your input about how we can make our spring athletic clothing line more original)고 말하는 것으로 보아 화자들은 의류 업계에 종사하고 있다는 것을 알 수 있다. 따라서 정답은 (B)이다.

> Paraphrasing 대화의 clothing line → 정답의 Fashion

39

What does the man suggest doing?

(A) Providing tours of a facility

(B) Opening a branch office

(C) Designing special fabric

(D) Installing brighter lights

남자는 무엇을 하자고 제안하는가?

(A) 시설 견학 제공

(B) 지점 개설

(C) 특수 직물 디자인

(D) 더 밝은 조명 설치

어휘 facility 시설 install 설치하다

해설 세부 사항 관련 - 남자의 제안 사항

남자가 첫 대사에서 직물에 인쇄할 수 있는 기하학 패턴을 디자인하는 것은 어떨지(How about designing some geometric patterns that we can have printed onto our fabric?) 묻고 있으므로 정답은 (C)이다.

40

What is the woman concerned about?

(A) A plan would be time-consuming.

(B) A color is too bright.

(C) Some sales figures have declined.

(D) Some supplies will be expensive.

여자는 무엇을 걱정하는가?

(A) 계획은 시간이 걸릴 것이다.

(B) 색상이 너무 밝다.

(C) 매출액이 감소했다.

(D) 물품이 비쌀 것이다.

어휘 time-consuming 시간이 걸리는 sales figure 매출액 decline 감소하다

해설 세부 사항 관련 - 여자의 우려 사항

여자가 마지막 대사에서 생산 일정에 한두 단계 더 추가될까 봐 걱정된다(I'm worried it would add a step or two to our production schedule)며 곧 연장이 불가능한 마감 기한이 여러 건 돌아온다(We have several hard deadlines coming up soon)고 말하는 것으로 보아, 작업이 늘어나 일정에 차질이 생겨 마감일에 영향을 미칠 것을 걱정하고 있으므로 정답은 (A)이다.

41-43 3인 대화

W-Br	Hi Yoon-Ho. Do you have a minute? **41 Anita and I need your assistance with our e-mails.**
M-Au	Sure. **41 How can I help?**
W-Br	**41 The system seems to be running very slow.** We've been experiencing long delays in receiving e-mails, right Anita?
W-Am	Yes. Since we have deadlines that are very time sensitive, can you look into this right away?
M-Au	You know, **42 several people have already called us at the IT Department about it this morning**—it's our top priority now.
W-Am	Thanks. **43 We're on our way to catch a flight now,** but could you please call us when it's all taken care of?

여1	안녕, 윤호. 잠시 시간 있어요? **아니타와 제가 이메일 때문에 도움이 필요해요.**
남	물론이죠. **어떻게 도와 드릴까요?**
여1	**시스템이 너무 느리게 작동하는 것 같아요.** 이메일 수신이 오래 지연되고 있어요, 맞죠, 아니타?
여2	네. 분초를 다투는 마감이 있어서 그런데, 지금 바로 봐 주실 수 있나요?
남	저기, **오늘 아침 벌써 여러 사람이 이 문제로 우리 IT부에 전화했어요.** 지금은 이 문제가 최우선 과제예요.
여2	고마워요. **지금 비행기 타러 가는 중인데,** 다 해결되면 전화 주실래요?

어휘 time sensitive 분초를 다투는 priority 우선 과제

41

What problem is being discussed?

(A) A company manual contains some errors.

(B) A shipment was not delivered on time.

(C) Some materials are missing from a cabinet.

(D) An e-mail system is not functioning properly.

어떤 문제가 논의되고 있는가?

(A) 회사 매뉴얼에 오류가 있다.

(B) 배송품이 제때 배달되지 않았다.

(C) 자료가 캐비닛에 없다.

(D) 이메일 시스템이 제대로 작동하지 않는다.

해설 전체 내용 관련 – 대화의 주제

첫 번째 여자가 첫 대사에서 아니타와 제가 이메일 때문에 도움이 필요하다(Anita and I need your assistance with our e-mails)고 했고 남자가 어떻게 도와 드릴지(How can I help?) 묻자 다시 첫 번째 여자가 시스템이 너무 느리게 작동하는 것 같다(The system seems to be running very slow)고 대답하고 있는 것으로 보아 화자들은 이메일 시스템의 작동과 관련한 문제에 대해 대화하고 있으므로 정답은 (D)이다.

▸▸ Paraphrasing 대화의 **be running very slow**
→ 정답의 **is not functioning properly**

42

Who most likely is the man?

(A) A computer technician

(B) A security guard

(C) A warehouse manager

(D) A sales representative

남자는 누구이겠는가?

(A) 컴퓨터 기술자

(B) 경비원

(C) 창고 관리자

(D) 영업 담당자

해설 전체 내용 관련 – 남자의 직업

남자가 두 번째 대사에서 오늘 아침 벌써 여러 사람이 이 문제로 우리 IT 부에 전화했다(several people have already called us at the IT Department about it this morning)고 하는 것으로 보아 남자는 IT 부서에서 근무하고 있으므로 정답은 (A)이다.

43

What are the women most likely planning to do next?

(A) Sign a contract

(B) Attend a training

(C) Go to the airport

(D) Revise a presentation

여자들은 다음에 무엇을 할 계획이겠는가?

(A) 계약 체결하기

(B) 교육 참석하기

(C) 공항으로 가기

(D) 프레젠테이션 수정하기

어휘 revise 수정하다

해설 세부 사항 관련 – 여자들이 다음에 할 일

두 번째 여자가 마지막 대사에서 지금 비행기 타러 가는 중(We're on our way to catch a flight now)이라고 말하고 있으므로 정답은 (C)이다.

▸▸ Paraphrasing 대화의 **are on our way to catch a flight**
→ 정답의 **Go to the airport**

44-46

W-Br ⁴⁴**Paniz Outdoor Tours. Can I help you?**

M-Cn I'm from Alderman Associates, and ⁴⁴**I'm calling to book a cycling tour of the city for my colleagues and me.** There are eight of us, and we'd like to go next Thursday.

W-Br I'm sorry— ⁴⁵**we'll be closed next Thursday. We're replacing all of our bikes**, and it'll take a few days to get them ready to ride.

M-Cn Oh, we work nearby, so we could go another time.

W-Br Great. So, what about the following Monday—June third?

M-Cn That works. We have a membership with you already, so you should have all of our information on file.

W-Br In that case, ⁴⁶**just tell me your membership number, and I'll make the reservation.**

여 **파니즈 야외 투어입니다. 도와 드릴까요?**

남 저는 올더먼 어소시에이츠 소속인데, **동료들과 저를 위해 시내 사이클 투어를 예약하려고 전화했어요.** 8명이고, 다음 주 목요일에 가고 싶습니다.

여 죄송합니다. **다음 주 목요일에는 저희가 문을 닫아요. 자전거를 모두 교체할 예정인데,** 탈 수 있게 자전거가 준비되려면 며칠 걸릴 거예요.

남 아, 근처에서 일하니까 다른 시간에 가면 돼요.

여 좋아요. 그 다음 월요일, 6월 3일은 어떠세요?

남 괜찮아요. 이미 회원권이 있으니, 우리 정보는 전부 정리돼 있을 겁니다.

여 그렇다면 **회원 번호만 알려 주시면 예약해 드릴게요.**

어휘 colleague 동료 replace 교체하다 on file (파일로) 정리되어

44

Where does the woman work?

(A) At an amusement park

(B) At a fitness center

(C) At a bicycle-tour company

(D) At an automobile dealership

여자는 어디에서 일하는가?

(A) 놀이 공원
(B) 헬스장
(C) 자전거 여행 회사
(D) 자동차 대리점

해설 전체 내용 관련 - 여자의 근무지

여자가 첫 대사에서 파니즈 야외 투어(Paniz Outdoor Tours)라고 전화를 받으며 무엇을 도울지(Can I help you?) 묻는 것으로 보아 여행사 직원임을 알 수 있고, 뒤이어 남자가 동료들과 나를 위해 시내 사이클 투어를 예약하려고 전화했다(I'm calling to book a cycling tour of the city for my colleagues and me)고 말하고 있으므로 정답은 (C)이다.

45

Why is the man unable to make a reservation for next Thursday?

(A) A calendar is fully booked.
(B) An employee is on vacation.
(C) Some roads will be closed.
(D) Some equipment will be replaced.

남자는 왜 다음 주 목요일에 예약할 수 없는가?

(A) 일정표에 예약이 꽉 찼다.
(B) 직원이 휴가 중이다.
(C) 도로가 폐쇄될 예정이다.
(D) 장비가 교체될 예정이다.

해설 세부 사항 관련 - 남자가 다음 주 목요일에 예약할 수 없는 이유

여자가 두 번째 대사에서 다음 주 목요일에는 문을 닫는다(we'll be closed next Thursday)며 자전거를 모두 교체할 예정(We're replacing all of our bikes)이라고 말하고 있으므로 정답은 (D)이다.

46

What will the man most likely do next?

(A) Pick up a brochure
(B) Make a down payment
(C) Provide a membership number
(D) Write a customer review

남자는 다음에 무엇을 하겠는가?

(A) 안내책자 가져가기
(B) 계약금 지불하기
(C) 회원 번호 제공하기
(D) 고객 후기 작성하기

어휘 down payment 계약금

해설 세부 사항 관련 - 남자가 다음에 할 일

여자가 마지막 대사에서 회원 번호만 알려 주면 예약해 주겠다(just tell me your membership number, and I'll make the reservation)며 남자에게 회원 번호를 요청하고 있는 것으로 보아 정답은 (C)이다.

47-49

M-Cn	Ms. Khan, [47] **this is James Wilson, one of the freelance photographers for your magazine.** I'm calling about the September issue.
W-Am	Right. I know we're using some of your photos for the special spread about homes in San Francisco.
M-Cn	Yes. But [48] **I have a few more shots I took this weekend when there was a beautiful sunset. Would you be interested in looking at those?**
W-Am	The issue is already being printed.
M-Cn	Oh, I see. Sorry to bother you, then.
W-Am	Actually, I'm glad you called. [49] **We're opening a position for assistant photo editor, and I wonder if you can come in for an interview.** I think you'd be great for the job.

남	칸 씨, **저는 제임스 윌슨이고 귀 잡지사의 프리랜서 사진작가예요.** 9월호 때문에 전화드렸어요.
여	그렇군요. 샌프란시스코의 집들에 관한 양면 특별 기사를 위해 우리가 작가님 사진 몇 장을 사용하고 있다고 알고 있어요.
남	네. 하지만 **일몰이 아름다웠던 이번 주말에 찍은 사진이 몇 장 더 있어요. 보시겠어요?**
여	그 호는 이미 인쇄 중이에요.
남	아, 그렇군요. 그렇다면 번거롭게 해 드려서 죄송해요.
여	실은 전화 주셔서 기뻐요. **사진 편집 보조 자리가 비어서, 면접을 보러 오실 수 있을지 모르겠네요.** 그 일에 아주 적합하실 것 같은데요.

어휘 issue (잡지·신문) 호 spread 양면 기사

47

Who is the man?

(A) A news reporter
(B) A photographer
(C) A fashion designer
(D) A translator

남자는 누구인가?

(A) 기자
(B) 사진작가
(C) 패션 디자이너
(D) 번역가

해설 전체 내용 관련 - 남자의 직업

남자가 첫 대사에서 귀 잡지사의 프리랜서 사진작가인 제임스 윌슨(this is James Wilson, one of the freelance photographers for your magazine)이라고 본인을 소개하고 있으므로 정답은 (B)이다.

48

Why does the woman say, "The issue is already being printed"?

(A) To apologize for an error
(B) To provide reassurance
(C) To indicate a schedule change
(D) To decline an offer

여자가 "그 호는 이미 인쇄 중이에요"라고 말하는 이유는 무엇인가?

(A) 오류에 대해 사과하려고
(B) 안심시키려고
(C) 일정 변경을 암시하려고
(D) 제안을 거절하려고

어휘 reassurance 안심시키는 것   decline 거절하다

해설 화자의 의도 파악 - 그 호는 이미 인쇄 중이라는 말의 의도

앞에서 남자가 일몰이 아름다웠던 이번 주말에 찍은 사진이 몇 장 더 있다 (I have a few more shots I took this weekend when there was a beautiful sunset)며 살펴볼 의향이 있는지(Would you be interested in looking at those?) 묻자 여자가 인용문을 언급한 것으로 보아, 해당 잡지에 사진을 추가하기에는 이미 늦었음을 알려 남자의 제안을 거절하려는 의도로 한 말임을 알 수 있다. 따라서 정답은 (D)이다.

49

What does the woman ask the man to do?

(A) Come in for an interview
(B) Appear in a feature story
(C) Travel for an assignment
(D) Post some information online

여자는 남자에게 무엇을 해 달라고 요청하는가?

(A) 면접 보러 오기
(B) 특집 기사에 나오기
(C) 업무차 출장 가기
(D) 온라인에 정보 게시하기

어휘 assignment 업무

해설 세부 사항 관련 - 여자의 요청 사항

여자가 마지막 대사에서 사진 편집 보조 자리가 비었는데 면접을 보러 올 수 있는지 궁금하다(We're opening a position for assistant photo editor, and I wonder if you can come in for an interview)고 말하고 있으므로 정답은 (A)이다.

50-52 3인 대화

M-Au	Emiko and Susan—⁵⁰could you give me an update on the negotiations with the city to purchase insurance through our company?
W-Am	Well, the city officials expressed interest in buying insurance for all of their emergency vehicles, including ambulances,

through us. ⁵¹**I sent them a quote, but unfortunately I'm still waiting to hear back**.

W-Br I've been working on the account with the city parks department, and ⁵¹**I have the same problem. They haven't committed yet, either.**

M-Au Hmm, ⁵²**we could offer them a reduced first-year rate.** That might motivate them to make a final decision quickly.

남	에미코, 수잔, **우리 회사 보험에 가입하도록 시와 협상하는 건과 관련하여 새로운 소식이 있으면 주시겠어요?**
여1	음, 시 공무원들이 구급차를 포함해 긴급 차량 전부를 우리 회사 보험에 가입하는 데 관심을 표했어요. **견적서를 보냈는데, 안타깝게도 아직 답변을 기다리고 있어요.**
여2	전 시립 공원 부서와 거래하는 업무를 하는데, **저도 같은 문제가 있어요. 그들도 아직 결정하지 않았어요.**
남	음, 그들에게 1년차 할인을 제공할 수 있어요. 그러면 최종 결정을 빨리 내리도록 동기 부여가 될 거예요.

어휘 negotiation 협상 purchase insurance 보험에 가입하다 emergency 응급 quote 견적서 account 거래 commit 결정하다

50

What kind of business do the speakers most likely work for?

(A) An automobile manufacturer
(B) An insurance company
(C) A county hospital
(D) A construction firm

화자들은 어떤 업종에서 일하겠는가?

(A) 자동차 제조업체
(B) 보험 회사
(C) 시립 병원
(D) 건설 회사

해설 전체 내용 관련 - 화자들의 근무 업종

남자가 첫 대사에서 우리 회사 보험에 가입하도록 시와 협상하는 건과 관련하여 새로운 소식이 있으면 줄 수 있는지(could you give me an update on the negotiations with the city to purchase insurance through our company?) 묻고 있는 것으로 보아 화자들이 보험 회사에 근무하고 있음을 알 수 있다. 따라서 정답은 (B)이다.

51

What problem do the women mention?

(A) A building site did not pass an inspection.
(B) A vehicle needs to be repaired.
(C) Potential clients have not made a decision.
(D) Some vendors are making late deliveries.

여자들은 어떤 문제를 언급하는가?

(A) 건축 부지가 검사를 통과하지 못했다.
(B) 차량을 수리해야 한다.
(C) 잠재 고객들이 결정을 내리지 않았다.
(D) 판매 업체들이 늦게 배송하고 있다.

어휘 vendor 판매 업체

해설 세부 사항 관련 - 여자들이 언급하는 문제점

첫 번째 여자가 견적서를 보냈는데 안타깝게도 아직 답변을 기다리고 있다 (I sent them a quote, but unfortunately I'm still waiting to hear back)고 했고, 두 번째 여자도 저도 같은 문제가 있다(I have the same problem)며 그들도 아직 결정을 하지 않았다(They haven't committed yet, either)고 말하고 있으므로 정답은 (C)이다.

> ▸▸ Paraphrasing 대화의 **haven't committed yet**
> → 정답의 **have not made a decision**

52

What does the man recommend?

(A) Offering a discount
(B) Changing suppliers
(C) Forming a committee
(D) Closing a branch

남자는 무엇을 권하는가?

(A) 할인 제공
(B) 납품 업체 변경
(C) 위원회 구성
(D) 지점 폐쇄

해설 세부 사항 관련 - 남자의 권유 사항

남자가 마지막에 그들에게 1년차 할인을 제공할 수 있다(we could offer them a reduced first-year rate)고 말하고 있으므로 정답은 (A)이다.

> ▸▸ Paraphrasing 대화의 **a reduced ~ rate**
> → 정답의 **a discount**

53-55

M-Cn Ms. Moreau, [53,54]**thank you for volunteering to participate in this product testing session.**

W-Am It sounds interesting. So [53]**I'll be testing out some new designs for drinking mugs?**

M-Cn Exactly. We want to test if our mugs are easier to drink from than traditional mugs. Before we begin, [54]**could you please sign this agreement form?** It states that we can use your comments in our marketing campaign.

W-Am Sure. But I have one question... Do you have different beverages available? I don't drink coffee.

M-Cn Oh, definitely—you'll have several to choose from. OK, now let's go join the other participants. [55]**Please follow me to Room B.**

남 모로 씨, **제품 테스트 세션에 자원해 참가해 주셔서 감사합니다.**

여 재미있겠어요. 그럼 제가 새 머그잔 디자인을 시험하는 건가요?

남 맞아요. 머그잔이 종전 머그잔보다 마시기 더 쉬운지 시험해 보고 싶어요. 시작하기 전에 **이 동의서에 서명하시겠어요?** 마케팅 캠페인에 선생님 의견을 활용할 수 있다고 명시되어 있어요.

여 그럼요. 그런데 한 가지 질문이 있어요… 다양한 음료가 있나요? 제가 커피를 안 마시거든요.

남 아, 물론이죠. 선택할 수 있는 음료가 몇 가지 있을 거예요. 자, 이제 가서 다른 참가자들과 합류하죠. **B호실로 따라오세요.**

어휘 participate in ~에 참여하다 agreement 동의 definitely 물론 participant 참가자

53

What has the woman volunteered to do?

(A) Try out some new products
(B) Purchase beverages for a luncheon
(C) Lead a workshop session
(D) Organize a hiring event

여자는 어떤 일을 하겠다고 자원했는가?

(A) 신제품 시험 사용
(B) 오찬에 쓸 음료 구입
(C) 워크숍 진행
(D) 채용 행사 준비

어휘 beverage 음료 organize 준비하다

해설 세부 사항 관련 - 여자가 자원한 일

남자가 첫 대사에서 여자에게 제품 테스트 세션에 자원해 참가해 줘서 감사하다(thank you for volunteering to participate in this product testing session)고 했고, 여자가 자신이 새 머그잔 디자인을 시험하는 것인지(I'll be testing out some new designs for drinking mugs?)를 묻고 있으므로 정답은 (A)이다.

> ▸▸ Paraphrasing 대화의 **testing out some new designs**
> → 정답의 **Try out some new products**

54

What does the man ask the woman to sign?

(A) An employee contract
(B) An attendance sheet
(C) A participant agreement
(D) A service estimate

남자는 여자에게 무엇에 서명해 달라고 요청하는가?

(A) 사원 계약서
(B) 출석부
(C) 참가자 동의서
(D) 용역 견적서

어휘 estimate 견적서

해설 세부 사항 관련 – 남자가 여자에게 서명을 요청한 것
남자가 첫 대사에서 여자에게 제품 테스트 세션에 자원해 참가해 줘서 감사하다(thank you for volunteering to participate in this product testing session)고 했고 두 번째 대사에서 동의서에 서명해 줄 것(could you please sign this agreement form?)을 요청하고 있으므로, 남자는 여자에게 참가자 동의서에 서명해 달라고 요청하고 있음을 알 수 있다. 따라서 정답은 (C)이다.

55

What will the woman most likely do next?

(A) Set up her computer
(B) Go to another room
(C) Have some lunch
(D) Make a phone call

여자는 다음에 무엇을 하겠는가?

(A) 컴퓨터 설치하기
(B) 다른 방으로 가기
(C) 점심 먹기
(D) 전화 걸기

해설 세부 사항 관련 – 여자가 다음에 할 일
남자가 마지막 대사에서 B호실로 자신을 따라오라(Please follow me to Room B)고 말하고 있으므로 정답은 (B)이다.

56-58

M-Cn	Hi Irina, ⁵⁶**are you all finished styling your client's hair?**
W-Br	Yes, I cut and blow dried it. She's all set. Now I'm going to sweep the floor and wash some towels.
M-Cn	Thanks. I wanted to mention something… ⁵⁷**It seems we're all using too much electricity every month. I'd like us all to start thinking of ways to reduce that expense.**
W-Br	Oh? I didn't realize that was an issue.
M-Cn	Well, ⁵⁷**the other salons I own spend about half of what this location does every month.**
W-Br	Hmm… they don't have as many clients, though.

M-Cn	True, but I still think we all need to make changes nonetheless. ⁵⁸**We'll discuss it further at the employee meeting later today.**

남	안녕하세요 이리나, **고객 헤어 스타일링은 다 끝냈나요?**
여	네, 자르고 드라이어로 말렸어요. 다 됐어요. 이제 바닥 쓸고 수건을 세탁하려고요.
남	고마워요. 한 가지 말하고 싶은 게 있는데… **우리 모두 매달 전기를 너무 많이 쓰는 것 같아요. 모두 비용을 줄일 수 있는 방법을 생각해 봤으면 해요.**
여	아? 그런 문제가 있는지 몰랐어요.
남	음, **제가 소유한 다른 살롱들은 매달 이 지점의 절반 정도를 소비해요.**
여	음… 하지만 거기는 고객이 여기만큼 많지 않잖아요.
남	그렇긴 하지만 그래도 우리 모두 변화가 필요하다고 생각해요. **오늘 이따가 있을 직원 회의 때 더 논의하려고요.**

어휘	electricity 전기 reduce 줄이다 expense 비용 realize 인지하다 location 지점 nonetheless 그래도

56

Where most likely are the speakers?

(A) At a hair salon
(B) At a catering hall
(C) At a laundry service
(D) At an energy company

화자들은 어디에 있겠는가?

(A) 미용실
(B) 급식실
(C) 세탁소
(D) 에너지 회사

해설 전체 내용 관련 – 대화의 장소
남자가 첫 대사에서 여자에게 고객 헤어 스타일링은 다 끝냈는지(are you all finished styling your client's hair?) 묻고 있는 것으로 보아 대화의 장소가 미용실임을 알 수 있다. 따라서 정답은 (A)이다.

57

Why does the woman say, "they don't have as many clients, though"?

(A) To express pride in her company's growth
(B) To explain why an expense is so high
(C) To suggest that a strategy should continue
(D) To question the accuracy of a client list

여자가 "하지만 거기는 고객이 여기만큼 많지 않잖아요"라고 말하는 이유는 무엇인가?

(A) 회사의 성장에 대한 자긍심을 피력하려고
(B) 비용이 많이 나가는 이유를 설명하려고
(C) 전략이 계속되어야 한다고 제안하려고
(D) 고객 목록의 정확성에 의문을 제기하려고

어휘 accuracy 정확성

해설 화자의 의도 파악 – 하지만 거기는 고객이 여기만큼 많지 않다는 말의 의도

앞에서 남자가 우리 모두 매달 전기를 너무 많이 쓰는 것 같다(It seems we're all using too much electricity every month)며 비용을 줄일 수 있는 방법을 생각해 봤으면 한다(I'd like us all to start ~ reduce that expense)고 말하며 자신이 소유한 다른 살롱들은 매달 이 지점의 절반 정도를 소비한다(the other salons I own spend ~ does every month)고 하자 여자가 인용문을 언급한 것으로 보아, 해당 지점이 다른 지점에 비해 전기 비용이 많이 나온다는 남자의 불만에 반박하기 위한 근거를 제시하려고 한 말임을 알 수 있다. 따라서 정답은 (B)이다.

58

What will happen later today?

(A) Some supplies will be delivered.

(B) An inspection will be conducted.

(C) An employee meeting will be held.

(D) An expense report will be submitted.

오늘 오후에 어떤 일이 일어날 것인가?

(A) 비품이 배송될 것이다.

(B) 점검이 있을 것이다.

(C) 직원 회의가 열릴 것이다.

(D) 지출 보고서가 제출될 것이다.

어휘 inspection 점검   submit 제출하다

해설 세부 사항 관련 – 오늘 오후에 있을 일

남자가 마지막 대사에서 오늘 이따가 있을 직원 회의 때 더 논의하겠다(We'll discuss it further at the employee meeting later today)고 말하고 있으므로 정답은 (C)이다.

59-61

> W-Am Thanks for meeting with me today, Diego. ⁵⁹**Our firm's been contracted by a ferry company to design a hydrogen-powered boat.** They're hoping to cut down on their carbon emissions with a boat that runs on clean energy.
>
> M-Cn Hmm. ⁶⁰**A hydrogen power source is going to need a lot of space. Since ferries usually transport cars, I'm concerned about where we'd place the hydrogen source.**
>
> W-Am Actually this ferry would give tours. So it won't be carrying vehicles, just passengers.
>
> M-Cn Then maybe we could store the hydrogen on the deck?
>
> W-Am Possibly. ⁶¹**Could you research that before we meet with the ferry company?**
>
> M-Cn ⁶¹**Absolutely.**

여 오늘 만나 주셔서 감사합니다, 디에고 씨. **우리 회사가 수소 동력 보트를 설계하기로 페리 회사와 계약을 체결했어요.** 그들은 청정 에너지로 운행하는 보트로 탄소 배출량을 줄이기를 바라고 있어요.

남 흠. **수소 전지는 공간이 많이 필요할 겁니다. 페리는 보통 차를 수송하니 수소 전지를 어디에 둘지 걱정이에요.**

여 사실 이 페리는 관광용이에요. 따라서 차량을 수송하지 않고 승객만 수송할 거예요.

남 그럼 수소를 갑판에 둘 수 있을까요?

여 그럴 수도 있죠. **페리 회사와 만나기 전에 그걸 좀 조사해 주실래요?**

남 **물론이죠.**

어휘 contract 계약하다   hydrogen 수소   emission 배출

59

Which industry do the speakers most likely work in?

(A) Tourism

(B) Agriculture

(C) Education

(D) Engineering

화자들은 어떤 업종에서 일하겠는가?

(A) 관광

(B) 농업

(C) 교육

(D) 엔지니어링

해설 전체 내용 관련 – 화자들의 근무 업종

여자가 첫 대사에서 우리 회사가 수소 동력 보트를 설계하기로 페리 회사와 계약을 체결했다(Our firm's been contracted by a ferry company to design a hydrogen-powered boat)고 말하고 있는 것으로 보아 정답은 (D)이다.

60

What does the man say he is concerned about?

(A) Expenses

(B) Safety

(C) Competition

(D) Space

남자는 무엇이 걱정이라고 말하는가?

(A) 비용

(B) 안전

(C) 경쟁

(D) 공간

해설 세부 사항 관련 – 남자의 우려 사항

남자가 첫 대사에서 수소 전지는 공간이 많이 필요할 것(A hydrogen power source is going to need a lot of space)이라면서 페리는 보통 차를 수송하니 수소 전지를 어디에 둘지 걱정이다(Since ferries usually transport cars, I'm concerned about where we'd place the hydrogen source)라고 말하고 있으므로 정답은 (D)이다.

61

What does the man agree to do?

(A) Apply for some funding

(B) Do some research

(C) Organize a business trip

(D) Assemble a work crew

남자는 무엇을 하기로 동의하는가?

(A) 지원금 신청

(B) 조사

(C) 출장 준비

(D) 작업반 구성

어휘 assemble 구성하다

해설 세부 사항 관련 - 남자가 동의한 일

여자가 마지막 대사에서 페리 회사와 만나기 전에 그것을 좀 조사해 달라(Could you research that before we meet with the ferry company?)고 요청하자 남자가 물론이죠(Absolutely)라고 동의하고 있으므로 정답은 (B)이다.

62-64 대화 + 표지판

M-Au	Dolores, thanks again for offering to drive to the technology seminar. I'm not very familiar with the city of Hartsville.
W-Am	It's no problem. ⁶²**I grew up in downtown Hartsville**, remember? I know the area well.
M-Au	Oh—that's right. Does it take long to get to the conference center from here? I know it's on Carter Lane.
W-Am	Well, usually not—but ⁶³**the traffic report earlier said that the exit to Carter Lane is closed for repairs. We'll have to take exit eight**. It'll take us about twenty minutes longer to get there.
M-Au	Well, in that case, ⁶⁴**I'd better call our coworkers and ask them to save us some seats**.
W-Am	Good idea!

남 돌로레스, 기술 세미나장까지 태워다 준다고 해서 다시 한번 고마워요. 제가 하츠빌 시는 잘 모르거든요.

여 문제없어요. **제가 하츠빌 시내에서 자랐잖아요**, 기억나요? 이곳을 잘 알죠.

남 아 참, 그렇죠. 여기서 회의장까지 가려면 오래 걸리나요? 카터 레인에 있다는 건 알아요.

여 글쎄요, 보통은 안 그런데, **아까 나온 교통 정보로는 카터 레인으로 가는 출구가 보수를 위해 폐쇄됐다고 하네요. 우리는 8번 출구로 나가야 해요**. 거기까지 가는 데 20분 정도 더 걸릴 거예요.

남 음, 그렇다면 **동료들에게 전화해서 우리 자리를 좀 맡아 달라고 부탁하는 게 좋겠어요**.

여 좋은 생각이에요!

어휘 familiar with ~을 잘 아는 repair 보수

HARTSVILLE EXITS →

Maple Road	Exit 5
Carter Lane	Exit 7
⁶³Berk Street	Exit 8
High Road	Exit 10

하츠빌 출구 →

메이플 로드	5번 출구
카터 레인	7번 출구
⁶³버크 스트리트	**8번 출구**
하이 로드	10번 출구

62

What does the woman remind the man about?

(A) She used to live in the area.

(B) She needs to stop at a store.

(C) She attended a seminar last year.

(D) She has just bought a new car.

여자는 남자에게 무엇을 일깨워 주는가?

(A) 그녀는 한때 그 지역에 살았다.

(B) 그녀는 가게에 들러야 한다.

(C) 그녀는 작년에 세미나에 참석했다.

(D) 그녀는 막 새 차를 샀다.

해설 세부 사항 관련 - 여자가 남자에게 일깨워 주는 것

여자가 첫 대사에서 하츠빌 시내에서 자랐다(I grew up in downtown Hartsville)고 말하고 있으므로 정답은 (A)이다.

▸▸ Paraphrasing 대화의 **grew up in**
→ 정답의 **used to live in**

63

Look at the graphic. Which exit will the speakers take?

(A) Maple Road

(B) Carter Lane

(C) Berk Street

(D) High Road

시각 정보에 의하면 화자들은 어느 출구로 나갈 것인가?

(A) 메이플 로드
(B) 카터 레인
(C) 버크 스트리트
(D) 하이 로드

해설 시각 정보 연계 – 화자들이 나갈 출구

여자가 두 번째 대사에서 아까 나온 교통 정보에 따르면 카터 레인으로 가는 출구가 보수를 위해 폐쇄됐다고 한다(the traffic report earlier said that the exit to Carter Lane is closed for repairs)면서 8번 출구로 나가야 한다(We'll have to take exit eight)고 말하고 있고, 표지판에 따르면 8번 출구는 버크 스트리트이므로 정답은 (C)이다.

64

What will the man ask his coworkers to do?

(A) Cancel a reservation
(B) Save some seats
(C) Sign in at an event
(D) Print some materials

남자는 동료들에게 무엇을 해 달라고 요청할 것인가?

(A) 예약 취소하기
(B) 좌석 맡아 두기
(C) 행사에 도착 서명하기
(D) 자료 인쇄하기

해설 세부 사항 관련 – 남자가 동료들에게 요청할 일

남자가 세 번째 대사에서 동료들에게 전화해서 우리 자리를 좀 맡아 달라고 부탁하는 게 좋겠다(I'd better call our coworkers and ask them to save us some seats)고 말하고 있으므로 정답은 (B)이다.

65-67 대화 + 재활용품 통

W-Br **⁶⁵Good work helping the office go paperless**, Kentaro. **You've scanned and shredded everything that had any personal student data, correct?**

M-Au Yes, so now **⁶⁶we can get rid of the rest of these old documents—class schedules, information sheets to parents—all of it can be recycled.** The bins are out back, right?

W-Br That's right, behind the gym. But **⁶⁷don't try to carry all these boxes; they're too heavy. I brought a cart over from the maintenance closet for you to use.**

여 사무실에서 문서를 없애도록 도와주시느라 수고하셨어요, 켄타로. 학생 개인 정보가 있는 건 전부 스캔해서 **파쇄했죠?**

남 네, 이제 **수업 시간표**와 학부모들에게 보내는 안내문 같은 이런 오래된 나머지 문서들을 모두 재활용품으로 치우면 돼요. 쓰레기통은 바깥 뒤쪽에 있죠?

여 맞아요, 체육관 뒤예요. 하지만 **이 상자들은 너무 무거우니 다들고 옮기려 하지 마세요. 쓰시도록 제가 정비용품 벽장에서 카트를 가져왔어요.**

어휘 shred 파쇄하다 get rid of ~을 치우다 maintenance 정비 closet 벽장

65

Where does the conversation most likely take place?

(A) At a hotel
(B) At an accounting firm
(C) At a doctor's office
(D) At a school

대화는 어디에서 이루어지겠는가?

(A) 호텔
(B) 회계 법인
(C) 진료실
(D) 학교

해설 전체 내용 관련 – 대화의 장소

여자가 첫 대사에서 사무실에서 문서를 없애도록 돕느라 수고했다(Good work helping the office go paperless)며 학생 개인 정보가 있는 것은 전부 스캔하고 파쇄했는지(You've scanned and shredded everything that had any personal student data, correct?)를 묻고 있다. 사무실에 학생 관련 자료가 있다는 점으로 보아 대화의 장소는 학교일 가능성이 높으므로 정답은 (D)이다.

66

Look at the graphic. Which bin will the man use?

(A) Bin 1
(B) Bin 2
(C) Bin 3
(D) Bin 4

시각 정보에 의하면 남자는 어떤 쓰레기통을 사용할 것인가?

(A) 1번 쓰레기통
(B) 2번 쓰레기통
(C) 3번 쓰레기통
(D) 4번 쓰레기통

해설 시각 정보 연계 - 남자가 사용할 쓰레기통

남자가 첫 대사에서 수업 시간표와 학부모들에게 보내는 안내문 같은 이런 오래된 나머지 문서들을 모두 재활용품으로 치우면 된다(we can get rid of the rest of these old documents—class schedules, information sheets to parents—all of it can be recycled)고 말하고 있으므로 남자가 버릴 물건들이 종이임을 알 수 있고, 시각 정보에 의하면 3번 재활용 통에 종이라고 표기되어 있으므로 정답은 (C)이다.

67

What does the woman suggest?

(A) Using a cart
(B) Waiting for a confirmation
(C) Giving an assignment to a colleague
(D) Rescheduling an appointment with a client

여자는 무엇을 제안하는가?

(A) 카트 사용
(B) 확인 대기
(C) 동료에게 과제 주기
(D) 고객과 약속 일정 다시 잡기

해설 세부 사항 관련 - 여자의 제안 사항

여자가 마지막 대사에서 이 상자들은 너무 무거우니 다 들고 옮기려 하지 말라(don't try to carry all these boxes; they're too heavy)면서, 쓰시도록 제가 정비용품 벽장에서 카트를 가져왔다(I brought a cart over from the maintenance closet for you to use)고 말하고 있으므로 정답은 (A)이다.

68-70 대화 + 초대장

W-Am Riccardo, **68could you take a look at this invitation? It's a draft I put together for our upcoming fund-raiser.** Your feedback would be helpful.

M-Au Sure. Hmm... It looks good, but **69we should have the live music start at the same time as dinner.** Otherwise, there'll be very little time for the band to perform.

W-Am You're right. Anything else?

M-Au **70Let's add a line at the bottom with the name of our organization, since we're sponsoring the event.**

W-Am OK, that's an easy addition.

여 리카르도, **이 초대장 좀 봐 주실래요? 곧 있을 모금 행사를 위해 작성한 초안이에요.** 의견 주시면 도움될 거예요.

남 물론이죠. 음… 좋아 보이는데, **저녁 식사와 동시에 라이브 음악 공연이 시작되게 해야 해요.** 그렇지 않으면 밴드가 공연할 시간이 거의 없을 거예요.

여 맞아요. 또 다른 건 없나요?

남 **우리가 행사를 후원하고 있으니 우리 단체 이름을 맨 아래에 한 줄 추가하죠.**

여 좋아요, 쉽게 추가할 수 있어요.

어휘 draft 초안 put together ~을 작성하다 fund-raiser 모금 행사 organization 단체

Invitation draft

Date:	Friday, August 10
Location:	Davis Botanical Garden
• 5:00 P.M.	Garden Tour
69• 6:00 P.M.	Dinner
• 7:00 P.M.	Live Music
• 8:00 P.M.	Speeches

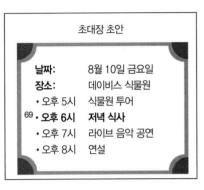

초대장 초안

날짜:	8월 10일 금요일
장소:	데이비스 식물원
• 오후 5시	식물원 투어
69 • 오후 6시	저녁 식사
• 오후 7시	라이브 음악 공연
• 오후 8시	연설

68

What type of event are the speakers organizing?

(A) An award ceremony
(B) A grand-opening celebration
(C) A foreign official's reception
(D) A fund-raiser

화자들은 어떤 종류의 행사를 준비하고 있는가?

(A) 시상식
(B) 개업 축하 행사
(C) 외국 관계자 환영회
(D) 모금 행사

해설 세부 사항 관련 - 화자들이 준비하고 있는 행사

여자가 첫 대사에서 초대장을 좀 봐 달라(could you take a look at this invitation?)면서 곧 있을 모금 행사를 위해 작성한 초안(It's a draft I put together for our upcoming fund-raiser)이라고 말하고 있는 것으로 보아 화자들은 모금 행사를 준비 중임을 알 수 있다. 따라서 정답은 (D)이다.

69

Look at the graphic. What time does the man think the music should begin?

(A) At 5:00 P.M.
(B) At 6:00 P.M.
(C) At 7:00 P.M.
(D) At 8:00 P.M.

시각 정보에 의하면 남자는 음악이 몇 시에 시작되어야 한다고 생각하는가?

(A) 오후 5시
(B) 오후 6시
(C) 오후 7시
(D) 오후 8시

해설 시각 정보 연계 – 남자가 음악이 시작되어야 한다고 생각하는 시간
남자가 첫 대사에서 저녁 식사와 동시에 라이브 음악 공연이 시작되게 해야 한다(we should have the live music start at the same time as dinner)고 말하고 있고, 초대장에 따르면 저녁 식사 시간은 오후 6시에 시작한다고 나와 있으므로 정답은 (B)이다.

70

What information does the man suggest adding to the invitation?

(A) The name of a sponsor
(B) The location of a concert hall
(C) A Web site address
(D) A list of performers

남자는 어떤 정보를 초대장에 추가하자고 제안하는가?

(A) 후원자 이름
(B) 콘서트홀 위치
(C) 웹사이트 주소
(D) 공연자 목록

해설 세부 사항 관련 – 남자가 초대장에 추가하자고 제안하는 정보
남자가 두 번째 대사에서 우리가 행사를 후원하고 있으니 우리 단체 이름을 맨 아래에 한 줄 추가하자(Let's add a line at the bottom with the name of our organization, since we're sponsoring the event)고 말하고 있으므로 정답은 (A)이다.

PART 4

71-73 방송

M-Cn You're listening to radio station WKXL. Turning to local business updates, [71]**Monday marked the grand opening of Starbright Corporation's new factory.** [72]**Starbright Corporation is a leading manufacturer of boots, athletic shoes, and sandals.** So far, the new factory has created 800 jobs in our community, with positions ranging from assembly line workers to department managers. To hear more about the company, [73]**please visit our radio station's Web site, where my video interview with Starbright's president has been posted.**

여러분은 지금 WKXL 라디오 방송을 듣고 계십니다. 지역 업체 소식으로 가죠. **월요일 스타브라이트사의 신규 공장이 문을 열었습니다. 스타브라이트사는 부츠와 운동화, 샌들을 만드는 대표적인 제조업체죠.** 지금까지 새 공장은 지역 사회에 일자리 800개를 창출했고, 그 직위는 조립라인 작업자부터 부서장까지 다양합니다. 회사에 대해 더 자세히 들으시려면 **제가 스타브라이트사 회장을 인터뷰한 동영상이 게시된 라디오 방송국 웹사이트를 방문하세요.**

어휘 manufacturer 제조업체 range from A to B (범위가) A에서 B에 이르다

71

What did Starbright Corporation recently do?

(A) It changed its company logo.
(B) It opened a new factory.
(C) It conducted a financial audit.
(D) It upgraded a product line.

스타브라이트사는 최근에 무엇을 했는가?

(A) 회사 로고를 바꿨다.
(B) 새로운 공장을 열었다.
(C) 재무 감사를 실시했다.
(D) 제품 라인을 개선했다.

어휘 audit 감사

해설 세부 사항 관련 – 스타브라이트사가 최근에 한 일
화자가 초반부에 월요일 스타브라이트사의 신규 공장이 문을 열었다(Monday marked the grand opening of Starbright Corporation's new factory)고 말하고 있으므로 정답은 (B)이다.

72

What type of product does Starbright Corporation make?

(A) Footwear
(B) Cosmetics
(C) Housewares
(D) Electronics

스타브라이트사는 어떤 종류의 제품을 생산하는가?

(A) 신발
(B) 화장품
(C) 가정용품
(D) 전자 제품

해설 세부 사항 관련 – 스타브라이트사가 생산하는 제품
화자가 중반부에 스타브라이트사는 부츠와 운동화, 샌들을 만드는 대표적인 제조업체(Starbright Corporation is a leading manufacturer of boots, athletic shoes, and sandals)라고 소개하고 있으므로 정답은 (A)이다.

▸▸ Paraphrasing 담화의 boots, athletic shoes, and sandals
→ 정답의 Footwear

73

What is available online?

(A) An application

(B) A schedule

(C) A video interview

(D) A virtual tour

온라인에서 무엇을 이용할 수 있는가?

(A) 신청서

(B) 일정

(C) **동영상 인터뷰**

(D) 가상 투어

해설 세부 사항 관련 - 온라인에서 이용 가능한 것

화자가 마지막에 자신이 스타브라이트사 회장을 인터뷰한 동영상이 게시된 라디오 방송국 웹사이트를 방문하라(please visit our radio station's Web site, where my video interview with Starbright's president has been posted)고 말하고 있으므로 정답은 (C)이다.

74-76 담화

W-Br **74Thank you all for coming to this celebration. 75I know I speak for everyone here at the newspaper when I say that I'm sad to see Mustafa Perez retire next week. For the past 30 years, he's been the photographer we've all relied on to capture photos that illustrate our news articles.** To honor his career, **76I've made a slideshow of some of the most impressive photos that Mustafa has taken.** Please look at the screen at the front of the room.

축하 행사에 참석해 주셔서 감사합니다. 다음 주에 무스타파 페레즈 씨가 은퇴해서 슬프다는 제 말이 여기 신문사에 계시는 모두를 대변한다는 것 압니다. 지난 30년 동안 그는 사진기자로 일했고 우리 모두는 뉴스 기사를 묘사하는 사진을 찍는 그에게 의존해 왔습니다. 그의 경력을 기리기 위해 **무스타파가 찍은 가장 인상적인 사진들을 슬라이드쇼로 만들었습니다.** 방 앞쪽에 있는 화면을 봐 주세요.

어휘 retire 은퇴하다   rely on ~에 의존하다   impressive 인상적인

74

What event is taking place?

(A) An orientation session

(B) A gallery opening

(C) An awards ceremony

(D) **A retirement party**

어떤 행사가 열리고 있는가?

(A) 오리엔테이션 세션

(B) 미술관 개관

(C) 시상식

(D) **은퇴 파티**

해설 전체 내용 관련 - 담화의 장소

화자가 도입부에 축하 행사에 참석해 줘서 감사하다(Thank you all for coming to this celebration)며 다음 주에 무스타파 페레즈 씨가 은퇴해서 슬프다는 말이 여기 신문사에 있는 모두를 대변한다는 것을 안다(I know I speak for everyone ~ Mustafa Perez retire next week)고 말하는 것으로 보아, 화자는 무스타파 페레즈 씨의 은퇴 축하 행사에서 말하고 있다는 것을 알 수 있다. 따라서 정답은 (D)이다.

75

What type of business does Mustafa Perez work for?

(A) An advertising agency

(B) An art gallery

(C) A newspaper publisher

(D) A camera shop

무스타파 페레즈는 어떤 업종에서 일하는가?

(A) 광고 대행사

(B) 미술관

(C) **신문사**

(D) 카메라점

해설 세부 사항 관련 - 무스타파 페레즈의 근무 업종

화자가 초반부에 다음 주에 무스타파 페레즈 씨가 은퇴해서 슬프다는 말이 여기 신문사에 있는 모두를 대변한다는 것을 안다(I know I speak for everyone ~ Mustafa Perez retire next week)고 했고, 지난 30년간 그가 사진기자로 일했고 우리는 뉴스 기사를 묘사하는 사진을 찍는 그에게 의존해 왔다(For the past 30 years, he's been the photographer ~ illustrate our news articles)고 말하고 있으므로 정답은 (C)이다.

76

What has the speaker created for the event?

(A) **A slideshow**

(B) A T-shirt design

(C) A Web site

(D) A brochure

화자가 행사를 위해 무엇을 만들었는가?

(A) **슬라이드쇼**

(B) 티셔츠 디자인

(C) 웹사이트

(D) 안내책자

해설 세부 사항 관련 - 화자가 행사를 위해 만든 것

화자가 후반부에 무스타파가 찍은 가장 인상적인 사진들을 슬라이드쇼로 만들었다(I've made a slideshow of some of the most impressive photos that Mustafa has taken)고 말하고 있으므로 정답은 (A)이다.

77-79 회의 발췌

M-Au **77The last point on our agenda is about maintaining a safe environment while making the medications we sell here at Tamarah**

Pharmaceuticals. ⁷⁸**If you're working in any of the laboratories, please make sure to turn on the room's exhaust fan.** It's especially important to keep the area well ventilated when working with some of the chemicals we use in our medications. We'd like to maintain our excellent safety record, so thank you in advance. ⁷⁹**The safety procedure handbook is on our internal company Web site** if you need more information.

마지막 안건은 안전한 환경을 유지하면서 여기 타마라 제약에서 판매하는 약을 만드는 것입니다. 실험실에서 작업하는 분은 반드시 방의 환기팬을 켜시기 바랍니다. 약물에 사용하는 화학 물질로 작업할 때 그 구역의 환기가 잘돼야 한다는 것이 특히 중요합니다. 회사의 우수한 안전 기록을 유지하고 싶으니, 미리 감사드립니다. 더 자세한 정보가 필요하시면 회사 내부 웹사이트에 안전 절차 편람이 있습니다.

어휘 medication 약 pharmaceutical 제약 exhaust fan 환기팬 ventilate 환기하다

77

What does the speaker's company produce?

(A) Medications
(B) Textbooks
(C) Exercise clothing
(D) Construction materials

화자의 회사는 무엇을 생산하는가?

(A) 약품
(B) 교재
(C) 운동복
(D) 건설 자재

해설 세부 사항 관련 – 화자의 회사가 생산하는 제품

화자가 도입부에 마지막 안건은 안전한 환경을 유지하면서 여기 타마라 제약에서 판매하는 약을 만드는 것(The last point on our agenda is about maintaining a safe environment while making the medications we sell here at Tamarah Pharmaceuticals)이라고 말하고 있으므로 정답은 (A)이다.

78

What are the listeners reminded to do?

(A) Recruit some staff
(B) Enter some data
(C) Attend some training sessions
(D) Turn on a fan

청자들은 무엇을 하라고 주의를 받는가?

(A) 직원 모집하기
(B) 데이터 입력하기
(C) 교육 세션에 참석하기
(D) 팬 켜기

해설 세부 사항 관련 – 청자들이 주의받은 사항

화자가 중반부에 실험실에서 작업할 경우 반드시 방의 환기팬을 켜기 바란다(If you're working in any of the laboratories, please make sure to turn on the room's exhaust fan)고 말하고 있으므로 정답은 (D)이다.

79

What can be found online?

(A) A product database
(B) An employee directory
(C) A handbook
(D) A contract

온라인에서 무엇을 찾을 수 있는가?

(A) 제품 데이터베이스
(B) 사원 명부
(C) 편람
(D) 계약서

해설 세부 사항 관련 – 온라인에서 찾을 수 있는 것

화자가 마지막에 회사 내부 웹사이트에 안전 절차 편람이 있다(The safety procedure handbook is on our internal company Web site)고 말하고 있으므로 정답은 (C)이다.

▸▸ Paraphrasing 담화의 our ~ Web site → 질문의 online

80-82 전화 메시지

W-Br Hi, Aisha. ⁸⁰**I'm here at the park for the farmers' market—I just set out the blueberries and strawberries that I'll be selling this morning.** Everything's ready to go... Though ⁸¹**I did accidentally forget to bring the tent that we use to shade the fruit. I know you're concerned about the fruit sitting out in the sun,** but it's supposed to be cloudy all day. Anyways, ⁸²**the real reason I called was to remind you to register us for the annual farmers' association competition.** I think we have a pretty good chance of winning the award for our strawberries.

안녕, 아이샤. 저는 농산물 직판장 때문에 공원에 왔어요. 오늘 아침에 판매할 블루베리와 딸기를 막 내놓았어요. 전부 준비됐는데… 제가 어쩌다 보니 과일 위로 햇빛을 가리는 데 쓸 텐트를 깜빡 잊고 안 가져왔어요. 과일이 햇빛을 받을까 봐 걱정되겠죠. 하지만 하루 종일 흐릴 거예요. 아무튼 제가 전화한 진짜 이유는 연례 농업인 협회 경연 대회에 우리가 등록해야 하니까 다시 알려 드리려고요. 저는 딸기로 우리가 상을 받을 가능성이 높다고 생각해요.

어휘 farmers' market 농산물 직판장 accidentally 실수로 shade 햇빛을 가리다 sit out in the sun 햇볕을 쬐다 register 등록하다 competition 경연 대회

80

What will the speaker do at a park?

(A) Watch a performance
(B) Sell fruit
(C) Plant trees
(D) Take photographs

화자는 공원에서 무엇을 할 것인가?

(A) 공연 관람하기
(B) 과일 판매하기
(C) 나무 심기
(D) 사진 찍기

해설 세부 사항 관련 – 화자가 공원에서 할 일

화자가 초반부에 농산물 직판장 때문에 공원에 와서 오늘 아침에 판매할 블루베리와 딸기를 막 내놓았다(I'm here at the park for the farmers' market—I just set out the blueberries and strawberries that I'll be selling this morning)고 말하는 것으로 보아 화자는 공원에서 과일을 팔 예정임을 알 수 있다. 따라서 정답은 (B)이다.

> ▸▸ **Paraphrasing** 담화의 blueberries and strawberries
> → 정답의 **fruit**

81

Why does the speaker say, "but it's supposed to be cloudy all day"?

(A) To ask for help
(B) To express frustration
(C) To reject the listener's suggestion
(D) To reassure the listener

화자가 "하지만 하루 종일 흐릴 거예요"라고 말하는 이유는 무엇인가?

(A) 도움을 요청하려고
(B) 좌절감을 표현하려고
(C) 청자의 제안을 거절하려고
(D) 청자를 안심시키려고

어휘 frustration 좌절감   reject 거절하다   reassure 안심시키다

해설 화자의 의도 파악 – 하지만 하루 종일 흐릴 것이라는 말의 의도

앞에서 화자가 어쩌다 보니 과일 위로 햇빛을 가리는 데 쓸 텐트를 깜빡 잊고 안 가져왔다(I did accidentally forget to bring the tent that we use to shade the fruit)면서 과일이 햇볕을 받을까 봐 당신이 걱정한다는 것을 안다(I know you're concerned about the fruit sitting out in the sun)고 한 뒤 인용문을 언급하고 있으므로, 비록 텐트를 가져오지 않았지만 흐린 날씨 덕에 과일이 햇볕에 노출될 일은 없을 것이므로 걱정할 필요가 없다는 의도로 한 말임을 알 수 있다. 따라서 정답은 (D)이다.

82

What does the speaker remind the listener to do?

(A) Register for a competition
(B) Purchase some supplies
(C) Prepare a shipment
(D) Speak to a customer

화자는 청자에게 무엇을 하라고 일깨워 주는가?

(A) 경연 대회에 등록하기
(B) 물품 구매하기
(C) 배송품 준비하기
(D) 고객과 이야기하기

해설 세부 사항 관련 – 화자가 청자에게 일깨워 주는 것

화자가 후반부에 전화를 건 진짜 이유는 연례 농업인 협회 경연 대회에 우리를 등록하라고 말하기 위한 것(the real reason I called was to remind you to register us for the annual farmers' association competition)이라고 말하고 있으므로 정답은 (A)이다.

83-85 공지

M-Au **⁸³Attention, Home Furniture factory employees.** The software program we use for clocking in and out isn't working. This means you cannot enter your hours electronically. Instead, **⁸⁴when your shift's over, please write your start and end time on the form that's on the receptionist's desk.** The form already includes your name and the machine you operate. I know this is a hassle, but it's only temporary—**⁸⁵the time-reporting software will be working when you get to the factory tomorrow morning.**

홈 퍼니처 공장 직원 여러분, 주목해 주세요. 우리가 출퇴근 시간을 기록하는 데 사용하는 소프트웨어 프로그램이 작동하지 않고 있습니다. 즉 컴퓨터로 출퇴근하신 시간을 입력할 수 없습니다. 대신 **근무가 끝나면 접수 담당자 책상 위에 있는 양식에 시작 시간과 종료 시간을 적으세요.** 양식에는 이미 사용자 이름과 사용자가 조작하는 기계가 포함되어 있습니다. 번거롭겠지만, 잠시 동안만입니다. **내일 아침 공장에 도착하면 시간 보고용 소프트웨어가 작동될 겁니다.**

어휘 clock in 출퇴근기에 출근 시간을 기록하다   clock out 출퇴근기에 퇴근 시간을 기록하다   electronically 컴퓨터로, 전자로   hassle 번거로움   temporary 잠시 동안의

83

Where is the announcement being made?

(A) At a technology firm
(B) At a repair shop
(C) At a factory
(D) At a law office

어디에서 나오는 공지인가?

(A) 기술 기업
(B) 수리점
(C) 공장
(D) 법률 사무소

해설 전체 내용 관련 – 공지의 장소

화자가 도입부에 홈 퍼니처 공장 직원 여러분, 주목해 주십시오(Attention, Home Furniture factory employees)라고 말하고 있는 것으로 보아

공지가 나오는 장소는 가구 공장임을 알 수 있다. 따라서 정답은 (C)이다.

84

Where should the listeners go at the end of their shifts?

(A) To the company cafeteria
(B) To the receptionist's desk
(C) To the locker room
(D) To the parking area

근무가 끝나면 청자들은 어디로 가야 하는가?

(A) 구내식당
(B) 접수 담당자 책상
(C) 탈의실
(D) 주차 구역

해설 세부 사항 관련 - 근무가 끝나고 청자들이 가야 할 장소

화자가 중반부에 근무가 끝나면 접수 담당자 책상 위에 있는 양식에 시작 시간과 종료 시간을 적으라(when your shift's over, please write your start and end time on the form that's on the receptionist's desk)고 요청하고 있으므로 정답은 (B)이다.

▸▸ Paraphrasing 담화의 when your shift's over
→ 질문의 at the end of their shifts

85

What will happen tomorrow?

(A) Some office furniture will be delivered.
(B) New board members will be elected.
(C) A city official will conduct an inspection.
(D) Some time-reporting software will be fixed.

내일 무슨 일이 일어날 것인가?

(A) 사무용 가구가 배달될 것이다.
(B) 새로운 이사진이 선출될 것이다.
(C) 시 공무원이 점검할 것이다.
(D) 시간 보고용 소프트웨어가 고쳐질 것이다.

해설 세부 사항 관련 - 내일 일어날 일

화자가 마지막에 내일 아침 공장에 도착하면 시간 보고용 소프트웨어가 작동될 것(the time-reporting software will be working when you get to the factory tomorrow morning)이라고 말하고 있는 것으로 보아 정답은 (D)이다.

86-88 회의 발췌

W-Am The final item on our agenda is the annual community health fair. As in previous years, ⁸⁶**our clinic will have a booth at the fair, where one of our nurses will be available to answer questions and give presentations about maintaining a healthy lifestyle.** ⁸⁷**In the past, Mary Jenkins has always managed our booth,** but, as you may know, Ms. Jenkins has retired. ⁸⁷**I want to tell you that working at the fair is a great way to give back to the community, so feel free to get in touch with me.** OK, let's end there. As promised, ⁸⁸**I brought in soup and sandwiches for everyone—the food's in the break room.**

안건 마지막 항목은 연례 지역 건강 박람회입니다. 예년과 마찬가지로 우리 병원에서는 박람회에 부스를 마련해 간호사 한 명이 질문에 답하고 건강한 생활 방식 유지에 관해 발표할 수 있게 됩니다. 예전에는 메리 젠킨스 씨가 항상 우리 부스를 관리해 왔지만, 아시다시피 젠킨스 씨는 은퇴하셨습니다. 박람회에서 일하는 건 지역 사회에 보답하는 훌륭한 방법이라는 점 말씀드리고 싶습니다. 그러니 언제든지 제게 연락하세요. 자, 이쯤해서 마무리합시다. 약속대로 모두를 위해 수프와 샌드위치를 가져왔어요. 음식은 휴게실에 있어요.

어휘 agenda 안건 maintain 유지하다 retire 은퇴하다

86

Where do the listeners work?

(A) At an employment agency
(B) At a sports arena
(C) At a conference center
(D) At a medical clinic

청자들은 어디에서 일하는가?

(A) 직업 소개소
(B) 스포츠 경기장
(C) 회의장
(D) 병원

해설 전체 내용 관련 - 청자들의 근무지

화자가 초반부에 우리 병원에서는 박람회에 부스를 마련해 간호사 한 명이 질문에 답하고 건강한 생활 방식 유지에 관해 발표할 수 있게 된다(our clinic will have a booth at the fair, where one of our nurses will be available to answer questions and give presentations about maintaining a healthy lifestyle)고 말하고 있으므로 정답은 (D)이다.

87

What does the speaker imply when she says, "Ms. Jenkins has retired"?

(A) A role needs to be filled.
(B) An e-mail will not be answered.
(C) A marketing strategy should be revised.
(D) A process will be less efficient.

화자가 "젠킨스 씨는 은퇴하셨습니다"라고 말하는 의도는 무엇인가?

(A) 역할을 맡아 해야 한다.
(B) 이메일에 회신이 없을 것이다.
(C) 마케팅 전략이 수정돼야 한다.
(D) 공정은 효율성이 떨어질 것이다.

어휘 fill 직무를 맡아 하다   revise 수정하다   efficient 효율적인

해설 화자의 의도 파악 - 젠킨스 씨는 은퇴했다는 말의 의도
앞에서 화자가 예전에는 메리 젠킨스 씨가 항상 우리 부스를 관리해 왔다(In the past, Mary Jenkins has always managed our booth)고 말한 뒤 인용문을 언급했고, 뒤이어 박람회에서 일하는 것은 지역 사회에 보답하는 훌륭한 방법이라는 점을 말씀드리고 싶고 언제든지 자신에게 연락하라(I want to tell you that working at the fair ~ get in touch with me)며 청자들에게 박람회에서 일하는 데 자원할 것을 권하고 있다. 따라서 인용문은 부스를 관리하던 사람이 현재 은퇴하고 없으며 그 역할을 맡아 대신해 줄 사람이 필요하다는 의도로 한 말이므로 정답은 (A)이다.

88
What will the listeners most likely do next?
(A) Check a schedule
(B) Complete a registration form
(C) **Eat a meal**
(D) Brainstorm some ideas

청자들은 다음에 무엇을 하겠는가?
(A) 일정 확인하기
(B) 등록서 작성하기
(C) **식사하기**
(D) 아이디어 브레인스토밍하기

해설 세부 사항 관련 - 청자들이 다음에 할 일
화자가 마지막에 모두를 위해 수프와 샌드위치를 가져왔으며 음식은 휴게실에 있다(I brought in soup and sandwiches for everyone—the food's in the break room)고 말하는 것으로 보아 청자들은 휴게실로 가 음식을 먹을 예정임을 알 수 있다. 따라서 정답은 (C)이다.

89-91 전화 메시지

M-Au Good morning, Martina. **⁸⁹I'm calling about our biggest client**, NVC Industries. A couple things... First, **⁸⁹thank you for sending me your slides for the advertising pitch you'll be delivering to them at the meeting on Friday.** **⁹⁰I know you expressed some hesitation about your particular approach... you have concerns that it might be a bit too bold.** Well, always remember that the advertising business is very competitive. Second, **⁹¹Isabel can make some recommendations about what to do while you're in Barcelona for the meeting with NVC Industries.** Make sure you see her before you travel there.

안녕하세요, 마티나. **우리 회사 최대 고객인 NVC 산업 때문에 전화드렸는데요.** 두어 가지… 우선, **금요일 회의에서 그쪽에 전달할 광고 홍보 슬라이드를 보내 줘서 고마워요.** **특이한 접근 방식에 대해 다소 망설였다는 것 알고 있어요… 너무 대담할지도 모른다고 걱정하신다고요.** 흠, 광고 업계는 경쟁이 아주 치열하다는 점 항상 명심하세요. 둘째, **당신이**

NVC 산업과의 회의를 위해 바르셀로나에 있는 동안 해야 할 일에 대해 이사벨이 몇 가지 의견을 줄 수 있어요. 그곳으로 가기 전에 그녀를 꼭 만나 보세요.

어휘 pitch 홍보, 권유   hesitation 망설임   particular 특이한
approach 접근 방식   bold 대담한   competitive 경쟁이 치열한

89
What is scheduled for Friday?
(A) A job fair
(B) A wellness workshop
(C) A client meeting
(D) An employee luncheon

금요일에 무엇이 예정되어 있는가?
(A) 취업 박람회
(B) 건강 워크숍
(C) **고객 회의**
(D) 직원 오찬

어휘 wellness 건강

해설 세부 사항 관련 - 금요일에 예정된 일
화자가 초반부에 우리 회사 최대 고객인 NVC 산업 때문에 전화했다(I'm calling about our biggest client, NVC Industries)며 금요일 회의에서 그쪽에 전달할 광고 홍보 슬라이드를 보내 줘서 고맙다(thank you for sending me your slides for the advertising pitch you'll be delivering to them at the meeting on Friday)고 말하고 있으므로, 금요일에는 NVC 산업이라는 고객을 상대로 회의가 열린다는 것을 알 수 있다. 따라서 정답은 (C)이다.

90
Why does the speaker say, "the advertising business is very competitive"?
(A) To explain a decision to retire
(B) To justify an employee's promotion
(C) To question the listener's abilities
(D) **To express confidence in an approach**

화자가 "광고 업계는 경쟁이 아주 치열하다"라고 말하는 이유는 무엇인가?
(A) 퇴직 결정을 해명하려고
(B) 직원 승진의 당위성을 설명하려고
(C) 청자의 역량에 의문을 제기하려고
(D) **접근 방식에 대한 신뢰를 표현하려고**

어휘 justify 당위성을 설명하다   ability 역량   confidence 신뢰

해설 화자의 의도 파악 - 광고 업계는 경쟁이 아주 치열하다는 말의 의도
앞에서 특이한 접근 방식에 대해 다소 망설였다는 것과 너무 대담할지도 몰라 걱정하고 있다는 것을 안다(I know you expressed some hesitation about your particular approach… you have concerns that it might be a bit too bold)고 말한 뒤 언급한 인용문에서 청자의 독특하고 대담한 접근 방식이 필요한 근거를 제시하고 있는 것으로 보아, 인용문은 청자의 방식에 대한 믿음을 표현하고자 한 말임을 알 수 있다. 따라서 정답은 (D)이다.

91

What does the speaker say about Isabel?

(A) She has recently joined the company.

(B) She can recommend some activities.

(C) She will approve expense reports.

(D) She used to work on the NVC Industries account.

화자는 이사벨에 대해 무엇을 말하는가?

(A) 최근에 입사했다.

(B) 몇 가지 활동을 권할 수 있다.

(C) 지출 보고서를 승인할 것이다.

(D) 한때 NVC 산업과 거래하는 업무를 했다.

해설 세부 사항 관련 - 화자가 이사벨에 대해 하는 말

화자가 후반부에 당신이 NVC 산업과의 회의를 위해 바르셀로나에 있는 동안 해야 할 일에 대해 이사벨이 몇 가지 의견을 줄 수 있다(Isabel can make some recommendations about what to do while you're in Barcelona for the meeting with NVC Industries)고 말하고 있으므로 정답은 (B)이다.

> ▸▸ Paraphrasing 담화의 **make some recommendations about what to do**
> → 정답의 **recommend some activities**

92-94 담화

M-Cn Hi, everyone. Now, ^{92, 93}**our goal has been to encourage our customers to try out the line of health drinks and energy bars we've recently started stocking at our store locations.** And ⁹³**to do this, we've been sending out weekly newsletters by e-mail to our customers.** Unfortunately, our analytics show that only ten percent of those e-mails are even opened. So, I'd like to try another strategy. ⁹⁴**I'd like to put together a team to create some videos about our groceries, and we can pick a few to post to our Web site.** Maybe some with testimonials from satisfied customers? Anyway, please send me an e-mail if you're interested in helping with this project.

여러분, 안녕하세요. 자, **우리 목표는 고객들에게 우리가 최근 매장에 들여놓기 시작한 건강 음료와 에너지 바를 먹어 보도록 만드는 것이었습니다. 이를 위해 매주 고객에게 이메일로 소식지를 발송하고 있죠.** 아쉽게도, 분석에 따르면 열어 본 이메일이 10퍼센트밖에 안 된다고 하네요. 그래서 저는 다른 전략을 시도하고 싶습니다. **제가 팀을 짜서 식료품에 관한 동영상들을 만들고 싶어요. 그러면 웹사이트에 올릴 동영상 몇 개를 고를 수 있죠.** 만족한 고객의 추천글을 함께 올릴 수도 있고요. 아무튼 이 프로젝트를 돕고 싶으면 제게 이메일을 보내세요.

어휘 stock 들여놓다 analytics 분석 testimonial 추천하는 글

92

What type of business does the speaker most likely work for?

(A) A television studio

(B) A hardware store

(C) A publishing company

(D) A grocery store

화자는 어떤 업종에서 일하겠는가?

(A) 텔레비전 스튜디오

(B) 철물점

(C) 출판사

(D) 식료품점

해설 전체 내용 관련 - 화자의 근무지

화자가 초반부에 우리 목표는 고객들에게 우리가 최근 매장에 들여놓기 시작한 건강 음료와 에너지 바를 먹어 보도록 만드는 것이었다(our goal has been to encourage our customers ~ started stocking at our store locations)고 말하고 있으므로 화자는 식품을 취급하는 상점에서 일하고 있음을 알 수 있다. 따라서 정답은 (D)이다.

93

What is the speaker concerned about?

(A) A business has lost customers.

(B) An advertising plan has not been effective.

(C) A stockroom is overcrowded.

(D) A Web site is not working.

화자는 무엇을 걱정하는가?

(A) 사업체가 고객들을 잃었다.

(B) 광고 계획이 효과가 없었다.

(C) 창고가 너무 혼잡하다.

(D) 웹사이트가 작동하지 않고 있다.

어휘 effective 효과적인 overcrowded 혼잡한

해설 세부 사항 관련 - 화자의 우려 사항

화자가 초반부에 우리 목표는 고객들에게 건강 음료와 에너지 바를 먹어 보도록 만드는 것이었다(our goal has been to encourage ~ health drinks and energy bars)며 이를 위해 매주 고객에게 이메일로 소식지를 발송하고 있다(to do this, we've been sending out ~ by e-mail to our customers)고 했고, 아쉽게도 분석에 따르면 열어 본 이메일이 10퍼센트밖에 안 된다고 한다(Unfortunately, our analytics show ~ are even opened)고 말하는 것으로 보아 건강 음료와 에너지 바를 홍보하기 위한 이메일이 효과를 발휘하지 못하고 있음을 알 수 있다. 따라서 정답은 (B)이다.

94

What does the speaker plan to do?

(A) Transfer to another location

(B) Offer discounts online

(C) Hire more employees

(D) Add videos to a Web site

화자는 무엇을 할 계획인가?

(A) 다른 지점으로 전근

(B) 온라인으로 할인 제공

(C) 인력 충원

(D) 웹사이트에 동영상 추가

어휘 transfer 전근하다

해설 세부 사항 관련 - 화자의 계획

화자가 후반부에 팀을 짜서 식료품에 관한 동영상들을 만들고 동영상 몇 개를 골라 웹사이트에 올리고 싶다(I'd like to put together a team to create some videos about our groceries, and we can pick a few to post to our Web site)고 말하고 있으므로 정답은 (D)이다.

▸▸ Paraphrasing 담화의 **post** → 정답의 **Add**

95-97 전화 메시지 + 목록

W-Am Hello, Mr. Harris. This is Nadia calling. 95 **I've been getting the paperwork ready for the vehicle you're purchasing from us.** When you come over to the dealership to pick up your car, you'll need to pay several fees. 96 **Please remember that the one hundred dollar fee must be paid in cash.** The other fees can be paid with your credit card. The car title will take a few days to process, and then will be mailed to your home address. And 97 **don't forget to take advantage of our free monthly car wash**—just use the service code provided on your contract.

안녕하세요, 해리스 씨. 나디아예요. **고객님이 구입하려는 차량에 대한 서류를 준비하고 있어요.** 대리점에 차를 가지러 오실 때 몇 가지 수수료를 내셔야 합니다. **100달러 수수료는 현금으로 지불해야 한다는 점 기억해 주세요.** 다른 수수료는 신용카드로 결제할 수 있고요. 자동차 등록증은 처리하는 데 며칠 걸리므로 우편을 통해 고객님의 집 주소로 발송됩니다. 그리고 **무료로 저희 월 세차 이용하시는 것 잊지 마세요.** 계약서에 제공된 서비스 코드만 사용하시면 됩니다.

어휘 purchase 구매하다 dealership 대리점 process 처리하다 take advantage of ~을 이용하다 registration 등록

List of Fees		Paid	Not paid
Filing:	$50.00	✓	
Contract processing:	$250.00		✓
Vehicle title:	$125.00		✓
96 Vehicle registration:	$100.00		✓

수수료 목록		지불	미지불
신청:	50달러	v	
계약 절차:	250달러		v
자동차 등록증:	125달러		v
96 자동차 번호 등록:	100달러		v

95

Who most likely is the speaker?

(A) A car salesperson

(B) An auto mechanic

(C) A car rental agent

(D) A vehicle inspector

화자는 누구이겠는가?

(A) 자동차 판매원

(B) 자동차 정비사

(C) 렌터카 업체 직원

(D) 자동차 검사원

어휘 mechanic 정비사

해설 전체 내용 관련 - 화자의 직업

화자가 초반부에 고객님이 구입하려는 차량에 대한 서류를 준비하고 있다(I've been getting the paperwork ready for the vehicle you're purchasing from us)고 말하고 있으므로 화자는 자동차를 판매하는 일을 하고 있음을 알 수 있다. 따라서 정답은 (A)이다.

96

Look at the graphic. Which fee must be paid in cash?

(A) Filing

(B) Contract processing

(C) Vehicle title

(D) Vehicle registration

시각 정보에 의하면 현금으로 지불해야 하는 수수료는 무엇인가?

(A) 신청

(B) 계약 절차

(C) 자동차 등록증

(D) 자동차 번호 등록

해설 시각 정보 연계 - 현금으로 지불해야 하는 수수료

화자가 중반부에 100달러 수수료는 현금으로 지불해야 한다는 점을 기억해 달라(Please remember that the one hundred dollar fee must be paid in cash)고 요청하고 있고, 목록에 따르면 수수료가 100달러인 항목은 자동차 번호 등록이므로 정답은 (D)이다.

97

What service does the speaker remind the listener about?

(A) Shuttle service

(B) Maintenance reminders

(C) Free car washes

(D) Replacement keys

화자는 청자에게 어떤 서비스를 다시 알려 주는가?

(A) 셔틀 서비스
(B) 정비 안내문
(C) 무료 세차
(D) 대체 키

어휘 maintenance 정비 reminder 안내문 replacement 대체

해설 세부 사항 관련 - 화자가 청자에게 알려 주는 서비스

화자가 후반부에 무료로 우리 월 세차를 이용하는 것을 잊지 말라(don't forget to take advantage of our free monthly car wash)고 말하고 있으므로 정답은 (C)이다.

98-100 회의 발췌 + 원 그래프

M-Cn **98At this staff meeting, I'd like to talk about some changes we'll be implementing here at Helgen's Music Shop**. First, to attract more customers, **99we're going to host a small talent contest in September**. I've recruited several local musicians to be the judges. Second, take a look at this chart from our annual sales report. Now, I'm not worried about the drums. But **100look at this instrument—we only sell twenty of them per year. That isn't very many, and they take a lot of time and effort to maintain**. So, after careful consideration, I've decided we're going to stop selling them.

이번 직원 회의에서는 여기 헬겐의 뮤직숍에서 우리가 시행하게 될 몇 가지 변경 사항에 대해 말씀드리고자 합니다. 우선, 고객을 더 많이 유치하기 위해 9월에 소규모 재능 경연 대회를 개최할 거예요. 제가 심사 위원으로 지역 음악가 몇 명을 선정했어요. 둘째, 연간 매출 보고서에서 이 차트를 살펴보세요. 자, 드럼은 걱정 안 됩니다. 하지만 이 악기를 보세요. 일 년에 20대밖에 못 팔았어요. 많다고 할 수 없죠. 게다가 유지하는 데 많은 시간과 노력이 필요해요. 그래서 저는 심사숙고 끝에 판매를 중단하기로 결정했습니다.

어휘 implement 시행하다 attract 유치하다 instrument 악기 maintain 유지하다 consideration 고려

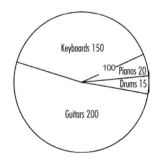

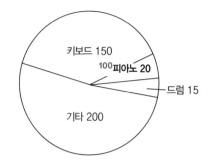

98
Who most likely is the speaker?

(A) A jazz singer
(B) A music teacher
(C) A shop manager
(D) A radio host

화자는 누구이겠는가?

(A) 재즈 가수
(B) 음악 교사
(C) 점장
(D) 라디오 진행자

해설 전체 내용 관련 - 화자의 직업

화자가 도입부에 이번 직원 회의에서는 여기 헬겐의 뮤직숍에서 우리가 시행하게 될 몇 가지 변경 사항에 대해 말하고자 한다(At this staff meeting, I'd like to talk about some changes we'll be implementing here at Helgen's Music Shop)고 말하고 있으므로 화자는 음악용품 매장에서 근무하고 있음을 알 수 있다. 따라서 정답은 (C)이다.

99
What event will take place in September?

(A) A music festival
(B) A press conference
(C) A charity dinner
(D) A talent contest

9월에 무슨 행사가 열릴 것인가?

(A) 음악 축제
(B) 기자 회견
(C) 자선 만찬
(D) 재능 경연 대회

어휘 charity 자선

해설 세부 사항 관련 - 9월에 열릴 행사

화자가 중반부에 9월에 소규모 재능 경연 대회를 개최할 것(we're going to host a small talent contest in September)이라고 말하고 있으므로 정답은 (D)이다.

100

Look at the graphic. Which type of instrument does the speaker focus on?

(A) Keyboards

(B) Pianos

(C) Drums

(D) Guitars

시각 정보에 의하면 화자는 어떤 악기에 초점을 맞추는가?

(A) 키보드

(B) 피아노

(C) 드럼

(D) 기타

해설 시각 정보 연계 – 화자가 중점을 두는 악기의 종류

화자가 후반부에 이 악기를 보자면 일 년에 20대밖에 못 팔았다(look at this instrument—we only sell twenty of them per year)고 했고, 이는 많다고 할 수 없는 수치이며 게다가 유지하는 데 많은 시간과 노력이 필요하다(That isn't very many, and they take a lot of time and effort to maintain)며 한 악기에 대해 집중적으로 언급하고 있다. 원 그래프에 따르면 판매량이 20대인 악기는 피아노이므로 정답은 (B)이다.

1 (A)	2 (A)	3 (C)	4 (D)	5 (B)
6 (D)	7 (B)	8 (A)	9 (C)	10 (A)
11 (A)	12 (C)	13 (A)	14 (B)	15 (A)
16 (A)	17 (A)	18 (C)	19 (C)	20 (A)
21 (C)	22 (C)	23 (B)	24 (C)	25 (C)
26 (A)	27 (B)	28 (C)	29 (A)	30 (C)
31 (B)	32 (A)	33 (D)	34 (A)	35 (B)
36 (A)	37 (C)	38 (C)	39 (D)	40 (C)
41 (C)	42 (D)	43 (B)	44 (C)	45 (B)
46 (A)	47 (D)	48 (C)	49 (C)	50 (B)
51 (C)	52 (D)	53 (C)	54 (C)	55 (A)
56 (C)	57 (B)	58 (C)	59 (A)	60 (C)
61 (D)	62 (D)	63 (B)	64 (C)	65 (A)
66 (B)	67 (D)	68 (B)	69 (B)	70 (C)
71 (B)	72 (A)	73 (D)	74 (A)	75 (D)
76 (C)	77 (C)	78 (B)	79 (D)	80 (C)
81 (B)	82 (A)	83 (B)	84 (D)	85 (A)
86 (B)	87 (A)	88 (C)	89 (C)	90 (D)
91 (A)	92 (D)	93 (C)	94 (B)	95 (C)
96 (A)	97 (B)	98 (D)	99 (C)	100 (B)

PART 1

1 W-Am

(A) He's leaning over a container.
(B) He's digging in a garden.
(C) He's replacing some floor tiles.
(D) He's trimming some trees.

(A) 남자가 통 위로 몸을 숙이고 있다.
(B) 남자가 정원을 파고 있다.
(C) 남자가 바닥 타일을 교체하고 있다.
(D) 남자가 가지를 치고 있다.

어휘 lean over ~위로 몸을 숙이다　dig 파다　replace 교체하다
　　　trim a tree 가지를 치다

해설 1인 등장 사진 - 사람의 동작/상태 묘사
(A) 정답. 남자가 통 위로 몸을 숙이고 있는(is leaning over a container) 모습이므로 정답.
(B) 동사 오답. 남자가 정원을 파고 있는(is digging in a garden) 모습이 아니므로 오답.

(C) 동사 오답. 남자가 바닥 타일을 교체하고 있는(is replacing some floor tiles) 모습이 아니므로 오답.
(D) 동사 오답. 남자가 가지를 치고 있는(is trimming some trees) 모습이 아니므로 오답.

---

2 M-Cn

(A) A customer is picking up some clothing at a dry cleaner's.
(B) A customer is trying on a jacket.
(C) A customer is handing a worker some cash.
(D) A worker is typing on a computer.

(A) 고객이 세탁소에서 옷을 찾고 있다.
(B) 고객이 재킷을 입어 보고 있다.
(C) 고객이 직원에게 현금을 건네고 있다.
(D) 직원이 컴퓨터로 타자를 치고 있다.

어휘 hand 건네다
해설 2인 이상 등장 사진 - 사람의 동작/상태 묘사
(A) 정답. 고객(a customer)이 세탁소에서 옷을 찾고 있는(is picking up some clothing at a dry cleaner's) 모습이므로 정답.
(B) 동사 오답. 고객(a customer)이 재킷을 입어 보고 있는(is trying on a jacket) 모습이 아니므로 오답.
(C) 동사 오답. 고객(a customer)이 직원에게 현금을 건네고 있는(is handing a worker some cash) 모습이 아니므로 오답.
(D) 동사 오답. 직원(a worker)이 컴퓨터로 타자를 치고 있는(is typing on a computer) 모습이 아니므로 오답.

---

3 M-Au

(A) She's paying for her meal.
(B) She's pouring a beverage.
(C) She's facing a refrigerated display case.
(D) She's ordering her lunch from a server.

(A) 여자가 식사비를 내고 있다.
(B) 여자가 음료를 따르고 있다.
(C) 여자가 냉장 진열장을 마주보고 있다.
(D) 여자가 웨이터에게 점심을 주문하고 있다.

어휘 pour 따르다　face 마주보다　refrigerated 냉장된

해설 1인 등장 사진 - 사람의 동작/상태 묘사

(A) 동사 오답. 여자가 식사비를 내고 있는(is paying for her meal) 모습이 아니므로 오답.

(B) 동사 오답. 여자가 음료를 따르고 있는(is pouring a beverage) 모습이 아니므로 오답.

(C) 정답. 여자가 냉장 진열장을 마주보고 있는(is facing a refrigerated display case) 모습이므로 정답.

(D) 동사 오답. 여자가 웨이터에게 점심을 주문하고 있는(is ordering her lunch from a server) 모습이 아니므로 오답.

---

4 W-Am

(A) He's putting vegetables into a bag.
(B) He's setting up a tent.
(C) The rear doors of a van are closed.
(D) **Some boxes have been stored inside a vehicle.**

(A) 남자가 봉지에 채소를 넣고 있다.
(B) 남자가 텐트를 치고 있다.
(C) 승합차 후문이 닫혀 있다.
(D) **상자들이 차량 안에 보관되어 있다.**

어휘 rear 뒤의   store 보관하다

해설 혼합 사진 - 사람/사물/풍경 혼합 묘사

(A) 동사 오답. 남자가 봉지에 채소를 넣고 있는(is putting vegetables into a bag) 모습이 아니므로 오답.

(B) 사진에 없는 명사를 이용한 오답. 사진에 텐트(a tent)의 모습이 보이지 않으므로 오답.

(C) 동사 오답. 승합차 후문(the rear doors of a van)이 닫혀 있는(are closed) 모습이 아니므로 오답.

(D) 정답. 상자들(some boxes)이 차량 안에 보관되어 있는(have been stored inside a vehicle) 모습이므로 정답.

---

5 M-Au

(A) The speaker is positioned next to a podium.
(B) **The man is drawing a graph on a presentation board.**
(C) One of the women is watching a video.
(D) One of the women is adjusting her glasses.

(A) 강연자가 연단 옆에 자리를 잡고 있다.
(B) **남자가 발표용 보드에 그래프를 그리고 있다.**
(C) 여자들 중 한 명이 동영상을 보고 있다.
(D) 여자들 중 한 명이 안경을 고쳐 쓰고 있다.

어휘 adjust 고쳐 쓰다

해설 2인 이상 등장 사진 - 사람의 동작/상태 묘사

(A) 사진에 없는 명사를 이용한 오답. 사진에 연단(a podium)의 모습이 보이지 않으므로 오답.

(B) 정답. 남자가 발표용 보드에 그래프를 그리고 있는(is drawing a graph on a presentation board) 모습이므로 정답.

(C) 동사 오답. 여자들 중 한 명(one of the women)이 동영상을 보고 있는(is watching a video) 모습이 아니므로 오답.

(D) 동사 오답. 여자들 중 한 명(one of the women)이 안경을 고쳐 쓰고 있는(is adjusting her glasses) 모습이 아니므로 오답.

---

6 W-Br

(A) Some chairs have been arranged on a balcony.
(B) A clock has been propped up on a shelf.
(C) Some place mats are laid out on a bench.
(D) **A light fixture is hanging above a dining area.**

(A) 의자들이 발코니에 정리되어 있다
(B) 시계를 선반 위에 받쳐 놓았다.
(C) 깔개들이 벤치 위에 펼쳐져 있다.
(D) **조명 기구가 식탁 공간 위에 걸려 있다.**

어휘 arrange 정리하다   prop up ~을 받치다   light fixture 조명 기구

해설 사물/풍경 사진 - 사물 묘사

(A) 위치 오답. 의자들(some chairs)이 발코니에 정리되어 있는(have been arranged on a balcony) 모습이 아니므로 오답.

(B) 동사 오답. 시계(a clock)가 선반 위에 받쳐져 있는(has been propped up on a shelf) 모습이 아니라 벽에 걸려 있는(is hanging on the wall) 모습이므로 오답.

(C) 사진에 없는 명사를 이용한 오답. 사진에 벤치(a bench)의 모습이 보이지 않으므로 오답.

(D) 정답. 조명 기구(a light fixture)가 식탁 공간 위에 걸려 있는(is hanging above a dining area) 모습이므로 정답.

PART 2

7

M-Cn Where is the closest coffee shop?
W-Br (A) From nine until five.
      (B) It's down the street.
      (C) Just a few office supplies.

    가장 가까운 커피숍이 어디죠?
    (A) 9시부터 5시까지요.
    (B) 길 따라 가면 있어요.
    (C) 사무용품 몇 개만요.

어휘 office supply 사무용품

해설 가장 가까운 커피숍의 위치를 묻는 Where 의문문
(A) 질문과 상관없는 오답. When 의문문에 대한 응답이므로 오답.
(B) 정답. 가장 가까운 커피숍의 위치를 묻는 질문에 길을 따라 가면 있다고 알려 주고 있으므로 정답.
(C) 질문과 상관없는 오답. What 의문문에 대한 응답이므로 오답.

8

M-Cn Would you like a morning or an afternoon appointment?
W-Am (A) The afternoon, please.
      (B) She was at her annual checkup.
      (C) I can bring in the paperwork.

    오전으로 예약하시겠어요, 오후로 예약하시겠어요?
    (A) 오후로 해 주세요.
    (B) 그녀는 연례 건강 검진을 받고 있었어요.
    (C) 제가 서류를 가져올 수 있어요.

어휘 appointment 예약 annual 연례의 checkup 건강 검진
     paperwork 서류 (작업)

해설 원하는 예약 시간을 묻는 선택 의문문
(A) 정답. 오전과 오후 중 원하는 예약 시간대를 묻는 질문에 오후로 해 달라며 둘 중 하나를 선택해 응답하고 있으므로 정답.
(B) 연상 단어 오답. 질문의 appointment에서 병원 진료를 연상하게 하는 checkup을 이용한 오답.
(C) 질문과 상관없는 오답.

9

W-Br Are you having trouble with your Internet connection, too?
M-Cn (A) He'll take a connecting flight to Paris.
      (B) We should double our order.
      (C) Yes, I can't access anything online.

    인터넷 연결도 문제가 있나요?
    (A) 그는 파리행 경유편을 탈 예정이에요.
    (B) 주문을 두 배로 해야겠어요.
    (C) 네, 온라인으로 어디에도 접속이 안 돼요.

어휘 access 접속하다

해설 인터넷 연결에 문제가 있는지 묻는 Be동사 의문문
(A) 파생어 오답. 질문의 connection과 파생어 관계인 connecting을 이용한 오답.
(B) 유사 발음 오답. 질문의 trouble과 부분적으로 발음이 유사한 double을 이용한 오답.
(C) 정답. 인터넷 연결에 문제가 있는지 묻는 질문에 네(Yes)라고 대답한 뒤, 온라인으로 어디에도 접속이 안 된다며 긍정 답변과 일관된 내용을 덧붙이고 있으므로 정답.

10

W-Am Who's that sitting in the lobby?
M-Au (A) That's the new summer intern.
      (B) The armchair is comfortable.
      (C) My hobby's photography.

    로비에 앉아 있는 사람 누군가요?
    (A) 새로 온 하계 인턴이에요.
    (B) 안락의자가 편하네요.
    (C) 제 취미는 사진 찍기예요.

어휘 comfortable 편한

해설 로비에 앉아 있는 사람을 묻는 Who 의문문
(A) 정답. 로비에 앉아 있는 사람이 누구인지 묻는 질문에 새로 온 하계 인턴이라고 알려 주고 있으므로 정답.
(B) 연상 단어 오답. 질문의 sitting에서 연상 가능한 armchair를 이용한 오답.
(C) 유사 발음 오답. 질문의 lobby와 부분적으로 발음이 유사한 hobby를 이용한 오답.

11

M-Au What did Simone say about the project proposal?
M-Cn (A) She said she liked it a lot.
      (B) The other projector's broken.
      (C) Right, I heard about them.

    시몬이 프로젝트 제안서에 대해 뭐라고 하던가요?
    (A) 그녀는 아주 마음에 든다고 했어요.
    (B) 다른 프로젝터가 고장났어요.
    (C) 네, 저도 들었어요.

어휘 proposal 제안서 broken 고장난

해설 시몬이 제안서에 대해 한 말을 묻는 What 의문문
(A) 정답. 시몬이 프로젝트 제안서에 대해 뭐라고 말했는지 묻는 질문에 그녀가 아주 마음에 든다고 했다고 응답하고 있으므로 정답.
(B) 파생어 오답. 질문의 project와 파생어 관계인 projector를 이용한 오답.
(C) Yes/No 불가 오답. What 의문문에는 Yes/No 응답이 불가능한데, Right도 일종의 Yes 응답이라고 볼 수 있으므로 오답.

12

M-Au Would you like a free ticket to tonight's play?

W-Br (A) Which team won?

(B) A short intermission.

(C) No thanks, I have plans.

오늘밤 연극 무료 입장권을 드릴까요?

(A) 어느 팀이 이겼어요?

(B) 잠깐 휴식 시간이에요.

(C) 고맙지만 괜찮아요, 선약이 있어요.

어휘 intermission (연극 등의) 중간 휴식 시간

해설 제안/권유의 의문문

(A) 질문과 상관없는 오답.

(B) 연상 단어 오답. 질문의 play에서 연상 가능한 intermission을 이용한 오답.

(C) 정답. 오늘밤 연극 무료 입장권을 받겠냐고 제안하는 질문에 사양하겠다(No thanks)고 거절한 뒤, 선약이 있다고 이유를 말하며 부정 답변과 일관된 내용을 덧붙이고 있으므로 정답.

13

W-Am Isn't that new restaurant supposed to open soon?

M-Cn (A) Yes, in a few more weeks.

(B) No, I prefer Italian food.

(C) A great lunch menu.

저 새 식당이 곧 문을 열지 않나요?

(A) 네, 몇 주 더 있으면요.

(B) 아니요, 저는 이탈리아 음식이 더 좋아요.

(C) 훌륭한 점심 메뉴예요.

어휘 be supposed to ~하기로 되어 있다

해설 새 식당이 곧 개점하는지 여부를 확인하는 부정 의문문

(A) 정답. 새 식당이 곧 문을 여는지 확인하는 질문에 네(Yes)라고 대답한 뒤, 몇 주 후라고 구체적인 시점을 알려 주며 긍정 답변과 일관된 내용을 덧붙이고 있으므로 정답.

(B) 연상 단어 오답. 질문의 restaurant에서 연상 가능한 Italian food를 이용한 오답.

(C) 연상 단어 오답. 질문의 restaurant에서 연상 가능한 lunch menu를 이용한 오답.

14

M-Cn Why is the flight delayed?

W-Am (A) The prices are all displayed.

(B) Because we're waiting for a storm to pass.

(C) Two hours and forty-five minutes.

왜 비행기가 연착하나요?

(A) 가격이 전부 표시되어 있어요.

(B) 폭풍이 지나가기를 기다리고 있어서요.

(C) 2시간 45분이요.

해설 비행기가 연착하는 이유를 묻는 Why 의문문

(A) 유사 발음 오답. 질문의 delayed와 부분적으로 발음이 유사한 displayed를 이용한 오답.

(B) 정답. 비행기가 연착하는 이유를 묻는 질문에 폭풍이 지나가기를 기다리고 있기 때문이라고 이유를 제시하고 있으므로 정답.

(C) 질문과 상관없는 오답. How long 의문문에 대한 응답이므로 오답.

15

M-Au Who's organizing the bowling league?

W-Br (A) It starts next spring.

(B) Stack the bowls on top of the plates.

(C) By alphabetical order.

볼링 리그를 누가 준비하고 있나요?

(A) 그것은 내년 봄에 시작해요.

(B) 그릇을 접시 위에 쌓으세요.

(C) 알파벳 순으로요.

어휘 organize 준비하다 stack 쌓다

해설 볼링 리그를 준비하는 사람을 묻는 Who 의문문

(A) 정답. 볼링 리그를 준비하는 사람이 누구인지 묻는 질문에 그것은 내년 봄에 시작한다며 아직 리그를 준비하는 사람이 정해지지 않았음을 우회적으로 알려 주고 있으므로 정답.

(B) 유사 발음 오답. 질문의 bowling과 부분적으로 발음이 유사한 bowls를 이용한 오답.

(C) 연상 단어 오답. 질문의 organizing을 '정리하다'라는 뜻으로 이해했을 경우 연상 가능한 alphabetical order를 이용한 오답.

16

W-Br Did you submit the expense reports?

M-Au (A) There's a lot of data to review.

(B) The team we saw last week.

(C) That's not as expensive as we thought.

경비 보고서 제출하셨어요?

(A) 검토할 자료가 많아요.

(B) 우리가 지난주에 봤던 팀이요.

(C) 우리가 생각했던 것만큼 비싸지 않네요.

어휘 submit 제출하다 expense 비용 expensive 비싼

해설 보고서 제출 여부를 확인하는 조동사(Did) 의문문

(A) 정답. 경비 보고서를 제출했는지 묻는 질문에 검토할 자료가 많다며 아직 제출하지 않았음을 우회적으로 알려 주고 있으므로 정답.

(B) 질문과 상관없는 오답.

(C) 파생어 오답. 질문의 expense와 파생어 관계인 expensive를 이용한 오답.

17

W-Br Aren't we all getting new business cards?

M-Cn (A) No, you have to request them.

(B) An upcoming conference.

(C) I just bought a birthday card.

우리 모두 새 명함을 받지 않나요?

(A) 아니요, 요청해야 해요.
(B) 곧 있을 회의예요.
(C) 저 방금 생일카드 샀어요.

어휘 business card 명함 upcoming 곧 있을

해설 모두가 새 명함을 받는지 여부를 확인하는 부정 의문문
(A) 정답. 모두가 새 명함을 받는지 여부를 확인하는 질문에 아니요(No)라고 대답한 뒤, 요청을 해야 받을 수 있다며 부정 답변과 일관된 내용을 덧붙이고 있으므로 정답.
(B) 질문과 상관없는 오답. What 의문문에 대한 응답이므로 오답.
(C) 파생어 오답. 질문의 cards와 파생어 관계인 card를 이용한 오답.

18

W-Am How many people did you interview?
M-Cn (A) The company newsletter.
　　　 (B) I've prepared some questions.
　　　 (C) Three candidates.

몇 명이나 면접을 보셨어요?
(A) 회사 소식지요.
(B) 몇 가지 질문을 준비했어요.
(C) 지원자 세 명이요.

어휘 candidate 지원자

해설 면접 인원수를 묻는 How many 의문문
(A) 연상 단어 오답. 질문의 interview에서 연상 가능한 company를 이용한 오답.
(B) 연상 단어 오답. 질문의 interview에서 연상 가능한 questions를 이용한 오답.
(C) 정답. 면접을 본 인원수를 묻는 질문에 지원자 세 명이라고 알려 주고 있으므로 정답.

19

W-Br Sales of our strawberry ice cream rose by ten percent last month.
M-Cn (A) Yes, it was very cold.
　　　 (B) Get the fruit from Fresh Fruits Farms.
　　　 (C) I had no idea it was so popular.

지난달 딸기 아이스크림 매출이 10퍼센트 올랐어요.
(A) 네, 아주 추웠어요.
(B) 신선 과일 농장에서 과일을 사세요.
(C) 이렇게 인기가 많을 줄은 몰랐어요.

어휘 popular 인기가 많은

해설 정보 전달의 평서문
(A) 연상 단어 오답. 평서문의 ice cream에서 연상 가능한 cold를 이용한 오답.
(B) 연상 단어 오답. 평서문의 strawberry에서 연상 가능한 fruit을 이용한 오답.
(C) 정답. 지난달 딸기 아이스크림 매출이 10퍼센트 올랐다는 평서문에 이렇게 인기가 많을 줄 몰랐다며 매출 상승 소식에 대한 소감을 말하고 있으므로 정답.

20

W-Am Can you help me log on to my computer?
M-Au (A) Sorry, you'll need to call Technical Support.
　　　 (B) A password with both letters and numbers.
　　　 (C) That's a useful software program.

제 컴퓨터에 접속하는 것 좀 도와주실래요?
(A) 죄송해요. 기술 지원부에 전화해야 해요.
(B) 문자와 숫자가 다 포함된 비밀번호예요.
(C) 그것은 유용한 소프트웨어 프로그램이에요.

어휘 letter 문자 useful 유용한

해설 부탁/요청의 의문문
(A) 정답. 컴퓨터에 접속하는 것을 도와 달라는 요청에 죄송하다(Sorry)라고 거절한 뒤, 기술 지원부에 전화해야 한다고 해결 방법을 알려 주고 있으므로 정답.
(B) 연상 단어 오답. 질문의 log on에서 연상 가능한 password를 이용한 오답.
(C) 연상 단어 오답. 질문의 computer에서 연상 가능한 software program을 이용한 오답.

21

M-Au What time do you think we'll leave the zoo?
W-Br (A) Please go through the west gate.
　　　 (B) Fifteen dollars for adults.
　　　 (C) Some of the exhibit lines are quite long.

우리가 동물원을 몇 시에 나갈 것 같아요?
(A) 서쪽 게이트로 가 주세요.
(B) 성인은 15달러입니다.
(C) 일부 전시관은 줄이 꽤 길어요.

어휘 exhibit 전시관

해설 동물원을 떠나는 시간을 묻는 What 의문문
(A) 연상 단어 오답. 질문의 leave에서 연상 가능한 gate를 이용한 오답.
(B) 연상 단어 오답. 질문의 zoo에서 입장료를 연상하게 하는 fifteen dollars를 이용한 오답.
(C) 정답. 동물원에서 나갈 시간에 대해서 묻는 질문에 일부 전시관은 줄이 꽤 길다며 동물원에 머무는 시간이 길어질 수 있다는 것을 우회적으로 응답하고 있으므로 정답.

22

M-Au The artist has signed the paintings, hasn't she?
W-Br (A) The opening ceremony.
　　　 (B) On both walls, please.
　　　 (C) Yes, she did.

화가가 그림에 서명했죠, 아닌가요?
(A) 개막식이요.
(B) 양쪽 벽에요.
(C) 네, 했어요.

해설 화가의 서명 여부를 확인하는 부가 의문문

(A) 질문과 상관없는 오답.

(B) 연상 단어 오답. 질문의 paintings에서 연상 가능한 walls를 이용한 오답.

(C) 정답. 화가가 그림에 서명했는지 여부를 확인하는 질문에 네(Yes)라고 대답한 뒤, 서명을 했다고 긍정 답변과 일관된 내용을 덧붙이고 있으므로 정답.

23

W-Am How do you like traveling by train?

M-Cn (A) I'm looking for a fitness trainer.

(B) Well, you know I hate flying.

(C) A round-trip ticket to Busan.

기차로 가는 건 어때세요?

(A) 저는 헬스 트레이너를 찾고 있어요.

(B) **어, 제가 비행기 타는 것을 싫어하는 거 아시잖아요.**

(C) 부산행 왕복표요.

어휘 look for ~을 찾다

해설 기차 여행에 대한 생각을 묻는 How 의문문

(A) 유사 발음 오답. 질문의 train과 부분적으로 발음이 유사한 trainer를 이용한 오답.

(B) 정답. 기차로 여행하는 것에 대해 어떻게 생각하는지 묻는 질문에 자신은 비행기 타기를 싫어한다는 점을 상기시키며 기차 여행을 선호한다는 것을 우회적으로 응답하고 있으므로 정답.

(C) 연상 단어 오답. 질문의 train에서 연상 가능한 round-trip ticket을 이용한 오답.

24

M-Au Would you take charge of planning Pablo's retirement party?

W-Am (A) Blue, red, and yellow.

(B) Turn the volume up please.

(C) What's the budget?

파블로의 은퇴 파티 기획을 맡아 주실래요?

(A) 파랑, 빨강, 노랑이요.

(B) 소리 좀 높여 주세요.

(C) **예산이 얼마죠?**

어휘 take charge of ~을 떠맡다   retirement 은퇴

해설 부탁/요청의 의문문

(A) 질문과 상관없는 오답.

(B) 질문과 상관없는 오답.

(C) 정답. 파블로의 은퇴 파티 기획을 맡아 달라는 요청에 예산이 얼마인지 파티 기획에 필요한 정보를 되물으며 수락의 의사를 간접적으로 표현하고 있으므로 정답.

25

M-Au You hired the new assistant director, didn't you?

W-Br (A) A wonderful new film.

(B) They were running a bit late.

(C) I haven't even met her yet…

새로 차장을 채용하셨죠, 아닌가요?

(A) 멋진 신작 영화예요.

(B) 그들은 좀 늦었어요.

(C) **아직 그녀를 만나지도 못했어요…**

해설 새로운 차장의 채용 여부를 확인하는 부가 의문문

(A) 연상 단어 오답. 질문의 director에서 연상 가능한 film을 이용한 오답.

(B) 질문과 상관없는 오답.

(C) 정답. 새로 차장을 채용했는지 여부를 확인하는 질문에 아직 그녀를 만나지도 못했다며 자신은 해당 업무와 관련이 없음을 우회적으로 나타내고 있으므로 정답.

26

W-Am Should we put the advertisement on the first page or the last page?

M-Cn (A) The first page, definitely.

(B) He bought a newspaper.

(C) Last year in August.

광고를 첫 페이지에 넣을까요, 아니면 마지막 페이지에 넣을까요?

(A) **물론 첫 페이지죠.**

(B) 그는 신문을 샀어요.

(C) 작년 8월이요.

어휘 definitely 물론

해설 광고를 삽입할 페이지를 묻는 선택 의문문

(A) 정답. 첫 페이지와 마지막 페이지 중 광고를 삽입할 페이지를 묻는 질문에 물론 첫 페이지라며 둘 중 하나를 선택해 응답하고 있으므로 정답.

(B) 연상 단어 오답. 질문의 advertisement와 page에서 연상 가능한 newspaper를 이용한 오답.

(C) 질문과 상관없는 오답. When 의문문에 대한 응답이므로 오답.

27

W-Am I've finished the building inspection.

W-Br (A) To my work e-mail address.

(B) Did you find any problems?

(C) On the seventh floor.

건물 점검을 마쳤습니다.

(A) 제 회사 이메일 주소로요.

(B) **무슨 문제라도 발견하셨나요?**

(C) 7층에요.

어휘 inspection 점검

해설 정보 전달의 평서문

(A) 연상 단어 오답. 평서문의 building에서 연상 가능한 address를 이용한 오답.

(B) 정답. 건물 점검을 마쳤다는 평서문에 무슨 문제라도 발견했는지 점검에 따른 결과를 묻고 있으므로 정답.

(C) 연상 단어 오답. 평서문의 building에서 연상 가능한 seventh floor를 이용한 오답.

28

M-Au　When is Pierre scheduled to pick up the steel pipe?

M-Cn　(A) No, I'm sorry about that.

　　　(B) That should be interesting.

　　　(C) Well, the truck is gone.

피에르가 언제 쇠파이프를 찾아올 예정인가요?

(A) 아니요, 죄송합니다.

(B) 재미있겠어요.

(C) 음, 트럭이 없네요.

해설 피에르가 쇠파이프를 찾아올 시점을 묻는 When 의문문

(A) Yes/No 불가 오답. When 의문문에는 Yes/No 응답이 불가능하므로 오답.

(B) 질문과 상관없는 오답.

(C) 정답. 피에르가 쇠파이프를 찾아올 시점을 묻는 질문에 트럭이 없다며 트럭이 돌아올 때까지는 물건을 찾으러 가지 못한다는 것을 간접적으로 응답하고 있으므로 정답.

29

W-Am　Why am I not authorized to download this software?

M-Cn　(A) You'd better check with your manager.

　　　(B) Two million so far.

　　　(C) Is he a famous author?

제게 왜 이 소프트웨어를 내려받을 권한이 없나요?

(A) 관리자에게 확인해 보는 게 좋겠어요.

(B) 지금까지 200만이요.

(C) 그는 유명한 작가인가요?

어휘 authorized 권한이 있는

해설 소프트웨어를 내려받을 권한이 없는 이유를 묻는 Why 의문문

(A) 정답. 자신에게 소프트웨어를 내려받을 권한이 없는 이유를 묻는 질문에 관리자에게 확인해 보는 게 좋겠다며 자신은 정확한 이유를 알지 못한다는 점을 우회적으로 응답하고 있으므로 정답.

(B) 질문과 상관없는 오답. How many 의문문에 대한 응답이므로 오답.

(C) 유사 발음 오답. 질문의 authorized와 부분적으로 발음이 유사한 author를 이용한 오답.

30

W-Br　Where do you park when you drive to Dr. Li's office?

W-Am　(A) An annual medical checkup.

　　　(B) She thought it was the best treatment.

　　　(C) It's more convenient to take the bus.

리 박사님 진료실에 갈 때 주차는 어디에 하세요?

(A) 해마다 받는 건강 검진이요.

(B) 그녀는 그게 최선의 치료라고 생각했어요.

(C) 버스를 타는 게 더 편해요.

어휘 medical checkup 건강 검진　treatment 치료　convenient 편한

해설 주차 장소를 묻는 Where 의문문

(A) 연상 단어 오답. 질문의 Dr. Li's office에서 연상 가능한 medical checkup을 이용한 오답.

(B) 연상 단어 오답. 질문의 Dr. Li's office에서 연상 가능한 treatment를 이용한 오답.

(C) 정답. 리 박사의 진료실에 차 타고 갈 때 주차하는 장소를 묻는 질문에 버스를 타는 게 더 편하다며 차를 가져가지 말 것을 우회적으로 권유하고 있으므로 정답.

31

M-Cn　Aren't we getting a digital sound system?

W-Br　(A) She was recently promoted to manager!

　　　(B) You know how long the approval process takes.

　　　(C) Because the store closes early tonight.

디지털 사운드 시스템을 마련하고 있지 않나요?

(A) 그녀는 최근에 매니저로 승진했어요!

(B) 승인 절차가 얼마나 오래 걸리는지 아시잖아요.

(C) 오늘밤에는 가게가 일찍 문을 닫아서요.

어휘 promote 승진시키다　approval 승인

해설 디지털 사운드 시스템의 마련 여부를 확인하는 부정 의문문

(A) 질문과 상관없는 오답.

(B) 정답. 디지털 사운드 시스템의 마련 여부를 확인하는 질문에 승인 절차가 얼마나 오래 걸리는지를 상기시키며 아직 시스템 확보 결정이 나지 않았음을 우회적으로 알려 주고 있으므로 정답.

(C) 질문과 상관없는 오답. Why 의문문에 대한 응답이므로 오답.

PART 3

32-34

M-Cn	Thank you for registering with the Zimmerman Staffing Agency, Ms. Vogel. **32 Why are you interested in finding a temporary position?**
W-Br	Well, **32 I moved here recently**, so I thought your agency would be a good place to find out about local companies. I don't have a business network here yet.
M-Cn	I see. **33 Your résumé says you have computer programming experience.** That skill's in high demand.
W-Br	Yes, I did programming for five years at my last job, so I'm very comfortable with it.
M-Cn	Excellent. We should be able to place you with an employer shortly. As part of the process though, **34 please come in on Wednesday to complete your paperwork.**
남	짐머만 채용 업체에 등록해 주셔서 감사합니다, 보겔 씨. **임시직을 구하는 데 관심 있으신 이유는요?**
여	음, 최근에 여기로 이사 와서 이 업체가 지역 회사들을 알아보기 좋은 곳일 것 같았어요. 아직 이곳에 업무 인맥이 없거든요.
남	그렇군요. **이력서를 보니 컴퓨터 프로그래밍 경력이 있으시네요.** 그 기술은 수요가 많아요.
여	네, 직전 직장에서 5년 동안 프로그래밍을 했어요. 그래서 아주 익숙해요.
남	잘됐네요. 곧 고용주를 구해 드릴 수 있을 겁니다. 그럼 그 과정의 일환으로 **수요일에 오셔서 서류를 작성해 주세요.**
어휘	staffing agency 채용 업체 temporary 임시의 demand 수요 comfortable with ~에 익숙한 place (집이나 직장을) 구해 주다

32

Why is the woman seeking a temporary position?

(A) To become familiar with local opportunities
(B) To gain experience in a new field
(C) To have more scheduling flexibility
(D) To focus on a specific project

여자는 왜 임시직을 구하는가?
(A) 지역의 취업 기회를 파악하려고
(B) 새로운 분야에서 경력을 쌓으려고
(C) 일정의 융통성을 더 확보하려고
(D) 특정 프로젝트에 집중하려고

어휘 become familiar with ~을 파악하다 flexibility 융통성

해설 세부 사항 관련 - 여자가 임시직을 구하는 이유

남자가 첫 대사에서 임시직을 구하는 데 관심 있는 이유(Why are you interested in finding a temporary position?)를 묻자, 여자가 첫 대사에서 최근에 여기로 이사 와서 이 업체가 지역 회사들을 알아보기 좋은 곳일 것 같았다(I moved here recently, ~ about local companies)며 아직 이곳에 업무 인맥이 없다(I don't have a business network here yet)고 이유를 말하고 있으므로 정답은 (A)이다.

33

What skill does the woman have?

(A) Accounting
(B) Event organizing
(C) Team management
(D) Computer programming

여자는 어떤 기술이 있는가?
(A) 회계
(B) 행사 준비
(C) 팀 관리
(D) 컴퓨터 프로그래밍

해설 세부 사항 관련 - 여자가 보유한 기술

남자가 두 번째 대사에서 여자에게 당신의 이력서를 보니 컴퓨터 프로그래밍 경력이 있다고 나와 있다(Your résumé says you have computer programming experience)고 말하고 있으므로 정답은 (D)이다.

34

Why does the man tell the woman to come in on Wednesday?

(A) To complete some paperwork
(B) To visit a job site
(C) To fill out a survey
(D) To present a certificate

남자는 왜 여자에게 수요일에 오라고 하는가?
(A) 서류를 작성하려고
(B) 작업 현장을 방문하려고
(C) 설문 조사서를 작성하려고
(D) 자격증을 제시하려고

어휘 certificate 자격증

해설 세부 사항 관련 - 남자가 여자에게 수요일에 오라고 한 이유

남자가 마지막 대사에서 수요일에 와서 서류를 작성해 달라(please come in on Wednesday to complete your paperwork)고 말하고 있으므로 정답은 (A)이다.

35-37

M-Au	Hi, Rosa. **35 I'd like you to attend the annual technology trade show in Montreal.** A lot of other electronics

companies will be there to showcase their latest products.

W-Am That's great! I appreciate the opportunity. ³⁶**Can I choose someone from my team to take with me? That way we'll be able to visit more presentations.**

M-Au Yes, that's a good idea. ³⁷**I'd recommend asking Taro to come with you. Why don't I call him to see if he can come to my office now and discuss it with us.**

남 안녕하세요, 로사. 몬트리올에서 열리는 연례 기술 무역 박람회에 참석하셨으면 해요. 다른 전자 회사들이 최신 제품을 선보이려고 많이 올 거예요.

여 좋아요! 기회를 주셔서 감사해요. **우리 팀에서 같이 갈 사람을 제가 선택할 수 있나요? 그러면 발표회에 더 많이 갈 수 있을 거예요.**

남 네, 좋은 생각이에요. **타로에게 같이 가자고 요청하시죠. 지금 타로에게 전화해서 제 사무실로 와서 같이 상의할 수 있는지 알아볼게요.**

어휘 annual 연례의 latest 최신의 appreciate 고맙게 생각하다 opportunity 기회 recommend 권하다

35

Why does the man ask Rosa to go to Montreal?

(A) To meet with a client
(B) To attend a trade show
(C) To train for a position
(D) To oversee a construction project

남자는 왜 로사에게 몬트리올에 가라고 요청하는가?

(A) 고객을 만나려고
(B) 무역 박람회에 참석하려고
(C) 직책 교육을 받으려고
(D) 건설 공사를 감독하려고

어휘 oversee 감독하다 construction project 건설 공사

해설 세부 사항 관련 - 남자가 로사에게 몬트리올에 가라고 요청하는 이유
남자가 첫 대사에서 여자에게 몬트리올에서 열리는 연례 기술 무역 박람회에 참석했으면 한다(I'd like you to attend the annual technology trade show in Montreal)고 말하고 있으므로 정답은 (B)이다.

36

What does the woman ask permission to do?

(A) Take a coworker
(B) Change a flight
(C) Postpone a deadline
(D) Increase an advertising budget

여자는 무엇을 하겠다고 허락을 구하는가?

(A) 동료 데려가기
(B) 항공편 변경하기
(C) 마감일 연기하기
(D) 광고 예산 늘리기

어휘 permission 허락 coworker 동료 postpone 연기하다 increase 늘리다

해설 세부 사항 관련 - 여자가 허락을 구하는 일
여자가 첫 대사에서 자신의 팀에서 같이 갈 사람을 선택해도 되는지(Can I choose someone from my team to take with me?)를 물으며 그러면 발표회에 더 많이 갈 수 있을 것(That way we'll be able to visit more presentations)이라고 말하고 있으므로 정답은 (A)이다.

> ▶▶ Paraphrasing 대화의 **someone from my team**
> → 정답의 **a coworker**

37

What will the man most likely do next?

(A) Prepare some sales data
(B) Order some business cards
(C) Make a phone call
(D) Go to lunch

남자는 다음에 무엇을 하겠는가?

(A) 매출 자료 작성하기
(B) 명함 주문하기
(C) 전화 걸기
(D) 점심 먹으러 가기

해설 세부 사항 관련 - 남자가 다음에 할 일
남자가 마지막 대사에서 타로에게 같이 가자고 요청할 것을 권한다(I'd recommend asking Taro to come with you)면서 지금 타로에게 전화해 사무실로 와서 같이 상의할 수 있는지 알아보겠다(Why don't I call him to see if he can come to my office now and discuss it with us)고 말하고 있으므로 정답은 (C)이다.

> ▶▶ Paraphrasing 대화의 **call him**
> → 정답의 **Make a phone call**

38-40 3인 대화

M-Au Well, Ms. Yamamoto, ³⁸**your x-rays look good. Your teeth and gums are healthy. We'll do a cleaning at your next appointment.**

W-Am Thank you, but I... I thought I was going to get my teeth cleaned today. I made an appointment for x-rays and a cleaning.

M-Au ³⁹**I'm... sorry. Whoever scheduled your appointment must not've explained our policy.** For new patients, the first visit is an inspection and x-rays.

W-Am I see. OK.

M-Au	⁴⁰**Ms. Petrova, please schedule a cleaning for Ms. Yamamoto.**
W-Br	Of course. Hmmm. Before I do that, ⁴⁰**I see in your file that we don't have your records from your previous dentist. Would you please fill out this form so we can request them?**
W-Am	Sure.

남	저, 야마모토 씨, **엑스레이는 괜찮아 보이네요. 치아와 잇몸은 건강합니다. 다음 예약 때 스케일링을 해 드릴게요.**
여1	감사합니다, 하지만 전⋯ 저는 오늘 치아 스케일링을 받는 줄 알았어요. 엑스레이와 스케일링을 예약했거든요.
남	**죄송합니다. 누가 예약을 잡았는지, 우리 방침을 설명하지 않았나 보네요.** 처음 오는 환자들은 첫 번째 방문에 검사와 엑스레이를 합니다.
여1	그렇군요. 알겠습니다.
남	**페트로바 씨, 야마모토 씨 스케일링 일정을 잡아 주세요.**
여2	물론이죠. 음. 그 전에, **서류철을 보니 이전 치과 의사의 기록이 저희한테 없네요. 저희가 기록을 요청할 수 있도록 이 양식을 작성해 주시겠어요?**
여1	그럼요.

어휘	gum 잇몸 appointment 예약 policy 방침 patient 환자 inspection 검사 previous 이전의 fill out ~을 작성하다

38

Who is the man?

(A) A lawyer
(B) An electrician
(C) A dentist
(D) A banker

남자는 누구인가?

(A) 변호사
(B) 전기 기술자
(C) 치과 의사
(D) 은행원

해설 전체 내용 관련 - 남자의 직업

남자가 첫 대사에서 엑스레이는 괜찮아 보인다(your x-rays look good)고 했고, 치아와 잇몸은 건강하다(Your teeth and gums are healthy)며 다음 예약 때 스케일링을 해 주겠다(We'll do a cleaning at your next appointment)고 말하는 것으로 보아 정답은 (C)이다.

39

Why does the man apologize?

(A) Some documents are missing.
(B) Some equipment is not working.
(C) An assistant is late.
(D) A policy was not explained.

남자는 왜 사과하는가?

(A) 문서가 누락되었다.
(B) 장비가 작동하지 않는다.
(C) 조수가 늦었다.
(D) **방침이 설명되지 않았다.**

어휘 equipment 장비

해설 세부 사항 관련 - 남자가 사과하는 이유

남자가 두 번째 대사에서 최송하다(I'm… sorry)고 사과하며 누가 예약을 잡았는지 우리 방침을 설명하지 않은 것 같다(Whoever scheduled your appointment must not've explained our policy)라고 말하고 있으므로 정답은 (D)이다.

40

Why is Ms. Yamamoto asked to fill out a form?

(A) To update her contact information
(B) To set up a payment plan
(C) To request some records
(D) To opt for paperless statements

야마모토 씨는 왜 양식 작성을 요청받는가?

(A) 연락처 정보를 수정하려고
(B) 결제 방식을 마련하려고
(C) **기록을 요청하려고**
(D) 전자 명세서를 선택하려고

어휘 opt for ~을 선택하다 statement 명세서

해설 세부 사항 관련 - 야마모토 씨가 양식 작성을 요청받은 이유

남자가 첫 대사에서 첫 번째 여자를 야마모토 씨(Ms. Yamamoto)라고 부르고 있으므로 첫 번째 여자가 야마모토임을 알 수 있고, 남자가 세 번째 대사에서 페트로바 씨(Ms. Petrova)를 부르며 야마모토 씨의 스케일링 일정을 잡아 달라(please schedule a cleaning for Ms. Yamamoto)고 하자 두 번째 여자가 대답하며 서류철을 보니 이전 치과 의사의 기록이 우리에게 없다(I see in your file that ~ previous dentist)면서 우리가 기록을 요청할 수 있도록 양식을 작성해 줄 것(Would you please fill out this form so we can request them?)을 첫 번째 여자에게 요청하고 있으므로 정답은 (C)이다.

41-43

M-Cn	Hi, I'm from the IT department. You wanted help setting up for a teleconference? I can answer any questions you have about the equipment.
W-Br	Thanks. This is an important meeting. ⁴¹**We're looking to finance a new project, and I'm going to present to some people we hope will become investors.**
M-Cn	OK, we'll make sure the technology will work smoothly.
W-Br	⁴²**This camera will automatically move to focus on whoever is speaking, right?**

M-Cn　Yes.

W-Br　But ⁴²**there will also be times that I want to control the camera manually. Can I do that?**

M-Cn　Sure, you can do that on the control panel. ⁴³**Let me demonstrate how it works.**

남　안녕하세요, IT 부서에서 왔어요. 전화 회의 준비를 도와 달라고 하셨죠? 장비에 관한 문의라면 무엇이든 답변해 드리겠습니다.

여　감사합니다. 이건 중요한 회의예요. **새 프로젝트에 필요한 자금을 확보하려고 하거든요. 그래서 우리가 투자자가 되길 바라는 사람들 앞에서 제가 발표할 예정이에요.**

남　네, 반드시 기술이 원활하게 작동되도록 하겠습니다.

여　**이 카메라는 말하는 사람에게 초점을 맞추도록 자동으로 움직이죠?**

남　네.

여　**하지만 카메라를 수동으로 제어하고 싶은 경우도 있을 텐데. 그렇게 할 수 있나요?**

남　물론이죠, 제어 패널에서 가능합니다. **어떻게 작동하는지 보여 드릴게요.**

어휘　equipment 장비　investor 투자자　manually 수동으로　demonstrate 보여 주다

41

Who will the woman give a presentation to?

(A) New employees

(B) Government officials

(C) Potential investors

(D) Board members

여자는 누구에게 발표할 것인가?

(A) 신입 사원

(B) 공무원

(C) **잠재 투자자**

(D) 이사진

어휘　potential 잠재적인　board member 이사

해설　세부 사항 관련 – 여자가 발표를 할 대상

여자가 첫 대사에서 새 프로젝트에 필요한 자금을 확보하려고 하는 중이라 우리가 투자자가 되길 바라는 사람들 앞에서 발표할 예정(We're looking to finance a new project, and I'm going to present to some people we hope will become investors)이라고 말하고 있으므로 정답은 (C)이다.

> ▸▸ Paraphrasing　대화의 **some people we hope will become investors** → 정답의 **Potential investors**

42

What does the woman ask the man about?

(A) Adjusting a microphone

(B) Turning on a monitor

(C) Connecting a speaker

(D) Using a camera

여자는 남자에게 무엇을 묻는가?

(A) 마이크 조정

(B) 모니터 켜기

(C) 스피커 연결

(D) **카메라 사용**

어휘　adjust 조정하다

해설　세부 사항 관련 – 여자가 남자에게 묻는 것

여자가 두 번째 대사에서 카메라가 말하는 사람에게 초점을 맞추도록 자동으로 움직이는지(This camera will automatically move to focus on whoever is speaking, right?)를 확인한 뒤, 세 번째 대사에서도 카메라를 수동으로 제어하고 싶은 경우도 있을 것(there will also be times that I want to control the camera manually)이라며 그렇게 할 수 있는지(Can I do that?) 카메라 이용과 관련된 질문을 연달아 하고 있으므로 정답은 (D)이다.

43

What will the man do next?

(A) Check a manual

(B) Give a demonstration

(C) Ask a colleague for help

(D) Look for a tool

남자는 다음에 무엇을 할 것인가?

(A) 사용 설명서 확인하기

(B) **시연하기**

(C) 동료에게 도움 요청하기

(D) 공구 찾기

해설　세부 사항 관련 – 남자가 다음에 할 일

남자가 마지막 대사에서 어떻게 작동하는지 보여 드리겠다(Let me demonstrate how it works)고 말하고 있으므로 정답은 (B)이다.

> ▸▸ Paraphrasing　대화의 **Let me demonstrate how it works** → 정답의 **Give a demonstration**

44-46

M-Au　Ms. Gupta, ⁴⁴**do you think you could divert a little more money to the spring catalog?**

W-Am　⁴⁴**Isn't your budget the same as last season's?**

M-Au **44It turns out the cost of photography will be higher this time.** Our spring footwear collection has lots of new colors and designs, and some old ones are being discontinued. About half of the photos from last season need to be replaced.

W-Am Oh, I didn't realize that.

M-Au **45We could try to find another photographer, but Stefan Vogel always does such a good job.**

W-Am And we should keep him. **46Let's look at the plans for the catalog this afternoon and see what revisions can be made.**

남 굽타 씨, 봄 카탈로그에 예산을 좀 더 유용해 주실 수 있으신가요?

여 예산은 지난 시즌과 같지 않나요?

남 이번에는 사진 비용이 더 많이 드는 걸로 나왔어요. 봄 신발 컬렉션은 새로운 색상과 디자인이 많고 예전 것들은 일부 단종되고 있어요. 지난 시즌 사진 중 절반 정도를 교체해야 해요.

여 아, 몰랐어요.

남 다른 사진작가를 물색해 볼 수도 있지만 스테판 보겔 씨가 늘 잘 해내고 있네요.

여 그러면 계속 써야죠. 오늘 오후에 카탈로그 안을 보고 어떤 수정이 가능한지 살펴보죠.

어휘 divert (돈·재료 등을) 전용[유용]하다 discontinue 단종하다 revision 수정

44

What is the man concerned about?

(A) Venue availability
(B) Product efficiency
(C) A project budget
(D) A guest list

남자는 무엇을 걱정하는가?
(A) 장소 이용 가능 여부
(B) 제품 효율
(C) 프로젝트 예산
(D) 손님 명단

어휘 availability 이용[입수] 가능함 efficiency 효율

해설 세부 사항 관련 – 남자의 우려 사항

남자가 첫 대사에서 봄 카탈로그에 예산을 좀 더 유용해 줄 수 있는지(do you think you could ~ money to the spring catalog?)를 묻자 여자가 예산이 지난 시즌과 같지 않은지(Isn't your budget the same as last season's?) 되물었고, 다시 남자가 이번에는 사진 비용이 더 많이 드는 것으로 나왔다(It turns out the cost of photography will be higher this time)고 말하는 것으로 보아 남자는 기존 예산을 초과하는 비용이 나올 것을 걱정하며 여자에게 도움을 청하고 있는 것으로 볼 수 있다. 따라서 정답은 (C)이다.

45

Who is Stefan Vogel?

(A) A furniture designer
(B) A photographer
(C) An accountant
(D) An event planner

스테판 보겔은 누구인가?
(A) 가구 디자이너
(B) 사진작가
(C) 회계사
(D) 행사 기획자

해설 세부 사항 관련 – 스테판 보겔의 직업

남자가 세 번째 대사에서 다른 사진작가를 물색해 볼 수도 있지만 스테판 보겔 씨가 늘 잘 해내고 있다(We could try to find ~ does such a good job)고 말하는 것으로 보아 스테판 보겔은 사진가임을 알 수 있다. 따라서 정답은 (B)이다.

46

What will the speakers do this afternoon?

(A) Review some plans
(B) Consult with a graphic designer
(C) Choose some colors
(D) Survey other team members

화자들은 오늘 오후에 무엇을 할 것인가?
(A) 안 검토
(B) 그래픽 디자이너와 협의
(C) 색상 선택
(D) 다른 팀원 조사

해설 세부 사항 관련 – 화자들이 오늘 오후에 할 일

여자가 마지막 대사에서 오늘 오후에 카탈로그 안을 보고 어떤 수정이 가능한지 살펴보자(Let's look at the plans for the catalog this afternoon and see what revisions can be made)고 말하고 있으므로 정답은 (A)이다.

47-49

M-Cn **47Did you hear about the smart screens that'll be installed in the guest rooms?**

W-Am I did. They're supposed to make it easier for guests to control the temperature in their rooms, schedule wake-up calls, order room service... things like that. **48And installation should only take an hour in each hotel room.**

M-Cn **48But they're going to be using power tools.** And the rooms are so close together.

W-Am The guest rooms are mostly soundproof. **49I just hope we have time to test the**

	screens out before our busy season in June. I don't want to deal with complaints about them not working.
남	객실에 설치된다는 스마트 스크린 얘기 들었어요?
여	들었어요. 손님들이 방 온도 조절, 모닝콜 예약, 룸서비스 주문 등등을 더 쉽게 할 수 있다고 하네요. 그리고 **각 호텔 객실에 설치하는 데 1시간밖에 안 걸려요.**
남	**하지만 전동 공구를 쓰겠죠. 게다가 방들이 서로 너무 가깝잖아요.**
여	객실은 대부분 방음이 돼요. **바쁜 시기인 6월 전에 우리가 스크린을 테스트할 시간이 있으면 좋겠어요.** 작동이 안 된다는 항의를 처리하고 싶진 않아요.

어휘	be supposed to ~하기로 되어 있다 temperature 온도 power tool 전동 공구 soundproof 방음이 되는 deal with ~을 처리하다

47

Where do the speakers work?

(A) At a hardware store

(B) At a construction site

(C) At a factory

(D) At a hotel

화자들은 어디에서 일하는가?

(A) 철물점

(B) 건설 현장

(C) 공장

(D) 호텔

해설 전체 내용 관련 – 화자들의 근무지

남자가 첫 대사에서 객실에 설치된다는 스마트 스크린에 대한 이야기를 들었는지(Did you hear about the smart screens that'll be installed in the guest rooms?)를 물으며 객실에 대해 말하는 것으로 보아 화자들이 호텔에서 일하고 있다는 것을 짐작할 수 있다. 따라서 정답은 (D)이다.

48

What does the man mean when he says, "And the rooms are so close together"?

(A) Some renovations will be finished quickly.

(B) A work schedule will be revised.

(C) Noise levels will be a problem.

(D) An architect should be consulted.

남자가 "게다가 방들이 서로 너무 가깝잖아요"라고 말하는 의도는 무엇인가?

(A) 보수 공사가 빨리 끝날 것이다.

(B) 작업 일정이 수정될 것이다.

(C) 소음 수준이 문제가 될 것이다.

(D) 건축가와 협의해야 한다.

어휘 revise 수정하다   architect 건축가

해설 화자의 의도 파악 – 게다가 방들이 서로 너무 가깝다는 말의 의도 앞에서 여자가 각 호텔 객실에 설치하는 데 1시간밖에 안 걸린다(And installation should only take an hour in each hotel room)고 하자 남자가 하지만 전동 공구를 쓸 것(But they're going to be using power tools)이라고 말한 뒤 인용문을 언급한 것으로 보아, 설치 작업에 사용될 전동 공구로 인해 가까운 객실들 사이에 소음이 발생할 것을 우려해 한 말임을 알 수 있다. 따라서 정답은 (C)이다.

49

What does the woman hope to do before June?

(A) Take inventory

(B) Order new uniforms

(C) Test out some technology

(D) Prepare for an inspection

여자는 6월 전에 무엇을 하고 싶어 하는가?

(A) 재고 조사

(B) 새 근무복 주문

(C) 기술 테스트

(D) 점검 준비

어휘 inventory 재고 (조사)   inspection 점검

해설 세부 사항 관련 – 여자가 6월 전에 하고 싶어 하는 일

여자가 마지막 대사에서 바쁜 시기인 6월 전에 우리가 스크린을 테스트할 시간이 있으면 좋겠다(I just hope we have time to test the screens out before our busy season in June)고 말하고 있으므로 정답은 (C)이다.

50-52

M-Au	Hi, Mei Ting. **50 Do you have any updates on how the designs are coming along for our new line of school backpacks?** The factory will need those to begin production.
W-Br	**51 I'm a bit frustrated, honestly. 52 The design team originally planned to meet this week to make final decisions about pocket sizes for the backpacks, but...** Irina's been at the School Supply Convention all week and Samir's out on vacation.
M-Au	So, **52 what are you planning to do?** The school year is starting in three months.
W-Br	I was hoping to get some advice from you, actually... since you used to lead the design team.

남	안녕, 메이 팅. **신제품 책가방 디자인이 어떻게 되어 가는지 소식 있나요?** 공장에서 생산을 시작하려면 그게 필요할 텐데요.

여　솔직히 좀 답답하네요. 원래 디자인 팀이 이번 주에 모여서 백팩 주머니 크기를 최종 결정할 계획이었어요. 그런데… 이리나는 일주일 내내 학용품 회의에 가 있고 사미르는 휴가를 떠났어요.

남　그럼 어쩔 참이에요? 석 달 후면 학기가 시작돼요.

여　실은 조언을 구하고 싶었어요… 예전에 디자인 팀을 이끌었잖아요.

| 어휘 | frustrated 답답한　decision 결정 |

50

What type of product are the speakers discussing?

(A) Pencils

(B) Backpacks

(C) Sneakers

(D) Folders

화자들은 어떤 제품에 대해 논의하고 있는가?

(A) 연필

(B) 백팩

(C) 운동화

(D) 폴더

해설　전체 내용 관련 - 화자들이 논의 중인 제품

남자가 첫 대사에서 신제품 책가방 디자인이 어떻게 되어 가는지에 대한 소식이 있는지(Do you have any updates on how the designs are coming along for our new line of school backpacks?)를 물으며 대화를 시작하고 있으므로 정답은 (B)이다.

51

What is the woman frustrated by?

(A) Some customers wrote a negative review.

(B) Some equipment is malfunctioning.

(C) Some team members are unavailable.

(D) Some packages have not arrived.

여자는 무엇 때문에 답답해하는가?

(A) 일부 고객이 부정적인 후기를 썼다.

(B) 일부 장비가 오작동하고 있다.

(C) 일부 팀원이 부재중이다.

(D) 일부 소포가 도착하지 않았다.

어휘　malfunction 오작동하다　unavailable 부재중인

해설　세부 사항 관련 - 여자가 답답함을 느끼는 이유

여자가 첫 대사에서 솔직히 좀 답답하다(I'm a bit frustrated, honestly)며 원래 디자인 팀이 이번 주에 모여 백팩 주머니 크기를 최종 결정할 계획이었는데 이리나는 일주일 내내 학용품 회의에 가 있고 사미르는 휴가를 떠났다(The design team originally planned to meet ~ Samir's out on vacation)고 말하고 있으므로 정답은 (C)이다.

52

Why does the man say, "The school year is starting in three months"?

(A) To request some time off from work

(B) To correct an error in a schedule

(C) To express interest in an assignment

(D) To emphasize the need for urgency

남자가 "석 달 후면 학기가 시작돼요"라고 말하는 이유는 무엇인가?

(A) 휴가를 신청하려고

(B) 일정표 오류를 바로잡으려고

(C) 업무에 관심을 표명하려고

(D) 시급한 필요성을 강조하려고

어휘　assignment 업무　emphasize 강조하다　urgency 시급함

해설　화자의 의도 파악 - 석 달 후면 학기가 시작된다는 말의 의도

앞에서 여자가 원래 디자인 팀이 이번 주에 모여 백팩 주머니 크기를 최종 결정할 계획이었는데 이리나는 일주일 내내 학용품 회의에 가 있고 사미르는 휴가를 떠났다(The design team originally planned to meet ~ Samir's out on vacation)고 하자 남자가 어쩔 계획(what are you planning to do?)인지 물으며 인용문을 언급한 것으로 보아, 디자인 팀의 업무가 일정보다 늦어지고 있는 것에 대해 일정이 촉박함을 상기시키며 신속하게 일을 진행해야 한다는 점을 강조하려는 의도로 한 말임을 알 수 있다. 따라서 정답은 (D)이다.

53-55 3인 대화

M-Au	Hello, I'm George from McKinnie Environmental Engineering.
W-Am	Hi, thanks for coming. As you can see, we manage a large forest here. **53 We provide lumber, plywood, and fiberboard for the construction and furniture industries. These trees are our business.**
M-Au	And **54 lately you've been noticing a problem?**
W-Br	Yes, several acres of pine on the other end of our property... the needles are all brown. They look really unhealthy. But we can't figure out what's wrong.
M-Au	**54 I'll try to determine the cause.** Might be a nutrient deficiency. First, **55 I'll conduct some soil tests. Can you show me to the site?** I'll follow you in my truck.

남　안녕하세요, 저는 맥키니 환경 공학의 조지예요.

여1　안녕하세요, 와 주셔서 고마워요. 보시다시피 저희는 이곳에서 광활한 숲을 관리하고 있어요. **건축과 가구 업계에 목재와 합판, 섬유판을 제공해요. 이 나무들이 저희 사업이죠.**

남　그런데 **최근에 문제가 발견됐다고요?**

여2 네, 부지 맞은편 끝에 있는 소나무 몇 에이커가… 솔잎이 모두 갈색이에요. 정말 병든 것 같아 보여요. 그런데 뭐가 잘못됐는지 알 수가 없어요.

남 **원인을 밝혀 보겠습니다.** 영양소 결핍일지도 몰라요. 먼저 **토양 검사를 좀 할게요. 현장으로 안내해 주시겠어요?** 저는 제 트럭으로 따라갈게요.

어휘 lumber 목재 plywood 합판 fiberboard 섬유판
determine 밝히다 cause 원인 nutrient 영양소
deficiency 결핍 soil 토양

53

What does the women's company sell?

(A) Construction vehicles
(B) Power tools
(C) Wood products
(D) Home appliances

여자들의 회사는 무엇을 판매하는가?

(A) 건설용 차량
(B) 전동 공구
(C) **목제품**
(D) 가전제품

해설 세부 사항 관련 – 여자들의 회사가 판매하는 제품

첫 번째 여자가 첫 대사에서 우리는 건축과 가구 업계에 목재와 합판, 섬유판을 제공한다(We provide lumber, plywood, and fiberboard for the construction and furniture industries)면서 이 나무들이 우리의 사업(These trees are our business)이라고 말하고 있으므로 정답은 (C)이다.

54

Why is the man visiting the company?

(A) To interview for a job
(B) To revise a contract
(C) To investigate a problem
(D) To make a complaint

남자는 왜 회사에 방문하는가?

(A) 구직 면접을 보려고
(B) 계약서를 수정하려고
(C) **문제를 조사하려고**
(D) 불만을 제기하려고

어휘 investigate 조사하다

해설 세부 사항 관련 – 남자가 회사에 방문하는 이유

남자가 두 번째 대사에서 최근에 문제가 발견됐는지(lately you've been noticing a problem?) 묻고 있고 세 번째 대사에서 원인을 밝혀 보겠다(I'll try to determine the cause)고 말하고 있으므로 남자는 여자들의 회사에 발생한 문제를 살펴보려고 방문한 것임을 알 수 있다. 따라서 정답은 (C)이다.

55

What does the man ask the women to do?

(A) Lead him to a specific location
(B) Provide him a discounted service
(C) Demonstrate a technical procedure
(D) Explain a company policy

남자는 여자들에게 무엇을 해 달라고 요청하는가?

(A) **특정 장소로 안내**
(B) 할인 서비스 제공
(C) 기술 절차 시연
(D) 회사 방침 설명

어휘 demonstrate 시연하다

해설 세부 사항 관련 – 남자가 여자들에게 요청하는 일

남자가 마지막 대사에서 먼저 토양 검사를 좀 하겠다(I'll conduct some soil tests)며 현장으로 안내해 줄 수 있는지(Can you show me to the site?) 묻고 있으므로 정답은 (A)이다.

▸▸ Paraphrasing 대화의 **show me to the site**
→ 정답의 **Lead him to a specific location**

56-58

M-Cn How can I help you?

W-Br Hello. I'm doing some renovating at home. **56 I'll be replacing all the pipes, the sink, and the bathtub in my bathroom.** The pipes are lead, and the other fixtures are cast iron. They're all very heavy.

M-Cn That's no problem. **57 We'll bring a dumpster out to your home, you fill it up with scrap, and then we'll come remove it when you're ready.**

W-Br OK. So, is payment determined by the number of days I keep the dumpster?

M-Cn No, **58 we'll weigh it before and after and charge you accordingly. Here's a list of charges by kilogram.**

남 어떻게 도와 드릴까요?

여 안녕하세요. 집을 좀 수리하고 있어요. **욕실에 있는 파이프 전부와 세면대, 욕조를 교체하려고 해요.** 파이프는 납이고 다른 설비는 주철이에요. 모두 아주 무거워요.

남 문제없어요. **저희가 대형 쓰레기통을 댁으로 가지고 가고 고객님이 고철로 통을 가득 채워 준비가 되면 저희가 그걸 치울 겁니다.**

여 네. 그럼 대금은 제가 대형 쓰레기통을 가지고 있는 일수에 따라 결정되나요?

남 아니요, **전후로 무게를 재서 그에 따라 청구합니다.** 여기 **킬로그램별 요금 목록입니다.**

어휘   lead 납   fixture 고정[붙박이] 세간   cast iron 주철
dumpster 대형 쓰레기통   scrap 고철   remove 치우다
weigh 무게를 재다   accordingly 그에 따라

56

What is the woman renovating?

(A) A kitchen

(B) A swimming pool

(C) A bathroom

(D) A garden

여자는 무엇을 수리하고 있는가?

(A) 주방

(B) 수영장

(C) **욕실**

(D) 정원

해설 세부 사항 관련 - 여자가 수리하는 것

여자가 첫 대사에서 욕실에 있는 파이프 전부와 세면대, 욕조를 교체하려고 한다(I'll be replacing all the pipes, the sink, and the bathtub in my bathroom)고 말하고 있으므로 정답은 (C)이다.

57

What service does the man's company provide?

(A) Landscaping

(B) Waste removal

(C) Safety inspections

(D) Concrete mixing

남자의 회사는 어떤 서비스를 제공하는가?

(A) 조경

(B) **폐기물 제거**

(C) 안전 점검

(D) 콘크리트 배합

어휘 removal 제거

해설 세부 사항 관련 - 남자의 회사가 제공하는 서비스

남자가 두 번째 대사에서 저희가 대형 쓰레기통을 댁으로 가지고 가고 고객님이 고철로 통을 가득 채워 준비가 되면 저희가 그것을 치울 것(We'll bring a dumpster out to your home, you fill it up with scrap, and then we'll come remove it when you're ready)이라고 말하는 것으로 보아 정답은 (B)이다.

▸▸ Paraphrasing   대화의 scrap → 정답의 **Waste**

58

According to the man, how is a cost determined?

(A) By number of workers

(B) By project duration

(C) By weight

(D) By area

남자의 말에 따르면, 비용은 어떻게 결정되는가?

(A) 작업자 수

(B) 프로젝트 기간

(C) **무게**

(D) 면적

어휘 duration 기간

해설 세부 사항 관련 - 비용 산정 방식

남자가 마지막 대사에서 전후로 무게를 재서 그에 따라 청구한다(we'll weigh it before and after and charge you accordingly)며 여기 킬로그램별 요금 목록이 있다(Here's a list of charges by kilogram)고 말하고 있으므로 정답은 (C)이다.

59-61

W-Am   **59 Finley Science Museum. Can I help you?**

M-Cn   Hi, I'm calling about the asteroid lecture at your planetarium this Friday. I represent a group of people with hearing impairments who'll be attending the lecture.

W-Am   Oh, yes. I've already been notified, and **60 I've hired a sign-language interpreter.** Your group has reserved seats on the right side of the theater, so they'll have a direct view of her.

M-Cn   Great, thank you. One more thing—**61 at similar events, there've been problems with the venue being too dark. Could you make sure there's a spotlight on the interpreter?**

W-Am   Absolutely—I'll be happy to arrange that.

여   **핀리 과학 박물관입니다. 도와 드릴까요?**

남   안녕하세요, 이번 주 금요일에 천문관에서 열리는 소행성 강의 때문에 전화드렸습니다. 저는 강의에 참석할 청각 장애인들을 대표해요.

여   아, 네. 이미 통보받아서 **수화 통역사를 고용했어요.** 일행의 좌석이 강당 오른쪽에 예약되어 있으니 통역사가 바로 보일 거예요.

남   잘됐네요, 감사합니다. 한 가지 더, **비슷한 행사에서 장소가 너무 어두워서 문제가 생긴 적이 있어요. 통역사에게 꼭 스포트라이트가 비치도록 해 주시겠어요?**

여   물론이죠. 기꺼이 그렇게 준비해 드리겠습니다.

어휘   asteroid 소행성   planetarium 천문관   impairment 장애   sign-language 수화   interpreter 통역사

59

Where does the woman work?

(A) At a museum
(B) At a movie theater
(C) At a newspaper office
(D) At a photography studio

여자는 어디에서 일하는가?

(A) 박물관
(B) 영화관
(C) 신문사
(D) 사진관

해설 전체 내용 관련 - 여자의 근무지

여자가 첫 대사에서 핀리 과학 박물관(Finley Science Museum)이라며 도와 드릴까요(Can I help you?)라고 묻고 있는 것으로 보아 여자는 박물관에서 근무하는 직원임을 알 수 있다. 따라서 정답은 (A)이다.

60

Who does the woman say she has hired?

(A) An engineer
(B) A musician
(C) An interpreter
(D) A scientist

여자는 누구를 고용했다고 말하는가?

(A) 기술자
(B) 음악가
(C) 통역사
(D) 과학자

해설 세부 사항 관련 - 여자가 고용했다고 말하는 사람

여자가 두 번째 대사에서 수화 통역사를 고용했다(I've hired a sign-language interpreter)고 말하고 있으므로 정답은 (C)이다.

61

What problem does the man mention?

(A) Traffic noise
(B) Late deliveries
(C) Uncomfortable seating
(D) Inadequate lighting

남자는 어떤 문제를 언급하는가?

(A) 교통 소음
(B) 늦은 배송
(C) 불편한 좌석
(D) 부족한 조명

어휘 inadequate 부족한

해설 세부 사항 관련 - 남자가 언급하는 문제

남자가 두 번째 대사에서 비슷한 행사에서 장소가 너무 어두워서 문제가 생긴 적이 있다(at similar events, there've been problems with the venue being too dark)며 통역사에게 꼭 스포트라이트가 비치도록

해 줄 수 있는지(Could you make sure there's a spotlight on the interpreter?)를 묻고 있는 것으로 보아 정답은 (D)이다.

62-64 대화 + 파일 캐비닛

W-Br Hi, Hiroshi, it's Natalia. **62 I know you're in the middle of completing the internal audit of our company's manufacturing processes, and I just wanted to know how that's going.**

M-Au Almost done. It all looks good so far. There was one thing... **63 I can't find the retired work instructions, you know, the old paper copies.**

W-Br **63 The old work instructions are all in the green filing cabinet in the office. The drawers are labeled.**

M-Au OK, great... **64 The new industry regulations are pretty strict, but, like I said, the processes that I've checked so far are all in compliance.**

여 안녕, 히로시, 나탈리아예요. 회사 제조 공정에 대한 내부 감사를 한창 마무리하고 있다고요. 어떻게 진행되고 있는지 알고 싶어서요.

남 거의 다 됐어요. 지금까지는 다 괜찮아 보여요. 한 가지가 있었는데… 폐기된 작업 지침서를 찾을 수가 없어요, 그러니까, 예전 종이 사본이요.

여 예전 작업 지침서는 모두 사무실 녹색 파일 캐비닛에 있어요. 서랍에 라벨이 붙어 있어요.

남 그렇군요, 좋아요… 새로운 산업 규정이 상당히 엄격한데도, 얘기했듯이 지금까지 점검한 공정은 모두 지켜지고 있어요.

어휘 audit 감사 retired 폐기된 work instructions 작업 지침 regulation 규정 strict 엄격한 in compliance (규칙 등을) 지키는 log 일지 inventory 재고

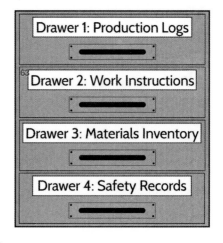

Drawer 1: Production Logs

Drawer 2: Work Instructions

Drawer 3: Materials Inventory

Drawer 4: Safety Records

서랍 1: 생산 일지
⁶³서랍 2: 작업 지침
서랍 3: 자재 재고
서랍 4: 안전 기록

62

Why is the woman calling?

(A) To compliment a staff member
(B) To schedule an appointment
(C) To criticize a policy
(D) To check on an assignment

여자는 왜 전화하는가?

(A) 직원을 칭찬하려고
(B) 약속을 잡으려고
(C) 방침을 비판하려고
(D) 업무를 확인하려고

어휘 compliment 칭찬하다 criticize 비판하다

해설 전체 내용 관련 - 전화의 목적

여자가 첫 대사에서 회사 제조 공정에 대한 내부 감사를 한창 마무리하고 있다는데 어떻게 진행되고 있는지 알고 싶다(I know you're in the middle of completing ~ know how that's going)고 말하고 있으므로 정답은 (D)이다.

63

Look at the graphic. Which drawer will the man probably check next?

(A) Drawer 1
(B) Drawer 2
(C) Drawer 3
(D) Drawer 4

시각 정보에 의하면 남자는 이후에 어떤 서랍을 확인할 것인가?

(A) 서랍 1
(B) 서랍 2
(C) 서랍 3
(D) 서랍 4

해설 시각 정보 연계 - 남자가 이후에 확인할 서랍

남자가 첫 대사에서 폐기된 작업 지침서, 즉 예전 종이 사본을 찾을 수가 없다(I can't find the retired work ~ the old paper copies)고 말하자 여자가 예전 작업 지침서는 모두 사무실 녹색 파일 캐비닛에 있다(The old work instructions are ~ in the office)며 서랍에 라벨이 붙어 있다(The drawers are labeled)고 덧붙이고 있다. 파일 캐비닛을 보면, 작업 지침이라는 라벨이 붙어 있는 서랍은 서랍 2이므로 정답은 (B)이다.

64

What does the man say about some processes?

(A) They are described in a training program.
(B) They take too long to complete.
(C) They meet regulations.
(D) They are easy to learn.

남자는 공정에 대해 무엇이라고 말하는가?

(A) 교육 프로그램에 기술되어 있다.
(B) 완료하는 데 너무 오래 걸린다.
(C) 규정을 지킨다.
(D) 배우기 쉽다.

해설 세부 사항 관련 - 남자가 공정에 대해 하는 말

남자가 마지막 대사에서 새로운 산업 규정이 상당히 엄격한데도, 얘기했듯이 지금까지 점검한 공정은 모두 지켜지고 있다(The new industry regulations ~ in compliance)고 말하고 있으므로 정답은 (C)이다.

> ▸▸ **Paraphrasing** 대화의 in compliance → 정답의 meet

65-67 대화 + 표

W-Am Hassan, ⁶⁵**thanks for your help motivating the other servers to collect surveys from customers.** We collected over four hundred responses. ⁶⁵**The owners are going to use the feedback to make some changes to the menu and the table settings.**
M-Au ⁶⁶**Your incentive of a bonus certainly helped persuade all the servers. I collected 63,** and I know I'm looking forward to having a little extra in my paycheck.
W-Am Any plans for how you're going to spend it?
M-Au Actually, ⁶⁷**my phone is really old, and I've been wanting to upgrade it. The extra cash will help with that.**

여	하산, 다른 웨이터들이 적극적으로 고객 설문 조사서를 회수하도록 도와줘서 고마워요. 400장이 넘는 답변을 회수했어요. 소유주들이 이 의견을 이용해 메뉴와 상차림을 바꿀 거예요.
남	보너스 인센티브가 웨이터 모두를 설득하는 데 확실히 도움이 됐어요. 저는 63장을 회수했는데, 월급에서 좀 더 받을 것으로 기대하고 있어요.
여	어떻게 쓸지 계획 있어요?
남	실은 제 핸드폰이 정말 오래돼서 더 좋은 걸로 바꾸고 싶었어요. 가욋돈이 도움이 되겠네요.

어휘	response 응답 persuade 설득하다 look forward to ~을 기대하다

TEST 3

Bonus per Surveys Collected	
$400	70+
[66] $300	60-69
$200	50-59
$100	40-49

회수한 설문 조사서별 보너스	
400달러	70+
[66] 300달러	60-69
200달러	50-59
100달러	40-49

65

Where do the speakers work?

(A) At a restaurant
(B) At a hotel
(C) At a travel agency
(D) At a marketing firm

화자들은 어디에서 일하는가?

(A) 식당
(B) 호텔
(C) 여행사
(D) 마케팅 회사

해설 전체 내용 관련 – 화자들의 근무지

여자가 첫 대사에서 다른 웨이터들이 적극적으로 고객 설문 조사서를 회수하도록 도와줘서 고맙다(thanks for your help ~ surveys from customers)며 소유주들이 이 의견을 이용해 메뉴와 상차림을 바꿀 것(The owners are going to ~ the menu and the table settings)이라고 말하는 것으로 보아 화자들은 식당에서 일하고 있음을 알 수 있다. 따라서 정답은 (A)이다.

66

Look at the graphic. How much extra money will the man receive in his next paycheck?

(A) $400
(B) $300
(C) $200
(D) $100

시각 정보에 의하면 남자는 다음 급여에서 얼마를 추가로 받을 것인가?

(A) 400달러
(B) 300달러
(C) 200달러
(D) 100달러

해설 시각 정보 연계 – 남자가 다음 급여에서 추가로 받을 돈

남자가 첫 대사에서 보너스 인센티브가 웨이터들을 설득하는 데 확실히 도움이 됐다(Your incentive of a bonus certainly helped persuade all the servers)고 말하는 것으로 보아 설문 조사서 회수 결과에 따라 보너스가 지급된다는 것을 알 수 있으며, 자신은 63장을 회수했다(I collected 63)고 말하고 있고 회수한 설문 조사서별 보너스 표에 따르면

60-69 구간은 300달러가 지급된다고 나와 있으므로 정답은 (B)이다.

67

What does the man say he will do with the extra money?

(A) Fix his car
(B) Give it to his parents
(C) Put it in the bank
(D) Buy a new phone

남자는 가욋돈으로 무엇을 할 것이라고 말하는가?

(A) 차 고치기
(B) 부모님께 드리기
(C) 은행에 예치하기
(D) 새 전화기 사기

해설 세부 사항 관련 – 남자가 가욋돈으로 할 것이라고 말하는 것

남자가 마지막 대사에서 핸드폰이 정말 오래돼서 더 좋은 것으로 바꾸고 싶었다(my phone is really old, and I've been wanting to upgrade it)며 가욋돈이 도움이 될 것(The extra cash will help with that)이라고 말하고 있으므로 정답은 (D)이다.

> ▸▸ Paraphrasing   대화의 upgrade → 정답의 Buy a new

68-70 대화 + 포스터

W-Am Satoshi, [68] I'm planning a staff party to celebrate Lena's promotion to director of marketing.

M-Cn That's a great idea. When are you thinking of having the party?

W-Am [69] Most people said they'd be available around five on March twenty-second. Does that work for you?

M-Cn Well, [69] I have tickets to a music festival that night, but the festival doesn't start until seven on the twenty-second, so I can come for a little while.

W-Am Great! [70] I'll make a reservation at the new restaurant on Baker Street right away. I know Lena has been wanting to try it.

여 사토시, 레나의 마케팅 부장 승진을 축하하려고 직원 파티를 계획하고 있어요.

남 좋은 생각이에요. 파티는 언제 열 생각이에요?

여 대부분이 3월 22일 5시쯤에 시간이 난다고 했어요. 그때 괜찮으세요?

남 음, 그날 밤 음악 축제 티켓이 있는데, 축제는 22일 7시에나 시작하니까 잠깐 갈 수 있어요.

여 잘됐네요! 베이커 가에 새로 생긴 식당으로 당장 예약해야겠어요. 레나가 한번 가 보고 싶어 했거든요.

Sunville Music Festival
Sunville City Park

Thursday, March 21, 7 P.M.–10 P.M.
⁶⁹ Friday, March 22, 7 P.M.–11 P.M.
Saturday, March 23, noon–11 P.M.
Sunday, March 24, noon–10 P.M.

선빌 음악 축제
선빌 시티 파크

목요일, 3월 21일, 오후 7–10시
⁶⁹ **금요일, 3월 22일, 오후 7–11시**
토요일, 3월 23일, 정오–오후 11시
일요일, 3월 24일, 정오–오후 10시

68

What is the woman planning a celebration for?

(A) A business merger
(B) A colleague's promotion
(C) A product launch
(D) A company anniversary

여자는 무엇을 위한 축하 행사를 계획하고 있는가?

(A) 업체 합병
(B) 동료의 승진
(C) 제품 출시
(D) 회사 기념일

어휘 merger 합병 anniversary 기념일

해설 세부 사항 관련 – 여자가 축하 행사를 계획하고 있는 이유

여자가 첫 대사에서 레나가 마케팅 부장으로 승진한 것을 축하하려고 직원 파티를 계획하고 있다(I'm planning a staff party to celebrate Lena's promotion to director of marketing)고 말하고 있으므로 정답은 (B)이다.

69

Look at the graphic. Which day is the man attending a music festival?

(A) On Thursday
(B) On Friday
(C) On Saturday
(D) On Sunday

시각 정보에 의하면 남자는 어느 요일에 음악 축제에 참가하는가?

(A) 목요일
(B) 금요일
(C) 토요일
(D) 일요일

해설 시각 정보 연계 – 남자가 음악 축제에 참가하는 요일

여자가 두 번째 대사에서 대부분이 3월 22일 5시쯤에 시간이 난다고 했다(Most people said they'd be available around five on March twenty-second)며 그때가 괜찮은지(Does that work for you?)를 묻자 남자가 그날 밤 음악 축제 티켓이 있다(I have tickets to a music festival that night)고 말하고 있으므로 남자는 3월 22일에 음악 축제에 참가할 예정임을 알 수 있다. 포스터에 따르면 3월 22일은 금요일이므로 정답은 (B)이다.

70

What does the woman say she will do next?

(A) Purchase a gift
(B) Decorate a room
(C) Make a reservation
(D) Send an invitation

여자는 다음에 무엇을 할 것이라고 말하는가?

(A) 선물 사기
(B) 방 장식하기
(C) 예약하기
(D) 초대장 발송하기

해설 세부 사항 관련 – 여자가 다음에 할 것이라고 말하는 일

여자가 마지막 대사에서 베이커 가에 새로 생긴 식당으로 당장 예약해야겠다(I'll make a reservation at the new restaurant on Baker Street right away)고 말하고 있으므로 정답은 (C)이다.

PART 4

71-73 안내 방송

M-Au ⁷¹ **Attention, passengers. On Monday, some of our major bus routes will begin departing from another part of the station.** All buses to Freeport, Johnstown, and Grant City will be leaving from gates 300 through 305 on the west side of the building. ⁷² **This change will help us to improve traffic flow.** ⁷³ **Since the new gates are a ten-minute walk from the ticket counter, we recommend allowing yourself extra time to walk there.**

승객 여러분께 알립니다. 월요일에 주요 버스 노선 일부가 역의 다른 구역에서 출발하기 시작합니다. 프리포트, 존스타운, 그랜트 시티로 가는 버스는 모두 건물 서쪽에 있는 300번에서 305번 게이트에서 출발합니다. 이번 변화는 교통 흐름을 개선하는 데 도움이 될 것입니다. 새

게이트들은 매표소에서 도보로 10분 거리에 있으므로, 걸어서 거기까지 가는 시간을 넉넉히 잡으시길 권합니다.

71

Where is the announcement most likely being made?

(A) At a train station

(B) At a bus station

(C) At an airport

(D) At a ferry terminal

어디에서 나오는 안내 방송이겠는가?

(A) 기차역

(B) 버스 정류장

(C) 공항

(D) 여객선 터미널

해설 전체 내용 관련 - 안내 방송의 장소

화자가 도입부에 승객 여러분께 알린다(Attention, passengers)면서 월요일에 주요 버스 노선 일부가 역의 다른 구역에서 출발하기 시작한다(On Monday, some of our major bus routes will begin departing from another part of the station)고 버스 운행에 관해 공지를 하고 있으므로 정답은 (B)이다.

72

Why is a change being made?

(A) It will improve traffic flow.

(B) It will keep prices low.

(C) It will increase energy efficiency.

(D) It will save staff time.

변경되는 이유는 무엇인가?

(A) 교통 흐름을 개선할 것이다.

(B) 가격이 저렴하게 유지될 것이다.

(C) 에너지 효율을 높일 것이다.

(D) 직원 시간이 절약될 것이다.

해설 세부 사항 관련 - 변경의 이유

화자가 중반부에 이번 변화로 교통 흐름을 개선하는 데 도움이 될 것(This change will help us to improve traffic flow)이라고 말하고 있으므로 정답은 (A)이다.

73

What does the speaker recommend?

(A) Filling out a survey

(B) Printing some tickets

(C) Checking online for updates

(D) Allowing extra time

화자는 무엇을 권하는가?

(A) 설문 조사서 작성하기

(B) 티켓 인쇄하기

(C) 온라인에서 새 소식 확인하기

(D) 시간 넉넉히 잡기

해설 세부 사항 관련 - 화자의 권고 사항

화자가 마지막에 새 게이트들은 매표소에서 도보로 10분 거리에 있으므로 걸어서 거기까지 가는 시간을 넉넉히 잡을 것을 권한다(Since the new gates are ~ extra time to walk there)고 말하고 있으므로 정답은 (D)이다.

74-76 담화

M-Cn Welcome! 74**Thank you for attending the grand opening of my new coffee shop.** We're featuring our very own signature coffee blend. 75**This coffee is distinct from all other blends on the market, because it has more caffeine than any other coffee,** thanks to our roasting process. It's not all about caffeine though—this coffee still has a rich, nutty flavor. I'm so confident of my new coffee, that 76**if any customers believe that it's not the strongest they've ever had, I'm offering a 100 percent money-back guarantee.** Enjoy!

어서 오세요! 새로 문을 여는 저의 커피숍 개업식에 참석해 주셔서 감사합니다. 저희는 저희만의 독특한 커피 블렌드를 선보입니다. 저희 로스팅 과정 덕분에 이 커피는 다른 어떤 커피보다 카페인이 많아 시중에 있는 모든 다른 블렌드와 구별됩니다. 하지만 카페인뿐만이 아닙니다. 이 커피에는 여전히 풍부한 견과류의 풍미가 있습니다. 새 커피에 제가 얼마나 자신이 있는지, 만약 어떤 고객이든 그것이 여태까지 맛본 커피 중 가장 진하지 않다고 생각하시면, 100퍼센트 환불을 보증합니다. 맛있게 드세요!

74

What event is taking place?

(A) A grand opening

(B) A focus group

(C) A food festival

(D) A sales workshop

어떤 행사가 열리고 있는가?

(A) 개업식

(B) 포커스 그룹

(C) 음식 축제

(D) 영업 워크숍

해설 세부 사항 관련 - 열리고 있는 행사

화자가 초반부에 새로 문을 여는 자신의 커피숍 개업식에 참석해 줘서 감사하다(Thank you for attending the grand opening of my new coffee shop)고 말하고 있으므로 정답은 (A)이다.

75

What does the speaker say is distinct about a coffee blend?

(A) It is locally sourced.

(B) It is available in glass bottles.

(C) It comes in several different flavors.

(D) It contains a lot of caffeine.

화자는 커피 블렌드가 어떤 점이 다르다고 말하는가?

(A) 현지 조달이다.

(B) 유리병에 담겨 있다.

(C) 여러 가지 맛이 있다.

(D) 카페인이 많이 들어 있다.

해설 세부 사항 관련 - 화자가 커피 블렌드가 다르다고 말하는 점

화자가 중반부에 다른 어떤 커피보다 카페인이 많아 시중에 있는 모든 다른 블렌드와 구별된다(This coffee is distinct from all other blends ~ any other coffee)고 말하고 있으므로 정답은 (D)이다.

▸▸ Paraphrasing   담화의 has → 정답의 contains

76

What is the speaker offering customers?

(A) Free delivery

(B) Two-day shipping

(C) A full refund

(D) A discount

화자는 고객들에게 무엇을 제공하는가?

(A) 무료 배송

(B) 2일 내 배송

(C) 전액 환불

(D) 할인

해설 세부 사항 관련 - 화자가 고객들에게 제공하는 것

화자가 후반부에 만약 어떤 고객이든 여태까지 맛본 커피 중 가장 진하지 않다고 생각하면 100퍼센트 환불을 보증한다(if any customers believe ~ 100 percent money-back guarantee)고 말하고 있으므로 정답은 (C)이다.

▸▸ Paraphrasing   담화의 a 100 percent money-back
guarantee → 정답의 A full refund

77-79 광고

W-Br If you're looking for a unique experience for the whole family, why not try a tour of Baxter's

Snack Food Factory? 77Each tour begins with a video about the history of Baxter's. Then, unlike most factory tours, we actually take you out on the factory floor. 78At the end of the tour, everyone receives a free bag of our delicious snacks. Tours are available every weekday, but 79if you want to see our production in action, be sure to come and visit us from Monday to Wednesday. We can't guarantee production will be running on Thursdays and Fridays!

온 가족이 함께하는 색다른 경험을 찾으신다면 백스터 스낵 푸드 공장을 둘러보는 건 어떨까요? 모든 견학은 백스터의 역사에 대한 동영상으로 시작합니다. 이후 대다수 공장 견학과 달리 실제로 공장 작업장까지 안내합니다. 견학을 마무리할 때 모두가 당사의 맛있는 간식이 담긴 가방을 무료로 받습니다. 매주 평일에 견학이 가능하지만, 생산이 진행되는 모습을 보시려면 꼭 월요일부터 수요일 사이에 방문해 주세요. 목요일과 금요일은 생산이 가동될지 장담할 수 없습니다!

어휘 unlike ~와 달리   factory floor 공장 작업장   in action 진행 중인

77

How does each tour begin?

(A) Refreshments are served.

(B) Safety equipment is explained.

(C) A video is shown.

(D) Maps are distributed.

모든 견학은 어떻게 시작하는가?

(A) 다과가 제공된다.

(B) 안전 장비를 설명한다.

(C) 동영상이 상영된다.

(D) 지도가 배포된다.

어휘 refreshments 다과   distribute 배포하다

해설 세부 사항 관련 - 견학이 시작되는 방식

화자가 초반부에 모든 견학은 백스터의 역사에 대한 동영상으로 시작한다(Each tour begins with a video about the history of Baxter's)고 말하고 있으므로 정답은(C)이다.

78

What kind of gift do participants receive?

(A) A discount coupon

(B) A bag of snacks

(C) A T-shirt

(D) A postcard

참가자들은 어떤 선물을 받는가?

(A) 할인 쿠폰

(B) 간식 가방

(C) 티셔츠

(D) 엽서

해설 세부 사항 관련 - 참가자들이 받는 선물

화자가 중반부에 견학을 마무리할 때 모두가 당사의 맛있는 간식이 담긴 가방을 무료로 받는다(At the end of the tour, everyone receives a free bag of our delicious snacks)고 말하고 있으므로 정답은 (B)이다.

79

What does the speaker warn the listeners about?

(A) How to pay for food

(B) What clothes to wear

(C) Where to park

(D) Which days to visit

화자는 청자들에게 무엇에 대해 주의를 주는가?

(A) 음식값 지불 방식

(B) 입는 옷

(C) 주차할 곳

(D) 방문하는 요일

해설 세부 사항 관련 - 화자가 청자들에게 주의를 주는 것

화자가 후반부에 생산이 진행되는 모습을 보려면 꼭 월요일부터 수요일 사이에 방문하라(if you want to see ~ visit us from Monday to Wednesday)며 목요일과 금요일은 생산이 가동될지 장담할 수 없다(We can't guarantee ~ on Thursdays and Fridays!)고 말하고 있으므로 정답은 (D)이다.

80-82 전화 메시지

W-Am Hello, ⁸⁰**this is Anna Messina from Messina Roofing, and I'm calling about the new roof for your house that you're remodeling.** ⁸¹**I've learned that when our representative, John, visited you last week, he only talked to you about the cost of the shingles and other materials.** But an official estimate includes parts and labor. It's important that we discuss this soon. ⁸²**I'll be in your area this afternoon and could stop by if that's convenient for you.** Please let me know when you have a chance.

안녕하세요, 메시나 루핑의 안나 메시나입니다. 고객님이 개조하는 집의 새 지붕 때문에 전화드렸어요. 지난주에 저희 직원인 존이 방문했을 때, 고객님께 지붕널과 기타 자재 비용만 이야기했던 걸 알게 됐습니다. 그러나 정식 견적에는 부품과 인건비도 포함됩니다. 곧 이 사안을 꼭 논의해야 하는데요. 오늘 오후에 제가 고객님 지역에 있을 예정이니, 고객님이 편하시다면 들를 수 있습니다. 기회 될 때 알려 주세요.

어휘 representative 직원 shingle 지붕널 estimate 견적(서) convenient 편리한

80

Where does the speaker work?

(A) At an architecture firm

(B) At an accounting firm

(C) At a roofing company

(D) At an auto repair shop

화자는 어디에서 일하는가?

(A) 건축 회사

(B) 회계 법인

(C) 지붕 시공 업체

(D) 자동차 정비소

해설 전체 내용 관련 - 화자의 근무지

화자가 초반부에 메시나 루핑의 안나 메시나인데 고객님이 개조하는 집의 새 지붕 때문에 전화했다(this is Anna Messina from Messina Roofing, and I'm calling about the new roof for your house that you're remodeling)고 말하고 있으므로 정답은 (C)이다.

81

Why does the speaker say, "an official estimate includes parts and labor"?

(A) To compare her company to another one

(B) To correct a colleague's mistake

(C) To complain about an expense

(D) To ask for help with a project

화자가 "정식 견적에는 부품과 인건비도 포함됩니다"라고 말하는 이유는 무엇인가?

(A) 자신의 회사를 다른 회사와 비교하려고

(B) 동료의 실수를 바로잡으려고

(C) 비용에 불만을 제기하려고

(D) 프로젝트에 도움을 요청하려고

해설 화자의 의도 파악 - 정식 견적에는 부품과 인건비도 포함된다는 말의 의도

앞에서 지난주에 저희 직원인 존이 방문했을 때 고객님께 지붕널과 기타 자재 비용만 이야기했다는 것을 알게 됐다(I've learned that ~ cost of the shingles and other materials)고 말한 뒤 인용문을 언급하고 있으므로, 직원이 일부 비용에 대해서만 언급하는 오류가 있었다는 점을 알리려는 의도로 한 말임을 알 수 있다. 따라서 정답은 (B)이다.

82

What does the speaker offer to do this afternoon?

(A) Visit the listener's home

(B) Update the listener's contact information

(C) Consult a financial advisor

(D) Post a job announcement

화자는 오늘 오후에 무엇을 하겠다고 제안하는가?

(A) 청자의 집 방문

(B) 청자의 연락처 수정

(C) 금융 상담사와 상담

(D) 채용 공고 게시

해설 세부 사항 관련 - 화자가 오늘 오후에 하겠다고 제안하는 일

화자가 후반부에 오늘 오후에 제가 고객님 지역에 있을 예정이니 고객님이 편하시다면 들를 수 있다(I'll be in your area this afternoon and could stop by if that's convenient for you)고 말하고 있으므로 정답은 (A)이다.

> ▸▸ Paraphrasing 담화의 stop by → 정답의 Visit

83-85 방송

> **M-Cn** Good evening, and welcome to the program. ⁸³**Today we're discussing using social media to promote your business.** As you know, there are many challenges in this area. In fact, ⁸⁴**setting goals for your company's use of social media is one of the most difficult, so that's what I'm going to help you with today.** I'll show you how creating goals based on your company's specific clientele will make it easier to adjust your social media presence. So, how do you do this? ⁸⁵**Joining me now in the studio is Li Zhao, the founder of the company Spacetime Services. I'll be speaking with Li about how she approached this task.**

> 안녕하세요, 프로그램을 시작합니다. **오늘은 소셜 미디어를 활용한 업체 홍보에 대해 논의하겠습니다.** 아시다시피 이 분야에는 난제가 많죠. 사실 **회사의 소셜 미디어 활용 목표를 설정하는 게 가장 어려운 일 중 하나입니다. 따라서 오늘 제가 바로 이 작업을 도와 드리려고 합니다.** 회사의 특정 고객층을 기반으로 어떻게 목표를 만들면 소셜 미디어에서 존재감을 더 쉽게 조정할 수 있는지 보여 드리겠습니다. 그럼, 어떻게 하면 될까요? **스페이스타임 서비스 사의 설립자인 리 자오 씨가 지금 스튜디오에 함께하고 계십니다. 리 씨가 어떤 방식으로 이 과제에 접근했는지 함께 이야기 나누겠습니다.**

> 어휘 promote 홍보하다 challenge 난제 clientele 고객층 adjust 조정하다 presence 존재감 founder 설립자

83

What is the broadcast about?

(A) Financing your company
(B) **Using social media**
(C) Recruiting staff
(D) Getting a business license

무엇에 관한 방송인가?

(A) 회사 자금 조달
(B) **소셜 미디어 활용**
(C) 직원 채용
(D) 사업자 등록증 취득

어휘 business license 사업자 등록증

해설 전체 내용 관련 - 방송의 주제

화자가 초반부에 오늘은 소셜 미디어를 활용한 업체 홍보에 대해 논의하겠다(Today we're discussing using social media to promote your business)고 말하고 있으므로 정답은 (B)이다.

84

What will the speaker help the listeners with today?

(A) Choosing a service
(B) Lowering costs
(C) Analyzing feedback
(D) **Setting goals**

화자는 오늘 청자들에게 어떤 도움을 줄 것인가?

(A) 서비스 선택
(B) 비용 절감
(C) 피드백 분석
(D) **목표 설정**

어휘 analyze 분석하다

해설 세부 사항 관련 - 화자가 오늘 청자들에게 줄 도움

화자가 중반부에 회사의 소셜 미디어 활용 목표를 설정하는 것이 가장 어려운 일 중 하나라서 오늘 제가 바로 이 작업을 도와 드리려고 한다(setting goals for your company's use of social media is one of the most difficult, so that's what I'm going to help you with today)고 말하고 있으므로 정답은 (D)이다.

85

What will most likely happen next?

(A) **The speaker will conduct an interview.**
(B) The speaker will give a weather update.
(C) An advertisement will play.
(D) A contest winner will be announced.

다음에 어떤 일이 있겠는가?

(A) **화자가 인터뷰를 할 것이다.**
(B) 화자가 날씨 정보를 전할 것이다.
(C) 광고가 나올 것이다.
(D) 대회 우승자가 발표될 것이다.

해설 세부 사항 관련 - 다음에 일어날 일

화자가 마지막에 스페이스타임 서비스 사의 설립자인 리 자오 씨가 지금 스튜디오에 함께하고 있다(Joining me now ~ Spacetime Services)며 리 씨가 어떤 방식으로 이 과제에 접근했는지 함께 이야기를 나누겠다(I'll be speaking with Li about how she approached this task)고 말하고 있으므로 정답은 (A)이다.

> ▸▸ Paraphrasing 담화의 be speaking with → 정답의 conduct an interview

86-88 회의 발췌

M-Au Hi, everyone. I've got some big news. **86 Our company has decided to move in an interesting direction, and it's going to affect us here in the marketing department.** As you know, we've had great success getting stores to carry our line of fine cotton bedding, such as sheets and blankets. **87 Now the company has decided to switch to using bamboo cloth for these products.** The fabric is soft and durable and also environmentally sustainable. Our job, of course, is to maintain and expand our markets for this new bedding. Now, **88 you may be worried that customers won't be happy with this change,** but I use these products. Let's look at some samples now.

여러분, 안녕하세요. 중요한 소식이 있어요. **회사에서 흥미로운 길로 들어서기로 결정했는데, 여기 마케팅부에 있는 우리들에게 영향을 미칠 겁니다.** 아시다시피, 자사의 시트와 담요 같은 고급 면 침구류를 취급할 매장을 구하는 데 우리가 대성공을 거뒀죠. **이제 회사는 이 제품들에 대나무 직물로 바꿔 사용하기로 결정했습니다.** 이 직물은 부드럽고 내구성이 뛰어나며 환경 측면에서 지속 가능합니다. 물론 우리가 할 일은 이 새로운 침구의 시장을 유지하고 확장하는 겁니다. 자, **고객들이 이 변화에 불만을 보일까 걱정되실 겁니다.** 하지만 제가 이 제품들을 쓰고 있어요. 이제 몇 가지 샘플을 봅시다.

어휘 affect 영향을 미치다 switch 바꾸다 durable 내구성이 뛰어난 environmentally 환경 측면에서 sustainable 지속 가능한 maintain 유지하다 expand 확장하다

86

Who most likely are the listeners?

(A) Potential investors

(B) Marketing specialists

(C) Quality control inspectors

(D) Product designers

청자들은 누구이겠는가?

(A) 잠재 투자자

(B) 마케팅 전문가

(C) 품질 관리 검사원

(D) 제품 설계자

해설 전체 내용 관련 – 청자들의 직업

화자가 초반부에 회사에서 흥미로운 길로 들어서기로 결정했는데 여기 마케팅부에 있는 우리들에게 영향을 미칠 것(Our company has decided to ~ in the marketing department)이라고 말하고 있으므로 청자들은 마케팅 부서의 직원들임을 알 수 있다. 따라서 정답은 (B)이다.

87

According to the speaker, what is the company going to change?

(A) The material it uses

(B) The financing it makes available

(C) The maintenance schedule for its equipment

(D) The publisher for its catalog

화자의 말에 따르면, 회사는 무엇을 바꿀 것인가?

(A) 사용하는 재료

(B) 이용할 수 있는 자금

(C) 장비 정비 일정

(D) 카탈로그 발행인

어휘 maintenance 정비

해설 세부 사항 관련 – 화자가 회사가 바꿀 것이라고 말하는 것

화자가 중반부에 이제 회사는 이 제품들에 대나무 직물로 바꿔서 사용하기로 결정했다(Now the company has decided to switch to using bamboo cloth for these products)고 말하고 있으므로 정답은 (A)이다.

88

Why does the speaker say, "but I use these products"?

(A) To reject an offer

(B) To correct an advertisement

(C) To provide reassurance

(D) To explain a decision

화자가 "하지만 제가 이 제품들을 쓰고 있어요"라고 말하는 이유는 무엇인가?

(A) 제안을 거절하려고

(B) 광고를 수정하려고

(C) 안심시키려고

(D) 결정을 설명하려고

어휘 reject 거절하다 reassurance 안심

해설 화자의 의도 파악 – 하지만 제가 이 제품들을 쓰고 있다는 말의 의도

앞에서 고객들이 이 변화에 불만을 보일까 걱정될 수도 있다(you may be worried that customers won't be happy with this change)고 말한 뒤 인용문을 언급한 것으로 보아, 제품의 질에 대한 확신을 줌으로써 청자들의 불안을 해소시키려는 의도로 한 말임을 알 수 있다. 따라서 정답은 (C)이다.

89-91 소개

M-Cn **89 Thanks for coming to this month's meeting of the Emery Bird Watching Club. 90 I'm very excited to welcome our guest speaker, author Kentaro Nakamura. He recently led a project in the Canadian wilderness where he spent six months researching bird migration patterns.** In his lecture tonight, he'll talk about the dangers of light pollution to migrating birds and what we can do to help. **⁹¹After the presentation, please join us in the library for some drinks and treats.**

이번 달 에머리 탐조 동아리 모임에 와 주셔서 감사합니다. 초청 연사인 작가 켄타로 나카무라 씨를 모시게 되어 무척 설레네요. 나카무라 씨는 최근 캐나다 야생에서 6개월을 보내면서 새의 이동 패턴을 연구하는 프로젝트를 이끌었죠. 오늘밤 강연에서는 이동 중인 새들에게 빛 공해가 미치는 위험과 우리가 도울 수 있는 일에 대해 이야기하시겠습니다. **발표가 끝나면 저희와 함께 도서관에서 음료와 간식을 드세요.**

어휘 recently 최근 wilderness 야생 migration 이동 pollution 공해

89

Where is the talk taking place?

(A) At an awards ceremony
(B) At an exhibit opening
(C) At a club meeting
(D) At a national park tour

담화는 어디에서 진행되고 있는가?

(A) 시상식
(B) 전시회 개회식
(C) 동아리 모임
(D) 국립공원 투어

해설 전체 내용 관련 - 담화의 장소

화자가 도입부에 이번 달 에머리 탐조 동아리 모임에 와 주셔서 감사하다(Thanks for coming to this month's meeting of the Emery Bird Watching Club)고 말하고 있으므로 정답은 (C)이다.

90

What did Kentaro Nakamura recently do?

(A) He published a book.
(B) He started a conservation society.
(C) He won a photography contest.
(D) He conducted a research project.

켄타로 나카무라 씨는 최근에 무엇을 했는가?

(A) 책을 출판했다.
(B) 보호 단체를 설립했다.
(C) 사진 공모전에서 우승했다
(D) 연구 프로젝트를 수행했다.

어휘 conservation 보호 society 단체

해설 세부 사항 관련 - 켄타로 나카무라 씨가 최근에 한 일

화자가 초반부에 초청 연사인 작가 켄타로 나카무라 씨를 모시게 되어 무척 설렌다(I'm very excited to ~ author Kentaro Nakamura)고 나카무라 씨를 소개하며 그가 최근 캐나다 야생에서 6개월을 보내면서 새의 이동 패턴을 연구하는 프로젝트를 이끌었다(He recently led a project ~ researching bird migration patterns)고 말하고 있으므로 정답은 (D)이다.

91

What are the listeners invited to do after the event?

(A) Enjoy some refreshments
(B) Sign up to volunteer
(C) Purchase some souvenirs
(D) Take some maps

행사 후에 청자들은 무엇을 하도록 권유받는가?

(A) 다과 즐기기
(B) 자원봉사 신청하기
(C) 기념품 구입하기
(D) 지도 가져가기

어휘 souvenir 기념품

해설 세부 사항 관련 - 행사 후에 청자들이 권유받은 일

화자가 마지막에 발표가 끝나면 저희와 함께 도서관에서 음료와 간식을 드시라(After the presentation, please join us in the library for some drinks and treats)고 권하고 있으므로 정답은 (A)이다.

> ▸▸ Paraphrasing 담화의 some drinks and treats
> → 정답의 some refreshments

92-94 회의 발췌

W-Br I'm glad to see everyone here for today's monthly team meeting. **⁹²I'm quite impressed with the number of sales this team has finalized this month.** Everyone met their quota—so congratulations! I read through your responses to the online questionnaire I posted. **⁹³Thanks for sharing your ideas about professional development.** Many people suggested improving our ability to create more-attractive slide presentations. I agree this'll be useful when you meet with prospective clients, so **⁹⁴I'd like to accommodate that request with an on-site training. A sign-up sheet has been posted in the employee break room.** Just a heads-up that we have a limited number of computers available.

오늘 월간 팀 회의에 모두 모이셔서 기쁩니다. **이 팀이 이번 달에 확정한 판매 수치를 봤는데 대단하더군요.** 모두 할당량을 채웠어요. 축하해요! 제가 올린 온라인 설문지에 대한 여러분의 답변을 쭉 읽었어요. **직무 능력 개발에 관한 여러분의 생각을 공유해 주셔서 감사해요.** 많은 분이 보기 좋게 슬라이드 프레젠테이션을 만드는 역량을 키우자고 제안했더군요. 잠재 고객을 만날 때 유용하다는 점에 저도 동의하기 때문에 **현장 교육을 통해 그 요청을 수용하고자 합니다. 직원 휴게실에 신청서가 게시됐습니다.** 다만 알려 드리고 싶은 것은 쓸 수 있는 컴퓨터 대수가 제한되어 있다는 겁니다.

어휘 quota 할당량 questionnaire 설문지 professional development 직무 능력 개발 prospective 예상되는, 장래의 accommodate 수용하다 heads-up 알림

92

What type of work do the listeners most likely do?

(A) Architectural planning

(B) Software design

(C) Therapy

(D) Sales

청자들은 어떤 종류의 일을 하겠는가?

(A) 건축 설계

(B) 소프트웨어 설계

(C) 치료

(D) 영업

해설 전체 내용 관련 - 청자들의 직종

화자가 초반부에 이 팀이 이번 달에 확정한 판매 수치를 봤는데 대단하다(I'm quite impressed with the number of sales this team has finalized this month)고 말하고 있는 것으로 보아 청자들은 판매를 담당하는 사람들임을 알 수 있다. 따라서 정답은 (D)이다.

93

What does the speaker thank the listeners for?

(A) Finalizing a business contract

(B) Preparing a presentation

(C) Sharing some ideas

(D) Meeting with some clients

화자는 청자들에게 무엇을 감사하는가?

(A) 사업 계약 마무리

(B) 발표 준비

(C) 아이디어 공유

(D) 고객 면담

해설 세부 사항 관련 - 화자가 청자들에게 감사하는 것

화자가 중반부에 직무 능력 개발에 관한 여러분의 생각을 공유해 줘서 감사하다(Thanks for sharing your ideas about professional development)고 말하고 있으므로 정답은 (C)이다.

94

Why does the speaker say, "we have a limited number of computers available"?

(A) To warn the listeners about a maintenance issue

(B) To encourage the listeners to sign up quickly

(C) To suggest that the listeners buy a device

(D) To remind the listeners about budget cuts

화자가 "쓸 수 있는 컴퓨터 대수가 제한되어 있다"라고 말하는 이유는 무엇인가?

(A) 청자들에게 정비 문제를 경고하려고

(B) 청자들이 빨리 신청하도록 유도하려고

(C) 청자들에게 기기를 구매하라고 제안하려고

(D) 청자들에게 예산 삭감을 알리려고

해설 화자의 의도 파악 - 쓸 수 있는 컴퓨터 대수가 제한되어 있다는 말의 의도

앞에서 현장 교육을 통해 그 요청을 수용하고자 한다(I'd like to accommodate that request with an on-site training)며 직원 휴게실에 신청서가 게시됐다(A sign-up sheet has been posted in the employee break room)고 말한 뒤 인용문을 언급하고 있으므로, 현장 교육 자리가 한정적이어서 참여를 원하는 사람은 신청을 서두를 것을 종용하려는 의도로 한 말임을 알 수 있다. 따라서 정답은 (B)이다.

95-97 전화 메시지 + 식당 배치도

W-Am Hello. This is Megumi from Fellmetric Limited. **95I'm calling about our company's anniversary dinner scheduled for this Friday at your hotel. 96We need audio equipment set up for the event host.** Looking at the dining room layout, I think it's best to set it up next to the table by the window that is farthest away from the buffet. One last thing—**97I've shipped a box of our company's branded vases to the hotel.** There should be enough for all the flower arrangements. Thanks.

안녕하세요. 펠메트릭 사의 메구미예요. **이번 주 금요일 호텔에서 열릴 예정인 우리 회사 기념일 저녁 식사 때문에 전화드렸어요. 행사 진행자를 위해 오디오 장비를 설치해야 해요.** 식당 배치도를 보니 뷔페에서 가장 먼 창가 테이블 옆에 설치하는 게 제일 좋을 것 같아요. 마지막으로 한 가지, **우리 회사 상표가 있는 꽃병 한 상자를 호텔로 보냈어요.** 전부 꽃꽂이하기에 충분한 양이 있을 거예요. 고마워요.

어휘 farthest 가장 먼 flower arrangement 꽃꽂이

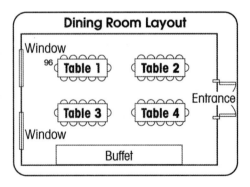

Dining Room Layout

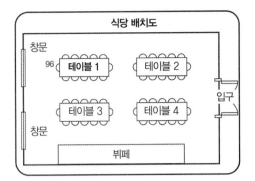

식당 배치도

창문

96 테이블 1　　테이블 2

입구

테이블 3　　테이블 4

창문

뷔페

95

What will take place this Friday?

(A) An industry award ceremony
(B) A fund-raising dinner
(C) A company anniversary event
(D) A holiday celebration

이번 주 금요일에 무슨 일이 있을 것인가?

(A) 산업상 시상식
(B) 모금 만찬
(C) 회사 기념일 행사
(D) 명절 축하 행사

해설 세부 사항 관련 - 이번 주 금요일에 일어날 일

화자가 초반부에 이번 주 금요일 호텔에서 열릴 예정인 우리 회사 기념일 저녁 식사 때문에 전화했다(I'm calling about our company's anniversary dinner scheduled for this Friday at your hotel)고 말하고 있으므로 정답은 (C)이다.

> ▸▸ Paraphrasing　담화의 our company's anniversary dinner
> → 정답의 A company anniversary event

96

Look at the graphic. Where does the speaker want some audio equipment?

(A) Next to table 1
(B) Next to table 2
(C) Next to table 3
(D) Next to table 4

시각 정보에 의하면 화자는 어디에 오디오 장비를 원하는가?

(A) 테이블 1 옆
(B) 테이블 2 옆
(C) 테이블 3 옆
(D) 테이블 4 옆

해설 시각 정보 연계 - 화자가 오디오 장비를 원하는 위치

화자가 중반부에 행사 진행자를 위해 오디오 장비를 설치해야 한다(We need audio equipment set up for the event host)며 식당 배치도를 보니 뷔페에서 가장 먼 창가 테이블 옆에 설치하는 것이 제일 좋을 것 같다(Looking at the dining room layout, ~ table by the window that is farthest away from the buffet)고 말하고 있고, 식당 배치도에 따르면 뷔페에서 가장 먼 창가 쪽의 테이블은 테이블 1이므로 정답은 (A)이다.

97

What has the speaker shipped to the hotel?

(A) Some tablecloths
(B) Some vases
(C) Some aprons
(D) Some glasses

화자는 호텔에 무엇을 보냈는가?

(A) 식탁보
(B) 꽃병
(C) 앞치마
(D) 유리잔

해설 세부 사항 관련 - 화자가 호텔에 보낸 것

화자가 후반부에 우리 회사 상표가 있는 꽃병 한 상자를 호텔로 보냈다(I've shipped a box of our company's branded vases to the hotel)고 말하고 있으므로 정답은 (B)이다.

98-100 담화 + 안건

W-Br 98Here are the topics we're going to cover in today's workshop on effective store management. 99I know interviewing is listed first on your agenda, but let's start with something more fun—setting up displays at your clothing stores. Displays are important because they have the biggest impact on how your store looks during business hours. From signage to lighting, there are many factors to consider. 100I'm going to show some photographs of displays, and let's see if we can identify which are the most effective, and why.

효과적인 매장 관리에 관한 오늘 워크숍에서 다룰 주제들입니다. 면접이 첫 번째 안건에 있는 건 알지만, 좀 더 재미있는 일부터 시작하죠. 의류 매장에 진열하는 것부터요. 진열은 영업 시간 동안 매장 외관에 가장 영향을 크게 미치므로 중요합니다. 간판부터 조명까지 고려해야 할 요소가 많아요. 진열 사진을 몇 장 보여 드릴 테니 어떤 것이 가장 효과적이며, 왜 효과적인지를 식별할 수 있는지 알아보죠.

어휘 effective 효과적인 agenda 안건 impact 영향 signage 간판 factor 요소 identify 식별하다

AGENDA TOPICS

1. Interviewing

2. Training

99 3. Displaying merchandise

4. Tracking inventory

```
┌─────────────────────────────┐
│         안건 주제             │
│   1. 면접                    │
│                             │
│   2. 교육                    │
│                             │
│ 99 3. 제품 진열              │
│                             │
│   4. 재고 추적                │
└─────────────────────────────┘
```

98

Who most likely are the listeners?

(A) Event planners

(B) Fashion designers

(C) Sales analysts

(D) Store managers

청자들은 누구이겠는가?

(A) 행사 기획자

(B) 패션 디자이너

(C) 매출 분석가

(D) 매장 관리자

해설 전체 내용 관련 – 청자들의 직업

화자가 도입부에 효과적인 매장 관리에 관한 오늘 워크숍에서 다룰 주제들(Here are the topics we're going to cover in today's workshop on effective store management)이라고 말하는 것으로 보아 청자들은 매장 관리를 맡고 있는 사람들임을 알 수 있다. 따라서 정답은 (D)이다.

99

Look at the graphic. Which topic does the speaker start the workshop with?

(A) Topic 1

(B) Topic 2

(C) Topic 3

(D) Topic 4

시각 정보에 의하면 화자는 어떤 주제로 워크숍을 시작하는가?

(A) 주제 1

(B) 주제 2

(C) 주제 3

(D) 주제 4

해설 시각 정보 연계 – 화자가 워크숍을 시작하는 주제

화자가 초반부에 면접이 첫 번째 안건에 있는 것은 알지만 좀 더 재미있는 의류 매장에 진열하는 것부터 시작하자(I know interviewing is listed first on your agenda, but let's start with something more fun—setting up displays at your clothing stores)고 제안하고 있고, 안건 주제에 따르면 제품 진열은 3번이므로 정답은 (C)이다.

100

What does the speaker say the listeners will do next?

(A) Introduce themselves

(B) Discuss some pictures

(C) Practice doing interviews

(D) Try out some software

화자는 청자들이 다음에 무엇을 할 것이라고 말하는가?

(A) 자기소개

(B) 사진에 관해 토론

(C) 면접 연습

(D) 소프트웨어 시험 사용

해설 세부 사항 관련 – 화자가 청자들이 다음에 할 것이라고 말하는 일

화자가 마지막에 진열 사진을 몇 장 보여 드릴테니 어떤 것이 가장 효과적이며 왜 효과적인지를 식별할 수 있는지 알아보자(I'm going to show some photographs of displays, and let's see if we can identify which are the most effective, and why)고 말하고 있으므로 정답은 (B)이다.

┌───┐
│ ▸▸ **Paraphrasing**   담화의 **photographs** → 정답의 **pictures** │
└───┘

기출 TEST 4

1 (A)	2 (D)	3 (C)	4 (B)	5 (C)
6 (C)	7 (B)	8 (B)	9 (A)	10 (C)
11 (C)	12 (B)	13 (C)	14 (C)	15 (B)
16 (A)	17 (C)	18 (A)	19 (A)	20 (C)
21 (C)	22 (A)	23 (A)	24 (C)	25 (C)
26 (A)	27 (C)	28 (B)	29 (C)	30 (C)
31 (A)	32 (B)	33 (A)	34 (D)	35 (D)
36 (B)	37 (B)	38 (C)	39 (A)	40 (D)
41 (D)	42 (A)	43 (A)	44 (A)	45 (B)
46 (B)	47 (D)	48 (B)	49 (A)	50 (C)
51 (B)	52 (A)	53 (C)	54 (A)	55 (B)
56 (D)	57 (B)	58 (A)	59 (D)	60 (C)
61 (D)	62 (B)	63 (B)	64 (C)	65 (B)
66 (C)	67 (B)	68 (B)	69 (C)	70 (A)
71 (A)	72 (C)	73 (B)	74 (C)	75 (D)
76 (A)	77 (B)	78 (C)	79 (D)	80 (C)
81 (B)	82 (A)	83 (D)	84 (C)	85 (A)
86 (D)	87 (C)	88 (B)	89 (D)	90 (B)
91 (D)	92 (A)	93 (D)	94 (B)	95 (C)
96 (D)	97 (B)	98 (D)	99 (B)	100 (C)

PART 1

1 W-Br

(A) She's kneeling in front of a chalkboard.
(B) She's sweeping a tile floor.
(C) She's signing a receipt.
(D) She's clearing off a countertop.

(A) 여자가 칠판 앞에 무릎을 꿇고 있다.
(B) 여자가 타일 바닥을 쓸고 있다.
(C) 여자가 영수증에 서명하고 있다.
(D) 여자가 조리대를 치우고 있다.

어휘 kneel 무릎을 꿇다 in front of ～ 앞에 chalkboard
칠판 sweep 쓸다 receipt 영수증 clear off ～을 치우다
countertop 조리대

해설 1인 등장 사진 – 사람의 동작/상태 묘사

(A) 정답. 여자가 칠판 앞에 무릎을 꿇고 있는(is kneeling in front of a chalkboard) 모습이므로 정답.
(B) 동사 오답. 여자가 타일 바닥을 쓸고 있는(is sweeping a tile floor) 모습이 아니므로 오답.

(C) 동사 오답. 여자가 영수증에 서명하고 있는(is signing a receipt) 모습이 아니므로 오답.
(D) 동사 오답. 여자가 조리대를 치우고 있는(is clearing off a countertop) 모습이 아니므로 오답.

2 M-Cn

(A) A man is polishing the floor.
(B) A man is unzipping a suitcase.
(C) A man is picking up a cushion.
(D) A man is drinking from a bottle.

(A) 남자가 마루를 닦고 있다.
(B) 남자가 여행 가방의 지퍼를 열고 있다.
(C) 남자가 쿠션을 집어 들고 있다.
(D) 남자가 병째로 마시고 있다.

어휘 polish 닦다 unzip 지퍼를 열다

해설 1인 등장 사진 – 사람의 동작/상태 묘사

(A) 동사 오답. 남자가 마루를 닦고 있는(is polishing the floor) 모습이 아니므로 오답.
(B) 동사 오답. 남자가 여행 가방의 지퍼를 열고 있는(is unzipping a suitcase) 모습이 아니므로 오답.
(C) 사진에 없는 명사를 이용한 오답. 사진에 쿠션(a cushion)의 모습이 보이지 않으므로 오답.
(D) 정답. 남자가 병째로 마시고 있는(is drinking from a bottle) 모습이므로 정답.

3 W-Br

(A) An announcer is setting down a microphone.
(B) Some workers are constructing a platform.
(C) There are some performers on a stage.
(D) Some musicians are unpacking their equipment.

(A) 아나운서가 마이크를 내려놓고 있다.
(B) 작업자들이 플랫폼을 세우고 있다.
(C) 공연자들이 무대 위에 있다.
(D) 음악가들이 장비를 꺼내고 있다.

어휘 construct 세우다, 건설하다 performer 공연자 unpack
꺼내다 equipment 장비

해설 2인 이상 등장 사진 - 사람의 동작/상태 묘사

(A) 동사 오답. 아나운서(an announcer)가 마이크를 내려놓고 있는(is setting down a microphone) 모습이 아니므로 오답.

(B) 동사 오답. 인부들(some workers)이 플랫폼을 세우고 있는(are constructing a platform) 모습이 아니므로 오답.

(C) 정답. 공연자들(some performers)이 무대 위에 있는(on a stage) 모습이므로 정답.

(D) 동사 오답. 음악가들(some musicians)이 장비를 꺼내고 있는(are unpacking their equipment) 모습이 아니므로 오답.

4 M-Au

(A) The woman is hanging up some posters.

(B) The woman is writing on a document.

(C) A laptop is being put away.

(D) A flowerpot is being stored on a shelf.

(A) 여자가 포스터들을 걸고 있다.

(B) 여자가 서류에 글을 쓰고 있다.

(C) 노트북이 치워지고 있다.

(D) 화분이 선반에 보관되고 있다.

어휘 hang up ~을 걸다　put away ~을 치우다　flowerpot 화분

해설 혼합 사진 - 사람/사물/풍경 혼합 묘사

(A) 사진에 없는 명사를 이용한 오답. 사진에 포스터(posters)의 모습이 보이지 않으므로 오답.

(B) 정답. 여자가 서류에 글을 쓰고 있는(is writing on a document) 모습이므로 정답.

(C) 동사 오답. 노트북(a laptop)이 치워지고 있는(is being put away) 모습이 아니므로 오답.

(D) 동사 오답. 화분(a flowerpot)이 선반에 보관되고 있는(is being stored on a shelf) 모습이 아니므로 오답.

5 W-Br

(A) The presenter is closing a window.

(B) The presenter is standing behind a podium.

(C) The audience is facing a screen.

(D) The audience is seated in a circle.

(A) 발표자가 창을 닫고 있다.

(B) 발표자가 연단 뒤에 서 있다.

(C) 청중이 스크린을 마주보고 있다.

(D) 청중이 둥그렇게 앉아 있다.

어휘 presenter 발표자　podium 연단　audience 청중

해설 2인 이상 등장 사진 - 사람의 동작/상태 묘사

(A) 사진에 없는 명사를 이용한 오답. 창문(a window)의 모습이 보이지 않으므로 오답.

(B) 사진에 없는 명사를 이용한 오답. 연단(a podium)의 모습이 보이지 않으므로 오답.

(C) 정답. 청중(the audience)이 스크린을 마주보고 있는(is facing a screen) 모습이므로 정답.

(D) 동사 오답. 청중(the audience)이 둥그렇게 앉아 있는(is seated in a circle) 모습이 아니므로 오답.

6 W-Am

(A) Some passengers are waiting on the walkway.

(B) Some bicycles are mounted on a bus.

(C) A bus is being driven down a road.

(D) A garage door has been opened.

(A) 승객들이 보도에서 기다리고 있다.

(B) 자전거들이 버스에 탑재되어 있다.

(C) 버스가 도로를 따라 운행되고 있다.

(D) 차고 문이 열려 있다.

어휘 passenger 승객　walkway 보도　mount 탑재하다　garage 차고

해설 혼합 사진 - 사람/사물/풍경 혼합 묘사

(A) 사진에 없는 명사를 이용한 오답. 보도에서 기다리고 있는(are waiting on the walkway) 승객들(some passengers)의 모습이 보이지 않으므로 오답.

(B) 위치 오답. 자전거들(some bicycles)이 버스에 탑재되어 있는(are mounted on a bus) 모습이 아니므로 오답.

(C) 정답. 버스(a bus)가 도로를 따라 운행되고 있는(is being driven down a road) 모습이므로 정답.

(D) 동사 오답. 차고 문(a garage door)이 열려 있는(has been opened) 모습이 아니므로 오답.

PART 2

7

W-Am　When are applications for the summer internship due?

M-Cn　(A) You did excellent work today!

　　(B) By October nineteenth.

　　(C) Yes, they do.

여름 인턴직 지원은 언제까지 해야 하나요?

(A) 오늘 정말 잘했어요!

(B) 10월 19일까지예요.

(C) 네, 그렇습니다.

어휘 application 지원(서) due ~하기로 되어 있는

해설 여름 인턴직 지원 마감 시점을 묻는 When 의문문

(A) 연상 단어 오답. 질문의 internship에서 연상 가능한 work를 이용한 오답.

(B) 정답. 여름 인턴직 지원을 언제까지 해야 하는지 묻는 질문에 10월 19일까지라고 알려 주고 있으므로 정답.

(C) Yes/No 불가 오답. When 의문문에는 Yes/No 응답이 불가능하므로 오답.

8

M-Au What ingredients are in this cake?

W-Am (A) Not that I'm aware of.

(B) Some dried fruits and nuts.

(C) Cookbooks are on the second floor.

이 케이크에는 어떤 재료가 들어 있나요?

(A) 제가 알기로는 아닙니다.

(B) 말린 과일과 견과류예요.

(C) 요리책은 2층에 있습니다.

어휘 ingredient 재료 aware of ~을 아는

해설 케이크의 재료를 묻는 What 의문문

(A) 질문과 상관없는 오답.

(B) 정답. 케이크에 어떤 재료가 들어 있는지 묻는 질문에 말린 과일과 견과류라며 구체적으로 응답하고 있으므로 정답.

(C) 연상 단어 오답. 질문의 ingredients와 cake에서 연상 가능한 cookbooks를 이용한 오답.

9

W-Br Who's in charge of training the new salespeople?

M-Cn (A) Mr. Lee's responsible for that.

(B) Can I pay with my credit card?

(C) There's a sales event at the store.

신입 영업 사원 교육은 누가 담당하죠?

(A) 이 씨가 맡고 있어요.

(B) 신용 카드로 결제할 수 있나요?

(C) 매장에서 할인 행사가 있어요.

어휘 in charge of ~을 담당하는 responsible for ~을 맡고 있는

해설 신입 영업 사원 교육 담당자를 묻는 Who 의문문

(A) 정답. 신입 영업 사원 교육을 누가 담당하고 있는지 묻는 질문에 이 씨가 맡고 있다고 응답하고 있으므로 정답.

(B) 연상 단어 오답. 질문의 charge를 '요금, 사용료'라는 뜻으로 들었을 때 연상 가능한 credit card를 이용한 오답.

(C) 연상 단어 오답. 질문의 salespeople에서 연상 가능한 a sales event를 이용한 오답.

10

W-Am What time is our flight to Hamburg?

M-Au (A) Business class.

(B) No, I've never been there.

(C) The travel agent sent an itinerary.

함부르크행 우리 비행기는 몇 시인가요?

(A) 비즈니스 클래스입니다.

(B) 아니요, 저는 안 가 봤어요.

(C) 여행사가 여행 일정을 보냈어요.

어휘 travel agent 여행사 itinerary 여행 일정

해설 비행기 출발 시각을 묻는 What 의문문

(A) 연상 단어 오답. 질문의 flight에서 연상 가능한 business class를 이용한 오답.

(B) Yes/No 불가 오답. What 의문문에는 Yes/No 응답이 불가능하므로 오답.

(C) 정답. 함부르크행 비행기의 출발 시각을 묻는 질문에 여행사가 여행 일정을 보냈다며, 일정표를 보면 비행 일정을 알 수 있음을 우회적으로 알려 주고 있으므로 정답.

11

W-Br Our new employees have been doing a great job.

M-Cn (A) Sure, that should be easy.

(B) A job announcement.

(C) I agree.

신입 사원들이 아주 잘하고 있어요.

(A) 그럼요, 쉬울 거예요.

(B) 채용 공고예요.

(C) 동감이에요.

어휘 job announcement 채용 공고

해설 의사 전달의 평서문

(A) 평서문과 상관없는 오답.

(B) 단어 반복 오답. 평서문의 job을 반복 이용한 오답.

(C) 정답. 신입 사원들이 아주 잘하고 있다는 평서문에 동감이라며 호응하고 있으므로 정답.

12

M-Cn Should we drive or take the train to the meeting?

W-Br (A) He cleaned the drain.

(B) I'd prefer to drive.

(C) A potential client.

회의에 차로 갈까요, 아니면 기차를 탈까요?

(A) 그가 배수관을 청소했어요.

(B) 저는 운전하는 게 더 좋아요.

(C) 잠재 고객이에요.

어휘 drain 배수관 prefer to ~하는 것을 더 선호하다 potential 잠재적인

해설 선호하는 교통수단을 묻는 선택 의문문

(A) 유사 발음 오답. 질문의 train과 부분적으로 발음이 유사한 drain을 이용한 오답.

(B) 정답. 회의에 가기 위해 선호하는 교통수단을 묻는 질문에 운전하는 것이 더 좋다며 둘 중 하나를 선택해 응답하고 있으므로 정답.

(C) 연상 단어 오답. 질문의 meeting에서 연상 가능한 potential client를 이용한 오답.

13

M-Cn The food at the Fairmont Café is delicious, isn't it?

M-Au (A) A table for two.
(B) The pasta, please.
(C) Yes, I like it a lot.

페어몬트 카페 음식이 맛있죠?
(A) 2인용 테이블이요.
(B) 파스타 주세요.
(C) 네, 아주 좋아해요.

어휘 delicious 맛있는

해설 음식점의 음식이 맛있는지 여부를 확인하는 부가 의문문

(A) 연상 단어 오답. 질문의 café에서 연상 가능한 table을 이용한 오답.

(B) 연상 단어 오답. 질문의 food에서 연상 가능한 pasta를 이용한 오답.

(C) 정답. 페어몬트 카페의 음식이 맛있는지를 확인하는 질문에 네(Yes)라고 대답한 뒤, 아주 좋아한다며 긍정 답변과 일관된 내용을 덧붙이고 있으므로 정답.

14

W-Br How long will it take to fix the air conditioner?

M-Cn (A) No, I don't have it.
(B) It will fit in the larger window.
(C) It should be ready soon.

에어컨을 고치는 데 얼마나 걸릴까요?
(A) 아니요, 저는 없어요.
(B) 더 큰 창에 맞을 겁니다.
(C) 곧 준비될 거예요.

어휘 fix 고치다 fit in ~에 맞다

해설 에어컨 수리에 걸리는 기간을 묻는 How long 의문문

(A) Yes/No 불가 오답. How long 의문문에는 Yes/No 응답이 불가능하므로 오답.

(B) 유사 발음 오답. 질문의 fix와 부분적으로 발음이 유사한 fit을 이용한 오답.

(C) 정답. 에어컨을 고치는 데 걸리는 기간을 묻는 질문에 곧 준비될 거라고 알려 주고 있으므로 정답.

15

M-Au We've seen a big increase in sales over the last month.

W-Br (A) It won't fit in my car.
(B) That's great news!
(C) An interesting television show.

지난달에 매출이 크게 늘었어요.
(A) 제 차에는 안 맞을 거예요.
(B) 좋은 소식이네요!
(C) 재미있는 텔레비전 쇼예요.

어휘 increase 증가

해설 정보 전달의 평서문

(A) 연상 단어 오답. 평서문의 big에서 연상 가능한 fit을 이용한 오답.

(B) 정답. 지난달에 매출이 크게 늘었다는 평서문에 좋은 소식이라며 호응하고 있으므로 정답.

(C) 평서문과 상관없는 오답. What 의문문에 어울리는 응답이므로 오답.

16

W-Br Shouldn't we move the desk closer to the window?

M-Au (A) Yes, that's a good idea.
(B) One of the adjustable chairs.
(C) There are some in the drawer.

책상을 창문 더 가까이로 옮겨야 하지 않을까요?
(A) 네, 좋은 생각이에요.
(B) 조절이 가능한 의자들 중 하나예요.
(C) 서랍 안에 몇 개 있어요.

어휘 adjustable 조절이 가능한

해설 제안/권유의 의문문

(A) 정답. 책상을 창문에 더 가까이 옮기자고 제안하는 질문에 네(Yes)라고 대답한 뒤, 좋은 생각이라며 긍정 답변과 일관된 내용을 덧붙이고 있으므로 정답.

(B) 연상 단어 오답. 질문의 desk에서 연상 가능한 chairs를 이용한 오답.

(C) 연상 단어 오답. 질문의 desk에서 연상 가능한 drawer를 이용한 오답.

17

M-Cn Why can't I access the reports folder anymore?

W-Br (A) Sixteen pages long.
(B) It's colder than usual in here.
(C) We were sent an e-mail about that.

보고서 폴더에 왜 더 이상 접속할 수 없는 건가요?
(A) 16페이지 분량이에요.
(B) 여기는 평소보다 더 춥네요.
(C) 우리는 그것에 관한 이메일을 받았어요.

어휘 access 접근하다, (컴퓨터에) 접속하다

해설 보고서 폴더에 접속할 수 없는 이유를 묻는 Why 의문문

(A) 연상 단어 오답. 질문의 reports에서 연상 가능한 pages를 이용한 오답.

(B) 유사 발음 오답. 질문의 folder와 부분적으로 발음이 유사한 colder를 이용한 오답.

(C) 정답. 보고서 폴더에 더 이상 접속할 수 없는 이유를 묻는 질문에 그것에 관한 이메일을 받았다며, 이메일을 보면 이유를 알 수 있음을 우회적으로 알려 주고 있으므로 정답.

18

M-Au Would you like to schedule an appointment for next week?

W-Br **(A) How about Thursday at ten?**
(B) Last year's train schedule.
(C) A new cancellation policy.

다음 주로 예약하시겠어요?

(A) 목요일 10시는 어떤가요?
(B) 작년 열차 시간표예요.
(C) 새로운 취소 규정이에요.

어휘 appointment 예약 cancellation 취소 policy 규정

해설 제안/권유의 의문문

(A) 정답. 다음 주로 예약을 잡을 것인지 제안하는 질문에 목요일 10시가 어떤지 물으며, 제안에 응해 예약 가능한 시간을 확인하고 있으므로 정답.

(B) 단어 반복 오답. 질문의 schedule을 반복 이용한 오답.

(C) 연상 단어 오답. 질문의 appointment에서 연상 가능한 cancellation을 이용한 오답.

19

M-Cn Why haven't the budget adjustments been made yet?

W-Br **(A) Because the accountant is on vacation.**
(B) I'll update the event calendar.
(C) How do I adjust the chair height?

왜 아직 예산 조정이 안 된 거죠?

(A) 회계사가 휴가 중이라서요.
(B) 행사 일정을 수정하겠습니다.
(C) 의자 높이는 어떻게 조절하나요?

어휘 budget 예산 adjustment 조정 accountant 회계사 height 높이

해설 예산 조정이 아직 되지 않은 이유를 묻는 Why 의문문

(A) 정답. 예산 조정이 아직 되지 않은 이유를 묻는 질문에 회계사가 휴가 중이라고 구체적인 이유를 제시하고 있으므로 정답.

(B) 연상 단어 오답. 질문의 adjustments에서 연상 가능한 update를 이용한 오답.

(C) 파생어 오답. 질문의 adjustments와 파생어 관계인 adjust를 이용한 오답.

20

M-Cn I think you should choose the black and white desk chairs.

M-Au (A) I'm certain it's at night.
(B) I printed a color copy.
(C) They're a bit expensive.

흑백 책상 의자를 선택하셔야 할 것 같아요.

(A) 분명히 밤이에요.
(B) 저는 컬러로 출력했어요.
(C) 그것들은 좀 비싸요.

어휘 choose 선택하다 expensive 비싼

해설 제안/권유의 평서문

(A) 평서문과 상관없는 오답. When 의문문에 대한 응답이므로 오답.

(B) 연상 단어 오답. 평서문의 black and white에서 연상 가능한 color를 이용한 오답.

(C) 정답. 흑백 책상 의자를 선택해야 할 것 같다고 권유하는 평서문에 그것들은 좀 비싸다는 이유를 들어 권유를 간접적으로 거절하고 있으므로 정답.

21

W-Br You're going to attend tomorrow's training session, right?

M-Cn (A) An attendance sheet.
(B) It departs this afternoon.
(C) Do you think that's necessary?

내일 교육 세션에 참석하시죠?

(A) 출석부예요.
(B) 오늘 오후에 출발해요.
(C) 그럴 필요가 있을까요?

어휘 attend 참석하다 attendance 출석, 참석 depart 출발하다 necessary 필요한

해설 교육 세션 참석 여부를 확인하는 부가 의문문

(A) 파생어 오답. 질문의 attend와 파생어 관계인 attendance를 이용한 오답.

(B) 질문과 상관없는 오답. When 의문문에 대한 응답이므로 오답.

(C) 정답. 내일 교육 세션에 참석할 것인지 묻는 질문에 그럴 필요가 있을지를 되물으며, 참석하지 않을 예정임을 우회적으로 표현하고 있으므로 정답.

22

W-Am Should I reserve the meeting room for one hour or two?

W-Br **(A) Our agenda is very short.**
(B) We could open the window.
(C) No, I haven't had a chance.

회의실을 한 시간을 예약해야 할까요, 아니면 두 시간을 예약해야 할까요?

(A) 우리 안건은 아주 짧아요.
(B) 창문을 열어도 되겠어요.
(C) 아니요, 저는 기회가 없었어요.

어휘 reserve 예약하다 agenda 안건

해설 회의실 예약 시간에 대해 묻는 선택 의문문

(A) 정답. 회의실을 얼마나 오래 예약할지 묻는 선택 의문문에 우리 안건은 아주 짧다며, 둘 중에 더 짧은 시간을 선호한다는 것을 간접적으로 알려 주고 있으므로 정답.
(B) 연상 단어 오답. 질문의 room에서 연상 가능한 window를 이용한 오답.
(C) 질문과 상관없는 오답.

23

M-Cn Does this factory use any recycled materials?

W-Am **(A) Not yet, but it's in our plans.**
(B) Please put on this protective hat.
(C) They're highly skilled workers.

이 공장에서는 재활용 재료를 사용하나요?
(A) 아직은 아니지만, 계획에 있어요.
(B) 이 방호용 모자를 써 주세요.
(C) 그들은 고도로 숙련된 작업자들입니다.

어휘 factory 공장 recycle 재활용하다 protective 방호용의 skilled 숙련된

해설 공장의 재활용 재료 사용 여부를 확인하는 조동사(Does) 의문문

(A) 정답. 공장이 재활용 재료를 사용하는지 여부를 묻는 질문에 아직은 아니다(Not yet)라고 대답한 뒤, 계획에 있다며 부정 답변과 일관된 내용을 덧붙이고 있으므로 정답.
(B) 연상 단어 오답. 질문의 factory에서 연상 가능한 protective hat을 이용한 오답.
(C) 연상 단어 오답. 질문의 factory에서 연상 가능한 workers를 이용한 오답.

24

M-Au Who's leading today's tour group?

W-Am (A) Please group the shirts by price.
(B) About two hours long.
(C) I just saw Alexi with them.

오늘 관광단은 누가 인솔하고 있나요?
(A) 셔츠를 가격별로 분류해 주세요.
(B) 두 시간 정도요.
(C) 방금 알렉시가 그들과 함께 있는 걸 봤어요.

어휘 group 분류하다

해설 관광단의 인솔자를 묻는 Who 의문문

(A) 단어 반복 오답. 질문의 group을 반복 이용한 오답.
(B) 질문과 상관없는 오답. How long 의문문에 대한 응답이므로 오답.
(C) 정답. 오늘 관광단을 인솔하는 사람이 누구인지 묻는 질문에 방금 알

렉시가 그들과 함께 있는 것을 봤다며 알렉시가 인솔자라는 것을 우회적으로 알려 주고 있으므로 정답.

25

W-Br Can you tell me the name of that band we liked at the music festival?

M-Cn (A) The lead guitarist.
(B) At eight o'clock tonight.
(C) I can't remember it either.

음악 축제에서 우리가 좋아했던 밴드 이름을 알려 주실래요?
(A) 리드 기타리스트예요.
(B) 오늘밤 8시예요.
(C) 저도 기억이 안 나요.

해설 부탁/요청의 의문문

(A) 연상 단어 오답. 질문의 band에서 연상 가능한 guitarist를 이용한 오답.
(B) 질문과 상관없는 오답. When 의문문에 대한 응답이므로 오답.
(C) 정답. 음악 축제에서 좋아했던 밴드 이름을 알려 달라는 요청에 자신도 기억이 나지 않는다고 응답하고 있으므로 정답.

26

W-Am When will you be available to start the position?

M-Cn (A) I still have a month left of school.
(B) It's been here since last winter.
(C) Of course I'd be willing to do that.

언제 그 직무를 시작하실 수 있나요?
(A) 아직 학교 수업이 한 달 남았어요.
(B) 그것은 작년 겨울부터 여기 있었어요.
(C) 물론 기꺼이 그렇게 하겠습니다.

어휘 available 시간이 있는

해설 직무 시작 가능 시점을 묻는 When 의문문

(A) 정답. 직무를 시작할 수 있는 시점을 묻는 질문에 아직 학교 수업이 한 달 남았다며, 한 달 뒤에나 직무를 시작할 수 있음을 간접적으로 표현하고 있으므로 정답.
(B) 질문과 상관없는 오답.
(C) Yes/No 불가 오답. When 의문문에는 Yes/No 응답이 불가능한데, Of course도 일종의 Yes 응답이라고 볼 수 있으므로 오답.

27

M-Au Isn't tomorrow's seminar about time management?

W-Am (A) I hired a property manager.
(B) Sure, we have plenty of time.
(C) No, that one's scheduled for next week.

내일 세미나는 시간 관리에 관한 것 아닌가요?
(A) 부동산 관리인을 고용했어요.
(B) 그럼요, 시간은 충분해요.
(C) 아니요, 그것은 다음 주로 일정이 잡혀 있어요.

어휘 management 관리 hire 고용하다 property 부동산 plenty of 많은

해설 세미나 주제가 시간 관리에 관한 것인지 확인하는 부정 의문문
(A) 파생어 오답. 질문의 management와 파생어 관계인 manager를 이용한 오답.
(B) 단어 반복 오답. 질문의 time을 반복 이용한 오답.
(C) 정답. 내일 세미나가 시간 관리에 관한 것이 맞는지 묻는 질문에 아니요(No)라고 대답한 뒤, 그것은 다음 주로 일정이 잡혀 있다고 구체적인 설명을 덧붙이고 있으므로 정답.

28

M-Cn Why is it so hot in this room?
M-Au (A) On the top shelf.
(B) Sorry, I just got here.
(C) We have enough room, thanks.

이 방은 왜 이렇게 덥죠?
(A) 맨 위 선반에요.
(B) 미안해요, 저는 방금 도착했어요.
(C) 우리는 공간이 충분해요, 고마워요.

어휘 room 공간

해설 방이 더운 이유를 묻는 Why 의문문
(A) 질문과 상관없는 오답. Where 의문문에 대한 응답이므로 오답.
(B) 정답. 방이 더운 이유를 묻는 질문에 미안하지만 방금 도착했다며, 이유를 알지 못해 답변을 할 수 없음을 우회적으로 표현하고 있으므로 정답.
(C) 단어 반복 오답. 질문의 room을 반복 이용한 오답.

29

W-Am Where's the main entrance to the museum?
M-Cn (A) It's not supposed to rain today.
(B) An exhibit on ancient Egypt.
(C) I see a long line of people over there.

박물관 정문은 어디인가요?
(A) 오늘은 비가 안 올 거예요.
(B) 고대 이집트에 관한 전시회예요.
(C) 저기 길게 줄 선 사람들이 보이네요.

어휘 main entrance 정문 be supposed to ~하기로 되어 있다 exhibit 전시회

해설 박물관 정문의 위치를 묻는 Where 의문문
(A) 질문과 상관없는 오답. 날씨를 묻는 질문에 대한 응답이므로 오답.
(B) 연상 단어 오답. 질문의 museum에서 연상 가능한 exhibit을 이용한 오답.
(C) 정답. 박물관 정문 위치를 묻는 질문에 저기 길게 줄 선 사람들이 보인다며 우회적으로 알려 주고 있으므로 정답.

30

W-Br How can we cut office expenses?
M-Au (A) It's on the fifth floor.
(B) I thought it was on sale.
(C) We use a lot of paper for printing.

어떻게 하면 사무실 경비를 줄일 수 있을까요?
(A) 5층에 있어요.
(B) 할인하는 줄 알았어요.
(C) 출력하느라 종이를 많이 써요.

어휘 expense 경비 a lot of 많은

해설 사무실 경비를 절감할 방법을 묻는 How 의문문
(A) 질문과 상관없는 오답. Where 의문문에 대한 응답이므로 오답.
(B) 질문과 상관없는 오답.
(C) 정답. 사무실 경비를 줄일 수 있는 방법을 묻는 질문에 출력하느라 종이를 많이 쓴다며, 인쇄 용지의 사용을 줄이면 경비를 절감할 수 있다는 점을 우회적으로 제안하고 있으므로 정답.

31

W-Am Have we ordered more of the lavender soap yet?
M-Cn **(A) It's not that popular with customers.**
(B) Actually, I'd like to try the soup.
(C) Put the painting in the lobby.

벌써 라벤더 비누를 더 주문했나요?
(A) 그건 손님들에게 그다지 인기가 없어요.
(B) 실은 그 수프를 먹어 보고 싶어요.
(C) 그 그림은 로비에 두세요.

어휘 popular 인기 있는 actually 실은

해설 라벤더 비누를 추가 주문했는지 묻는 조동사(Have) 의문문
(A) 정답. 라벤더 비누를 더 주문했는지 묻는 질문에 그것은 손님들에게 그다지 인기가 없다며, 추가 주문하지 않았음을 우회적으로 알리고 있으므로 정답.
(B) 유사 발음 오답. 질문의 soap와 부분적으로 발음이 유사한 soup를 이용한 오답.
(C) 질문과 상관없는 오답. Where 의문문에 대한 응답이므로 오답.

PART 3

32-34

M-Cn Hello, you've reached Custom Gifts. How can I help you?

W-Br I'd like to order 200 mugs with my café's logo. **32 We're doing some promotional giveaways for the grand opening of our second location,** so I'll need them by next Friday.

M-Cn	Oh, that's soon. But ³³**I can make this an express order so we'll make that deadline.** It'll cost a bit extra. And you'll have to e-mail us your logo.
W-Br	OK, that's fine. ³⁴**Can you tell me what color mugs are available?** I'd like to give customers a choice.

남	안녕하세요. 맞춤 선물입니다. 무엇을 도와 드릴까요?
여	제 카페 로고가 있는 머그잔 200개를 주문하고 싶어요. **두 번째 지점 개업식에 맞춰 판촉용 증정품을 만들려고 하니** 다음 주 금요일까지는 필요해요.
남	아, 금방이네요. 하지만 **급행 주문으로 할 수 있으니 마감일을 맞춰 드릴게요.** 그건 비용이 좀 더 들어요. 그리고 로고를 이메일로 보내 주셔야 합니다.
여	네, 좋아요. **머그잔 색상은 어떤 것이 가능한지 알려 주시겠어요?** 고객에게 선택권을 주고 싶어요.

어휘	reach (전화 등으로) 연락하다 custom 맞춤의, 주문 제작한 promotional 판촉의 giveaway 증정품 express order 급행 주문 make a deadline 마감일을 맞추다 available 이용 가능한

32

What is the woman preparing for?

(A) A holiday raffle
(B) A grand opening
(C) A retirement party
(D) A charity event

여자는 무엇을 준비하고 있는가?
(A) 휴일 맞이 경품 추첨
(B) 개업식
(C) 은퇴 파티
(D) 자선 행사

어휘 raffle (복권·경품 등) 추첨   retirement 은퇴   charity 자선

해설 세부 사항 관련 – 여자가 준비하고 있는 것

여자가 첫 대사에서 두 번째 지점 개업식에 맞춰 판촉용 증정품을 만들려고 한다(We're doing some promotional giveaways for the grand opening of our second location)고 했으므로 정답은 (B)이다.

33

What does the man say he can do?

(A) Rush an order
(B) Apply a discount
(C) Include some free samples
(D) Set up a product display

남자는 자신이 무엇을 할 수 있다고 말하는가?

(A) 주문을 서둘러 처리하기
(B) 할인 적용하기
(C) 무료 샘플 포함하기
(D) 제품 전시 준비하기

어휘 rush 서두르다   apply 적용하다

해설 세부 사항 관련 – 남자가 자신이 할 수 있다고 말한 것

남자가 두 번째 대사에서 급행 주문으로 할 수 있으니 마감일을 맞추겠다(I can make this an express order so we'll make that deadline)고 했으므로 정답은 (A)이다.

> ▶▶ Paraphrasing   대화의 **make this an express order**
> → 정답의 **Rush an order**

34

What does the woman ask about?

(A) Payment methods
(B) Store hours
(C) Return policies
(D) Color options

여자는 무엇에 대해 물어보는가?
(A) 결제 방법
(B) 매장 영업 시간
(C) 반품 규정
(D) 색상 선택 사항

어휘 payment 결제   policy 규정

해설 세부 사항 관련 – 여자의 문의 사항

여자가 마지막 대사에서 머그잔 색상은 어떤 것이 가능한지 알려 줄 수 있는지(Can you tell me what color mugs are available?) 묻고 있으므로 정답은 (D)이다.

35-37

M-Au	Hi, Paloma?
W-Br	Yes, this is Paloma.
M-Au	Hi, it's Takumi Sato, from the International Orchestra.
W-Br	It's good to hear from you, Mr. Sato.
M-Au	³⁵**The committee and I listened to the recordings you gave us. Your performances at the Galveston Festival were fantastic.**
W-Br	Oh, I'm glad you liked them.
M-Au	³⁶**We also enjoyed your interview. We've decided to offer you the position.**

W-Br That's wonderful! There's one thing I should let you know about, though. ³⁷**I saw that rehearsals for the next season begin in July, but I'll be traveling in Japan during the first week of July. Will that be a problem?**

남	여보세요, 팔로마 씨죠?
여	네, 팔로마예요.
남	안녕하세요, 국제 오케스트라의 타쿠미 사토입니다.
여	사토 씨, 소식 들으니 반갑네요.
남	**위원회와 제가 당신이 준 녹음을 들었는데요. 갤버스턴 축제에서 하신 공연은 굉장했어요.**
여	아, 맘에 드셨다니 다행이네요.
남	면접도 즐거웠고요. **팔로마 씨께 그 직책을 제안하기로 결정했습니다.**
여	정말 기뻐요! 하지만 한 가지 알려 드려야 할 게 있어요. **다음 시즌 리허설이 7월에 시작한다고 알고 있는데, 제가 7월 첫째 주에 일본을 여행할 예정이에요. 문제가 될까요?**

어휘 committee 위원회 performance 공연 decide 결정하다

35

What most likely is the woman's profession?

(A) Sound engineer
(B) Travel agent
(C) Actor
(D) Musician

여자의 직업은 무엇이겠는가?

(A) 음향 엔지니어
(B) 여행사 직원
(C) 배우
(D) 음악가

해설 전체 내용 관련 – 여자의 직업

남자가 세 번째 대사에서 여자에게 위원회와 제가 당신이 준 녹음을 들었다(The committee and I listened to the recordings you gave us)면서, 갤버스턴 축제에서 하신 공연이 굉장했다(Your performances at the Galveston Festival were fantastic)고 말하고 있는 것으로 보아 여자는 공연에서 음악을 연주하는 사람임을 알 수 있다. 따라서 정답은 (D)이다.

36

Why is the man calling?

(A) To ask the woman for a favor
(B) To offer the woman a job
(C) To purchase some tickets
(D) To recommend a colleague

남자는 왜 전화하고 있는가?

(A) 여자에게 부탁하려고
(B) 여자에게 일자리를 제의하려고
(C) 티켓을 사려고
(D) 동료를 추천하려고

어휘 ask for a favor 부탁하다 purchase 사다 recommend 추천하다 colleague 동료

해설 세부 사항 관련 – 남자가 전화한 이유

남자가 네 번째 대사에서 당신과의 면접이 즐거웠다(We also enjoyed your interview)면서 당신에게 그 직책을 제안하기로 결정했다(We've decided to offer you the position)고 말하고 있으므로 정답은 (B)이다.

▶▶ Paraphrasing   대화의 **offer you the position**
→ 정답의 **offer the woman a job**

37

According to the woman, what might cause a problem?

(A) A billing error
(B) A schedule conflict
(C) A visa requirement
(D) A mechanical failure

여자의 말에 따르면, 무엇이 문제가 될 수 있는가?

(A) 청구서 발송 오류
(B) 일정 겹침
(C) 비자 요건
(D) 기계 고장

어휘 billing 청구서 발송 schedule conflict 일정 겹침 requirement 요건 mechanical 기계의 failure 고장

해설 세부 사항 관련 – 여자가 문제가 될 수 있는지 묻는 것

여자가 마지막 대사에서 다음 시즌 리허설이 7월에 시작한다고 알고 있는데, 제가 7월 첫째 주에 일본을 여행할 예정이다(I saw that rehearsals for the next season begin in July, but I'll be traveling in Japan during the first week of July)라면서, 이 점이 문제가 될지(Will that be a problem?) 묻고 있는 것으로 보아 리허설과 자신의 일본 여행 일정이 겹쳐 문제를 일으킬 가능성에 대해 우려하고 있음을 알 수 있다. 따라서 정답은 (B)이다.

38-40 3인 대화

M-Cn	Hi, Emiko and Fatima. ³⁸**Thanks for coming in early to set up for this evening's event. This is the first time JMA Technologies is hosting their annual fund-raiser here**, and I think it'll really increase our hotel's visibility.
W-Br	Of course. What do you need?

M-Cn Well, ³⁹**JMA has a new AV equipment request. Initially, they wanted only a podium and microphone, but now they'd also like a projector and a screen.**

W-Br I can set that up now.

M-Cn Thanks, Emiko. ⁴⁰**Fatima, while she's working on that, can you make sure the place settings on the tables are all in order?**

W-Am ⁴⁰**Sure—let me get the seating chart layout so I can check each table against it.**

남 안녕하세요, 에미코, 파티마. **오늘 저녁 행사 준비를 위해 일찍 와 주셔서 고마워요.** JMA 테크놀로지에서 이곳에서 연례 모금 행사를 개최하는 건 이번이 처음이라 우리 호텔이 한층 눈길을 끌 수 있을 것 같아요.

여1 물론이죠. 필요하신 게 뭔가요?

남 **JMA가 새로 시청각 장비를 요청했어요. 처음에는 연단과 마이크만 원했는데 지금은 프로젝터와 스크린도 원하네요.**

여1 제가 지금 설치할 수 있어요.

남 고마워요, 에미코. **파티마, 에미코가 그 일을 하는 동안, 테이블 위 개인별 식기 세트가 모두 제대로인지 확인해 주실래요?**

여2 그러죠, 좌석 배치도를 주시면 각 테이블을 배치도와 대조할게요.

어휘 host 개최하다 annual 연례의 fund-raiser 모금 행사 visibility 눈길 끌기, 가시성 AV equipment (AV = audio and visual) 시청각 장비 initially 처음에는 podium 연단 place setting 개인별 식기 세트 in order 제대로 된

38

What kind of event is taking place?

(A) A trade show
(B) A job fair
(C) A fund-raiser
(D) A grand opening

어떤 행사가 열리는가?

(A) 무역 박람회
(B) 채용 박람회
(C) **모금 행사**
(D) 개업식

해설 세부 사항 관련 – 행사의 종류

남자가 첫 대사에서 오늘 저녁 행사 준비를 위해 일찍 와 줘서 고맙다(Thanks for coming in early to set up for this evening's event)고 했고, JMA 테크놀로지가 이곳에서 연례 모금 행사를 개최하는 것은 이번이 처음(This is the first time JMA Technologies is hosting their annual fund-raiser here)이라고 했으므로 오늘 저녁 열리는 행사는 모금 행사임을 알 수 있다. 따라서 정답은 (C)이다.

39

According to the man, what did a client request?

(A) Projection equipment
(B) Vegetarian meals
(C) Additional parking
(D) An earlier start time

남자의 말에 따르면, 고객은 무엇을 요청했는가?

(A) **영사 장비**
(B) 채식주의자용 식사
(C) 추가 주차 장소
(D) 더 이른 개시 시간

어휘 projection 영사 vegetarian 채식의 additional 추가의

해설 세부 사항 관련 – 남자가 고객이 요청했다고 말한 것

남자가 두 번째 대사에서 JMA가 새로 시청각 장비를 요청했다(JMA has a new AV equipment request)고 했고, 처음에는 연단과 마이크만 원했는데 지금은 프로젝터와 스크린도 원한다(Initially, they wanted only a podium and microphone, but now they'd also like a projector and a screen)고 말하고 있으므로 정답은 (A)이다.

> ▶▶ Paraphrasing 대화의 **a projector**
> → 정답의 **Projection equipment**

40

What will Fatima do next?

(A) Locate some keys
(B) Process a payment
(C) Make a phone call
(D) Check some seating arrangements

파티마는 다음에 무엇을 할 것인가?

(A) 열쇠 찾기
(B) 지급 처리
(C) 전화 걸기
(D) **좌석 배치 확인하기**

어휘 locate 찾다 process 처리하다 arrangement 배치

해설 세부 사항 관련 – 파티마가 다음에 할 일

남자가 세 번째 대사에서 파티마(Fatima)를 호명하며 에미코가 그 일을 하는 동안 테이블 위 개인별 식기 세트가 모두 제대로인지 확인해 줄 것(while she's working on that, can you make sure the place settings on the tables are all in order?)을 요청했고, 두 번째 여자인 파티마가 그러겠다(Sure)고 응하며 좌석 배치도를 주면 각 테이블을 배치도와 대조하겠다(let me get the seating chart layout so I can check each table against it)고 대답했으므로 파티마는 좌석 배치를 점검할 것임을 알 수 있다. 따라서 정답은 (D)이다.

> ▶▶ Paraphrasing 대화의 **let me get the seating chart layout so I can check each table against it**
> → 정답의 **Check some seating arrangements**

41-43

M-Cn	Hi, **41, 42I think I lost my mobile phone while I was shopping here yesterday. The last time I remember using it was in the frozen food aisle.** Has anyone turned in a phone?
W-Br	**42Let me check. What does it look like?**
M-Cn	It has a green protector case with a picture of a motorcycle on the back.
W-Br	Ah, here it is.
M-Cn	Thank you so much. Oh. **43How much are these canned peaches?** I forgot to buy them when I was here yesterday.
W-Br	**43They're two dollars.**

남	안녕하세요. **어제 여기서 장을 보다가 핸드폰을 잃어버린 것 같아요. 제 기억에 마지막으로 핸드폰을 사용한 건 냉동식품 코너였어요.** 핸드폰을 돌려준 사람이 있나요?
여	**확인해 볼게요. 어떻게 생겼나요?**
남	뒷면에 오토바이 사진이 있는 녹색 보호 케이스가 있어요.
여	아, 여기 있어요.
남	정말 감사합니다. 참. **이 복숭아 통조림 얼마죠?** 어제 여기 왔을 때 깜빡 잊고 못 샀어요.
여	**2달러예요.**

어휘 aisle 통로 turn in ~을 돌려주다, 인도하다

41

Where is the conversation most likely taking place?

(A) At a vegetable farm

(B) At an electronics store

(C) At a motorcycle repair shop

(D) At a grocery store

대화는 어디에서 이루어지겠는가?
(A) 채소 농장
(B) 전자 제품 매장
(C) 오토바이 수리점
(D) 식료품점

해설 전체 내용 관련 - 대화의 장소

남자가 첫 대사에서 어제 여기서 장을 보다가 핸드폰을 잃어버린 것 같다(I think I lost my mobile phone while I was shopping here yesterday)고 했고, 기억에 마지막으로 핸드폰을 사용한 것은 냉동식품 코너였다(The last time I remember using it was in the frozen food aisle)고 말하고 있으므로 정답은 (D)이다.

42

What does the woman ask the man to do?

(A) Describe a phone

(B) Show a receipt

(C) Contact a manufacturer

(D) Speak to a mechanic

여자는 남자에게 무엇을 해 달라고 요청하는가?
(A) 전화기 묘사하기
(B) 영수증 제시하기
(C) 제조 업체에 문의하기
(D) 정비사에게 이야기하기

어휘 describe 묘사하다 receipt 영수증 manufacturer 제조 업체 mechanic 정비사

해설 세부 사항 관련 - 여자가 남자에게 요청한 일

남자가 첫 대사에서 어제 여기서 장을 보다가 핸드폰을 잃어버린 것 같다(I think I lost my mobile phone while I was shopping here yesterday)고 하자 여자가 확인해 보겠다(Let me check)면서 어떻게 생겼는지(What does it look like?)를 묻고 있는 것으로 보아 여자는 남자에게 핸드폰의 생김새를 설명해 달라고 요청하고 있음을 알 수 있다. 따라서 정답은 (A)이다.

43

What information does the woman give the man?

(A) The price of an item

(B) The name of a supervisor

(C) The location of a product

(D) The size of an order

여자는 남자에게 어떤 정보를 주는가?
(A) 품목의 가격
(B) 관리자 이름
(C) 제품의 위치
(D) 주문의 규모

어휘 supervisor 관리자

해설 세부 사항 관련 - 여자가 남자에게 주는 정보

남자가 세 번째 대사에서 이 복숭아 통조림이 얼마인지(How much are these canned peaches?) 묻자 여자가 뒤이어 2달러(They're two dollars)라고 답하고 있으므로 정답은 (A)이다.

44-46

W-Br	Hey, Omar. **44I know we'd planned to meet today to review résumés for the open junior accountant position,** but I'm just swamped.
M-Cn	Oh, what's going on?
W-Br	Well, you know I have to finish the quarterly tax filings for two of my top clients... so **45could we review the résumés tomorrow?**

TEST 4

M-Cn	It won't take that long. ⁴⁵ I've already gone through them and separated out the candidates with the accounting experience we're looking for. We just need to decide who to interview.
W-Br	OK. But ⁴⁶ I'll have to leave right at five o'clock, because I have a dentist appointment after work.
여	안녕하세요, 오마르. **오늘 만나서 공석인 하급회계사 이력서를 검토하기로 한 건 아는데**, 그냥 눈코 뜰 새 없이 바쁘네요.
남	저런, 무슨 일이에요?
여	음, 제가 최고 고객 두 사람을 위해 분기 세금 신고를 끝내야 하는 거 아시죠… 그래서 **이력서는 내일 검토해도 될까요?**
남	그렇게 오래 걸리진 않을 겁니다. 제가 이미 검토해서 우리가 찾고 있는 회계 경험이 있는 지원자들을 분류해 놓았어요. 면접 볼 사람만 결정하면 돼요.
여	좋아요. 하지만 퇴근 후에 치과 예약이 있어서 저는 5시에 바로 나가야 해요.

어휘	swamped 눈코 뜰 새 없이 바쁜 quarterly 분기의 tax filing 세금 신고 separate out ~을 분류[분리]하다 candidate 지원자 appointment 예약

44

What field do the speakers most likely work in?

(A) Accounting

(B) Engineering

(C) Education

(D) Agriculture

화자들은 어떤 분야에서 일하겠는가?

(A) 회계

(B) 엔지니어링

(C) 교육

(D) 농업

어휘 agriculture 농업

해설 전체 내용 관련 – 화자들의 직종

여자가 첫 대사에서 오늘 만나서 공석인 하급회계사 이력서를 검토하기로 한 것을 알고 있다(I know we'd planned to meet today to review résumés for the open junior accountant position)고 말하고 있는 것으로 보아 화자들은 회계 관련 업종에서 근무하고 있음을 알 수 있다. 따라서 정답은 (A)이다.

45

Why does the man say, "It won't take that long"?

(A) To request the woman's permission

(B) To convince the woman to meet

(C) To decline an invitation

(D) To express surprise about a decision

남자가 "그렇게 오래 걸리진 않을 겁니다"라고 말하는 이유는 무엇인가?

(A) 여자의 허락을 구하려고

(B) 만나자고 여자를 설득하려고

(C) 초대를 거절하려고

(D) 결정에 놀라움을 표현하려고

어휘 permission 허락 convince 설득하다 decline 거절하다 decision 결정

해설 화자의 의도 파악 – 그렇게 오래 걸리지는 않을 것이라는 말의 의도

앞에서 여자가 이력서를 내일 검토해도 될지(could we review the résumés tomorrow?) 묻자, 남자가 인용문을 언급하며 이미 검토를 마쳐 우리가 찾고 있는 회계 경험이 있는 지원자들을 분류해 놓았다(I've already gone through them and separated out the candidates with the accounting experience we're looking for)면서 면접 볼 사람만 결정하면 된다(We just need to decide who to interview)고 여자를 설득하고 있는 것으로 보아 이력서를 검토하는 데 많은 시간이 필요하지 않다는 의도로 한 말임을 알 수 있다. 따라서 정답은 (B)이다.

46

What does the woman say she will do after work?

(A) Pack for a business trip

(B) Go to a dental appointment

(C) Pick up a food order

(D) Attend a retirement party

여자는 퇴근 후에 무엇을 할 것이라고 말하는가?

(A) 출장을 위해 짐 꾸리기

(B) 치과 예약에 가기

(C) 주문한 음식 찾아오기

(D) 은퇴 파티에 참석하기

어휘 retirement 은퇴

해설 세부 사항 관련 – 여자가 퇴근 후에 할 것이라고 말하는 일

여자가 마지막 대사에서 퇴근 후에 치과 예약이 있어서 5시에 바로 나가야 한다(I'll have to leave right at five o'clock, because I have a dentist appointment after work)고 말하고 있으므로 정답은 (B)이다.

> ▸▸ Paraphrasing 대화의 **have a dentist appointment**
> → 정답의 **Go to a dental appointment**

47-49

M-Cn	Irina, ⁴⁷ **do you have the results from our latest employee satisfaction survey?**
W-Br	Yes, and ⁴⁷ **based on the comments, the majority of our employees want us to make the company more environmentally friendly.** Apparently, they feel that we don't do enough to promote recycling efforts.

M-Cn Hmm, ⁴⁸**that reminds me about an article I read recently**. It said that eco-friendly companies tend to have higher employee satisfaction rates.

W-Br In that case, ⁴⁹**why don't we bring in an outside consultant?** We can hire someone who's an expert on finding ways to promote sustainability.

남 이리나, **최근에 실시한 직원 만족도 설문 조사 결과가 나왔나요?**

여 네, 그리고 **의견을 토대로 보면 직원 대다수는 회사가 좀 더 환경친화적으로 되길 바라네요.** 보아하니 직원들은 우리가 재활용 활동을 충분히 장려하지 않는다고 생각하는 듯해요.

남 음, **최근에 읽은 기사가 생각나네요.** 환경친화적인 회사들이 직원 만족도가 더 높은 경향이 있다고 하더군요.

여 그렇다면 **외부 컨설턴트를 데려오는 게 어때요?** 지속 가능성을 고취할 방법을 찾는 데 전문가인 사람을 고용하면 돼요.

어휘 satisfaction 만족(도) survey (설문) 조사 majority 대다수 environmentally friendly 환경친화적인 apparently 보아하니 promote 장려[고취]하다 effort 활동 article 기사 recently 최근 satisfaction rate 만족도 expert 전문가 sustainability 지속 가능성

47

According to the woman, what do the results of a survey indicate about a company?

(A) It should create an employee award.
(B) It should provide free transportation.
(C) Its employees are happy with a training program.
(D) Its employees are concerned about the environment.

여자의 말에 따르면, 조사 결과는 회사에 관해 무엇을 명시하는가?

(A) 직원상을 신설해야 한다.
(B) 무료 교통편을 제공해야 한다.
(C) 직원들이 교육 프로그램에 만족한다.
(D) 직원들이 환경에 관심이 있다.

어휘 transportation 교통(편) concerned about ~에 관심을 가지는 environment 환경

해설 세부 사항 관련 – 여자가 조사 결과가 회사에 관해 명시하는 것이라고 말하는 것

남자가 첫 대사에서 여자에게 최근에 실시한 직원 만족도 설문 조사 결과가 나왔는지(do you have the results from our latest employee satisfaction survey?) 물으며 회사에 관한 설문 조사 결과에 대해 언급하자, 여자가 의견을 토대로 보면 직원 대다수는 회사가 좀 더 환경친화적으로 되길 바라고 있다(based on the comments, the majority of our employees want us to make the company more environmentally friendly)고 응답하고 있으므로 정답은 (D)이다.

48

What does the man say he did recently?

(A) He accepted a job offer.
(B) He read an article.
(C) He downloaded a schedule.
(D) He met a sales goal.

남자는 최근에 무엇을 했다고 말하는가?

(A) 일자리 제의를 수락했다.
(B) 기사를 읽었다.
(C) 일정을 내려받았다.
(D) 판매 목표를 달성했다.

어휘 accept 수락하다 meet a goal 목표를 달성하다

해설 세부 사항 관련 – 남자가 최근에 했다고 말하는 것

남자가 두 번째 대사에서 최근에 읽은 기사가 생각난다(that reminds me about an article I read recently)고 말하고 있으므로 정답은 (B)이다.

49

What does the woman suggest?

(A) Hiring a consultant
(B) Changing a venue
(C) Modifying a production process
(D) Recruiting volunteers

여자는 무엇을 제안하는가?

(A) 컨설턴트 채용
(B) 장소 변경
(C) 생산 공정 수정
(D) 자원봉사자 모집

어휘 venue (행사 등이 열리는) 장소 modify 수정하다 recruit 모집하다 volunteer 자원봉사자

해설 세부 사항 관련 – 여자의 제안 사항

여자가 마지막 대사에서 외부 컨설턴트를 데려오는 게 어떨지(why don't we bring in an outside consultant?) 묻고 있으므로 정답은 (A)이다.

▸▸ Paraphrasing 대화의 **bring in an outside consultant** → 정답의 **Hiring a consultant**

50-52

M-Au Sofia, ⁵⁰**how was the graphic design conference in Sacramento?**

W-Am Very good. I especially enjoyed the sessions on customer service. I think it'll help me serve our clients better.

M-Au Great! By the way, have you seen the latest expense report for our design department?

W-Am Not yet. Why?

M-Au　We've already exceeded our quarterly budget. We really need to restrict our spending now. So ⁵¹ **I'm asking everyone to come up with ideas for cutting our department's expenses. Could you write up some ideas by two o'clock today?**

W-Am　That'll be quite challenging.

M-Au　I know you just got back, but this is important.

W-Am　OK. ⁵² **I'll talk to my assistant and have her clear my schedule for the rest of the morning.**

남　소피아, 새크라멘토에서 **열린 그래픽 디자인 회의는 어땠어요?**

여　아주 좋았어요. 특히 고객 서비스에 관한 세션이 좋았어요. 고객을 더 잘 모시는 데 도움이 될 것 같아요.

남　잘됐군요! 그건 그렇고, 우리 디자인부의 최근 경비 보고서 보셨어요?

여　아직이요. 왜요?

남　이미 분기 예산을 초과했어요. 현재 지출을 꼭 제한해야 해요. 그래서 우리 **부서의 경비를 줄일 수 있는 아이디어를 생각하라고 모두에게 부탁하고 있어요. 오늘 2시까지 아이디어를 적어 내시겠어요?**

여　상당히 어렵겠는데요.

남　방금 복귀했다는 건 알지만, 이 일은 중요해요.

여　좋아요. **비서와 상의해서 나머지 오전 시간 일정을 비워 두라고 할게요.**

어휘　especially 특히　expense 경비　exceed 초과하다　quarterly 분기의　budget 예산　restrict 제한하다　spending 지출　come up with ~을 생각해 내다　cut 줄이다, 삭감하다　challenging 어려운

50

What type of event did the woman attend?

(A) A theater performance
(B) A grand opening
(C) A professional conference
(D) A retirement party

여자는 어떤 종류의 행사에 참석했는가?

(A) 연극 공연
(B) 개업식
(C) **직업 관련 회의**
(D) 은퇴 파티

해설　세부 사항 관련 - 여자가 참석한 행사의 종류

남자가 첫 대사에서 여자에게 새크라멘토에서 열린 그래픽 디자인 회의는 어땠는지(how was the graphic design conference in Sacramento?) 묻고 있는 것으로 보아 여자가 최근에 그래픽 디자인 회의에 참석했다는 것을 알 수 있다. 따라서 정답은 (C)이다.

51

What does the woman imply when she says, "That'll be quite challenging"?

(A) She wants to apply for a new position.
(B) She does not think she can meet a deadline.
(C) She will need additional funding for a project.
(D) She admires a colleague's plan.

여자가 "상당히 어렵겠는데요"라고 말하는 의도는 무엇인가?

(A) 새로운 직책에 지원하고 싶다.
(B) **마감일을 맞출 수 없다고 생각한다.**
(C) 프로젝트에 추가 자금이 필요하다.
(D) 동료의 계획에 감탄한다.

어휘　meet a deadline 마감일을 맞추다　additional 추가의　admire 감탄하다　colleague 동료

해설　화자의 의도 파악 - 상당히 어렵겠다는 말의 의도

앞에서 남자가 우리 부서의 경비를 줄일 수 있는 아이디어를 생각하라고 모두에게 부탁하고 있다(I'm asking everyone to come up with ideas for cutting our department's expenses)면서 오늘 2시까지 아이디어를 적어 내 달라고(Could you write up some ideas by two o'clock today?) 요청하자 여자가 인용문을 언급했으므로 남자가 요구한 시간까지 일을 끝내는 것이 힘들겠다는 의도로 볼 수 있다. 따라서 정답은 (B)이다.

52

What does the woman say she will do now?

(A) Speak with her assistant
(B) Print out her résumé
(C) Order some food
(D) Make travel arrangements

여자는 지금 무엇을 할 것이라고 하는가?

(A) **비서에게 이야기하기**
(B) 자신의 이력서 출력하기
(C) 음식 주문하기
(D) 출장 준비하기

어휘　make an arrangement 준비[처리]하다

해설　세부 사항 관련 - 여자가 지금 하겠다고 말하는 것

여자가 마지막 대사에서 비서와 상의해서 나머지 오전 시간 일정을 비워 두라고 하겠다(I'll talk to my assistant and have her clear my schedule for the rest of the morning)고 말하고 있으므로 정답은 (A)이다.

> ▸▸ Paraphrasing　대화의 **talk to my assistant**
> → 정답의 **Speak with her assistant**

53-55

W-Br　⁵³ **This is Springfield Community Center. How can I help you?**

M-Au Hi, ⁵³**I'm with the local historical club. We're looking for a place for our monthly meetings.**

W-Br OK. We have a few rooms that community organizations can reserve. When are your meetings held?

M-Au The first Saturday of each month.

W-Br Oh, ⁵⁴**that's a very popular time. You'll have to reserve the space well in advance.**

M-Au No problem. I'll do that. Also, ⁵⁵**I saw that you have a message board at the front of the building. Can groups use it to advertise their events?**

W-Br Yes. Notices can be posted a week in advance.

여 스프링필드 주민 센터입니다. 무엇을 도와 드릴까요?

남 안녕하세요. 저는 지역 역사 동아리 회원이에요. 월례 모임을 위한 장소를 찾고 있어요.

여 그러시군요. 지역 단체들이 예약할 수 있는 방이 몇 개 있어요. 모임이 언제 열리나요?

남 매달 첫째 토요일이에요.

여 아, 많이들 찾는 시간이네요. 한참 전에 장소를 미리 예약해야 할 거예요.

남 문제없어요. 그렇게 할게요. 또 건물 앞쪽에 안내판이 있는 걸 봤어요. 단체들이 게시판을 이용해 행사를 알릴 수 있나요?

여 네. 공지는 일주일 전에 게시할 수 있어요.

어휘 community center 주민 센터 organization 조직, 단체 reserve 예약하다 well in advance 한참 전에 미리 message board 게시판 advertise 널리 알리다

53

Why is the man calling the Springfield Community Center?

(A) He is looking for a backpack.
(B) He is researching a historical place.
(C) He is asking about a meeting space.
(D) He is interested in joining a club.

남자는 왜 스프링필드 주민 센터에 전화하고 있는가?

(A) 배낭을 찾고 있다.
(B) 역사적인 장소를 연구하고 있다.
(C) 모임 장소에 대해 묻고 있다.
(D) 동아리에 가입하고 싶어 한다.

해설 전체 내용 관련 - 남자가 전화한 이유

여자가 첫 대사에서 스프링필드 주민 센터(This is Springfield Community Center)라고 전화를 받으며 무엇을 도울지(How can I help you?) 묻자, 남자가 지역 역사 동아리 회원(I'm with the local historical club)이라고 자신을 소개하며 월례 모임을 위한 장소를 찾고 있다(We're looking for a place for our monthly meetings)고 말하고 있으므로 정답은 (C)이다.

> ▸▸ Paraphrasing 대화의 **a place for our monthly meetings** → 정답의 **a meeting space**

54

What does the woman warn the man about?

(A) A busy time of the month
(B) An early store closing
(C) The cost of an event
(D) A missing document

여자는 남자에게 무엇을 충고하는가?

(A) 한 달 중 붐비는 시간
(B) 매장 조기 폐점
(C) 행사 비용
(D) 누락된 문서

해설 세부 사항 관련 - 여자가 남자에게 충고하는 것

여자가 세 번째 대사에서 많이들 찾는 시간(that's a very popular time)이라면서 한참 전에 미리 예약해야 할 것(You'll have to reserve the space well in advance)이라고 알려 주고 있으므로 정답은 (A)이다.

> ▸▸ Paraphrasing 대화의 **popular time** → 정답의 **busy time**

55

What does the man ask about using?

(A) A library
(B) A message board
(C) A mobile phone
(D) A projector

남자는 무엇의 사용에 관해 묻는가?

(A) 도서관
(B) 게시판
(C) 핸드폰
(D) 프로젝터

해설 세부 사항 관련 - 남자가 사용에 관해 묻는 것

남자가 마지막 대사에서 건물 앞쪽에 게시판이 있는 것을 봤다(I saw that you have a message board at the front of the building)며 단체들이 게시판을 이용해 행사를 알릴 수 있는지(Can groups use it to advertise their events?) 묻고 있으므로 정답은 (B)이다.

56-58

W-Am Hi, ^{56, 57}**I'm calling because I'm redesigning a hotel lobby for a client, and I'd like the reception countertop to be made of stone.**

M-Cn ⁵⁷**We have slabs of granite and marble here in our showroom. You can stop by and choose the one you want.**

W-Am Great—I'll be there this afternoon. Also... how long will it take before the countertop's installed?

M-Cn For a basic rectangular shape, it takes a week to cut it to size, polish it, and install it. [58]**If you have the exact length and width, we can get started as soon as you make your selection.**

W-Am I'll bring the dimensions.

여 안녕하세요. **고객을 위해 호텔 로비를 다시 꾸미려고 하는데, 접수 카운터를 돌로 만들고 싶어서 전화드렸어요.**

남 저희 전시장에 화강암과 대리석 판이 있습니다. 잠시 들러서 원하시는 것을 고르세요.

여 좋아요. 오늘 오후에 그리로 갈게요. 또… 카운터가 설치되는 데 얼마나 걸릴까요?

남 기본 직사각형 모양은 크기대로 자르고, 광택을 내고, 설치하는 데 일주일 정도 걸립니다. **정확한 길이와 너비가 있으면 선택하시는 대로 바로 시작할 수 있습니다.**

여 치수를 갖고 갈게요.

어휘 reception 접수 slab 판 granite 화강암 marble 대리석 install 설치하다 rectangular 직사각형의 polish 광택을 내다 exact 정확한 length 길이 width 너비 dimension 치수

56

Who most likely is the woman?

(A) A cafeteria manager
(B) A hotel receptionist
(C) A laboratory technician
(D) An interior designer

여자는 누구이겠는가?
(A) 구내식당 관리자
(B) 호텔 접수원
(C) 연구실 기사
(D) 인테리어 디자이너

해설 전체 내용 관련 – 여자의 직업

여자가 첫 대사에서 자신이 고객을 위해 호텔 로비를 다시 꾸미려 하고 있다(I'm calling because I'm redesigning a hotel lobby for a client)고 말한 것으로 보아 여자는 인테리어 디자이너임을 알 수 있다. 따라서 정답은 (D)이다.

57

Why will the woman visit the man's business this afternoon?

(A) To perform an inspection
(B) To select a product
(C) To learn a new skill
(D) To interview for a job

여자는 왜 오늘 오후에 남자의 업체를 방문하는가?
(A) 점검하려고
(B) 제품을 선택하려고
(C) 새로운 기술을 습득하려고
(D) 취업 면접을 보려고

어휘 inspection 점검

해설 세부 사항 관련 – 여자가 오늘 오후에 남자의 업체를 방문하는 이유

여자가 첫 대사에서 고객을 위해 호텔 로비를 다시 꾸미려고 하는데, 접수 카운터를 돌로 만들고 싶어서 전화했다(I'm calling because I'm redesigning a hotel lobby for a client, and I'd like the reception countertop to be made of stone)고 하자, 남자가 뒤이어 우리 전시장에 화강암과 대리석 판이 있다(We have slabs of granite and marble here in our showroom)며 방문해서 원하는 것을 고르라(You can stop by and choose the one you want)고 제안하고 있으므로 여자는 호텔 실내 장식에 필요한 석자재를 선택하기 위해 남자의 업체를 방문할 것임을 알 수 있다. 따라서 정답은 (B)이다.

> ▸▸ **Paraphrasing** 대화의 **choose** → 정답의 **select**

58

What does the man recommend that the woman bring?

(A) Some measurements
(B) Some photographs
(C) A handbook
(D) A business card

남자는 여자에게 무엇을 가져오라고 권하는가?
(A) 치수
(B) 사진
(C) 안내서
(D) 명함

어휘 measurement 치수, 측정

해설 세부 사항 관련 – 남자가 여자에게 가져오라고 권하는 것

남자가 마지막 대사에서 정확한 길이와 너비가 있으면 선택하자마자 바로 시작할 수 있다(If you have the exact length and width, we can get started as soon as you make your selection)고 알려 주고 있으므로 정답은 (A)이다.

> ▸▸ **Paraphrasing** 대화의 **the ~ length and width** → 정답의 **Some measurements**

59-61 3인 대화

> **W-Am** Congratulations! As top employees at NGR Industries, you've been selected for our Future Leaders Program. [59]**In this program, you'll be rotating through jobs in each division to learn everything about our company.** Now my colleague, Ms. Park, will continue.

W-Br Thanks, Margaret. ⁵⁹**This rotational program is critical to becoming a successful manager here.** Oh... there's a question in the back?

M-Cn Yes, thank you, Ms. Park. ⁶⁰**I was wondering how long we'll spend in each department.**

W-Br You'll work in one department for about two months and then move to another area. ⁶¹**Preferences for first assignments will be taken into consideration. You may indicate your preference on the form in front of you.**

여1 축하해요! NGR 산업의 최고 직원으로 여러분은 NGR 미래의 지도자 프로그램에 선정되셨어요. **이 프로그램에서는 각 부서를 순환 근무하면서 우리 회사에 대한 모든 것을 배우게 됩니다.** 이제 제 동료인 박 씨가 계속 말씀드리겠습니다.

여2 고마워요, 마가렛. **이곳에서 관리자로 성공하려면 이 순환 프로그램이 정말 중요하죠.** 아… 뒤쪽에 질문 있으신가요?

남 네, 감사합니다, 박 씨. **각 부서에서 얼마나 오래 근무하는지 궁금해서요.**

여2 한 부서에서 두 달 정도 근무한 다음 다른 구역으로 옮기게 됩니다. **첫 업무에 대한 선호도가 고려돼요. 앞에 있는 양식에 선호도를 표시할 수 있어요.**

어휘 rotate 순환하다 division 부서 critical 매우 중요한 preference 선호도 assignment 업무, 과제 take into consideration 고려하다

59

Who most likely are the program participants?

(A) Sales recruiters
(B) Prospective clients
(C) Building inspectors
(D) Management trainees

프로그램 참여자는 누구이겠는가?

(A) 영업 사원 모집 전문가
(B) 잠재 고객
(C) 건축물 조사관
(D) 관리직 연수생

어휘 prospective 잠재적인 inspector 조사관 trainee 연수생

해설 세부 사항 관련 – 프로그램 참여자의 신분

첫 번째 여자가 첫 대사에서 이 프로그램에서는 각 부서를 순환 근무하면서 우리 회사에 대한 모든 것을 배우게 된다(In this program, you'll be rotating through jobs in each division to learn everything about our company)고 프로그램을 소개했고, 두 번째 여자가 뒤이어 이곳에서 관리자로 성공하려면 이 순환 프로그램이 정말 중요하다(This rotational program is critical to becoming a successful manager here)고 했으므로 대화에서 언급되고 있는 프로그램은 관리자가 되기 위한 연수 과정임을 알 수 있다. 따라서 정답은 (D)이다.

60

What does the man ask about?

(A) An office location
(B) A budget amount
(C) A length of time
(D) A list of attendees

남자는 무엇에 대해 묻는가?

(A) 사무실 위치
(B) 예산액
(C) 기간
(D) 참석자 명단

어휘 budget 예산 length 기간 attendee 참석자

해설 세부 사항 관련 – 남자의 문의 사항

남자가 각 부서에서 얼마나 오래 근무하는지 궁금하다(I was wondering how long we'll spend in each department)고 묻고 있으므로 정답은 (C)이다.

▸▸ Paraphrasing 대화의 how long → 정답의 A length of time

61

How should the participants communicate a request?

(A) By making a phone call
(B) By speaking with Ms. Park
(C) By sending an e-mail
(D) By filling out a form

참가자는 요청 사항을 어떻게 전해야 하는가?

(A) 전화를 걸어서
(B) 박 씨에게 이야기해서
(C) 이메일을 보내서
(D) 양식을 작성해서

어휘 fill out ~을 작성하다

해설 세부 사항 관련 – 참가자가 요청 사항을 전하는 방법

두 번째 여자가 마지막 대사에서 첫 업무에 대한 선호도가 고려될 것(Preferences for first assignments will be taken into consideration)이며 앞에 있는 양식에 선호도를 표시하면 된다(You may indicate your preference on the form in front of you)고 말하고 있으므로 선호하는 업무에 대한 요청은 양식을 작성해 전할 수 있음을 알 수 있다. 따라서 정답은 (D)이다.

▸▸ Paraphrasing 대화의 indicate ~ on the form → 정답의 filling out a form

62-64 대화 + 모델 목록

W-Br ⁶²**Welcome to Smith's Sports Equipment and More.** How may I help you?

M-Au Hi, uh, my brother and I often go biking in the mountains, and I'd like to buy an exterior bike rack for my car.

W-Br	I can help you with that. We have several sizes available. ⁶³**What carrying capacity do you need?**
M-Au	Something small... ⁶³**one that can carry up to two bikes**, but no more.
W-Br	Here's a list of our models. We have just what you need.
M-Au	OK. ⁶⁴**Is it difficult to attach to the car? I hope it's not too complicated.**
W-Br	Don't worry. It comes with detailed, step-by-step instructions to install it.

여	**스미스 스포츠 장비에 오신 것을 환영합니다.** 무엇을 도와드릴까요?
남	안녕하세요, 어, 남동생과 종종 산으로 자전거를 타러 가는데, 차 외부에 부착할 자전거 고정대를 사고 싶어요.
여	제가 도와 드릴게요. 몇 가지 사이즈가 있는데요. **운반 용량은 어느 정도 필요하세요?**
남	작은 것… **자전거 2대까지 운반할 수 있는 것으로요,** 그 이상은 아니고요.
여	여기 모델 목록이에요. 고객님께 딱 필요한 게 있어요.
남	좋아요. **차에 부착하기가 어려운가요? 너무 복잡하지 않으면 좋겠어요.**
여	걱정하지 마세요. 자세한 단계별 설치 설명서가 함께 제공돼요.

| 어휘 | exterior 외부(의) bike rack 자전거 고정대 capacity 용량 attach 부착하다 complicated 복잡한 instructions (사용) 설명서 install 설치하다 |

Model	Capacity
Country	1
⁶³Classic	1-2
Premier	3-4
Deluxe	5

모델	용량
컨트리	1
⁶³클래식	1-2
프리미어	3-4
디럭스	5

62

What kind of products does the woman's store sell?

(A) Kitchen appliances
(B) **Sporting goods**
(C) Luggage
(D) Bathroom furnishings

여자의 매장에서는 어떤 제품을 판매하는가?

(A) 주방기기
(B) **스포츠용품**
(C) 여행 가방
(D) 욕실 비품

어휘 appliance 기기 furnishings 비품

해설 세부 사항 관련 – 여자의 매장에서 판매하는 제품의 종류

여자가 첫 대사에서 스미스 스포츠 장비에 오신 것을 환영한다(Welcome to Smith's Sports Equipment and More)고 했으므로 여자는 스포츠 장비 판매점의 점원임을 알 수 있다. 따라서 정답은 (B)이다.

63

Look at the graphic. Which model will the man buy?

(A) Country
(B) **Classic**
(C) Premier
(D) Deluxe

시각 정보에 의하면 남자는 어떤 모델을 살 것인가?

(A) 컨트리
(B) **클래식**
(C) 프리미어
(D) 디럭스

해설 시각 정보 연계 – 남자가 사려는 모델

여자가 두 번째 대사에서 운반 용량은 어느 정도 필요한지(What carrying capacity do you need?) 묻자 남자가 자전거 2대까지 운반할 수 있는 것으로 그 이상은 필요 없다(one that can carry up to two bikes, but no more)고 말하고 있다. 모델 목록에 따르면 용량이 2대인 것은 클래식이라고 나와 있으므로 정답은 (B)이다.

64

What is the man concerned about?

(A) A price
(B) A warranty
(C) **The installation**
(D) The quality

남자는 무엇을 걱정하는가?

(A) 가격
(B) 보증
(C) **설치**
(D) 품질

어휘 warranty 보증 installation 설치

해설 세부 사항 관련 – 남자의 우려 사항

남자가 마지막 대사에서 차에 부착하기가 어려운지(Is it difficult to attach to the car?) 물으며 너무 복잡하지 않았으면 좋겠다(I hope it's not too complicated)고 말하고 있는 것으로 보아 남자는 장비를 설치하는 일을 걱정하고 있음을 알 수 있다. 따라서 정답은 (C)이다.

> ▸▸ Paraphrasing 대화의 **attach to the car**
> → 정답의 **installation**

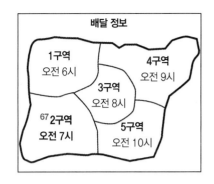

M-Au	Hello. ⁶⁵**This is Vogel's Laundry Service.**
W-Br	Hi. I'm calling from the Happy Stay Hotel on Forbes Avenue. ⁶⁵**We're looking for an outside service to wash the hotel's bedding and towels,** and I've heard good things about you.
M-Au	I'm glad to hear that. Our customers will tell you that we're very trustworthy— ⁶⁶**we're known for our reliable service.**
W-Br	So... ⁶⁷**what time would you be delivering our clean linens each day?**
M-Au	⁶⁷**It depends on the location. If you take a look at the online delivery map, you'll see that you're in Zone 2.**
W-Br	Oh, I see it now. That would work. The housekeeping staff doesn't start until nine o'clock, so that gives us plenty of time.

남	안녕하세요. **보겔 세탁소입니다.**
여	안녕하세요. 포브스 가에 있는 해피 스테이 호텔에서 전화 드립니다. **호텔의 침구와 수건을 세탁할 외부 서비스 업체를 찾고 있는데,** 거기가 평이 좋더군요.
남	그 말을 들으니 반갑네요. 고객님들이 저희가 아주 믿음직하다고 얘기하곤 하시죠. **저희는 믿을 수 있는 서비스로 유명하거든요.**
여	그럼… **매일 세탁이 끝난 침구와 수건을 몇 시에 배달해 주실 건가요?**
남	**위치에 따라 다릅니다. 온라인 배달 지도를 보시면 귀사는 2구역에 있다는 것을 알 수 있어요.**
여	아, 이제 보이네요. 괜찮을 것 같아요. 객실 담당 직원은 9시가 되어야 일을 시작하니까, 그러면 시간이 넉넉할 거예요.

어휘	laundry 세탁 bedding 침구 trustworthy 믿음직한 reliable 믿을 수 있는 housekeeping staff (호텔) 객실 담당 직원 plenty of 넉넉한

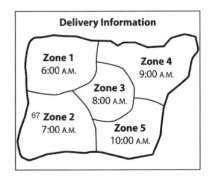

Delivery Information

Zone 1 6:00 A.M.
Zone 4 9:00 A.M.
Zone 3 8:00 A.M.
⁶⁷ Zone 2 7:00 A.M.
Zone 5 10:00 A.M.

65

What type of business is the woman calling?

(A) A catering company
(B) A laundry service
(C) A flower shop
(D) A furniture store

여자는 어떤 종류의 업체에 전화하고 있는가?

(A) 출장 요리 업체
(B) 세탁 서비스 업체
(C) 꽃집
(D) 가구점

해설 전체 내용 관련 – 여자가 전화하고 있는 업체

남자가 첫 대사에서 보겔 세탁소(This is Vogel's Laundry Service)라고 하며 전화를 받았고, 여자가 뒤이어 호텔의 침구와 수건을 세탁할 외부 서비스 업체를 찾고 있다(We're looking for an outside service to wash the hotel's bedding and towels)고 말하고 있으므로 정답은 (B)이다.

66

What does the man say his company is known for?

(A) Its prices
(B) Its locations
(C) Its reliability
(D) Its products

남자는 자신의 업체가 무엇으로 유명하다고 말하는가?

(A) 가격
(B) 위치
(C) 신뢰성
(D) 제품

해설 세부 사항 관련 – 남자가 자신의 업체가 유명하다고 말하는 것

남자가 두 번째 대사에서 우리는 믿을 수 있는 서비스로 유명하다(we're known for our reliable service)고 말하고 있으므로 정답은 (C)이다.

67

Look at the graphic. What time will the delivery be made?

(A) 6:00 A.M.
(B) 7:00 A.M.
(C) 8:00 A.M.
(D) 9:00 A.M.

시각 정보에 의하면 배달은 몇 시에 이루어질 것인가?

(A) 오전 6시
(B) 오전 7시
(C) 오전 8시
(D) 오전 9시

해설 시각 정보 연계 - 배달이 이루어질 시간

여자가 두 번째 대화에서 매일 세탁이 끝난 침구와 수건을 몇 시에 배달해 주는지(what time would you be delivering our clean linens each day?) 묻자, 남자가 위치에 따라 다르다(It depends on the location)고 알려 주며 온라인 배달 지도를 보면 귀사는 2구역에 있다는 것을 알 수 있다(If you take a look at the online delivery map, you'll see that you're in Zone 2)고 설명하고 있다. 지도에 따르면 2구역은 배송 시간이 오전 7시라고 나와 있으므로 정답은 (B)이다.

68-70 대화 + 일정표

W-Am	Hello, Midtown Health Clinic.
M-Au	Hi. [68]**I have an appointment scheduled with Dr. Miller for two o'clock on Wednesday, but I need to change it. I have an important client meeting I need to attend.**
W-Am	OK. What time would you be able to come in?
M-Au	Well, [69]**I get out of work at five o'clock, so any time after that is fine.**
W-Am	[69]**Dr. Miller doesn't have anything past four o'clock this week. But there's an opening at five thirty on Friday with a different doctor?**
M-Au	OK, that's fine.
W-Am	Great. [70]**Let me ask you a few questions to be sure that none of your information has changed.**

여	안녕하세요, 미드타운 병원입니다.
남	안녕하세요. **수요일 2시에 밀러 박사님과 예약이 잡혀 있는데, 바꿔야겠어요. 참석해야 할 중요한 고객 회의가 있어서요.**
여	좋아요. 몇 시에 올 수 있으세요?
남	음, **5시에 퇴근하니까 그 이후에는 아무때나 괜찮아요.**
여	**이번 주에 밀러 박사님은 4시 이후에 진료가 없어요. 하지만 금요일 5시 30분에 다른 의사 선생님 일정이 비네요?**
남	네, 좋습니다.
여	잘됐네요. **고객님 정보가 변경되지 않았는지 확인차 몇 가지 여쭐게요.**

어휘	attend 참석하다 past 지나서

Doctor	Work Hours (Monday-Friday)
Dr. Fontana	8:00 A.M.-5:00 P.M.
Dr. Miller	10:00 A.M.-4:00 P.M.
[69]Dr. Smith	10:00 A.M.-6:00 P.M.
Dr. Yang	8:00 A.M.-3:00 P.M.

의사	근무 시간(월-금)
폰타나 박사	오전 8시-오후 5시
밀러 박사	오전 10시-오후 4시
[69]**스미스 박사**	**오전 10시-오후 6시**
양 박사	오전 8시-오후 3시

68

Why does the man want to change an appointment?

(A) His car broke down.
(B) He has to attend a meeting.
(C) He has a family event.
(D) He has to wait for a delivery.

남자는 왜 예약을 바꾸고 싶어 하는가?

(A) 차가 고장났다.
(B) 회의에 참석해야 한다.
(C) 가족 행사가 있다.
(D) 배송을 기다려야 한다.

어휘 break down 고장나다   delivery 배송

해설 세부 사항 관련 - 남자가 예약을 바꾸려는 이유

남자가 첫 대사에서 수요일 2시에 밀러 박사님과 예약이 잡혀 있는데, 바꿔야겠다(I have an appointment scheduled with Dr. Miller for two o'clock on Wednesday, but I need to change it)면서 참석해야 할 중요한 고객 회의가 있다(I have an important client meeting I need to attend)고 이유를 말하고 있으므로 정답은 (B)이다.

69

Look at the graphic. Who will the man see on Friday?

(A) Dr. Fontana
(B) Dr. Miller
(C) Dr. Smith
(D) Dr. Yang

시각 정보에 의하면 남자는 금요일에 누구를 만날 것인가?

(A) 폰타나 박사
(B) 밀러 박사
(C) 스미스 박사
(D) 양 박사

해설 시각 정보 연계 - 남자가 금요일에 만날 사람

남자가 두 번째 대사에서 5시에 퇴근하니까 그 이후에는 아무때나 괜찮다 (I get out of work at five o'clock, so any time after that is fine)고 말하자, 여자가 이번 주에 밀러 박사님은 4시 이후에 진료가 없다(Dr. Miller doesn't have anything past four o'clock this week)면서 하지만 금요일 5시 30분에 다른 의사 선생님 일정이 비어 있다(But there's an opening at five thirty on Friday with a different doctor?)고 알려 주고 있다. 일정표에 따르면 오후 5시 이후에 진료를 보는 의사는 스미스 박사뿐이므로 정답은 (C)이다.

70

What will the man most likely do next?

(A) Answer some questions
(B) Visit a Web site
(C) Make a payment
(D) Drive to an office

남자는 다음에 무엇을 하겠는가?

(A) 질문에 대답
(B) 웹사이트 방문
(C) 결제
(D) 사무실까지 운전

해설 세부 사항 관련 - 남자가 다음에 할 일

여자가 마지막 대사에서 남자에게 고객님의 정보가 변경되지 않았는지 확인차 몇 가지 묻겠다(Let me ask you a few questions to be sure that none of your information has changed)고 했으므로 남자는 여자가 묻는 질문에 대답할 것임을 알 수 있다. 따라서 정답은 (A)이다.

PART 4

71-73 녹음 메시지

W-Am **⁷¹Hello, Fairview Apartment residents.** This is your property manager. **⁷²Due to repairs to the main water line along Chasman Boulevard, water service to all units at Fairview will be temporarily shut off on July fifteenth.** I estimate that regular service will resume fully by five o'clock, though **⁷³I recommend checking the building's social media page periodically. There'll be updates posted about possible delays.** Thank you in advance for your patience and understanding.

안녕하세요, 페어뷰 아파트 주민 여러분. 저는 건물 관리자입니다. 채스먼 대로변에 있는 주 수도관 보수 공사 때문에 7월 15일 페어뷰의 모든 가구에 수도 서비스가 일시 중단됩니다. 5시까지는 정규 서비스가 온전히 재개되리라 예상하지만, 주기적으로 건물의 소셜 미디어 페이지를 확인하시기를 권합니다. 혹시 있을지 모르는 지연에 대한 최신 정보가 게시됩니다. 안내와 이해에 미리 감사드립니다.

어휘 property 건물, 부동산 repair 수리 temporarily 일시로 estimate 예상하다 resume 재개되다 periodically 주기적으로 patience 인내

71

Who are the listeners?

(A) Residents in an apartment building
(B) Employees in an office building
(C) Visitors to a historical site
(D) Guests in a hotel

청자들은 누구인가?

(A) 아파트 주민
(B) 사무용 건물의 직원
(C) 사적지 방문자
(D) 호텔 투숙객

어휘 historical site 사적지

해설 전체 내용 관련 - 청자들의 신분

화자가 도입부에 청자들에게 인사(Hello)하며 페어뷰 아파트 주민 여러분(Fairview Apartment residents)이라고 부르고 있으므로 정답은 (A)이다.

72

What service does the speaker say will be unavailable?

(A) Telephone
(B) Electric
(C) Water
(D) Natural gas

화자는 어떤 서비스를 이용할 수 없을 것이라고 말하는가?

(A) 전화
(B) 전기
(C) 수도
(D) 천연가스

해설 세부 사항 관련 - 화자가 이용할 수 없다고 말하는 서비스

화자가 초반부에 채스먼 대로변에 있는 주 수도관 보수 공사 때문에 7월 15일 페어뷰의 모든 가구에 수도 서비스가 일시 중단된다(Due to repairs to the main water line along Chasman Boulevard, water service to all units at Fairview will be temporarily shut off on July fifteenth)고 했으므로 정답은 (C)이다.

73

According to the speaker, why should the listeners go online?

(A) To download software
(B) To check for status updates
(C) To register a complaint
(D) To view a price list

화자의 말에 따르면, 청자들은 왜 인터넷에 접속해야 하는가?

(A) 소프트웨어를 내려받으려고
(B) 상황에 관한 최신 정보를 확인하려고
(C) 불만을 표현하려고
(D) 가격표를 보려고

어휘 status 상황 register (감정을) 표하다, 나타내다

해설 세부 사항 관련 - 화자가 청자들이 인터넷에 접속해야 한다고 말하는 이유

화자가 후반부에 주기적으로 건물의 소셜 미디어 페이지를 확인하기를 권한다(I recommend checking the building's social media page periodically)면서, 혹시 있을지 모르는 지연에 대한 최신 정보가 게시된다(There'll be updates posted about possible delays)고 알려 주고 있으므로 정답은 (B)이다.

74-76 공지

> W-Br ⁷⁴**Before we begin tonight's dinner shift, I have some announcements.** ⁷⁵**Our grilled tuna dish was so popular last night that we actually sold out of it for the rest of the weekend. Please let diners know that it's not available.** Also, we'll be dividing up the servers this evening—half of you will be working in the main dining room, and the rest of you will be in the special-events room for a private party. ⁷⁶**It's going to be a busy evening, so I encourage you to help each other provide great service for our customers.**

> 오늘 저녁 식사 근무를 시작하기 전에 몇 가지 공지 사항이 있어요. 어젯밤에 참치구이가 너무 인기가 많아서 실은 남은 주말 판매분이 다 팔렸어요. 손님들께 참치구이는 안 된다고 알려 주세요. 또 오늘 저녁에는 웨이터를 나눌 예정입니다. 절반은 메인 식당에서 일하고 나머지 절반은 비공개 파티가 열리는 특별 행사 룸에서 일할 겁니다. 바쁜 저녁이 될 테니 서로 도와서 손님들께 좋은 서비스를 제공해 주세요.

> 어휘 shift (교대) 근무 divide 나누다 server 웨이터 encourage 권장하다

74

Where does the announcement most likely take place?

(A) At a train station
(B) At a convention center
(C) At a restaurant
(D) At an outdoor market

어디에서 발표되는 공지이겠는가?

(A) 기차역
(B) 컨벤션 센터
(C) 식당
(D) 노천 시장

해설 전체 내용 관련 - 공지의 장소

화자가 도입부에 오늘 저녁 식사 근무를 시작하기 전에 몇 가지 공지 사항이 있다(Before we begin tonight's dinner shift, I have some announcements)고 말하는 것으로 보아 화자는 식당 직원들을 대상으로 공지를 하는 중임을 알 수 있다. 따라서 정답은 (C)이다.

75

According to the speaker, what should customers be told?

(A) The Wi-Fi is not working.
(B) A room is closed for renovations.
(C) A schedule has been changed.
(D) An item is unavailable.

화자의 말에 따르면, 고객에게 무엇을 알려야 하는가?

(A) 와이파이가 작동하지 않는다.
(B) 수리 때문에 룸이 폐쇄되었다.
(C) 일정이 변경되었다.
(D) 어떤 품목을 이용할 수 없다.

해설 세부 사항 관련 - 화자가 고객에게 알려야 한다고 말하는 것

화자가 초반부에 어젯밤에 참치구이가 너무 인기가 많아서 남은 주말 판매분이 다 팔렸다(Our grilled tuna dish was so popular last night that we actually sold out of it for the rest of the weekend)면서 손님들께 참치구이는 안 된다고 알려 주라(Please let diners know that it's not available)고 말하고 있으므로 정답은 (D)이다.

76

What does the speaker encourage the listeners to do?

(A) Work together
(B) Arrive early
(C) Take extra shifts
(D) Greet customers

화자는 청자들에게 무엇을 하라고 권장하는가?

(A) 협력하기
(B) 일찍 도착하기
(C) 추가 근무하기
(D) 고객 맞이하기

해설 세부 사항 관련 - 화자가 청자들에게 권장하는 것

화자가 마지막에 바쁜 저녁이 될 테니 서로 도와서 손님들께 좋은 서비스를 제공할 것(It's going to be a busy evening, so I encourage you to help each other provide great service for our customers)을 권하고 있으므로 정답은 (A)이다.

> ▸▸ Paraphrasing 담화의 help each other
> → 정답의 Work together

W-Am Good morning! **77 I really appreciate this opportunity to talk to you about investing in our company. After hearing my presentation, you'll see that our latest product is a worthwhile investment. 78 Cygni Fashions has been selling business suits for more than 30 years.** Last summer, when the weather was unusually hot, we decided to design suits that would be comfortable to wear when it's hot outside. People who wear these suits remain cool, regardless of the temperature. Now, these suits have become so popular that we cannot keep up with the demand. **79 With your investment, we'll be able to purchase some advanced machinery that would allow us to triple our production.**

안녕하세요! 당사 투자 건에 대해 이야기할 수 있는 기회를 주셔서 정말 감사합니다. 제 발표를 듣고 나면 당사 최신 제품이 투자할 가치가 있다는 것을 알게 되실 겁니다. 시그니 패션은 30년 넘게 정장을 판매해 왔습니다. 지난 여름은 날씨가 유난히 더워서 당사는 밖이 더울 때도 입기 편한 양복을 디자인하기로 결정했습니다. 이 양복을 입은 사람은 기온에 상관없이 시원하게 지냅니다. 이제 이 양복은 매우 인기가 많아져서 수요를 따라잡을 수가 없습니다. 여러분이 투자하시면 당사는 생산량을 3배 늘릴 수 있는 첨단 기계를 구입할 수 있을 것입니다.

어휘 appreciate 감사하다 opportunity 기회 worthwhile 가치가 있는 unusually 유난히 comfortable 편안한 regardless of ~에 상관없이 temperature 기온 keep up with ~을 따라잡다 demand 수요 triple 3배 늘리다

77

Who most likely are the listeners?
(A) Building contractors
(B) Potential investors
(C) Fashion models
(D) News reporters

청자들은 누구이겠는가?
(A) 건축 도급업자
(B) 잠재 투자자
(C) 패션 모델
(D) 기자

어휘 contractor 도급업자 potential 잠재적인

해설 전체 내용 관련 – 청자들의 신분
화자가 초반부에 당사 투자 건에 대해 이야기할 수 있는 기회를 줘서 정말 감사하다(I really appreciate this opportunity to talk to you about investing in our company)고 했고, 발표를 듣고 나면 당사 최신 제품이 투자할 가치가 있다는 걸 알게 될 것(After hearing my presentation, you'll see that our latest product is a worthwhile investment)이라고 말하고 있으므로 정답은 (B)이다.

78

What type of clothing does the company sell?
(A) Swimwear
(B) Hats
(C) Business suits
(D) Athletic shoes

회사는 어떤 종류의 의류를 판매하는가?
(A) 수영복
(B) 모자
(C) 정장
(D) 운동화

해설 세부 사항 관련 – 회사가 판매하는 의류의 종류
화자가 중반부에 시그니 패션은 30년 넘게 정장을 판매해 왔다(Cygni Fashions has been selling business suits for more than 30 years)고 말하고 있으므로 정답은 (C)이다.

79

What does the speaker's company hope to purchase?
(A) A new software program
(B) A larger storage facility
(C) Some delivery trucks
(D) Some manufacturing equipment

화자의 회사는 무엇을 구입하기를 원하는가?
(A) 새로운 소프트웨어 프로그램
(B) 더 넓은 저장 시설
(C) 배송 트럭
(D) 제조 장비

어휘 facility 시설 manufacturing 제조

해설 세부 사항 관련 – 화자의 회사가 구입하기를 원하는 것
화자가 마지막에 여러분이 투자하면 당사는 생산량을 3배 늘릴 수 있는 첨단 기계를 구입할 수 있을 것(With your investment, we'll be able to purchase some advanced machinery that would allow us to triple our production)이라고 말하고 있으므로 정답은 (D)이다.

▶▶ Paraphrasing 담화의 machinery → 정답의 equipment

M-Cn I'm Thomas Ortiz, head of Human Resources here at Hamilton Power. On behalf of the company, **80 I want to welcome you all to your new jobs. As you know, this is our most advanced power plant, and we provide electricity to over a half-million homes. 81 I'm sure you're all eager to go to your workstations. But there is a lot of paperwork to fill out.** I'll be going over it with you in a moment But first, **82 I'd like to take your pictures for your ID badges.** They'll be ready for you after lunch.

저는 해밀턴 파워의 인사부장 토마스 오티즈입니다. 회사를 대표해서 **새로운 직장에 오신 여러분 모두를 환영합니다.** 아시다시피 이곳은 최첨단 발전소로, 당사는 50만이 넘는 가정에 전기를 공급하고 있습니다. 여러분 모두 작업 장소에 몹시 가고 싶을 텐데요. 하지만 작성해야 할 서류가 많습니다. 곧 여러분과 함께 다시 살펴볼게요. 하지만 먼저 **신분증용 사진부터 찍었으면 합니다.** 신분증은 점심 식사 후에 준비될 거예요.

어휘 on behalf of ~을 대표해 advanced 첨단의
power plant 발전소 electricity 전기 eager to 몹시 ~하고 싶은 workstation 작업 장소 fill out ~을 작성하다 go over ~을 살펴보다

80

What industry do the listeners most likely work in?

(A) Construction
(B) Retail
(C) Energy
(D) Broadcast

청자들은 어떤 업종에서 일하겠는가?

(A) 건축
(B) 소매
(C) 에너지
(D) 방송

해설 전체 내용 관련 - 청자들의 근무 분야

화자가 초반부에 새로운 직장에 오신 여러분 모두를 환영한다(I want to welcome you all to your new jobs)면서, 이곳은 최첨단 발전소로 당사는 50만이 넘는 가정에 전기를 공급하고 있다(this is our most advanced power plant, and we provide electricity to over a half-million homes)고 말하고 있으므로 청자들의 근무지는 전력 발전소임을 알 수 있다. 따라서 정답은 (C)이다.

▸▸ Paraphrasing   담화의 **power & electricity**
→ 정답의 **Energy**

81

What does the speaker imply when he says, "But there is a lot of paperwork to fill out"?

(A) The listeners may have to work overtime.
(B) **The listeners will not begin work immediately.**
(C) A permit will be difficult to obtain.
(D) Additional help is needed for a project.

화자가 "하지만 작성해야 할 서류가 많습니다"라고 말하는 의도는 무엇인가?

(A) 청자들은 초과 근무를 해야 할 수도 있다.
(B) **청자들은 당장 일을 시작하지 않을 것이다.**
(C) 허가를 얻기 어려울 것이다.
(D) 프로젝트에 추가 지원이 필요하다.

어휘 work overtime 초과 근무를 하다 immediately 당장 permit 허가(증) obtain 얻다

해설 화자의 의도 파악 - 하지만 작성해야 할 서류가 많다는 말의 의도

앞에서 여러분 모두 작업 장소에 몹시 가고 싶을 것(I'm sure you're all eager to go to your workstations)이라고 말한 뒤 인용문을 언급한 것으로 보아, 아직 작성해야 할 서류들이 남아 있어서 당장 작업장으로 가서 작업을 시작하지는 않을 것이라는 의도로 한 말임을 알 수 있다. 따라서 정답은 (B)이다.

82

What will the speaker do next?

(A) **Take some photographs**
(B) Look at a model home
(C) Collect some viewer feedback
(D) Go to the cafeteria

화자는 다음에 무엇을 할 것인가?

(A) **사진 찍기**
(B) 모델 하우스 보기
(C) 시청자 의견 수렴하기
(D) 구내식당에 가기

어휘 viewer 시청자

해설 세부 사항 관련 - 화자가 다음에 할 일

화자가 후반부에 신분증용 사진부터 찍었으면 한다(I'd like to take your pictures for your ID badges)고 말하고 있으므로 정답은 (A)이다.

▸▸ Paraphrasing   담화의 **take your pictures**
→ 정답의 **Take some photographs**

83-85 전화 메시지

M-Au Hi, Mario. **83**I'm calling about tonight. I know you plan to be at the product launch in Holtsville to announce the release of our new smartphone. **84**You mentioned that you're taking the red subway line to that event. Well, I just found out that the subway line is closed unexpectedly for repairs. So, I wanted to let you know, I'll be driving to Holtsville from the office. Now, I have to make one stop on the way. **85**I have to pick up the promotional materials that'll be handed out to attendees—those phone cases with our company logo. But there's plenty of time to pick the cases up and still make it to the product launch before it starts.

안녕하세요, 마리오. **오늘밤 일 때문에 전화해요.** 당신이 새 스마트폰의 출시를 알리기 위해 홀츠빌에서 열리는 제품 출시 행사에 간다고 알고 있어요. 그 행사에 빨간색 지하철 노선으로 간다고 하셨잖아요. 흠, 방금 알아보니 지하철이 수리 때문에 예기치 않게 폐쇄됐다고 하네요. 그래서 제가 사무실에서 홀츠빌까지 운전해서 간다는 걸 알려 드리고 싶었어요. 저, 가는 길에 한 군데 들러야 해요. **참석자들에게 나눠줄 판촉물을 찾으**

러 가야 해요. 우리 로고가 있는 핸드폰 케이스예요. 하지만 시간이 넉넉하니까 케이스를 찾고도 제품 출시 시작 전에 도착할 거예요.

> 어휘 launch 출시 release 출시 unexpectedly 예기치 않게
> repair 수리 promotional 판촉의 hand out ~을 나눠주다
> attendee 참석자 make it 제시간에 도착하다

83

According to the speaker, what event will be held tonight?

(A) An anniversary party
(B) A press conference
(C) A board meeting
(D) A product launch

화자의 말에 따르면, 오늘밤에 어떤 행사가 열릴 것인가?

(A) 기념일 파티
(B) 기자 회견
(C) 이사회
(D) **제품 출시**

해설 세부 사항 관련 - 화자가 오늘밤에 열린다고 말한 행사

화자가 초반부에 오늘밤 일 때문에 전화한다(I'm calling about tonight)면서, 청자가 새 스마트폰의 출시를 알리기 위해 홀츠빌에서 열리는 제품 출시 행사에 갈 계획임을 알고 있다(I know you plan to be at the product launch in Holtsville to announce the release of our new smartphone)고 말하고 있으므로 정답은 (D)이다.

84

Why does the speaker say, "I'll be driving to Holtsville from the office"?

(A) To correct a mistake
(B) To provide an excuse
(C) To make an offer
(D) To request directions

화자가 "제가 사무실에서 홀츠빌까지 운전해서 간다"라고 말하는 이유는 무엇인가?

(A) 오류를 바로잡으려고
(B) 변명하려고
(C) **제안하려고**
(D) 길 안내를 요청하려고

해설 화자의 의도 파악 - 제가 사무실에서 홀츠빌까지 운전해서 간다는 말의 의도

화자가 초반부에 당신이 그 행사에 빨간색 지하철 노선으로 간다고 말했다(You mentioned that you're taking the red subway line to that event)면서 지하철이 수리 때문에 예기치 않게 폐쇄됐다는 것을 알게 되었다(Well, I just found out that the subway line is closed unexpectedly for repairs)고 덧붙이며 그래서 당신에게 알리고 싶었다(So, I wanted to let you know)고 말한 뒤 인용문을 언급한 것으로 보아, 청자가 지하철을 타고 이동하기는 불가능하게 되었고 본인이 홀츠빌까지 운전해서 갈 것이므로 태워 주겠다는 제안을 하려는 의도로 한 말임을 알 수 있다. 따라서 정답은 (C)이다.

85

What does the speaker say he needs to pick up?

(A) Some promotional materials
(B) Some refreshments
(C) Customer surveys
(D) Event programs

화자는 자신이 무엇을 찾아야 한다고 말하는가?

(A) **판촉물**
(B) 다과
(C) 고객 설문 조사서
(D) 행사 프로그램

어휘 refreshments 다과

해설 세부 사항 관련 - 화자가 찾아야 한다고 말한 것

화자가 후반부에 참석자들에게 나눠줄 판촉물을 찾으러 가야 한다(I have to pick up the promotional materials that'll be handed out to attendees)고 말하고 있으므로 정답은 (A)이다.

86-88 소개

> M-Cn **86 Welcome to this computer security workshop, hosted by the IT Department.** This workshop is intended to be interactive, so please ask questions at any time. We scheduled the workshop because **87 several employees' computers have recently become infected with a virus**, and they had to be fixed. OK, so the first thing I'm going to show you is how to update your security software. **88 Please open the program by clicking on the icon on the right-hand side of your computer screen.**

> **IT 부서에서 주최하는 컴퓨터 보안 워크숍에 오신 것을 환영합니다.** 본 워크숍은 대화형으로 할 계획이므로 언제든지 질문하세요. **몇몇 직원의 컴퓨터가 최근 바이러스에 감염되어** 고쳐야 했기 때문에 워크숍 일정을 잡았습니다. 자, 먼저 보여 드릴 것은 보안 소프트웨어를 업데이트하는 방법인데요. **컴퓨터 화면 오른쪽에 있는 아이콘을 클릭해서 프로그램을 여세요.**

> 어휘 security 보안 intend to ~하려고 의도[계획]하다
> interactive 대화형의 recently 최근에 infect 감염시키다
> fix 고치다

86

Which department does the speaker most likely work for?

(A) Product Development
(B) Research
(C) Engineering
(D) Information Technology

화자는 어느 부서에서 근무하겠는가?
(A) 제품 개발
(B) 연구
(C) 엔지니어링
(D) 정보 기술

해설 전체 내용 관련 - 화자의 근무 부서

화자가 도입부에 IT 부서에서 주최하는 컴퓨터 보안 워크숍에 온 것을 환영한다(Welcome to this computer security workshop, hosted by the IT Department)고 말하고 있으므로 정답은 (D)이다.

▸▸ **Paraphrasing** 담화의 **IT** → 정답의 **Information Technology**

87

What does the speaker say recently happened?

(A) Some certification classes began.
(B) Name badges were handed out.
(C) **A virus infected some computers.**
(D) A manager retired.

화자는 최근에 무슨 일이 있었다고 말하는가?
(A) 자격증 수업이 시작되었다.
(B) 명찰이 배부되었다.
(C) 바이러스가 일부 컴퓨터를 감염시켰다.
(D) 관리자가 퇴직했다.

어휘 certification 자격(증) retire 퇴직[은퇴]하다

해설 세부 사항 관련 - 화자가 최근에 있었다고 말한 일

화자가 중반부에 몇몇 직원의 컴퓨터가 최근 바이러스에 감염되었다(several employees' computers have recently become infected with a virus)고 말하고 있으므로 정답은 (C)이다.

88

What does the speaker ask the listeners to do?

(A) Sign an attendance sheet
(B) **Open a software program**
(C) Submit some photos
(D) View a slideshow

화자는 청자들에게 무엇을 해 달라고 요청하는가?
(A) 출석부에 서명하기
(B) 소프트웨어 프로그램 열기
(C) 사진 제출하기
(D) 슬라이드쇼 보기

어휘 attendance 출석

해설 세부 사항 관련 - 화자의 요청 사항

화자가 마지막에 컴퓨터 화면 오른쪽에 있는 아이콘을 클릭해서 프로그램을 열라(Please open the program by clicking on the icon on the right-hand side of your computer screen)고 요청하고 있으므로 정답은 (B)이다.

89-91 회의 발췌

M-Au OK, let's get started—there's a lot to cover! First, [89]**I want to thank the Web design team for joining this weekly check-in of our editorial staff and reporters.** An online organization like ours relies heavily on the support of its design and technical staff. Today [89]**I'd like to discuss adding a section to the site that features our most popular news stories.** [90]**Many other news sites already have a popular stories section. I'm concerned that we're not keeping up with them, and it could affect our readership.** Now, [91]**I realize you're all busy, but I don't think this will involve too much work.** Plus, remember, we have technology interns starting next week.

좋습니다, 시작하죠. 다뤄야 할 사안이 많아요! 먼저 편집진과 기자들의 주간 점검 회의에 참여해 주신 웹 디자인팀에게 감사드려요. 저희 같은 온라인 조직은 디자인과 기술 인력의 지원에 크게 의존하고 있죠. 오늘 저는 가장 인기 있는 뉴스 기사를 특집으로 다루는 섹션을 사이트에 추가하는 문제를 논의하고 싶어요. 다른 많은 뉴스 사이트에는 이미 인기 기사 섹션이 있어요. 우리가 그들을 따라잡지 못하고 있어서 독자 수에 영향을 미칠까 봐 걱정돼요. 다들 바쁘시겠지만, 일이 그렇게 많지는 않을 것 같아요. 그리고 기억하세요. 다음 주부터 기술직 인턴들이 온다는 걸요.

어휘 check-in 점검 organization 조직 rely on ~에 의존하다 heavily 크게 feature (특집으로) 다루다 concerned 걱정하는 keep up with ~을 따라잡다 affect 영향을 미치다 readership 독자 수

89

Where do the listeners most likely work?

(A) At a software development company
(B) At a book publishing company
(C) At a graphic design firm
(D) **At a news Web site**

청자들은 어디에서 일하겠는가?
(A) 소프트웨어 개발 회사
(B) 서적 출판사
(C) 그래픽 디자인 회사
(D) 뉴스 웹사이트

해설 전체 내용 관련 - 청자들의 근무지

화자가 초반부에 편집진과 기자들의 주간 점검 회의에 참여해 준 웹 디자인팀에게 감사한다(I want to thank the Web design team for joining this weekly check-in of our editorial staff and reporters)고 했고, 담화 중반부에서 가장 인기 있는 뉴스 기사를 특집으로 다루는 섹션을 사이트에 추가하는 문제를 논의하고 싶다(I'd like to discuss adding a section to the site that features our most popular news stories)고 한 것으로 보아 청자들은 뉴스를 주로 다루는 온라인 조직에서 일하고 있음을 알 수 있다. 따라서 정답은 (D)이다.

90

What is the speaker concerned about?

(A) Addressing a customer complaint
(B) Keeping up with competitors
(C) Exceeding an annual budget
(D) Improving employee productivity

화자는 무엇을 걱정하는가?

(A) 고객 불만 사항 해결
(B) 경쟁사 따라잡기
(C) 연간 예산 초과
(D) 직원 생산성 향상

어휘 address 해결하다 competitor 경쟁사 exceed 초과하다
annual 연간의 budget 예산 improve 향상시키다
productivity 생산성

해설 세부 사항 관련 - 화자의 우려 사항

화자가 중반부에 다른 많은 뉴스 사이트에는 이미 인기 기사 섹션이 있다
(Many other news sites already have a popular stories section)
면서, 우리가 그들을 따라잡지 못하고 있어서 독자 수에 영향을 미칠까
봐 걱정된다(I'm concerned that we're not keeping up with them,
and it could affect our readership)고 말하고 있으므로 정답은 (B)
이다.

91

What does the speaker imply when he says, "we
have technology interns starting next week"?

(A) A task must be finished soon.
(B) An assignment should be delayed.
(C) Volunteers are needed to greet interns.
(D) Interns can assist with a new project.

화자가 "다음 주부터 기술직 인턴들이 온다"라고 말하는 의도는 무엇인가?

(A) 일을 빨리 끝내야 한다.
(B) 업무가 연기되어야 한다.
(C) 인턴들을 맞이하려면 자원봉사자가 필요하다.
(D) 인턴들이 새로운 프로젝트를 도울 수 있다.

어휘 assignment 업무, 과제

해설 화자의 의도 파악 - 다음 주부터 기술직 인턴들이 온다는 말의 의도

화자가 후반부에 다들 바쁘겠지만 일이 그렇게 많지는 않을 것 같다(I
realize you're all busy, but I don't think this will involve too
much work)고 말한 뒤 인용문을 언급한 것으로 보아, 다음 주에 기술직
인턴들이 합류해 일을 도울 것이므로 업무 부담이 줄어들 것이라는 의도로
한 말임을 알 수 있다. 따라서 정답은 (D)이다.

92-94 방송

M-Cn Hello. ⁹²**This is Jie Liu, reporting live from
the Benton Public Library.** ⁹³**Starting next week,
the library will be undergoing major renovations.**
A new section will be added to the east side of
this building. The addition will include a larger
children's section and a computer lab. ⁹⁴**The library
will be open during the renovations, though
you may want to bring earplugs to wear. Susan
Anderson, the head librarian, warns that the
construction will be noisy.** And now, back to the
studio.

안녕하세요. 지에 리우입니다. 벤턴 공공 도서관에서 생방송으로 보도하
고 있는데요. 다음 주부터 도서관에서 대대적인 수리가 진행될 예정입니
다. 이 건물 동쪽에 새로운 구역이 추가됩니다. 추가된 구역에는 더 넓
은 어린이 구역과 컴퓨터실이 포함됩니다. 수리하는 동안 도서관은 문을
열겠지만, 귀마개를 가져와서 써야 할 수도 있습니다. 도서관장인 수잔
앤더슨은 공사로 시끄러울 거라고 경고하고 있습니다. 자, 다시 스튜디
오 나와 주세요.

어휘 undergo 진행하다 renovation 수리 earplug 귀마개
head librarian 도서관장 construction 공사

92

Where is the speaker?

(A) At a public library
(B) At a history museum
(C) At a community center
(D) At a sports arena

화자는 어디에 있는가?

(A) 공공 도서관
(B) 역사 박물관
(C) 주민 센터
(D) 스포츠 경기장

해설 전체 내용 관련 - 화자가 있는 장소

화자가 도입부에 벤턴 공공 도서관에서 생방송으로 보도하고 있는 지에 리
우(This is Jie Liu, reporting live from the Benton Public Library)
라고 자신을 소개하고 있으므로 정답은 (A)이다.

93

What will happen next week?

(A) A new exhibit will be set up.
(B) A fund-raiser will take place.
(C) A local election will be held.
(D) A construction project will begin.

다음 주에 무슨 일이 있을 것인가?

(A) 새로운 전시회가 준비된다.
(B) 모금 행사가 있다.
(C) 지방 선거가 있다.
(D) 공사 프로젝트가 시작된다.

어휘 exhibit 전시회 fund-raiser 모금 행사 election 선거

해설 세부 사항 관련 - 다음 주에 일어날 일

화자가 초반부에 다음 주부터 도서관에서 대대적인 수리가 진행될 예정(Starting next week, the library will be undergoing major renovations)이라고 말하고 있으므로 정답은 (D)이다.

> ▸▸ Paraphrasing 담화의 major renovations
> → 정답의 A construction project

94

What are visitors encouraged to do?

(A) Park on a side street
(B) Wear ear protection
(C) Donate money
(D) Take photographs

방문객들은 무엇을 하도록 권고받는가?

(A) 골목에 주차하기
(B) 귀 보호 장비 착용하기
(C) 돈 기부하기
(D) 사진 찍기

어휘 donate 기부하다

해설 세부 사항 관련 - 방문객들이 권고받은 일

화자가 후반부에 수리하는 동안 도서관은 문을 열겠지만 귀마개를 가져와서 써야 할 수도 있다(The library will be open during the renovations, though you may want to bring earplugs to wear)면서 도서관장인 수잔 앤더슨은 공사로 시끄러울 거라고 경고하고 있다(Susan Anderson, the head librarian, warns that the construction will be noisy)고 했으므로 정답은 (B)이다.

> ▸▸ Paraphrasing 담화의 earplugs → 정답의 ear protection

95-97 안내 방송 + 매장 지도

W-Br Attention shoppers! ⁹⁵Thanks for coming to Link Office Superstore's annual sale. We offer the best prices in town on office supplies, desks, and chairs. There are a lot of people here for our special deals today, so lines for the cashiers are rather long. ⁹⁶To help speed up the checkout process, please use the express lane located near the exit if you're buying five items or fewer. Also, ⁹⁷if you're purchasing a large item and need help moving it, just let one of the employees know and they'll help you bring the item to your vehicle.

쇼핑객 여러분! 링크 오피스 슈퍼스토어 연례 할인 행사에 와 주셔서 감사합니다. 저희는 사무용품, 책상, 의자를 시내 최고의 가격으로 제공하고 있습니다. 오늘 특별 할인 행사에 많은 분이 오셔서 계산원 줄이 좀 깁니다. 계산 과정의 속도를 높이기 위해, 5개 이하 품목을 구입하시려는 경우 출구 근처에 있는 빠른 계산대를 이용하세요. 또한 대형 품목을

구입하고 이동에 도움이 필요하신 경우, 직원 중 한 명에게 알려 주시면 해당 품목을 차량까지 옮기는 것을 도와 드리겠습니다.

어휘 annual 연례의 purchase 구입하다 vehicle 차량

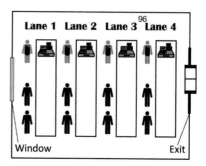

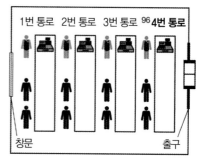

95

Where is the announcement being made?

(A) At a supermarket
(B) At a clothing store
(C) At an office supply store
(D) At a home garden center

어디에서 나오는 안내 방송인가?

(A) 슈퍼마켓
(B) 옷가게
(C) 사무용품 매장
(D) 가정 원예 센터

해설 전체 내용 관련 - 안내 방송 장소

화자가 초반부에 링크 오피스 슈퍼스토어 연례 할인 행사에 와 주셔서 감사하다(Thanks for coming to Link Office Superstore's annual sale)면서, 저희는 사무용품, 책상, 의자를 시내 최고의 가격으로 제공하고 있다(We offer the best prices in town on office supplies, desks, and chairs)고 말하고 있으므로 정답은 (C)이다.

96

Look at the graphic. Which lane is the express lane?

(A) Lane 1
(B) Lane 2
(C) Lane 3
(D) Lane 4

시각 정보에 의하면 빠른 계산대는 어느 통로인가?

(A) 1번 통로
(B) 2번 통로
(C) 3번 통로
(D) 4번 통로

해설 시각 정보 연계 – 빠른 계산대의 번호

화자가 중반부에 계산 과정의 속도를 높이기 위해 5개 이하 품목을 구입할 경우 출구 근처에 있는 빠른 계산대를 이용하라(To help speed up the checkout process, please use the express lane located near the exit if you're buying five items or fewer)고 말하고 있고, 매장 지도에 따르면 출구 근처의 통로는 4번 통로이므로 정답은 (D)이다.

97

According to the speaker, what can the listeners receive assistance with?

(A) Checking a price
(B) Moving large items
(C) Getting a refund
(D) Locating some merchandise

화자의 말에 따르면, 청자들은 무엇에 대해 도움을 받을 수 있는가?

(A) 가격 확인
(B) 대형 품목 옮기기
(C) 환불받기
(D) 물품의 위치 찾기

어휘 locate 찾다 merchandise 물품

해설 세부 사항 관련 – 화자가 청자들이 도움을 받을 수 있다고 말하는 것
화자가 마지막에 대형 품목을 구입하고 이동에 도움이 필요할 경우 직원 중 한 명에게 알려 주면 해당 품목을 차량까지 옮기는 것을 도와 드리겠다 (if you're purchasing a large item and need help moving it, just let one of the employees know and they'll help you bring the item to your vehicle)고 말하고 있으므로 정답은 (B)이다.

98-100 담화 + 달력

M-Cn **98 Thanks for coming to today's painting class at the Lightdale Community Center. I hope you enjoyed learning some of the techniques I showed you. 99 If you could collect your brushes and paints and leave them right here on this table, it'll make my cleanup easier.** And before you go, I want to remind everyone about the other great events here at the center. There's a copy of the schedule at the door. **100 I recommend the Mystery Book Club meeting, because there will be a special guest that night**—the author Gerard Messina will be reading from his latest novel.

오늘 라이트데일 주민 센터에서 열린 회화 강좌에 참석해 주셔서 감사합니다. 제가 보여 드린 몇 가지 기법을 즐겁게 배우셨기를 바랍니다. 붓과 물감을 모아서 여기 이 탁자 위에 두시면 제가 청소하기가 더 쉽겠습니다. 그리고 가시기 전에 여러분 모두에게 이 센터에서 열리는 다른 멋진 행사들에 대해 다시 알려 드리고자 하는데요. 문에 일정표 사본이 있습니다. 저는 탐정 소설 동호회 모임을 추천합니다. 그날 밤 특별 초대 손님이 오시거든요. 작가 제라드 메시나 씨가 자신의 최신작 소설을 낭독할 예정입니다.

어휘 cleanup 청소 recommend 추천하다

June				
Mon.	Tues.	Wed.	Thurs.	Fri.
5 Painting Class	6	7 Guitar Lessons	8	9 Pottery Class
12	13 100 Mystery Book Club	14	15 Movie Night	16 Knitting Circle

6월				
월	화	수	목	금
5 회화 강좌	6	7 기타 강좌	8	9 도자기 강좌
12	13 100 탐정 소설 동호회	14	15 영화의 밤	16 뜨개질 취미반

98

Who most likely is the speaker?

(A) A musician
(B) An actor
(C) A writing instructor
(D) An art teacher

화자는 누구이겠는가?

(A) 음악가
(B) 배우
(C) 글쓰기 강사
(D) 미술 교사

TEST 4

화자가 도입부에 오늘 라이트데일 주민 센터에서 열린 회화 강좌에 참석해 주셔서 감사하다(Thanks for coming to today's painting class at the Lightdale Community Center)며, 제가 보여 드린 몇 가지 기법을 즐겁게 배우셨기를 바란다(I hope you enjoyed learning some of the techniques I showed you)고 말하고 있으므로 정답은 (D)이다.

▸▸ Paraphrasing   담화의 painting → 정답의 art

99

What are the listeners asked to do?

(A) Arrive early
(B) Help clean an area
(C) Silence mobile phones
(D) Provide feedback

청자들은 무엇을 하도록 요청받는가?

(A) 일찍 도착하기
(B) 공간 청소 돕기
(C) 핸드폰 무음으로 설정하기
(D) 의견 제공하기

화자가 중반부에 붓과 물감을 모아서 여기 이 탁자 위에 두면 제가 청소하기가 더 쉽겠다(If you could collect your brushes and paints and leave them right here on this table, it'll make my cleanup easier)고 부탁하고 있으므로 정답은 (B)이다.

100

Look at the graphic. On which date will there be a special guest?

(A) June 7
(B) June 9
(C) June 13
(D) June 15

시각 정보에 의하면 특별 초대 손님은 어떤 날짜에 오는가?

(A) 6월 7일
(B) 6월 9일
(C) 6월 13일
(D) 6월 15일

화자가 후반부에 탐정 소설 동호회 모임을 추천하는데 그날 밤 특별 초대 손님이 오기 때문(I recommend the Mystery Book Club meeting, because there will be a special guest that night)이라고 말하고 있고, 달력에 따르면 탐정 소설 동호회가 있는 날은 6월 13일 화요일이므로 정답은 (C)이다.

기출 TEST 5

1 (D)	**2** (C)	**3** (C)	**4** (A)	**5** (D)
6 (B)	**7** (B)	**8** (B)	**9** (A)	**10** (B)
11 (C)	**12** (B)	**13** (B)	**14** (B)	**15** (C)
16 (A)	**17** (B)	**18** (B)	**19** (C)	**20** (C)
21 (A)	**22** (A)	**23** (A)	**24** (B)	**25** (C)
26 (C)	**27** (B)	**28** (A)	**29** (C)	**30** (B)
31 (A)	**32** (A)	**33** (C)	**34** (B)	**35** (B)
36 (D)	**37** (C)	**38** (C)	**39** (B)	**40** (A)
41 (B)	**42** (D)	**43** (A)	**44** (C)	**45** (D)
46 (C)	**47** (A)	**48** (D)	**49** (C)	**50** (A)
51 (B)	**52** (D)	**53** (C)	**54** (A)	**55** (B)
56 (C)	**57** (A)	**58** (D)	**59** (D)	**60** (C)
61 (B)	**62** (A)	**63** (B)	**64** (B)	**65** (A)
66 (B)	**67** (D)	**68** (A)	**69** (D)	**70** (C)
71 (B)	**72** (D)	**73** (A)	**74** (A)	**75** (C)
76 (B)	**77** (C)	**78** (A)	**79** (C)	**80** (B)
81 (B)	**82** (A)	**83** (C)	**84** (B)	**85** (D)
86 (D)	**87** (B)	**88** (C)	**89** (D)	**90** (C)
91 (A)	**92** (B)	**93** (C)	**94** (C)	**95** (D)
96 (C)	**97** (A)	**98** (C)	**99** (D)	**100** (C)

PART 1

1 M-Au

(A) The people are watching a presentation.
(B) Some books are being placed on a cart.
(C) The people are kneeling in front of a shelf.
(D) The people are visiting a library.

(A) 사람들이 발표를 보고 있다.
(B) 책들을 카트에 싣고 있다.
(C) 사람들이 선반 앞에 무릎을 꿇고 있다.
(D) **사람들이 도서관을 방문하고 있다.**

어휘 kneel 무릎을 꿇다

해설 혼합 사진 - 사람/사물/풍경 혼합 묘사
(A) 동사 오답. 사람들이 발표를 보고 있는(are watching a presentation) 모습이 아니므로 오답.
(B) 사진에 없는 명사를 이용한 오답. 사진에 카트(a cart)의 모습이 보이지 않으므로 오답.

(C) 동사 오답. 사람들이 선반 앞에 무릎을 꿇고 있는(are kneeling in front of a shelf) 모습이 아니므로 오답.
(D) 정답. 사람들이 도서관을 방문하고 있는(are visiting a library) 모습이므로 정답.

2 W-Am

(A) The women are facing each other.
(B) The women are walking together.
(C) **One of the women is removing an item from her purse.**
(D) One of the women is drinking from a coffee cup.

(A) 여자들이 서로 마주보고 있다.
(B) 여자들이 함께 걷고 있다.
(C) **여자들 중 한 명이 핸드백에서 물건을 꺼내고 있다.**
(D) 여자들 중 한 명이 커피잔으로 마시고 있다.

어휘 remove 꺼내다 purse 핸드백

해설 2인 이상 등장 사진 - 사람의 동작/상태 묘사
(A) 동사 오답. 여자들이 서로 마주보고 있는(are facing each other) 모습이 아니므로 오답.
(B) 동사 오답. 여자들이 함께 걷고 있는(are walking together) 모습이 아니므로 오답.
(C) 정답. 여자들 중 한 명(one of the women)이 핸드백에서 물건을 꺼내고 있는(is removing an item from her purse) 모습이므로 정답.
(D) 동사 오답. 여자들 중 한 명(one of the women)이 커피잔으로 마시고 있는(is drinking from a coffee cup) 모습이 아니므로 오답.

3 W-Br

(A) One of the men is emptying out a plastic bag.
(B) They're waiting in line at a checkout counter.
(C) **One of the men is pointing at some flowers.**
(D) They're selecting some fruits and vegetables.

(A) 남자들 중 한 명이 비닐봉지를 비우고 있다.
(B) 사람들이 계산대에서 줄을 서서 기다리고 있다.
(C) **남자들 중 한 명이 꽃들을 가리키고 있다.**
(D) 사람들이 과일과 채소를 고르고 있다.

어휘 empty out ~을 몽땅 비우다

TEST 5 **119**

해설 2인 이상 등장 사진 - 사람의 동작/상태 묘사

(A) 동사 오답. 남자들 중 한 명(one of the men)이 비닐봉지를 비우고 있는(is emptying out a plastic bag) 모습이 아니므로 오답.

(B) 사진에 없는 명사를 이용한 오답. 사진에 계산대(a checkout counter)의 모습이 보이지 않으므로 오답.

(C) 정답. 남자들 중 한 명(one of the men)이 꽃들을 가리키고 있는(is pointing at some flowers) 모습이므로 정답.

(D) 사진에 없는 명사를 이용한 오답. 사진에 과일과 채소(some fruits and vegetables)의 모습이 보이지 않으므로 오답.

---

4 W-Am

(A) Some plants have been arranged in a row.
(B) The woman is leaning against a windowsill.
(C) Some cabinets have been opened at a workstation.
(D) The woman is reading a billboard.

(A) 식물들이 일렬로 배열되어 있다.
(B) 여자가 창틀에 기대어 있다.
(C) 작업대에 캐비닛들이 열려 있다.
(D) 여자가 광고판을 읽고 있다.

어휘 arrange 배열하다   windowsill 창틀   lean against ~에 기대다
workstation 작업대   billboard 광고판

해설 혼합 사진 - 사람/사물/풍경 혼합 묘사

(A) 정답. 식물들(some plants)이 일렬로 배열되어 있는(have been arranged in a row) 모습이므로 정답.

(B) 동사 오답. 여자가 창틀에 기대어 있는(is leaning against a windowsill) 모습이 아니므로 오답.

(C) 동사 오답. 작업대에(at a workstation) 캐비닛들(some cabinets)이 열려 있는(have been opened) 모습이 아니므로 오답.

(D) 동사 오답. 여자가 광고판을 읽고 있는(is reading a billboard) 모습이 아니므로 오답.

---

5 M-Au

(A) A house overlooks a fishing pier.
(B) Ducks are swimming in a lake.
(C) A bridge crosses over a river.
(D) Some trees border a pond.

(A) 집에서 낚시터가 내려다보인다.
(B) 오리들이 호수에서 헤엄치고 있다.
(C) 다리가 강을 가로지른다.
(D) 나무들이 연못에 접해 있다.

어휘 fishing pier 낚시터   border ~에 접하다

해설 사물/풍경 사진 – 풍경 묘사

(A) 사진에 없는 명사를 이용한 오답. 사진에 낚시터(a fishing pier)의 모습이 보이지 않으므로 오답.

(B) 사진에 없는 명사를 이용한 오답. 사진에 오리들(ducks)의 모습이 보이지 않으므로 오답.

(C) 사진에 없는 명사를 이용한 오답. 사진에 다리(a bridge)의 모습이 보이지 않으므로 오답.

(D) 정답. 나무들(some trees)이 연못에 접해 있는(border a pond) 모습이므로 정답.

---

6 M-Cn

(A) One of the women is picking up a suitcase.
(B) One of the women is holding a notebook under her arm.
(C) One of the women is standing in the doorway.
(D) One of the women is posting a sign on the wall.

(A) 여자들 중 한 명이 여행 가방을 집어 들고 있다.
(B) 여자들 중 한 명이 겨드랑이에 노트를 끼고 있다.
(C) 여자들 중 한 명이 출입구에 서 있다.
(D) 여자들 중 한 명이 벽에 팻말을 붙이고 있다.

해설 2인 이상 등장 사진 - 사람의 동작/상태 묘사

(A) 사진에 없는 명사를 이용한 오답. 사진에 여행 가방(a suitcase)의 모습이 보이지 않으므로 오답.

(B) 정답. 여자들 중 한 명(one of the women)이 겨드랑이에 노트를 끼고 있는(is holding a notebook under her arm) 모습이므로 정답.

(C) 동사 오답. 여자들 중 한 명(one of the women)이 출입구에 서 있는(is standing in the doorway) 모습이 아니므로 오답.

(D) 동사 오답. 여자들 중 한 명(one of the women)이 벽에 팻말을 붙이고 있는(is posting a sign on the wall) 모습이 아니므로 오답.

PART 2

7

M-Au Where is the parking garage?
W-Am (A) The local park is nice.
       (B) Behind the office building.
       (C) During his commute to work.

주차장이 어디죠?

(A) 지역 공원이 근사해요.

(B) 사무실 건물 뒤에요.

(C) 그가 출근하는 동안에요.

어휘 commute to work 출[통]근하다

해설 주차장의 위치를 묻는 Where 의문문

(A) 유사 발음 오답. 질문의 parking과 부분적으로 발음이 유사한 park를 이용한 오답.

(B) 정답. 주차장의 위치를 묻는 질문에 사무실 건물 뒤라고 구체적인 위치를 알려 주고 있으므로 정답.

(C) 질문과 상관없는 오답. When 의문문에 대한 응답이므로 오답.

8

W-Br　When will the design team meet?

W-Am　(A) No, I ordered five.

　　　　(B) Sometime next month.

　　　　(C) On top of the cabinet.

디자인 팀은 언제 모이나요?

(A) 아니요, 저는 다섯 개 주문했어요

(B) 다음 달쯤이요.

(C) 캐비닛 위에요.

해설 디자인 팀이 모이는 시기를 묻는 When 의문문

(A) Yes/No 불가 오답. When 의문문에는 Yes/No 응답이 불가능하므로 오답.

(B) 정답. 디자인 팀이 모이는 시기를 묻는 질문에 다음 달쯤이라고 응답하고 있으므로 정답.

(C) 질문과 상관없는 오답. Where 의문문에 대한 응답이므로 오답.

9

W-Am　Should we consider Anita for the accountant position?

M-Au　(A) Yes, we're reviewing her application now.

　　　　(B) Down the hall to the right.

　　　　(C) The box is open.

회계사 직에 아니타를 고려해야 할까요?

(A) 네, 우리가 지금 지원서를 검토하고 있어요.

(B) 복도를 따라 오른쪽이에요.

(C) 상자는 열려 있어요.

어휘 accountant 회계사　application 지원(서)

해설 제안/권유의 의문문

(A) 정답. 회계사 직에 아니타를 고려해야 할지 묻는 질문에 네(Yes)라고 대답한 뒤, 지금 지원서를 검토하고 있다며 긍정 답변과 일관된 내용을 덧붙이고 있으므로 정답.

(B) 질문과 상관없는 오답. Where 의문문에 대한 응답이므로 오답.

(C) 질문과 상관없는 오답.

10

M-Cn　What are they building near the shopping center?

W-Br　(A) On the eighteenth floor.

　　　　(B) An apartment complex.

　　　　(C) I shop there on the weekends.

쇼핑센터 근처에 뭘 짓고 있나요?

(A) 18층이에요.

(B) 아파트 단지요.

(C) 저는 주말에 거기서 쇼핑해요.

해설 건축 중인 건물을 묻는 What 의문문

(A) 질문과 상관없는 오답. Where 의문문에 대한 응답이므로 오답.

(B) 정답. 쇼핑센터 근처에 짓고 있는 건물이 무엇인지 묻는 질문에 아파트 단지라고 건물의 종류를 알려 주고 있으므로 정답.

(C) 파생어 오답. 질문의 shopping과 파생어 관계인 shop을 이용한 오답.

11

W-Am　How did you like the meal?

M-Cn　(A) I like that idea.

　　　　(B) By taxicab.

　　　　(C) It was excellent.

식사는 어땠어요?

(A) 그 아이디어 마음에 드네요.

(B) 택시로요.

(C) 아주 좋았어요.

해설 식사 소감을 묻는 How 의문문

(A) 단어 반복 오답. 질문의 like를 반복 이용한 오답.

(B) 연상 단어 오답. 질문의 How를 교통수단을 묻는 뜻으로 이해했을 경우 연상 가능한 taxicab을 이용한 오답.

(C) 정답. 식사가 어땠는지 묻는 질문에 아주 좋았다며 소감을 말하고 있으므로 정답.

12

W-Br　Why did the manager e-mail you?

W-Am　(A) Yes, I'm sure.

　　　　(B) Because she wants me to work late.

　　　　(C) Do you have any stamps?

매니저가 왜 당신에게 이메일을 보냈죠?

(A) 네, 확실해요.

(B) 제가 늦게까지 일했으면 해서요.

(C) 우표 있어요?

해설 매니저가 이메일을 보낸 이유를 묻는 Why 의문문

(A) Yes/No 불가 오답. Why 의문문에는 Yes/No 응답이 불가능하므로 오답.

(B) 정답. 매니저가 이메일을 보낸 이유를 묻는 질문에 매니저(she)가 자신이 늦게까지 일하기를 원하기 때문이라고 이유를 제시하고 있으므로 정답.

(C) 연상 단어 오답. 질문의 e-mail에서 연상 가능한 stamps를 이용한 오답.

13

M-Cn Will the prototype be ready in time for the trade show?

M-Au (A) That's a wonderful TV show.
(B) Yes, it'll be finished.
(C) It's in Chicago this year.

무역 박람회에 맞춰 시제품이 준비될까요?
(A) 정말 멋진 TV 쇼예요.
(B) 네, 완성될 거예요.
(C) 올해는 시카고에서 있어요.

어휘 prototype 시제품   in time 시간 맞춰

해설 무역 박람회에 맞춰 시제품이 준비될지 여부를 묻는 조동사(Will) 의문문
(A) 단어 반복 오답. 질문의 show를 반복 이용한 오답.
(B) 정답. 무역 박람회에 맞춰 시제품이 준비될 여부를 묻는 질문에 네 (Yes)라고 대답한 뒤, 완성될 것이라며 긍정 답변과 일관된 내용을 덧붙이고 있으므로 정답.
(C) 질문과 상관없는 오답. Where 의문문에 대한 응답이므로 오답.

14

M-Cn Our office building is locked on the weekends, isn't it?

W-Br (A) Right down Franklin Boulevard.
(B) Just bring your employee badge.
(C) To visit with some friends.

우리 사무실 건물은 주말에 잠그지 않나요?
(A) 프랭클린 대로를 따라 바로요.
(B) 사원증만 가져오세요.
(C) 친구 몇 명과 함께 방문하려고요.

해설 주말에 사무실이 잠기는지 여부를 확인하는 부가 의문문
(A) 질문과 상관없는 오답. Where 의문문에 대한 응답이므로 오답.
(B) 정답. 사무실 건물이 주말에 잠기는지 여부를 확인하는 질문에 사원증만 가져오라며 사원증이 있으면 사무실에 출입이 허용된다는 것을 우회적으로 알려 주고 있으므로 정답.
(C) 연상 단어 오답. 질문의 building에서 연상 가능한 visit을 이용한 오답.

15

W-Am Can't you deliver both of these orders during the same trip?

M-Au (A) It arrived in good condition.
(B) Actually, we had a very nice trip.
(C) Sure, they go to the same part of town.

한 번 이동할 때 이 두 가지 주문품을 모두 배달할 수는 없나요?
(A) 그것은 좋은 상태로 도착했어요.
(B) 사실 여행은 아주 좋았어요.
(C) 그럼요, 시내 같은 동네로 가요.

해설 두 주문품을 한 번에 배송할 수 있는지 여부를 확인하는 부정 의문문
(A) 연상 단어 오답. 질문의 deliver에서 연상 가능한 arrived를 이용한 오답.
(B) 단어 반복 오답. 질문의 trip을 반복 이용한 오답.
(C) 정답. 한 번 이동할 때 두 가지 주문품을 모두 배달할 수 있는지 여부를 확인하는 질문에 그렇다(Sure)고 대답한 뒤, 같은 동네로 간다며 긍정 답변과 일관된 내용을 덧붙이고 있으므로 정답.

16

M-Au Do you want to purchase a laptop or desktop computer?

W-Br (A) I have the model number here.
(B) Yes, in the top drawer.
(C) At the new furniture store.

노트북을 사시겠어요, 아니면 데스크탑을 사시겠어요?
(A) 여기 모델 번호가 있어요.
(B) 네, 맨 위 서랍 안에요.
(C) 새 가구점에서요.

어휘 purchase 사다

해설 구입을 원하는 컴퓨터의 종류를 묻는 선택 의문문
(A) 정답. 노트북과 데스크탑 중 사고 싶어 하는 컴퓨터의 종류를 묻는 질문에 여기 모델 번호가 있다며 구입하고자 하는 컴퓨터의 종류를 알 수 있는 정보를 제시하면서 간접적으로 응답하고 있으므로 정답.
(B) 단어 반복 오답. 질문의 laptop과 desktop의 top을 반복 이용한 오답.
(C) 연상 단어 오답. 질문의 purchase에서 연상 가능한 store를 이용한 오답.

17

W-Am What did you think of the company newsletter?

M-Au (A) About two pages long.
(B) It had some interesting articles.
(C) Please seal the envelope.

회사 사보 어땠어요?
(A) 두 페이지 정도 돼요.
(B) 흥미로운 기사가 몇 개 있었어요.
(C) 봉투를 봉해 주세요.

해설 회사 사보에 대한 의견을 묻는 What 의문문
(A) 질문과 상관없는 오답. How long 의문문에 대한 응답이므로 오답.
(B) 정답. 회사 사보에 대해 어떻게 생각하는지 묻는 질문에 흥미로운 기사가 몇 개 있었다며 사보를 읽은 뒤의 소감을 말하고 있으므로 정답.
(C) 연상 단어 오답. 질문의 newsletter에서 연상 가능한 envelope를 이용한 오답.

18

W-Br　Can I help you move your furniture?

M-Cn　(A) He bought a desk last week.

　　　　(B) I think I can manage on my own.

　　　　(C) The furniture store on Grove Street.

가구 옮기는 것 좀 도와 드릴까요?

(A) 그는 지난주에 책상을 샀어요.

(B) 혼자 할 수 있을 거예요.

(C) 그로브 가에 있는 가구점이에요.

해설　제안/권유의 의문문

(A) 연상 단어 오답. 질문의 furniture에서 연상 가능한 desk를 이용한 오답.

(B) 정답. 가구 옮기는 것을 도와주겠다고 제안하는 질문에 혼자 할 수 있을 것 같다고 우회적으로 거절하고 있으므로 정답.

(C) 단어 반복 오답. 질문의 furniture를 반복 이용한 오답.

19

M-Au　Why did Mr. Harrison resign from his position?

W-Am　(A) Two weeks ago.

　　　　(B) It's just been signed.

　　　　(C) He found a different job.

해리슨 씨는 왜 사직했나요?

(A) 2주 전이에요.

(B) 방금 계약됐어요.

(C) 그는 다른 직장을 찾았어요.

어휘　resign 사직하다

해설　해리슨 씨가 사직한 이유를 묻는 Why 의문문

(A) 질문과 상관없는 오답. When 의문문에 대한 응답이므로 오답.

(B) 유사 발음 오답. 질문의 resign과 부분적으로 발음이 유사한 signed를 이용한 오답.

(C) 정답. 해리슨 씨가 사직한 이유를 묻는 질문에 그가 다른 직장을 찾았다며 이유를 제시하고 있으므로 정답.

20

M-Cn　Which client are we meeting with tomorrow morning?

M-Au　(A) They talked about the upcoming merger.

　　　　(B) Just a light breakfast.

　　　　(C) The Greendale Company representative.

내일 아침에 만나는 고객은 누구죠?

(A) 그들은 다가오는 합병에 대해 이야기했어요.

(B) 가벼운 아침 식사만요.

(C) 그린데일 회사 직원이에요.

어휘　merger 합병　representative 직원

해설　내일 아침에 만날 고객이 누구인지 묻는 Which 의문문

(A) 질문과 상관없는 오답. What 의문문에 대한 응답이므로 오답.

(B) 연상 단어 오답. 질문의 morning에서 연상 가능한 breakfast를 이용한 오답.

(C) 정답. 내일 아침에 만날 고객이 누구인지 묻는 질문에 그린데일 회사 직원이라고 구체적으로 응답하고 있으므로 정답.

21

W-Br　Weren't those lightbulbs replaced recently?

M-Cn　(A) Yes, we just changed them.

　　　　(B) Actually, this isn't very heavy.

　　　　(C) It's on Fourth Street.

저 전구들은 최근에 교체되지 않았나요?

(A) 네, 우리가 조금 전에 바꿨어요.

(B) 사실 이건 별로 무겁지 않아요.

(C) 4번 가에 있어요.

어휘　lightbulb 전구　replace 교체하다　recently 최근에

해설　전구의 최근 교체 여부를 확인하는 부정 의문문

(A) 정답. 전구들이 최근에 교체되었는지 여부를 묻는 질문에 네(Yes)라고 대답한 뒤, 우리가 조금 전에 바꿨다며 긍정 답변과 일관된 내용을 덧붙이고 있으므로 정답.

(B) 연상 단어 오답. 질문의 lightbulbs의 light에서 연상 가능한 heavy를 이용한 오답.

(C) 질문과 상관없는 오답. Where 의문문에 대한 응답이므로 오답.

22

W-Am　Who knows how to start the conference call?

M-Cn　(A) Alyssa can do it.

　　　　(B) The conference registration fee.

　　　　(C) Yes, we've got them all.

전화 회의 시작할 줄 아는 사람 있어요?

(A) 알리사가 할 수 있어요.

(B) 회의 등록비예요.

(C) 네, 전부 갖고 있어요.

어휘　conference call 전화 회의

해설　전화 회의를 시작할 줄 아는 사람을 묻는 Who 의문문

(A) 정답. 전화 회의를 시작할 줄 아는 사람이 누구인지 묻는 질문에 알리사가 할 수 있다고 알려 주고 있으므로 정답.

(B) 단어 반복 오답. 질문의 conference를 반복 이용한 오답.

(C) Yes/No 불가 오답. Who 의문문에는 Yes/No 응답이 불가능하므로 오답.

23

W-Br   What should I do with the extra training
materials?

M-Au   (A) Leave them on my desk.
(B) No, they shouldn't.
(C) Around four thirty.

추가 교육 자료는 어떻게 해야 하나요?
(A) 제 책상 위에 두세요.
(B) 아니요, 안 돼요.
(C) 4시 30분쯤이요.

해설 추가 교육 자료의 처리 방법을 묻는 What 의문문
(A) 정답. 추가 교육 자료를 어떻게 해야 할지 묻는 질문에 제 책상 위에
두라고 알려 주고 있으므로 정답.
(B) Yes/No 불가 오답. What 의문문에는 Yes/No 응답이 불가능하므로
오답.
(C) 질문과 상관없는 오답. When 의문문에 대한 응답이므로 오답.

24

M-Cn   It's raining quite hard outside.

W-Br   (A) With an umbrella.
(B) I can drive you to the store.
(C) Yes, that was difficult.

밖에 비가 참 세차게 오네요.
(A) 우산으로요.
(B) 제가 매장까지 태워다 드릴 수 있어요.
(C) 네, 어려웠어요.

해설 정보 전달의 평서문
(A) 연상 단어 오답. 평서문의 raining에서 연상 가능한 umbrella를 이
용한 오답.
(B) 정답. 밖에 비가 세차게 온다는 평서문에 제가 매장까지 태워다 줄 수
있다며 폭우로 인한 곤란함에 대한 해결책을 제안하고 있으므로 정답.
(C) 연상 단어 오답. 평서문의 hard에서 연상 가능한 difficult를 이용한
오답.

25

W-Br   How many servers do we need waiting tables
on Saturday?

M-Cn   (A) Yes, you can leave it on the floor.
(B) At eleven o'clock.
(C) We have a party of 25 coming in.

토요일에 테이블에서 시중들 웨이터가 몇 명이나 필요하죠?
(A) 네, 바닥에 두셔도 돼요.
(B) 11시예요.
(C) 단체 손님이 25명 와요.

해설 필요한 웨이터의 수를 묻는 How many 의문문
(A) Yes/No 불가 오답. How many 의문문에는 Yes/No 응답이 불가능
하므로 오답.
(B) 질문과 상관없는 오답. When 의문문에 대한 응답이므로 오답.
(C) 정답. 토요일에 테이블에서 시중들 웨이터가 몇 명 필요한지 묻는 질
문에 단체 손님 25명이 온다며 필요한 웨이터의 수를 가늠할 수 있는
정보를 간접적으로 제시하고 있으므로 정답.

26

W-Am   George, will you call our clients back?

M-Cn   (A) The information pack.
(B) Yes, she'll be back soon.
(C) Anna left them a message.

조지, 고객들에게 다시 전화하실래요?
(A) 정보 꾸러미예요.
(B) 네, 그녀는 곧 돌아올 거예요.
(C) 애나가 그들에게 메시지를 남겼어요.

해설 부탁/요청의 의문문
(A) 유사 발음 오답. 질문의 back과 부분적으로 발음이 유사한 pack을
이용한 오답.
(B) 단어 반복 오답. 질문의 back을 반복 이용한 오답.
(C) 정답. 고객들에게 다시 전화해 달라고 요청하는 질문에 애나가 그들에
게 메시지를 남겼다며 자신이 다시 전화할 필요가 없음을 우회적으로
응답하고 있으므로 정답.

27

M-Au   Our quarterly sales results were lower than
expected.

W-Br   (A) It's an easy hiking trail.
(B) We do have a new competitor.
(C) A quarter of an hour.

분기 매출 실적이 예상보다 저조했어요.
(A) 수월한 등산로예요.
(B) 우리에게 새로운 경쟁 업체가 있죠.
(C) 15분이요.

어휘 quarterly 분기의   than expected 예상보다   competitor 경쟁
업체

해설 정보 전달의 평서문
(A) 평서문과 상관없는 오답.
(B) 정답. 분기 매출 실적이 예상보다 저조했다는 평서문에 우리에게 새
로운 경쟁 업체가 생겼다며 매출이 저조한 이유를 제시하고 있으므로
정답.
(C) 파생어 오답. 평서문의 quarterly와 파생어 관계인 quarter를 이용
한 오답.

28

M-Cn When do you want to work on this new project?

W-Am (A) I haven't been trained yet.
(B) Yes, he got a full-time job.
(C) I completely agree with you.

언제 이 새 프로젝트를 진행하고 싶으세요?
(A) 저는 아직 교육을 못 받았어요.
(B) 네, 그는 정규직 일자리를 얻었어요.
(C) 전적으로 동의해요.

해설 새 프로젝트를 진행하길 원하는 시점을 묻는 When 의문문

(A) 정답. 새 프로젝트를 진행하기를 원하는 시점을 묻는 질문에 아직 교육을 못 받았다며 교육을 받을 때까지는 일을 진행하지 않을 것임을 우회적으로 응답하고 있으므로 정답.
(B) Yes/No 불가 오답. When 의문문에는 Yes/No 응답이 불가능하므로 오답.
(C) 질문과 상관없는 오답.

29

W-Br I'll be happy to take pictures at the company retreat.

M-Cn (A) Some coffee and desserts.
(B) Yes, a digital camera.
(C) They hired a photographer.

회사 수련회에서 제가 기꺼이 사진을 찍을게요.
(A) 커피와 디저트요.
(B) 네, 디지털 카메라예요.
(C) 그들이 사진작가를 고용했어요.

해설 제안/권유의 평서문

(A) 평서문과 상관없는 오답.
(B) 연상 단어 오답. 평서문의 pictures에서 연상 가능한 camera를 이용한 오답.
(C) 정답. 회사 수련회에서 자신이 사진을 찍겠다는 제안에 사진작가를 고용했다며 우회적으로 거절하고 있으므로 정답.

30

M-Au These all-weather tires are very expensive.

W-Br (A) A fifteen-minute drive.
(B) They'll last for a long time.
(C) Let me turn it on for you.

이 전천후 타이어는 아주 비싸네요.
(A) 차로 15분이에요.
(B) 오래갈 거예요.
(C) 제가 켜 드릴게요.

어휘 all-weather 전천후 expensive 비싼

해설 의사 전달의 평서문

(A) 연상 단어 오답. 평서문의 tires에서 연상 가능한 drive를 이용한 오답.
(B) 정답. 전천후 타이어가 아주 비싸다고 평가하는 평서문에 오래갈 것이라며 납득할 만한 이유를 제시하고 있으므로 정답.
(C) 평서문과 상관없는 오답.

31

M-Au Why aren't the trainees in the computer lab now?

W-Am (A) Didn't you get a copy of the updated schedule?
(B) Yes, at the next station.
(C) There's a repair shop on Lancaster Avenue.

지금 컴퓨터실에 왜 수습 직원들이 없죠?
(A) 수정된 일정표 사본 못 받으셨어요?
(B) 네, 다음 역에서요.
(C) 랭커스터 가에 수리점이 있어요.

어휘 repair 수리

해설 컴퓨터실에 수습 직원들이 없는 이유를 묻는 Why 의문문

(A) 정답. 컴퓨터실에 수습 직원들이 없는 이유를 묻는 질문에 수정된 일정표 사본을 못 받았느냐고 되물으며 일정이 바뀌었음을 우회적으로 알려 주고 있으므로 정답.
(B) 연상 단어 오답. 질문의 trainees를 train으로 잘못 들었을 경우 연상 가능한 station을 이용한 오답.
(C) 질문과 상관없는 오답.

PART 3

32-34

W-Br Hi! Welcome to Gonzalez and Partners.

M-Cn Hi, [32] **I'm from Federov Portraits. I'm here to take the staff photos for the firm's Web site.**

W-Br Oh, great—we've reserved a conference room down the hall for the photo shoot.

M-Cn Thank you. There's just one thing... [33] **I have some heavy lighting equipment to bring in from my truck, and the only free parking space was several rows back. Do you have a cart I can use or ...**

W-Br I don't, but [34] **take this parking pass.** You can use it to park in the VIP spot right by the front door.

M-Cn Thanks, I'll do that now.

여	안녕하세요! 곤잘레스 앤 파트너스에 오신 것을 환영합니다.
남	안녕하세요, **페데로프 인물 사진에서 왔습니다. 회사 웹사이트용 직원 사진을 찍으러 왔어요.**
여	아, 잘됐네요. 사진 촬영을 위해 복도 저쪽에 있는 회의실을 예약해 뒀어요.
남	감사합니다. 한 가지만요⋯ **트럭에서 무거운 조명 장비를 가져와야 하는데, 유일한 무료 주차 공간이 몇 줄 뒤에 있었어요. 제가 쓸 만한 카트가 있나요, 아니면⋯**
여	없어요, 하지만 **이 주차권을 받으세요.** 이걸로 정문 바로 옆에 있는 VIP 공간에 주차하시면 돼요.
남	고마워요, 지금 할게요.

어휘	portrait 인물 사진 reserve 예약하다 row 줄

32

Who most likely is the man?

(A) A photographer
(B) A journalist
(C) A florist
(D) A caterer

남자는 누구이겠는가?
(A) 사진작가
(B) 기자
(C) 꽃집 주인
(D) 급식업자

해설 전체 내용 관련 - 남자의 직업
남자가 첫 대사에서 페데로프 인물 사진에서 왔다(I'm from Federov Portraits)고 자신을 소개하며 회사 웹사이트용 직원 사진을 찍으러 왔다 (I'm here to take the staff photos for the firm's Web site)고 말하고 있으므로 정답은 (A)이다.

33

What is the man concerned about?

(A) Contacting his assistant
(B) Locating a conference room
(C) Moving some equipment
(D) Printing a document

남자는 무엇을 걱정하는가?
(A) 조수에게 연락하기
(B) 회의실 찾기
(C) 장비 옮기기
(D) 문서 출력하기

어휘 locate 찾다

해설 세부 사항 관련 - 남자가 걱정하는 것
남자가 두 번째 대사에서 트럭에서 무거운 조명 장비를 가져와야 하는데 유일한 무료 주차 공간이 몇 줄 뒤에 있었다(I have some heavy lighting equipment ~ was several rows back)며 쓸 만한 카트가 있는지(Do you have a cart I can use or) 묻고 있는 것으로 보아 조명 장

비를 가져오는 일을 걱정하고 있다는 것을 알 수 있다. 따라서 정답은 (C) 이다.

34

What does the woman give the man?

(A) Some keys
(B) A parking pass
(C) A mobile phone charger
(D) A cart

여자는 남자에게 무엇을 주는가?
(A) 열쇠
(B) 주차권
(C) 핸드폰 충전기
(D) 카트

해설 세부 사항 관련 - 여자가 남자에게 주는 것
여자가 세 번째 대사에서 이 주차권을 받으라(take this parking pass) 며 남자에게 주차권을 건네고 있으므로 정답은 (B)이다.

35-37 3인 대화

M-Cn	Hi, Barbara and Nancy. **35 Now that our design's been selected for the new parking area at the airport, we can move forward to the next step.** Barbara, do you have any updates?
W-Am	Yes, so now **36 we need to consider residents in the surrounding neighborhoods. A preliminary survey showed their biggest concern is the potential increase in traffic.**
M-Cn	Nancy, **37 do we have a meeting set up at city hall for residents to discuss those concerns with us?**
W-Br	Yes, on October second, but in a new location. **37 The room at city hall was too small for this purpose, so it'll be held at the high school auditorium instead.**

남	안녕, 바바라, 낸시. 이제 **공항에 들어설 새 주차 구역에 우리 설계가 선정됐으니, 다음 단계로 넘어갈 수 있겠군요.** 바바라, 새로운 소식 있나요?
여1	네, 그래서 이제는 **인근 지역의 주민들을 고려해야 해요. 예비 설문 조사 결과 주민들이 가장 걱정하는 건 교통량이 늘어날지도 모른다는 거예요.**
남	낸시, **주민들이 그런 우려에 대해 시청에서 우리와 토론할 수 있는 회의가 마련됐나요?**
여2	네, 10월 2일이에요. 하지만 새로운 장소예요. **이 목적으로 쓰기엔 시청에 있는 방이 너무 작아서 대신 고등학교 강당에서 열릴 거예요.**

어휘 preliminary 예비의 potential 잠재적인 increase
증가 purpose 목적 auditorium 강당

35

What will be constructed at an airport?

(A) A runway

(B) A parking area

(C) A storage facility

(D) A fueling station

공항에 무엇이 건설될 것인가?

(A) 활주로

(B) 주차 구역

(C) 보관 시설

(D) 주유소

해설 세부 사항 관련 - 공항에 건설되는 것

남자가 첫 대사에서 이제 공항에 들어설 새 주차 구역에 우리 설계가 선정됐으니 다음 단계로 넘어갈 수 있겠다(Now that our design's been selected ~ we can move forward to the next step)고 말하고 있으므로 공항에 새로운 주차 구역이 건설될 것임을 알 수 있다. 따라서 정답은 (B)이다.

36

What is the residents' biggest concern?

(A) Money

(B) Safety

(C) Noise

(D) Traffic

주민들은 무엇을 가장 걱정하는가?

(A) 돈

(B) 안전

(C) 소음

(D) 교통

해설 세부 사항 관련 - 주민들이 가장 걱정하는 것

첫 번째 여자가 첫 대사에서 인근 지역의 주민들을 고려해야 한다(we need to consider residents in the surrounding neighborhoods)며 예비 설문 조사 결과 주민들이 가장 걱정하는 것은 교통량이 늘어날지도 모른다는 것(A preliminary survey showed their biggest concern is the potential increase in traffic)이라고 말하고 있으므로 정답은 (D)이다.

37

Why has a new meeting location been chosen?

(A) It is available on the weekend.

(B) It is closer to public transportation.

(C) It provides more space.

(D) It costs less to rent.

왜 새로운 회의 장소가 선정되었는가?

(A) 주말에 이용할 수 있다.

(B) 대중교통과 더 가깝다.

(C) 공간이 더 넓다.

(D) 임대료가 더 저렴하다.

해설 세부 사항 관련 - 새로운 회의 장소가 선정된 이유

남자가 두 번째 대사에서 주민들이 우려에 대해 시청에서 우리와 토론할 수 있는 회의가 마련됐는지(do we have a meeting set up at city hall ~ concerns with us?)를 묻자 두 번째 여자가 그 목적으로 쓰기에는 시청에 있는 방이 너무 작아서 대신 고등학교 강당에서 열릴 것(The room at city hall was too small ~ high school auditorium instead)이라고 말하고 있으므로 원래 회의 장소였던 시청에 비해 새 회의 장소인 고등학교 강당이 더 넓다는 것을 알 수 있다. 정답은 (C)이다.

38-40

M-Au	Thanks for coming to see me, Helen. How are things going in your new position?
W-Am	Great, Taro—thanks for asking. ³⁸**The management training that Human Resources provided was very helpful.**
M-Au	Good. Since ³⁸**you're now part of the management team,** ³⁹**I requested a corporate credit card for you.** It just came in—here it is.
W-Am	Thanks. I should use this for small day-to-day expenses in my department, like office supplies, right?
M-Au	Correct. By the way, for bigger expenses, like when you're traveling to a conference, you'll need to fill out an expense form when you return. So ⁴⁰**it's a good idea to save all your receipts.**

남 와 줘서 고마워요, 헬렌. 새 직책은 어때요?

여 좋아요, 타로. 물어봐 줘서 고마워요. **인사과에서 제공한 경영 교육이 크게 도움이 됐어요.**

남 잘됐군요. **이제 경영진의 일원이 되셨으므로 당신의 법인 카드를 신청했어요.** 방금 들어왔어요. 여기요.

여 고마워요. 부서에서 사무용품 같은 소소한 일상 경비에 이걸 써야 하는 거 맞죠?

남 맞아요. 그런데 회의차 출장 갈 때처럼 더 큰 비용의 경우 돌아와서 비용 양식을 작성해야 할 겁니다. 그러니 **영수증을 전부 챙겨 두는 게 좋아요.**

어휘 management 경영 corporate 법인의

38

Who most likely is the woman?

(A) An event organizer
(B) A marketing consultant
(C) A department manager
(D) A travel agent

여자는 누구이겠는가?

(A) 행사 주최자
(B) 마케팅 컨설턴트
(C) **부서장**
(D) 여행사 직원

해설 전체 내용 관련 - 여자의 직업

여자가 첫 대사에서 인사과에서 제공한 경영 교육이 크게 도움이 됐다
(The management training that Human Resources provided
was very helpful)고 했고, 뒤이어 남자가 여자에게 이제 경영진의 일원
이 되었다(you're now part of the management team)고 말하고 있
으므로 정답은 (C)이다.

39

What did the man order for the woman?

(A) A computer tablet
(B) A credit card
(C) Some furniture
(D) Some office supplies

남자는 여자를 위해 무엇을 주문했는가?

(A) 태블릿
(B) **신용카드**
(C) 가구
(D) 사무용품

해설 세부 사항 관련 - 남자가 여자를 위해 주문한 것

남자가 두 번째 대사에서 당신의 법인 카드를 신청했다(I requested a
corporate credit card for you)고 말하고 있으므로 정답은 (B)이다.

40

What does the man suggest the woman do?

(A) Save receipts
(B) Return a handbook
(C) E-mail a client
(D) Consult with a supervisor

남자는 여자에게 무엇을 하라고 권하는가?

(A) **영수증 챙기기**
(B) 편람 반납하기
(C) 고객에게 이메일 보내기
(D) 상사와 의논하기

해설 세부 사항 관련 - 남자가 여자에게 권하는 일

남자가 마지막 대사에서 영수증을 전부 챙겨 두는 게 좋다(it's a good
idea to save all your receipts)고 말하고 있으므로 정답은 (A)이다.

41-43

M-Cn	Hey, Martina. [41] **I'm going to a conference in Los Angeles next week.**
W-Am	Oh, that's where I'm from!
M-Cn	That's why I mentioned it. I'll probably be too busy with the conference to see any sights, but at least I can eat some good food while I'm there. [42] **I was hoping you could recommend some restaurants to try.**
W-Am	Of course! Do you know where your hotel is located? That way I can recommend places that are nearby.
M-Cn	I don't remember. But [43] **the address must be in the confirmation e-mail from the hotel. Let me pull it up right now.**

남	안녕, 마르티나. **저 다음 주에 로스앤젤레스에서 열리는 회의에 가요.**
여	아, 거기 제 고향이에요!
남	그래서 얘기했죠. 회의로 너무 바빠서 관광은 못하겠지만, 거기 있는 동안 최소한 좋은 음식은 먹을 수 있어요. **가 볼 만한 식당 좀 추천해 줬으면 했거든요.**
여	그럼요! 호텔이 어디 있는지 아세요? 그럼 가까운 데로 추천해 줄 수 있거든요.
남	기억이 안 나네요. 하지만 **호텔에서 보낸 확인 이메일에 주소가 있을 거예요. 지금 바로 열어 볼게요.**

어휘	recommend 추천하다 pull up (정보를 찾기 위해 핸드폰 등을) 열다

41

What will the man do next week?

(A) Meet with some customers
(B) Attend a conference
(C) Go on vacation
(D) Move to another city

남자는 다음 주에 무엇을 할 것인가?

(A) 고객들과 만나기
(B) **회의 참석하기**
(C) 휴가 가기
(D) 다른 도시로 이사하기

해설 세부 사항 관련 - 남자가 다음 주에 할 일

남자가 첫 대사에서 다음 주에 로스앤젤레스에서 열리는 회의에 간다(I'm
going to a conference in Los Angeles next week)고 말하고 있으므
로 정답은 (B)이다.

▸▸ Paraphrasing 대화의 **going to a conference**
→ 정답의 **Attend a conference**

42

What does the man want the woman to recommend?

(A) City tours
(B) Transportation services
(C) Hotels
(D) Restaurants

남자는 여자가 무엇을 추천하기를 바라는가?

(A) 시내 관광
(B) 교통 서비스
(C) 호텔
(D) 식당

해설 세부 사항 관련 - 남자가 여자가 추천하기를 바라는 것

남자가 두 번째 대사에서 가 볼 만한 식당을 좀 추천해 줬으면 했다(I was hoping you could recommend some restaurants to try)고 말하고 있으므로 정답은 (D)이다.

43

What does the man say he will do next?

(A) Look up an address
(B) Check a bus route
(C) Pack some equipment
(D) Activate a credit card

남자는 다음에 무엇을 할 것이라고 말하는가?

(A) 주소 찾아보기
(B) 버스 노선 확인하기
(C) 장비 포장하기
(D) 신용카드 활성화하기

어휘 look up (정보를) 찾아보다   activate 활성화하다

해설 세부 사항 관련 - 남자가 다음에 할 것이라고 말하는 일

남자가 마지막 대사에서 호텔에서 보낸 확인 이메일에 주소가 있을 것(the address must be in the confirmation e-mail from the hotel)이라며 지금 바로 열어 보겠다(Let me pull it up right now)고 말하고 있으므로 남자는 이메일에서 주소를 찾아볼 것임을 알 수 있다. 따라서 정답은 (A)이다.

44-46

> W-Br ⁴⁴**I wanted to talk about the results from the online customer questionnaires we sent out last week.** I know you've been exceptionally busy, Mario, but have you had a chance to look at the data?
>
> M-Cn Yes. In fact, I just finished the report. I'll present it to the sales department later today.
>
> W-Br Already? Fantastic! ⁴⁵**Did you want me to look it over before the meeting?**
>
> M-Cn The report's only half a page long.

> W-Br Ah, OK... Oh, ⁴⁶**I wanted to remind you to book us a table at your cousin's restaurant.** The sales team wants to go there after the meeting tomorrow.
>
> M-Cn Sure, I'll do that now.

> 여 지난주에 발송한 온라인 고객 설문 결과 건으로 얘기하려고요. 마리오, 유난히 바빴던 건 알지만, 자료를 볼 겨를이 있었나요?
>
> 남 네. 실은 방금 보고서를 끝냈어요. 오늘 이따가 영업부에 주려고요.
>
> 여 벌써요? 굉장하네요! 회의 전에 제가 한번 검토할까요?
>
> 남 보고서가 반 페이지밖에 안 돼요.
>
> 여 아, 그렇군요… 어, 일러 주고 싶었는데, 당신 사촌네 식당에 우리 자리를 예약해야 해요. 영업팀에서 내일 회의 후에 거기 가고 싶어 하거든요.
>
> 남 네, 지금 할게요.

어휘 questionnaire 설문   exceptionally 유난히

44

What does the woman want to discuss?

(A) Job candidates
(B) Vendor selections
(C) Customer survey results
(D) Computer system updates

여자는 무엇을 의논하고 싶어 하는가?

(A) 입사 지원자
(B) 판매 업체 선정
(C) 고객 설문 결과
(D) 컴퓨터 시스템 업데이트

해설 세부 사항 관련 - 여자가 의논하고 싶어 하는 것

여자가 첫 대사에서 지난주에 발송한 온라인 고객 설문 결과 건으로 얘기하려 한다(I wanted to talk about the results from the online customer questionnaires we sent out last week)고 말하고 있으므로 정답은 (C)이다.

> ▸▸ Paraphrasing 대화의 customer questionnaires
> → 정답의 Customer survey

45

Why does the man say, "The report's only half a page long"?

(A) To confirm some details
(B) To express disappointment
(C) To ask for another assignment
(D) To refuse an offer

남자가 "보고서가 반 페이지밖에 안 돼요"라고 말하는 이유는 무엇인가?

(A) 세부 사항을 확인하려고
(B) 실망감을 나타내려고
(C) 다른 과제를 요청하려고
(D) 제안을 거절하려고

해설 화자의 의도 파악 – 보고서가 반 페이지밖에 안 된다는 말의 의도

앞에서 여자가 회의 전에 자신이 한번 검토하길 원하는지(Did you want me to look it over before the meeting?) 묻는 말에 남자가 인용문을 언급한 것이므로, 보고서가 짧아 여자가 미리 검토해 줄 필요가 없다고 거절하려는 의도로 한 말임을 알 수 있다. 따라서 정답은 (D)이다.

46

What does the woman remind the man about?

(A) Checking a social media account

(B) Unpacking some equipment

(C) Making a reservation

(D) Going to a print shop

여자는 남자에게 무엇을 상기시키는가?

(A) 소셜 미디어 계정 확인

(B) 장비 꺼내기

(C) 예약하기

(D) 인쇄소 가기

해설 세부 사항 관련 – 여자가 남자에게 상기시키는 것

여자가 세 번째 대사에서 당신 사촌네 식당에 우리 자리를 예약해야 한다고 일러 주고 싶었다(I wanted to remind you to book us a table at your cousin's restaurant)고 말하고 있으므로 정답은 (C)이다.

> ▸▸ Paraphrasing 대화의 **book us a table**
> → 정답의 **Making a reservation**

47-49

M-Au **⁴⁷Mount Alifan Department of Parks and Recreation.** How can I help you?

W-Am Hello, **⁴⁸I read about your tree planting initiative, and I wanted to learn more about it.**

M-Au Sure. Our department is now offering residents the opportunity to have a tree planted on their street in honor of someone special. It's part of our city's new beautification project.

W-Am That's great. How can I make a request to do this?

M-Au **⁴⁹You'll need to fill out an online request form from our Web site.** After you put in all your information and submit the form, you'll receive weekly e-mail updates.

남 **마운트 앨리펀 공원 휴양부입니다.** 어떻게 도와 드릴까요?

여 안녕하세요, **나무 심기 계획에 대해 읽었는데 더 알고 싶어요.**

남 물론이죠. 저희 부서는 지금 주민들에게 거리에 나무를 심어 특별한 사람을 기릴 수 있는 기회를 드리고 있어요. 우리 시의 새로운 미화 프로젝트의 일환입니다.

여 훌륭하네요. 하려면 어떻게 요청하나요?

남 **웹사이트에서 온라인 요청 양식을 작성해야 합니다.** 모든 정보를 입력하고 양식을 제출하면 매주 이메일로 새 소식을 받으실 겁니다.

어휘 initiative 계획 opportunity 기회 in honor of ~을 기리기 위해 beautification 미화

47

What city department does the man work in?

(A) Parks and Recreation

(B) Water Management

(C) Transportation

(D) Education

남자는 시청 어느 부서에서 일하는가?

(A) 공원 휴양

(B) 물 관리

(C) 교통

(D) 교육

해설 전체 내용 관련 – 남자가 근무하는 시청의 부서

남자가 첫 대사에서 마운트 앨리펀 공원 휴양부(Mount Alifan Department of Parks and Recreation)라고 소속을 밝히고 있으므로 정답은 (A)이다.

48

Why is the woman calling?

(A) To report a fallen tree

(B) To ask about city-job openings

(C) To find out the cost of a project

(D) To inquire about a tree planting program

여자는 왜 전화하는가?

(A) 쓰러진 나무를 신고하려고

(B) 시 일자리를 문의하려고

(C) 프로젝트 비용을 파악하려고

(D) 나무 심기 프로그램에 관해 문의하려고

해설 세부 사항 관련 – 여자가 전화하는 이유

여자가 첫 대사에서 나무 심기 계획에 대해 읽었는데 더 알고 싶다(I read about your tree planting initiative, and I wanted to learn more about it)며 나무 심기에 대한 정보를 요청하고 있으므로 정답은 (D)이다.

> ▸▸ Paraphrasing 대화의 **your tree planting initiative**
> → 정답의 **a tree planting program**

49

What does the man tell the woman to do?

(A) Review a policy

(B) Make an appointment

(C) Complete an online form

(D) Contact a different office

남자는 여자에게 무엇을 하라고 말하는가?

(A) 정책 검토
(B) 예약
(C) 온라인 양식 작성
(D) 다른 사무실로 연락

해설 세부 사항 관련 – 남자가 여자에게 하라고 한 일

남자가 마지막 대사에서 웹사이트에서 온라인 요청 양식을 작성해야 한다(You'll need to fill out an online request form from our Web site)고 말하고 있으므로 정답은 (C)이다.

> ▸▸ Paraphrasing 대화의 **fill out an online request form**
> → 정답의 **Complete an online form**

50-52

W-Br	Rohan, I have a question about the production of our new model KT17 wireless headphones. **⁵⁰I just reviewed the quarterly sales report.** They're selling even better than we expected.
M-Au	Yeah, I've heard consumer demand is increasing for those.
W-Br	That's what I wanted to discuss. **⁵¹Do you think we'll need to hire some temporary workers for the factory floor?** I'm concerned that we won't be able keep up with the demand over the holidays.
M-Au	**⁵²We do have a lot of existing inventory ready to ship,** so we may not need to hire more people. **⁵²I'll get an exact count of how many KT17 headphones are available for shipment and let you know this afternoon.**

여	로한, 신모델인 KT17 무선 헤드폰 생산에 관해 질문이 있어요. **방금 분기 판매 보고서를 검토했는데요.** 우리가 예상했던 것보다 훨씬 잘 팔리고 있네요.
남	네, 소비자 수요가 늘고 있다고 들었어요.
여	제가 얘기하려던 게 그거예요. **공장 작업장에 임시직 직원을 몇 명 채용해야 할까요?** 연휴 동안 수요를 따라가지 못할까 걱정이에요.
남	**출고 대기 중인 기존 재고가 많으니까** 사람을 더 채용하지 않아도 돼요. **출고할 수 있는 KT17 헤드폰이 몇 대인지 정확히 계산해서 오늘 오후에 알려 드릴게요.**

어휘	consumer demand 소비자 수요 increase 늘다 temporary 임시의 keep up with ~을 따라가다 existing 기존의 ship (상품을) 출고하다

50

What did the woman recently review?

(A) A sales report
(B) An assembly line
(C) Some online brochures
(D) Some assembly directions

여자는 최근에 무엇을 검토했는가?

(A) 판매 보고서
(B) 조립 라인
(C) 온라인 안내책자
(D) 조립 지침

해설 세부 사항 관련 – 여자가 최근에 검토한 것

여자가 첫 대사에서 방금 분기 판매 보고서를 검토했다(I just reviewed the quarterly sales report)고 말하고 있으므로 정답은 (A)이다.

51

What does the woman ask the man about?

(A) Packaging additional shipments
(B) Hiring temporary employees
(C) Changing a deadline
(D) Sending a press release

여자는 남자에게 무엇을 묻는가?

(A) 추가 출고품 포장
(B) 임시직 직원 채용
(C) 마감일 변경
(D) 보도 자료 발송

해설 세부 사항 관련 – 여자가 남자에게 묻는 것

여자가 두 번째 대사에서 공장 작업장에 임시직 직원을 몇 명 채용해야 할지(Do you think we'll need to hire some temporary workers for the factory floor?)를 묻고 있으므로 정답은 (B)이다.

> ▸▸ Paraphrasing 대화의 **temporary workers**
> → 정답의 **temporary employees**

52

What information will the man provide this afternoon?

(A) Overtime schedules
(B) Design improvements
(C) Production costs
(D) Inventory status

남자는 오늘 오후에 어떤 정보를 제공할 것인가?

(A) 잔업 일정
(B) 디자인 개선
(C) 제조 원가
(D) 재고 현황

어휘 status 현황

해설 세부 사항 관련 - 남자가 오늘 오후에 제공할 정보

남자가 마지막 대사에서 출고 대기 중인 기존 재고가 많다(We do have a lot of existing inventory ready to ship)고 했고 출고할 수 있는 KT17 헤드폰이 몇 대인지 정확히 계산해서 오늘 오후에 알려 주겠다(I'll get an exact count of how many ~ let you know this afternoon)며 출고 가능한 재고 물량을 파악하겠다고 말하고 있으므로 정답은 (D)이다.

53-55

M-Au	Miss Chaudry, I'm glad I caught you before you left for the day. ⁵⁴**About our meeting tomorrow...**
W-Br	Yes, it's in the afternoon, right? ⁵³**We have to go over your designs for the new advertising campaign for Softwell Shoes.**
M-Au	I'm sorry, but ⁵⁴**unfortunately I need to reschedule. I forgot that I have a doctor's appointment.**
W-Br	Hmm. Since we're presenting our ideas to the Softwell representative next week, we should discuss them soon. Are you free in the morning instead? At ten o'clock?
M-Au	Yes, that works.
W-Br	OK, great. Oh, and ⁵⁵**could you post the images in the shared folder?** I'd like to look at them in advance.
M-Au	⁵⁵**Sure. I'll take care of that now.**

남	초드리 씨, 퇴근하시기 전에 만나서 다행이에요. **내일 회의 말인데요…**
여	네, 오후에 하죠? **소프트웰 슈즈의 새 광고 캠페인을 위한 당신 디자인을 검토해야 해요.**
남	죄송하지만, **아쉽게도 일정을 변경해야 할 것 같습니다. 병원 예약이 있는 걸 깜빡했어요.**
여	음. 다음 주에 소프트웰 담당자에게 아이디어를 발표하니까 곧 논의해야 해요. 대신 오전에는 시간이 있으세요? 10시?
남	네, 괜찮아요.
여	좋아요, 잘됐네요. 아, 그리고 **공유 폴더에 이미지 올려 주실래요?** 미리 보고 싶네요.
남	**물론이죠. 지금 처리할게요.**

어휘	unfortunately 아쉽게도 representative 담당자 in advance 미리 take care of ~을 처리하다

53

What project are the speakers working on?

(A) A news article
(B) A training session
(C) An advertising campaign
(D) A research experiment

화자들은 어떤 프로젝트를 작업중인가?

(A) 뉴스 기사
(B) 교육 세션
(C) 광고 캠페인
(D) 연구 실험

어휘 experiment 실험

해설 세부 사항 관련 - 화자들이 작업 중인 프로젝트

여자가 첫 대사에서 소프트웰 슈즈의 새 광고 캠페인을 위한 당신의 디자인을 검토해야 한다(We have to go over your designs for the new advertising campaign for Softwell Shoes)고 말하고 있으므로 정답은 (C)이다.

54

What problem does the man mention?

(A) He has a scheduling conflict.
(B) He missed a presentation.
(C) Some data is unavailable.
(D) There are errors in a report.

남자는 어떤 문제를 언급하는가?

(A) 일정이 겹친다.
(B) 발표를 놓쳤다.
(C) 데이터를 구할 수 없다.
(D) 보고서에 오류가 있다.

어휘 scheduling conflict 일정 겹침

해설 세부 사항 관련 - 남자가 언급하는 문제

남자가 첫 대사에서 여자에게 내일 회의(About our meeting tomorrow)를 언급했고, 두 번째 대사에서 아쉽게도 일정을 변경해야 할 것 같다(unfortunately I need to reschedule)며 병원 예약이 있는 것을 깜빡했다(I forgot that I have a doctor's appointment)고 말하고 있으므로 정답은 (A)이다.

55

What will the man do next?

(A) Make a phone call
(B) Share some images
(C) Change a password
(D) Edit a document

남자는 다음에 무엇을 할 것인가?

(A) 전화 통화
(B) 이미지 공유
(C) 비밀번호 변경
(D) 문서 편집

해설 세부 사항 관련 - 남자가 다음에 할 일

여자가 세 번째 대사에서 공유 폴더에 이미지를 올려 줄 것(could you post the images in the shared folder?)을 요청하자 남자가 물론(Sure)이라고 대답하며 지금 처리하겠다(I'll take care of that now)고 덧붙이고 있으므로 정답은 (B)이다.

56-58 3인 대화

> **W-Am** ⁵⁶**Welcome, everyone, to your second day of training to be an industrial fabric worker. You did a great job running the sewing machines yesterday.** Before we get started, do you have any questions?
>
> **M-Au** This isn't about the training, but... ⁵⁷**this morning, my security badge didn't work.** The guard had to let me into the factory.
>
> **W-Am** OK, I'll follow up with you about that later. Any other questions?
>
> **W-Br** Miss Park? Yesterday you showed us how to make a castle knot on the machine. Could we practice that?
>
> **W-Am** Of course. ⁵⁸**Let's practice that knot—it's essential to sewing almost all shirts. Turn on your sewing machines.**

여1 어서 오세요, 여러분. 산업용 직물 직공이 되기 위한 이틀째 교육입니다. 어제 재봉틀을 아주 잘 쓰셨는데요. 시작하기 전에 질문 있으신가요?

남 교육에 관한 건 아니지만… 오늘 아침에 보안증이 작동하지 않았어요. 경비원이 공장에 들여보내 줘야 했어요.

여1 그렇군요, 그 문제는 나중에 조치할게요. 또 질문 있으세요?

여2 박 선생님? 어제 재봉틀로 캐슬 매듭 만드는 방법을 보여 주셨는데요. 연습할 수 있을까요?

여1 물론이죠. 그 매듭을 연습해 봅시다. 거의 모든 셔츠를 재봉할 때 꼭 필요하죠. 재봉틀 전원을 켜세요.

어휘 sewing machine 재봉틀   follow up 후속 조치를 하다   essential 꼭 필요한

56

Where does the conversation most likely take place?

(A) At a hotel
(B) At a flower farm
(C) At a clothing factory
(D) At a ferry station

대화는 어디에서 이루어지겠는가?

(A) 호텔
(B) 화훼 농장
(C) 의류 공장
(D) 여객선 터미널

해설 전체 내용 관련 – 대화의 장소

첫 번째 여자가 첫 대사에서 여러분 모두 산업용 직물 직공이 되기 위한 이틀째 교육에 온 것을 환영한다(Welcome, everyone, ~ to be an industrial fabric worker)고 했고, 어제 재봉틀을 아주 잘 쓰셨다(You did a great job running the sewing machines yesterday)고 하는 것으로 보아 직물을 다루는 공장에서 말하고 있음을 알 수 있다. 따라서 정답은 (C)이다.

57

What did the man have a problem with this morning?

(A) An identification badge
(B) A parking pass
(C) A time card
(D) A uniform

남자는 오늘 아침에 무엇으로 문제를 겪었는가?

(A) 신분증
(B) 주차권
(C) 근무 시간 기록 카드
(D) 유니폼

해설 세부 사항 관련 – 남자가 오늘 아침에 겪은 문제

남자가 첫 대사에서 오늘 아침에 보안증이 작동하지 않았다(this morning, my security badge didn't work)고 말하고 있으므로 정답은 (A)이다.

58

What will the speakers most likely do next?

(A) Fill out some forms
(B) Tour a facility
(C) Watch a video
(D) Practice a skill

화자들은 다음에 무엇을 하겠는가?

(A) 양식 작성
(B) 시설 견학
(C) 동영상 시청
(D) 기술 연습

해설 세부 사항 관련 – 화자들이 다음에 할 일

첫 번째 여자가 마지막 대사에서 매듭을 연습해 보자(Let's practice that knot)며 거의 모든 셔츠를 재봉할 때 꼭 필요하다(it's essential to sewing almost all shirts)고 했고 재봉틀 전원을 켜라(Turn on your sewing machines)고 말하고 있으므로 재봉틀로 매듭 만드는 방법을 연습할 것임을 알 수 있다. 따라서 정답은 (D)이다.

59-61

M-Cn	Hi Dolores, ^{59, 60}I know we were supposed to review applications for a medical assistant today, but I'm still working on my presentation for the international surgeons' conference next week.
W-Br	⁶⁰No problem. I've presented at that conference before. ⁶⁰You'll need to be prepared.
M-Cn	So... should we reschedule for next week?
W-Br	Actually, ⁶¹why don't we just postpone hiring someone until next month?
M-Cn	⁶¹That would work better for me. But don't we need someone sooner?
W-Br	No. Jerome just told me he could stay until we find his replacement.

남	안녕 돌로레스, 오늘 의료 보조원 지원서를 검토하기로 한 거 알아요. 그런데 다음 주에 있을 국제 외과의 회의에서 할 발표를 아직도 작업하고 있어요.
여	괜찮아요. 제가 전에 그 회의에서 발표해 봤거든요. 준비 잘해야 해요.
남	그럼… 다음 주로 일정을 다시 잡을까요?
여	실은 다음 달로 채용을 미루는 게 어떨까요?
남	저한텐 그게 나아요. 하지만 더 빨리 사람이 필요하지 않나요?
여	아니요. 제롬이 좀 전에 우리가 후임을 찾을 때까지 있을 수 있다고 얘기했어요

어휘 be supposed to ~하기로 되어 있다 application 지원(서) surgeon 외과의 postpone 연기하다 replacement 후임

59

What field do the speakers most likely work in?

(A) Education
(B) Finance
(C) Law
(D) Medicine

화자들은 어느 분야에서 일하겠는가?

(A) 교육
(B) 금융
(C) 법
(D) 의료

해설 전체 내용 관련 - 화자들의 근무 업종

남자가 첫 대사에서 오늘 의료 보조원 지원서를 검토하기로 한 것은 알지만 다음 주에 있을 국제 외과의 회의에서 할 발표를 아직도 작업하고 있다(I know we were supposed to review ~ the international surgeons' conference next week)고 말하는 것으로 보아 화자들은 의료 업계에 종사하고 있다는 것을 알 수 있다. 따라서 정답은 (D)이다.

60

What does the woman mean when she says, "I've presented at that conference before"?

(A) She has a lot of professional experience.
(B) She dislikes giving presentations.
(C) She understands the man's situation.
(D) She has completed a requirement.

여자가 "제가 전에 그 회의에서 발표해 봤거든요"라고 말하는 의도는 무엇인가?

(A) 직종 관련 경험이 많다.
(B) 발표하기 싫어한다.
(C) 남자의 상황을 이해한다.
(D) 요구 사항을 완료했다.

해설 화자의 의도 파악 - 제가 전에 그 회의에서 발표해 봤다는 말의 의도

앞에서 남자가 오늘 의료 보조원 지원서를 검토하기로 한 것은 알지만 다음 주에 있을 국제 외과의 회의에서 할 발표를 아직도 작업하고 있다(I know we were supposed to review ~ the international surgeons' conference next week)며 발표 준비 때문에 여자와의 업무 일정을 맞추기 힘들다고 말하자 여자가 괜찮다(No problem)고 안심시키며 인용문을 언급했고 뒤이어 준비를 잘해야 한다(You'll need to be prepared)고 격려하는 것으로 보아, 자신도 같은 경험을 한 적이 있어 남자의 상황을 잘 안다는 공감을 표하려는 의도로 볼 수 있다. 따라서 정답은 (C)이다.

61

What do the speakers agree to do?

(A) Temporarily close an office
(B) Postpone hiring an employee
(C) Work on a presentation together
(D) Contact some clients

화자들은 무엇을 하기로 동의하는가?

(A) 임시 휴업
(B) 직원 채용 연기
(C) 함께 발표 준비
(D) 고객들에게 연락

해설 세부 사항 관련 - 화자들이 동의하는 일

여자가 두 번째 대사에서 다음 달로 채용을 미루는 게 어떨지(why don't we just postpone hiring someone until next month?)를 제안하자 남자도 저한테는 그게 더 좋다(That would work better for me)며 동의하고 있으므로 정답은 (B)이다.

62-64 대화 + 카탈로그 페이지

W-Am	Thanks for calling Rose Mound Pottery. How can I help you?
M-Au	⁶²I'm interested in ordering some dishes that I saw in your catalog for my new restaurant. They're the ones with the large star in the middle and smaller ones around the edge.

134

W-Am Yes, I know the ones you mean. Did you notice that pattern's a limited edition?

M-Au Oh no. I hope they're still available. [63]**The grand opening for my restaurant is in May.**

W-Am Yes, they're still in stock. But I know [64]**that pattern will be discontinued at the end of the year. They'll be hard to replace after that.**

M-Au I'm glad you told me. Then I'll order extra ones now.

여　로즈 마운드 도자기에 전화 주셔서 감사합니다. 어떻게 도와 드릴까요?

남　새 식당용으로 카탈로그에서 본 접시들을 주문하고 싶은데요. 가운데에 큰 별이 있고 가장자리에 작은 별들이 있는 접시예요.

여　네, 어떤 접시를 말씀하시는지 알겠어요. 그 무늬는 한정판인데, 아셨나요?

남　이런. 지금도 구할 수 있으면 좋겠네요. **식당 개점이 5월이에요.**

여　네, 아직 재고가 있어요. 그런데 제가 알기로 **그 무늬는 연말에 단종될 예정이에요. 그 이후에는 대체하기 어려울 거예요.**

남　알려 주셔서 다행이에요. 그렇다면 지금 여분을 주문할게요.

어휘　in stock 재고가 있는　discontinue 단종시키다 replace 대체하다

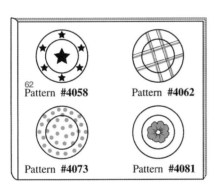

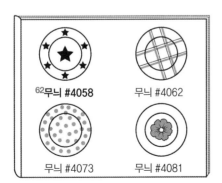

62

Look at the graphic. Which dish pattern is the man interested in?

(A) #4058
(B) #4062
(C) #4073
(D) #4081

시각 정보에 의하면 남자는 어떤 접시 무늬에 관심이 있는가?

(A) 4058번
(B) 4062번
(C) 4073번
(D) 4081번

해설　시각 정보 연계 - 남자가 관심 있는 접시 무늬

남자가 첫 대사에서 새 식당용으로 카탈로그에서 본 접시들을 주문하고 싶다(I'm interested in ordering ~ for my new restaurant)며 가운데에 큰 별이 있고 가장자리에 작은 별들이 있는 접시(They're the ones with the large star in the middle and smaller ones around the edge)라고 말하고 있고, 카탈로그 페이지에 따르면 별 무늬 접시는 4058번이므로 정답은 (A)이다.

63

According to the man, what will happen in May?

(A) A store will take inventory.
(B) A new restaurant will open.
(C) A product line will launch.
(D) A factory will move to a new location.

남자의 말에 따르면, 5월에 무슨 일이 있을 것인가?

(A) 매장에서 재고를 조사한다.
(B) 새 식당이 문을 연다.
(C) 제품군이 출시된다.
(D) 공장이 새 장소로 이전한다.

어휘　take inventory 재고를 조사하다

해설　세부 사항 관련 - 남자가 5월에 있을 것이라고 말하는 일

남자가 두 번째 대사에서 식당 개점이 5월(The grand opening for my restaurant is in May)이라고 말하고 있으므로 정답은 (B)이다.

64

What problem does the woman mention?

(A) Some shipping fees will increase.
(B) Some items will become unavailable.
(C) Some items were damaged during shipping.
(D) Some catalogs contain inaccurate information.

여자는 어떤 문제를 언급하는가?

(A) 배송비가 인상될 것이다.
(B) 품목을 구할 수 없게 된다.
(C) 품목이 배송 중에 파손됐다.
(D) 카탈로그에 잘못된 정보가 있다.

어휘　inaccurate 잘못된

여자가 세 번째 대사에서 그 무늬는 연말에 단종될 예정(that pattern will be discontinued at the end of the year)이라고 했고, 그 이후에는 대체하기 어려울 것(They'll be hard to replace after that)이라고 말하고 있으므로 정답은 (B)이다.

65-67 대화 + 표 확인증

M-Cn	⁶⁵**Taggert Railways.** How may I help you?
W-Br	Good morning. I have a question about a reservation for a trip to San Francisco. The confirmation code is 0146H.
M-Cn	OK, let me look it up. I see you have three tickets.
W-Br	That's right. ⁶⁶**I was wondering if there's a train leaving a day earlier, but at the same time.**
M-Cn	Let me check... ⁶⁶**Yes there is**, and the tickets are the same price.
W-Br	Perfect. ⁶⁶**Then I'd like to make that change.**
M-Cn	OK. ⁶⁷**Should I use the e-mail associated with your original reservation to send you the new information?**
W-Br	⁶⁷**Yes, please.**

남	**태거트 철도입니다.** 어떻게 도와 드릴까요?
여	안녕하세요. 샌프란시스코행 예약에 관해 궁금한 게 있어요. 확인 코드는 0146H예요.
남	찾아볼게요. 표를 석 장 갖고 계시네요.
여	맞아요. **하루 전 같은 시간에 출발하는 기차가 있는지 궁금해서요.**
남	확인해 볼게요… **네, 있네요,** 그리고 표가 같은 가격이에요.
여	딱 좋네요. **그럼 그걸로 바꿀래요.**
남	알겠습니다. **원래 예약과 연계된 이메일을 사용해서 새로운 정보를 보낼까요?**
여	**네, 그렇게 해 주세요.**

어휘 associated with ~와 연계된

Ticket Confirmation Code: 0146H	
Number of Passengers	3
Date	June ⁶⁶22
Departure Time	11 A.M.
Price per Ticket	$14
Total Price	$42

표 확인 코드: 0146H	
승객 수	3
날짜	6월 ⁶⁶22일
출발 시간	오전 11시
표당 가격	14달러
총 금액	42달러

65

What type of business is the woman calling?

(A) A railway company
(B) A bus company
(C) An airline
(D) A ferry service

여자는 어떤 업체에 전화를 걸고 있는가?

(A) 철도 회사
(B) 버스 회사
(C) 항공사
(D) 여객선 서비스 업체

해설 전체 내용 관련 - 여자가 전화를 건 업체

남자가 첫 대사에서 태거트 철도(Taggert Railways)라고 전화를 받고 있으므로 여자는 철도 회사에 전화를 걸고 있음을 알 수 있다. 따라서 정답은 (A)이다.

66

Look at the graphic. What number will be updated?

(A) 3
(B) 22
(C) 11
(D) 14

시각 정보에 의하면 어떤 숫자가 수정되겠는가?

(A) 3
(B) 22
(C) 11
(D) 14

해설 시각 정보 연계 - 수정될 숫자

여자가 두 번째 대사에서 하루 전 같은 시간에 출발하는 기차가 있는지 궁금하다(I was wondering if there's a train leaving a day earlier, but at the same time)고 하자 남자가 있다(Yes there is)고 대답했고, 여자가 뒤이어 그럼 그것으로 바꾸겠다(Then I'd like to make that change)고 말하고 있으므로 여자가 출발할 날짜가 하루 전으로 변경될 것임을 알 수 있다. 표 확인증에 따르면 출발 날짜는 6월 22일로 나와 있으므로 변경될 숫자는 22이다. 따라서 정답은 (B)이다.

67

What will the man most likely do next?

(A) Collect some money
(B) Check a seat assignment
(C) Make an announcement
(D) Send an e-mail

남자는 다음에 무엇을 하겠는가?

(A) 수금하기
(B) 좌석 배정 확인하기
(C) 공지하기
(D) 이메일 보내기

어휘 assignment 배정

해설 세부 사항 관련 - 남자가 다음에 할 일

남자가 네 번째 대사에서 원래 예약과 연계된 이메일을 사용해서 새로운 정보를 보내 줄지(Should I use the e-mail ~ send you the new information?)를 묻자 여자가 그렇게 해 달라(Yes, please)고 응답하고 있으므로 남자는 곧 여자에게 이메일을 보낼 것임을 알 수 있다. 따라서 정답은 (D)이다.

68-70 대화 + 비교 차트

M-Au Margaret, ⁶⁸**do you have any plastic zip ties?** We used some to tie cables together when we installed the servers last week.

W-Am Sure, they're on my desk. Need help with anything?

M-Au No, I just need them to fasten some electronic trackers to my luggage. ⁶⁹**I'm flying to Shanghai tomorrow for a week to meet the new clients**, and I want to be able to keep track of my suitcases while I'm traveling.

W-Am I need one of those. I misplace my keys all the time. How'd you decide which one to buy?

M-Au ⁷⁰**The most important feature for me is battery life, so I bought the one with the longest-lasting battery.**

남 마가렛, **플라스틱 케이블 타이 있어요?** 지난주에 서버 설치할 때 케이블 묶느라 몇 개 썼잖아요.

여 네, 제 책상 위에 있어요. 도와 드려요?

남 아니요, 그냥 전자 위치 추적기를 제 가방에 고정하느라 필요해요. **일주일 일정으로 새 고객들을 만나러 내일 비행기로 상하이에 가는데**, 여행하는 동안 여행 가방의 위치를 추적하고 싶어서요.

여 저도 하나 필요해요. 열쇠를 늘 엉뚱한 데 두고 못 찾거든요. 어떤 걸 살지는 어떻게 결정하셨어요?

남 **저한테 가장 중요한 기능은 배터리 수명이라서 배터리가 가장 오래가는 걸로 샀어요.**

어휘 install 설치하다 fasten 고정하다 keep track of ~을 추적하다 misplace 엉뚱한 곳에 두고 못 찾다 feature 기능

Electronic Trackers	
Brand	**Battery Life**
Beep It	6 months
Filez	4 months
Loc Pro	⁷⁰2 years
XMarks	1 year

전자 위치 추적기	
브랜드	**배터리 수명**
빕 잇	6개월
파일즈	4개월
록 프로	⁷⁰2년
X마크스	1년

68

What does the man ask the woman for?

(A) Some plastic ties
(B) Some computer cables
(C) An Internet password
(D) A storage room key

남자는 여자에게 무엇을 요청하는가?

(A) 플라스틱 케이블 타이
(B) 컴퓨터 케이블
(C) 인터넷 비밀번호
(D) 창고 열쇠

해설 세부 사항 관련 - 남자가 여자에게 요청하는 것

남자가 첫 대사에서 여자에게 플라스틱 케이블 타이가 있는지(do you have any plastic zip ties?)를 묻고 있으므로 정답은 (A)이다.

69

What is the man doing tomorrow?

(A) Inspecting a factory
(B) Upgrading a company database
(C) Leading a tour
(D) Going on a business trip

남자는 내일 무엇을 하는가?

(A) 공장 점검
(B) 회사 데이터베이스 업그레이드
(C) 견학 인솔
(D) 출장

해설 세부 사항 관련 - 남자가 내일 할 일

남자가 두 번째 대사에서 일주일 일정으로 새 고객들을 만나러 내일 비행기로 상하이에 간다(I'm flying to Shanghai tomorrow for a week to meet the new clients)고 말하고 있으므로 정답은 (D)이다.

▸▸ Paraphrasing 대화의 **flying to ~ to meet the new clients**
→ 정답의 **Going on a business trip**

70

Look at the graphic. Which brand did the man buy?

(A) Beep It
(B) Filez
(C) Loc Pro
(D) XMarks

시각 정보에 의하면 남자는 어떤 브랜드를 샀는가?

(A) 빕 잇
(B) 파일즈
(C) 록 프로
(D) X마크스

해설 시각 정보 연계 - 남자가 구입한 브랜드

남자가 마지막 대사에서 내게 가장 중요한 기능은 배터리 수명이라서 배터리가 가장 오래가는 것으로 샀다(The most important feature ~ the one with the longest-lasting battery)고 말하고 있고, 비교 차트에 따르면 배터리 수명이 가장 긴 브랜드는 록 프로이므로 정답은 (C)이다.

PART 4

71-73 광고

> M-Cn Are you looking for a location to host your next company event? Well, look no further than Mirelli's. ⁷¹**With our delicious food and private dining rooms, Mirelli's is the perfect place for everything from small to large business gatherings.** But that's not the only reason to choose Mirelli's. ⁷²**We're famous for our friendly waitstaff.** They are always ready to help! Planning to hold an event with food at your office? No problem—we'll bring the food to you. ⁷³**You can view our catering packages on our Web site.**

> 다음 회사 행사를 주최할 장소를 찾고 계신가요? 자, 미렐리스만 보시면 됩니다. 맛있는 음식과 전용 식당이 있는 미렐리스는 소규모 회사 모임에서 대규모 회사 모임까지 모든 모임에 완벽한 장소입니다. 하지만 이것이 미렐리스를 선택하는 유일한 이유는 아닙니다. 저희는 친절한 종업원들로 유명합니다. 그들은 언제나 도울 준비가 되어 있습니다! 사무실에서 음식을 차리고 행사를 열 계획이신가요? 문제없습니다. 저희가 음식을 가져다 드리겠습니다. 저희 웹사이트에서 출장 요리 패키지를 보실 수 있습니다.

> 어휘 waitstaff 종업원들 catering 출장 요리(업)

71

What is most likely being advertised?

(A) A convention center
(B) A restaurant
(C) A supermarket
(D) A shipping company

무엇이 광고되고 있겠는가?

(A) 컨벤션 센터
(B) 식당
(C) 슈퍼마켓
(D) 운송 회사

해설 전체 내용 관련 - 광고되고 있는 것

화자가 초반부에 맛있는 음식과 전용 식당이 있는 미렐리스는 소규모 회사 모임에서 대규모 회사 모임까지 모든 모임에 완벽한 장소(With our delicious food and private dining rooms, ~ business gatherings)라고 광고하고 있으므로 정답은 (B)이다.

72

What is the business famous for?

(A) Its prices
(B) Its location
(C) Its history
(D) Its staff

업체는 무엇으로 유명한가?

(A) 가격
(B) 위치
(C) 역사
(D) 직원

해설 세부 사항 관련 - 업체가 유명한 것

화자가 중반부에 저희는 친절한 종업원들로 유명하다(We're famous for our friendly waitstaff)고 말하고 있으므로 정답은 (D)이다.

73

What does the speaker say is on a Web site?

(A) Some catering options
(B) Some driving directions
(C) Current discounts
(D) Business hours

화자는 웹사이트에 무엇이 있다고 말하는가?

(A) 출장 요리 선택 사항
(B) 운전해서 오는 길 안내
(C) 현재 할인
(D) 영업 시간

해설 세부 사항 관련 - 화자가 웹사이트에 있다고 말하는 것

화자가 마지막에 저희 웹사이트에서 출장 요리 패키지를 보실 수 있다(You can view our catering packages on our Web site)고 말하고 있으므로 정답은 (A)이다.

M-Au **74I have an update about the video game you've been working hard to develop.** As you know, we'll be partnering with a video game publishing company to get our product on the market. **75I just received their initial contract. And I'm pleased to say, the terms they are proposing are quite favorable—we're promised a payment as soon as we sign on. 76Our legal team wants to make sure the programmers are happy before they negotiate some other provisions in the contract. I'll send you the document later.**

여러분이 열심히 개발한 비디오 게임 관련해서 새 소식이 있어요. 아시다시피, 비디오 게임 퍼블리싱 회사와 제휴해 우리 제품을 출시할 텐데요. 방금 그쪽에서 보낸 계약서 초안을 받았어요. 그리고 이렇게 말하게 되어서 기쁜데요, 그들이 제안한 조건이 꽤 유리해요. 우리가 서명하는 즉시 지불이 보장되거든요. 법무팀에서는 계약서의 다른 조항들을 협상하기 전에 프로그래머들이 만족하는지 확인했으면 해요. 이따가 서류를 보내 드리죠.

어휘 contract 계약(서) terms (계약) 조건 favorable 유리한 provision 조항

74

Who most likely are the listeners?

(A) Product developers
(B) Investment bankers
(C) Book publishers
(D) Building contractors

청자들은 누구이겠는가?

(A) 제품 개발자
(B) 투자 은행 직원
(C) 서적 출판인
(D) 건설 도급 업자

해설 전체 내용 관련 – 청자들의 직업

화자가 도입부에 여러분이 열심히 개발한 비디오 게임 관련해서 새 소식이 있다(I have an update about the video game you've been working hard to develop)고 말하는 것으로 보아 청자들은 게임 개발자임을 알 수 있다. 따라서 정답은 (A)이다.

75

What does the speaker say is favorable about a contract?

(A) There is 24-hour service call availability.
(B) There is an extended warranty.
(C) There is an immediate payment.
(D) There is a low interest rate.

화자는 계약에서 무엇이 유리하다고 말하는가?

(A) 24시간 호출 서비스가 가능하다.
(B) 보증 연장이 있다.
(C) 즉시 지불한다.
(D) 금리가 낮다.

어휘 extended 연장된 warranty 보증

해설 세부 사항 관련 – 화자가 계약에서 유리하다고 말하는 것

화자가 중반부에 방금 그쪽에서 보낸 계약서 초안을 받았다(I just received their initial contract)고 계약에 대해 언급하며, 그들이 제안한 조건이 꽤 유리하다고 말하게 되어 기쁘다(I'm pleased to say, the terms they are proposing are quite favorable)면서 우리가 서명하는 즉시 지불이 보장된다(we're promised a payment as soon as we sign on)고 설명하고 있으므로 정답은 (C)이다.

▸▸ Paraphrasing 담화의 **as soon as**
→ 정답의 **immediate**

76

What does the speaker imply when he says, "I'll send you the document later"?

(A) He is having computer problems.
(B) He wants the listeners' opinions.
(C) He has missed a deadline.
(D) He is almost finished with some work.

화자가 "이따가 서류를 보내 드리죠"라고 말하는 의도는 무엇인가?

(A) 컴퓨터에 문제가 있다.
(B) 청자들의 의견을 원한다.
(C) 마감일을 놓쳤다.
(D) 일을 거의 끝냈다.

해설 화자의 의도 파악 – 이따가 서류를 보내 드리겠다는 말의 의도

화자가 앞에서 법무팀에서는 계약서의 다른 조항들을 협상하기 전에 프로그래머들이 만족하는지 확인했으면 한다(Our legal team wants to make sure ~ some other provisions in the contract)고 말한 뒤 인용문을 언급하고 있으므로, 프로그래머인 청자들이 화자가 보내 주는 서류의 내용을 살펴보고 나서 계약과 관련해 의견을 제시해 줄 것을 요청하려는 의도로 한 말임을 알 수 있다. 따라서 정답은 (B)이다.

W-Br **77Thank you for joining me on this tour of our solar panel manufacturing plant.** Here at Nature's Solar Energy, Incorporated, we believe our customers should have the chance to see the production of the solar panels that power their homes and businesses. Before we begin, I want to remind you about our main safety rule. **78Make sure you wear the hard hats we provided and keep them on at all times.** OK, **79our first stop will be in the showroom. I'll show you the latest models of**

our solar panels so you understand exactly how they work.

이번 태양열 전지판 제조 공장 견학에 함께해 주셔서 감사합니다. 네이처스 태양 에너지 사는 가정과 업체에 전력을 공급하는 태양열 전지판이 생산되는 모습을 고객님들이 보실 기회가 있어야 한다고 믿습니다. 시작하기 전에 당사의 주요 안전 수칙을 다시 알려 드리고자 합니다. **저희가 제공한 안전모를 꼭 쓰시되 항상 쓰고 다니세요.** 자, **처음 들를 곳은 전시장입니다.** 태양열 전지판이 작동하는 방식을 정확히 이해하실 수 있도록 **최신 모델 태양열 전지판을 보여 드리겠습니다.**

어휘 manufacturing 제조 hard hat 안전모

77

Where is the tour taking place?

(A) At an art gallery
(B) At a construction site
(C) **At a solar-panel factory**
(D) At a car-part warehouse

견학은 어디에서 진행되고 있는가?
(A) 미술관
(B) 건설 현장
(C) **태양열 전지판 공장**
(D) 자동차 부품 창고

해설 전체 내용 관련 - 견학 장소
화자가 도입부에 이번 태양열 전지판 제조 공장 견학에 함께해 주셔서 감사하다(Thank you for joining me on this tour of our solar panel manufacturing plant)고 말하고 있으므로 정답은 (C)이다.

▸▸ Paraphrasing 담화의 **manufacturing plant**
→ 정답의 **factory**

78

What does the speaker remind the listeners to do?

(A) **Wear protective hats**
(B) Follow posted signs
(C) Stay together as a group
(D) Store personal belongings

화자는 청자들에게 무엇을 하라고 일러 주는가?
(A) **보호모 착용하기**
(B) 게시된 표지판 따라가기
(C) 단체로 함께 움직이기
(D) 개인 소지품 보관하기

해설 세부 사항 관련 - 화자가 청자들에게 하라고 일러 주는 것
화자가 중반부에 저희가 제공한 안전모를 꼭 쓰시되 항상 쓰고 다니라(Make sure you wear the hard hats we provided and keep them on at all times)고 말하고 있으므로 정답은 (A)이다.

▸▸ Paraphrasing 담화의 **hard hats**
→ 정답의 **protective hats**

79

What will the listeners see first on the tour?

(A) A map of the grounds
(B) An informational video
(C) **Some product models**
(D) Some historic photographs

청자들은 견학에서 무엇을 가장 먼저 볼 것인가?
(A) 부지 지도
(B) 정보 제공 동영상
(C) **제품 모델**
(D) 역사적 사진

해설 세부 사항 관련 - 청자들이 견학에서 가장 먼저 볼 것
화자가 후반부에 처음 들를 곳은 전시장(our first stop will be in the showroom)이라고 말한 뒤 최신 모델 태양열 전지판을 보여 드리겠다(I'll show you the latest models of our solar panels)고 말하고 있으므로, 청자들이 가장 처음 보게 될 것은 최신 모델 태양열 전지판임을 알 수 있다. 따라서 정답은 (C)이다.

80-82 방송

M-Cn Thanks for tuning in to *Business World*! **80 On today's episode, we'll be taking a deep dive into the topic of making a career change.** Transitioning to a new industry can be challenging. **81 It's important to highlight any transferable skills you have to offer.** What abilities do you currently possess that could be useful in a new role, and how can you promote them on professional networking sites? To help us explore this, **82 So-Hee Chung, chief executive officer of the popular job search app, Zantage, is joining us in the studio today.** Welcome, So-Hee.

〈비즈니스 월드〉를 청취해 주셔서 감사합니다! **오늘 회차에서는 진로 변경의 주제를 심도 있게 다루도록 하겠습니다.** 새로운 업종으로 전환하기가 어려울 수도 있는데요. **제공해야 할 이전 가능한 기술을 강조하는 게 중요하죠.** 지금 가지고 있는 역량 중 새로운 역할에 유용할 수 있는 능력은 무엇이며, 어떻게 하면 이 역량들을 업계 교류 현장에서 홍보할 수 있을까요? 이 문제를 알아보는 데 도움을 주기 위해 **인기 구직 앱인 잔타지의 CEO 정소희 씨가 오늘 스튜디오에 저희와 함께합니다.** 소희 씨, 어서 오세요.

어휘 transition 전환하다 challenging 어려운 transferable 이전 가능한 explore 알아보다

80

What is the focus of the episode?

(A) Improving training programs

(B) Changing careers

(C) Designing Web sites

(D) Increasing sales

이 회차의 초점은 무엇인가?

(A) 교육 프로그램 개선

(B) 진로 변경

(C) 웹사이트 설계

(D) 매출 증대

해설 전체 내용 관련 - 방송의 주제

화자가 초반부에 오늘 회차에서는 진로 변경의 주제를 심도 있게 다루도록 하겠다(On today's episode, we'll be taking a deep dive into the topic of making a career change)고 말하고 있으므로 정답은 (B)이다.

> ▸▸ Paraphrasing   담화의 **making a career change**
> → 정답의 **Changing careers**

81

What does the speaker say is important?

(A) Complying with industry regulations

(B) Emphasizing transferable skills

(C) Offering promotional discounts

(D) Attending networking events

화자는 무엇이 중요하다고 말하는가?

(A) 업계 규정 준수

(B) 이전 가능한 기술 강조

(C) 판촉용 할인 제공

(D) 교류 행사 참석

어휘 comply with ~을 준수하다   regulation 규정

해설 세부 사항 관련 - 화자가 중요하다고 말하는 것

화자가 중반부에 제공해야 할 이전 가능한 기술을 강조하는 것이 중요하다(It's important to highlight any transferable skills you have to offer)고 말하고 있으므로 정답은 (B)이다.

> ▸▸ Paraphrasing   담화의 **highlight**
> → 정답의 **Emphasizing**

82

Who is So-Hee Chung?

(A) A company executive

(B) A government official

(C) A news reporter

(D) A financial analyst

정소희는 누구인가?

(A) 회사 임원

(B) 공무원

(C) 보도 기자

(D) 금융 분석가

해설 세부 사항 관련 - 정소희의 직업

화자가 후반부에 인기 구직 앱인 잔타지의 CEO 정소희 씨가 오늘 스튜디오에 저희와 함께한다(So-Hee Chung, chief executive officer ~ us in the studio today)고 말하고 있으므로 정답은 (A)이다.

> ▸▸ Paraphrasing   담화의 **chief executive officer**
> → 정답의 **A company executive**

83-85 전화 메시지

W-Am Hello, ⁸³**this is Adriana Ortiz... set designer from the Summer Theater.** We met last week. ⁸³**Since you're directing the new play we're featuring,** I'd like to get together to discuss some ideas I have. I've read the script and started sketching possible backgrounds we could use. ⁸⁴**You mentioned being concerned about the short amount of time we have for creating a set.** Well, we have a large team. And there are lots of props in storage. ⁸⁵**I'm going out of town to see some relatives tomorrow,** but if you're free to meet this weekend, my schedule's flexible then.

안녕하세요, **여름 극장 무대 디자이너 아드리아나 오티즈예요**··· 지난주에 만났죠. 이번에 **저희가 선보이는 신작 연극을 연출하신다니,** 모여서 제가 갖고 있는 아이디어에 대해 논의하고 싶어요. 제가 대본을 읽고 우리가 쓸 만한 어울리는 배경 스케치를 시작했어요. **무대 만들 시간이 짧아서 걱정이라고 말씀하셨는데요.** 음, 저희는 대규모 팀이 있어요. 게다가 창고에 소품도 많고요. **전 내일 친척들을 만나러 시외로 나가는데** 그래도 이번 주말에 시간 괜찮으시면 제 일정을 바꿀 수 있어요.

어휘 possible 어울리는   props 소품   relative 친척   flexible 바꿀 수 있는

83

What is the message mainly about?

(A) Scheduling auditions

(B) Purchasing tickets

(C) Designing a set

(D) Revising a script

주로 무엇에 관한 메시지인가?

(A) 오디션 일정 조율

(B) 티켓 구매

(C) 무대 디자인

(D) 대본 수정

어휘 purchase 구매하다   revise 수정하다

화자가 초반부에 여름 극장 무대 디자이너 아드리아나 오티즈(this is Adriana Ortiz… set designer from the Summer Theater)라고 자신을 소개했고, 이번에 저희가 선보이는 신작 연극을 연출하신다니 모여서 제가 갖고 있는 아이디어에 대해 논의하고 싶다(Since you're directing the new play ~ to discuss some ideas I have)며 제가 대본을 읽고 우리가 쓸 만한 어울리는 배경 스케치를 시작했다(I've read the script ~ backgrounds we could use)고 말하는 것으로 보아, 화자는 극장의 무대 디자이너로서 신작 연극의 무대 디자인에 대해 이야기하고 있음을 알 수 있다. 따라서 정답은 (C)이다.

84

Why does the speaker say, "we have a large team"?

(A) To make a complaint

(B) To provide reassurance

(C) To express surprise

(D) To refuse an offer

화자가 "저희는 대규모 팀이 있어요"라고 말하는 이유는 무엇인가?

(A) 항의하려고

(B) 안심시키려고

(C) 놀라움을 표명하려고

(D) 제안을 거절하려고

해설 화자의 의도 파악 - 저희는 대규모 팀이 있다는 말의 의도

앞에서 세트 만들 시간이 짧아서 걱정이라고 말씀하셨다(You mentioned being concerned about the short amount of time we have for creating a set)고 말한 뒤 인용문을 언급한 것으로 보아, 일할 수 있는 인력이 많으므로 작업 시간이 짧은 점에 대해서는 걱정하지 않아도 된다고 청자를 안심시키려고 한 말임을 알 수 있다. 따라서 정답은 (B)이다.

85

Why is the speaker unable to meet tomorrow?

(A) Her car needs repairs.

(B) She is moving to a new apartment.

(C) She is going hiking.

(D) She is visiting family.

화자는 왜 내일 만날 수 없는가?

(A) 차를 수리해야 한다.

(B) 새 아파트로 이사한다.

(C) 등산을 간다.

(D) 가족을 방문한다.

해설 세부 사항 관련 - 화자가 내일 만날 수 없는 이유

화자가 후반부에 내일 친척들을 만나러 시외로 나간다(I'm going out of town to see some relatives tomorrow)고 말하고 있으므로 정답은 (D)이다.

> ▸▸ Paraphrasing 담화의 **see some relatives**
> → 정답의 **is visiting family**

86-88 담화

W-Br Welcome to Cornerway Industries. **[86]I'm Sunita Yadav, Coordinator of the Internship Program. I'm sure you'll find your summer experience here rewarding!** Before we begin the first training session, we have to take care of some administrative matters. **[87]As you entered the room, you received a packet of documents.** It includes information about logging into your e-mail and submitting time sheets. I'll briefly go over those procedures now. Then, **[88]in an hour, you'll head to the security office to get identification badges.** You'll need those to enter and exit the building.

코너웨이 인더스트리에 오신 것을 환영합니다. **저는 인턴십 프로그램 책임 진행자 수니타 야다브입니다. 이곳에서 체험하는 여름 프로그램은 틀림없이 보람 있을 겁니다!** 첫 번째 교육 세션을 시작하기 전에 몇 가지 행정 문제를 처리해야 하는데요. **방에 들어오실 때 서류 꾸러미를 받으셨죠.** 거기에 이메일 로그인과 근무 시간 기록부 제출에 대한 정보가 있어요. 이제 그 절차들을 간략히 살펴볼게요. 그런 다음 **한 시간 뒤에 경비실에 가서 신분증을 받을 겁니다.** 건물을 드나들려면 신분증이 필요해요.

어휘 rewarding 보람 있는 administrative 행정의 time sheet 근무 시간 기록부 procedure 절차

86

Who most likely are the listeners?

(A) Board members

(B) Government officials

(C) Clients

(D) Interns

청자들은 누구이겠는가?

(A) 이사

(B) 공무원

(C) 고객

(D) 인턴

해설 전체 내용 관련 - 청자들의 직업

화자가 초반부에 인턴십 프로그램 책임 진행자 수니타 야다브(I'm Sunita Yadav, Coordinator of the Internship Program)라고 자신을 소개하며 이곳에서 체험하는 여름 프로그램은 틀림없이 보람 있을 것(I'm sure you'll find your summer experience here rewarding!)이라고 말하는 것으로 보아 청자들은 인턴십 프로그램 참가자들임을 알 수 있다. 따라서 정답은 (D)이다.

87

What did the listeners receive?

(A) An event ticket

(B) An information packet

(C) A project invoice

(D) An annual report

청자들은 무엇을 받았는가?

(A) 행사 티켓

(B) 정보 꾸러미

(C) 프로젝트 송장

(D) 연차 보고서

해설 세부 사항 관련 - 청자들이 받은 것

화자가 중반부에 방에 들어오실 때 서류 꾸러미를 받으셨다(As you entered the room, you received a packet of documents)고 말하고 있으므로 정답은 (B)이다.

> ▸▸ Paraphrasing   담화의 **a packet of documents**
> → 정답의 **An information packet**

88

According to the speaker, what will the listeners do in an hour?

(A) Have lunch

(B) Join a conference call

(C) Get security badges

(D) Take a building tour

화자의 말에 따르면, 청자들은 한 시간 후에 무엇을 할 것인가?

(A) 점심 먹기

(B) 전화 회의 참여하기

(C) 보안증 받기

(D) 건물 둘러보기

해설 세부 사항 관련 - 화자가 청자들이 한 시간 후에 할 일이라고 말하는 것

화자가 후반부에 한 시간 뒤에 경비실에 가서 신분증을 받을 것(in an hour, you'll head to the security office to get identification badges)이라고 말하고 있으므로 정답은 (C)이다.

> ▸▸ Paraphrasing   담화의 **identification badges**
> → 정답의 **security badges**

89-91 회의 발췌

W-Am **⁸⁹Last month, I went to a conference** that allowed me the opportunity to meet other small business owners from the region and have discussions with them. A number of helpful ideas were exchanged. For example, **⁹⁰several speakers pointed out that it can be difficult for customers to navigate corporate Web sites, especially when looking for information like a phone number they**

can call when they need service. I've asked the IT department to redesign our Web site to make it more navigable. **⁹¹If you'll look up here, I'll demonstrate the new layout that'll go live in a few weeks.**

지난달에 회의에 다녀왔는데, 지역 내 다른 소상공인들을 만나 함께 논의할 기회가 있었습니다. 유용한 아이디어를 많이 교환했어요. 예를 들어, 몇몇 강연자들은 고객이 기업 웹사이트를 탐색하기 어려울 수 있다고 지적했어요. 특히 서비스가 필요할 때 전화할 수 있는 전화번호 같은 정보를 찾을 때 말이죠. IT 부서에 쉽게 탐색할 수 있도록 웹사이트를 다시 설계해 달라고 요청했습니다. 여기 보시면, 몇 주 후에 가동될 새로운 설계를 보여 드리겠습니다.

어휘 navigable (웹사이트에서) 이동하기 쉬운 demonstrate 보여 주다

89

What did the speaker do last month?

(A) She relocated to another building.

(B) She hired additional employees.

(C) She organized a luncheon.

(D) She attended a conference.

화자는 지난달에 무엇을 했는가?

(A) 다른 건물로 옮겼다.

(B) 직원을 추가로 고용했다.

(C) 오찬을 준비했다.

(D) 회의에 참석했다.

어휘 relocate 이전하다 organize 준비하다

해설 세부 사항 관련 - 화자가 지난달에 한 일

화자가 도입부에 지난달에 회의에 다녀왔다(Last month, I went to a conference)고 말하고 있으므로 정답은 (D)이다.

> ▸▸ Paraphrasing   담화의 **went to a conference**
> → 정답의 **attended a conference**

90

What do some customers have trouble locating?

(A) Delivery schedules

(B) Password requirements

(C) Contact information

(D) Account archives

고객들은 무엇을 찾는 데 어려움을 겪는가?

(A) 배송 일정

(B) 비밀번호 요건

(C) 연락처

(D) 계정 아카이브

해설 세부 사항 관련 - 고객들이 찾느라 어려움을 겪는 것

화자가 중반부에 몇몇 강연자들은 고객이 특히 서비스가 필요할 때 전화할 수 있는 전화번호 같은 정보를 찾을 때 기업 웹사이트를 탐색하기 어려

울 수 있다고 지적했다(several speakers pointed out that ~ like a phone number they can call when they need service)고 말하고 있으므로 정답은 (C)이다.

> ▸▸ **Paraphrasing**　담화의 **information like a phone number**
> → 정답의 **Contact information**

91

What will the speaker do next?

(A) Give a demonstration

(B) Introduce a guest

(C) Distribute some documents

(D) Hand out some awards

화자는 다음에 무엇을 할 것인가?

(A) 시연하기

(B) 초대 손님 소개하기

(C) 문서 배포하기

(D) 상 나눠주기

해설　세부 사항 관련 - 화자가 다음에 할 일

화자가 마지막에 여기 보시면 몇 주 후에 가동될 새로운 설계를 보여 드리겠다(If you'll look up here, I'll demonstrate the new layout that'll go live in a few weeks)고 말하고 있으므로 정답은 (A)이다.

> ▸▸ **Paraphrasing**　담화의 **demonstrate**
> → 정답의 **Give a demonstration**

92-94 담화

> M-Au Thank you all for coming to this town hall meeting. ⁹²**I'm the mayor of Madison**, and the first topic on our agenda is tourism. ⁹³**We're all very excited that the documentary about our historic town center, which was filmed here last year, is a box office success!** My office has already received hundreds of inquiries from travel agencies around the world asking about hotel capacity and tour buses—good news for local businesses. However, ⁹⁴**some people are wondering about the damage that the influx of tourists on their streets may cause. And they do have a point.** ==Those roads weren't designed for traffic.==

> 시청 회의에 참석해 주셔서 모든 분께 감사합니다. **저는 매디슨 시장입니다.** 안건에 오른 첫 번째 주제는 관광입니다. **지난해 이곳에서 촬영된 유서 깊은 중심가에 관한 다큐멘터리가 흥행에 성공해서 우리 모두 기쁩니다!** 제 사무실에서 전 세계 여행사로부터 호텔 수용 인원과 관광 버스에 대한 문의를 벌써 수백 건 받았습니다. 지역 업체에겐 반가운 소식이죠. 하지만 **일각에선 거리에 관광객이 몰려오면 피해가 생기지 않을까 걱정합니다. 정말이지 일리가 있습니다.** ==그 도로들은 차량용으로 설계된 게 아니니까요.==

어휘 capacity 수용 인원　influx 유입

92

Who is the speaker?

(A) A real-estate developer

(B) A city official

(C) A history professor

(D) A television reporter

화자는 누구인가?

(A) 부동산 개발업자

(B) 시 공무원

(C) 역사학 교수

(D) 텔레비전 기자

해설　전체 내용 관련 - 화자의 직업

화자가 초반부에 자신을 매디슨 시장(I'm the mayor of Madison)이라고 소개하고 있으므로 정답은 (B)이다.

> ▸▸ **Paraphrasing**　담화의 **mayor** → 정답의 **A city official**

93

What happened last year in Madison?

(A) An international hotel convention was held.

(B) A national sports event was hosted.

(C) A documentary movie was filmed.

(D) A historic landmark was named.

지난해 매디슨에서는 무슨 일이 있었는가?

(A) 국제 호텔 회의가 열렸다.

(B) 전국 체육 행사가 열렸다.

(C) 다큐멘터리 영화가 촬영되었다.

(D) 역사적 건물에 이름을 붙였다.

해설　세부 사항 관련 - 지난해 매디슨에서 있었던 일

화자가 중반부에 지난해 이곳에서 촬영된 유서 깊은 중심가에 관한 다큐멘터리가 흥행에 성공해서 우리 모두 기쁘다(We're all very excited that the documentary ~ filmed here last year, is a box office success!)고 말하는 것으로 보아 작년에 다큐멘터리가 촬영되었음을 알 수 있다. 따라서 정답은 (C)이다.

94

Why does the speaker say, "Those roads weren't designed for traffic"?

(A) To make a complaint

(B) To show surprise

(C) To express concern

(D) To offer an apology

화자가 "그 도로들은 차량용으로 설계된 게 아니니까요"라고 말하는 이유는 무엇인가?

(A) 항의하려고
(B) 놀라움을 나타내려고
(C) 우려를 표명하려고
(D) 사과하려고

해설 화자의 의도 파악 - 차량용으로 설계된 도로들이 아니라는 말의 의도 앞에서 일각에서는 거리에 관광객이 몰려오면 피해가 생기지 않을까 걱정한다(some people are wondering ~ on their streets may cause)며 정말이지 일리가 있다(And they do have a point)고 말한 뒤 인용문을 통해 일부 사람들이 걱정하는 이유를 구체적으로 지적하고 있는 것으로 보아, 제기되고 있는 일각의 우려에 공감을 표현하려는 의도로 한 말임을 알 수 있다. 따라서 정답은 (C)이다.

95-97 안내 방송 + 매장 배치도

W-Br Attention, book lovers! The Regal Reader bookstore is excited to announce the beginning of its summer author series. [95]**Join us this Friday when renowned author Karima Samir will visit the store** to read from her books, sign copies, and chat with customers. [96]**Stop by our history aisle to find her latest book about fascinating North Africa.** And [97]**make sure you enter our annual drawing while you're here to win a five-dollar gift card for our café!** Use it to purchase any of our freshly brewed coffees or homemade pastries.

애서가 여러분, 안내 말씀을 드립니다! 리걸 리더 서점에서 설레는 마음으로 여름 작가 시리즈 시작을 알립니다. **이번 주 금요일, 저명 작가 카리마 사미르 씨가 서점을 방문해** 자신의 책 일부를 낭독하고, 책에 사인하고, 고객과 이야기를 나눌 예정이니, 저희와 함께하시기 바랍니다. **역사 코너에 들러 사미르 씨가 최근 발간한 매혹적인 북아프리카에 관한 책을 찾아보세요.** 그리고 **이곳에 머무는 동안 연례 추첨에 참여해 이곳 카페에서 쓸 수 있는 5달러 기프트 카드를 꼭 타 가세요!** 갓 내린 커피나 수제 빵을 구매할 때 사용하세요.

어휘 renowned 저명한 aisle 통로 drawing 추첨

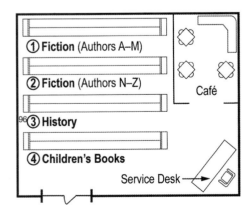

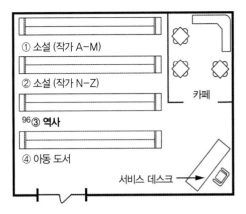

95

According to the speaker, what will happen this Friday?

(A) A delivery will arrive.
(B) A holiday sale will begin.
(C) An employee will retire.
(D) An author will visit.

화자의 말에 따르면, 이번 주 금요일에 무슨 일이 있을 것인가?

(A) 배송품이 도착할 것이다.
(B) 휴일 할인 판매를 시작할 것이다.
(C) 직원이 퇴직할 것이다.
(D) 작가가 방문할 것이다.

해설 세부 사항 관련 - 화자가 이번 주 금요일에 있을 것이라고 말하는 일
화자가 초반부에 이번 주 금요일에 저명 작가 카리마 사미르 씨가 서점을 방문할 것(Join us this Friday when renowned author Karima Samir will visit the store)이라고 말하고 있으므로 정답은 (D)이다.

96

Look at the graphic. Which aisle does the speaker direct the listeners to?

(A) Aisle 1
(B) Aisle 2
(C) Aisle 3
(D) Aisle 4

시각 정보에 의하면 화자는 청자들을 어느 코너로 안내하는가?

(A) 1번 코너
(B) 2번 코너
(C) 3번 코너
(D) 4번 코너

해설 시각 정보 연계 - 화자가 청자들을 안내하는 코너
화자가 중반부에 역사 코너에 들러 사미르 씨가 최근 발간한 매혹적인 북아프리카에 관한 책을 찾아보라(Stop by our history aisle to find her latest book about fascinating North Africa)고 말하고 있고, 매장 배치도에 따르면 역사 코너는 3번 코너이므로 정답은 (C)이다.

97

What can the listeners win?

(A) A gift card
(B) A book
(C) A free membership
(D) A calendar

청자들은 무엇을 획득할 수 있는가?

(A) 기프트 카드
(B) 책
(C) 무료 회원권
(D) 달력

해설 세부 사항 관련 – 청자들이 받을 수 있는 것

화자가 후반부에 이곳에 머무는 동안 연례 추첨에 참여해 카페에서 쓸 수 있는 5달러 기프트 카드를 꼭 타 가라(make sure you enter our ~ to win a five-dollar gift card for our café!)고 권유하고 있는 것으로 보아 청자들이 기프트 카드에 당첨될 수 있다는 것을 알 수 있다. 따라서 정답은 (A)이다.

98-100 전화 메시지 + 공지

> **M-Cn** Hello Ms. Kapoor. My name's Mark Giordano. **98I'm a forklift operator in the Shipping Department.** I'm calling because I'm supposed to complete the training session on refueling equipment, but I need to change my date. I signed up for the session on January twenty-third, but **99our department just received notice that a large order will ship out at the end of the month.** I'll have a lot of work to do earlier in the day all month, so **100I can only attend the session that starts at three P.M. Could you reschedule me?** Please let me know.

> 안녕하세요 카푸어 씨. 제 이름은 마크 조르다노예요. **배송부 지게차 기사입니다.** 급유 장비 교육을 수료해야 하는데 날짜를 바꿔야 해서 전화드려요. 1월 23일 세션에 등록했는데, **1월 말에 대량 주문이 출하된다는 공지를 방금 부서에서 받았습니다.** 한 달 내내 오전에는 할 일이 많아서 **오후 3시에 시작하는 세션에만 참석할 수 있어요. 제 일정을 다시 잡아 주시겠어요?** 알려 주세요.

> 어휘 forklift 지게차 be supposed to ~하기로 되어 있다

Refueling Equipment

Sign up for one of these sessions:

January 14: 2 P.M.–5 P.M.

January 23: 10 A.M.–1 P.M.

January 26:[100] 3 P.M.–6 P.M.

January 31: 9 A.M.–12 noon

급유 장비

다음 세션 중 하나를 신청하세요:

1월 14일: 오후 2–5시

1월 23일: 오전 10시–오후 1시

1월 26일: [100]**오후 3–6시**

1월 31일: 오전 9시–정오 12시

98

Where does the speaker most likely work?

(A) At a boat dock
(B) At an auto repair shop
(C) At a warehouse
(D) At a job training school

화자는 어디에서 일하겠는가?

(A) 보트 선착장
(B) 자동차 정비소
(C) 창고
(D) 직업 훈련 학교

해설 전체 내용 관련 – 화자의 근무지

화자가 초반부에 자신을 배송부의 지게차 기사(I'm a forklift operator in the Shipping Department)라고 소개하고 있는 것으로 보아 화자는 물류 창고에서 물품을 선적 및 운반하는 일을 하고 있음을 알 수 있다. 따라서 정답은 (C)이다.

99

What will the speaker's department be doing at the end of the month?

(A) Fixing some equipment
(B) Attending a trade show
(C) Interviewing job candidates
(D) Preparing a large order

화자의 부서는 월말에 무엇을 할 것인가?

(A) 장비 수리
(B) 무역 박람회 참석
(C) 입사 지원자 면접
(D) 대량 주문 준비

해설 세부 사항 관련 – 화자의 부서가 월말에 할 일

화자가 중반부에 월말에 대량 주문이 출하된다는 공지를 방금 부서에서 받았다(our department just received notice that a large order will ship out at the end of the month)고 말하고 있으므로 정답은 (D)이다.

100

Look at the graphic. Which session does the man request to attend?

(A) January 14
(B) January 23
(C) January 26
(D) January 31

시각 정보에 의하면 남자는 어느 세션에 참석하겠다고 요청하는가?

(A) 1월 14일
(B) 1월 23일
(C) 1월 26일
(D) 1월 31일

해설 시각 정보 연계 – 남자가 참석하겠다고 요청하는 세션

남자가 후반부에 오후 3시에 시작하는 세션에만 참석할 수 있다(I can only attend the session that starts at three P.M.)며 일정을 다시 잡아 줄 수 있는지(Could you reschedule me?) 요청하고 있고, 공지에 따르면 오후 3시에 시작하는 세션은 1월 26일자 세션이므로 정답은 (C)이다.

기출 TEST 6

1 (B)	2 (A)	3 (C)	4 (D)	5 (C)
6 (A)	7 (A)	8 (C)	9 (C)	10 (C)
11 (A)	12 (B)	13 (A)	14 (C)	15 (B)
16 (B)	17 (A)	18 (C)	19 (B)	20 (B)
21 (C)	22 (B)	23 (B)	24 (C)	25 (B)
26 (B)	27 (C)	28 (A)	29 (C)	30 (A)
31 (B)	32 (B)	33 (C)	34 (A)	35 (C)
36 (D)	37 (A)	38 (D)	39 (B)	40 (D)
41 (B)	42 (C)	43 (D)	44 (A)	45 (C)
46 (D)	47 (D)	48 (A)	49 (C)	50 (C)
51 (B)	52 (D)	53 (C)	54 (A)	55 (B)
56 (B)	57 (D)	58 (B)	59 (A)	60 (A)
61 (B)	62 (D)	63 (C)	64 (C)	65 (D)
66 (C)	67 (B)	68 (C)	69 (A)	70 (D)
71 (C)	72 (B)	73 (D)	74 (A)	75 (C)
76 (B)	77 (C)	78 (D)	79 (A)	80 (C)
81 (C)	82 (A)	83 (A)	84 (D)	85 (C)
86 (B)	87 (C)	88 (C)	89 (B)	90 (D)
91 (C)	92 (B)	93 (A)	94 (D)	95 (A)
96 (C)	97 (D)	98 (B)	99 (A)	100 (C)

PART 1

1   M-Cn

(A) She's looking out a window.
(B) She's taking an item out of a refrigerator.
(C) She's grabbing a handful of carrots.
(D) She's putting some items in a bag.

(A) 여자가 창밖을 내다보고 있다.
(B) 여자가 냉장고에서 물건을 꺼내고 있다.
(C) 여자가 당근을 한 움큼 움켜쥐고 있다.
(D) 여자가 가방에 물건들을 넣고 있다.

어휘 refrigerator 냉장고 grab 움켜쥐다 a handful of 한 움큼의

해설 1인 등장 사진 - 사람의 동작/상태 묘사

(A) 동사 오답. 여자가 창밖을 내다보고 있는(is looking out a window) 모습이 아니므로 오답.
(B) 정답. 여자가 냉장고에서 물건을 꺼내고 있는(is taking an item out of a refrigerator) 모습이므로 정답.
(C) 동사 오답. 여자가 당근을 한 움큼 움켜쥐고 있는(is grabbing a handful of carrots) 모습이 아니므로 오답.

(D) 동사 오답. 여자가 가방에 물건들을 넣고 있는(is putting some items in a bag) 모습이 아니므로 오답.

2   W-Am

(A) One of the women is tying her shoe.
(B) One of the women is wearing a hat.
(C) One of the women is standing near a park bench.
(D) One of the women is carrying a computer up some stairs.

(A) 여자들 중 한 명이 신발끈을 묶고 있다.
(B) 여자들 중 한 명이 모자를 쓰고 있다.
(C) 여자들 중 한 명이 공원 벤치 근처에 서 있다.
(D) 여자들 중 한 명이 컴퓨터를 들고 계단을 오르고 있다.

어휘 stairs 계단

해설 2인 이상 등장 사진 - 사람의 동작/상태 묘사

(A) 정답. 여자들 중 한 명(one of the women)이 신발끈을 묶고 있는(is tying her shoe) 모습이므로 정답.
(B) 동사 오답. 모자를 쓰고 있는(is wearing a hat) 여자의 모습이 보이지 않으므로 오답.
(C) 동사 오답. 공원 벤치 근처에 서 있는(is standing near a park bench) 여자의 모습이 보이지 않으므로 오답.
(D) 동사 오답. 컴퓨터를 들고 계단을 오르고 있는(is carrying a computer up some stairs) 여자의 모습이 보이지 않으므로 오답.

3   M-Au

(A) The man is setting a clock.
(B) The man is reaching for a box.
(C) The man is posting some information.
(D) The woman is handing some food to the man.

(A) 남자가 시계를 맞추고 있다.
(B) 남자가 상자를 향해 손을 뻗고 있다.
(C) 남자가 정보를 게시하고 있다.
(D) 여자가 남자에게 음식을 건네고 있다.

어휘 set a clock 시계를 맞추다 reach for ~을 향해 손을 뻗다 hand 건네다

해설 2인 이상 등장 사진 - 사람의 동작/상태 묘사
(A) 동사 오답. 남자가 시계를 맞추고 있는(is setting a clock) 모습이 아니므로 오답.
(B) 동사 오답. 남자가 상자를 향해 손을 뻗고 있는(is reaching for a box) 모습이 아니므로 오답.
(C) 정답. 남자가 정보를 게시하고 있는(is posting some information) 모습이므로 정답.
(D) 동사 오답. 여자가 남자에게 음식을 건네고 있는(is handing some food to the man) 모습이 아니므로 오답.

4 W-Br

(A) He's twisting some wires.
(B) He's pruning a bush next to a building.
(C) He's lifting a block.
(D) **He's spreading cement with a shovel.**

(A) 남자가 전선을 꼬고 있다.
(B) 남자가 건물 옆에 있는 관목 가지를 치고 있다.
(C) 남자가 블록을 들어올리고 있다.
(D) **남자가 삽으로 시멘트를 펴고 있다.**

어휘 wire 전선   prune 가지치기하다   bush 관목   shovel 삽

해설 1인 등장 사진 - 사람의 동작/상태 묘사
(A) 동사 오답. 남자가 전선을 꼬고 있는(is twisting some wires) 모습이 아니므로 오답.
(B) 동사 오답. 남자가 건물 옆에 있는 관목 가지를 치고 있는(is pruning a bush next to a building) 모습이 아니므로 오답.
(C) 사진에 없는 명사를 이용한 오답. 사진에 블록(a block)의 모습이 보이지 않으므로 오답.
(D) 정답. 남자가 삽으로 시멘트를 펴고 있는(is spreading cement with a shovel) 모습이므로 정답.

5 W-Am

(A) The women are facing a desk.
(B) One of the women is holding a jacket.
(C) **A drawer has been left open.**
(D) Some folders have been placed on top of a file cabinet.

(A) 여자들이 책상을 마주보고 있다.
(B) 여자들 중 한 명이 재킷을 들고 있다.
(C) **서랍이 열려 있다.**
(D) 폴더들이 파일 캐비닛 위에 놓여 있다.

어휘 face 마주보다   drawer 서랍

해설 혼합 사진 - 사람/사물/풍경 혼합 묘사
(A) 동사 오답. 여자들이 책상을 마주보고 있는(are facing a desk) 모습이 아니므로 오답.
(B) 동사 오답. 여자들 중 한 명(one of the women)이 재킷을 들고 있는(is holding a jacket) 모습이 아니므로 오답.
(C) 정답. 서랍(a drawer)이 열려 있는(has been left open) 모습이므로 정답.
(D) 위치 오답. 폴더들(some folders)이 파일 캐비닛 위에 놓여 있는(have been placed on top of a file cabinet) 모습이 아니므로 오답.

6 M-Au

(A) **Some cups have been lined up on shelves.**
(B) A fruit basket has been emptied.
(C) Some pots are being filled with water.
(D) Some coffee has been spilled on the counter.

(A) **컵들이 선반에 정렬되어 있다.**
(B) 과일 바구니가 비어 있다.
(C) 냄비들에 물을 채우고 있다.
(D) 커피가 조리대 위에 엎질러져 있다.

어휘 shelf 선반   empty 비우다   spill 엎지르다

해설 사물/풍경 사진 - 사물 묘사
(A) 정답. 컵들(some cups)이 선반에 정렬되어 있는(have been lined up on shelves) 모습이므로 정답.
(B) 동사 오답. 과일 바구니(a fruit basket)가 비어 있는(has been emptied) 모습이 아니라 과일로 가득 차 있는(has been filled with some fruit) 모습이므로 오답.
(C) 동사 오답. 냄비들(some pots)이 물로 채워지고 있는(are being filled with water) 모습이 아니므로 오답.
(D) 동사 오답. 커피(some coffee)가 조리대 위에 엎질러져 있는(has been spilled on the counter) 모습이 아니므로 오답.

PART 2

7
W-Br   Who made changes to the budget proposal?
M-Cn   (A) The associate director.
       (B) Additional funding.
       (C) A range of menu options.

누가 예산안을 변경했나요?
(A) 차장님이에요.
(B) 추가 자금입니다.
(C) 다양한 메뉴 항목이요.

어휘 budget proposal 예산안 additional 추가의 a range of 다양한

해설 예산안을 변경한 사람을 묻는 Who 의문문
(A) 정답. 예산안을 변경한 사람이 누구인지 묻는 질문에 차장님이라고 알려 주고 있으므로 정답.
(B) 연상 단어 오답. 질문의 budget에서 연상 가능한 funding을 이용한 오답.
(C) 질문과 상관없는 오답. What 의문문에 대한 응답이므로 오답.

8
M-Au When are they delivering the manuals?
W-Am (A) Because they're busy.
(B) The new cover design.
(C) On Wednesday.

그들은 언제 설명서를 배달하나요?
(A) 그들이 바빠서요.
(B) 새로운 표지 디자인이에요.
(C) 수요일이요.

해설 설명서의 배송 시기를 묻는 When 의문문
(A) 질문과 상관없는 오답. Why 의문문에 대한 응답이므로 오답.
(B) 연상 단어 오답. 질문의 manuals에서 연상 가능한 cover design을 이용한 오답.
(C) 정답. 설명서를 배달하는 시기를 묻는 질문에 수요일이라고 알려 주고 있으므로 정답.

9
W-Br How much does it cost to rent this retail space?
W-Am (A) By living close to work.
(B) The desk measures five feet long.
(C) The fee is 200 dollars.

이 소매 공간을 빌리려면 비용이 얼마인가요?
(A) 직장과 가까운 곳에 살아서요.
(B) 책상은 길이 5피트예요.
(C) 요금은 200달러예요.

어휘 retail 소매 measure 측정해 보니 ~이다

해설 공간의 대여 비용을 묻는 How much 의문문
(A) 질문과 상관없는 오답. How 의문문에 대한 응답이므로 오답.
(B) 연상 단어 오답. 질문의 space에서 공간의 크기를 연상하게 하는 five feet long을 이용한 오답.
(C) 정답. 소매 공간을 빌리는 데 드는 비용을 묻는 질문에 요금이 200달러라며 구체적인 액수로 응답하고 있으므로 정답.

10
W-Br Where is the store manager?
M-Au (A) Some items from the back room.
(B) No, I'm not a manager.
(C) She went out for lunch.

점장은 어디 있죠?
(A) 안쪽 방에서 가져온 물품들이에요.
(B) 아니요, 저는 점장이 아니에요.
(C) 점심 먹으러 나갔어요.

해설 점장이 있는 장소를 묻는 Where 의문문
(A) 연상 단어 오답. 질문의 store에서 연상 가능한 items를 이용한 오답.
(B) Yes/No 불가 오답. Where 의문문에는 Yes/No 응답이 불가능하므로 오답.
(C) 정답. 점장이 있는 장소를 묻는 질문에 점심을 먹으러 나갔다면서 점장이 매장 내에 있지 않다는 점을 간접적으로 알려 주고 있으므로 정답.

11
W-Am Should I turn off my computer or leave it on?
M-Au (A) Please turn it off.
(B) How did you sleep?
(C) The yellow one.

제 컴퓨터를 끌까요, 아니면 켜 둘까요?
(A) 꺼 주세요.
(B) 잘 잤어요?
(C) 노란 거요.

어휘 turn off 끄다

해설 컴퓨터의 전원을 어떤 상태로 둘지 묻는 선택 의문문
(A) 정답. 컴퓨터의 전원을 어떤 상태로 둘지 묻는 질문에 꺼 달라며 둘 중 하나를 선택해 응답하고 있으므로 정답.
(B) 질문과 상관없는 오답.
(C) 질문과 상관없는 오답. Which 의문문에 대한 응답이므로 오답.

12
M-Cn Who has attended a public speaking workshop before?
W-Am (A) Next Monday.
(B) I think Julia has.
(C) A copy from the public library.

전에 연설 워크숍에 참석해 보신 분?
(A) 다음 주 월요일이요.
(B) 줄리아가 그런 것 같아요.
(C) 공공 도서관 책이에요.

해설 워크숍 참석 경험이 있는 사람을 묻는 Who 의문문
(A) 질문과 상관없는 오답. When 의문문에 대한 응답이므로 오답.
(B) 정답. 전에 연설 워크숍에 참석해 본 경험이 있는 사람을 묻는 질문에 줄리아가 그런 것 같다고 알려 주고 있으므로 정답.

(C) 단어 반복 오답. 질문의 public을 반복 이용한 오답.

13

W-Br Why is Min-Soo selling his car?

M-Cn (A) He's buying a new one.
(B) Twenty years ago.
(C) The next stop, please.

민수는 왜 차를 팔죠?
(A) 그는 새것을 산대요.
(B) 20년 전이에요.
(C) 다음 정거장이요.

해설 민수가 차를 파는 이유를 묻는 Why 의문문
(A) 정답. 민수가 자신의 차를 파는 이유를 묻는 질문에 그가 새 차를 산다고 이유를 제시하고 있으므로 정답.
(B) 질문과 상관없는 오답. When 의문문에 대한 응답이므로 오답.
(C) 질문과 상관없는 오답. Where 의문문에 대한 응답이므로 오답.

14

W-Am When should we call the client in Beijing?

M-Cn (A) That's what I heard.
(B) I usually take a direct flight.
(C) It's only five A.M. there now.

베이징에 있는 거래처에 언제 전화하면 될까요?
(A) 저는 그렇게 들었어요.
(B) 저는 보통 직항편을 타요.
(C) 거기는 이제 겨우 새벽 5시예요.

어휘 direct flight 직항편

해설 거래처에 전화할 시점을 묻는 When 의문문
(A) 질문과 상관없는 오답.
(B) 연상 단어 오답. 질문의 Beijing에서 연상 가능한 flight을 이용한 오답.
(C) 정답. 베이징에 있는 거래처에 전화할 시점을 묻는 질문에 거기는 이제 겨우 새벽 5시라며 아직 전화를 걸기에 적절한 때가 아님을 우회적으로 응답하고 있으므로 정답.

15

M-Cn Where should we set up the packaging machine?

W-Br (A) Many small parts.
(B) By the loading dock.
(C) Overnight delivery.

포장 기계는 어디에 설치해야 할까요?
(A) 수많은 작은 부품들이요.
(B) 하역장 옆이요.
(C) 익일 배송입니다.

어휘 loading dock 하역장 overnight delivery 익일 배송

해설 기계를 설치할 장소를 묻는 Where 의문문
(A) 질문과 상관없는 오답. What 의문문에 대한 응답이므로 오답.
(B) 정답. 포장 기계를 설치할 장소를 묻는 질문에 하역장 옆이라고 구체적인 위치로 응답하고 있으므로 정답
(C) 질문과 상관없는 오답.

16

W-Br Who will we purchase costumes from?

W-Am (A) In the rehearsal hall, I think.
(B) It's cheaper to make them ourselves.
(C) I'm excited about the performance!

의상은 누구한테 살 건가요?
(A) 리허설 홀에 있는 것 같아요.
(B) 우리가 직접 만드는 게 더 싸요.
(C) 공연이 기대돼요!

어휘 purchase 사다 cheap 싼 performance 공연

해설 의상의 구매처를 묻는 Who 의문문
(A) 연상 단어 오답. 질문의 costumes에서 연상 가능한 rehearsal을 이용한 오답.
(B) 정답. 누구에게서 의상을 구입할지 묻는 질문에 우리가 직접 만드는 것이 더 싸다며 의상을 구입하지 않을 것임을 우회적으로 알리고 있으므로 정답.
(C) 연상 단어 오답. 질문의 costumes에서 연상 가능한 performance를 이용한 오답.

17

W-Am Isn't the building inspector coming this afternoon?

M-Au (A) No, he'll be here next week.
(B) It's a beautiful building.
(C) Some updated safety regulations.

오늘 오후에 건축물 검사원이 오지 않나요?
(A) 아니요, 다음 주에 와요.
(B) 멋진 건물이에요.
(C) 수정된 안전 규정이에요.

어휘 building inspector 건축물 검사원 safety 안전 regulation 규정

해설 건축물 검사원의 방문 여부를 확인하는 부정 의문문
(A) 정답. 오늘 오후에 건축물 검사원이 방문하는지 여부를 묻는 질문에 아니요(No)라고 대답한 뒤, 다음 주에 온다며 부정 답변과 일관된 내용을 덧붙였으므로 정답.
(B) 단어 반복 오답. 질문의 building을 반복 이용한 오답.
(C) 연상 단어 오답. 질문의 building inspector에서 연상 가능한 safety regulations를 이용한 오답.

18

M-Cn Do you have an appointment to see Ms. Singh?

W-Am (A) The event calendar.

(B) Thanks, I'll be right back.

(C) Oh, we're old friends.

싱 씨와 만나기로 약속하셨나요?

(A) 행사 일정표예요.

(B) 고마워요, 금방 올게요.

(C) 아, 우리는 오랜 친구예요.

어휘 appointment 약속

해설 싱 씨와 미팅 약속이 있는지 여부를 묻는 조동사(Do) 의문문

(A) 연상 단어 오답. 질문의 appointment에서 연상 가능한 calendar를 이용한 오답.

(B) 질문과 상관없는 오답.

(C) 정답. 싱 씨와 미팅 약속이 있는지 여부를 묻는 질문에 우리는 오랜 친구라면서 따로 약속이 잡혀 있지 않다는 것을 우회적으로 알려 주고 있으므로 정답.

19

M-Cn I could let you know when we have a job opening.

W-Br (A) It opens at ten o'clock on weekdays.

(B) OK, here's my e-mail address.

(C) I don't have the right set of keys.

일자리가 나면 알려 드릴 수 있어요.

(A) 평일에는 10시에 문을 엽니다.

(B) 좋아요, 제 이메일 주소예요.

(C) 맞는 열쇠 꾸러미가 없어요.

해설 제안/권유의 평서문

(A) 파생어 오답. 평서문의 opening과 파생어 관계인 opens를 이용한 오답.

(B) 정답. 일자리가 나면 알려 줄 수 있다는 제안에 대해 좋다(OK)고 대답한 뒤, 여기 제 이메일 주소가 있다고 연락처를 알려 주며 긍정 답변과 일관된 내용을 덧붙였으므로 정답.

(C) 연상 단어 오답. 평서문의 opening에서 연상 가능한 keys를 이용한 오답.

20

M-Au What kind of business are you interested in launching?

W-Am (A) I'm very aware of that.

(B) One that sells clothes and accessories.

(C) Yes, many different hobbies.

어떤 사업을 시작하려고 관심을 두고 있나요?

(A) 저도 잘 알고 있습니다.

(B) 옷과 장신구를 파는 사업이요.

(C) 네, 다양한 취미들이요.

어휘 be aware of ~을 알다

해설 관심 있는 사업의 종류를 묻는 What 의문문

(A) 질문과 상관없는 오답.

(B) 정답. 시작하려고 관심을 둔 사업의 종류를 묻는 질문에 옷과 장신구를 파는 사업이라고 구체적으로 응답하고 있으므로 정답.

(C) Yes/No 불가 오답. What 의문문에는 Yes/No 응답이 불가능하므로 오답.

21

W-Am When did this pharmaceutical company move to this larger facility?

M-Au (A) In several pharmacies.

(B) By offering more sessions.

(C) About a year ago.

이 제약 회사는 언제 이 큰 시설로 옮겼나요?

(A) 여러 약국이에요.

(B) 더 많은 세션을 제공해서요.

(C) 1년 전쯤에요.

어휘 pharmaceutical 제약의 pharmacy 약국

해설 회사의 이전 시점을 묻는 When 의문문

(A) 파생어 오답. 질문의 pharmaceutical과 파생어 관계인 pharmacies를 이용한 오답.

(B) 질문과 상관없는 오답. How 의문문에 대한 응답이므로 오답.

(C) 정답. 제약 회사가 큰 시설로 이전한 시점을 묻는 질문에 1년 전쯤이라고 응답하고 있으므로 정답.

22

M-Cn Ms. Johnson will be coming to today's meeting.

M-Au (A) It was a pleasure to meet you.

(B) Actually, it's been rescheduled.

(C) Every few hours.

존슨 씨가 오늘 회의에 오십니다.

(A) 만나서 반가웠어요.

(B) 실은 일정이 변경되었어요.

(C) 몇 시간마다요.

어휘 reschedule 일정을 바꾸다

해설 정보 전달의 평서문

(A) 파생어 오답. 평서문의 meeting과 파생어 관계인 meet를 이용한 오답.

(B) 정답. 존슨 씨가 오늘 회의에 온다는 평서문에 실은 일정이 변경되었다며 존슨 씨가 오늘 오지 않을 것임을 우회적으로 알려 주고 있으므로 정답.

(C) 질문과 상관없는 오답. How often 의문문에 대한 응답이므로 오답.

23

W-Am I'll need to update the software, right?

M-Cn (A) I like that fabric, too.

(B) **Yes, it's easy to do.**

(C) The machine in the warehouse.

제가 소프트웨어를 업데이트해야겠죠?

(A) 저도 그 옷감이 마음에 들어요.

(B) **네, 쉽게 할 수 있어요.**

(C) 창고에 있는 기계요.

어휘 warehouse 창고

해설 소프트웨어 업데이트의 실행 여부를 확인하는 부가 의문문

(A) 질문과 상관없는 오답.

(B) 정답. 자신이 소프트웨어를 업데이트해야 하는지 여부를 확인하는 질문에 네(Yes)라고 대답한 뒤, 쉽게 할 수 있다고 격려하며 긍정 답변과 일관된 내용을 덧붙였으므로 정답.

(C) 유사 발음 오답. 질문의 software와 부분적으로 발음이 유사한 warehouse를 이용한 오답.

24

M-Au Where's the museum's sculpture exhibit?

W-Am (A) It's a large database.

(B) A course on ancient cultures.

(C) **I'm going that way now.**

미술관 조각 전시회는 어디죠?

(A) 대규모 데이터베이스입니다.

(B) 고대 문화 강좌예요.

(C) **제가 지금 그리로 가요.**

어휘 sculpture 조각 exhibit 전시회 ancient 고대의

해설 전시회의 위치를 묻는 Where 의문문

(A) 연상 단어 오답. 질문의 sculpture에서 연상 가능한 large를 이용한 오답.

(B) 연상 단어 오답. 질문의 museum에서 연상 가능한 cultures를 이용한 오답.

(C) 정답. 미술관 조각 전시회의 위치를 묻는 질문에 제가 지금 그리고 간다면서 자신이 직접 안내할 것임을 간접적으로 표현하고 있으므로 정답.

25

M-Cn Why don't we interview the two candidates together?

W-Am (A) Multiple references.

(B) **That's a great suggestion.**

(C) It went well, thank you.

두 지원자를 함께 면접하는 게 어때요?

(A) 복수의 추천서요.

(B) **좋은 제안이에요.**

(C) 잘됐어요, 고마워요.

어휘 candidate 지원자, 후보 reference 추천서 suggestion 제안

해설 제안/권유의 의문문

(A) 연상 단어 오답. 질문의 candidates에서 연상 가능한 references를 이용한 오답.

(B) 정답. 두 지원자를 함께 면접하자고 제안하는 질문에 좋은 제안이라고 호응하고 있으므로 정답.

(C) 질문과 상관없는 오답. How 의문문에 대한 응답이므로 오답.

26

M-Cn This research report is unusually long.

M-Au (A) For three to six months.

(B) **I typed up a summary page.**

(C) No, I don't have a measuring stick.

이 연구 보고서는 유난히 기네요.

(A) 3개월에서 6개월 동안요.

(B) **제가 컴퓨터로 요약 페이지를 작성했어요.**

(C) 아니요, 저는 자가 없어요.

어휘 unusually 유난히 type up 컴퓨터로 작성하다 summary 요약 measuring stick 자

해설 정보 전달의 평서문

(A) 평서문과 상관없는 오답. How long 의문문에 대한 응답이므로 오답.

(B) 정답. 연구 보고서가 유난히 길다는 평서문에 제가 컴퓨터로 요약 페이지를 작성했다며 긴 보고서 대신 간략한 요약본을 보면 된다는 해결책을 우회적으로 제시하고 있으므로 정답.

(C) 연상 단어 오답. 평서문의 long에서 연상 가능한 measuring stick을 이용한 오답.

27

W-Am We reserved a booth at the festival, didn't we?

W-Br (A) That sounds like a fair price.

(B) Round-trip tickets to Rome, please.

(C) **Yes, it was done last week.**

축제 때 부스를 예약했죠?

(A) 적당한 가격 같군요.

(B) 로마행 왕복표 주세요.

(C) **네, 지난주에 했어요.**

어휘 reserve 예약하다 fair 적당한 round-trip 왕복의

해설 부스 예약 여부를 확인하는 부가 의문문

(A) 연상 단어 오답. 질문의 reserved에서 연상 가능한 price를 이용한 오답.

(B) 연상 단어 오답. 질문의 reserved에서 연상 가능한 tickets를 이용한 오답.

(C) 정답. 축제 때 부스를 예약했는지 여부를 확인하는 질문에 네(Yes)라고 대답한 뒤, 지난주에 했다며 긍정 답변과 일관된 내용을 덧붙였으므로 정답.

28

M-Cn Could you help me draw up a contract?

W-Am (A) I have no legal expertise.

(B) Those pencil drawings should be framed.

(C) It looks like a compact vehicle.

계약서 작성 좀 도와주실래요?

(A) 저는 법률 전문 지식이 없어요.

(B) 저 연필화들은 액자에 넣어야 해요.

(C) 소형차 같네요.

어휘 draw up 작성하다   contract 계약(서)   legal 법률의
expertise 전문 지식   vehicle 차량

해설 부탁/요청의 의문문

(A) 정답. 계약서 작성을 도와 달라는 요청에 법률 전문 지식이 없다며 간접적으로 거절하고 있으므로 정답.

(B) 파생어 오답. 질문의 draw와 파생어 관계인 drawings를 이용한 오답.

(C) 유사 발음 오답. 질문의 contract와 부분적으로 발음이 유사한 compact를 이용한 오답.

29

W-Br What are your dinner specials this evening?

M-Au (A) At the corner of Main Street and Linden Avenue.

(B) That table is reserved.

(C) Your server will be with you momentarily.

오늘 저녁 특선 요리는 뭔가요?

(A) 메인 가와 린덴 대로 모퉁이에요.

(B) 저 테이블은 예약됐습니다.

(C) 웨이터가 곧 올 겁니다.

어휘 server 웨이터   momentarily 곧

해설 특선 요리를 묻는 What 의문문

(A) 질문과 상관없는 오답. Where 의문문에 대한 응답이므로 오답.

(B) 연상 단어 오답. 질문의 dinner에서 연상 가능한 table을 이용한 오답.

(C) 정답. 오늘 저녁 특선 요리를 묻는 질문에 웨이터가 곧 올 것이라며 웨이터가 질문에 대한 답을 말해 줄 것임을 우회적으로 알려 주고 있으므로 정답.

30

M-Au Have you signed up to access your medical records online?

W-Br (A) It's not a requirement, is it?

(B) I'll hang up the sign.

(C) Another recording studio, I think.

온라인으로 의료 기록에 접속하기 위해 등록하셨나요?

(A) 꼭 해야 하는 건 아니죠?

(B) 제가 표지판을 걸게요.

(C) 다른 녹음실인 것 같아요.

어휘 access 접속하다   medical record 의료 기록   requirement
필수로 해야 하는 것   hang up 걸다

해설 온라인 의료 기록 열람을 위한 등록 여부를 묻는 조동사(Have) 의문문

(A) 정답. 온라인으로 의료 기록에 접속하기 위해 등록했는지 여부를 묻는 질문에 꼭 해야 하는 건 아니지 않냐고 되물으며 아직 등록하지 않았음을 우회적으로 알리고 있으므로 정답.

(B) 파생어 오답. 질문의 signed와 파생어 관계인 sign을 이용한 오답.

(C) 파생어 오답. 질문의 records와 파생어 관계인 recording을 이용한 오답.

31

W-Am Didn't the office manager order more company letterhead?

M-Cn (A) The lunch caterer should be arriving by eleven.

(B) I have some that you can use.

(C) We haven't confirmed the hotel reservation yet.

사무장이 회사 이름과 주소가 인쇄된 편지지를 더 주문하지 않았나요?

(A) 점심 요식업체가 11시까지는 도착해야 합니다.

(B) 쓰실 수 있는 게 저한테 좀 있어요.

(C) 아직 호텔 예약을 확인하지 않았어요.

어휘 letterhead 회사 이름과 주소가 인쇄된 편지지   caterer 요식업체
confirm 확인하다   reservation 예약

해설 사무장의 회사 편지지 추가 주문 여부를 확인하는 부정 의문문

(A) 질문과 상관없는 오답. When 의문문에 대한 응답이므로 오답.

(B) 정답. 사무장이 회사 이름과 주소가 인쇄된 편지지를 더 주문했는지 여부를 묻는 질문에 쓸 수 있는 것이 자신에게 좀 남아 있다며 아직 추가로 편지지를 주문하지 않았음을 우회적으로 응답하고 있으므로 정답.

(C) 질문과 상관없는 오답.

PART 3

32-34

W-Br You've reached the customer service department of Handel's Label Company.

M-Cn My name's Taro Nakamura. **[32] I'm the owner of a small cosmetics company,** and we recently started manufacturing a lip moisturizer. **[33] We placed a large rush order with you last week. We were supposed to get the labels yesterday, but they haven't come yet.**

W-Br Sorry for the delay, Mr. Nakamura. **[34] What is your order number?**

M-Cn It's BX856.

W-Br There's a note here that we're having issues with transportation due to the construction on roads in your area. But your order will be delivered this afternoon.

여	헨델 라벨 사 고객 서비스부입니다.
남	제 이름은 타로 나카무라인데요. **작은 화장품 회사 사장인데**, 최근에 입술 보습제를 제조하기 시작했어요. **우리는 지난주에 대량의 급행 주문을 했어요. 어제 라벨을 받기로 했는데 아직 안 왔어요.**
여	늦어서 죄송합니다, 나카무라 씨. **주문 번호가 어떻게 되나요?**
남	BX856입니다.
여	계시는 지역이 도로 공사 때문에 운송에 문제가 있다는 메모가 여기 있네요. 주문품은 오늘 오후에 배송될 거예요.

어휘 recently 최근 manufacture 제조하다 moisturizer 보습제 be supposed to ~하기로 되어 있다 issue 문제 transportation 운송 due to ~ 때문에 construction 공사 deliver 배송하다

32

What kind of business does the man own?

(A) A laundry service
(B) A cosmetics company
(C) A public relations firm
(D) A beverage manufacturer

남자는 어떤 종류의 업체를 소유하고 있는가?

(A) 세탁 서비스 업체
(B) 화장품 회사
(C) 홍보 회사
(D) 음료 제조 업체

어휘 public relations 홍보 beverage 음료 manufacturer 제조업체

해설 세부 사항 관련 - 남자가 소유하고 있는 업체

남자가 첫 대사에서 작은 화장품 회사의 사장(I'm the owner of a small cosmetics company)이라고 본인을 소개하고 있으므로 정답은 (B)이다.

33

What does the man want to know?

(A) Who to contact about a purchase
(B) Where to send some documents
(C) When a delivery will arrive
(D) How to use a product

남자는 무엇을 알고 싶어 하는가?

(A) 구매 문의 대상자
(B) 문서 발송처
(C) 배송품 도착 시간
(D) 제품 사용법

어휘 purchase 구매

해설 세부 사항 관련 - 남자가 알고 싶어 하는 것

남자가 첫 대사에서 지난주에 대량의 급행 주문을 했다(We placed a large rush order with you last week)면서 어제 라벨을 받기로 했는데 아직 안 왔다(We were supposed to get the labels yesterday, but they haven't come yet)고 말하고 있는 것으로 보아, 주문한 물품의 배송 상황 및 일정을 확인하고자 한다는 것을 알 수 있다. 따라서 정답은 (C)이다.

34

What does the woman ask the man to provide?

(A) An order number
(B) A return mailing address
(C) A signed contract
(D) An online payment

여자는 남자에게 무엇을 달라고 요청하는가?

(A) 주문 번호
(B) 반송 우편 주소
(C) 서명된 계약서
(D) 온라인 결제

해설 세부 사항 관련 - 여자가 남자에게 달라고 요청한 것

여자가 두 번째 대사에서 주문 번호가 어떻게 되는지(What is your order number?)를 묻고 있으므로 정답은 (A)이다.

35-37

W-Am Jerome, [36]**did you look at the options for in-flight entertainment? One of the options is e-books!**

M-Cn Oh, really? [36]**Are there any good books listed?**

W-Am Yes, actually. There are quite a few best sellers... and you can read them right on the screen in front of your seat.

M-Cn Interesting. But [35]**this is a short flight; what happens when we land and I haven't finished the book?**

W-Am Apparently, [37]**if you provide your e-mail address, the airline will send you a link so you can download the book to your personal electronic device. That's so convenient!**

여	제롬, 기내 즐길 거리 선택 항목들 봤어요? 선택 항목들 중 하나가 전자책이에요!
남	아, 정말요? 좋은 책들이 있나요?
여	네, 정말요. 베스트셀러가 꽤 있고… 좌석 바로 앞에 있는 화면에서 읽을 수 있어요.
남	흥미롭네요. 하지만 **이번은 짧은 비행이에요. 착륙할 때 내가 책을 다 읽지 못했으면 어쩌죠?**
여	듣자 하니, 이메일 주소를 알려 주면 항공사에서 링크를 보내서 책을 개인 전자기기에 내려받을 수 있대요. 아주 편리해요!

어휘	entertainment 즐길 거리 apparently 듣자[보아] 하니 electronic device 전자기기 convenient 편리한

35

Where most likely are the speakers?

(A) On a bus
(B) On a train
(C) On an airplane
(D) On a boat

화자들은 어디에 있겠는가?

(A) 버스
(B) 열차
(C) 비행기
(D) 배

해설 전체 내용 관련 – 대화의 장소

남자가 두 번째 대사에서 이번 비행은 짧은데 착륙할 때 책을 다 읽지 못했으면 어쩌냐(this is a short flight; what happens when we land and I haven't finished the book?)고 묻고 있는 것으로 보아 화자들은 현재 기내에서 대화 중임을 알 수 있다. 따라서 정답은 (C)이다.

36

What type of entertainment are the speakers discussing?

(A) Music
(B) Games
(C) Movies
(D) Books

화자들은 어떤 종류의 즐길 거리에 대해 논의하고 있는가?

(A) 음악
(B) 게임
(C) 영화
(D) 책

해설 세부 사항 관련 – 화자들이 이야기하고 있는 즐길 거리

여자가 첫 대사에서 기내 즐길 거리 선택 항목들을 봤는지(did you look at the options for in-flight entertainment?) 물으며 선택 항목들 중 하나가 전자책(One of the options is e-books!)이라고 했고, 뒤이어 남자도 좋은 책들이 있는지(Are there any good books listed?) 물으며 책에 대한 대화를 이어 가고 있으므로 정답은 (D)이다.

37

What does the woman say is convenient?

(A) Being able to download an item
(B) Taking a direct route
(C) Having reclining seats
(D) Selecting meal options online

여자는 무엇이 편리하다고 말하는가?

(A) 품목 내려받기 가능
(B) 직항로 이용
(C) 등받이가 젖혀지는 좌석 있음
(D) 온라인으로 식사 선택

어휘 recline 의자 등받이를 젖히다

해설 세부 사항 관련 – 여자가 편리하다고 말하는 것

여자가 마지막 대사에서 이메일 주소를 알려 주면 항공사에서 링크를 보내 책을 개인 전자기기에 내려받을 수 있다(if you provide your e-mail address, the airline will send you a link so you can download the book to your personal electronic device)고 말하며, 아주 편리하다(That's so convenient!)고 덧붙이고 있으므로 정답은 (A)이다.

38-40

M-Au	Thanks for inviting me to visit. As I said on the phone, [38]**I'm looking for a local farm to supply vegetables for my restaurant.**
W-Am	Sure. [38]**You can sample some of our seasonal produce when I show you around today.**
M-Au	Great. [39]**I'm concerned about variety,** though. How wide is your selection of vegetables?
W-Am	Well... we are constrained by what can be grown here in season. [40]**Let's tour the property now. I'll show you what we grow.**

남	방문하도록 초대해 주셔서 감사합니다. 전화로 말씀드렸듯이, **제 식당에 채소를 공급할 지역 농장을 찾고 있어요.**
여	좋아요. **오늘 제가 안내할 때 저희 제철 농산물 몇 가지를 시식해 보실 수 있어요.**
남	잘됐네요. 하지만 **종류가 다양한지 걱정돼요.** 채소가 얼마나 다양하게 구비돼 있나요?
여	아… 철따라 이곳에서 재배될 수 있는 것에 제약을 받죠. **이제 부지를 둘러보죠. 저희가 기르는 것들을 보여 드릴게요.**

어휘	sample 시식[시음]하다 produce 농산물 concerned 걱정하는 variety 다양성 selection 구비, 구색 constrain 제약하다 property 부지

38

What industry does the woman most likely work in?

(A) Landscaping
(B) Health care
(C) Event planning
(D) Agriculture

여자는 어떤 업계에서 일하겠는가?

(A) 조경
(B) 의료
(C) 행사 기획
(D) 농업

어휘 landscaping 조경   agriculture 농업

해설 전체 내용 관련 - 여자의 근무 업종

남자가 첫 대사에서 제 식당에 채소를 공급할 지역 농장을 찾고 있다(I'm looking for a local farm to supply vegetables for my restaurant)고 하자, 여자가 오늘 제가 안내할 때 제철 농산물 몇 가지를 시식해 보실 수 있다(You can sample some of our seasonal produce ~ today)고 말하고 있으므로 여자는 농작물을 생산하는 농장에서 일하고 있다는 것을 알 수 있다. 따라서 정답은 (D)이다.

39

What does the man say he is concerned about?

(A) Cost
(B) Variety
(C) Service dates
(D) Location

남자는 무엇이 걱정된다고 말하는가?

(A) 가격
(B) 종류
(C) 서비스 일자
(D) 위치

해설 세부 사항 관련 - 남자의 우려 사항

남자가 두 번째 대사에서 종류가 다양한지 걱정된다(I'm concerned about variety)고 말하고 있으므로 정답은 (B)이다.

40

What will the speakers do next?

(A) Look at a slideshow
(B) Have a meal
(C) Discuss an estimate
(D) Go on a tour

화자들은 다음에 무엇을 하겠는가?

(A) 슬라이드 쇼 보기
(B) 식사하기
(C) 견적 논의하기
(D) 둘러보기

어휘 estimate 견적(서)

해설 세부 사항 관련 - 화자들이 다음에 할 일

여자가 마지막 대사에서 이제 부지를 둘러보자(Let's tour the property now)고 제안하며, 저희가 기르는 것들을 보여 드리겠다(I'll show you what we grow)고 말하고 있으므로 정답은 (D)이다.

41-43

M-Cn	Hi, Elise. **41 Did you see the feedback from the focus group about our company's latest fitness trackers?**
W-Br	**41 No, did the customers like the new features that were added?**
M-Cn	Overall they did. They liked the fact that the new tracker is water resistant and can be worn while swimming. But **42 there were complaints about the battery life**.
W-Br	Yes, **42 I was sure customers would complain about that. The battery life on the older model was seven days, and this one is only five.**
M-Cn	Right. Then **43 we need to create good marketing materials for this new tracker that emphasize the improved features.** This will help us to sell the new product.

남	안녕, 엘리제. **우리 회사의 최신 건강 추적 장치에 대한 포커스 그룹의 의견 보셨어요?**
여	**아뇨, 고객들이 새로 추가된 기능을 좋아했나요?**
남	대체로 좋아했어요. 그들은 새 추적 장치에 방수 기능이 있어 수영할 때도 찰 수 있다는 점을 마음에 들어했어요. 하지만 **배터리 수명에는 불만이 있었어요.**
여	네, **고객들이 그것을 불평할 것으로 확신했어요. 구형 모델의 배터리 수명은 7일인데, 이번 모델은 5일밖에 안 되니까요.**
남	맞아요. 그렇다면 **이 신형 추적 장치를 위해 개선된 기능을 강조하는 좋은 마케팅 자료를 만들어야 해요.** 그렇게 하면 신제품 판매에 도움이 될 겁니다.

어휘	focus group 포커스 그룹(시장 조사를 위해 각계각층에서 선별된 소수 집단) feature 기능 overall 대체로 water resistant 방수 기능이 있는 complaint 불만 emphasize 강조하다 improved 개선된

41

What product are the speakers discussing?

(A) Cameras
(B) Fitness trackers
(C) Wireless speakers
(D) Mobile phones

화자들은 어떤 제품을 논의하고 있는가?
(A) 카메라
(B) 건강 추적 장치
(C) 무선 스피커
(D) 핸드폰

해설 전체 내용 관련 - 화자들이 논의 중인 제품
남자가 첫 대사에서 우리 회사의 최신 건강 추적 장치에 대한 포커스 그룹의 의견을 봤는지(Did you see the feedback ~ fitness trackers?) 묻자, 여자가 안 봤다(No)며 고객들이 새로 추가된 기능을 좋아하는지(did the customers like the new features that were added?) 물으면서 건강 추적 장치에 대한 대화를 이어 가고 있으므로 정답은 (B)이다.

42

What complaint did customers have about the product?

(A) It was unavailable in stores.
(B) The price was too high.
(C) **The battery life was short.**
(D) Some features were difficult to use.

고객들은 제품에 어떤 불만이 있는가?
(A) 매장에서 구할 수 없었다.
(B) 가격이 너무 비쌌다.
(C) 배터리 수명이 짧았다.
(D) 일부 기능이 사용하기 어려웠다.

어휘 unavailable 구할 수 없는

해설 세부 사항 관련 - 고객들이 제품에 갖고 있는 불만
남자가 두 번째 대사에서 배터리 수명에 불만이 있었다(there were complaints about the battery life)고 하자, 뒤이어 여자가 고객들이 그것을 불평할 것으로 확신했다(I was sure customers would complain about that)며 구형 모델의 배터리 수명은 7일인데 이번 모델은 5일밖에 안 된다(The battery life ~ this one is only five)고 말하고 있는 것으로 보아, 고객들은 짧은 배터리 수명에 불만이 있음을 알 수 있다. 따라서 정답은 (C)이다.

43

What does the man suggest doing?

(A) Revising a budget
(B) Postponing a product launch
(C) Visiting a manufacturing plant
(D) **Creating a good marketing campaign**

남자는 무엇을 하자고 제안하는가?
(A) 예산 수정
(B) 제품 출시 연기
(C) 제조 공장 방문
(D) 좋은 마케팅 전략 고안

어휘 revise 수정하다 postpone 연기하다 manufacturing plant 제조 공장 marketing campaign 마케팅 전략

해설 세부 사항 관련 - 남자의 제안 사항
남자가 마지막 대사에서 이 신형 추적 장치를 위해 개선된 기능을 강조하는 좋은 마케팅 자료를 만들어야 한다(we need to create good marketing materials for this new tracker that emphasize the improved features)고 제안하고 있으므로 정답은 (D)이다.

44-46 3인 대화

W-Am **44 We're making progress setting up our tour bus company, but finding the right drivers will be very important.**

W-Br You're right. **44 Should we use a recruitment agency?**

M-Au We could, but I was thinking... **45 you know I used to work at the Blue Eagle Hotel?**

W-Br Yes.

M-Au Well, the hotel had a lot of airport shuttle bus drivers. I have their contact info.

W-Am Great. Maybe they'll come work for us. **46 Why don't you reach out to them?**

M-Au **46 I will, but after our meeting with the insurance company. Remember they'll be here in twenty minutes.** I hope we can negotiate a good package to insure our drivers.

여1 관광버스 회사를 설립하는 일에 진전이 있지만, 적합한 운전기사를 찾는 게 아주 중요할 거예요.
여2 맞아요. 채용 정보 회사를 이용해야 할까요?
남 그래도 되지만, 제 생각엔… 제가 예전에 블루 이글 호텔에서 일했던 거 아시죠?
여2 네.
남 저, 그 호텔에는 공항 셔틀버스 운전기사가 많았어요. 저한테 연락처가 있어요.
여1 잘됐네요. 우리 회사로 일하러 올 수도 있잖아요. 연락해 보는 게 어때요?
남 그럴게요, 하지만 보험 회사와 회의부터 끝내고요. 20분 뒤면 그들이 여기 오니까 기억하세요. 협상해서 운전기사들을 괜찮은 보험 상품에 가입시켰으면 좋겠어요.

어휘 make progress 진전을 이루다 recruitment agency 채용 정보 회사 used to 예전에 ~하다 reach out 연락해 보다 insurance 보험 negotiate 협상하다 insure 보험에 가입시키다

44

What is the topic of the conversation?

(A) **Recruiting staff**
(B) Marketing a product
(C) Repairing a vehicle
(D) Booking a tour

대화의 주제는 무엇인가?

(A) 직원 모집
(B) 제품 마케팅
(C) 차량 수리
(D) 투어 예약

해설 전체 내용 관련 - 대화의 주제

첫 번째 여자가 첫 대사에서 관광버스 회사를 설립하는 일에 진전이 있지만 적합한 운전기사를 찾는 게 아주 중요할 것(We're making progress setting up ~ will be very important)이라고 말하자, 두 번째 여자가 채용 정보 회사를 이용해야 할지(Should we use a recruitment agency?)를 물어보며 인력 채용에 대한 대화를 이어 가고 있으므로 정답은 (A)이다.

> ▸▸ Paraphrasing   대화의 finding the right drivers
>   → 정답의 Recruiting staff

45

Where does the man say he used to work?

(A) At a driving school
(B) At an automobile factory
(C) At a hotel
(D) At an airport

남자는 예전에 어디에서 일했다고 말하는가?

(A) 자동차 운전 학원
(B) 자동차 공장
(C) 호텔
(D) 공항

해설 세부 사항 관련 - 남자의 이전 근무지

남자가 첫 대사에서 자신이 예전에 블루 이글 호텔에서 일했던 것을 아는지(you know I used to work at the Blue Eagle Hotel?) 묻고 있는 것으로 보아 정답은 (C)이다.

46

Who will the speakers meet with next?

(A) A real estate agent
(B) A delivery person
(C) Lawyers
(D) Insurance agents

화자들은 다음에 누구를 만나겠는가?

(A) 부동산 중개업자
(B) 배달 기사
(C) 변호사
(D) 보험 설계사

어휘 real estate 부동산

해설 세부 사항 관련 - 화자들이 다음에 만날 사람

첫 번째 여자가 두 번째 대사에서 그들(운전기사들)에게 연락해 보는 게 어떨지(Why don't you reach out to them?)를 제안하자, 남자가 보험 회사와 회의부터 끝낸 뒤에 하겠다(I will, but after our meeting with the insurance company)며 20분 뒤면 그들이 여기 오는 것을 기억하라(Remember they'll be here in twenty minutes)고 말하고 있으므로

화자들은 곧 보험 회사 직원들과 만나 회의를 할 것임을 알 수 있다. 따라서 정답은 (D)이다.

47-49

W-Br	⁴⁷**I bought this phone here a few months ago, and the fingerprint recognition feature has stopped working.**
M-Cn	You can still unlock your phone with your pass code, but it doesn't recognize your fingerprint anymore, correct?
W-Br	That's right. If it makes a difference, ⁴⁸**I paid extra for the extended warranty**.
M-Cn	That's good. I can replace it if I can't figure out how to fix it. Give me a few minutes while I check. And ⁴⁹**feel free to look at our accessories while you're waiting.**

여	몇 달 전에 여기서 이 전화기를 샀는데 지문 인식 기능이 작동을 멈췄어요.
남	비밀번호로 전화기 잠금을 해제할 수는 있지만, 더 이상 지문을 인식하지 못하네요, 맞죠?
여	맞아요. 혹시 차이가 있을까 말씀드리는데, 저는 추가 비용을 내고 보증 기간을 연장했어요.
남	잘됐네요. 고치는 방법을 알아내지 못하면 교체해 드릴게요. 확인하는 동안 잠시 기다리세요. 기다리시는 동안 주변 기기들을 마음껏 둘러보세요.

어휘   fingerprint 지문 recognition 인식 feature 기능 extended 연장된 warranty 보증 (기간) replace 교체하다 figure out 알아내다 fix 고치다 feel free to 마음껏 ~하다

47

What problem does the woman have?

(A) She lost her keys.
(B) Her phone screen has cracked.
(C) She injured her finger.
(D) Her phone is malfunctioning.

여자에게 어떤 문제가 있는가?

(A) 열쇠를 잃어버렸다.
(B) 전화기 화면이 깨졌다.
(C) 손가락을 다쳤다.
(D) 전화기가 고장 났다.

어휘 crack 깨지다 injure 다치다 malfunction 고장 나다

해설 세부 사항 관련 - 여자의 문제점

여자가 첫 대사에서 몇 달 전에 여기서 이 전화기를 샀는데 지문 인식 기능이 작동을 멈췄다(I bought this phone here a few months ago, and the fingerprint recognition feature has stopped working)고 말하고 있으므로 정답은 (D)이다.

48

What did the woman pay extra for?

(A) An extended warranty
(B) Twenty-four-hour assistance
(C) Express service
(D) A personalized design

여자는 무엇을 위해 추가 비용을 지불했는가?

(A) 보증 기간 연장
(B) 24시간 지원
(C) 급행 서비스
(D) 개인 맞춤 디자인

어휘 assistance 지원 express 급행의 personalized 개인 맞춤의

해설 세부 사항 관련 - 여자의 추가 비용 지불 목적

여자가 두 번째 대사에서 추가 비용을 내고 보증 기간을 연장했다(I paid extra for the extended warranty)고 말하고 있으므로 정답은 (A)이다.

49

What does the man suggest the woman do?

(A) Fill out a refund request
(B) Call another store
(C) Look at some accessories
(D) Change a pass code

남자는 여자에게 무엇을 하라고 권하는가?

(A) 환불 요청서 작성하기
(B) 다른 매장에 전화하기
(C) 주변 기기 보기
(D) 비밀번호 바꾸기

어휘 fill out 작성하다

해설 세부 사항 관련 - 남자가 여자에게 권한 일

남자가 마지막 대사에서 기다리는 동안 주변 기기들을 마음껏 둘러보라 (feel free to look at our accessories while you're waiting)고 권하고 있으므로 정답은 (C)이다.

50-52

M-Au	I got your message, Rita.
W-Br	Since 50**you're the factory manager,** I wanted to run something by you. 51**I think we should consider changing our lumber supplier. Ebson Lumber Mill sells very high-quality wood that would be perfect for the wood flooring we produce.**
M-Au	What's the difference in cost?
W-Br	Actually, none. The mill is much closer

to our factory, so the higher price of the wood would be canceled out by the lower shipping costs. And we'd have a higher-quality product.

M-Au	52**Can you ask the mill to send us some samples?** I'd like to see them.

남	메시지 받았어요, 리타.
여	**공장장이시니까** 같이 의논하고 싶었어요. **목재 납품업체 교체를 고려해야 할 것 같아요. 엡슨 제재소가 우리가 생산하는 나무바닥에 안성맞춤인 아주 고품질 목재를 판매해요.**
남	가격 차이요?
여	사실 없어요. 그 제재소가 우리 공장과 훨씬 가까워서, 목재 가격이 더 비싸도 배송비가 낮아 상쇄될 거예요. 게다가 우린 더 고품질 제품을 갖게 되고요.
남	**제재소에 샘플 좀 보내 달라고 부탁하실래요?** 샘플을 보고 싶네요.

어휘 run by ~와 의논하다 lumber 목재 supplier 납품업체
lumber mill 제재소 cancel out 상쇄하다

50

Who is the man?

(A) A software designer
(B) A landscape architect
(C) A factory supervisor
(D) A furniture store clerk

남자는 누구인가?

(A) 소프트웨어 디자이너
(B) 조경사
(C) 공장 관리자
(D) 가구점 직원

해설 전체 내용 관련 - 남자의 직업

여자가 첫 대사에서 남자에게 당신이 공장장(you're the factory manager)이라고 말하고 있으므로 정답은 (C)이다.

51

What reason does the woman give for making a change?

(A) The business hours would be more convenient.
(B) The quality of materials would be better.
(C) A discount is being offered.
(D) Fewer workers would be needed.

여자가 교체의 이유로 내세운 것은 무엇인가?

(A) 근무 시간이 더 편할 것이다.
(B) 재료의 품질이 더 좋을 것이다.
(C) 할인이 제공되고 있다.
(D) 인력이 더 적게 필요할 것이다.

어휘 convenient 편리한

해설 세부 사항 관련 - 여자가 교체의 이유로 내세운 것
여자가 첫 대사에서 목재 납품업체 교체를 고려해야 할 것 같다(I think we should consider changing our lumber supplier)며, 엡슨 제재소가 우리가 생산하는 나무마루에 안성맞춤인 아주 고품질 목재를 판매한다(Ebson Lumber Mill sells very high-quality wood that would be perfect for the wood flooring we produce)고 말하고 있으므로 정답은 (B)이다.

52

What does the man ask the woman to do?

(A) Visit a work site

(B) Send a contract

(C) Make a counteroffer

(D) Request some samples

남자는 여자에게 무엇을 해 달라고 요청하는가?
(A) 작업장 방문
(B) 계약서 발송
(C) 대안 제시
(D) 샘플 요청

어휘 counteroffer 대안 (제시)

해설 세부 사항 관련 - 남자가 여자에게 요청한 일
남자가 마지막 대사에서 제재소에 샘플을 보내 달라고 부탁할 것(Can you ask the mill to send us some samples?)을 요청하고 있으므로 정답은 (D)이다.

▶▶ Paraphrasing 대화의 ask the mill to send us some samples
→ 정답의 Request some samples

53-55

W-Br	Miguel, ⁵³do you have a minute to chat about the upcoming trade show in Los Angeles?
M-Cn	Sure, what's up?
W-Br	⁵⁴All I have left to do is to send specific instructions to the event organizers about setting up our booth.
M-Cn	OK, I'm nearly ready too, but I still need to print those extra business cards we talked about. ⁵⁵I know you said the print shop is having a sale this week, so I'll head over there after work.
W-Br	The office supply store has a sale.
M-Cn	Ahh... thanks. Good thing I mentioned it!

여	미겔, 로스앤젤레스에서 곧 있을 무역 박람회 건으로 잠깐 얘기 좀 하려는데 시간 있어요?

남	그럼요, 무슨 일이에요?
여	제가 할 일은 부스 설치에 대한 구체적인 지침을 행사 주최자에게 보내는 일만 남았어요.
남	네, 저도 거의 준비가 다 됐지만, 우리가 얘기했던 여분의 명함을 인쇄해야 해요. 이번 주에 인쇄소가 할인한다고 얘기하셨던 거 알아요. 그래서 퇴근하고 그쪽으로 가려고요.
여	사무용품점에서 할인해요.
남	아… 고마워요. 얘기하길 잘했네요!

어휘 upcoming 곧 있을 specific 구체적인 instruction 지침 organizer 주최자 nearly 거의 head 가다

53

What are the speakers preparing for?

(A) A client visit

(B) An employee orientation

(C) A trade show

(D) A fund-raising event

화자들은 무엇을 준비하고 있는가?
(A) 고객 방문
(B) 직원 오리엔테이션
(C) 무역 박람회
(D) 모금 행사

어휘 fund-raising 모금

해설 세부 사항 관련 - 화자들이 준비하고 있는 일
여자가 첫 대사에서 로스앤젤레스에서 곧 있을 무역 박람회 건으로 잠깐 얘기할 시간이 있는지(do you have a minute to chat about the upcoming trade show in Los Angeles?)를 묻고 있는 것으로 보아 정답은 (C)이다.

54

What does the woman say she needs to do?

(A) Send some instructions

(B) Make a reservation

(C) Order some badges

(D) Write a speech

여자는 자신이 무엇을 해야 한다고 말하는가?
(A) 지침 발송
(B) 예약
(C) 배지 주문
(D) 연설문 작성

어휘 reservation 예약

해설 세부 사항 관련 - 여자가 자신이 해야 한다고 말하는 일
여자가 두 번째 대사에서 제가 할 일은 부스 설치에 대한 구체적인 지침을 행사 주최자에게 보내는 일만 남았다(All I have left to do is to send specific instructions to the event organizers about setting up our booth)고 말하고 있으므로 정답은 (A)이다.

55

Why does the woman say, "The office supply store has a sale"?

(A) To extend an invitation
(B) To make a correction
(C) To express satisfaction
(D) To explain a decision

여자가 "사무용품점에서 할인해요"라고 말하는 이유는 무엇인가?

(A) 초대장을 주려고
(B) 바로잡으려고
(C) 만족감을 나타내려고
(D) 결정을 설명하려고

어휘 extend 주다　correction 정정[수정]　satisfaction 만족(감)
　　　decision 결정

해설 화자의 의도 파악 – 사무용품점에서 할인한다는 말의 의도

앞에서 남자가 이번 주에 인쇄소가 할인한다고 말했던 것을 알고 있어서 퇴근하고 그쪽으로 가려 한다(I know you said the print shop ~ head over there after work)고 말하자 여자가 인용문을 언급한다. 할인하는 곳은 남자가 말한 인쇄소가 아니라 사무용품점이라는 말은 남자가 잘못 알고 있는 부분을 정정해 주려는 의도라고 볼 수 있다. 따라서 정답은 (B)이다.

56-58 3인 대화

> M-Au　**56 Have you heard about the new robots that'll help us out organizing packages?** They just arrived.
>
> W-Br　Oh, yes... **56 the robots to help us sort the shipments.** Wait—**57 that's a surprise. I wasn't expecting them until the end of the month!**
>
> W-Am　**57 That's what I thought, too! They must have moved up the date** so we can start using them sooner.
>
> W-Br　And that means we'll probably get trained on how to use them next week. Remember when they trained us on the new scanners last year?
>
> M-Au　Yes, but **58 we didn't get very much detailed information about how to use the scanners. It was very general.**

남　포장 상자 정리를 도와줄 새 로봇에 대해 들어 보셨나요? 방금 도착했어요.

여1　아… 네… 선적물 분류를 도와줄 로봇이죠. 잠깐만요, 의외네요. 이번 달 말이나 돼야 도착할 줄 알았는데!

여2　저도 그렇게 생각했죠! 우리가 더 빨리 쓸 수 있도록 날짜를 앞당긴 게 틀림없어요.

여1　그럼 다음 주에 사용법에 대한 교육을 받겠군요. 작년에 새 스캐너 건으로 교육했던 거 기억나요?

남　네, 하지만 스캐너 사용법에 대한 자세한 정보를 별로 얻지는 못했죠. 너무 대충 했어요.

어휘　organize 정리하다　shipment 선적(물)

56

Which department do the speakers most likely work in?

(A) Human Resources
(B) Shipping
(C) Information Technology
(D) Sales

화자들은 어느 부서에서 일하겠는가?

(A) 인사
(B) 배송
(C) 정보 기술
(D) 영업

해설 전체 내용 관련 – 화자들의 근무 부서

남자가 첫 대사에서 포장 상자 정리를 도와줄 새 로봇에 대해 들어 봤는지(Have you heard about the new robots that'll help us out organizing packages?) 묻자 첫 번째 여자가 선적물 분류를 도와줄 로봇(the robots to help us sort the shipments)이라고 언급하고 있는 것으로 보아, 화자들은 물품을 정리하고 선적하는 배송 관련 부서에서 일하고 있음을 알 수 있다. 따라서 정답은 (B)이다.

57

Why are the women surprised?

(A) An event was canceled.
(B) A coworker retired on short notice.
(C) Some business hours were changed.
(D) Some equipment arrived early.

여자들은 왜 놀라는가?

(A) 행사가 취소되었다.
(B) 동료가 갑작스럽게 퇴직했다.
(C) 영업 시간이 변경되었다.
(D) 장비가 일찍 도착했다.

어휘　retire 퇴직하다　on short notice 갑작스럽게

해설 세부 사항 관련 – 여자들이 놀란 이유

첫 번째 여자가 첫 대사에서 의외(that's a surprise)라고 놀라움을 표현하며 이번 달 말이나 돼야 도착할 줄 알았다(I wasn't expecting them until the end of the month!)고 하자, 두 번째 여자가 저도 그렇게 생각했다(That's what I thought, too!)며 날짜를 앞당긴 게 틀림없다(They must have moved up the date)고 말하고 있으므로 로봇이 원래 일정보다 미리 도착해서 놀랐음을 알 수 있다. 따라서 정답은 (D)이다.

58

What complaint does the man have about a previous training?

(A) It was not offered to all workers.

(B) It was not detailed enough.

(C) It did not include lunch.

(D) It was not held during work hours.

남자는 이전 교육에 어떤 불만이 있는가?

(A) 모든 직원에게 제공되지 않았다.

(B) 충분히 상세하지 않았다.

(C) 점심 식사가 포함되지 않았다.

(D) 근무 시간에 실시되지 않았다.

해설 세부 사항 관련 - 남자가 이전 교육에 갖고 있는 불만

남자가 마지막 대사에서 스캐너 사용법에 대한 자세한 정보를 별로 얻지 못했다(we didn't get very much detailed information about how to use the scanners)며 너무 대충 했다(It was very general)고 말하고 있는 것으로 보아 정답은 (B)이다.

59-61

W-Am	Hi, Mr. Rashad. I just stopped by to let you know I won't be renewing my lease. **⁵⁹I'm going to rent an apartment that's closer to my job... I'm tired of driving so far to work.**
M-Au	I'm sorry you're leaving—you're an excellent tenant. **⁶⁰When will you be moving out?**
W-Am	**⁶⁰The middle of next month. The contract requires that I pay rent for the full month, though, right?**
M-Au	Well, I should be able to lease that unit pretty quickly. I'll let you know what happens.
W-Am	All right. Thanks.
M-Au	Oh, and, **⁶¹there's a form you'll need to fill out to make your notice official. I have it right here...**

여	안녕하세요, 라샤드 씨. 임대 계약을 갱신하지 않을 거라고 알려 드리고자 들렀어요. **직장에서 더 가까운 아파트를 임대하려고요… 회사까지 멀리 운전해서 다니느라 지쳐서요.**
남	떠나신다니 아쉽네요, 더할 나위 없이 좋은 세입자신데. **언제 이사하세요?**
여	**다음 달 중순이요. 계약상 꼬박 한 달 치 월세를 다 내야 하는 거 맞죠?**
남	어, 그 아파트를 빨리 임대할 수 있을 것 같아요. 어떻게 되는지 알려 드릴게요.
여	알겠습니다. 고마워요.
남	아, 그리고 **정식으로 통지하려면 작성해야 할 양식이 있어요. 지금 여기 갖고 있어요…**

어휘 renew 갱신하다 tenant 세입자 contract 계약(서)
fill out 작성하다

59

Why does the woman want to move out of her current apartment?

(A) It is far from her workplace.

(B) It is too small.

(C) It is in a noisy area.

(D) It is too expensive.

여자는 왜 현재 아파트에서 이사하려고 하는가?

(A) 직장에서 멀다.

(B) 너무 작다.

(C) 시끄러운 지역에 있다.

(D) 너무 비싸다.

어휘 expensive 비싼

해설 세부 사항 관련 - 여자가 현재 아파트에서 이사하려는 이유

여자가 첫 대사에서 직장에서 더 가까운 아파트를 임대하려고 한다(I'm going to rent an apartment that's closer to my job)면서 회사까지 멀리 운전해서 다니느라 지쳤다(I'm tired of driving so far to work)고 말하고 있으므로 정답은 (A)이다.

60

What does the man mean when he says, "I should be able to lease that unit pretty quickly"?

(A) A rental payment will likely be reduced.

(B) Investing in a property would be profitable.

(C) Some renovations will not take long.

(D) An apartment has a modern layout.

남자가 "그 아파트를 빨리 임대할 수 있을 것 같아요"라고 말하는 의도는 무엇인가?

(A) 임대료가 줄어들 것 같다.

(B) 부동산에 투자하면 수익이 날 것이다.

(C) 수리가 오래 걸리지 않을 것이다.

(D) 아파트 구조가 현대적이다.

어휘 reduce 줄이다 property 부동산 profitable 수익이 나는
renovation 수리

해설 화자의 의도 파악 - 그 아파트를 빨리 임대할 수 있을 것 같다는 말의 의도

앞에서 남자가 언제 이사하는지(When will you be moving out?) 묻자 여자가 다음 달 중순(The middle of next month)이라고 대답하며 계약상 꼬박 한 달 치 월세를 다 내야 하는 게 맞는지(The contract requires that I pay rent for the full month, though, right?) 확인하는 질문에 남자가 인용문을 언급한 것으로 보아, 여자가 중순에 이사한 뒤 새로운 세입자를 빨리 찾아 임대하게 되면 한 달 치 월세를 다 내지 않아도 될 수 있다는 의도로 한 말임을 알 수 있다. 따라서 정답은 (A)이다.

61

What will the woman most likely do next?

(A) Post an advertisement
(B) Complete a form
(C) Order some supplies
(D) Provide a reference

여자는 다음에 무엇을 하겠는가?

(A) 광고 게재
(B) 양식 작성
(C) 물품 주문
(D) 추천서 제공

해설 세부 사항 관련 – 여자가 다음에 할 일

남자가 마지막 대사에서 정식으로 통지하려면 작성해야 할 양식이 있다(there's a form you'll need to fill out to make your notice official)면서 지금 여기 갖고 있다(I have it right here)고 양식을 건네고 있으므로 정답은 (B)이다.

▸▸ **Paraphrasing** 대화의 **fill out** → 정답의 **Complete**

62-64 대화 + 재고 목록

M-Cn	Hi, Geeta, this is Ming. ⁶²**Sorry to call you on your day off, but I need someone to fill in for Stefan tomorrow at the bookstore. He injured his ankle playing basketball.**
W-Am	Sure, I can take Stefan's shift. Happy to help out.
M-Cn	Thanks! Also, I have another favor to ask.
W-Am	Of course. What is it?
M-Cn	Well, I was checking our cookbook inventory. ⁶³**We only have seven copies of the book we need for the author event later this month.** I'm worried seven won't be enough.
W-Am	I see. I can definitely order more.
M-Cn	Thanks! ⁶⁴**I think the author's going to draw a big crowd. She's pretty well-known and was recently on TV.**

남 안녕하세요, 기타, 밍이에요. **쉬는 날 전화해서 미안한데, 내일 서점에서 스테판을 대신할 사람이 필요해요. 스테판이 농구를 하다가 발목을 다쳤어요.**

여 그럼요, 스테판 근무를 대신할 수 있어요. 기꺼이 도울게요.

남 고마워요! 부탁이 하나 더 있어요.

여 그럼요. 뭔데요?

남 어, 요리책 재고를 조사하고 있었어요. **이번 달 말에 있을 저자 행사에 필요한 책이 7권밖에 없네요.** 7권으로는 부족할까 봐 걱정이에요.

여 그렇군요. 제가 꼭 더 주문할게요.

남 고마워요! 제 생각엔 저자가 사람을 많이 모을 것 같아요. 꽤 유명한데다 최근에 TV에 나왔거든요.

어휘 fill in for ~을 대신하다 injure 다치다 shift (교대) 근무
inventory 재고 definitely 꼭 recently 최근에

Book Title	Copies In Stock
Cooking with Kids	6
Delicious Dinners	9
⁶³*Easy Meals at Home*	7
Extraordinary Desserts	5

도서 제목	재고 부수
〈아이들과 함께하는 요리〉	6
〈맛있는 정찬〉	9
⁶³〈간편한 집밥〉	7
〈특별한 디저트〉	5

62

Why does the man ask the woman to work an extra shift?

(A) The store needs cleaning.
(B) A sale will happen soon.
(C) A shipment is arriving.
(D) A coworker has an injury.

남자는 왜 여자에게 추가 근무를 요청하는가?

(A) 매장을 청소해야 한다.
(B) 곧 할인 기간이다.
(C) 배송품이 도착할 것이다.
(D) 동료가 부상을 입었다.

해설 세부 사항 관련 – 남자가 여자에게 추가 근무를 요청하는 이유

남자가 첫 대사에서 쉬는 날 전화해서 미안한데, 내일 서점에서 스테판을 대신할 사람이 필요하다(Sorry to call you on your day off, but I need someone to fill in for Stefan tomorrow at the bookstore)면서 스테판이 농구를 하다가 발목을 다쳤다(He injured his ankle playing basketball)고 말하고 있으므로 정답은 (D)이다.

63

Look at the graphic. Which book is needed for an upcoming event?

(A) *Cooking with Kids*
(B) *Delicious Dinners*
(C) *Easy Meals at Home*
(D) *Extraordinary Desserts*

시각 정보에 의하면 곧 있을 행사에 어떤 책이 필요한가?

(A) 〈아이들과 함께하는 요리〉
(B) 〈맛있는 정찬〉
(C) 〈간편한 집밥〉
(D) 〈특별한 디저트〉

해설 시각 정보 연계 – 곧 있을 행사에 필요한 책

남자가 세 번째 대사에서 이번 달 말에 있을 저자 행사에 필요한 책이 7권밖에 없다(We only have seven copies of the book we need for the author event later this month)고 말하는데, 재고 목록에 따르면 7권 남아 있는 책은 〈간편한 집밥〉이므로 정답은 (C)이다.

64

Why does the man expect an event to be crowded?

(A) It is on a holiday weekend.

(B) It was advertised on television.

(C) An author is well-known.

(D) Free food will be served.

남자는 왜 행사가 붐빌 것으로 예상하는가?

(A) 휴일 주말에 열린다.

(B) 텔레비전에 광고되었다.

(C) 저자가 유명하다.

(D) 무료 음식이 제공된다.

해설 세부 사항 관련 – 남자가 행사가 붐빌 것으로 예상하는 이유

남자가 마지막 대사에서 저자가 사람을 많이 모을 것 같다(I think the author's going to draw a big crowd)며 저자가 꽤 유명한데다 최근에 TV에 나왔다(She's pretty well-known and was recently on TV)고 말하고 있으므로 정답은 (C)이다.

65-67 대화 + 좌석 배치도

W-Br	Hi, Yuri. 65 **Did you hear the East Lake Band is going to play a concert in town?**
M-Au	Yes! And 65 **now they have a great new guitarist. Simone Travers recently started playing with them.**
W-Br	Five of us from the marketing department plan to go together. Would you like to join us?
M-Au	That sounds like fun. Where are you going to sit?
W-Br	We thought about getting tickets for outdoor seating, but that'd be a problem if it rains. 66 **Would the balcony be OK with you?**
M-Au	66 **Sure.** And 67 **I'd be happy to drive. My car has room for everyone.**

여	안녕, 유리. **이스트 레이크 밴드가 시내에서 콘서트를 연다는 소식 들었어요?**
남	네! 그리고 **이젠 밴드에 훌륭한 기타리스트가 있죠. 시몬 트래버스가 최근에 그들과 함께 연주하기 시작했어요.**
여	마케팅부 직원 5명이 함께 갈 계획이에요. 같이 갈래요?
남	재미있겠어요. 어디에 앉을 거예요?

여	야외 좌석 표를 구하려고 했는데, 비가 오면 큰일이잖아요. **발코니석 괜찮아요?**
남	**물론이죠.** 그리고 운전은 제가 할게요. 제 차에 다 탈 공간이 있어요.

어휘	room 공간

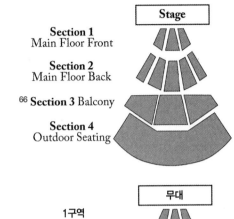

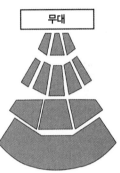

65

What did the East Lake Band recently do?

(A) They won a music award.

(B) They went on a national tour.

(C) They released a new recording.

(D) They added a new member to the group.

이스트 레이크 밴드는 최근에 무엇을 했는가?

(A) 음악상을 받았다.

(B) 전국 순회공연을 떠났다.

(C) 새 음반을 발매했다.

(D) 그룹에 새 멤버를 추가했다.

해설 세부 사항 관련 – 이스트 레이크 밴드가 최근 한 일

여자가 첫 대사에서 이스트 레이크 밴드가 시내에서 콘서트를 연다는 소식을 들었는지(Did you hear the East Lake Band is going to play a concert in town?) 묻자, 남자가 이제 밴드에 훌륭한 새 기타리스트가 있다(now they have a great new guitarist)며 시몬 트래버스가 최근에 그들과 함께 연주하기 시작했다(Simone Travers recently started playing with them)고 말하고 있으므로 정답은 (D)이다.

66

Look at the graphic. Where do the speakers plan to sit?

(A) In Section 1
(B) In Section 2
(C) In Section 3
(D) In Section 4

시각 정보에 의하면 화자들은 어디에 앉을 계획인가?

(A) 1구역
(B) 2구역
(C) 3구역
(D) 4구역

해설 시각 정보 연계 - 화자들이 앉을 곳

여자가 세 번째 대사에서 발코니석이 괜찮은지(Would the balcony be OK with you?) 묻자 남자가 물론이다(Sure)라고 대답하고 있으므로 화자들은 발코니석 구역에 앉을 것임을 알 수 있다. 좌석 배치도에 따르면 발코니석은 3구역이므로 정답은 (C)이다.

67

What does the man offer to do?

(A) Pick up some tickets
(B) Provide transportation
(C) Bring some umbrellas
(D) Make a dinner reservation

남자는 무엇을 하겠다고 제안하는가?

(A) 표 찾아오기
(B) 교통편 제공하기
(C) 우산 가져오기
(D) 저녁 식사 예약하기

어휘 transportation 교통(편)

해설 세부 사항 관련 - 남자의 제안 사항

남자가 마지막 대사에서 운전은 제가 하겠다(I'd be happy to drive)면서 제 차에 다 탈 공간이 있다(My car has room for everyone)고 말하고 있으므로 정답은 (B)이다.

> Paraphrasing 대화의 car → 정답의 transportation

68-70 대화 + 일정표

M-Cn	Natalia, I have a favor to ask. [68]**I have an important video call with the London office on Monday. I'll be interviewing some job candidates there.**
W-Br	OK. How can I help?
M-Cn	Well, [69]**I want to use Meeting Room B. And due to the different international time zones, I need the morning slot. I saw that you have that time booked already.**
W-Br	OK. I understand. In that case, [69]**I'll move**

---

my meeting to the afternoon instead. And [70]that's actually good because it'll give me extra time to improve the presentation I'm preparing.

남	나탈리아, 부탁이 있어요. **월요일에 런던 사무소와 중요한 영상 통화가 있어요. 거기서 구직자 몇 명을 면접해요.**
여	네. 어떻게 도와 드릴까요?
남	음, **B회의실을 쓰고 싶어요. 그리고 국가 간 시간대가 달라서 아침 시간대가 필요해요. 당신이 벌써 그 시간을 예약해 놓았더군요.**
여	네. 잘 알겠어요. 그렇다면 **제 회의를 오후로 옮길게요. 그러면 제가 준비하고 있는 프레젠테이션을 개선할 시간이 더 생기니까 실은 그게 좋아요.**

어휘 job candidate 구직자 improve 개선하다

Natalia's Schedule

	Monday	Tuesday	Wednesday
9–11 A.M.	[69]Budget Meeting Room B	Team Meeting Room A	Contract Meeting Lawyer's office
1–3 P.M.	Training Meeting Room C	Client Meeting Video call	
3–5 P.M.			

나탈리아 일정

	월	화	수
오전 9–11시	[69] 예산 회의 B회의실	팀 회의 A회의실	계약 회의 변호사 사무실
오후 1–3시	교육 회의 C회의실	고객 회의 영상 통화	
오후 3–5시			

68

What does the man plan to do during his meeting?

(A) Resolve a security issue
(B) Review a travel policy
(C) Conduct some job interviews
(D) Compare some software packages

남자는 회의 중에 무엇을 할 계획인가?

(A) 보안 문제 해결
(B) 출장 규정 검토
(C) 취업 면접 실시
(D) 소프트웨어 패키지 비교

어휘 resolve 해결하다 security 보안 conduct 실시하다 compare 비교하다

해설 세부 사항 관련 – 남자가 회의 중에 하려고 하는 일

남자가 첫 대사에서 월요일에 런던 사무소와 중요한 영상 통화가 있다(I have an important video call with the London office on Monday)며 거기서 구직자 몇 명을 면접할 것(I'll be interviewing some job candidates there)이라고 말하고 있으므로 정답은 (C)이다.

> ▶ Paraphrasing   대화의 be interviewing some job candidates → 정답의 Conduct some job interviews

69

Look at the graphic. Which one of the woman's meetings will be changed?

(A) Budget Meeting
(B) Training Meeting
(C) Team Meeting
(D) Contract Meeting

시각 정보에 의하면 여자의 회의들 중 어떤 것이 변경되는가?
(A) 예산 회의
(B) 교육 회의
(C) 팀 회의
(D) 계약 회의

해설 시각 정보 연계 – 여자의 회의들 중 변경되는 것

남자가 두 번째 대사에서 B회의실을 쓰고 싶다(I want to use Meeting Room B)고 했고 국가 간 시간대가 달라서 아침 시간대가 필요하다(due to the different international time zones, I need the morning slot)면서 당신이 벌써 그 시간을 예약해 놓았다(I saw that you have that time booked already)고 말하자 여자가 제 회의를 오후로 옮기겠다(I'll move my meeting to the afternoon instead)고 말하고 있으므로 여자는 B회의실에서의 오전 회의를 오후로 변경할 것임을 알 수 있다. 여자의 일정표에 따르면 오전에 B회의실에서 열리는 회의는 예산 회의이므로 정답은 (A)이다

70

What does the woman say she would like to improve?

(A) Her technical knowledge
(B) Her organizational skills
(C) A training manual
(D) A presentation

여자는 무엇을 개선하고 싶다고 말하는가?
(A) 기술 지식
(B) 조직화 기술
(C) 교육 매뉴얼
(D) 프레젠테이션

어휘 organizational 조직화에 관한

해설 세부 사항 관련 – 여자가 개선하고 싶다고 말하는 것

여자가 마지막 대사에서 그러면 제가 준비하고 있는 프레젠테이션을 개선할 시간이 더 생기니까 실은 그게 좋다(that's actually good because it'll give me extra time to improve the presentation I'm preparing)고 말하는 것으로 보아 정답은 (D)이다.

PART 4

71-73 전화 메시지

> **W-Br** Hello. This is the Chesterfield Community Center. [71] **We're calling to inform you about a change to our Movie Night event, originally planned for this Tuesday.** Unfortunately, another event had been booked at the community center for the same day. As a result, [72] **Movie Night has been rescheduled for this upcoming weekend, at nine P.M. on Saturday.** If you're no longer able to attend, we're happy to refund your ticket. [73] **You can request this refund by calling our office at 555-0126.**

> 여보세요. 체스터필드 주민 센터입니다. 당초 이번 주 화요일에 계획됐던 영화의 밤 행사 변경 사항을 알리기 위해 전화드립니다. 아쉽게도 같은 날 주민 센터에 다른 행사가 예약돼 있었습니다. 따라서 영화의 밤은 오는 주말인 토요일 오후 9시로 일정이 변경되었습니다. 더는 참석하실 수 없다면 기꺼이 표를 환불해 드리겠습니다. 저희 사무실에 555-0126으로 전화해서 환불을 요청하실 수 있습니다.

> 어휘 originally 당초   unfortunately 아쉽게도

71

Why has the Movie Night event been rescheduled?

(A) A projector is not available.
(B) A nearby road is being repaired.
(C) The space is double booked.
(D) The event organizer is ill.

영화의 밤 행사 일정은 왜 변경되었는가?
(A) 프로젝터를 사용할 수 없다.
(B) 인근 도로가 보수 중이다.
(C) 공간이 이중으로 예약됐다.
(D) 행사 주최자가 아프다.

어휘 repair 보수하다   organizer 주최자

해설 세부 사항 관련 – 영화의 밤 행사 일정이 변경된 이유

화자가 초반부에 당초 이번 주 화요일에 계획됐던 영화의 밤 행사 변경 사항을 알리기 위해 전화한다(We're calling to inform you about a change ~ for this Tuesday)며, 아쉽게도 같은 날 주민 센터에 다른 행사가 예약돼 있었다(Unfortunately, another event had been booked ~ the same day)고 말하고 있으므로 정답은 (C)이다.

72

When will the event be held?

(A) Tomorrow
(B) This weekend
(C) In two weeks
(D) In one month

행사는 언제 열리는가?

(A) 내일

(B) 이번 주말

(C) 2주 후

(D) 1달 후

해설 세부 사항 관련 - 행사가 열리는 시점

화자가 중반부에 영화의 밤은 오는 주말인 토요일 오후 9시로 일정이 변경되었다(Movie Night has been rescheduled for this upcoming weekend, at nine P.M. on Saturday)고 말하고 있으므로 정답은 (B)이다.

73

How can the listener request a refund?

(A) By mailing a ticket

(B) By visiting an office

(C) By completing an online form

(D) By making a phone call

청자는 어떻게 환불을 요청할 수 있는가?

(A) 표를 우편으로 보내서

(B) 사무실을 방문해서

(C) 온라인 양식을 작성해서

(D) 전화를 걸어서

해설 세부 사항 관련 - 환불 요청 방법

화자가 마지막에 저희 사무실에 555-0126으로 전화하면 환불을 요청할 수 있다(You can request this refund by calling our office at 555-0126)고 말하고 있으므로 정답은 (D)이다.

> ▸▸ Paraphrasing 담화의 calling our office
> → 정답의 making a phone call

74-76 담화

W-Am ⁷⁴Welcome to Canyon River National Park. I'm Marisol, and I'll be training you in your new role as park rangers. Each of you will be assigned one area of the park. Your duties will vary, but ⁷⁵one task you need to complete every day is to check your assigned area for hazardous conditions. For example, if you come across any fallen branches blocking the trails or roadways, you need to report them right away. Now—before I show you the grounds, ⁷⁶let me give you your uniforms. Please make sure that you wear them at all times on the premises.

캐니언 리버 국립공원에 오신 것을 환영합니다. 저는 마리솔이고, 공원 경비원으로서 여러분이 새로 맡을 역할에 대해 교육하려고 합니다. 여러분 각자에게 공원의 한 구역이 배정됩니다. 업무는 다양하지만 **매일 수행해야 할 한 가지 작업은 배정된 구역에서 위험한 상황을 확인하는 겁니다.** 예를 들어 오솔길이나 도로를 막고 있는 떨어진 나뭇가지를 발견하면 즉시 보고해야 합니다. 이제 구내로 안내하기 전에 **단체복부터 드**

릴게요. 구내에서는 항상 단체복을 착용하기 바랍니다.

어휘 park ranger 공원 경비원 assign 배정하다 hazardous 위험한 trail 오솔길 premises 구내, 부지

74

Who most likely is the speaker?

(A) A park ranger

(B) A travel agent

(C) A landscaper

(D) A building inspector

화자는 누구이겠는가?

(A) 공원 경비원

(B) 여행사 직원

(C) 조경업자

(D) 건축물 검사원

해설 전체 내용 관련 - 화자의 직업

화자가 도입부에 캐니언 리버 국립공원에 오신 것을 환영한다(Welcome to Canyon River National Park)면서, 저는 마리솔이고 공원 경비원으로서 여러분이 새로 맡을 역할에 대해 교육하려고 한다(I'm Marisol, and I'll be training you in your new role as park rangers)고 말하는 것으로 보아 화자는 공원에서 근무하는 경비원일 가능성이 높다. 따라서 정답은 (A)이다.

75

What are the listeners asked to check for?

(A) Expired identification cards

(B) Local construction regulations

(C) Hazardous outdoor conditions

(D) Sudden price increases

청자들은 무엇을 확인하라고 요청받는가?

(A) 유효 기간이 지난 신분증

(B) 지역 건축 규정

(C) 위험한 실외 상황

(D) 가격 급등

어휘 expire 기한이 끝나다 identification card 신분증 regulation 규정 increase 상승

해설 세부 사항 관련 - 청자들이 확인하라고 요청받은 사항

화자가 중반부에 매일 수행해야 할 한 가지 작업은 배정된 구역에서 위험한 상황을 확인하는 것(one task you need to complete every day is to check your assigned area for hazardous conditions)이라고 말하고 있으므로 정답은 (C)이다.

76

What does the speaker distribute?

(A) Maps

(B) Uniforms

(C) Visitor passes

(D) Employee handbooks

화자는 무엇을 나눠주는가?

(A) 지도
(B) 단체복
(C) 방문자 출입증
(D) 직원 편람

해설 세부 사항 관련 - 화자가 나눠주는 것

화자가 후반부에 단체복을 주겠다(let me give you your uniforms)고 말하고 있으므로 정답은 (B)이다.

77-79 회의 발췌

M-Au Hi, everyone. **77 I'm excited to announce that we're going to try out a change to our work arrangements.** Staff will be able to work from home one day a week. Whenever you do work from home, you must be reachable by phone and e-mail during our business hours. Now, I know many of you have asked for this change for a long time. **78 You should know that Human Resources will be monitoring productivity to determine whether these new work arrangements are a good idea.** This is only a trial period. **79 I'll be sending you a policy document that will explain everything in detail.** Check your e-mail later today.

안녕하세요, 여러분. **근무 제도에 변화를 시도한다고 발표하게 되어 기쁘네요.** 직원들은 일주일에 하루 집에서 일할 수 있을 것입니다. 집에서 일할 때마다 업무 시간에는 전화와 이메일로 연락이 닿아야 합니다. 자, 많은 분들이 오랫동안 이 변화를 요청해 왔다는 걸 압니다. **인사부에서 생산성을 주시하면서 이 새로운 근무 제도가 좋은 아이디어인지 여부를 판단한다는 사실, 명심하셔야 합니다.** 이번은 단지 시험 기간입니다. 모든 사항을 자세히 설명한 규정 문서를 보내 드리겠습니다. 오늘 이따가 이메일을 확인해 보세요.

어휘 work arrangement 근무 제도 reachable 연락이 닿는 productivity 생산성 determine 판단하다 policy 정책

77

Who is the speaker addressing?

(A) Potential investors
(B) Tourists
(C) Staff members
(D) Job applicants

화자는 누구에게 이야기하는가?

(A) 잠재 투자자
(B) 관광객
(C) 직원
(D) 입사 지원자

어휘 potential 잠재적인 applicant 지원자

해설 전체 내용 관련 - 청자의 신분

화자가 초반부에 근무 제도에 변화를 시도한다고 발표하게 되어 기쁘다(I'm excited to announce that we're going to try out a change to our work arrangements)며 변경된 근무 제도에 대해 언급하고 있는 것으로 보아 직원들을 대상으로 이야기하고 있다는 것을 알 수 있다. 따라서 정답은 (C)이다.

78

Why does the speaker say, "This is only a trial period"?

(A) To correct a colleague's statement
(B) To apologize for a meeting conflict
(C) To express surprise about a policy
(D) To encourage the listeners to remain productive

화자가 "이번은 단지 시험 기간입니다"라고 말하는 이유는 무엇인가?

(A) 동료의 설명을 수정하려고
(B) 회의 일정이 겹쳐서 사과하려고
(C) 정책에 놀라움을 피력하려고
(D) 청자들이 생산성을 유지하도록 독려하려고

어휘 conflict 일정 겹침

해설 화자의 의도 파악 - 이번은 단지 시험 기간이라는 말의 의도

앞에서 인사부에서 생산성을 주시하면서 이 새로운 근무 제도가 좋은 아이디어인지 여부를 판단한다는 사실을 명심해야 한다(You should know that Human Resources will be monitoring productivity to determine whether these new work arrangements are a good idea)고 말한 뒤 인용문을 언급한 것으로 보아, 새로 시도하는 근무 제도는 아직 확정된 것이 아니므로 효율적이라고 판명되기 위해서는 시험 기간 동안 직원들의 생산성이 잘 유지되어야 한다는 의도로 한 말임을 알 수 있다. 따라서 정답은 (D)이다.

79

What will the speaker do later?

(A) Send a document
(B) Make a phone call
(C) Leave for a business trip
(D) Introduce some managers

화자는 나중에 무엇을 하겠는가?

(A) 문서 전송하기
(B) 전화 걸기
(C) 출장 떠나기
(D) 관리자들 소개하기

해설 세부 사항 관련 - 화자가 나중에 할 일

화자가 후반부에 모든 사항을 자세히 설명한 규정 문서를 보내 드리겠다(I'll be sending you a policy document that will explain everything in detail)고 말하고 있으므로 정답은 (A)이다.

M-Cn Welcome to the KXS Radio afternoon update. **⁸⁰The traffic is heavy this afternoon because of the season's opening game at the baseball stadium.** But the good news is, **⁸¹we're giving away tickets to next week's game! Call our radio station for a chance to win.** The sixth caller will win the tickets! And **⁸²after today's game, we will have an exclusive interview with the coach of our city's baseball team.** Stay tuned!

KXS 라디오 오후 최신 소식입니다. **오늘 오후 야구장에서 열리는 시즌 개막전 때문에 교통이 혼잡합니다.** 하지만 좋은 소식이 있는데요, **저희가 다음 주 경기 티켓을 나눠 드립니다! 라디오 방송국에 전화해서 당첨 기회를 잡으세요.** 여섯 번째로 전화하는 사람이 표를 차지합니다! 그리고 **오늘 경기가 끝나면 우리 시 야구팀 코치와 단독 인터뷰를 진행합니다.** 채널 고정하세요!

어휘 exclusive 단독의

80

According to the speaker, what is causing traffic?

(A) Some bad weather
(B) Some construction projects
(C) **A sporting event**
(D) A city festival

화자의 말에 따르면, 무엇이 교통량을 유발하는가?

(A) 악천후
(B) 건설 공사
(C) **스포츠 행사**
(D) 도시 축제

해설 세부 사항 관련 - 화자가 교통량의 발생 원인이라고 말하는 것

화자가 초반부에 오늘 오후 야구장에서 열리는 시즌 개막전 때문에 교통이 혼잡하다(The traffic is heavy this afternoon because of the season's opening game at the baseball stadium)고 말하고 있으므로 정답은 (C)이다.

▶▶ Paraphrasing 담화의 the season's opening game at the baseball stadium
→ 정답의 A sporting event

81

Why should the listeners call the radio station?

(A) To ask a question
(B) To request a song
(C) **To win some tickets**
(D) To sign up as a volunteer

청자들은 왜 라디오 방송국에 전화해야 하는가?

(A) 질문하려고
(B) 곡을 신청하려고
(C) **표를 얻으려고**
(D) 자원봉사자로 등록하려고

해설 세부 사항 관련 - 청자들이 라디오 방송국에 전화해야 하는 이유

화자가 중반부에 다음 주 경기 티켓을 나눠준다(we're giving away tickets to next week's game!)면서 라디오 방송국에 전화해서 당첨 기회를 잡으라(Call our radio station for a chance to win)고 말하고 있으므로 정답은 (C)이다.

82

What does the speaker say will be broadcast later?

(A) **An interview**
(B) A political debate
(C) A comedy show
(D) A concert

화자는 나중에 무엇이 방송된다고 말하는가?

(A) **인터뷰**
(B) 정치 토론
(C) 코미디 쇼
(D) 콘서트

해설 세부 사항 관련 - 화자가 나중에 방송된다고 말하는 것

화자가 후반부에 오늘 경기가 끝나면 우리 시 야구팀 코치와 단독 인터뷰를 진행한다(after today's game, we will have an exclusive interview with the coach of our city's baseball team)고 말하고 있으므로 정답은 (A)이다.

W-Br Good evening, everyone. **⁸³Tonight's event is very important for our restaurant. To prepare for our official grand opening next week, we've invited people from neighboring businesses here. ⁸⁴This is a great opportunity to get some feedback on our service and menu.** Remember, several local business leaders will be here tonight. As you know, word-of-mouth recommendations are our best advertising tool. Hosts, **⁸⁵I'd like you to distribute surveys to guests after their meals.** Any feedback they have for us will help make this restaurant a success.

모두 안녕하세요. **오늘밤 행사는 우리 식당에 무척 중요합니다. 다음 주에 있을 공식 개업식을 준비하기 위해, 인근 업체 사람들을 여기로 초대했습니다. 서비스와 메뉴에 대한 반응을 얻을 수 있는 좋은 기회죠.** 명심하세요. 지역 업체 지도자 몇 분이 오늘밤 이곳에 옵니다. 아시다시피 입소문 추천이 최고의 광고 수단이죠. 진행자 여러분, **식사 후에 손님들에게 설문지를 나눠주셨으면 합니다.** 우리에 대한 그들의 어떤 의견도

이 식당을 성공시키는 데 도움이 될 겁니다.

어휘 neighboring 인근의 opportunity 기회
word-of-mouth 입소문으로 전달되는 recommendation
추천 distribute 나눠주다 survey 설문지

83

What is the talk mainly about?

(A) A business opening
(B) A company anniversary
(C) A new advertising service
(D) A renovation project

주로 무엇에 관한 담화인가?

(A) 개업
(B) 회사 기념일
(C) 새로운 광고 서비스
(D) 보수 공사

어휘 anniversary 기념일 renovation 보수

해설 전체 내용 관련 - 담화의 주제

화자가 초반부에 오늘밤 행사는 우리 식당에 무척 중요하다(Tonight's event is very important for our restaurant)고 했고, 다음 주에 있을 공식 개업식을 준비하기 위해 인근 업체 사람들을 여기로 초대했다(To prepare for our official grand opening next week, we've invited people from neighboring businesses here)며 식당의 개업 준비에 관해 이야기하고 있으므로 정답은 (A)이다.

84

What does the speaker mean when she says, "several local business leaders will be here tonight"?

(A) Extra staff is needed.
(B) An event will be televised.
(C) A larger venue should be reserved.
(D) Employees should provide good service.

화자가 "지역 업체 지도자 몇 분이 오늘밤 이곳에 옵니다"라고 말하는 의도는 무엇인가?
(A) 직원이 추가로 필요하다.
(B) 행사가 텔레비전으로 방송될 예정이다.
(C) 더 넓은 장소를 예약해야 한다.
(D) 직원들이 좋은 서비스를 제공해야 한다.

어휘 televise 텔레비전으로 방송하다 venue 장소

해설 화자의 의도 파악 - 지역 업체 지도자 몇 분이 오늘밤 이곳에 온다는 말의 의도

앞에서 서비스와 메뉴에 대한 반응을 얻을 수 있는 좋은 기회(This is a great opportunity to get some feedback on our service and menu)라고 말한 뒤 인용문을 언급하고 있으므로, 중요 인물들에게 훌륭한 서비스를 제공해 식당에 대해 좋은 인상을 줘야 한다는 의도로 한 말임을 알 수 있다. 따라서 정답은 (D)이다.

85

What does the speaker ask some of the listeners to do?

(A) Arrive early
(B) Check a schedule
(C) Hand out some surveys
(D) Consult a manager about problems

화자는 일부 청자들에게 무엇을 해 달라고 요청하는가?
(A) 일찍 도착
(B) 일정 확인
(C) 설문지 배포
(D) 문제점에 관해 관리자에게 문의

해설 세부 사항 관련 - 화자의 요청 사항

화자가 후반부에 식사 후에 손님들에게 설문지를 나눠주었으면 한다(I'd like you to distribute surveys to guests after their meals)고 말하고 있으므로 정답은 (C)이다.

▸▸ Paraphrasing 담화의 distribute → 정답의 Hand out

86-88 전화 메시지

M-Au Hi, Madoka. I'm calling you about some details of your trip to London next week. **86 Your flight is on Monday morning at... uh... four A.M. I couldn't find a later flight. 87 Adriana Lopez from the London office will meet you at the airport. She's my counterpart over there. Adriana will assist with your local itinerary and has already booked your hotel.** Oh, and one last thing... since this is your first trip since joining our company, **88 you'll soon be receiving log-in credentials for a travel expense tracking application.** You can download the app on your phone and load your receipts onto it.

안녕하세요, 마도카. 다음 주 런던 출장 세부 사항 때문에 전화드려요. **월요일 오전… 어… 4시 비행기예요. 더 늦은 항공편을 구할 수가 없었어요. 런던 사무소의 아드리아나 로페즈가 공항에 마중 나올 거예요. 그녀가 거기서 제 역할을 하거든요. 아드리아나가 현지 일정을 도와드릴 텐데 호텔은 벌써 예약했습니다.** 아, 그리고 마지막으로 한 가지 더 말씀드리면… 입사 후 첫 번째 출장이므로 **곧 출장 경비 추적 애플리케이션에 로그인할 수 있는 인증서를 받게 됩니다.** 핸드폰으로 앱을 내려받으면 영수증을 앱에 올릴 수 있어요.

어휘 counterpart 서로 비슷한 역할을 하는 사람 itinerary 여행 일정 credential 인증서 receipt 영수증

86

Why does the speaker say, "I couldn't find a later flight"?

(A) To refuse an invitation
(B) To apologize for an inconvenience
(C) To suggest canceling a trip
(D) To ask for help

화자가 "더 늦은 항공편을 구할 수가 없었어요"라고 말하는 이유는 무엇인가?

(A) 초대를 거절하려고
(B) 불편에 대해 사과하려고
(C) 여행 취소를 제안하려고
(D) 도움을 요청하려고

어휘 refuse 거절하다   inconvenience 불편

해설 화자의 의도 파악 – 더 늦은 항공편을 구할 수가 없었다는 말의 의도
앞에서 당신의 항공편은 월요일 오전 4시(Your flight is on Monday morning at… uh… four A.M.)라고 말한 뒤 인용문을 언급한 것으로 보아, 너무 이른 시간에 출발하는 항공편밖에 구하지 못해 미안하다는 의도로 한 말임을 알 수 있다. 따라서 정답은 (B)이다.

87

Who most likely is Adriana Lopez?

(A) A repair technician
(B) An airline pilot
(C) An administrative assistant
(D) A city official

아드리아나 로페즈는 누구이겠는가?

(A) 수리 기술자
(B) 항공기 조종사
(C) 사무 보조
(D) 시 공무원

어휘 administrative 사무의

해설 세부 사항 관련 – 아드리아나 로페즈의 직업
화자가 중반부에 런던 사무소의 아드리아나 로페즈가 공항에 마중 나올 것(Adriana Lopez from the London office will meet you at the airport)이라고 했고, 그녀가 거기서 제 역할을 한다(She's my counterpart over there)면서 아드리아나가 현지 일정을 도와 드릴 것이고 호텔은 벌써 예약했다(Adriana will assist with your local itinerary and has already booked your hotel)고 말하는 것으로 보아 아드리아나는 업무를 보조하는 사람임을 알 수 있다. 따라서 정답은 (C)이다.

88

What does the speaker say the listener will receive?

(A) A client file
(B) A list of restaurants
(C) Some log-in credentials
(D) Some promotional materials

화자는 청자가 무엇을 받을 것이라고 말하는가?

(A) 고객 파일
(B) 식당 목록
(C) 로그인 인증서
(D) 판촉물

해설 세부 사항 관련 – 화자가 청자가 받을 것이라고 말하는 것
화자가 후반부에 곧 출장 경비 추적 애플리케이션에 로그인할 수 있는 인증서를 받게 될 것(you'll soon be receiving log-in credentials for a travel expense tracking application)이라고 말하고 있으므로 정답은 (C)이다.

89-91 담화

M-Cn **89 Welcome to this seminar, which focuses on one of the most challenging aspects of starting a new business—locating investors.** Without start-up funds, your business may never get off the ground. **90 As a first step, I suggest compiling a list of firms that specialize in investing in your industry.** But there's much more to know, of course. Maryam Farooq, founder of multiple information technology companies, has been particularly good at securing investment funding. **91 She's here to answer questions and break down how she did it.**

이번 세미나에 잘 오셨습니다. 이 세미나는 새로 사업을 시작할 때 가장 어려운 측면 중 하나인 투자자 찾기에 주력합니다. 창업 자금 없이는 사업을 시작할 수 없죠. **첫 번째 단계로 귀사의 업종에 전문으로 투자하는 회사 목록을 작성하실 것을 제안합니다.** 하지만 물론 알아야 할 것이 더 많습니다. 정보 기술 기업을 여럿 창업한 마리암 파루크 씨는 특히 투자 자금 확보에 능했습니다. **파루크 씨가 와서 질문에 대답하고 어떻게 해냈는지 분석해 드립니다.**

어휘 challenging 어려운 aspect 측면 locate 찾다
get off the ground (순조롭게) 시작하다 compile 작성하다
specialize in ~을 전문으로 하다 break down 분석하다

89

What is the topic of the seminar?

(A) Choosing an advertising strategy
(B) Finding investors
(C) Leading focus groups
(D) Creating a budget

세미나의 주제는 무엇인가?

(A) 광고 전략 선택하기
(B) 투자자 찾기
(C) 포커스 그룹 이끌기
(D) 예산안 짜기

어휘 strategy 전략 budget 예산(안)

해설 전체 내용 관련 - 담화의 주제

화자가 도입부에 이번 세미나에 오신 것을 환영하며 이 세미나는 새로 사업을 시작할 때 가장 어려운 측면 중 하나인 투자자 찾기에 주력한다(Welcome to this seminar, which focuses on one of the most challenging aspects of starting a new business—locating investors)고 세미나의 주제를 밝히고 있으므로 정답은 (B)이다.

> ▸▸ Paraphrasing 담화의 locating → 정답의 Finding

90

What does the speaker recommend the listeners do first?

(A) Get employee input
(B) Hire a consultant
(C) Revise a plan
(D) Make a list

화자는 청자들에게 무엇을 먼저 하라고 권하는가?

(A) 직원 의견 받기
(B) 컨설턴트 채용하기
(C) 계획 수정하기
(D) 목록 만들기

어휘 revise 수정하다

해설 세부 사항 관련 - 화자가 청자들에게 먼저 하라고 권하는 일

화자가 중반부에 첫 번째 단계로 귀사의 업종에 전문으로 투자하는 회사 목록을 작성할 것을 제안한다(As a first step, I suggest compiling a list of firms that specialize in investing in your industry)고 말하고 있으므로 정답은 (D)이다.

> ▸▸ Paraphrasing 담화의 compiling a list → 정답의 Make a list

91

What will most likely happen next?

(A) A video will be shown.
(B) Information packets will be distributed.
(C) Some questions will be answered.
(D) There will be a lunch break.

다음에 어떤 일이 있겠는가?

(A) 동영상이 상영될 것이다.
(B) 정보 꾸러미가 배포될 것이다.
(C) 질문에 답할 것이다.
(D) 점심시간이 있을 것이다.

해설 세부 사항 관련 - 다음에 일어날 일

화자가 마지막에 파루크 씨가 와서 질문에 대답하고 어떻게 해냈는지 분석해 드린다(She's here to answer questions and break down how she did it)고 말하고 있으므로 정답은 (C)이다.

92-94 회의 발췌

W-Br Today's sales meeting is packed to capacity, and for good reason. **92 Gerard has delivered on his promise to craft a new strategy that'll enable us to broaden our market share in the Scandinavian region. As you'll soon see, his four-step approach is going to be critical to increasing our sales.** **93 Looks like he'll need a few minutes to get his computer up and running.** So while we wait, **94 let me remind you about the mentoring program that management is implementing.** It provides an opportunity to guide our new employees during their transitional period. **94 We need seasoned staff to participate as mentors, so be sure to sign up!**

오늘 영업 인원이 꽉 찼는데 그럴 만한 이유가 있어요. 제라드는 스칸디나비아 지역에서 시장 점유율을 넓힐 수 있는 새로운 전략을 세우겠다는 자신의 약속을 지켰습니다. 곧 알게 되겠지만, 그의 4단계 접근법은 매출 증대에 아주 중요할 겁니다. 그가 컴퓨터를 켜서 작동시키려면 몇 분 정도 걸릴 것 같네요. 그래서 기다리는 동안 경영진이 실시하고 있는 멘토링 프로그램에 대해 알려 드리겠습니다. 이 프로그램은 과도기에 있는 신입 사원들을 지도할 기회를 제공합니다. 멘토로 참여할 노련한 직원들이 필요하니 꼭 신청하세요!

어휘 be packed to capacity 만원이다 deliver on one's promise 약속을 이행하다 craft 만들다 broaden 넓히다 market share 시장 점유율 approach 접근(법) implement 실시하다 transitional 과도기의 seasoned 노련한 participate 참여하다

92

What is the purpose of the meeting?

(A) To celebrate a recent contract
(B) To explain a new sales strategy
(C) To introduce a new employee
(D) To address employee concerns

회의의 목적은 무엇인가?

(A) 최근 따낸 계약을 축하하려고
(B) 새로운 영업 전략을 설명하려고
(C) 신입 사원을 소개하려고
(D) 직원 우려를 해소하려고

어휘 address 해소하다

해설 전체 내용 관련 - 회의의 목적

화자가 초반부에 제라드는 스칸디나비아 지역에서 시장 점유율을 넓힐 수 있는 새로운 전략을 세우겠다는 자신의 약속을 지켰다(Gerard has delivered ~ in the Scandinavian region)면서 곧 알게 되겠지만 그의 4단계 접근법은 매출 증대에 아주 중요할 것(As you'll soon see, his four-step approach ~ increasing our sales)이라고 한 것으로 보아, 이 회의는 제라드가 세운 새로운 전략을 소개하려는 것임을 알 수 있다. 따라서 정답은 (B)이다.

93

What is causing a delay?

(A) A computer is being set up.

(B) A microphone stopped working.

(C) Some additional chairs are needed.

(D) The speaker misplaced some notes.

무엇이 지연을 초래하고 있는가?

(A) 컴퓨터를 준비하고 있다.

(B) 마이크가 작동을 멈췄다.

(C) 의자가 추가로 필요하다.

(D) 화자가 메모 둔 곳을 잊어버렸다.

어휘 misplace 둔 곳을 잊다

해설 세부 사항 관련 - 지연의 원인

화자가 중반부에 그가 컴퓨터를 켜서 작동시키려면 몇 분 정도 걸릴 것 같다(Looks like he'll need a few minutes to get his computer up and running)고 말하고 있으므로 정답은 (A)이다.

> ▸▸ **Paraphrasing** 담화의 get his computer up and running
> → 정답의 A computer is being set up

94

What are the listeners encouraged to sign up for?

(A) A staff feedback session

(B) A conference presentation

(C) A health initiative

(D) A mentoring program

청자들이 무엇을 신청하라고 권유받는가?

(A) 직원 의견 회의

(B) 회의 발표

(C) 건강 계획

(D) 멘토링 프로그램

어휘 initiative 계획

해설 세부 사항 관련 - 청자들이 신청하라고 권유받은 일

화자가 후반부에 경영진이 실시하고 있는 멘토링 프로그램에 대해 알려주겠다(let me remind you about the mentoring program that management is implementing)며 멘토로 참여할 노련한 직원들이 필요하니 꼭 신청하라(We need seasoned staff to participate as mentors, so be sure to sign up!)고 권유하고 있으므로 정답은 (D)이다.

95-97 전화 메시지 + 쿠폰

W-Am Hey, Hassan. It's Emiko. ⁹⁵**I'm calling about the retirement party we're planning for Dmitry next Friday.** Everyone from the accounting department is coming plus a few from sales, so ⁹⁶**we'll have a total of ten people. I made the reservation at the barbecue restaurant and even**

found a coupon that'll save us a lot of money since we have such a big group. Uh... ⁹⁷**did you place the cake order with the bakery yet?** Dmitry said he loves strawberry cake, and I want his retirement party to be perfect.

안녕, 하산. 에미코예요. 다음 주 금요일로 계획하고 있는 드미트리 은퇴 파티 때문에 전화해요. 경리부 사람들이 다 오는데다가 영업부에서 몇 명 더 오니까 총 10명이 와요. 바비큐 식당에 예약했는데 인원이 많아서 돈을 많이 절약할 수 있는 쿠폰까지 발견했어요. 어… 벌써 제과점에 케이크 주문했나요? 드미트리는 딸기 케이크를 좋아한다고 했으니 은퇴 파티가 완벽했으면 해서요.

어휘 retirement 은퇴

Southern Barbecue Restaurant
Coupon

Groups 3–5	10% off
Groups 5–9	15% off
⁹⁶Groups 10–15	20% off
Groups 16–20	25% off

서던 바비큐 식당
쿠폰

단체 3–5인	10% 할인
단체 5–9인	15% 할인
⁹⁶**단체 10–15인**	**20% 할인**
단체 16–20인	25% 할인

95

What type of event will take place on Friday?

(A) A retirement party

(B) A graduation celebration

(C) A cooking competition

(D) An award ceremony

금요일에 어떤 종류의 행사가 열리는가?

(A) 은퇴 파티

(B) 졸업 축하연

(C) 요리 경연 대회

(D) 시상식

해설 세부 사항 관련 - 금요일에 열릴 행사

화자가 초반부에 다음 주 금요일로 계획하고 있는 드미트리 은퇴 파티 때문에 전화한다(I'm calling about the retirement party we're planning for Dmitry next Friday)고 말하고 있으므로 정답은 (A)이다.

96

Look at the graphic. Which discount will be applied?

(A) 10%
(B) 15%
(C) 20%
(D) 25%

시각 정보에 의하면 어떤 할인이 적용될 것인가?

(A) 10%
(B) 15%
(C) 20%
(D) 25%

해설 시각 정보 연계 - 적용될 할인율

화자가 중반부에 총 10명이 온다(we'll have a total of ten people)면서 바비큐 식당에 예약했는데 인원이 많아 돈을 많이 절약할 수 있는 쿠폰까지 발견했다(I made the reservation ~ since we have such a big group)고 말하고 있고, 쿠폰에 따르면 10명인 단체는 20퍼센트를 할인받을 수 있으므로 정답은 (C)이다.

97

What does the speaker ask the listener?

(A) Who will decorate a space
(B) What type of gift will be purchased
(C) If an event should be rescheduled
(D) If an order has been placed

화자는 청자에게 무엇을 묻는가?

(A) 공간을 장식할 사람
(B) 구입할 선물 종류
(C) 행사 일정을 변경해야 하는지 여부
(D) 주문 여부

어휘 purchase 구매하다

해설 세부 사항 관련 - 화자가 청자에게 묻는 것

화자가 후반부에 제과점에 케이크를 주문했는지(did you place the cake order with the bakery yet?) 묻고 있으므로 정답은 (D)이다.

98-100 회의 발췌 + 안건 목록

M-Cn **⁹⁸I want to talk about our company's charitable giving program.** As you know, employees can make a donation to an approved organization, and the company will match that amount. **⁹⁹This year, we've expanded our list of approved organizations from 15 to 25.** We've selected organizations in the community that will benefit the most from our contributions. And **¹⁰⁰our company has been recognized for its philanthropy. In fact, it was featured last month in an article in the magazine *Business Effect*. I'll post a link to that on our Web site after this meeting.**

저는 우리 회사의 자선 기부 프로그램에 대해 얘기하려고 합니다. 아시다시피 직원은 인가받은 단체에 기부할 수 있고, 회사는 그 액수에 맞추어 기부할 것입니다. 올해는 인가받은 기관 목록을 15개에서 25개로 확대했어요. 지역 사회에서 우리의 기부로 가장 혜택을 많이 받을 기관들을 선정했죠. 그리고 우리 회사는 자선 활동으로 인정받고 있습니다. 실은 지난달 그것이 〈비즈니스 이펙트〉지 기사에 실렸어요. 회의가 끝나면 기사 링크를 회사 웹사이트에 올리겠습니다.

어휘 charitable 자선의 donation 기부 approved 인가받은 expand 늘리다 benefit 혜택받다 contribution 기부 philanthropy 자선 (활동) performance review 인사 고과 public relations 홍보 transformation 전환

Agenda	
Speaker	**Topic**
William Schmidt	Staff performance review
⁹⁸Paul Cohen	Corporate giving campaign
Jung-Soo Park	Public relations program
Santiago Reyes	IT transformation initiative

안건	
발표자	**주제**
윌리엄 슈미트	직원 인사 고과
⁹⁸폴 코헨	회사 기부 활동
박정수	홍보 프로그램
산티아고 레이예스	IT 전환 계획

98

Look at the graphic. Who most likely is the speaker?

(A) William Schmidt
(B) Paul Cohen
(C) Jung-Soo Park
(D) Santiago Reyes

시각 정보에 의하면 화자는 누구이겠는가?

(A) 윌리엄 슈미트
(B) 폴 코헨
(C) 박정수
(D) 산티아고 레이예스

해설 시각 정보 연계 - 화자의 이름

화자가 도입부에 저는 우리 회사의 자선 기부 프로그램에 대해 얘기하려고 한다(I want to talk about our company's charitable giving program)고 말하고 있고, 안건 목록에 따르면 회사 기부 활동의 발표자는 폴 코헨이므로 정답은 (B)이다.

TEST 6

99

According to the speaker, what is different about a program this year?

(A) A list of organizations is longer.

(B) A deadline has been extended.

(C) More employees are assigned to help.

(D) An operating budget has been increased.

화자의 말에 따르면, 올해 프로그램의 차이점은?

(A) 단체 목록이 더 길다.

(B) 기한이 연장되었다.

(C) 돕기 위해 더 많은 직원이 배정되었다.

(D) 운영 예산이 증액되었다.

어휘 extend 연장하다 assign 배치하다

해설 세부 사항 관련 – 화자가 말하는 올해 프로그램의 차이점

화자가 중반부에 올해는 인가받은 기관 목록을 15개에서 25개로 확대했다(This year, we've expanded our list of approved organizations from 15 to 25)고 말하고 있으므로 정답은 (A)이다.

100

What will the speaker make available to the listeners?

(A) A research report

(B) A training video

(C) A magazine article

(D) A corporate calendar

화자는 청자들에게 무엇을 제공할 것인가?

(A) 연구 보고서

(B) 교육용 동영상

(C) 잡지 기사

(D) 회사 달력

해설 세부 사항 관련 – 화자가 청자들에게 제공할 것

화자가 후반부에 우리 회사는 자선 활동으로 인정받고 있다(our company has been recognized for its philanthropy)고 했고 실은 지난달 〈비즈니스 이펙트〉지 기사에 실렸다(In fact, it was featured last month in an article in the magazine *Business Effect*)면서 회의가 끝나면 기사 링크를 회사 웹사이트에 올리겠다(I'll post a link to that on our Web site after this meeting)고 말하고 있으므로 정답은 (C)이다.

기출 TEST 7

1 (A)	2 (C)	3 (C)	4 (C)	5 (A)
6 (B)	7 (A)	8 (C)	9 (C)	10 (A)
11 (B)	12 (B)	13 (C)	14 (A)	15 (A)
16 (B)	17 (A)	18 (C)	19 (C)	20 (A)
21 (B)	22 (B)	23 (B)	24 (A)	25 (C)
26 (B)	27 (C)	28 (B)	29 (B)	30 (B)
31 (C)	32 (B)	33 (D)	34 (B)	35 (B)
36 (A)	37 (A)	38 (C)	39 (B)	40 (B)
41 (A)	42 (C)	43 (B)	44 (D)	45 (B)
46 (A)	47 (A)	48 (B)	49 (D)	50 (B)
51 (C)	52 (D)	53 (B)	54 (A)	55 (D)
56 (D)	57 (C)	58 (B)	59 (B)	60 (D)
61 (B)	62 (D)	63 (B)	64 (C)	65 (B)
66 (A)	67 (B)	68 (A)	69 (B)	70 (C)
71 (C)	72 (D)	73 (B)	74 (B)	75 (B)
76 (A)	77 (B)	78 (D)	79 (A)	80 (B)
81 (D)	82 (A)	83 (D)	84 (C)	85 (B)
86 (C)	87 (D)	88 (D)	89 (B)	90 (B)
91 (A)	92 (C)	93 (B)	94 (A)	95 (B)
96 (A)	97 (D)	98 (B)	99 (B)	100 (A)

PART 1

1 W-Am

(A) She's plugging in a fan.
(B) She's packing up some equipment.
(C) She's bending down to tie her shoe.
(D) She's entering a storeroom.

(A) 여자가 선풍기 플러그를 꽂고 있다.
(B) 여자가 장비를 챙기고 있다.
(C) 여자가 몸을 구부려 신발끈을 매고 있다.
(D) 여자가 창고로 들어가고 있다.

어휘 plug in 플러그를 꽂다 fan 선풍기 pack up (짐 따위를) 챙기다
　　 equipment 장비 bend down 몸을 구부리다 storeroom 창고

해설 1인 등장 사진 – 사람의 동작/상태 묘사
(A) 정답. 여자가 선풍기 플러그를 꽂고 있는(is plugging in a fan) 모습이므로 정답.
(B) 동사 오답. 여자가 장비를 챙기고 있는(is packing up some equipment) 모습이 아니므로 오답.

(C) 동사 오답. 여자가 몸을 구부려 신발끈을 매고 있는(is bending down to tie her shoe) 모습이 아니므로 오답.
(D) 동사 오답. 여자가 창고로 들어가고 있는(is entering a storeroom) 모습이 아니므로 오답.

---

2 W-Br

(A) They're carrying trays of food.
(B) They're walking into a building.
(C) They're approaching a sign in a parking area.
(D) They're opening the doors of a vehicle.

(A) 사람들이 음식 쟁반을 나르고 있다.
(B) 사람들이 건물 안으로 걸어가고 있다.
(C) 사람들이 주차 구역의 표지판에 다가가고 있다.
(D) 사람들이 차량의 문을 열고 있다.

어휘 tray 쟁반 approach 다가가다 vehicle 차량

해설 2인 이상 등장 사진 – 사람의 동작/상태 묘사
(A) 사진에 없는 명사를 이용한 오답. 사진에 음식 쟁반(trays of food)의 모습이 보이지 않으므로 오답.
(B) 사진에 없는 명사를 이용한 오답. 사진에 건물(a building)의 모습이 보이지 않으므로 오답.
(C) 정답. 사람들이 주차 구역의 표지판에 다가가고 있는(are approaching a sign in a parking area) 모습이므로 정답.
(D) 동사 오답. 사람들이 차량의 문을 열고 있는(are opening the doors of a vehicle) 모습이 아니므로 오답.

---

3 M-Au

(A) They're carrying a ladder.
(B) They're putting away some rope.
(C) They're installing a roof on a house.
(D) They're organizing boxes of materials.

(A) 사람들이 사다리를 나르고 있다.
(B) 사람들이 밧줄을 치우고 있다.
(C) 사람들이 집에 지붕을 시공하고 있다.
(D) 사람들이 자재 상자를 정리하고 있다.

어휘 ladder 사다리 install 시공하다 organize 정리하다
　　 materials 자재

해설 2인 이상 등장 사진 - 사람의 동작/상태 묘사
(A) 사진에 없는 명사를 이용한 오답. 사진에 사다리(a ladder)의 모습이 보이지 않으므로 오답.
(B) 동사 오답. 사람들이 밧줄을 치우고 있는(are putting away some rope) 모습이 아니므로 오답.
(C) 정답. 사람들이 집에 지붕을 시공하고 있는(are installing a roof on a house) 모습이므로 정답.
(D) 사진에 없는 명사를 이용한 오답. 사진에 상자(boxes)의 모습이 보이지 않으므로 오답.

4 W-Br

(A) A step stool has been set in a corner.
(B) A woman is reaching for a light switch.
(C) Some binders have been lined up on a shelf.
(D) A woman is connecting a monitor to a keyboard.

(A) 계단식 의자가 구석에 놓여 있다.
(B) 여자가 전등 스위치를 향해 손을 뻗고 있다.
(C) 바인더들이 선반에 정렬되어 있다.
(D) 여자가 모니터를 키보드에 연결하고 있다.

어휘 step stool 계단식 의자 reach (손이나 팔을) 뻗다 shelf 선반 connect 연결하다

해설 혼합 사진 - 사람/사물/풍경 혼합 묘사
(A) 위치 오답. 계단식 의자(a step stool)가 구석에 놓여 있는(has been set in a corner) 모습이 아니므로 오답.
(B) 동사 오답. 여자가 전등 스위치를 향해 손을 뻗고 있는(is reaching for a light switch) 모습이 아니므로 오답.
(C) 정답. 바인더들(some binders)이 선반에 정렬되어 있는(have been lined up on a shelf) 모습이므로 정답.
(D) 동사 오답. 여자가 모니터를 키보드에 연결하고 있는(is connecting a monitor to a keyboard) 모습이 아니므로 오답.

5 W-Am

(A) Some pillows have been placed on a bed.
(B) Some lamps are hanging from the ceiling.
(C) Some bed linens are piled on the floor.
(D) Some chairs are next to a nightstand.

(A) 베개들이 침대 위에 놓여 있다.
(B) 램프들이 천장에 매달려 있다.
(C) 이부자리가 바닥에 쌓여 있다.
(D) 의자들이 침실용 탁자 옆에 있다.

어휘 pillow 베개 hang 매달리다 ceiling 천장 bed linen 이부자리 nightstand 침실용 탁자

해설 사물/풍경 사진 - 사물 묘사
(A) 정답. 베개들(some pillows)이 침대 위에 놓여 있는(have been placed on a bed) 모습이므로 정답.
(B) 위치 오답. 램프들(some lamps)이 천장에 매달려 있는(are hanging from the ceiling) 모습이 아니므로 오답.
(C) 위치 오답. 이부자리(some bed linens)가 바닥에 쌓여 있는(are piled on the floor) 모습이 아니므로 오답.
(D) 위치 오답. 의자들(some chairs)이 침실용 탁자 옆에 있는(are next to a nightstand) 모습이 아니므로 오답.

6 W-Br

(A) There are some passengers boarding a boat.
(B) There's a deck overlooking a lake.
(C) A motorboat is passing under a bridge.
(D) Some people are diving off a pier.

(A) 승객들이 배에 타고 있다.
(B) 호수가 내려다보이는 데크가 있다.
(C) 모터보트가 다리 아래를 지나가고 있다.
(D) 사람들이 부두에서 다이빙하고 있다.

어휘 passenger 승객 board (배·기차 등에) 타다 overlook 내려다보다 pier 부두

해설 혼합 사진 - 사람/사물/풍경 혼합 묘사
(A) 동사 오답. 배에 타고 있는(boarding a boat) 승객들(some passengers)의 모습이 보이지 않으므로 오답.
(B) 정답. 호수가 내려다보이는(overlooking a lake) 데크(a deck)가 있는 모습이므로 정답.
(C) 사진에 없는 명사를 이용한 오답. 사진에 다리(a bridge)의 모습이 보이지 않으므로 오답.
(D) 동사 오답. 부두에서 다이빙하고 있는(are diving off a pier) 사람들의 모습이 보이지 않으므로 오답.

PART 2

7

W-Br Who is coming to the meeting?
M-Cn (A) The department managers.
(B) About the budget report.
(C) It starts at noon.

누가 회의에 오나요?
(A) **부서장들이요.**
(B) 예산 보고서에 관해서요.
(C) 정오에 시작합니다.

어휘 budget 예산

해설 회의에 참석할 사람을 묻는 Who 의문문
(A) 정답. 회의에 참석할 사람을 묻는 질문에 부서장들이라고 명확하게 응답하고 있으므로 정답.
(B) 연상 단어 오답. 질문의 meeting에서 회의 안건을 연상하게 하는 budget report를 이용한 오답.
(C) 질문과 상관없는 오답. When 의문문에 대한 응답이므로 오답.

8

W-Br I like having lots of plants in the office.
M-Cn (A) Try the file cabinet.
       (B) I already made plans for next week.
       (C) Yeah, I do too.

저는 사무실에 화초가 많은 게 좋아요.
(A) 파일 캐비닛을 보세요.
(B) 저는 벌써 다음 주 계획을 짰어요.
(C) **네, 저도 그래요.**

해설 의사 전달의 평서문
(A) 연상 단어 오답. 평서문의 office에서 연상 가능한 file cabinet을 이용한 오답.
(B) 유사 발음 오답. 평서문의 plants와 부분적으로 발음이 유사한 plans를 이용한 오답.
(C) 정답. 사무실에 화초가 많은 게 좋다는 평서문에 네(Yeah)라고 호응한 뒤, 저도 그렇다며 긍정 답변과 일관된 내용을 덧붙였으므로 정답.

9

W-Br When will the training manager arrive?
M-Au (A) Let me get my umbrella.
       (B) Of course I will.
       (C) At four thirty this afternoon.

교육부장은 언제 도착하나요?
(A) 우산 좀 가져올게요.
(B) 물론 그럴게요.
(C) **오늘 오후 4시 30분이요.**

해설 교육부장의 도착 시점을 묻는 When 의문문
(A) 연상 단어 오답. 질문의 training을 raining으로 잘못 들었을 경우 연상 가능한 umbrella를 이용한 오답.
(B) Yes/No 불가 오답. When 의문문에는 Yes/No 응답이 불가능한데, Of course도 일종의 Yes 응답이라고 볼 수 있으므로 오답.
(C) 정답. 교육부장이 도착하는 시점을 묻는 질문에 오늘 오후 4시 30분이라고 구체적으로 응답하고 있으므로 정답.

10

M-Cn Isn't there a pharmacy on Fifteenth Street?
W-Br (A) Yes, it's near the bank.
       (B) A prescription refill.
       (C) No, they're locally grown.

15번 가에 약국이 없나요?
(A) **있어요, 은행 근처예요.**
(B) 기존 처방전대로요.
(C) 아뇨, 그것들은 지역에서 재배됩니다.

어휘 pharmacy 약국   prescription refill 기존 처방전대로 처방하는 것

해설 15번 가에 약국이 있는지 여부를 확인하는 부정 의문문
(A) 정답. 15번 가에 약국이 있는지 여부를 묻는 질문에 있다(Yes)라고 대답한 뒤, 은행 근처라고 구체적인 위치를 알려 주고 있으므로 정답.
(B) 연상 단어 오답. 질문의 pharmacy에서 연상 가능한 prescription을 이용한 오답.
(C) 질문과 상관없는 오답.

11

M-Au Where is this shipment of supplies going?
W-Br (A) Not until five o'clock.
       (B) It's going to Texas.
       (C) We met on the ship.

이 비품 수송품은 어디로 가나요?
(A) 5시까지는 안 됩니다.
(B) **텍사스로 가요.**
(C) 우리는 배에서 만났어요.

어휘 shipment 수송(품)   supplies 비품

해설 수송품의 배송지를 묻는 Where 의문문
(A) 질문과 상관없는 오답. When 의문문에 대한 응답이므로 오답.
(B) 정답. 비품 수송품이 보내지는 곳을 묻는 질문에 텍사스로 간다고 장소로 응답하고 있으므로 정답.
(C) 유사 발음 오답. 질문의 shipment와 부분적으로 발음이 유사한 ship을 이용한 오답.

12

M-Au The new Peruvian restaurant is great, isn't it?
W-Am (A) No, it's at gate eighteen.
       (B) Yeah, the food is delicious.
       (C) A table for two, please.

새로 생긴 페루 식당 정말 괜찮지 않나요?
(A) 아뇨, 18번 게이트에 있어요.
(B) **네, 음식이 맛있어요.**
(C) 2인용 테이블로 주세요.

어휘 peruvian 페루의; 페루 사람

해설 새로운 식당이 마음에 드는지 확인하는 부가 의문문
(A) 유사 발음 오답. 질문의 great와 부분적으로 발음이 유사한 gate를 이용한 오답.

(B) 정답. 새로 생긴 페루 식당이 마음에 드는지 확인하는 질문에 네 (Yeah)라고 대답한 뒤, 음식이 맛있다며 긍정 답변과 일관된 내용을 덧붙였으므로 정답.

(C) 연상 단어 오답. 질문의 restaurant에서 연상 가능한 table을 이용한 오답.

13

M-Au How did your presentation for the client go?
W-Br (A) Our biggest customers.
(B) Can I join you?
(C) It went very well.

고객 프레젠테이션은 어떻게 됐나요?
(A) 우리 최대 고객이에요.
(B) 저도 같이 가도 돼요?
(C) 아주 좋았어요.

해설 프레젠테이션의 결과를 묻는 How 의문문

(A) 연상 단어 오답. 질문의 client에서 연상 가능한 customers를 이용한 오답.

(B) 질문과 상관없는 오답.

(C) 정답. 고객 프레젠테이션의 결과가 어떻게 되었는지 묻는 질문에 아주 좋았다고 알려 주고 있으므로 정답.

14

M-Au Please arrive ten minutes before your scheduled appointment.
W-Am (A) OK, is there parking nearby?
(B) She made several good points.
(C) But we ordered ten boxes.

예정된 약속 시간 10분 전에 도착해 주세요.
(A) 그럴게요, 근처에 주차할 곳이 있나요?
(B) 그녀는 몇 가지 좋은 지적을 했어요.
(C) 하지만 우리는 10상자를 주문했어요.

어휘 scheduled 예정된 appointment 약속, 예약 make a good point 좋은 지적을 하다

해설 부탁/요청의 평서문

(A) 정답. 예정된 약속 시간 10분 전에 도착할 것을 요청하는 평서문에 그 러겠다(OK)고 대답한 뒤, 근처에 주차할 곳이 있는지를 물으며 약속 장소에 오는 것과 관련된 내용을 묻고 있으므로 정답.

(B) 유사 발음 오답. 평서문의 appointment와 부분적으로 발음이 유사한 points를 이용한 오답.

(C) 단어 반복 오답. 평서문의 ten을 반복 이용한 오답.

15

M-Au Do you want to talk after your conference call?
W-Br (A) Actually, my call was canceled.
(B) Some new employees.
(C) The client in Chicago.

전화 회의 후에 얘기하시겠어요?
(A) 실은 회의가 취소됐어요.
(B) 신입 사원 몇 명이요.
(C) 시카고에 있는 고객이에요.

어휘 conference call 전화 회의 cancel 취소하다 employee 사원

해설 전화 회의 후 대화 의사를 묻는 조동사(Do) 의문문

(A) 정답. 전화 회의 후에 대화하기를 원하는지 묻는 질문에 실은 회의가 취소되었다며 전화 회의가 끝나기를 기다릴 필요가 없다는 것을 간접 적으로 알려 주고 있으므로 정답.

(B) 질문과 상관없는 오답. Who 의문문에 대한 응답이므로 오답.

(C) 질문과 상관없는 오답. Who 의문문에 대한 응답이므로 오답.

16

M-Au Why is Maria out of the office today?
M-Cn (A) About two thousand square meters.
(B) Because she's picking up some clients.
(C) It's next to the marketing department.

마리아가 오늘 왜 사무실에 없나요?
(A) 2천 제곱미터 정도요.
(B) 고객 몇 명을 태우러 갔거든요.
(C) 마케팅부 옆에 있어요.

해설 마리아가 사무실에 없는 이유를 묻는 Why 의문문

(A) 질문과 상관없는 오답. How big 의문문에 대한 응답이므로 오답.

(B) 정답. 마리아가 오늘 사무실에 없는 이유를 묻는 질문에 고객 몇 명을 태우러 갔기 때문이라고 구체적인 이유를 제시하고 있으므로 정답.

(C) 질문과 상관없는 오답. Where 의문문에 대한 응답이므로 오답.

17

W-Am There's heavy traffic on the highway.
M-Cn (A) I hope I don't miss my plane.
(B) I'm doing well, thanks.
(C) The box is very light.

고속도로에 차가 많이 막히네요.
(A) 비행기를 놓치지 않았으면 좋겠어요.
(B) 잘 지내고 있어요, 고마워요.
(C) 상자가 아주 가볍네요.

어휘 heavy traffic 교통 체증

해설 정보 전달의 평서문

(A) 정답. 고속도로에 차가 많이 막힌다는 평서문에 비행기를 놓치지 않았 으면 좋겠다며 전달받은 정보에 근거해 일어날 가능성이 있는 결과에 대해 언급하고 있으므로 정답.

(B) 평서문과 상관없는 오답. How 의문문에 대한 응답이므로 오답.

(C) 연상 단어 오답. 평서문의 heavy에서 연상 가능한 light을 이용한 오답.

18

W-Br Did John send the expense sheet by e-mail or regular mail?

M-Au   (A) In the printer.
　　　　　(B) Yes, it's very expensive.
　　　　　(C) Probably by e-mail.

존이 경비 내역서를 이메일로 보냈나요, 일반 우편으로 보냈나요?
(A) 인쇄소예요.
(B) 네, 아주 비싸요.
(C) 아마 이메일로요.

어휘 expense 비용   expensive 비싼

해설 문서 발송 경로를 묻는 선택 의문문
(A) 연상 단어 오답. 질문의 sheet에서 연상 가능한 printer를 이용한 오답.
(B) 유사 발음 오답. 질문의 expense와 부분적으로 발음이 유사한 expensive를 이용한 오답.
(C) 정답. 존이 경비 내역서를 보낸 경로를 묻는 질문에 아마 이메일로 보냈을 것이라며 둘 중 하나를 선택해 응답하고 있으므로 정답.

19

W-Br   Why don't we invite an author to speak at our bookstore?
M-Au   (A) I'll check the storage room.
　　　　　(B) Some microphones and loudspeakers.
　　　　　(C) My friend just had a novel published.

저자를 초대해 우리 서점에서 강연하도록 하면 어때요?
(A) 제가 창고를 확인해 볼게요.
(B) 마이크와 확성기요.
(C) 제 친구가 얼마 전에 소설을 출판했어요.

어휘 loudspeaker 확성기   novel 소설   publish 출판하다

해설 제안/권유의 의문문
(A) 유사 발음 오답. 질문의 bookstore와 부분적으로 발음이 유사한 storage를 이용한 오답.
(B) 연상 단어 오답. 질문의 speak에서 연상 가능한 microphones와 loudspeakers를 이용한 오답.
(C) 정답. 저자를 초대해 우리 서점에서 강연하도록 하자고 제안하는 질문에 제 친구가 얼마 전에 소설을 출판했다며 제안에 찬성하는 의사를 우회적으로 표현하고 있으므로 정답.

20

W-Am   What documents should I bring on my first day of work?
M-Cn   (A) The ones in the welcome packet.
　　　　　(B) The first Monday in August.
　　　　　(C) Sure, I'll make 30 copies.

출근 첫날에 어떤 서류를 가져가야 하나요?
(A) 환영 패키지에 있는 것들이요.
(B) 8월 첫째 월요일이요.
(C) 물론이죠, 30부 복사할게요.

어휘 welcome packet 환영 패키지(신입 사원에게 주는 정보 꾸러미)

해설 첫 출근일에 구비할 서류를 묻는 What 의문문
(A) 정답. 출근 첫날에 가져가야 하는 서류를 묻는 질문에 환영 패키지에 있는 것들이라고 필요한 서류의 목록을 알 수 있는 곳을 간접적으로 알려 주고 있으므로 정답.
(B) 질문과 상관없는 오답. When 의문문에 대한 응답이므로 오답.
(C) Yes/No 불가 오답. What 의문문에는 Yes/No 응답이 불가능한데, Sure도 일종의 Yes 응답이라고 볼 수 있으므로 오답.

21

M-Au   We completed the training course, right?
W-Br   (A) To Paris in the spring.
　　　　　(B) No, there's still one session left.
　　　　　(C) Platform Seven.

우리는 교육 과정을 수료했죠?
(A) 봄에 파리로요.
(B) 아뇨, 아직 한 회 남았어요.
(C) 7번 플랫폼이요.

어휘 complete 수료하다

해설 교육 과정 수료 여부를 확인하는 부가 의문문
(A) 질문과 상관없는 오답. Where 의문문에 대한 응답이므로 오답.
(B) 정답. 우리가 교육 과정을 수료했는지 묻는 질문에 아니요(No)라고 대답한 뒤, 아직 한 회 남아 있다며 부정 답변과 일관된 내용을 덧붙였으므로 정답.
(C) 연상 단어 오답. 질문의 training을 train으로 잘못 들었을 경우 연상 가능한 platform을 이용한 오답.

22

M-Cn   How can I get to the mail room?
W-Am   (A) Only a few more packages.
　　　　　(B) I'm on my way there now.
　　　　　(C) Yes, there's enough room.

우편물실에 어떻게 가나요?
(A) 소포 몇 개만 더요.
(B) 제가 지금 그리로 가는 중이에요.
(C) 네, 공간이 충분해요.

어휘 package 소포   room 공간

해설 우편물실에 가는 방법을 묻는 How 의문문
(A) 연상 단어 오답. 질문의 mail room에서 연상 가능한 packages를 이용한 오답.
(B) 정답. 우편물실에 가는 방법을 묻는 질문에 제가 지금 그리로 가는 중이라며 가는 길을 직접 안내해 줄 수 있음을 우회적으로 제안하고 있으므로 정답.
(C) Yes/No 불가 오답. How 의문문에는 Yes/No 응답이 불가능하므로 오답.

TEST 7

23

W-Br Didn't you register for the webinar?

M-Au (A) Some of the latest research findings.

(B) No, I'm busy at that time.

(C) This cash register is closed.

웹 세미나에 등록 안 하셨어요?

(A) 최근 연구 결과 중 일부예요.

(B) 아뇨, 그 시간에 바빠요.

(C) 이 금전 등록기는 마감했어요.

어휘 register for ~에 등록하다   webinar 웹 세미나   research findings 연구 결과   cash register 금전 등록기

해설 웹 세미나에 등록했는지 여부를 확인하는 부정 의문문

(A) 연상 단어 오답. 질문의 webinar에서 세미나 주제를 연상하게 하는 research findings를 이용한 오답.

(B) 정답. 웹 세미나에 등록했는지 묻는 질문에 아니요(No)라고 대답한 뒤, 그 시간에 바쁘다며 부정 답변과 일관된 내용인 등록하지 않은 이유를 덧붙이고 있으므로 정답.

(C) 단어 반복 오답. 질문의 register를 반복 이용한 오답.

24

W-Am Is there a fee to use my credit card abroad?

M-Au (A) There's no additional charge.

(B) A twelve-hour plane ride.

(C) Right—it expires soon.

해외에서 신용카드를 사용하면 수수료가 있나요?

(A) 추가 요금은 없습니다.

(B) 12시간 비행이에요.

(C) 맞아요, 곧 만기예요.

어휘 abroad 해외에서   additional 추가의   charge 요금   expire 만기가 되다

해설 신용카드의 수수료 부과 여부를 묻는 Be동사 의문문

(A) 정답. 해외에서 신용카드를 사용할 경우 수수료가 있는지 묻는 질문에 추가 요금은 없다며 수수료가 따로 부과되지 않는다고 응답하고 있으므로 정답.

(B) 질문과 상관없는 오답. How long 의문문에 대한 응답이므로 오답.

(C) 연상 단어 오답. 질문의 credit card에서 카드의 유효 기간을 연상하게 하는 expires를 이용한 오답.

25

M-Cn Are you taking the train or riding the bus to work?

W-Br (A) Usually, they're on schedule.

(B) No, it's a project for work.

(C) My car's back from the repair shop!

출근할 때 기차를 타시나요, 아니면 버스를 타시나요?

(A) 보통은 예정대로 운영됩니다.

(B) 아뇨, 작업 프로젝트예요.

(C) 제 차가 정비소에서 돌아왔어요!

해설 통근 수단을 묻는 선택 의문문

(A) 연상 단어 오답. 질문의 train과 bus에서 연상 가능한 on schedule을 이용한 오답.

(B) Yes/No 불가 오답. 문장과 문장을 연결하는 경우를 제외하고는 선택 의문문에는 Yes/No 응답이 불가능하므로 오답.

(C) 정답. 통근할 때 이용하는 교통수단을 묻는 질문에 제 차가 정비소에서 돌아왔다며 차를 이용해 출퇴근하고 있다는 것을 우회적으로 알려 주고 있으므로 정답.

26

M-Cn Would you like a tour of the new automobile factory this afternoon?

W-Am (A) A manufacturing process.

(B) I was there on Monday.

(C) It's the old model.

오늘 오후에 새 자동차 공장을 둘러보시겠어요?

(A) 제조 공정이요.

(B) 월요일에 거기 갔었어요.

(C) 그건 오래된 모델이에요.

어휘 manufacturing process 제조 공정

해설 제안/권유의 의문문

(A) 연상 단어 오답. 질문의 factory에서 연상 가능한 manufacturing을 이용한 오답.

(B) 정답. 오늘 오후에 새 자동차 공장을 둘러볼 것을 제안하는 질문에 월요일에 거기 갔었다는 이유를 들어 제안을 거절하는 의사를 우회적으로 표현하고 있으므로 정답.

(C) 연상 단어 오답. 질문의 new에서 연상 가능한 old를 이용한 오답.

27

M-Cn Who ordered the cake for Miguel's retirement party?

W-Br (A) We need to replace that tire.

(B) No, it's at eight o'clock.

(C) We're serving ice cream instead.

미겔의 은퇴 파티용 케이크를 누가 주문했나요?

(A) 저 타이어를 교체해야 해요.

(B) 아뇨, 8시예요.

(C) 대신 아이스크림을 내려고요.

어휘 retirement 은퇴   replace 교체하다

해설 케이크를 주문한 사람을 묻는 Who 의문문

(A) 유사 발음 오답. 질문의 retirement와 부분적으로 발음이 유사한 tire를 이용한 오답.

(B) Yes/No 불가 오답. Who 의문문에는 Yes/No 응답이 불가능하므로 오답.

(C) 정답. 미겔의 은퇴 파티용 케이크를 주문한 사람을 묻는 질문에 대신 아이스크림을 내려고 한다며 케이크를 주문하지 않았다는 것을 우회적으로 알려 주고 있으므로 정답.

28

M-Au Where is Mr. Watanabe's office?

W-Am (A) Only on weekdays.

(B) **All directors are on the fifth floor.**

(C) A lot of modern equipment.

와타나베 씨의 사무실은 어디에 있나요?

(A) 평일만요.

(B) 이사님들은 모두 5층에 계세요.

(C) 수많은 현대식 장비들요.

어휘 director 이사   equipment 장비

해설 와타나베 씨의 사무실 위치를 묻는 Where 의문문

(A) 질문과 상관없는 오답. When 의문문에 대한 응답이므로 오답.

(B) 정답. 와타나베 씨의 사무실이 있는 위치를 묻는 질문에 이사님들은 모두 5층에 계신다며 간접적으로 알려 주고 있으므로 정답.

(C) 질문과 상관없는 오답. What 의문문에 대한 응답이므로 오답.

29

M-Cn When will you start looking for a new apartment?

W-Br (A) Turn the knob on the side.

(B) **My job transfer has been canceled.**

(C) No more than two bedrooms.

언제부터 새 아파트를 구하실 건가요?

(A) 옆에 있는 손잡이를 돌리세요.

(B) 이직이 취소됐어요.

(C) 침실은 두 개밖에 없어요.

어휘 knob 손잡이   job transfer 이직   cancel 취소하다   no more than ~밖에 없다

해설 새 아파트를 구할 시기를 묻는 When 의문문

(A) 질문과 상관없는 오답.

(B) 정답. 새 아파트를 구하기 시작할 시기를 묻는 질문에 이직이 취소되었다며 새 아파트를 구할 필요가 없음을 우회적으로 알려 주고 있으므로 정답.

(C) 연상 단어 오답. 질문의 apartment에서 연상 가능한 bedrooms를 이용한 오답.

30

W-Am Let's get extra screws in case we need more.

M-Au (A) He just started a new career.

(B) **The store closed half an hour ago.**

(C) That piece of wood is the perfect size.

더 필요한 경우에 대비해서 나사를 더 구합시다.

(A) 그는 막 새로운 일을 시작했어요.

(B) 가게가 30분 전에 문을 닫았어요.

(C) 저 나무토막이 딱 맞는 크기예요.

어휘 screw 나사   in case ~한 경우에 대비해

해설 제안/권유의 평서문

(A) 평서문과 상관없는 오답.

(B) 정답. 더 필요한 경우에 대비해서 나사를 더 구하자는 제안에 대해 가게가 30분 전에 문을 닫았다며 제안대로 나사를 더 구입하는 것이 불가능하다는 것을 우회적으로 알리고 있으므로 정답.

(C) 연상 단어 오답. 평서문의 screws에서 연상 가능한 wood를 이용한 오답.

31

W-Br Which radio advertisement did the focus group like best?

M-Au (A) That's the best decision.

(B) An increased advertising budget.

(C) **There was a problem with the sound system.**

포커스 그룹은 어떤 라디오 광고를 제일 좋아했나요?

(A) 그게 최선의 결정입니다.

(B) 늘어난 광고 예산이요.

(C) 음향 시스템에 문제가 있었어요.

어휘 advertisement 광고   decision 결정   increased 늘어난   budget 예산

해설 포커스 그룹이 가장 선호했던 라디오 광고를 묻는 Which 의문문

(A) 단어 반복 오답. 질문의 best를 반복 이용한 오답.

(B) 파생어 오답. 질문의 advertisement와 파생어 관계인 advertising을 이용한 오답.

(C) 정답. 포커스 그룹이 제일 좋아했던 라디오 광고를 묻는 질문에 음향 시스템에 문제가 있었다며 포커스 그룹이 선호했던 광고를 파악할 수 없었다는 점을 우회적으로 알리고 있으므로 정답.

PART 3

32-34

W-Am Hi, my name is Min Zhou. ³²**I'm here for my ten o'clock appointment.**

M-Cn Hmm... ³²**with Dr. Farooq, yes, I see.** It looks like this is your first visit here, so ³³**I'll give you some paperwork to fill out.**

W-Am Actually, ³³**I got an e-mail about that ahead of time and filled everything out online.** You should already have it.

M-Cn Perfect, thank you. In that case, you can take a seat, and the doctor will be with you shortly.

W-Am Oh... I just realized... ³⁴**I forgot some X-rays in my car. I'll quickly run back to the parking garage.**

M-Cn OK, no problem.

여	안녕하세요, 제 이름은 민주예요. **10시에 예약이 있어서 왔어요.**
남	음… **파루크 선생님과요, 네, 알겠습니다.** 여기 처음 오신 것 같으니 **작성하실 서류를 드릴게요.**
여	실은 사전에 이메일을 받았고 온라인으로 모두 작성했어요. 벌써 받으셨을 거예요.
남	좋습니다, 감사합니다. 그렇다면 자리에 앉으세요. 의사 선생님이 금방 오실 거예요.
여	아… 방금 생각났어요. **차에 엑스레이 몇 장을 두고 왔네요. 빨리 주차장으로 다시 갈게요.**
남	네, 그렇게 하세요.

어휘	appointment 예약 fill out ~을 작성하다 shortly 금방 realize 깨닫다 parking garage 주차장

32

Where most likely are the speakers?

(A) At a fitness center
(B) At a doctor's office
(C) At a pharmacy
(D) At a bank

화자들은 어디에 있겠는가?

(A) 헬스장
(B) 병원
(C) 약국
(D) 은행

해설 전체 내용 관련 - 대화의 장소

여자가 첫 대사에서 10시에 예약이 있어서 왔다(I'm here for my ten o'clock appointment)고 하자 남자가 뒤이어 파루크 선생님과의 예약이 확인되었다(with Dr. Farooq, yes, I see)고 대답하고 있는 것으로 보아 화자들은 병원에서 대화를 나누고 있다는 것을 알 수 있다. 따라서 정답은 (B)이다.

33

What did the woman do in advance?

(A) She checked some business hours.
(B) She made a list of questions.
(C) She paid for a service online.
(D) She completed some forms.

여자는 무엇을 미리 했는가?

(A) 영업 시간을 확인했다.
(B) 질문 목록을 작성했다.
(C) 온라인으로 서비스 비용을 지불했다.
(D) 몇 가지 양식을 작성했다.

어휘 complete 작성하다

해설 세부 사항 관련 - 여자가 미리 한 일

남자가 첫 대사에서 작성하실 서류를 드리겠다(I'll give you some paperwork to fill out)고 하자 여자가 사전에 이메일을 받았고 온라인으로 모두 작성했다(I got an e-mail about that ahead of time and filled everything out online)고 말하고 있으므로 여자는 이미 서류 작성을 완료했다는 것을 알 수 있다. 따라서 정답은 (D)이다.

▸▸ Paraphrasing 대화의 filled ~ out → 정답의 completed ~

34

What does the woman say she will do?

(A) Get her coat
(B) Return to a parking garage
(C) Look through a magazine
(D) Connect to the Internet

여자는 무엇을 할 것이라고 말하는가?

(A) 코트 가져오기
(B) 주차장으로 다시 가기
(C) 잡지 훑어보기
(D) 인터넷에 연결하기

해설 세부 사항 관련 - 여자가 할 것이라고 말하는 일

여자가 마지막 대사에서 차에 엑스레이 몇 장을 두고 왔다(I forgot some X-rays in my car)며 빨리 주차장으로 다시 가겠다(I'll quickly run back to the parking garage)고 말하고 있으므로 정답은 (B)이다.

▸▸ Paraphrasing 대화의 **run back to the parking garage**
→ 정답의 **Return to a parking garage**

35-37

M-Cn	35 **Welcome to Mandy's. Would you prefer to dine out on the patio or indoors?**
W-Am	The patio, please.
M-Cn	OK. Follow me.
W-Am	Oh... Do you think I could get a bigger table? 36 **Two of my friends will be joining me in a few minutes.**
M-Cn	Of course. While you wait for your friends, take a look at our menu. 37 **Today's specials are maple waffles and a strawberry-mango smoothie.**
W-Am	37 **They both sound great.**
M-Cn	37 **Just so you know, everyone likes the waffles.** They're selling quickly.

남	맨디스에 잘 오셨습니다. 테라스에서 식사하시겠어요, 아니면 실내에서 식사하시겠어요?
여	테라스로 할래요.
남	좋습니다. 따라오세요.
여	저… 좀 더 큰 테이블로 할 수 있을까요? 곧 친구 둘이 합석하거든요.
남	물론이죠. 친구분들을 기다리는 동안, 메뉴를 보세요. **오늘의 특별 요리는 메이플 와플과 딸기 망고 스무디입니다.**

여	둘 다 맛있겠는데요.
남	참고로 말씀드리면 다들 와플을 좋아해요. <mark>빨리 팔려 나가고 있어요.</mark>

어휘	patio 테라스 just so you know 참고로 말씀드리면

35

Where most likely are the speakers?

(A) At a farm

(B) At a restaurant

(C) At a grocery store

(D) At a catering company

화자들은 어디에 있겠는가?

(A) 농장

(B) 식당

(C) 식료품점

(D) 급식업체

해설 전체 내용 관련 – 대화의 장소

남자가 첫 대사에서 맨디스에 잘 오셨다(Welcome to Mandy's)고 환영하며, 테라스에서 식사할지 아니면 실내에서 식사할지(Would you prefer to dine out on the patio or indoors?)를 묻고 있으므로 남자는 식당 직원임을 알 수 있다. 따라서 정답은 (B)이다.

36

What does the woman say will happen soon?

(A) Some friends will join her.

(B) She will apply for a job.

(C) She will pay her bill.

(D) An anniversary will be celebrated.

여자는 곧 무슨 일이 있을 것이라고 말하는가?

(A) 친구들이 합석할 것이다.

(B) 취업 지원서를 낼 것이다.

(C) 계산할 것이다.

(D) 기념일을 축하할 것이다.

어휘 anniversary 기념일

해설 세부 사항 관련 – 여자가 곧 일어날 일이라고 말하는 것

여자가 두 번째 대사에서 곧 친구 둘이 합석한다(Two of my friends will be joining me in a few minutes)고 말하고 있으므로 정답은 (A)이다.

37

What does the man imply when he says, "They're selling quickly"?

(A) An item may be unavailable soon.

(B) An item is not expensive.

(C) A delivery should be made immediately.

(D) Some help will be needed.

남자가 "빨리 팔려 나가고 있어요"라고 말하는 의도는 무엇인가?

(A) 곧 어떤 품목을 이용하지 못할 수도 있다.

(B) 품목이 비싸지 않다.

(C) 배송이 즉시 이루어져야 한다.

(D) 도움이 필요할 것이다.

해설 화자의 의도 파악 – 빨리 팔려 나가고 있다는 말의 의도

앞에서 남자가 오늘의 특별 요리는 메이플 와플과 딸기 망고 스무디(Today's specials are maple waffles and a strawberry-mango smoothie)라고 알려 주었고 여자가 둘 다 맛있겠다(They both sound great)고 반응하자 남자가 다시 참고로 말하면 다들 와플을 좋아한다(Just so you know, everyone likes the waffles)고 말하며 인용문을 언급한 것으로 보아, 와플이 인기가 많아 금세 매진될 수도 있다는 점을 알리려는 의도로 한 말임을 알 수 있다. 따라서 정답은 (A)이다.

38-40

M-Au	**38 Do you need help finding your gate?**
W-Br	**38 No—my flight takes off from gate C-11.** But I do need some help—**39 my suitcase just broke!**
M-Au	Oh no! I'm so sorry to hear that.
W-Br	Do you happen to have any tape that I could use to temporarily patch it up?
M-Au	**40 We do have some packing tape in our storage closet. I'll go get the key to it from another gate attendant.**

남	게이트 찾으시는 것을 도와 드릴까요?
여	아뇨. 제 비행기는 C-11 게이트에서 이륙해요. 그런데 정말 도움이 필요해요. **방금 제 여행 가방이 망가졌어요!**
남	저런! 안타깝네요.
여	임시로 대충 수선하는 데 쓸 수 있는 테이프가 혹시 있나요?
남	**창고 벽장에 포장용 테이프가 몇 개 있어요. 제가 다른 게이트 안내원한테 가서 열쇠를 가져올게요.**

어휘	take off 이륙하다 temporarily 임시로 patch up ~을 대충 수선하다 closet 벽장 attendant 안내원

38

Where does the man most likely work?

(A) At a ferry terminal

(B) At a bus depot

(C) At an airport

(D) At a train station

남자는 어디에서 일하겠는가?

(A) 여객선 터미널

(B) 버스 터미널

(C) 공항

(D) 기차역

어휘 depot 터미널

해설 전체 내용 관련 – 남자의 근무지

남자가 첫 대사에서 게이트 찾는 데 도움이 필요한지(Do you need help finding your gate?) 묻자 여자가 거절(No)하며 자신의 비행기는 C-11 게이트에서 이륙한다(my flight takes off from gate C-11)고 말하고 있는 것으로 보아 대화 장소는 공항이고 남자는 공항에서 일하는 직원임을 알 수 있다. 따라서 정답은 (C)이다.

39

What problem does the woman have?

(A) Her colleague is late.
(B) Her suitcase is broken.
(C) A security line is long.
(D) She lost her ticket.

여자에게 어떤 문제가 있는가?

(A) 동료가 늦었다.
(B) 여행 가방이 망가졌다.
(C) 보안 검색 줄이 길다.
(D) 표를 잃어버렸다.

해설 세부 사항 관련 – 여자가 겪고 있는 문제

여자가 첫 대사에서 방금 제 여행 가방이 망가졌다(my suitcase just broke!)고 말하고 있으므로 정답은 (B)이다.

40

What will the man borrow from one of his coworkers?

(A) A pen
(B) A key
(C) A jacket
(D) A mobile phone

남자는 동료 중 한 명에게 무엇을 빌리겠는가?

(A) 펜
(B) 열쇠
(C) 재킷
(D) 핸드폰

해설 세부 사항 관련 – 남자가 동료 중 한 명에게 빌릴 물건

남자가 마지막 대사에서 창고 벽장에 포장용 테이프가 몇 개 있다(We do have some packing tape in our storage closet)면서, 제가 다른 게이트 안내원한테 가서 열쇠를 가져오겠다(I'll go get the key to it from another gate attendant)고 말하고 있으므로 정답은 (B)이다.

41-43 3인 대화

W-Br Insook, I have to say, the Builders Trade Show has been extremely interesting. I'm glad that our boss decided to send us this year.

W-Am [41] Our construction business is going to benefit a lot from all this helpful

information. Oh, let's look at this booth about textile concrete.

M-Cn Hi! I can answer any questions you have. [42] I'm Yang Liu, and I'm part of the sales team at Innovative Construction Materials.

W-Am What is textile concrete? Never heard of it.

M-Cn Well, it's lighter, less expensive to make, and much stronger than regular reinforced concrete. [43] We're having a product demonstration this afternoon.

W-Br [43] I have a conference call at three, but Insook, you should attend.

W-Am [43] OK, I will!

여1 인숙 씨, 정말이지 건설업체 무역 박람회는 대단히 흥미롭네요. 사장님이 올해 우리를 보내기로 결정하셔서 다행이에요.

여2 우리 건설 사업은 이 온갖 유용한 정보에서 많은 도움을 받을 거예요. 아, 섬유 콘크리트에 관한 이 부스를 둘러봐요.

남 안녕하세요! 어떤 질문에도 대답해 드리겠습니다. 저는 혁신 건축 자재 영업팀의 양 리우라고 합니다.

여2 섬유 콘크리트? 처음 들어 보네요.

남 어, 일반 철근 콘크리트보다 가볍고 제작비도 저렴하고 훨씬 강합니다. 오늘 오후에 제품 시연회가 있어요.

여1 저는 3시에 전화 회의가 있지만, 인숙 씨는 참석하세요.

여2 좋아요, 그럴게요!

어휘 extremely 대단히 expensive 비싼 reinforced concrete 철근 콘크리트 demonstration 시연(회)

41

Where do the women work?

(A) At a construction company
(B) At an automotive factory
(C) At a chemical plant
(D) At an interior design firm

여자들은 어디에서 일하는가?

(A) 건설 회사
(B) 자동차 공장
(C) 화학 공장
(D) 인테리어 디자인 회사

해설 전체 내용 관련 – 여자들의 근무지

두 번째 여자가 첫 대사에서 첫 번째 여자에게 우리 건설 사업이 이 온갖 유용한 정보에서 많은 도움을 받을 것(Our construction business is going to benefit a lot from all this helpful information)이라고 말하고 있으므로 두 여자는 건설업에 종사하고 있음을 알 수 있다. 따라서 정답은 (A)이다.

42

What is the man's job?

(A) Warehouse manager
(B) Computer engineer
(C) Sales representative
(D) Building inspector

남자의 직업은 무엇인가?

(A) 창고 관리자
(B) 컴퓨터 엔지니어
(C) 영업 사원
(D) 건축물 검사원

해설 전체 내용 관련 – 남자의 직업

남자가 첫 대사에서 저는 혁신 건축자재 영업팀의 양 리우(I'm Yang Liu, and I'm part of the sales team at Innovative Construction Materials)라고 소개하고 있으므로 남자는 건축자재 회사의 영업 사원임을 알 수 있다. 따라서 정답은 (C)이다.

43

What does Insook plan to do in the afternoon?

(A) Finalize a contract
(B) Watch a demonstration
(C) Visit a property
(D) Meet with potential investors

인숙은 오후에 무엇을 할 계획인가?

(A) 계약서 마무리하기
(B) 시연 보기
(C) 건물 방문하기
(D) 잠재 투자자들 만나기

어휘 finalize 마무리하다 property 건물 potential 잠재적인

해설 세부 사항 관련 – 인숙이 오후에 하려고 계획한 일

남자가 마지막 대사에서 오늘 오후에 제품 시연회가 있다(We're having a product demonstration this afternoon)고 했고, 첫 번째 여자가 자신은 3시에 전화 회의가 있지만 인숙 씨에게 참석하라(I have a conference call at three, but Insook, you should attend)고 하자 두 번째 여자가 좋다(OK)고 수락하며 그러겠다(I will!)고 대답하고 있으므로 두 번째 여자가 인숙이고, 인숙은 오후에 남자의 회사 제품 시연회에 참석할 것임을 알 수 있다. 따라서 정답은 (B)이다.

44-46

W-Am Freemont Real Estate. This is So-Hee. How can I help you?

M-Cn Hi, **44I'm moving to Freemont next month and am looking to rent an apartment. I'd really like to live on the waterfront. Would your agency be able to help me?**

W-Am Absolutely. There's a beautiful new building right on the water where we've found apartments for a few clients recently. They're filling up fast, though, so **45I'd suggest setting up an appointment with me as soon as you can.**

M-Cn I'd like to, but I don't know my schedule just yet. **46I'll give you a call back within the next week to set up a tour.**

여 프리몬트 부동산입니다. 저는 소희예요. 무엇을 도와 드릴까요?

남 안녕하세요, **다음 달에 프리몬트로 이사해서 아파트를 임대하려고 하는데요. 꼭 해안가에서 살고 싶어요. 거기 중개소에서 도움 주실 수 있을까요?**

여 물론이죠. 바로 물가에 멋진 신축 건물이 있어요. 최근 고객 몇 분을 위해 그곳에 아파트를 찾아 드렸죠. 그래도 금방 다 차니까 **가능한 한 빨리 약속을 잡으시길 권해요.**

남 그러고 싶지만 아직 제 일정을 알 수 없네요. **다음 주 안으로 다시 전화해서 둘러볼 일정을 잡을게요.**

어휘 waterfront 해안가 recently 최근에

44

Why is the man calling?

(A) To hire a moving truck
(B) To schedule a job interview
(C) To make a payment
(D) To ask about renting an apartment

남자는 왜 전화하는가?

(A) 이사용 트럭을 빌리려고
(B) 취업 면접 일정을 잡으려고
(C) 대금을 지불하려고
(D) 아파트 임대에 관해 문의하려고

어휘 hire 빌리다

해설 전체 내용 관련 – 남자가 전화한 이유

남자가 첫 대사에서 다음 달에 프리몬트로 이사해서 아파트를 임대하려고 한다(I'm moving to Freemont next month and am looking to rent an apartment)고 했고, 꼭 해안가에서 살고 싶다(I'd really like to live on the waterfront)며 거기 중개소에서 도움을 줄 수 있는지(Would your agency be able to help me?)를 묻고 있으므로 정답은 (D)이다.

45

What does the woman suggest the man do soon?

(A) Create an online account
(B) Schedule an appointment
(C) Take some measurements
(D) Review a contract

여자는 남자에게 무엇을 빨리 하라고 권하는가?

(A) 온라인 계정 만들기
(B) 예약 일정 잡기
(C) 측정하기
(D) 계약서 검토하기

어휘 measurement 측정 contract 계약(서)

해설 세부 사항 관련 - 여자가 남자에게 권하는 일

여자가 두 번째 대사에서 가능한 한 빨리 약속을 잡길 권한다(I'd suggest setting up an appointment with me as soon as you can)고 말하고 있으므로 정답은 (B)이다.

> ▸▸ Paraphrasing 대화의 **setting up an appointment**
> → 정답의 **Schedule an appointment**

46

What does the man say he will do?

(A) Call back next week
(B) Write a report
(C) Use another agency
(D) Contact some references

남자는 무엇을 할 것이라고 말하는가?

(A) 다음 주에 다시 전화
(B) 보고서 작성
(C) 다른 중개소 이용
(D) 추천인들에게 연락

어휘 reference 추천인, 신원 보증인

해설 세부 사항 관련 - 남자가 할 것이라고 말하는 일

남자가 마지막 대사에서 다음 주 안으로 다시 전화해서 둘러볼 일정을 잡겠다(I'll give you a call back within the next week to set up a tour)고 말하고 있으므로 정답은 (A)이다.

47-49

M-Au	Good morning, Ms. Zhang. ⁴⁷**Sorry I'm late to work—traffic was really slow this morning.** Everyone's driving carefully because of the rain.
W-Am	No problem, Richard. The store's been pretty quiet today. I just hope the stormy weather doesn't delay the delivery truck!
M-Au	Are we expecting a delivery?
W-Am	⁴⁸**I'm replacing the two desktop computers in our office. The new ones are supposed to arrive today.** In fact, I was going to ask you to help me set them up.
M-Au	I'd be happy to. By the way, ⁴⁹**what are you doing with the old computers? I know of an electronics recycling center. They even pick up!**

W-Am	Wonderful! ⁴⁹**Could you give them a call?**
M-Au	⁴⁹**Sure.**

남	안녕하세요, 장 씨. 늦게 출근해서 죄송해요. 오늘 아침은 차가 많이 막혔어요. 비 때문에 다들 조심해서 운전하고 있어요.
여	괜찮아요, 리처드. 오늘은 가게가 꽤 조용하네요. 폭풍우 때문에 배송 트럭이 늦지 않기만 바란답니다!
남	배송 올 게 있나요?
여	사무실에 있는 데스크톱 컴퓨터 두 대를 교체하려고 해요. 새것이 오늘 도착하기로 되어 있어요. 실은 설치하는 일을 도와 달라고 부탁하려던 참이었어요.
남	기꺼이 할게요. 그런데 오래된 컴퓨터는 어떻게 하시려고요? 제가 전자 제품 재활용 센터를 하나 알고 있어요. 거기서 가지러도 와요!
여	좋네요! 거기 전화 좀 해 줄래요?
남	그럴게요.

어휘 replace 교체하다 electronics 전자 제품

47

Why was the man late to work?

(A) He was stuck in traffic.
(B) He missed a train.
(C) He had a doctor's appointment.
(D) He woke up late.

남자는 왜 직장에 지각했는가?

(A) 길이 막혀서 꼼짝 못했다.
(B) 기차를 놓쳤다.
(C) 병원 예약이 있었다.
(D) 늦게 일어났다.

어휘 stuck in traffic 길이 막혀서 꼼짝 못하는

해설 세부 사항 관련 - 남자가 직장에 지각한 이유

남자가 첫 대사에서 늦게 출근해서 죄송하다(Sorry I'm late to work)며 오늘 아침은 차가 많이 막혔다(traffic was really slow this morning)고 말하고 있으므로 정답은 (A)이다.

> ▸▸ Paraphrasing 대화의 **traffic was really slow**
> → 정답의 **was stuck in traffic**

48

What is scheduled to be delivered today?

(A) Company uniforms
(B) Desktop computers
(C) Cleaning supplies
(D) Informational brochures

오늘 배송 예정인 것은 무엇인가?

(A) 회사 단체복
(B) 데스크톱 컴퓨터
(C) 청소용품
(D) 안내책자

여자가 두 번째 대사에서 사무실에 있는 데스크톱 컴퓨터 두 대를 교체하려고 한다(I'm replacing the two desktop computers in our office)면서, 새것이 오늘 도착하기로 되어 있다(The new ones are supposed to arrive today)고 말하고 있으므로 정답은 (B)이다.

49

What business will the man call?

(A) A plumbing service
(B) A catering company
(C) An automotive repair company
(D) An electronics recycling center

남자는 어떤 업체에 전화할 것인가?
(A) 배관 서비스
(B) 급식업체
(C) 자동차 수리업체
(D) 전자 제품 재활용 센터

어휘 plumbing 배관

해설 세부 사항 관련 - 남자가 전화할 업체

남자가 세 번째 대사에서 오래된 컴퓨터는 어떻게 할 것(what are you doing with the old computers?)인지 물으며 제가 전자 제품 재활용 센터를 하나 알고 있다(I know of an electronics recycling center)고 하자, 여자가 거기에 전화해 줄 것(Could you give them a call?)을 요청했고 남자가 뒤이어 그러겠다(Sure)고 수락했으므로 남자는 곧 전자 제품 재활용 센터에 전화할 것임을 알 수 있다. 따라서 정답은 (D)이다.

50-52 3인 대화

W-Br Good morning, Hiroshi and Carlos. ⁵⁰**I'd like to talk to both of you about your current project.**

M-Au Sure, Ms. Park. ⁵⁰**Right now, we're designing the denim line: jeans, of course, but also some jackets.**

W-Br That's why I wanted to talk to you. ⁵¹**The product management team has actually decided to use a new fabric for this line. It's a cotton and wool blend.**

M-Cn Really! That's interesting. Hmm... ⁵¹**the wool should increase the warmth of our denim items, which is good.**

M-Au You're right. But... I'm worried about whether this change will affect our deadlines.

W-Br ⁵²**I'm going to review the new project plan with you now—I have it right here.**

여 안녕하세요, 히로시, 카를로스. **현재 진행 중인 프로젝트에 대해 두 분과 이야기하고 싶어요.**

남1 물론이죠, 박 선생님. **지금 저희는 데님 제품군을 디자인하고 있어요. 청바지는 물론 재킷도요.**

여 그것 때문에 여러분과 얘기하고 싶었어요. 실은 **제품 관리팀이 이 제품군에 새 직물을 사용하기로 결정했어요. 면과 모직 혼방이에요.**

남2 정말인가요! 별일이네요. 음… **모직은 데님 용품의 보온성을 높이니까, 그건 좋군요.**

남1 맞아요. 하지만… 이번 변경으로 마감일에 영향을 미치지는 않을지 걱정되네요.

여 **지금 여러분과 함께 새 프로젝트 계획을 검토하려고요. 바로 여기 제가 갖고 있어요.**

어휘 decide 결정하다 increase 높이다 warmth 보온성

50

Who most likely is the woman?

(A) A client
(B) A supervisor
(C) An intern
(D) A vendor

여자는 누구이겠는가?
(A) 고객
(B) 관리자
(C) 인턴
(D) 판매업자

어휘 supervisor 관리자 vendor 판매업자

해설 전체 내용 관련 - 여자의 신분

여자가 첫 대사에서 현재 진행 중인 프로젝트에 대해 두 분과 이야기하고 싶다(I'd like to talk to both of you about your current project)고 하자, 첫 번째 남자가 지금 저희는 데님 제품군인 청바지는 물론 재킷도 디자인하고 있다(we're designing the denim line: jeans, of course, but also some jackets)고 수행 중인 프로젝트의 진행 상황에 대해 보고하고 있는 것으로 보아 여자는 관리자임을 알 수 있다. 따라서 정답은 (B)이다.

51

What is a benefit of a new material?

(A) It is strong.
(B) It is lightweight.
(C) It is warm.
(D) It is soft.

신소재의 이점은 무엇인가?
(A) 튼튼하다.
(B) 가볍다.
(C) 따뜻하다.
(D) 부드럽다.

해설 세부 사항 관련 - 신소재의 이점

여자가 두 번째 대사에서 실은 제품 관리팀이 이 제품군에 새 직물을 사용하기로 결정했다(The product management team has actually decided to use a new fabric for this line)며 면과 모직 혼방(It's a cotton and wool blend)이라고 알리자, 두 번째 남자가 모직은 데님 용

품의 보온성을 높이니까, 그건 좋다(the wool should increase the warmth of our denim items, which is good)고 말하고 있으므로 모직이 혼방된 신소재는 보온성이 높다는 장점이 있음을 알 수 있다. 따라서 정답은 (C)이다.

52

What will the speakers do next?

(A) Contact a colleague
(B) Plan a celebration
(C) Look at some samples
(D) Review a document

화자들은 다음에 무엇을 하겠는가?

(A) 동료에게 연락
(B) 기념행사 계획
(C) 샘플 검사
(D) 문서 검토

해설 세부 사항 관련 – 화자들이 다음에 할 일

여자가 마지막 대사에서 지금 여러분과 함께 새 프로젝트 계획을 검토하려 한다(I'm going to review the new project plan with you now)며 바로 여기 제가 갖고 있다(I have it right here)고 말하고 있으므로 정답은 (D)이다.

53-55

> W-Am ⁵³**I just received the proposed contract from the Westerly Hotel for hosting our conference there. I just need your approval on it.**
>
> M-Au We used that hotel for last year's conference and got good feedback from most people who went.
>
> W-Am Right, and the contract includes the room block as well, so ⁵⁴**our attendees will receive a discounted price on their hotel rooms.**
>
> M-Au OK. If you could leave the contract on my desk, I'll take a look a little later.
>
> W-Am Thanks. ⁵⁵**We'll need to sign the agreement by the end of the week.**

> 여 방금 웨스털리 호텔에서 우리 회의를 주최하겠다는 가계약서를 받았어요. 승인만 하시면 돼요.
>
> 남 작년 회의에 그 호텔을 사용했는데 거기 갔던 참석자 대다수가 좋은 반응을 보였어요.
>
> 여 맞습니다. 그리고 계약서에는 단체 예약 객실도 포함되어 있어서 **참석자들은 호텔 객실에 대해 가격 할인을 받게 됩니다.**
>
> 남 좋아요. 계약서를 제 책상 위에 놓아 두시면, 잠시 후에 볼게요.
>
> 여 감사합니다. **이번 주 안에는 계약을 체결해야 합니다.**

어휘 proposed contract 가계약서 approval 승인 room block 호텔에서 회의 및 참석자를 위해 단체 예약하는 객실 attendee 참석자 sign an agreement 계약을 체결하다

53

What type of event are the speakers discussing?

(A) A holiday party
(B) A conference
(C) A grand opening
(D) A job fair

화자들은 어떤 종류의 행사에 대해 논의하고 있는가?

(A) 휴가철 파티
(B) 회의
(C) 개업식
(D) 채용 박람회

해설 세부 사항 관련 – 화자들이 논의 중인 행사

여자가 첫 대사에서 방금 웨스털리 호텔에서 우리 회의를 주최하겠다는 가계약서를 받았다(I just received the proposed contract from the Westerly Hotel for hosting our conference there)며 승인만 하시면 된다(I just need your approval on it)고 회의 장소 계약과 관련된 내용을 언급하고 있으므로 정답은 (B)이다.

54

What does the woman say attendees will receive?

(A) A discounted rate
(B) A raffle ticket
(C) Free transportation
(D) A city map

여자는 참석자들이 무엇을 받을 것이라고 말하는가?

(A) 할인 요금
(B) 경품 응모권
(C) 무료 교통편
(D) 도시 지도

어휘 rate 요금 raffle ticket 경품 응모권

해설 세부 사항 관련 – 여자가 참석자들이 받을 것이라고 말한 것

여자가 두 번째 대사에서 참석자들은 호텔 객실에 대해 가격 할인을 받게 된다(our attendees will receive a discounted price on their hotel rooms)고 말하고 있으므로 정답은 (A)이다.

> ▶ Paraphrasing 대화의 a discounted price
> → 정답의 A discounted rate

55

What do the speakers need to do soon?

(A) Write a short speech
(B) Submit a budget report
(C) Notify some employees
(D) Sign a contract

화자들은 곧 무엇을 해야 하는가?

(A) 짧은 연설문 작성
(B) 예산 보고서 제출
(C) 직원들에게 통보
(D) 계약 체결

어휘 submit 제출하다 budget 예산 notify 통보하다

해설 세부 사항 관련 - 화자들이 곧 해야 할 일

여자가 마지막 대사에서 이번 주 안에는 계약을 체결해야 한다(We'll need to sign the agreement by the end of the week)고 말하고 있으므로 정답은 (D)이다.

56-58

W-Br	Hi, Sam. ⁵⁶**Can you give me an update on the phone case your team's designing for the Parker SI16 mobile phone?**
M-Cn	Sure. You said to experiment, so ⁵⁷**we tried something new: a case that's environmentally friendly. It's made of 100 percent recycled materials. What do you think?**
W-Br	Our clients are interested in environmentally friendly products.
M-Cn	Good. ⁵⁸**We hope to have some designs ready to present at the managers' meeting that's happening on Friday.**

여	안녕하세요, 샘. 파커 SI16 핸드폰용으로 팀에서 디자인하고 있는 전화 케이스 관련해서 새로운 소식 좀 알려 주실래요?
남	물론이죠. 실험해 보라고 하셔서 새로운 것을 시도했는데, 친환경적인 케이스예요. 100퍼센트 재활용 재료로 만들어졌어요. 어떻게 생각하세요?
여	우리 고객들은 친환경적인 제품에 관심이 있어요.
남	잘됐네요. 금요일 매니저 회의에서 발표하도록 디자인이 준비되면 좋겠어요.

어휘	experiment (새로운 방법 등을) 실험하다 environmentally friendly 친환경적인 recycled 재활용된

56

Who most likely is the man?

(A) An advertising executive
(B) A factory manager
(C) A customer service representative
(D) A product designer

남자는 누구이겠는가?

(A) 광고 담당 임원
(B) 공장장
(C) 고객 서비스 담당자
(D) 제품 디자이너

해설 전체 내용 관련 - 남자의 직업

여자가 첫 대사에서 남자에게 파커 SI16 핸드폰용으로 당신의 팀에서 디자인하고 있는 전화 케이스 관련해서 새로운 소식을 알려 줄 수 있는지 (Can you give me an update on the phone case your team's designing for the Parker SI16 mobile phone?)를 묻고 있는 것으로 보아 정답은 (D)이다.

57

What does the woman imply when she says, "Our clients are interested in environmentally friendly products"?

(A) She is frustrated with her clients.
(B) She is surprised by some feedback.
(C) She approves of the man's idea.
(D) She thinks the man is unfamiliar with a topic.

여자가 "우리 고객들은 친환경적인 제품에 관심이 있어요"라고 말하는 의도는 무엇인가?

(A) 고객들 때문에 낙담했다.
(B) 일부 반응에 놀랐다.
(C) 남자의 아이디어에 찬성한다.
(D) 남자가 논제를 잘 모른다고 생각한다.

어휘 frustrated 낙담한 approve 찬성하다 unfamiliar with ~을 잘 모르는

해설 화자의 의도 파악 - 우리 고객들은 친환경적인 제품에 관심이 있다는 말의 의도

앞에서 남자가 새로운 것을 시도했는데 친환경적인 케이스(we tried something new: a case that's environmentally friendly)이고 100 퍼센트 재활용 재료로 만들어졌다(It's made of 100 percent recycled materials)면서 어떻게 생각하는지(What do you think?)를 묻자, 여자가 인용문을 언급한 것으로 보아, 남자가 새로 시도한 친환경 제품이 고객들의 관심사에 속한다는 점을 근거로 남자의 아이디어에 공감하려는 의도로 한 말임을 알 수 있다. 따라서 정답은 (C)이다.

58

What does the man say will take place on Friday?

(A) An awards ceremony
(B) A managers' meeting
(C) A safety inspection
(D) A training class

남자는 금요일에 무슨 일이 있다고 말하는가?

(A) 시상식
(B) 매니저 회의
(C) 안전 점검
(D) 교육 강좌

어휘 inspection 점검

해설 세부 사항 관련 - 남자가 금요일에 일어날 일이라고 말하는 것

남자가 마지막 대사에서 금요일 매니저 회의에서 발표하도록 디자인이 준비되길 바라고 있다(We hope to have some designs ready to present at the managers' meeting that's happening on Friday)고 말하고 있으므로 정답은 (B)이다.

M-Au	⁵⁹**Welcome to Marston Paints. I'm the manager here.** How can I help you today?
W-Br	Hi. ⁶⁰**Last week I bought an office building nearby**, and I'm planning to have all the interior walls repainted.
M-Au	Welcome to the neighborhood! Have you decided on a color for your walls?
W-Br	Not yet. I was hoping you would have some samples?
M-Au	Sure. You know, ⁶¹**we also have a mobile phone application that you might find useful.**
W-Br	How so?
M-Au	⁶¹**It'll help you visualize what your office will look like with different-colored walls.** Just take a picture of the space and upload it to the app. You'll be prompted to enter different color codes to see what it would look like.

남	마스턴 페인트에 잘 오셨습니다. 저는 여기 매니저인데요. 오늘 제가 어떻게 도와 드릴까요?
여	안녕하세요. 지난주에 근처에 있는 업무용 건물을 구입했는데, 내부 벽을 전부 새로 칠할 계획이에요.
남	이 동네에 오신 걸 환영합니다! 벽 색상은 정하셨나요?
여	아직이요. 여기 샘플이 있었으면 했거든요?
남	물론이죠. 그런데 저희는 핸드폰 애플리케이션도 있어서 유용하실 겁니다.
여	어째서 그런가요?
남	벽이 다른 색상일 때 사무실이 어떤 모습일지 마음속에 그려 보는 데 도움이 될 겁니다. 공간을 사진으로 찍어 앱에 올리기만 하면 됩니다. 어떤 모습이 될지 보려면 다른 색상 코드를 입력하라는 메시지가 표시돼요.

어휘	visualize 마음속에 그려 보다　prompt 사용자에게 메시지를 보내다

59

Who is the man?
(A) An art gallery owner
(B) A store manager
(C) A hair stylist
(D) A real estate agent

남자는 누구인가?
(A) 미술관 주인
(B) 매장 매니저
(C) 헤어 스타일리스트
(D) 부동산 중개업자

해설　전체 내용 관련 – 남자의 직업

남자가 첫 대사에서 마스턴 페인트에 잘 오셨다(Welcome to Marston Paints)며 저는 여기 매니저(I'm the manager here)라고 자신을 소개하고 있으므로 남자는 페인트 가게의 매니저임을 알 수 있다. 따라서 정답은 (B)이다.

60

What does the woman say happened last week?
(A) She visited some relatives.
(B) She received a raise.
(C) She gave a presentation.
(D) She purchased a building.

여자는 지난주에 무슨 일이 있었다고 말하는가?
(A) 친척들을 방문했다.
(B) 봉급이 인상되었다.
(C) 프레젠테이션을 했다.
(D) 건물을 구입했다.

어휘　relative 친척　raise (임금 등의) 인상, 상승　purchase 구입하다

해설　세부 사항 관련 – 여자가 지난주에 일어났다고 말하는 일

여자가 첫 대사에서 지난주에 근처에 있는 업무용 건물을 구입했다(Last week I bought an office building nearby)고 말하고 있으므로 정답은 (D)이다.

> ▸▸ Paraphrasing　대화의 bought
> → 정답의 purchased

61

What does the man recommend doing?
(A) Postponing a project
(B) Using a mobile phone application
(C) Creating some promotional flyers
(D) Ordering some name tags

남자는 무엇을 하라고 권하는가?
(A) 프로젝트 연기
(B) 핸드폰 애플리케이션 사용
(C) 판촉 전단 제작
(D) 명찰 주문

어휘　postpone 연기하다　flyer 전단

해설　세부 사항 관련 – 남자가 권하는 일

남자가 세 번째 대사에서 저희는 핸드폰 애플리케이션도 있는데 유용하실 것(we also have a mobile phone application that you might find useful)이라고 자사의 핸드폰 앱을 소개했고, 마지막 대사에서 벽이 다른 색상일 때 사무실이 어떤 모습이 될지 마음속에 그려 보는 데 도움이 될 것(It'll help you visualize what your office will look like with different-colored walls)이라며 핸드폰 앱이 어떻게 도움이 되는지를 설명하고 있는 것으로 보아 정답은 (B)이다.

M-Au Simone, ⁶²I know you wanted me to add music to the video you uploaded. But when I went to work on it, the video file wouldn't open. I wonder if there's something wrong with it.

W-Br ⁶³You mean the one for the Riverton City promotional video? It's odd that it's not working. I got an e-mail earlier about that video. I'm about to answer it, so I'll ask her to send another copy of the file.

M-Au Thanks. We have to finish the video by Friday. ⁶⁴The annual Riverton City Cultural Festival is this weekend, and they're planning to debut it there.

남 시몬, 올리신 동영상에 음악을 추가해 달라고 하셨죠. 그런데 막상 작업을 하려고 하니 동영상 파일이 열리지 않네요. 무슨 문제가 있는 것 같아요.

여 리버턴 시티 홍보 동영상 말씀이시죠? 작동하지 않는다니 이상하네요. 아까 그 동영상 관련 이메일을 받았어요. 곧 답장할 참이니 그녀에게 파일 한 부를 더 보내 달라고 부탁할게요.

남 고마워요. 금요일까지 동영상을 마무리해야 해요. 해마다 열리는 리버턴 시티 문화 축제가 이번 주말인데, 거기서 선보일 계획이거든요.

어휘 promotional 홍보하는 odd 이상한 annual 해마다 열리는 debut 선보이다

Inbox:		
From	Subject	Received
Claudine Li	Nature documentary	12:45 P.M.
⁶³Elise Choi	Riverton promotional video	1:10 P.M.
Anya Lundly	Training schedule	2:25 P.M.
Madoka Ito	Location suggestions	3:50 P.M.

받은 메일함:		
발신	제목	수신
클로딘 리	자연 다큐	오후 12:45
⁶³일리스 최	리버턴 홍보 동영상	오후 1:10
아냐 런들리	교육 일정	오후 2:25
마도카 이토	장소 제안	오후 3:50

62

What problem are the speakers mainly discussing?
(A) An event venue is unavailable.
(B) A project deadline has passed.
(C) A document contains spelling errors.
(D) A video file is not working.

화자들은 주로 어떤 문제를 논의하고 있는가?
(A) 행사장을 이용할 수 없다.
(B) 프로젝트 마감일이 지났다.
(C) 문서에 철자 오류가 있다.
(D) 동영상 파일이 작동하지 않는다.

어휘 venue (행사 등을 위한) 장소 unavailable 이용할 수 없는 contain 들어 있다

해설 전체 내용 관련 - 대화의 주제

남자가 첫 대사에서 올리신 동영상에 음악을 추가해 달라고 하셨다(I know you wanted me to add music to the video you uploaded)고 했고 그런데 막상 작업을 하려고 하니 동영상 파일이 열리지 않는다(But when I went to work on it, the video file wouldn't open)면서 무슨 문제가 있는 것 같다(I wonder if there's something wrong with it)고 문제점을 알리고 있으므로 정답은 (D)이다.

▸▸ Paraphrasing 대화의 the video file wouldn't open
→ 정답의 A video file is not working

63

Look at the graphic. Whose e-mail does the woman mention?
(A) Claudine Li's
(B) Elise Choi's
(C) Anya Lundly's
(D) Madoka Ito's

시각 정보에 의하면 여자는 누구의 이메일을 언급하는가?
(A) 클로딘 리
(B) 일리스 최
(C) 아냐 런들리
(D) 마도카 이토

해설 시각 정보 연계 - 여자가 언급한 이메일의 발신인

여자가 첫 대사에서 리버턴 시티 홍보 동영상을 말씀하시는 것인지(You mean the one for the Riverton City promotional video?)를 묻고 있고, 받은 메일함에 따르면 리버턴 홍보 동영상이라는 제목의 이메일은 일리스 최가 보낸 것이므로 정답은 (B)이다.

64

What event will happen this weekend?
(A) A local election
(B) A corporate fund-raiser
(C) A city festival
(D) A sports competition

이번 주말에 무슨 행사가 있겠는가?

(A) 지방 선거

(B) 기업 모금 행사

(C) 시 축제

(D) 스포츠 경기

어휘 fund-raiser 모금 행사   competition 경기

해설 세부 사항 관련 – 이번 주말에 열릴 행사

남자가 마지막 대사에서 해마다 열리는 리버턴 시티 문화 축제가 이번 주말(The annual Riverton City Cultural Festival is this weekend)이라고 말하고 있으므로 정답은 (C)이다.

65-67 대화 + 웹페이지

M-Au	Mei Ting, have you ordered the new shopping bags for our store yet? **65 Since we've recently updated our logo, the bags should have our new logo on them.**
W-Am	Let's look at our options online... We want the same type of bags we use now, right— the large plastic bags?
M-Au	**66 What about switching to large paper bags? It's easier to see our logo on the paper bags, so it'd be a better way to promote our store.**
W-Am	**66 Good point. I'll order the large ones, then.**
M-Au	And while you're doing that, **67 I'll stock the displays. The shelves are looking a little empty.**

남	메이 팅, 우리 매장에 쓸 새 쇼핑백을 벌써 주문하셨어요? **최근에 로고를 수정했으니 쇼핑백에 새 로고가 있어야 해요.**
여	온라인으로 옵션을 살펴봐요… 지금 사용하는 것과 같은 종류의 백, 그러니까 대형 비닐백이 필요한 거죠?
남	**대형 종이백으로 바꾸는 건 어떨까요? 종이백이 로고가 더 잘 보일 테니까 매장을 홍보하기에 더 나은 방법이 될 거예요.**
여	**좋은 지적이네요. 그럼 큰 걸로 주문할게요.**
남	그럼 그렇게 하는 사이에 **저는 진열품을 채울게요. 선반이 좀 비어 보여요.**

어휘	recently 최근 promote 홍보하다 stock 채우다 empty 빈

65

What does the man say the store has recently done?

(A) Replaced some equipment

(B) Updated a company logo

(C) Installed a security system

(D) Painted some shelving units

남자는 가게에서 최근에 무엇을 했다고 말하는가?

(A) 장비 교체

(B) 회사 로고 수정

(C) 보안 시스템 설치

(D) 선반 장치 도색

어휘 replace 교체하다   install 설치하다

해설 세부 사항 관련 – 남자가 최근에 가게에서 했다고 말하는 것

남자가 첫 대사에서 최근에 로고를 수정했으니 쇼핑백에는 새 로고가 있어야 한다(Since we've recently updated our logo, the bags should have our new logo on them)고 말하고 있는 것으로 보아 가게에서 최근에 로고를 수정했다는 것을 알 수 있다. 따라서 정답은 (B)이다.

66

Look at the graphic. Which item will the store order?

(A) Item 231

(B) Item 498

(C) Item 540

(D) Item 762

시각 정보에 의하면 가게는 어떤 상품을 주문할 것인가?

(A) 품번 231
(B) 품번 498
(C) 품번 540
(D) 품번 762

해설 **시각 정보 연계 - 가게에서 주문할 상품**

남자가 두 번째 대사에서 대형 종이백으로 바꾸는 건 어떨지(What about switching to large paper bags?)를 물으며 종이백이 로고가 더 잘 보일 테니까 매장을 홍보하기에 더 나은 방법이 될 것(It's easier to see our logo on the paper bags, so it'd be a better way to promote our store)이라고 하자, 여자가 좋은 지적(Good point)이라면서 그럼 큰 것으로 주문하겠다(I'll order the large ones, then)고 했으므로 대형 종이백을 주문할 것임을 알 수 있다. 웹페이지에 따르면 대형 종이백은 품목 231번이므로 정답은 (A)이다.

67

What does the man say he will do next?

(A) Print a receipt
(B) Stock some shelves
(C) Finalize a schedule
(D) Find a credit card

남자는 다음에 무엇을 할 것이라고 말하는가?

(A) 영수증 출력하기
(B) 선반 채우기
(C) 일정 확정하기
(D) 신용 카드 찾기

어휘 receipt 영수증 finalize 확정하다

해설 **세부 사항 관련 - 남자가 다음에 할 것이라고 말하는 일**

남자가 마지막 대사에서 진열품을 채우겠다(I'll stock the displays)면서 선반이 좀 비어 보인다(The shelves are looking a little empty)고 했으므로 정답은 (B)이다.

68-70 대화 + 지도

M-Cn　Hey, Anya... I sent you a map with several office buildings. I also attached some photos and the dimensions of the rooms. [68] **What do you think about one of these for our new law offices?**

W-Am　Well, the one closest to the courthouse would be very convenient.

M-Cn　Actually, [69] **I think the one across the street from the library is better for our legal firm.** It's still on the same street as the courthouse, and I like the layout more.

W-Am　That sounds good. [70] **Can you call Emiko and Satoshi and see when they're free?** I'd like them to go see the offices with us.

남　안녕하세요, 아냐… 업무용 건물 몇 동이 있는 지도를 보냈어요. 사진 몇 장과 방 치수도 첨부했고요. **우리 새 법률 사무소로 이 건물들 중 하나는 어때요?**

여　음, 법원에서 가장 가까운 곳이 아주 편하겠네요.

남　사실 제 생각에는 도서관 건너편에 있는 건물이 우리 법률 사무소로 더 나을 것 같아요. 이곳도 법원과 같은 거리에 있고, 배치가 더 마음에 들어서요.

여　좋아요. 에미코와 사토시에게 전화해서 언제 시간이 되는지 알아봐 줄래요? 그들이 우리와 함께 사무실을 보러 갔으면 해요.

어휘　attach 첨부하다　dimension 치수　courthouse 법원
convenient 편한

68

Who most likely are the speakers?

(A) Lawyers
(B) Bakers
(C) Accountants
(D) Doctors

화자들은 누구이겠는가?

(A) 변호사
(B) 제빵사
(C) 회계사
(D) 의사

해설 **전체 내용 관련 - 화자들의 직업**

남자가 첫 대사에서 여자에게 우리 새 법률 사무소로 이 건물들 중 하나는 어떤지(What do you think about one of these for our new law offices?)라고 묻고 있는 것으로 보아 화자들은 법률 사무소에서 근무하고 있음을 알 수 있다. 따라서 정답은 (A)이다.

69

Look at the graphic. Which building does the man say he likes?

(A) Building 1
(B) Building 2
(C) Building 3
(D) Building 4

시각 정보에 의하면 남자는 어떤 건물이 마음에 든다고 말하는가?

(A) 건물 1
(B) 건물 2
(C) 건물 3
(D) 건물 4

해설 시각 정보 연계 - 남자가 마음에 든다고 말하는 건물

남자가 두 번째 대사에서 제 생각에는 도서관 건너편에 있는 건물이 우리 법률 사무소로 더 나을 것 같다(I think the one across the street from the library is better for our legal firm)고 말하고 있고, 지도에 따르면 도서관 건너편에 있는 건물은 건물 2이므로 정답은 (B)이다.

70

What does the woman ask the man to do?

(A) E-mail a real estate agent
(B) Make a lunch reservation
(C) Contact some colleagues
(D) Upload some photographs

여자는 남자에게 무엇을 해 달라고 요청하는가?

(A) 부동산 중개업자에게 이메일 보내기
(B) 점심 예약하기
(C) 동료들에게 연락하기
(D) 사진 올리기

어휘 reservation 예약 colleague 동료

해설 세부 사항 관련 - 여자의 요청 사항

여자가 마지막 대사에서 에미코와 사토시에게 전화해서 언제 시간이 되는지 알아봐 줄 수 있는지(Can you call Emiko and Satoshi and see when they're free?)를 묻고 있으므로 정답은 (C)이다.

> ▶ Paraphrasing   대화의 call Emiko and Satoshi
> → 정답의 Contact some Colleagues

PART 4

71-73 전화 메시지

W-Am Hi, Kavi. This is Anna. I just got off the phone with a candidate for the strategy director position. [71]**I'd like to bring him in for an interview, but I want to check with you about the cost. Will you approve travel expenses for him to come here?** [72]**He doesn't live locally—he'd be flying in from**

Chicago. I'd like to make these arrangements quickly, if possible. [73]**I just e-mailed you a cost estimate.** Can you let me know what you think?

안녕, 카비. 안나예요. 방금 전략 본부장직 지원자와 통화했어요. **면접에 부르고 싶은데, 비용에 관해서 당신과 상의하고 싶어요. 그가 이곳에 오는 여비를 승인해 주시겠어요?** 그는 이 지역에 살지 않아요. 시카고에서 비행기로 올 거예요. 가능하면 빨리 이 일을 처리하고 싶어요. **방금 비용 견적서를 이메일로 보냈어요.** 어떻게 생각하시는지 말씀해 주시겠어요?

어휘 candidate 지원자 strategy 전략 approve 승인하다 expense 비용 locally 지역에 make an arrangement 처리하다 estimate 견적(서)

71

Why is the speaker calling?

(A) To explain a schedule change
(B) To discuss an upcoming conference
(C) To request approval for an expense
(D) To confirm an e-mail address

화자는 왜 전화하는가?

(A) 일정표 변경을 설명하려고
(B) 곧 있을 회의에 관해 논의하려고
(C) 비용 승인을 요청하려고
(D) 이메일 주소를 확인하려고

어휘 upcoming 곧 있을 approval 승인

해설 전체 내용 관련 - 전화의 이유

화자가 초반부에 남자를 면접에 부르고 싶은데 비용에 관해서 당신과 상의하고 싶다(I'd like to bring him in for an interview, but I want to check with you about the cost)면서, 그가 이곳에 오는 여비를 승인해 줄 수 있는지(Will you approve travel expenses for him to come here?)를 묻고 있으므로 정답은 (C)이다.

72

What does the speaker say about a job candidate?

(A) He requires additional training.
(B) He has good references.
(C) He speaks several languages.
(D) He does not live in the area.

화자는 일자리 지원자에 대해 무엇이라고 말하는가?

(A) 추가 교육이 필요하다.
(B) 추천서가 좋다.
(C) 여러 언어를 구사한다.
(D) 이 지역에 살지 않는다.

어휘 additional 추가의 reference 추천서, 추천인

해설 세부 사항 관련 - 화자가 일자리 지원자에 대해 말하는 것

화자가 중반부에 그는 이 지역에 살지 않는다(He doesn't live locally)며, 시카고에서 비행기로 올 것(he'd be flying in from Chicago)이라고 말하고 있으므로 정답은 (D)이다.

73

What did the speaker send in an e-mail?

(A) A résumé

(B) A cost estimate

(C) A meeting agenda

(D) A tour itinerary

화자는 이메일로 무엇을 보냈는가?

(A) 이력서

(B) 비용 견적서

(C) 회의 안건

(D) 관광 일정

어휘 agenda 안건   itinerary 여행 일정

해설 세부 사항 관련 - 화자가 이메일로 보낸 것

화자가 후반부에 방금 비용 견적서를 이메일로 보냈다(I just e-mailed you a cost estimate)고 했으므로 정답은 (B)이다.

74-76   안내 방송

M-Au ⁷⁴**Attention, passengers. The conductor will soon make his way through the train to check tickets.** Please have them ready. ⁷⁵**If you have an e-ticket on your smartphone, please make sure you set your screen brightness to high.** The conductor will be using an electronic scanner to read the tickets, and the scanner won't be able to read your ticket code if the light on your phone's screen is too low. Also, ⁷⁶**this is a fully booked train**, so you shouldn't leave any belongings on the seat next to you.

승객 여러분께 알립니다. 잠시 후 승무원이 기차를 쭉 통과하면서 기차표를 확인할 예정입니다. 기차표를 준비해 주세요. **스마트폰에 전자표가 있는 경우 화면 밝기를 높게 설정하십시오.** 차장이 전자 스캐너를 사용해 표를 읽는데, 핸드폰 화면의 조도가 너무 낮으면 스캐너가 표 코드를 읽을 수 없습니다. 또한 **이 열차는 예약이 꽉 찼으므로 옆 좌석에 소지품을 두시면 안 됩니다.**

어휘 conductor 승무원   brightness 밝기   fully booked 예약이 꽉 찬   belongings 소지품

74

Where are the listeners?

(A) In an airport

(B) On a train

(C) At a theater

(D) On a ferry

청자들은 어디에 있는가?

(A) 공항

(B) 기차

(C) 극장

(D) 여객선

해설 전체 내용 관련 - 안내 방송의 장소

화자가 도입부에 승객 여러분께 알린다(Attention, passengers)면서, 잠시 후 승무원이 기차를 쭉 통과하면서 기차표를 확인할 예정(The conductor will soon make his way through the train to check tickets)이라고 했으므로 정답은 (B)이다.

75

What are the listeners with e-tickets asked to do?

(A) Check their seat numbers

(B) Increase their screen's brightness

(C) Come to the front of the line

(D) Download a mobile application

전자표를 가지고 있는 청자들은 무엇을 하라고 요청받는가?

(A) 좌석 번호 확인하기

(B) 화면 밝기 높이기

(C) 줄 앞쪽으로 오기

(D) 모바일 애플리케이션 내려받기

어휘 increase 높이다

해설 세부 사항 관련 - 전자표를 가지고 있는 청자들이 요청받은 일

화자가 중반부에 스마트폰에 전자표가 있는 경우 화면 밝기를 높게 설정해 달라(If you have an e-ticket on your smartphone, please make sure you set your screen brightness to high)고 요청하고 있으므로 정답은 (B)이다.

76

Why does the speaker say, "you shouldn't leave any belongings on the seat next to you"?

(A) To ask the listeners to clear space

(B) To remind the listeners about forgotten items

(C) To explain safety regulations

(D) To clarify the checked baggage policy

화자가 "옆 좌석에 소지품을 두시면 안 됩니다"라고 말하는 이유는 무엇인가?

(A) 청자들에게 공간을 비워 두라고 요청하려고

(B) 청자들에게 잊은 물건에 대해 상기시키려고

(C) 안전 수칙을 설명하려고

(D) 위탁 수하물 규정을 명확하게 설명하려고

어휘 regulation 수칙   clarify 명확하게 설명하다   baggage 수하물   policy 규정

해설 화자의 의도 파악 - 옆 좌석에 소지품을 두면 안 된다는 말의 의도

앞에서 이 열차는 예약이 꽉 찼다(this is a fully booked train)고 말한 뒤 인용문을 언급하고 있으므로, 좌석이 모두 판매가 되어 승객이 앉을 것이기 때문에 좌석을 비워 두라고 요청하려는 의도로 한 말임을 알 수 있다.

따라서 정답은 (A)이다.

77-79 전화 메시지

W-Br Hello, my name's Darya, and ⁷⁷**I heard a radio advertisement about your bicycle shop. It said that you offer bicycle repair demonstrations. Would you consider doing that at a corporate health fair?** ⁷⁸**My company recently launched a new health initiative,** and one thing we'd like to do is encourage employees to cycle to work. We'd provide you with a booth, and you'd bring the bike and tools. ⁷⁹**I also encourage you to bring some cycling accessories—such as helmets and water bottles—to display.**

안녕하세요, 저는 다리아인데, 자전거 가게 라디오 광고를 들었어요. 자전거 수리 시연을 하신다고 하던데요. 기업 건강 박람회에서 하는 걸 고려해 보시겠어요? 저희 회사는 최근에 새로운 건강 프로그램을 시작했는데, 한 가지 하고 싶은 것은 직원들에게 자전거로 출근하도록 권장하는 거예요. 저희가 그쪽에 부스를 제공하면 자전거와 용구를 가지고 오시면 됩니다. 전시할 수 있도록 헬멧이나 물병 같은 자전거 부대용품도 가지고 오시길 권합니다.

어휘 repair 수리 demonstration 시연(회) consider -ing ~하는 것을 고려하다 corporate 기업의 fair 박람회 initiative (문제 해결이나 목표 달성을 위한) 프로그램, 계획 encourage 권장하다 accessory 부대용품, 액세서리

77

Why is the speaker calling?
(A) To reschedule an inspection
(B) To request a demonstration
(C) To book a vacation package
(D) To change an order

화자는 왜 전화하는가?
(A) 점검 일정을 바꾸려고
(B) 시연을 요청하려고
(C) 휴가 패키지를 예약하려고
(D) 주문을 변경하려고

어휘 inspection 점검

해설 전체 내용 관련 - 전화의 이유

화자가 초반부에 자전거 가게 라디오 광고를 들었다(I heard a radio advertisement about your bicycle shop)고 했고 자전거 수리 시연을 한다고 하던데(It said that you offer bicycle repair demonstrations)라고 하면서, 기업 건강 박람회에서 하는 것을 고려해 보겠는지(Would you consider doing that at a corporate health fair?)를 묻고 있는 것으로 보아 정답은 (B)이다.

78

What has the speaker's company recently done?
(A) It changed its hours of operation.
(B) It hired additional staff.
(C) It moved to a new location.
(D) It started a health program.

화자의 회사는 최근에 무엇을 했는가?
(A) 운영 시간을 변경했다.
(B) 추가로 직원을 채용했다.
(C) 새로운 장소로 이전했다.
(D) 건강 프로그램을 시작했다.

해설 세부 사항 관련 - 화자의 회사에서 최근에 한 일

화자가 중반부에 저희 회사는 최근에 새로운 건강 프로그램을 시작했다(My company recently launched a new health initiative)고 했으므로 정답은 (D)이다.

▸▸ Paraphrasing 담화의 launched a new health initiative
→ 정답의 started a health program

79

What does the speaker encourage the listener to do?
(A) Display some products
(B) Offer some coupons
(C) Create a handbook
(D) Expedite a delivery

화자는 청자에게 무엇을 하라고 권장하는가?
(A) 제품 전시
(B) 쿠폰 제공
(C) 안내책자 제작
(D) 신속하게 배송 처리

어휘 expedite 신속하게 처리하다

해설 세부 사항 관련 - 화자의 권장 사항

화자가 마지막에 전시할 수 있도록 헬멧이나 물병 같은 자전거 부대용품도 가지고 오시길 권한다(I also encourage you to bring some cycling accessories—such as helmets and water bottles—to display)고 말하고 있으므로 정답은 (A)이다.

80-82 회의 발췌

M-Cn ⁸⁰**So, this meeting is for everyone—cooks, servers, hosts, cleaners—because we all need to work together as a team.** Today is an important day. So, first of all, ⁸¹**thank you all for coming in extra early to help prepare for our grand opening.** I appreciate it. Second thing I'd like to mention: ⁸²**tomorrow, a journalist from the local newspaper—her name is Ingrid Vogel—has made a reservation for six o'clock.** Ms. Vogel will be writing an article about her experience here and rating the food we serve, so take good care of her. A positive review in the paper will definitely be good for future business.

자, 이번 회의는 요리사, 웨이터, 진행자, 청소원 등 모두를 위한 회의입니다. 우리 모두는 한 팀으로 협력해야 하기 때문이죠. 오늘은 중요한 날입니다. 먼저 **개업식 준비를 돕기 위해 각별히 일찍 와 주셔서 감사합니다.** 감사해요. 두 번째로 말씀드리고 싶은 것은 **내일 지역 신문사의 잉그리드 보겔이라는 기자가 6시에 예약했습니다.** 보겔 씨는 이곳에서 자신의 경험에 대한 기사를 쓰고 우리가 제공하는 음식을 평가할 예정이니 잘 대접하세요. 그 신문에 긍정적인 후기가 실리면 앞으로 영업에 분명 좋을 겁니다.

어휘 prepare for ~을 준비하다　appreciate 감사하다　make a reservation 예약하다　article 기사　experience 경험　rate 평가하다　positive 긍정적인　definitely 분명

80

Where do the listeners most likely work?

(A) At a health food store
(B) At a restaurant
(C) At a spice factory
(D) At a vegetable farm

청자들은 어디에서 일하겠는가?
(A) 건강식품 매장
(B) 식당
(C) 향신료 공장
(D) 채소 농장

해설 전체 내용 관련 - 청자들의 근무지

화자가 도입부에 이번 회의는 요리사, 웨이터, 진행자, 청소원 등 모두를 위한 회의(this meeting is for everyone—cooks, servers, hosts, cleaners)라면서 청자들을 지칭하고 있는 것으로 보아 이들은 식당에서 근무하는 사람들임을 알 수 있다. 따라서 정답은 (B)이다.

81

What are the listeners preparing for today?

(A) A seasonal sale
(B) A cooking class
(C) A baking contest
(D) A grand opening

청자들은 오늘 무엇을 준비하는가?
(A) 계절 할인
(B) 요리 교실
(C) 제빵 경연 대회
(D) 개업식

해설 세부 사항 관련 - 청자들이 오늘 준비하는 것

화자가 초반부에 개업식 준비를 돕기 위해 각별히 일찍 와 주셔서 감사하다(thank you all for coming in extra early to help prepare for our grand opening)고 말하고 있으므로 정답은 (D)이다.

82

Who is Ingrid Vogel?

(A) A newspaper journalist
(B) A health inspector
(C) A famous chef
(D) An interior decorator

잉그리드 보겔은 누구인가?
(A) 신문기자
(B) 위생 검사원
(C) 유명 요리사
(D) 실내 장식가

어휘 inspector 검사원

해설 세부 사항 관련 - 잉그리드 보겔의 직업

화자가 중반부에 내일 지역 신문사의 잉그리드 보겔이라는 기자가 6시에 예약했다(tomorrow, a journalist from the local newspaper ~ a reservation for six o'clock)고 말하고 있으므로 정답은 (A)이다.

83-85 견학 정보

W-Br ⁸³**Welcome to this tour of Jenson Manufacturing. Our town is known for the glasswork that has been produced for centuries by the many factories here.** In fact, decorative glass is still the town's main source of income. ⁸⁴**While products from all the factories are known locally,** we ship to customers all over the world. Today, you'll see our skilled artisans at work and learn about the history of their craft. After the tour, you may want to visit our gift shop, where you'll find many of the items produced here. ⁸⁵**Be sure to hold on to your tour ticket. It qualifies you for ten percent off anything you buy today.**

젠슨 제조에 견학 오신 것을 환영합니다. 우리 마을은 이곳의 많은 공장에서 수 세기에 걸쳐 생산된 유리 제품으로 유명합니다. 사실, 장식용 유리는 여전히 마을의 주요 수입원이죠. **모든 공장에서 나온 제품이 현지에서 유명하지만** 저희는 전 세계 고객들에게 출하하고 있습니다. 오늘 숙련된 장인들이 작업하는 모습을 보시고 그들의 공예 역사에 관해 배우겠습니다. 견학이 끝나고 선물 가게를 방문하시면 이곳에서 생산되는 많은 상품들을 볼 수 있습니다. **견학 티켓을 꼭 가지고 계세요.** 그것이 있으면 **오늘 사시는 어떤 물건이든 10퍼센트 할인을 받으실 수 있습니다.**

어휘 manufacturing 제조　income 수입　ship 출하하다　skilled 숙련된　artisan 장인　qualify ~에 대한 자격을 주다

83

Where is the tour taking place?

(A) At an art museum
(B) At a pottery workshop
(C) At a clothing design studio
(D) At a glass factory

견학은 어디에서 진행되고 있는가?

(A) 미술관
(B) 도자기 워크숍
(C) 의류 디자인 스튜디오
(D) 유리 공장

어휘 pottery 도자기

해설 전체 내용 관련 - 견학의 장소
화자가 도입부에 젠슨 제조에 견학 오신 것을 환영한다(Welcome to this tour of Jenson Manufacturing)고 했으므로 공장임을 알 수 있고, 우리 마을은 이곳의 많은 공장에서 수 세기에 걸쳐 생산된 유리 제품으로 유명하다(Our town is known for the glasswork ~ by the many factories here)고 한 것으로 보아 공장이 유리를 다루는 곳임을 짐작할 수 있다. 따라서 정답은 (D)이다.

84

Why does the speaker say, "we ship to customers all over the world"?

(A) To reassure the listeners about a service
(B) To explain why a storage area is large
(C) To emphasize the popularity of some products
(D) To make a suggestion for a gift

화자가 "저희는 전 세계 고객들에게 출하하고 있습니다"라고 말하는 이유는 무엇인가?

(A) 서비스 관련하여 청자들을 안심시키려고
(B) 보관 구역이 넓은 이유를 설명하려고
(C) 일부 제품의 인기를 강조하려고
(D) 선물을 추천하려고

어휘 reassure 안심시키다 emphasize 강조하다 popularity 인기 make a suggestion 추천하다

해설 화자의 의도 파악 - 저희는 전 세계 고객들에게 출하하고 있다는 말의 의도
앞에서 모든 공장에서 나온 제품이 현지에서 유명하지만(While products from all the factories are known locally)이라고 말한 뒤 인용문을 언급한 것으로 보아, 자사의 제품은 현지에서만 인지도가 있는 타사의 제품에 비해 해외로 수출할 정도로 인기가 좋다는 점을 알리려는 의도로 한 말임을 알 수 있다. 따라서 정답은 (C)이다.

85

What does the speaker say is available to the listeners?

(A) An event calendar
(B) A discount on a purchase
(C) A subscription to a newsletter
(D) Entry in a prize drawing

화자는 청자들에게 무엇을 이용할 수 있다고 말하는가?

(A) 행사 일정표
(B) 구매품 할인
(C) 소식지 구독
(D) 경품 추첨 기회

어휘 purchase 구매(품) subscription 구독 entry (참여할 수 있는) 기회 drawing 추첨

해설 세부 사항 관련 - 화자가 청자들에게 이용할 수 있다고 말하는 것
화자가 마지막에 견학 티켓을 꼭 가지고 있을 것(Be sure to hold on to your tour ticket)을 권고하며, 그것이 있으면 오늘 사는 어떤 물건이든 10퍼센트 할인을 받을 수 있다(It qualifies you for ten percent off anything you buy today)고 말하고 있으므로 정답은 (B)이다.

> ▶▶ Paraphrasing   담화의 **ten percent off anything you buy**
> → 정답의 **A discount on a purchase**

86-88 담화

W-Am Welcome back, everyone. On behalf of the city's business development council, I'm pleased you could attend today's workshop for small business start-ups. Again, **86the council exists with the sole purpose of getting you the resources that you need to successfully launch your new business.** So, this is the second workshop in a three-part series. **87During our initial session on March fifteenth, you worked on constructing a careful and detailed business proposal.** Those proposals you submitted were a good start. Today, **88we're fortunate to have a number of seasoned business mentors who've volunteered their time to assist you with strategies for securing financing. In a few minutes, you'll meet with them in small groups.**

어서 오세요, 여러분. 시의 기업 발전 협의회를 대표해서 오늘 중소기업 창업 워크숍에 참석해 주셔서 기쁩니다. 다시 한번 말씀드리지만 **협의회의 유일한 목적은 여러분이 새로운 사업을 성공적으로 시작하는 데 필요한 자원을 드리고자 합니다.** 이번은 3부로 이루어진 시리즈 중 두 번째 워크숍입니다. **3월 15일에 있었던 첫 번째 세션에서 여러분은 꼼꼼하고 상세한 사업 제안서를 작성했습니다.** 여러분이 제출한 제안서들은 훌륭한 출발이었습니다. **다행하게도 오늘 재정 확보 전략을 돕기 위해 시간을 내 자원한 노련한 비즈니스 멘토들이 많이 오십니다. 몇 분 후 소집단을 꾸려 멘토들을 만나겠습니다.**

어휘 on behalf of ~을 대표하여 development 발전 business start-up 창업 exist 존재하다 purpose 목적 resource 자원 initial 첫 번째의 business proposal 사업 제안서 submit 제출하다 fortunate 다행인 seasoned 노련한 volunteer 자원하다 strategy 전략 secure 확보하다

86

What is the purpose of the speaker's organization?

(A) To advise businesses about mergers

(B) To arrange travel for executives

(C) To share resources with new business owners

(D) To recruit volunteers for a research study

화자가 속한 조직의 목적은 무엇인가?

(A) 업체들에게 합병에 대해 조언

(B) 임원을 위한 출장 준비

(C) 신규 업주들과 자원 공유

(D) 연구를 위한 지원자 모집

어휘 merger 합병 executive 임원

해설 세부 사항 관련 - 화자가 속한 조직의 목적

화자가 초반부에 협의회의 유일한 목적은 여러분이 새로운 사업을 성공적으로 시작하는 데 필요한 자원을 드리고자 함(the council exists with the sole purpose ~ successfully launch your new business)이라고 말하고 있으므로 정답은 (C)이다.

87

What did the listeners do on March 15?

(A) They signed some documents.

(B) They purchased some materials.

(C) They downloaded some software.

(D) They wrote some proposals.

청자들은 3월 15일에 무엇을 했는가?

(A) 서류에 서명했다.

(B) 재료를 구입했다.

(C) 소프트웨어를 내려받았다.

(D) 제안서를 썼다.

어휘 purchase 구입하다

해설 세부 사항 관련 - 청자들이 3월 15일에 한 일

화자가 중반부에 3월 15일에 있었던 첫 번째 세션에서 여러분은 꼼꼼하고 상세한 사업 제안서를 작성했다(During our initial session on March fifteenth, you worked on constructing a careful and detailed business proposal)고 말하고 있으므로 정답은 (D)이다.

▸▸ Paraphrasing 담화의 **worked on constructing a ~ proposal** → 정답의 **wrote some proposals**

88

What will the listeners do in a few minutes?

(A) Congratulate a colleague

(B) Vote on a policy change

(C) Create an advertisement

(D) Meet with mentors

청자들은 몇 분 후에 무엇을 하겠는가?

(A) 동료 축하하기

(B) 정책 변경에 대해 투표하기

(C) 광고 만들기

(D) 멘토 만나기

해설 세부 사항 관련 - 청자들이 몇 분 후 할 일

화자가 후반부에 다행히도 오늘 재정 확보 전략을 돕기 위해 시간을 내 자원한 노련한 비즈니스 멘토들이 많이 온다(we're fortunate to have a number of seasoned business mentors ~ for securing financing)면서, 몇 분 후 소집단을 꾸려 멘토들을 만나겠다(In a few minutes, you'll meet with them in small groups)고 말하고 있으므로 정답은 (D)이다.

89-91 회의 발췌

> M-Au Now let's talk about our new initiative. **89 Retaining quality personnel is now a top priority for our company.** We're hoping that competitive salaries and benefits packages will help us recruit and keep talented staff. So, **90 we recently brought in Helen Liu. Helen is a human resources consultant who'll spend the next few months helping us restructure our compensation program.** **91 Currently, she's requesting staff feedback about pay and benefits. To that end, she's created a questionnaire that will be sent out later today.** I know everyone's busy right now, but this affects all of us.

> 이제 새로운 프로그램에 대해 이야기해 봅시다. **우수한 인력을 계속 보유하는 것이 지금 회사의 최우선 과제입니다.** 경쟁력 있는 급여와 복리 후생이 유능한 직원들을 채용하고 유지하는 데 도움이 됐으면 하죠. 그래서 **최근 헬렌 리우를 영입했습니다. 헬렌은 인사 자문으로, 앞으로 몇 달 동안 보상 프로그램을 조정하도록 도와줄 겁니다.** 현재 헬렌은 직원들에게 급여와 복리 후생에 대한 의견을 요청하고 있어요. 이를 위해 헬렌이 오늘 이따가 발송될 설문지를 작성했습니다. 지금 다들 바쁜 건 알지만 이건 우리 모두에게 영향을 미치는 일입니다.

> 어휘 initiative 프로그램 retain 계속 보유하다 quality 우수한 personnel 인력 priority 우선 과제 competitive 경쟁력 있는 benefits 복리 후생 restructure 조정하다 compensation 보상 questionnaire 설문지 affect 영향을 미치다

89

What does the speaker say is a top priority?

(A) Increasing product sales

(B) Keeping quality employees

(C) Improving worker efficiency

(D) Lowering manufacturing costs

화자는 무엇이 최우선이라고 말하는가?

(A) 제품 판매 증가

(B) 우수 직원 유지

(C) 직원 효율 개선

(D) 제조 비용 낮추기

어휘 increase 증가하다 improve 개선하다 efficiency 효율, 능률 lower 낮추다

해설 세부 사항 관련 - 화자가 최우선이라고 말하는 것

화자가 초반부에 우수한 인력을 계속 보유하는 것이 지금 회사의 최우선 과제(Retaining quality personnel is now a top priority for our company)라고 말하고 있으므로 정답은 (B)이다.

> ▸▸ Paraphrasing 담화의 retaining quality personnel
> → 정답의 Keeping quality employees

90

Who is Helen Liu?

(A) A company spokesperson
(B) A human resources consultant
(C) A digital marketing expert
(D) A course instructor

헬렌 리우는 누구인가?
(A) 회사 대변인
(B) 인사 자문
(C) 디지털 마케팅 전문가
(D) 강사

어휘 spokesperson 대변인 expert 전문가

해설 세부 사항 관련 - 헬렌 리우의 직업

화자가 중반부에 최근 헬렌 리우를 영입했다(we recently brought in Helen Liu)고 언급하며, 헬렌은 인사 자문으로 앞으로 몇 달 동안 보상 프로그램을 조정하도록 도와줄 것(Helen is a human resources consultant ~ our compensation program)이라고 소개하고 있으므로 정답은 (B)이다.

91

Why does the speaker say, "this affects all of us"?

(A) To encourage participation
(B) To congratulate a team
(C) To discourage future errors
(D) To apologize for a delay

화자가 "이건 우리 모두에게 영향을 미치는 일입니다"라고 말하는 이유는 무엇인가?
(A) 참여를 독려하려고
(B) 팀을 축하하려고
(C) 향후 오류 발생을 막으려고
(D) 지연에 대해 사과하려고

어휘 discourage 막다 apologize for ~에 대해 사과하다

해설 화자의 의도 파악 - 이건 우리 모두에게 영향을 미치는 일입니다라는 말의 의도

앞에서 현재 헬렌은 직원들에게 급여와 복리 후생에 대한 의견을 요청하고 있다(she's requesting staff feedback about pay and benefits)고 했고 이를 위해 헬렌이 오늘 이따가 발송될 설문지를 작성했다(To that end, she's created a questionnaire that will be sent out later today)면서 지금 다들 바쁜 건 안다(I know everyone's busy right now)고 말한 뒤 인용문을 언급한 것으로 보아, 직원들의 의견을 파악하기 위한 설문지를 작성하는 일은 모두에게 영향력을 미치는 중요한 일이므로

바쁘더라도 요청에 응해 달라는 의도로 한 말임을 알 수 있다. 따라서 정답은 (A)이다.

92-94 담화

> M-Cn ⁹²I'm here from Tarmo Advertising to present the new marketing campaign my team and I propose for your electronic tablet device, Soft-Palm 51. ⁹³Let me begin with a recommendation, that you target a slightly older, more sophisticated age segment than you have in the past. Your products are already popular among younger customers, and Soft-Palm 51 is an opportunity to expand your brand to midcareer professionals. ⁹⁴With its compact, light design, Soft-Palm 51 has the portability that business travelers need. This is the key selling point.
>
> 저는 타르모 광고 소속으로 귀사의 전자 태블릿 기기인 소프트-팜 51을 위해 저희 팀과 제가 제안하는 새로운 마케팅 캠페인을 발표하기 위해 여기 왔습니다. 우선 귀사가 과거보다 조금 나이가 많고, 더 교양 있는 연령층을 목표로 삼으라는 권고로 시작하겠습니다. 귀사의 제품은 이미 젊은 고객들 사이에 인기가 있으므로 소프트-팜 51은 귀사의 브랜드를 중견 전문직 종사자로 확장할 수 있는 기회입니다. 소프트-팜 51은 작고 가벼운 디자인으로 출장 다니는 사람들에게 필요한 휴대성을 갖추고 있습니다. 이것이 판매에 유리한 핵심 장점입니다.
>
> 어휘 recommendation 권고 slightly 조금 sophisticated 교양 있는 segment 부분 opportunity 기회 expand 확장하다 midcareer 중견(의) portability 휴대성 selling point 판매에 유리한 장점

92

What is the purpose of the talk?

(A) To demonstrate a work process
(B) To choose a job applicant
(C) To present a marketing plan
(D) To review some sales reports

담화의 목적은 무엇인가?
(A) 작업 과정 시연
(B) 입사 지원자 선정
(C) 마케팅 계획 제시
(D) 판매 보고서 검토

해설 전체 내용 관련 - 담화의 목적

화자가 도입부에 저는 타르모 광고 소속으로 귀사의 전자 태블릿 기기인 소프트-팜 51을 위해 저희 팀과 제가 제안하는 새로운 마케팅 캠페인을 발표하기 위해 여기 왔다(I'm here from Tarmo Advertising to present the new marketing campaign ~ Soft-Palm 51)고 말하고 있으므로 정답은 (C)이다.

93

What does the speaker say about the company's current customers?

(A) They are unhappy with a service.
(B) They live mainly in cities.
(C) Many of them work in technology.
(D) Many of them are young.

화자는 회사의 현재 고객들에 대해 무엇을 말하는가?

(A) 서비스에 만족하지 않는다.
(B) 주로 도시에 산다.
(C) 다수가 기술 분야에서 일한다.
(D) 다수가 젊다.

어휘 mainly 주로

해설 세부 사항 관련 - 화자가 회사의 현재 고객들에 대해 하는 말

화자가 중반부에 우선 귀사가 과거보다 조금 나이가 많고 더 교양 있는 연령층을 목표로 삼으라는 권고로 시작하겠다(Let me begin with a recommendation, that you target a slightly older, more sophisticated age segment than you have in the past)고 말하고 있고, 귀사의 제품은 이미 젊은 고객들 사이에 인기가 있다(Your products are already popular among younger customers)고 말하는 것으로 보아 회사의 기존 고객들은 젊은 연령층임을 알 수 있다. 따라서 정답은 (D)이다.

94

What feature of Soft-Palm 51 does the speaker emphasize?

(A) It is easy to carry.
(B) It is less expensive than expected.
(C) It is energy efficient.
(D) It is faster than previous models.

화자는 소프트-팜 51의 어떤 특징을 강조하는가?

(A) 휴대가 간편하다.
(B) 예상보다 저렴하다.
(C) 에너지 효율이 좋다.
(D) 이전 모델보다 빠르다.

어휘 expensive 비싼 efficient 효율적인 previous 이전의

해설 세부 사항 관련 - 화자가 강조하는 소프트-팜 51의 특징

화자가 후반부에 소프트-팜 51은 작고 가벼운 디자인으로 출장 다니는 사람들에게 필요한 휴대성을 갖추고 있다(With its compact, light design, Soft-Palm 51 has the portability that business travelers need)고 말하고 있으므로 정답은 (A)이다.

> ▸▸ Paraphrasing 담화의 has the portability
> → 정답의 is easy to carry

95-97 방송 + 도표

W-Am This is the six o'clock update from NCK News with Patricia Sullivan. First, the traffic report:

95-97

95a traffic light on Samson Road isn't working, and it's causing a lengthy delay. A maintenance crew is currently fixing the light, so repairs are expected to be done within the hour. Until then, **96taking an alternate route home is advisable.** Next in weather: right now it's rainy and cold. **97Tomorrow's weather will be excellent; we're expecting a sunny day with no chance of rain. And that's good, because our local football team plays tomorrow at noon.** Stay tuned for the seven o'clock update.

NCK 뉴스 패트리샤 설리번이 전하는 6시 최신 정보입니다. 먼저 교통 정보입니다. 95샘슨 로의 신호등이 작동하지 않아 오래 지체되고 있습니다. 현재 정비팀이 신호등을 고치고 있으니 한 시간 내에 수리가 완료되리라 예상합니다. 그때까지는 96다른 길로 귀가하는 것이 바람직하겠습니다. 다음은 날씨입니다. 지금 비가 오고 추운데요. 97내일 날씨는 쾌청하겠습니다. 맑은 날씨로 비가 올 확률은 없겠습니다. 내일 정오에 우리 지역 축구팀이 경기를 하니 좋은 소식이네요. 7시에 최신 정보가 있으니 채널 고정하세요.

어휘 traffic light 신호등 lengthy 오랜 maintenance 정비 fix 고치다 repair 수리 be expected to ~하리라 예상되다 alternate 다른 advisable 바람직한 chance 확률 stay tuned 채널을 고정하다

Monday	Tuesday	Wednesday	97 Thursday

월	화	수	97목

95

What is causing a delay?

(A) A holiday parade
(B) A broken traffic light
(C) An icy road
(D) A fallen tree

무엇이 지체를 유발하는가?

(A) 휴일 퍼레이드
(B) 고장 난 신호등
(C) 빙판길
(D) 쓰러진 나무

해설 세부 사항 관련 - 지체의 원인

화자가 초반부에 샘슨 로의 신호등이 작동하지 않아 오래 지체되고 있다 (a traffic light on Samson Road isn't working, and it's causing a lengthy delay)고 말하고 있으므로 정답은 (B)이다.

> ▸▸ Paraphrasing 담화의 isn't working → 정답의 broken

96

What does the speaker advise the listeners to do?

(A) Take an alternate route home
(B) Take public transportation
(C) Drive carefully
(D) Postpone travel

화자는 청자들에게 무엇을 하라고 조언하는가?

(A) 다른 길로 집에 가기
(B) 대중교통 이용하기
(C) 조심해서 운전하기
(D) 여행 미루기

어휘 postpone 미루다

해설 세부 사항 관련 - 화자의 조언

화자가 중반부에 다른 길로 귀가하는 것이 바람직하겠다(taking an alternate route home is advisable)고 말하고 있으므로 정답은 (A)이다.

97

Look at the graphic. When will a sporting event take place?

(A) On Monday
(B) On Tuesday
(C) On Wednesday
(D) On Thursday

시각 정보에 의하면 스포츠 경기는 언제 열리는가?

(A) 월요일
(B) 화요일
(C) 수요일
(D) 목요일

해설 시각 정보 연계 - 스포츠 경기가 열리는 때

화자가 후반부에 내일 날씨는 쾌청하며 맑은 날씨로 비가 올 확률은 없겠다(Tomorrow's weather will be excellent; we're expecting a sunny day with no chance of rain)면서 내일 정오에 지역 축구팀이 경기를 하니 좋은 소식(And that's good, because our local football team plays tomorrow at noon)이라고 말하고 있고, 도표에 따르면 목요일에 날이 맑으므로 목요일에 축구 경기가 열린다는 것을 알 수 있다. 따라서 정답은 (D)이다.

98-100 회의 발췌 + 일정표

> W-Br **98 Welcome to our quarterly meeting. There's a lot of engineering business to discuss.**

> The first item is our Fall Lecture Series, which will start next month. We have an excellent lineup this year. **99 I'm especially excited about our October speaker, who will be talking about bridge design and materials.** OK, the next item on the agenda is elections. **100 We need to choose a new board member, so Luisa is passing around ballots now.**

> 분기 회의에 오신 것을 환영합니다. 엔지니어링 업무에 대해 논의할 게 많습니다. 첫 번째 항목은 다음 달에 시작하는 가을 강의 시리즈입니다. 올해는 구성이 탁월합니다. 저는 특히 10월 강사가 기대되는데요, 다리 설계와 자재에 대해 이야기하실 예정입니다. 자, 다음 안건 항목은 선거입니다. 이사를 새로 뽑아야 해서 루이사가 지금 투표용지를 나누어 드리고 있습니다.

> 어휘 quarterly 분기의 agenda 안건 election 선거 board member 이사 ballot 투표용지

Fall Lecture Series	
Date	**Name**
September 19	Jung-Hoon Kim
99 October 17	Mei Na Zhang
November 14	Maryam Alaoui
December 15	Isamu Nakamura

가을 강의 시리즈	
날짜	**이름**
9월 19일	김정훈
99 10월 17일	메이 나 장
11월 14일	마리암 알라위
12월 15일	이사무 나카무라

98

Who most likely are the listeners?

(A) Librarians
(B) Engineers
(C) Politicians
(D) Biologists

청자들은 누구이겠는가?

(A) 사서
(B) 엔지니어
(C) 정치인
(D) 생물학자

해설 전체 내용 관련 - 청자들의 직업

화자가 도입부에 분기 회의에 오신 것을 환영한다(Welcome to our quarterly meeting)며 엔지니어링 업무에 대해 논의할 게 많다(There's a lot of engineering business to discuss)고 말하고 있는 것으로 보아 회의에 참여한 청자들은 엔지니어임을 알 수 있다. 따라서 정답은 (B)이다.

99

Look at the graphic. Which lecturer is the speaker excited to hear?

(A) Jung-Hoon Kim

(B) Mei Na Zhang

(C) Maryam Alaoui

(D) Isamu Nakamura

시각 정보에 의하면 화자는 어떤 강사의 강연을 기대하는가?

(A) 김정훈

(B) 메이 나 장

(C) 마리암 알라위

(D) 이사무 나카무라

해설 시각 정보 연계 – 화자가 기대하는 강연의 강사

화자가 중반부에 저는 특히 10월 강사가 기대되는데 다리 설계와 자재에 대해 이야기하실 예정(I'm especially excited about our October speaker, who will be talking about bridge design and materials)이라고 말하고 있고, 일정표에 따르면 10월에 강의할 강사는 메이 나 장이므로 정답은 (B)이다.

100

What will the listeners most likely do next?

(A) Vote for a board member

(B) Share a meal

(C) Participate in a workshop

(D) Pay membership fees

청자들은 다음에 무엇을 하겠는가?

(A) 투표로 이사 선출하기

(B) 같이 식사하기

(C) 워크숍 참가하기

(D) 회비 납부하기

어휘 participate in ~에 참가하다

해설 세부 사항 관련 – 청자들이 다음에 할 일

화자가 마지막에 이사를 새로 뽑아야 해서 루이사가 지금 투표용지를 나누어 드리고 있다(We need to ~, so Luisa is passing around ballots now)고 말하고 있는 것으로 보아 청자들은 새로 선출할 이사를 위한 투표를 할 것임을 알 수 있다. 따라서 정답은 (A)이다.

> ▸▸ Paraphrasing 담화의 **choose a new board member**
> → 정답의 **Vote for a board member**

ETS TEST 8

1 (D)	**2** (A)	**3** (B)	**4** (C)	**5** (B)
6 (D)	**7** (C)	**8** (C)	**9** (B)	**10** (B)
11 (B)	**12** (C)	**13** (C)	**14** (A)	**15** (A)
16 (C)	**17** (A)	**18** (B)	**19** (A)	**20** (A)
21 (B)	**22** (B)	**23** (C)	**24** (C)	**25** (A)
26 (A)	**27** (C)	**28** (A)	**29** (B)	**30** (C)
31 (B)	**32** (A)	**33** (B)	**34** (D)	**35** (D)
36 (A)	**37** (C)	**38** (C)	**39** (B)	**40** (D)
41 (A)	**42** (B)	**43** (A)	**44** (A)	**45** (C)
46 (B)	**47** (A)	**48** (A)	**49** (D)	**50** (B)
51 (C)	**52** (D)	**53** (B)	**54** (D)	**55** (C)
56 (A)	**57** (C)	**58** (D)	**59** (B)	**60** (B)
61 (C)	**62** (B)	**63** (B)	**64** (D)	**65** (A)
66 (D)	**67** (B)	**68** (B)	**69** (B)	**70** (D)
71 (A)	**72** (D)	**73** (B)	**74** (C)	**75** (D)
76 (A)	**77** (C)	**78** (D)	**79** (A)	**80** (D)
81 (B)	**82** (B)	**83** (C)	**84** (A)	**85** (C)
86 (D)	**87** (A)	**88** (B)	**89** (D)	**90** (D)
91 (C)	**92** (D)	**93** (B)	**94** (D)	**95** (A)
96 (B)	**97** (C)	**98** (A)	**99** (A)	**100** (D)

PART 1

1 M-Au

(A) The people are decorating a wall.
(B) The man is using a napkin.
(C) One of the women is serving food.
(D) The people are looking at some menus.

(A) 사람들이 벽을 장식하고 있다.
(B) 남자가 냅킨을 사용하고 있다.
(C) 여자들 중 한 명이 음식을 갖다주고 있다.
(D) 사람들이 메뉴를 보고 있다.

해설 2인 이상 등장 사진 – 사람의 동작/상태 묘사

(A) 동사 오답. 사람들이 벽을 장식하고 있는(are decorating a wall) 모습이 아니므로 오답.
(B) 동사 오답. 남자가 냅킨을 사용하고 있는(is using a napkin) 모습이 아니므로 오답.
(C) 사진에 없는 명사를 이용한 오답. 사진에 음식(food)의 모습이 보이지 않으므로 오답.
(D) 정답. 사람들이 메뉴를 보고 있는(are looking at some menus) 모습이므로 정답.

2 W-Br

(A) The woman is standing on a stool.
(B) The woman is replacing a lightbulb.
(C) The woman is installing a bookshelf.
(D) The woman is climbing a staircase.

(A) 여자가 의자 위에 서 있다.
(B) 여자가 전구를 교체하고 있다.
(C) 여자가 책장을 설치하고 있다.
(D) 여자가 계단을 오르고 있다.

어휘 replace 교체하다 lightbulb 전구 install 설치하다
staircase 계단

해설 1인 등장 사진 – 사람의 동작/상태 묘사

(A) 정답. 여자가 의자 위에 서 있는(is standing on a stool) 모습이므로 정답.
(B) 동사 오답. 여자가 전구를 교체하고 있는(is replacing a lightbulb) 모습이 아니므로 오답.
(C) 동사 오답. 여자가 책장을 설치하고 있는(is installing a bookshelf) 모습이 아니므로 오답.
(D) 사진에 없는 명사를 이용한 오답. 사진에 계단(a staircase)의 모습이 보이지 않으므로 오답.

3 W-Am

(A) Some people are planting some trees.
(B) Some people are strolling on a path.
(C) Some people are getting on a train.
(D) Some people are jogging on a beach.

(A) 사람들이 나무를 심고 있다.
(B) 사람들이 길에서 거닐고 있다.
(C) 사람들이 기차를 타고 있다.
(D) 사람들이 해변에서 조깅을 하고 있다.

어휘 stroll 거닐다

해설 2인 이상 등장 사진 – 사람의 동작/상태 묘사

(A) 동사 오답. 사람들이 나무를 심고 있는(are planting some trees) 모습이 아니므로 오답.
(B) 정답. 사람들이 길에서 거닐고 있는(are strolling on a path) 모습이므로 정답.

(C) 사진에 없는 명사를 이용한 오답. 사진에 기차(a train)의 모습이 보이지 않으므로 오답.

(D) 사진에 없는 명사를 이용한 오답. 사진에 해변(a beach)의 모습이 보이지 않으므로 오답.

4 M-Cn

(A) The men are facing each other.
(B) The men are crossing a street.
(C) **The men have stopped on a walkway.**
(D) The men have left their suitcases open.

(A) 남자들이 서로 마주보고 있다.
(B) 남자들이 길을 건너고 있다.
(C) **남자들이 보도에 멈춰 섰다.**
(D) 남자들이 여행 가방을 열어 놓고 있다.

해설 2인 이상 등장 사진 – 사람의 동작/상태 묘사

(A) 동사 오답. 남자들이 서로 마주보고 있는(are facing each other) 모습이 아니므로 오답.

(B) 동사 오답. 남자들이 길을 건너고 있는(are crossing a street) 모습이 아니므로 오답.

(C) 정답. 남자들이 보도에 멈춰 서 있는(have stopped on a walkway) 모습이므로 정답.

(D) 동사 오답. 남자들이 여행 가방을 열어 놓고 있는(have left their suitcases open) 모습이 아니므로 오답.

5 W-Br

(A) Some leaves have been swept into a pile.
(B) **Some furniture has been stacked near a fence.**
(C) An umbrella has fallen on the ground.
(D) A bicycle has been chained to a pole.

(A) 쓸어 모은 나뭇잎들이 쌓여 있다
(B) **가구들이 울타리 근처에 쌓여 있다.**
(C) 우산이 땅에 떨어져 있다.
(D) 자전거가 체인으로 기둥에 묶여 있다.

어휘 pile 쌓아 올린 것 stack 쌓다

해설 사물/풍경 사진 – 풍경 묘사

(A) 동사 오답. 나뭇잎들(some leaves)이 비질이 되어 쌓여 있는(have been swept into a pile) 모습이 아니므로 오답.

(B) 정답. 가구들(some furniture)이 울타리 근처에 쌓여 있는(has been stacked near a fence) 모습이므로 정답.

(C) 사진에 없는 명사를 이용한 오답. 사진에 우산(an umbrella)의 모습이 보이지 않으므로 오답.

(D) 사진에 없는 명사를 이용한 오답. 사진에 자전거(a bicycle)의 모습이 보이지 않으므로 오답.

6 M-Au

(A) A man is walking into a garden area.
(B) The entrance to a building has been blocked by boxes.
(C) One of the women is refilling a copy machine with paper.
(D) **Some notices have been posted to a bulletin board.**

(A) 남자가 정원으로 걸어 들어가고 있다.
(B) 건물 출입구가 상자들로 막혀 있다.
(C) 여자들 중 한 명이 복사기에 종이를 다시 채우고 있다.
(D) **공고문들이 게시판에 붙어 있다.**

어휘 entrance 출입구 bulletin board 게시판

해설 혼합 사진 – 사람/사물/풍경 혼합 묘사

(A) 동사 오답. 정원으로 걸어 들어가고 있는(is walking into a garden area) 남자의 모습이 보이지 않으므로 오답.

(B) 사진에 없는 명사를 이용한 오답. 사진에 상자들(boxes)의 모습이 보이지 않으므로 오답.

(C) 동사 오답. 여자들 중 한 명(one of the women)이 복사기에 종이를 다시 채우고 있는(is refilling a copy machine with paper) 모습이 아니므로 오답.

(D) 정답. 공고문들(some notices)이 게시판에 붙어 있는(have been posted to a bulletin board) 모습이므로 정답.

PART 2

7

W-Br Who is covering Maria's shift at the clinic on Saturday?

M-Au (A) Yes, click on the check box.
(B) Cover the pot on the stove.
(C) **Alexi is going to do it.**

토요일에 병원에서 마리아 대신 누가 근무하나요?
(A) 네, 확인란을 클릭하세요.
(B) 가스레인지 위에 있는 냄비의 뚜껑을 덮으세요.
(C) **알렉시가 할 거예요.**

어휘 shift (교대) 근무

해설 마리아 대신 근무할 사람을 묻는 Who 의문문

(A) Yes/No 불가 오답. Who 의문문에는 Yes/No 응답이 불가능하므로 오답.

(B) 파생어 오답. 질문의 covering과 파생어 관계인 cover를 이용한 오답.

(C) 정답. 토요일에 병원에서 마리아 대신 근무할 사람이 누구인지 묻는 질문에 알렉시가 할 거라고 응답하고 있으므로 정답.

8

M-Cn Would you like to meet the new clients?

W-Am (A) It was made of wood.

(B) The new setup process.

(C) Sure, I have some time right now.

신규 고객들을 만나 보시겠어요?

(A) 그건 나무로 만들었어요.

(B) 새로운 설정 절차예요.

(C) 네, 지금 시간 돼요.

해설 제안/권유의 의문문

(A) 유사 발음 오답. 질문의 would와 부분적으로 발음이 유사한 wood를 이용한 오답.

(B) 단어 반복 오답. 질문의 new를 반복 이용한 오답.

(C) 정답. 신규 고객들을 만나 보겠냐고 제안하는 질문에 네(Sure)라고 대답한 뒤, 지금 시간이 된다며 긍정 답변과 일관된 내용을 덧붙였으므로 정답.

9

M-Cn Here's my presentation proposal.

M-Au (A) About an hour ago.

(B) Thanks, I'll look over it shortly.

(C) Did you like your present?

제 발표 제안서예요.

(A) 한 시간 전쯤이에요.

(B) 고마워요, 금방 훑어볼게요.

(C) 선물 마음에 들었어요?

어휘 proposal 제안(서) shortly 금방

해설 정보 전달의 평서문

(A) 평서문과 상관없는 오답. When 의문문에 대한 응답이므로 오답.

(B) 정답. 제 발표 제안서라고 제안서를 건네주며 말하는 평서문에 고맙다(Thanks)고 대답한 뒤, 금방 훑어보겠다며 제안서의 후속 처리에 대한 내용을 덧붙였으므로 정답.

(C) 유사 발음 오답. 평서문의 presentation과 부분적으로 발음이 유사한 present를 이용한 오답.

10

W-Am Do the city buses stop in the front or the back of the city hall building?

W-Br (A) A city council meeting.

(B) There's a stop in the front.

(C) A monthly bus pass.

시내버스가 시청 앞에 서나요, 아니면 뒤쪽에 서나요?

(A) 시 의회 회의예요.

(B) 앞에 정거장이 있어요.

(C) 한 달 버스 이용권이요.

해설 버스의 정차 위치를 묻는 선택 의문문

(A) 단어 반복 오답. 질문의 city를 반복 이용한 오답.

(B) 정답. 시청 앞과 뒤쪽 중 시내버스가 정차하는 위치를 묻는 질문에 앞에 정거장이 있다며 둘 중 하나를 선택해 응답하고 있으므로 정답.

(C) 파생어 오답. 질문의 buses와 파생어 관계인 bus를 이용한 오답.

11

M-Cn Why is the ceremony being moved indoors?

W-Am (A) It was nice seeing her there.

(B) Because there's rain in the forecast.

(C) I'll hold the door for you.

왜 기념식을 실내로 옮기는 거죠?

(A) 거기서 그녀를 만나 반가웠어요.

(B) 일기 예보에 비가 온다고 해서요.

(C) 제가 문을 잡아 드릴게요.

어휘 forecast 일기 예보

해설 기념식을 실내로 옮기는 이유를 묻는 Why 의문문

(A) 질문과 상관없는 오답. 질문에 3인칭 대명사 she로 지칭할 인물이 언급된 적이 없으므로 오답.

(B) 정답. 기념식을 실내로 옮기는 이유를 묻는 질문에 일기 예보에 비가 온다고 했기 때문이라고 이유를 제시하고 있으므로 정답.

(C) 유사 발음 오답. 질문의 indoors와 부분적으로 발음이 유사한 door를 이용한 오답.

12

W-Br I just love the taste of coffee, don't you?

M-Cn (A) About five minutes ago.

(B) A teaspoon of sugar.

(C) I always drink tea.

저는 커피 맛이 정말 좋아요, 당신은요?

(A) 약 5분 전이에요.

(B) 설탕 1작은술요.

(C) 저는 항상 차를 마셔요.

해설 커피를 좋아하는지 여부를 확인하는 부정 의문문

(A) 질문과 상관없는 오답. When 의문문에 대한 응답이므로 오답.

(B) 연상 단어 오답. 질문의 coffee에서 연상 가능한 sugar를 이용한 오답.

(C) 정답. 커피를 좋아하는지 여부를 확인하는 질문에 저는 항상 차를 마신다며 커피를 좋아하지 않는다고 우회적으로 응답하고 있으므로 정답.

13

W-Am Are you interested in a freelance translation job?

M-Au (A) An interest-free loan.
(B) Please don't touch the walls.
(C) No, I'm too busy these days.

프리랜서 번역 일에 관심 있으세요?
(A) 무이자 대출이요.
(B) 벽에 손 대지 마세요.
(C) 아뇨, 요즘 너무 바빠요.

어휘 translation 번역 interest 이자

해설 프리랜서 번역 일에 관심이 있는지 묻는 Be동사 의문문
(A) 파생어 오답. 질문의 interested와 파생어 관계인 interest를 이용한 오답.
(B) 질문과 상관없는 오답.
(C) 정답. 프리랜서 번역 일에 관심이 있는지 묻는 질문에 아니요(No)라고 대답한 뒤, 요즘 너무 바쁘다며 부정 답변과 일관된 내용을 덧붙였으므로 정답.

14

M-Au Could you send me this month's maintenance schedule?

W-Br (A) I'd be happy to.
(B) No, he left in January.
(C) You should use the stairs.

이번 달 정비 일정 좀 보내 주실래요?
(A) 기꺼이 그러죠.
(B) 아뇨, 그는 1월에 나갔어요.
(C) 계단을 이용하셔야 해요.

어휘 maintenance 정비

해설 부탁/요청의 의문문
(A) 정답. 이번 달 정비 일정을 보내 달라는 요청에 기꺼이 그러겠다고 요청에 응하고 있으므로 정답.
(B) 연상 단어 오답. 질문의 schedule에서 연상 가능한 January를 이용한 오답.
(C) 질문과 상관없는 오답.

15

W-Am Doesn't our firm reimburse travel expenses?

M-Cn (A) Yes, but only flight and hotel.
(B) No, Friday doesn't work.
(C) It's arriving at Gate 206.

우리 회사는 출장 경비를 환급하지 않나요?
(A) 네, 하지만 항공편과 호텔만요.
(B) 아뇨, 금요일은 안 돼요.
(C) 206번 게이트에 도착해요.

어휘 reimburse 환급하다

해설 출장 경비의 환급 여부를 확인하는 부정 의문문
(A) 정답. 회사가 출장 경비를 환급해 주는지 여부를 확인하는 질문에 네(Yes)라고 대답한 뒤, 하지만 항공편과 호텔에 한해서만이라고 부연 설명을 덧붙이고 있고 이는 긍정 답변과 일관된 내용이므로 정답.
(B) 질문과 상관없는 오답.
(C) 연상 단어 오답. 질문의 travel에서 연상 가능한 arriving을 이용한 오답.

16

M-Au I need to stop at the pharmacy on my way to work.

W-Am (A) It's a large dairy farm.
(B) Her résumé was very impressive.
(C) Oh, could you buy something for me?

출근길에 약국에 들러야 해요.
(A) 큰 낙농장이에요.
(B) 그녀의 이력서는 무척 인상 깊었어요.
(C) 아, 뭐 좀 사다 줄래요?

어휘 pharmacy 약국 impressive 인상 깊은

해설 정보 전달의 평서문
(A) 유사 발음 오답. 평서문의 pharmacy와 부분적으로 발음이 유사한 farm을 이용한 오답.
(B) 연상 단어 오답. 평서문의 work에서 연상 가능한 résumé를 이용한 오답.
(C) 정답. 출근길에 약국에 들러야 한다는 평서문에 뭘 좀 사다 줄 수 있는지 물으며 약국 방문 시 해 줄 일을 부탁하고 있으므로 정답.

17

M-Cn Why are we meeting to discuss the budget?

W-Br (A) Have you seen last quarter's sales figures?
(B) Next Tuesday at two o'clock.
(C) I'd like to, but it's expensive.

우리가 왜 예산을 논의하러 모이나요?
(A) 지난 분기 매출액 보셨나요?
(B) 다음 주 화요일 2시예요.
(C) 그러고 싶지만 비싸요.

어휘 budget 예산 sales figures 매출액 expensive 비싼

해설 예산안 논의를 위해 모이는 이유를 묻는 Why 의문문
(A) 정답. 예산을 논의하기 위해 모이는 이유를 묻는 질문에 지난 분기의 매출액을 보았는지 되물으며 우회적으로 단서를 제시하고 있으므로 정답.
(B) 질문과 상관없는 오답. When 의문문에 대한 응답이므로 오답.
(C) 연상 단어 오답. 질문의 budget에서 연상 가능한 expensive를 이용한 오답.

18

W-Am When does your flight land in Los Angeles?
M-Au (A) Yes, it's finished.
(B) I'm flying into San Francisco.
(C) They bought a plot of land.

당신 비행기는 언제 로스앤젤레스에 착륙하나요?
(A) 네, 끝났어요.
(B) 저는 샌프란시스코로 가요.
(C) 그들은 토지 한 필지를 샀어요.

해설 비행기의 착륙 시점을 묻는 When 의문문
(A) Yes/No 불가 오답. When 의문문에는 Yes/No 응답이 불가능하므로 오답.
(B) 정답. 비행기가 로스앤젤레스에 착륙하는 시점을 묻는 질문에 저는 샌프란시스코로 간다며 로스앤젤레스로 가는 비행기를 타지 않는다는 것을 우회적으로 알려 주고 있으므로 정답.
(C) 단어 반복 오답. 질문의 land를 반복 이용한 오답.

19

M-Au How do I sign up for the accounting webinar?
W-Br (A) You can do that online.
(B) No, it's not too far.
(C) I like the Web design.

회계 웹 세미나에 등록하려면 어떻게 해야 하나요?
(A) 온라인으로 하면 돼요.
(B) 아뇨, 그다지 멀지 않아요.
(C) 웹 디자인이 마음에 드네요.

어휘 sign up for ~에 등록하다

해설 웹 세미나 등록 방법을 묻는 How 의문문
(A) 정답. 회계 웹 세미나에 등록하는 방법을 묻는 질문에 온라인으로 하면 된다고 알려 주고 있으므로 정답.
(B) Yes/No 불가 오답. How 의문문에는 Yes/No 응답이 불가능하므로 오답.
(C) 파생어 오답. 질문의 webinar와 파생 관계인 Web을 이용한 오답.

20

M-Cn What kind of food should I bring to the company picnic?
W-Am (A) They hired a catering service this year.
(B) Yes, Barbara will be at the meeting.
(C) A park on Grand Street.

회사 야유회에 어떤 음식을 가져갈까요?
(A) 올해는 급식업체를 고용했어요.
(B) 네, 바바라가 회의에 참석할 거예요.
(C) 그랜드 가에 있는 공원이에요.

해설 야유회에 가져갈 음식의 종류를 묻는 What 의문문
(A) 정답. 회사 야유회에 어떤 음식을 가져갈지 묻는 질문에 올해는 급식 업체를 고용했다며 따로 음식을 가져올 필요가 없다는 것을 간접적으로 알려 주고 있으므로 정답.
(B) Yes/No 불가 오답. What 의문문에는 Yes/No 응답이 불가능하므로 오답.
(C) 연상 단어 오답. 질문의 picnic에서 연상 가능한 park를 이용한 오답.

21

W-Am Where did you put my copy of our project proposal?
W-Br (A) Actually, only the charts are in color.
(B) It's in the file cabinet.
(C) The company newsletter.

제 프로젝트 제안서 사본 어디에 두셨어요?
(A) 실은 차트만 컬러예요.
(B) 파일 캐비닛에 있어요.
(C) 회사 소식지예요.

해설 프로젝트 제안서 사본을 둔 장소를 묻는 Where 의문문
(A) 연상 단어 오답. 질문의 proposal에서 연상 가능한 charts를 이용한 오답.
(B) 정답. 자신의 프로젝트 제안서 사본을 둔 장소를 묻는 질문에 파일 캐비닛에 있다고 구체적인 위치를 알려 주고 있으므로 정답.
(C) 연상 단어 오답. 질문의 copy에서 연상 가능한 newsletter를 이용한 오답.

22

W-Am How many more deliveries are we expecting today?
M-Au (A) It was a great turnout.
(B) I can wait for them if you need to leave.
(C) No, it should be less than that.

오늘 배송이 얼마나 더 올까요?
(A) 참가자 수가 엄청났어요.
(B) 퇴근해야 하시면 제가 기다릴게요.
(C) 아뇨, 그것보다 적을 거예요.

어휘 turnout 참가자 수

해설 남은 배송 건수를 묻는 How many 의문문
(A) 연상 단어 오답. 질문의 How many에서 연상 가능한 turnout을 이용한 오답.
(B) 정답. 오늘 배송이 얼마나 더 올지 묻는 질문에 퇴근해야 하시면 제가 기다리겠다며, 업무가 끝날 시간을 알고 싶어 하는 상대의 의도를 파악해 자신이 일을 대신 처리해 주겠다고 제안하고 있으므로 정답.
(C) Yes/No 불가 오답. How many 의문문에는 Yes/No 응답이 불가능하므로 오답.

23

W-Br When are we handing out the employee survey?

M-Cn (A) On a scale of one to ten.

(B) Have a seat in the front row.

(C) Probably at the end of the quarter.

직원 설문 조사서는 언제 배포하나요?

(A) 1부터 10까지 척도로요.

(B) 앞줄에 앉으세요.

(C) 아마 분기 말일 거예요.

어휘 hand out ~을 배포하다 scale 척도

해설 직원 설문 조사서 배포 시기를 묻는 When 의문문

(A) 연상 단어 오답. 질문의 survey에서 연상 가능한 scale을 이용한 오답.

(B) 질문과 상관없는 오답.

(C) 정답. 직원 설문 조사서를 배포할 시기를 묻는 질문에 아마 분기 말일 것이라고 응답하고 있으므로 정답.

24

M-Au Would you like me to send you samples of the fabrics we have available?

W-Br (A) The hotel room is available.

(B) They built a brick wall around the garden.

(C) I saw the pictures on your Web site.

저희가 갖고 있는 원단 견본을 보내 드릴까요?

(A) 호텔 객실은 이용할 수 있어요.

(B) 그들은 정원 둘레에 벽돌담을 쌓았어요.

(C) 웹사이트에서 사진을 봤어요.

어휘 available 이용할 수 있는

해설 제안/권유의 의문문

(A) 단어 반복 오답. 질문의 available을 반복 이용한 오답.

(B) 유사 발음 오답. 질문의 fabrics와 부분적으로 발음이 유사한 brick을 이용한 오답.

(C) 정답. 갖고 있는 원단 견본을 보내 주겠다고 제안하는 질문에 웹사이트에서 사진을 봤다고 대답하며 우회적으로 제안을 거절하고 있으므로 정답.

25

M-Au Her contract ends next month, doesn't it?

W-Am (A) I'm sure it will get renewed.

(B) Please sign at the bottom.

(C) The employee orientation.

그녀의 계약은 다음 달에 끝나죠?

(A) 분명 갱신될 거예요.

(B) 하단에 서명해 주세요.

(C) 직원 오리엔테이션이에요.

어휘 contract 계약 renew 갱신하다

해설 계약 만료 여부를 확인하는 부가 의문문

(A) 정답. 그녀의 계약이 다음 달에 끝나는지 여부를 확인하는 질문에 분명 갱신될 것이라며 계약 만료 여부와 관련된 내용으로 응답하고 있으

으로 정답.

(B) 연상 단어 오답. 질문의 contract에서 연상 가능한 sign을 이용한 오답.

(C) 질문과 상관없는 오답.

26

W-Br Should we open the store at eight thirty or nine on Saturday?

M-Au (A) Since it's a holiday, let's open later.

(B) I've never been there before.

(C) That sign on the door.

토요일 8시 30분이나 9시에 가게를 열까요?

(A) 휴일이니까 더 늦게 열어요.

(B) 거기는 한 번도 안 가 봤어요.

(C) 문에 붙어 있는 저 표지판이요.

해설 매장의 개점 시간을 묻는 선택 의문문

(A) 정답. 토요일 8시 30분과 9시 중 매장 문을 열 시간을 묻는 질문에 휴일이니까 더 늦게 열자고 두 선택지를 제외한 제3의 안을 제시하고 있으므로 정답.

(B) 연상 단어 오답. 질문의 store에서 연상 가능한 have never been there를 이용한 오답.

(C) 연상 단어 오답. 질문의 open에서 연상 가능한 door를 이용한 오답.

27

M-Cn What kinds of audiobooks do you listen to?

W-Br (A) Could you turn the volume down please?

(B) Yes, an auto repair shop.

(C) I like mystery novels.

어떤 종류의 오디오북을 들으시나요?

(A) 소리 좀 줄여 주시겠어요?

(B) 네, 자동차 정비소예요.

(C) 저는 추리 소설을 좋아해요.

해설 즐겨 듣는 오디오북의 종류를 묻는 What 의문문

(A) 연상 단어 오답. 질문의 listen에서 연상 가능한 volume을 이용한 오답.

(B) Yes/No 불가 오답. What 의문문에는 Yes/No 응답이 불가능하므로 오답.

(C) 정답. 어떤 종류의 오디오북을 듣는지 묻는 질문에 추리 소설을 좋아한다며 구체적으로 응답하고 있으므로 정답.

28

M-Au How long will it take to receive a confirmation e-mail?

W-Br (A) It shouldn't take more than a few minutes.

(B) The construction noise is getting worse.

(C) The color will fade in direct sunlight.

TEST 8

확인 이메일을 받으려면 얼마나 걸릴까요?
(A) 몇 분밖에 안 걸려요.
(B) 공사 소음이 점점 심해지고 있어요.
(C) 직사광선을 받으면 색이 바래요.

어휘 confirmation 확인 fade (색이) 바래다

해설 확인 이메일을 받는 데 걸리는 시간을 묻는 How long 의문문
(A) 정답. 확인 이메일을 받는 데 걸리는 시간을 묻는 질문에 몇 분밖에 안 걸린다고 알려 주고 있으므로 정답.
(B) 유사 발음 오답. 질문의 confirmation과 부분적으로 발음이 유사한 construction을 이용한 오답.
(C) 질문과 상관없는 오답.

29

W-Br Where should I have the workers stack the cases when they arrive?
M-Cn (A) Tomorrow at the latest.
　　 (B) I'll be there to supervise.
　　 (C) It was a challenging legal case.

작업자들이 도착하면 어디에 상자를 쌓으라고 할까요?
(A) 늦어도 내일까지요.
(B) 제가 그리로 가서 지시할게요.
(C) 어려운 소송이었어요.

어휘 supervise 지시하다

해설 상자를 쌓을 장소를 묻는 Where 의문문
(A) 질문과 상관 없는 오답. When 의문문에 대한 응답이므로 오답.
(B) 정답. 인부들이 도착하면 상자를 쌓도록 할 장소를 묻는 질문에 제가 그리로 가서 지시하겠다며 상자 적재 장소에 대해 신경 쓰지 않아도 된다는 것을 우회적으로 표현하고 있으므로 정답.
(C) 유사 발음 오답. 질문의 cases와 부분적으로 발음이 유사한 case를 이용한 오답.

30

W-Am Would offering more specialty breads attract more customers?
M-Cn (A) Please turn off the lights.
　　 (B) No thanks, I've already eaten.
　　 (C) That could get expensive.

특제 빵을 추가 제공하면 고객을 더 많이 끌 수 있을까요?
(A) 불을 꺼 주세요.
(B) 괜찮아요, 저는 벌써 먹었어요.
(C) 그럼 비싸질 수도 있어요.

어휘 attract 끌다

해설 특제 빵의 추가 제공 효과 여부를 묻는 조동사(Would) 의문문
(A) 질문과 상관없는 오답.
(B) 연상 단어 오답. 질문의 breads에서 연상 가능한 eaten을 이용한 오답.

(C) 정답. 특제 빵을 추가 제공하면 더 많은 고객을 유치할 수 있을지 묻는 질문에 그러면 비싸질 수도 있다고 역효과의 가능성에 대해 언급하며 부정적인 의견을 내고 있으므로 정답.

31

W-Am Who's going with you to the technology convention?
M-Au (A) Thanks, I'd appreciate that.
　　 (B) Management budgeted for only one attendee.
　　 (C) It's a great product.

기술 컨벤션에 누구와 함께 가세요?
(A) 고마워요, 그렇게 해 주시면 감사하죠.
(B) 경영진에서 참석자 한 사람 예산만 배분했어요.
(C) 정말 좋은 제품이에요.

어휘 budget 예산을 배분하다 attendee 참석자

해설 컨벤션 동행자를 묻는 Who 의문문
(A) 질문과 상관없는 오답.
(B) 정답. 기술 컨벤션에 함께 갈 사람이 누구인지 묻는 질문에 경영진에서 참석자 한 사람을 위한 예산만 배분했다며 동행자가 없음을 간접적으로 알려 주고 있으므로 정답.
(C) 연상 단어 오답. 질문의 technology에서 연상 가능한 product를 이용한 오답.

PART 3

32-34

M-Cn 32 **Welcome to the Trellisville Museum of Art.** How can I help you?

W-Am 33 **I'd like an all-day pass, please.**

M-Cn Sure. Just so you know, 33 **we've introduced resident and nonresident prices for the museum. Do you happen to be a resident of Trellisville?**

W-Am 33 **Yes, I've lived here for more than twenty years.**

M-Cn Wonderful. 34 **All I need to see is a piece of ID with your address.**

W-Am OK, here's my driver's license.

남 **어서 오세요. 트렐리스빌 미술관입니다.** 어떻게 도와 드릴까요?

여 **일일 이용권 한 장 주세요.**

남 네. 참고로, **박물관에서 거주자와 비거주자 요금을 도입했습니다. 혹시 트렐리스빌 주민이신가요?**

여 네, **여기서 20년 넘게 살고 있어요.**

남 　잘됐어요. **주소가 적힌 신분증만 보여 주세요.**

여 　알겠습니다, 제 운전면허증이에요.

어휘 introduce 도입하다

32

Where are the speakers?

(A) At a museum

(B) At a public library

(C) At an art supply shop

(D) At a botanical garden

화자들은 어디에 있는가?

(A) 박물관

(B) 공공 도서관

(C) 미술용품 매장

(D) 식물원

해설 전체 내용 관련 - 대화의 장소

남자가 첫 대사에서 트렐리스빌 미술관에 오신 것을 환영한다(Welcome to the Trellisville Museum of Art)고 말하고 있으므로 정답은 (A)이다.

33

What type of pass does the woman qualify for?

(A) Student

(B) Local resident

(C) Senior citizen

(D) Tour group

여자는 어떤 종류의 이용권을 받을 자격이 되는가?

(A) 학생

(B) 지역 주민

(C) 어르신

(D) 단체 관광

해설 세부 사항 관련 - 여자가 자격이 되는 이용권

여자가 첫 대사에서 일일 이용권 한 장을 구입하겠다(I'd like an all-day pass, please)고 하자 남자가 박물관에서 거주자와 비거주자 요금을 도입했다(we've introduced resident and nonresident prices for the museum)고 소개하며 혹시 트렐리스빌에 사는지(Do you happen to be a resident of Trellisville?)를 물었고 여자가 네(Yes)라고 대답한 뒤, 여기서 20년 넘게 살고 있다(I've lived here for more than twenty years)고 말하고 있으므로 여자는 지역 거주자 이용권을 받을 자격이 된다는 것을 알 수 있다. 따라서 정답은 (B)이다.

34

What will the man check?

(A) A ticket

(B) A receipt

(C) An event schedule

(D) An identification card

남자는 무엇을 확인할 것인가?

(A) 표

(B) 영수증

(C) 행사 일정

(D) 신분증

해설 세부 사항 관련 - 남자가 확인할 것

남자가 세 번째 대사에서 주소가 적힌 신분증만 보여 주면 된다(All I need to see is a piece of ID with your address)고 말하고 있으므로 정답은 (D)이다.

▸▸ Paraphrasing 대화의 **a piece of ID**
→ 정답의 **An identification card**

35-37

W-Br	Hello, [35] **I'm calling from Dr. Park's office. This is a courtesy reminder that you have an annual health checkup on Friday at two thirty** P.M.
M-Cn	Oh, I completely forgot about that. But... uh... my car needs to be repaired, and I'm taking it to the mechanic on Friday. [36] **Could I reschedule for next week?**
W-Br	Let's see... It looks like we have only one appointment available at ten A.M. next Wednesday.
M-Cn	I'll take it.
W-Br	OK. It's scheduled. When you come, [37] **I hope you'll enjoy our new waiting room. We've recently remodeled it to make it more comfortable.**

여	안녕하세요, 박 선생님 진료실에서 전화드렸습니다. 금요일 오후 2시 30분에 연간 건강 검진을 받으셔야 해서 서비스 차원에서 알려 드립니다.
남	아, 까맣게 잊고 있었네요. 하지만… 어… 차를 수리해야 해서 금요일에 정비사한테 갖다주려고 해요. **다음 주로 일정을 바꿀 수 있을까요?**
여	볼게요… 다음 주 수요일에는 오전 10시에만 예약이 가능한 것 같습니다.
남	그걸로 할게요.
여	네, 예약됐어요. 오시면 새로 바뀐 대기실이 마음에 드시길 바랍니다. 최근에 좀 더 편안하게 개조했거든요.

어휘	courtesy 서비스의 repair 수리하다 comfortable 편안한

35

What type of business does the woman work for?

(A) A construction company

(B) A real estate agency

(C) A law firm

(D) A medical office

여자는 어떤 종류의 업체에서 일하는가?

(A) 건설 회사

(B) 부동산 중개업소

(C) 법무 법인

(D) 진료소

해설 전체 내용 관련 - 여자의 근무지

여자가 첫 대사에서 박 선생님 진료실에서 전화드렸다(I'm calling from Dr. Park's office)면서 금요일 오후 2시 30분에 연간 건강 검진을 받으셔야 해서 서비스 차원에서 알려 드린다(This is a courtesy reminder ~ health checkup on Friday at two thirty P.M.)고 말하는 것으로 보아 병원에서 일하고 있음을 알 수 있다. 따라서 정답은 (D)이다.

36

What does the man ask the woman to do?

(A) Reschedule an appointment

(B) Forward a telephone call

(C) Send an invoice

(D) Provide a refund

남자는 여자에게 무엇을 해 달라고 요청하는가?

(A) 예약 일정 변경하기

(B) 전화 돌리기

(C) 송장 발송하기

(D) 환불해 주기

해설 세부 사항 관련 - 남자의 요청 사항

남자가 첫 대사에서 여자에게 다음 주로 일정을 바꿀 수 있을지(Could I reschedule for next week?) 묻고 있으므로 정답은 (A)이다.

37

What does the woman say a business has recently done?

(A) It has updated a payment system.

(B) It has purchased new equipment.

(C) It has renovated a room.

(D) It has hired temporary staff.

여자는 업체가 최근에 무엇을 했다고 말하는가?

(A) 결제 시스템을 개선했다.

(B) 새로운 장비를 구입했다.

(C) 방을 개조했다.

(D) 임시직 직원을 채용했다.

어휘 temporary 임시의

해설 세부 사항 관련 - 여자가 최근에 업체가 했다고 말하는 일

여자가 마지막 대사에서 새로 바뀐 대기실이 마음에 들길 바란다(I hope

you'll enjoy our new waiting room)며 최근에 좀 더 편안하게 개조했다(We've recently remodeled it to make it more comfortable)고 말하고 있으므로 정답은 (C)이다.

> ▸▸ Paraphrasing   대화의 remodeled
> → 정답의 renovated

38-40

W-Am	Excuse me, sir. Are you part of the road crew that's working here? I'm wondering why I can't turn on to this street.
M-Cn	**38 The street will be blocked off until five P.M. while we put in some charging stations for electric cars.** Once they're installed, people will be able to charge their cars while they're parked here.
W-Am	But **39 I'm already late for a recording session, and this street has the closest parking spots to the music studio. Plus, I have to carry my guitars there.**
M-Cn	I'm sorry, but **40 if you go to the next block, there are some open spots there.**

여	실례합니다. 여기서 작업 중인 도로 작업반이신가요? 왜 이 도로에 들어올 수 없는지 궁금해서요.
남	전기차 충전소를 설치하는 동안 오후 5시까지 도로가 차단됩니다. 충전소가 설치되면 여기 주차하는 동안 차를 충전할 수 있게 됩니다.
여	하지만 저는 이미 녹음 시간에 늦었고, 음악 스튜디오에서 가장 가까운 주차장이 이 도로에 있어요. 게다가 거기까지 기타들을 들고 가야 하거든요.
남	죄송하지만, 다음 블록으로 가시면 비어 있는 곳이 몇 군데 있어요.

어휘	install 설치하다

38

Why is a street blocked off?

(A) A tree is being removed.

(B) A car is being towed.

(C) Some charging stations are being installed.

(D) Some holes are being filled.

도로는 왜 차단되었는가?

(A) 나무가 제거되고 있다.

(B) 차가 견인되고 있다.

(C) 충전소가 설치되고 있다.

(D) 구덩이를 메우고 있다.

해설 세부 사항 관련 - 도로가 차단된 이유

남자가 첫 대사에서 전기차 충전소를 설치하는 동안 오후 5시까지 도로가 차단된다(The street will be blocked off until five P.M. while we put in some charging stations for electric cars)고 말하고 있으므로 정답은 (C)이다.

> ▸▸ **Paraphrasing** 대화의 **put in** → 정답의 **installed**

39
What most likely is the woman's profession?
(A) Auto mechanic
(B) Musician
(C) Park ranger
(D) Teacher

여자의 직업은 무엇이겠는가?
(A) 자동차 정비사
(B) 음악가
(C) 공원 경비원
(D) 교사

해설 전체 내용 관련 - 여자의 직업

여자가 두 번째 대사에서 저는 이미 녹음 시간에 늦었고 음악 스튜디오에서 가장 가까운 주차장이 이 도로에 있다(I'm already late for a recording session ~ to the music studio)며 게다가 거기까지 기타들을 들고 가야 한다(Plus, I have to carry my guitars there)고 말하는 것으로 보아 정답은 (B)이다.

40
What does the man suggest the woman do?
(A) Purchase an electric car
(B) File a complaint
(C) Postpone a meeting
(D) Drive to another location

남자는 여자에게 무엇을 하라고 권하는가?
(A) 전기차 구입하기
(B) 민원 제기하기
(C) 회의 연기하기
(D) 운전해서 다른 장소로 가기

해설 세부 사항 관련 - 남자의 권장 사항

남자가 마지막 대사에서 다음 블록으로 가시면 비어 있는 곳이 몇 군데 있다(if you go to the next block, there are some open spots there)고 말하고 있으므로 정답은 (D)이다.

> ▸▸ **Paraphrasing** 대화의 **go to the next block**
> → 정답의 **Drive to another location**

41-43

M-Au	Good morning, Ms. Osman. I arrived a little early, so ⁴¹**I already swept the aisles and I'm in the process of restocking the frozen foods section. Is there anything else you need me to do to get the store ready for the day?**

W-Br	⁴²,⁴³**Can you also open up the second cash register?**
M-Au	Sure, ⁴³**I'll do that as soon as I finish restocking the frozen vegetables.**
W-Br	OK... Remember, though, we open at seven.
M-Au	Got it. I just have a few boxes of vegetables left.

남	안녕하세요, 오스만 씨. 제가 조금 일찍 도착해서 벌써 통로는 쓸었고 냉동식품 코너를 다시 채워 넣고 있어요. 오늘 매장을 준비하기 위해 제가 해야 할 일이 또 있나요?
여	두 번째 금전 등록기도 열어 두시겠어요?
남	그럼요, 냉동 채소를 다 다시 채워 넣으면 바로 할게요.
여	좋아요… 하지만 기억하세요. 우리는 7시에 문을 열어요.
남	알겠습니다. 채소 몇 상자만 남았어요.

어휘 restock 다시 채워 넣다   cash register 금전 등록기

41
Where do the speakers work?
(A) At a grocery store
(B) At a cooking school
(C) At a restaurant
(D) At a food-processing plant

화자들은 어디에서 일하는가?
(A) 식료품점
(B) 요리 학교
(C) 식당
(D) 식품 가공 공장

해설 전체 내용 관련 - 화자들의 근무지

남자가 첫 대사에서 벌써 통로는 쓸었고 냉동식품 코너를 다시 채워 넣고 있다(I already swept the aisles and I'm in the process of restocking the frozen foods section)며 오늘 매장을 준비하기 위해 제가 해야 할 일이 또 있는지(Is there anything else you need me to do to get the store ready for the day?) 묻고 있는 것으로 보아 화자들은 식료품 매장에서 일하고 있음을 알 수 있다. 따라서 정답은 (A)이다.

42
What does the woman ask the man to do?
(A) Make some deliveries
(B) Open a cash register
(C) Label some products
(D) Clean some machinery

여자는 남자에게 무엇을 해 달라고 요청하는가?
(A) 배송하기
(B) 금전 등록기 열기
(C) 제품에 라벨 붙이기
(D) 기계 청소하기

여	그런 것 같아요. 하지만 **경쟁이 꽤 치열해요. 이 그래픽 디자이너직에 자격 있는 사람들이 많이 지원해서 다음 면접을 진짜 잘 봐야 해요.**
남	틀림없이 잘 하실 거예요. **2차 인터뷰가 언제죠?**
여	**목요일이에요. 제가 공장에 가면 그쪽에서 안내할 거예요.**

| 어휘 | competition 경쟁   qualified 자격 있는 |

43

What does the woman imply when she says, "we open at seven"?

(A) The man must work quickly.

(B) The man should take a break.

(C) The man unlocked the doors too early.

(D) The man is mistaken about a schedule.

여자가 "우리는 7시에 문을 열어요"라고 말하는 의도는 무엇인가?

(A) 남자가 빨리 일해야 한다.

(B) 남자가 쉬어야 한다.

(C) 남자가 문을 너무 일찍 열었다.

(D) 남자가 일정을 착각하고 있다.

해설 화자의 의도 파악 – 우리는 7시에 문을 연다는 말의 의도

앞에서 여자가 두 번째 금전 등록기도 열어 줄 수 있는지(Can you also open up the second cash register?) 묻자 남자가 냉동 채소를 다 다시 채워 넣으면 바로 하겠다(I'll do that as soon as I finish restocking the frozen vegetables)고 대답한 데 대해 여자가 인용문을 언급하고 있는 것으로 보아, 매장 개점 시간이 얼마 남지 않았으므로 여자가 요청한 일을 서둘러 끝내라고 재촉하려는 의도로 한 말임을 알 수 있다. 따라서 정답은 (A)이다.

44-46

M-Cn	[44]**How'd the interview for the graphic designer position with Hackley Motors go?**
W-Am	[44]**Very well! They called me back for a second interview.**
M-Cn	Wow, they must've really liked you.
W-Am	I think so. But [45]**there's quite a bit of competition. A lot of qualified people are applying for this graphic designer position, so I really need to do well in the next round of interviews.**
M-Cn	I'm sure you'll do great. [46]**When's the second interview?**
W-Am	[46]**Thursday. I'll be visiting the factory and they'll show me around.**

남	**해클리 자동차 그래픽 디자이너직 면접은 어떻게 됐어요?**
여	**아주 잘 봤어요! 2차 면접을 보라고 다시 전화가 왔어요.**
남	와, 정말 마음에 들었나 봐요.

44

Who most likely is the woman?

(A) A graphic designer

(B) A sales person

(C) An auto mechanic

(D) A human resources executive

여자는 누구이겠는가?

(A) 그래픽 디자이너

(B) 영업 사원

(C) 자동차 정비사

(D) 인사 담당 임원

해설 전체 내용 관련 – 여자의 직업

남자가 첫 대사에서 해클리 자동차 그래픽 디자이너직 면접이 어떻게 됐는지(How'd the interview for the graphic designer position with Hackley Motors go?) 묻자 여자가 아주 잘 봤다(Very well!)며 2차 면접을 보라고 다시 전화가 왔다(They called me back for a second interview)고 대답하고 있는 것으로 보아 여자는 그래픽 디자이너직 구직자이므로 정답은 (A)이다.

45

Why is the woman worried she might not be offered a job?

(A) She missed an application deadline.

(B) She has limited experience.

(C) She is competing with other qualified candidates.

(D) She did not perform well in a telephone interview.

여자는 왜 일자리를 제안받지 못할까 봐 걱정하는가?

(A) 지원서 접수 마감일을 놓쳤다.

(B) 경력이 부족하다.

(C) 다른 적격 후보자들과 경쟁하고 있다.

(D) 전화 면접을 잘 보지 못했다.

해설 세부 사항 관련 – 여자가 일자리를 제안받지 못할까 봐 걱정하는 이유

여자가 두 번째 대사에서 경쟁이 꽤 치열하다(there's quite a bit of competition)며 이 그래픽 디자이너직에 자격 있는 사람들이 많이 지원해서 다음 면접을 진짜 잘 봐야 한다(A lot of qualified people are applying ~ the next round of interviews)고 말하는 것으로 보아 정답은 (C)이다.

46

What does the woman say she will do on Thursday?

(A) Call a recruiter
(B) Tour a factory
(C) Sign a contract
(D) Update a résumé

여자는 목요일에 무엇을 할 것이라고 말하는가?

(A) 채용 담당자에게 전화
(B) 공장 견학
(C) 계약 체결
(D) 이력서 수정

해설 세부 사항 관련 - 여자가 목요일에 할 것이라고 말하는 일

남자가 세 번째 대사에서 2차 인터뷰가 언제인지(When's the second interview?) 묻자 여자가 목요일(Thursday)이라고 대답하며 제가 공장에 가면 그쪽에서 안내할 것(I'll be visiting the factory and they'll show me around)이라고 말하고 있으므로 정답은 (B)이다.

▸▸ Paraphrasing 대화의 **show ~ around** → 정답의 **Tour**

47-49 3인 대화

W-Am	**⁴⁷Welcome to Sandelman's Rare Books.** How can I help you?
M-Au	Hi, **⁴⁸I have this first edition book that I'd like to know the value of. I called yesterday to confirm that you do book appraisals here**…
W-Am	Yes, my colleague, Margaret, assesses the value of books.
W-Br	Hi, ⁴⁹I'm Margaret. I see that your book is in… fair condition. Where do you store it?
M-Au	⁴⁹I keep it on my bookcase at home.
W-Br	I ask because it looks like it's got some sun damage. ⁴⁹**It's a good idea to use a plastic cover to protect a book like this from exposure to the sunlight. We have some near the entrance** with the other maintenance products, if you're interested.

여1	어서 오세요. 샌들맨 희귀 도서입니다. 어떻게 도와 드릴까요?
남	안녕하세요. 저한테 이 초판본이 있는데 가치를 알고 싶어요. 여기서 도서 감정을 하는지 확인하려고 어제 전화했어요…
여1	네, 제 동료 마가렛이 책의 가치를 평가합니다.
여2	안녕하세요. 마가렛이에요. 책 상태가… 괜찮아 보이네요. 어디에 보관하시나요?
남	집에 있는 책장에 보관해요.
여2	햇빛에 좀 손상된 것 같아서 여쭤봤어요. 이런 책은 햇빛에 노출되지 않도록 비닐 덮개를 씌우는 게 좋아요. 관심 있으시면 몇 가지가 입구 근처에 다른 관리 제품들과 같이 있어요.

어휘 appraisal 평가, 감정 colleague 동료 protect 보호하다 exposure 노출 maintenance 유지

47

Where does the conversation take place?

(A) At a bookshop
(B) At a supermarket
(C) At a furniture store
(D) At a craft store

대화는 어디에서 이루어지는가?

(A) 서점
(B) 슈퍼마켓
(C) 가구점
(D) 공예품 매장

해설 전체 내용 관련 - 대화의 장소

첫 번째 여자가 첫 대사에서 샌들맨 희귀 도서에 오신 것을 환영한다(Welcome to Sandelman's Rare Books)고 말하는 것으로 보아 대화가 이루어지고 있는 장소는 도서를 다루는 곳이므로 정답은 (A)이다.

48

What is the purpose of the man's visit?

(A) To have an item appraised
(B) To film a commercial
(C) To deliver some supplies
(D) To conduct some repairs

남자가 방문한 목적은 무엇인가?

(A) 물품을 평가받으려고
(B) 광고를 촬영하려고
(C) 물품을 배송하려고
(D) 수리하려고

어휘 appraise 평가하다 commercial 광고

해설 세부 사항 관련 - 남자의 방문 목적

남자가 첫 대사에서 저한테 이 초판본이 있는데 가치를 알고 싶다(I have this first edition book that I'd like to know the value of)며 여기서 도서 감정을 하는지 확인하려고 전화했다(I called yesterday to confirm that you do book appraisals here)고 말하는 것으로 보아 자신이 소장하고 있는 초판본 도서를 감정받기 위해 방문한 것임을 알 수 있다. 따라서 정답은 (A)이다.

49

According to Margaret, what can be found by the entrance?

(A) A shopping basket
(B) A brochure
(C) A light switch
(D) A plastic cover

마가렛의 말에 따르면, 입구 옆에서 무엇을 찾을 수 있는가?
(A) 장바구니
(B) 안내책자
(C) 조명 스위치
(D) 비닐 덮개

해설 세부 사항 관련 - 마가렛이 입구 옆에서 찾을 수 있다고 말하는 것
두 번째 여자가 첫 대사에서 마가렛(I'm Margaret)이라고 자신을 소개
하면서 책의 상태가 괜찮아 보인다(I see that your book is in… fair
condition)며 어디에 보관하는지(Where do you store it?) 물었고 남자
가 집에 있는 책장에 보관한다(I keep it on my bookcase at home)고
대답하자 뒤이어 마가렛이 이런 책은 햇빛에 노출되지 않도록 비닐 덮개
를 씌우는 게 좋다(It's a good idea to use a plastic cover ~ to the
sunlight)고 조언하면서 입구 근처에 몇 가지가 비치되어 있다(We have
some near the entrance)고 알려 주고 있으므로 정답은 (D)이다.

50-52

W-Br	Hi. ⁵⁰**I'm here to pick up a package. I found this notice on my door indicating I missed a delivery.**
M-Cn	OK, ⁵⁰**let me check my computer**. Hmm, apparently the postal carrier tried to deliver it three times, but no one was home to sign for it.
W-Br	Oh no! ⁵¹**I've been away on business the last two weeks**. I just saw the notice yesterday.
M-Cn	I'm sorry, but it's already been returned to the sender.
W-Br	I understand. Is there any way to avoid this in the future?
M-Cn	⁵²**I'd suggest downloading our mobile application.** Then you can track packages and receive delivery notifications online.

여	안녕하세요. **소포를 찾으러 왔어요. 문에 제가 배달을 못 받았다는 안내장이 붙어 있었어요.**
남	알겠습니다, **컴퓨터로 확인해 볼게요.** 음, 집배원이 세 번이나 배달하려고 했는데 집에 수령했다고 서명할 사람이 아무도 없었나 보네요.
여	아 이런! **지난 2주 동안 출장을 갔거든요.** 어제야 안내장을 봤네요.
남	죄송하지만 이미 발송인에게 반송됐네요.
여	알겠습니다. 앞으로 이런 일을 피할 방법이 있을까요?
남	**모바일 애플리케이션을 다운로드하세요.** 그러면 온라인으로 소포를 추적하고 배달 통지를 받을 수 있습니다.

어휘	apparently 보아하니 sign for ~을 수령했다고 서명하다 avoid 피하다 notification 통지

50

Where does the man most likely work?

(A) At a hotel
(B) At a post office
(C) At a travel agency
(D) At an office supply store

남자는 어디에서 일하겠는가?
(A) 호텔
(B) 우체국
(C) 여행사
(D) 사무용품점

해설 전체 내용 관련 - 남자의 근무지
여자가 첫 대사에서 소포를 찾으러 왔다(I'm here to pick up a
package)며 문에 제가 배달을 못 받았다는 안내장이 붙어 있었다(I
found this notice on my door indicating I missed a delivery)고 하
자 남자가 컴퓨터로 확인해 보겠다(let me check my computer)며 여
자를 응대하고 있는 것으로 보아 정답은 (B)이다.

51

Why was the woman unavailable for two weeks?

(A) She was on vacation.
(B) She was moving to a new location.
(C) She was traveling for business.
(D) She was without phone service.

여자는 왜 2주 동안 없었는가?
(A) 휴가 중이었다.
(B) 새로운 장소로 이사 중이었다.
(C) 출장 중이었다.
(D) 전화가 끊겼다.

해설 세부 사항 관련 - 여자가 2주 동안 없었던 이유
여자가 두 번째 대사에서 지난 2주 동안 출장을 가 있었다(I've been
away on business the last two weeks)고 말하고 있으므로 정답은
(C)이다.

▶▶ Paraphrasing	대화의 **have been away on business** → 정답의 **was traveling for business**

52

What does the man recommend doing?

(A) Filing a complaint
(B) Visiting another location
(C) Making reservations online
(D) Downloading a mobile application

남자는 무엇을 하라고 권하는가?
(A) 민원 제기
(B) 다른 장소 방문
(C) 온라인으로 예약
(D) 모바일 애플리케이션 다운로드

해설 세부 사항 관련 - 남자의 추천 사항

남자가 마지막 대사에서 모바일 애플리케이션을 다운로드하라(I'd suggest downloading our mobile application)고 제안하고 있으므로 정답은 (D)이다.

53-55 3인 대화

> M-Cn **53Great work, both of you, on the new visitor brochure for Silverton. The pictures you selected for it really highlight the town nicely.**
>
> W-Am Thanks. Now we can spend time focusing on other ways that our committee can promote tourism in Silverton. **54,55Priyanka and I have a suggestion.**
>
> W-Br Right. **54We think it'd be a good idea to offer walking tours of the city center as a way to teach visitors about our town's history. 55We could ask for volunteers to run the tours. I can post a notice about it around town.**
>
> 남 실버톤 방문자를 위한 새 안내 책자를 만드느라 두 분 다 수고 많으셨습니다. 여러분이 그것을 위해 선택한 사진들이 정말 도시를 멋지게 부각시키고 있어요.
>
> 여1 감사합니다. 이제 우리는 위원회가 실버톤 관광업을 진흥할 수 있는 다른 방법들에 집중하면서 시간을 보낼 수 있겠어요. **프리얀카와 제가 생각한 게 있어요.**
>
> 여2 맞아요. **방문객들에게 우리 도시의 역사를 가르치는 방안으로 도심 도보 관광을 제공하는 게 좋을 것 같아요. 자원봉사자들에게 관광을 진행하라고 요청할 수도 있고요. 제가 시내 곳곳에 공지를 붙일 수 있어요.**
>
> 어휘 brochure 안내책자

53

According to the speakers, what has recently been completed?

(A) A map

(B) A brochure

(C) A hiking trail

(D) A memorial statue

화자들의 말에 따르면, 최근에 무엇이 완성되었는가?

(A) 지도

(B) 안내 책자

(C) 등산로

(D) 기념 동상

어휘 memorial 기념하는

해설 세부 사항 관련 - 화자들이 최근에 완성되었다고 말하는 것

남자가 첫 대사에서 실버톤 방문자를 위한 새 안내 책자를 만드느라 두 분 다 수고 많았다(Great work, both of you, on the new visitor

54

What do the women suggest doing?

(A) Expanding parking areas

(B) Organizing an art festival

(C) Changing a bus route

(D) Offering walking tours

여자들은 무엇을 하자고 제안하는가?

(A) 주차 구역 확장

(B) 예술제 개최

(C) 버스 노선 변경

(D) 도보 관광 제공

해설 세부 사항 관련 - 여자들의 제안 사항

첫 번째 여자가 첫 대사에서 프리얀카와 제가 생각한 게 있다(Priyanka and I have a suggestion)고 했고 뒤이어 두 번째 여자가 방문객들에게 우리 도시의 역사를 가르치는 방안으로 도심 도보 관광을 제공하는 게 좋을 것 같다(We think it'd be a good idea ~ about our town's history)고 말하고 있으므로 정답은 (D)이다.

55

Why will Priyanka post a public notice?

(A) To identify ticket sale locations

(B) To encourage people to vote

(C) To request volunteers

(D) To announce some winners

프리얀카는 왜 공고를 붙이겠는가?

(A) 티켓 판매 장소를 표시하려고

(B) 사람들에게 투표를 독려하려고

(C) 자원봉사자들을 요청하려고

(D) 수상자를 발표하려고

해설 세부 사항 관련 - 프리얀카가 공고를 붙이려는 이유

첫 번째 여자가 첫 대사에서 프리얀카와 제가 생각한 게 있다(Priyanka and I have a suggestion)고 한 뒤 두 번째 여자가 말을 이어받고 있으므로 두 번째 여자가 프리얀카임을 알 수 있고, 프리얀카가 자원봉사자들에게 관광을 진행하라고 요청할 수도 있다(We could ask for volunteers to run the tours)며 제가 시내 곳곳에 공지를 붙이겠다(I can post a notice about it around town)고 말하고 있으므로 공지 게시는 자원봉사자들을 구하기 위한 것임을 알 수 있다. 따라서 정답은 (C)이다.

> ▸▸Paraphrasing 대화의 ask for → 정답의 request

56-58

> W-Am Enzo, **56have you looked at the latest production numbers for the Shimmer Bright moisturizing lotion?**

M-Cn	Yes, our production is up by nearly twenty percent. And not only for the lotion, but also for some of the lip glosses and nail polishes.
W-Am	That's great to hear! I was wondering how it was going since we upgraded the assembly line machinery.
M-Cn	⁵⁷ **The new machinery has definitely sped up the manufacturing process.**
W-Am	I have a meeting tomorrow with the management team. ⁵⁸**Do you think you could prepare a status report that I could share at the meeting?**
M-Cn	I'd be happy to.

여	엔조 씨, **시머 브라이트 보습 로션 최근 생산 수치 보셨어요?**
남	네, 생산량이 20퍼센트 가까이 늘었어요. 게다가 로션뿐 아니라 립글로스와 매니큐어도요.
여	반가운 소식이네요! 조립 라인 기계를 개선한 뒤로 어떻게 돼 가는지 궁금했거든요.
남	**새 기계가 확실히 제조 공정 속도를 높였어요.**
여	내일 경영진과 회의가 있는데요. **회의에서 공유하게끔 현황 보고서를 준비해 주실 수 있을까요?**
남	기꺼이 할게요.

어휘	nail polish 매니큐어 status report 현황 보고서

56

Where do the speakers most likely work?

(A) At a cosmetics company
(B) At a home appliance outlet
(C) At an art supply store
(D) At a textile factory

화자들은 어디에서 일하겠는가?

(A) **화장품 회사**
(B) 가전제품 판매점
(C) 미술용품 매장
(D) 직물 공장

해설 전체 내용 관련 - 화자들의 근무지

여자가 첫 대사에서 시머 브라이트 보습 로션의 최근 생산 수치를 보았는지(have you looked at the latest production numbers for the Shimmer Bright moisturizing lotion?) 물으며 화장품 생산과 관련된 내용을 언급하고 있는 것으로 보아 정답은 (A)이다.

> ▸ Paraphrasing 대화의 **moisturizing lotion**
> → 정답의 **cosmetics**

57

What does the man say about some new machinery?

(A) It requires very little maintenance.
(B) It is easy to learn how to use.
(C) **It has made a process faster.**
(D) It has not been installed yet.

남자는 새 기계에 대해 무엇이라고 말하는가?

(A) 정비가 거의 필요 없다.
(B) 사용법을 배우기 쉽다.
(C) **공정 속도를 높였다.**
(D) 아직 설치되지 않았다.

해설 세부 사항 관련 - 남자가 새 기계에 대해 말하는 것

남자가 두 번째 대사에서 새 기계가 확실히 제조 공정 속도를 높였다 (The new machinery has definitely sped up the manufacturing process)고 말하고 있으므로 정답은 (C)이다.

> ▸ Paraphrasing 대화의 **has ~ sped up the manufacturing process** → 정답의 **has made a process faster**

58

What does the woman ask the man to prepare?

(A) A price list
(B) A meeting invitation
(C) A handbook
(D) A report

여자는 남자에게 무엇을 준비하라고 요청하는가?

(A) 가격표
(B) 회의 초대장
(C) 편람
(D) **보고서**

해설 세부 사항 관련 - 여자가 남자에게 준비하라고 요청한 것

여자가 세 번째 대사에서 회의에서 공유하게끔 현황 보고서를 준비해 줄수 있겠냐고(Do you think you could prepare a status report that I could share at the meeting?) 요청하고 있으므로 정답은 (D)이다.

59-61

M-Au	Hi Mary. ⁵⁹**I'm sorry I didn't make it to the biotech conference last week. I needed to finish an important project.**
W-Br	No problem. You know, I met a reporter at the conference.... She's really interested in our company's new medical device. She's going to interview me about it this week for a science magazine.
M-Au	⁶⁰**That'll make the marketing department happy.** You should reach out to one of our coworkers in that department.
W-Br	That's a good idea. I'll talk to Megumi Ito.

M-Au So ⁶¹how did your conference presentation go? I know you were worried about attendance. You said you probably prepared too many materials for a small crowd.

W-Br Actually, I ran out of handouts!

M-Au Nice!

남 안녕 메리. 지난주 생명 공학 회의에 참석하지 못해서 죄송해요. 중요한 프로젝트를 끝내야 했어요.

여 괜찮아요. 저기, 회의에서 기자를 만났는데요…. 우리 회사의 새 의료 기기에 관심이 많았어요. 과학 잡지에 실으려고 이번 주에 그 건으로 절 인터뷰하겠대요.

남 마케팅부에서 좋아하겠네요. 그 부서 동료 한 명에게 연락해 보세요.

여 좋은 생각이에요. 메구미 이토에게 얘기할게요

남 그래서 회의 발표는 어땠어요? 참석자 수를 걱정하셨다는 거 알아요. 인원은 적은데 자료를 너무 많이 준비한 것 같다고 얘기하셨잖아요.

여 실은 유인물이 다 떨어졌어요!

남 잘됐네요!

어휘 device 기기, 장치 reach out to ~에게 연락하다
attendance 참가자 수 run out of ~이 다 떨어지다

59

Why did the man miss a conference?

(A) His plane was delayed.

(B) He was busy with a project.

(C) He was not feeling well.

(D) He missed a registration deadline.

남자는 왜 회의에 빠졌는가?
(A) 비행기가 연착했다.
(B) 프로젝트 때문에 바빴다.
(C) 몸이 안 좋았다.
(D) 등록 마감일을 놓쳤다.

해설 세부 사항 관련 - 남자가 회의에 빠진 이유

남자가 첫 대사에서 지난주 생명 공학 회의에 참석하지 못해서 죄송하다(I'm sorry I didn't make it to the biotech conference last week)며 중요한 프로젝트를 끝내야 했다(I needed to finish an important project)고 이유를 말하고 있으므로 정답은 (B)이다.

▸▸ Paraphrasing 대화의 needed to finish an important project → 정답의 was busy with a project

60

What does the man recommend the woman do?

(A) Edit a press release

(B) Consult with a coworker

(C) Hire a marketing expert

(D) Review a departmental budget

남자는 여자에게 무엇을 하라고 권하는가?
(A) 보도 자료 편집
(B) 동료와 의논
(C) 마케팅 전문가 채용
(D) 부서 예산 검토

어휘 press release 보도 자료 expert 전문가

해설 세부 사항 관련 - 남자의 권유 사항

남자가 두 번째 대사에서 마케팅부에서 좋아하겠다(That'll make the marketing department happy)며 그 부서의 동료 한 명에게 연락해 보라(You should reach out to one of our coworkers in that department)고 말하고 있으므로 정답은 (B)이다.

▸▸ Paraphrasing 대화의 reach out to one of our coworkers → 정답의 Consult with a coworker

61

What does the woman mean when she says, "I ran out of handouts"?

(A) She was unprepared for a presentation.

(B) A coworker made an error.

(C) A presentation was well attended.

(D) Some information can only be found online.

여자가 "유인물이 다 떨어졌어요"라고 말하는 의도는 무엇인가?
(A) 그녀는 발표 준비가 되지 않았다.
(B) 동료가 실수했다.
(C) 발표회에 참석자가 많았다.
(D) 일부 정보는 온라인에서만 찾을 수 있다.

해설 화자의 의도 파악 - 유인물이 다 떨어졌다는 말의 의도

앞에서 남자가 회의 발표는 어땠는지(how did your conference presentation go?) 물으며 여자가 참석자 수를 걱정했다는 것을 안다(I know you were worried about attendance)고 했고 인원은 적은데 자료를 너무 많이 준비한 것 같다고 얘기했었다(You said you probably prepared too many materials for a small crowd)고 말하자 여자가 인용문을 언급한 것으로 보아, 우려했던 것과는 달리 유인물이 소진될 정도로 발표회의 참석률이 좋았다고 말하려는 것임을 알 수 있다. 따라서 정답은 (C)이다.

62-64 대화 + 열차 시간표

W-Am Hi, Alberto. ⁶²I couldn't get us tickets next to each other, but we can ask the train conductor about switching our seats when we get on board.

M-Au Oh, good. ⁶³That way we can prepare for our meeting this afternoon. These could be really important clients for us. If they sign this contract, it'll definitely expand our business in that region.

W-Am You're right. I'll ask right away if we can switch. Let's see... ⁶⁴our train leaves at

	nine twenty-four. **Why don't we head over to the platform now?**
M-Au	Sounds good.

여	안녕, 알베르토. 나란히 붙어 있는 표를 못 구했어요. 하지만 탈 때 자리 교환에 관해 승무원에게 물어보면 돼요.
남	아, 잘됐네요. 그러면 **오늘 오후에 있을 회의를 준비할 수 있어요. 이들은 우리한테 정말 중요한 고객이 될 수도 있어요.** 그들이 이 계약을 체결한다면, 틀림없이 그 지역에서 우리 사업이 확장될 거예요.
여	맞아요. 바꿀 수 있는지 바로 물어볼게요. 어디 보자… **우리 기차는 9시 24분에 출발해요. 지금 플랫폼으로 가는 게 어때요?**
남	좋아요.

어휘	conductor 승무원 sign a contract 계약을 체결하다 definitely 틀림없이 expand 확장하다

Destination	Platform	Departure time
Shanghai	3	8:28
Hong Kong	9	8:47
Beijing	12	9:15
Guangzhou	64 17	9:24

목적지	플랫폼	출발 시간
상하이	3	8:28
홍콩	9	8:47
베이징	12	9:15
광저우	64 17	9:24

62

What will the speakers ask about?

(A) A refund

(B) A seat change

(C) Food options

(D) Internet access

화자들은 무엇에 관해 질문할 것인가?

(A) 환불

(B) **좌석 변경**

(C) 음식 선택 사항

(D) 인터넷 접속

해설 세부 사항 관련 – 화자들이 문의할 것

여자가 첫 대사에서 나란히 붙어 있는 표는 못 구했지만 탈 때 자리 교환에 관해 승무원에게 물어보면 된다(I couldn't get us tickets ~ switching our seats when we get on board)고 말하고 있으므로 정답은 (B)이다.

> ▸▸ Paraphrasing 대화의 **switching our seats**
> → 정답의 **A seat change**

63

What do the speakers want to prepare for?

(A) An employee interview

(B) A meeting with potential clients

(C) An annual safety inspection

(D) A product-testing session

화자들은 무엇을 준비하고 싶어 하는가?

(A) 직원 면담

(B) **잠재 고객들과의 회의**

(C) 연간 안전 점검

(D) 제품 검사 세션

해설 세부 사항 관련 – 화자들이 준비하기를 원하는 것

남자가 첫 대사에서 오늘 오후에 있을 회의를 준비할 수 있겠다(That way we can prepare for our meeting this afternoon)며 이들은 우리한테 정말 중요한 고객이 될 수도 있다(These could be really important clients for us)고 말하고 있으므로 정답은 (B)이다.

> ▸▸ Paraphrasing 대화의 **could be ~ clients**
> → 정답의 **potential clients**

64

Look at the graphic. What platform will speakers go to?

(A) Platform 3

(B) Platform 9

(C) Platform 12

(D) Platform 17

시각 정보에 의하면 화자들은 어느 플랫폼으로 가겠는가?

(A) 3번 플랫폼

(B) 9번 플랫폼

(C) 12번 플랫폼

(D) **17번 플랫폼**

해설 시각 정보 연계 – 화자들이 향할 플랫폼

여자가 두 번째 대사에서 우리 기차는 9시 24분에 출발한다(our train leaves at nine twenty-four)며 지금 플랫폼으로 가자(Why don't we head over to the platform now?)고 제안하고 있고, 열차 시간표에 따르면 9시 24분에 출발하는 열차는 17번 플랫폼이라고 나와 있으므로 정답은 (D)이다.

65-67 대화 + 지도

M-Cn	Hey, Lisa… **65 I just talked to the property manager, and she's very happy with the new trees and flowers we planted.**
W-Am	Great! **66 Does that mean we're done for the day?**
M-Cn	Almost. **66 We just have to water the new plants and pack up our tools. Can you do that, though? I need to head across town to the bank to make a deposit.**

W-Am OK.

M-Cn Oh, and ⁶⁷ **please put up our promotional sign.** The property manager is fine with that. ⁶⁷ **Can you put it up at the intersection of Hill Lane and Meadow Street?**

W-Am Sure, I'll do that.

남 저기, 리사… **방금 부동산 관리인과 얘기했는데, 우리가 새로 심은 나무와 꽃들이 아주 마음에 든대요.**

여 **다행이네요! 그럼 오늘 일은 끝난 건가요?**

남 거의요. 새 식물들에 물 주고 도구만 챙기면 돼요. 하실 수 있죠? 저는 입금하러 시내 건너편에 있는 은행에 가야 하거든요.

여 알겠어요.

남 아, 그리고 홍보 표지판을 세워 주세요. 부동산 관리인이 괜찮다고 했어요. 힐 레인과 메도우 가 교차로에 세워 주실래요?

여 그럼요, 그렇게 할게요.

어휘 property 부동산 done for the day 오늘 일을 끝낸 make a deposit 입금하다 promotional 홍보의 intersection 교차로

Property Map

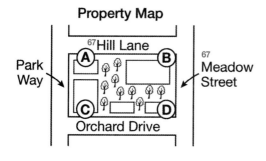

부동산 지도

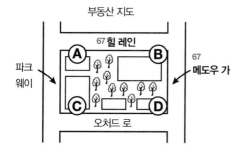

65

Who most likely are the speakers?

(A) Landscapers
(B) Photographers
(C) Architects
(D) Real estate agents

화자들은 누구이겠는가?

(A) 조경사
(B) 사진작가
(C) 건축가
(D) 부동산 중개업자

해설 전체 내용 관련 - 화자들의 직업

남자가 첫 대사에서 방금 부동산 관리인과 얘기했는데 우리가 새로 심은 나무와 꽃들을 아주 마음에 들어 한다(I just talked to the property manager ~ new trees and flowers we planted)고 말하고 있으므로 화자들은 조경 일을 하는 사람들임을 알 수 있다. 따라서 정답은 (A)이다.

66

What will the man do after he leaves?

(A) Have a vehicle repaired
(B) E-mail a contract
(C) Return some equipment
(D) Go to a bank

남자는 떠난 뒤 무엇을 하겠는가?

(A) 차량 수리 맡기기
(B) 계약서 이메일로 보내기
(C) 장비 반납하기
(D) 은행 가기

해설 세부 사항 관련 - 남자가 떠난 뒤 할 일

여자가 첫 대사에서 오늘 일은 끝난 것인지(Does that mean we're done for the day?) 묻자 남자가 새 식물들에 물을 주고 도구만 챙기면 된다(We just have to water the new plants and pack up our tools)며 여자에게 할 수 있겠는지(Can you do that, though?)를 물으면서 자신은 입금하러 시내 건너편에 있는 은행에 가야 한다(I need to head across town to the bank to make a deposit)고 말하고 있으므로 정답은 (D)이다.

▸▸ Paraphrasing 대화의 head ~ to the bank
→ 정답의 Go to a bank

67

Look at the graphic. Where will the woman put up a sign?

(A) At location A
(B) At location B
(C) At location C
(D) At location D

시각 정보에 의하면 여자는 표지판을 어디에 세울 것인가?

(A) A 위치
(B) B 위치
(C) C 위치
(D) D 위치

해설 시각 정보 연계 - 여자가 표지판을 세울 위치

남자가 세 번째 대사에서 여자에게 홍보 표지판을 세워 달라(please put up our promotional sign)고 부탁하며 표지판을 힐 레인과 메도우 가의 교차로에 세워 줄 것(Can you put it up at the intersection of Hill

TEST 8

Lane and Meadow Street?)을 요청하고 있고, 지도에 따르면 힐 레인과 메도우 가의 교차로는 B 위치이므로 여자는 B 위치에 홍보 표지판을 세울 것임을 알 수 있다. 따라서 정답은 (B)이다.

68-70 대화 + 일람표

M-Au	[68]**This is customer service for the *Portsville Times*.** How can I help you?
W-Am	Hi! [68]**I'm calling to subscribe to your paper. My best friend recommended it.**
M-Au	Well, please tell your friend that we appreciate her recommendation. Now, we have several options to choose from— are you interested in having the paper delivered to your house?
W-Am	No, that's not necessary. [69]**I prefer to read articles on my tablet computer.**
M-Au	All right, [69]**sounds like you just need online access, then.** Our digital subscription is nine dollars a month.
W-Am	That's perfect.
M-Au	OK. [70]**I'll just need your credit card information to begin processing your subscription.**

남	〈포츠빌 타임즈〉 고객 서비스입니다. 어떻게 도와 드릴까요?
여	안녕하세요! 신문을 구독하려고 전화드렸어요. 단짝이 추천해 줬어요.
남	음, 친구분께 추천 감사하다고 전해 주세요. 자, 선택할 수 있는 몇 가지 옵션이 있어요. 신문을 댁으로 배달해 드리는 게 좋을까요?
여	아뇨, 그럴 필요는 없어요. 저는 태블릿에서 기사를 읽는 게 더 좋아요.
남	알겠습니다, 그럼 온라인 접속만 필요하신 것 같군요. 디지털 구독료는 한 달에 9달러예요.
여	딱 적당하네요.
남	좋습니다. 구독 처리를 시작하려면 신용카드 정보만 있으면 됩니다.

어휘	subscribe to ~을 구독하다 subscription 구독

Subscription Options and Monthly Rates

Option 1: Print and online access	$14
Option 2: [69]Online access only	$9
Option 3: Weekend delivery (print only)	$8
Option 4: Student rate (online only)	$5

구독 옵션 및 월 요금

옵션 1: 종이 신문과 온라인 접속	14달러
옵션 2: [69]온라인 접속만	**9달러**
옵션 3: 주말 배달 (종이 신문만)	8달러
옵션 4: 학생 요금 (온라인만)	5달러

68

Who recommended that the woman subscribe to the *Portsville Times*?

(A) A professor
(B) A friend
(C) A colleague
(D) A relative

여자에게 〈포츠빌 타임즈〉를 구독하라고 권한 사람은 누구인가?

(A) 교수
(B) 친구
(C) 동료
(D) 친척

해설 세부 사항 관련 – 여자에게 포츠빌 타임즈의 구독을 권한 사람

남자가 첫 대사에서 〈포츠빌 타임즈〉 고객 서비스(This is customer service for the *Portsville Times*)라고 전화를 받고 있고, 여자가 뒤이어 신문을 구독하려고 전화했다(I'm calling to subscribe to your paper)며 단짝이 추천해 줬다(My best friend recommended it)고 말하고 있으므로 여자에게 〈포츠빌 타임즈〉의 구독을 권한 사람은 친구임을 알 수 있다. 따라서 정답은 (B)이다.

69

Look at the graphic. Which subscription option does the man recommend?

(A) Option 1
(B) Option 2
(C) Option 3
(D) Option 4

시각 정보에 의하면 남자는 어떤 구독 옵션을 추천하는가?

(A) 옵션 1
(B) 옵션 2
(C) 옵션 3
(D) 옵션 4

해설 시각 정보 연계 – 남자가 추천하는 구독 옵션

여자가 두 번째 대사에서 저는 태블릿에서 기사를 읽는 것을 선호한다(I prefer to read articles on my tablet computer)고 하자 남자가 그럼 온라인 접속만 필요하신 것 같다(sounds like you just need online access, then)고 권하며 디지털 구독료는 한 달에 9달러(Our digital subscription is nine dollars a month)라고 안내하고 있고, 일람표에 따르면 온라인 접속만 되며 월 요금 9달러짜리는 옵션 2이므로 정답은 (B)이다.

70

What will the man most likely do next?

(A) Confirm an address

(B) Choose a password

(C) Provide a discount code

(D) Process a payment

남자는 다음에 무엇을 하겠는가?

(A) 주소 확인

(B) 비밀번호 선택

(C) 할인 코드 제공

(D) 결제 처리

해설 세부 사항 관련 – 남자가 다음에 할 일

남자가 마지막 대사에서 구독 처리를 시작하려면 신용카드 정보만 있으면 된다(I'll just need your credit card information to begin processing your subscription)고 안내하고 있는 것으로 보아 여자에게 신용카드 정보를 받아 결제를 진행하려는 것임을 알 수 있다. 따라서 정답은 (D)이다.

PART 4

71-73 전화 메시지

M-Au Hi, **71this is Alexi from Petrov Roofing Company**. I just heard back from my supplier. Unfortunately, **72the estimate I gave you yesterday for the new roof shingles was a little low. The ones you chose are actually 39 dollars per bundle. That's more than what I quoted.** So, I just wanted to get your approval for this new price before I put in the order. And **73I recommend that we order soon, since the rainy season's only a month away.** Once the rain starts, it'll take more time to install the new roof.

안녕하세요, **페트로프 지붕 시공 회사 알렉시입니다.** 방금 납품업체에서 연락을 받았는데요. 아쉽게도 **제가 어제 드린 새 지붕널 견적이 좀 낮게 잡혔어요. 고객님이 고른 것은 실제로 한 묶음당 39달러입니다. 제가 견적 낸 가격보다 더 비싸죠.** 그래서 발주하기 전에 고객님께 이 새 가격을 승인받고 싶었어요. 그리고 **장마철이 한 달밖에 안 남았으니까 빨리 주문하는 게 좋을 것 같아요.** 비가 내리기 시작하면 새 지붕을 설치하는 데 시간이 더 걸릴 거예요.

어휘 supplier 납품업체 estimate 견적(서) shingle 지붕널 bundle 묶음 quote 견적을 내다 approval 승인

71

Where does the speaker work?

(A) At a roofing company

(B) At a catering company

(C) At a community park headquarters

(D) At an interior-design firm

화자는 어디에서 일하는가?

(A) 지붕 시공 회사

(B) 급식 회사

(C) 근린공원 본부

(D) 인테리어 디자인 업체

해설 전체 내용 관련 – 화자의 근무지

화자가 초반부에 페트로프 지붕 시공 회사의 알렉시(this is Alexi from Petrov Roofing Company)라고 자신을 소개하고 있으므로 정답은 (A)이다.

72

What information was incorrect?

(A) An order number

(B) A file name

(C) An address

(D) A price

어떤 정보가 정확하지 않은가?

(A) 주문 번호

(B) 파일명

(C) 주소

(D) 가격

해설 세부 사항 관련 – 정확하지 않은 정보

화자가 중반부에 제가 어제 드린 새 지붕널 견적이 좀 낮게 잡혔다(the estimate I gave you yesterday for the new roof shingles was a little low)고 했고 고객님이 고른 것은 실제로 한 묶음당 39달러(The ones you chose are actually 39 dollars per bundle)라고 가격 정보를 정정하며 제가 견적 낸 가격보다 더 비싸다(That's more than what I quoted)고 설명하고 있으므로 정답은 (D)이다.

▸▸ Paraphrasing 담화의 **estimate** → 정답의 **price**

73

Why does the speaker recommend placing an order soon?

(A) A material is in high demand.

(B) The rainy season is coming.

(C) Some new fees will be introduced.

(D) A permit is about to expire.

화자는 왜 빨리 주문하라고 권하는가?

(A) 자재 수요가 많다.

(B) 장마철이 다가오고 있다.

(C) 새로운 요금이 도입될 예정이다.

(D) 허가증이 곧 만료된다.

어휘 permit 허가(증) expire 만료되다

해설 세부 사항 관련 – 화자가 빨리 주문하라고 권하는 이유

화자가 후반부에 장마철이 한 달밖에 안 남았으니까 빨리 주문하는 게 좋을 것 같다(I recommend that we order soon, since the rainy season's only a month away)고 말하고 있으므로 정답은 (B)이다.

▸▸ Paraphrasing   담화의 the rainy season's only a month
away → 정답의 The rainy season is coming

74-76 담화

> W-Am ⁷⁴**Thanks for attending today's seminar for new real estate agents.** As people just joining the industry, ⁷⁵**it's very important that you learn how to create a memorable property advertisement.** The way you describe a house or apartment can determine how quickly the property sells. I've invited a guest speaker to discuss this very point. ⁷⁶**Insook Lee has recently won our county's agent of the year award,** and she attributes her success in large part to the fact that she has mastered the art of writing a great description. Insook, welcome, and thank you for joining us today.

오늘 신규 부동산 중개업자를 위한 세미나에 참석해 주셔서 감사합니다. 여러분은 막 이 업계에 합류하시므로 **기억에 남는 부동산 광고 제작 방법을 배우는 게 매우 중요합니다.** 주택이나 아파트를 어떻게 묘사하는지에 따라 부동산이 얼마나 빨리 팔리는지가 결정될 수도 있습니다. 바로 이 점을 설명하기 위해 초청 연사를 모셨습니다. **이인숙 씨는 최근 우리 카운티에서 올해의 중개인상을 수상하셨는데,** 훌륭한 묘사 기술에 통달한 것이 성공에 큰 힘이 됐다고 합니다. 인숙 씨, 어서 오세요, 오늘 함께해 주셔서 감사합니다.

어휘 real estate 부동산   memorable 기억할 만한   describe 묘사하다   attribute A to B A를 B 덕분으로 돌리다

74
Who are the listeners?
(A) Artists
(B) Journalists
(C) **Real estate agents**
(D) Sales representatives

청자들은 누구인가?
(A) 예술가
(B) 기자
(C) **부동산 중개업자**
(D) 영업 담당자

해설 전체 내용 관련 - 청자들의 직업
화자가 도입부에 오늘 신규 부동산 중개업자를 위한 세미나에 참석해 주셔서 감사하다(Thanks for attending today's seminar for new real estate agents)고 말하는 것으로 보아 정답은 (C)이다.

75
What does the speaker say the listeners should learn to do?

(A) Manage their time
(B) Negotiate prices
(C) Give memorable presentations
(D) **Create effective advertisements**

화자는 청자들이 무엇을 배워야 한다고 말하는가?
(A) 시간 관리하기
(B) 가격 협상하기
(C) 기억에 남는 발표 하기
(D) **효과적인 광고 만들기**

어휘 memorable 기억에 남는   effective 효과적인

해설 세부 사항 관련 - 화자가 청자들이 배워야 한다고 말하는 것
화자가 초반부에 기억에 남는 부동산 광고 제작 방법을 배우는 것이 매우 중요하다(it's very important that you learn how to create a memorable property advertisement)고 말하고 있으므로 정답은 (D)이다.

▸▸ Paraphrasing   담화의 a memorable ~ advertisement
→ 정답의 effective advertisements

76
What does the speaker mention about Insook Lee?
(A) **She has won an award.**
(B) She is on a lecture tour.
(C) She hosts a popular podcast.
(D) She recently started a company.

화자는 이인숙에 관해 무엇을 언급하는가?
(A) **상을 받았다.**
(B) 순회 강연을 하고 있다.
(C) 인기 팟캐스트를 진행한다.
(D) 최근에 회사를 차렸다.

해설 세부 사항 관련 - 화자가 이인숙에 관해 언급하는 것
화자가 후반부에 이인숙 씨는 최근 우리 카운티에서 올해의 중개인상을 수상했다(Insook Lee has recently won our county's agent of the year award)고 소개하고 있으므로 정답은 (A)이다.

77-79 방송

> M-Cn In local news, town officials are ready to take action on the untimely degradation of some of our town's main roads. Since ⁷⁷**the Bellville shopping mall opened last January,** there has been significantly more traffic on the streets leading to the mall. ⁷⁸**City officials have received numerous complaints from citizens about large cracks and potholes in the roads, which can be damaging to cars.** ⁷⁹**The city council has invited a few concrete engineers to their next meeting,** which will be open to the public. The engineers will share their expertise on the options available for

upgrading our roads, and the city council will vote on a budget for the project.

> 지역 소식입니다. 시 공무원들은 시 주요 도로 일부가 너무 빨리 훼손된 것에 조치를 취할 준비가 되어 있습니다. **지난 1월 벨빌 쇼핑몰이 문을 연 후, 몰로 이어지는 도로에 교통량이 크게 늘었습니다. 시 공무원들은 도로에 생긴 커다란 균열과 패인 곳으로 자동차가 훼손될 수 있다는 시민들의 민원을 많이 받았습니다. 시 의회는 다음 회의에 콘크리트 기술자 몇 명을 초청했는데**, 회의는 일반에 공개될 예정입니다. 기술자들이 도로 개선에 활용할 수 있는 선택 사항들에 관해 전문 지식을 공유하면, 시 의회가 프로젝트를 위한 예산안을 의결할 것입니다.

> 어휘 untimely 너무 이른 degradation 훼손 significantly 크게 numerous 많은 crack 균열 pothole 패인 곳 expertise 전문 지식

77

What happened last January?
(A) There was an election.
(B) There was a snowstorm.
(C) A shopping mall opened.
(D) A bridge was closed.

지난 1월에 어떤 일이 있었는가?
(A) 선거가 있었다.
(B) 눈보라가 쳤다.
(C) 쇼핑몰이 문을 열었다.
(D) 다리가 폐쇄됐다.

해설 세부 사항 관련 – 지난 1월에 있었던 일
화자가 초반부에 지난 1월에 벨빌 쇼핑몰이 문을 열었다(the Bellville shopping mall opened last January)고 말하고 있으므로 정답은 (C)이다.

78

Why have some citizens complained?
(A) A toll has increased.
(B) Traffic lights are badly timed.
(C) There is not enough parking.
(D) The roads are in poor condition.

시민들은 왜 불평했는가?
(A) 통행료가 올랐다.
(B) 신호등 시간이 맞지 않는다.
(C) 주차 공간이 넉넉하지 않다.
(D) 도로 상태가 좋지 않다.

해설 세부 사항 관련 – 시민들이 불평한 이유
화자가 중반부에 시 공무원들이 도로에 생긴 커다란 균열과 패인 곳으로 자동차가 훼손될 수 있다는 시민들의 민원을 많이 받았다(City officials have received numerous complaints ~ which can be damaging to cars)고 말하고 있으므로 정답은 (D)이다.

▸▸ Paraphrasing 담화의 **large cracks and potholes**
→ 정답의 **in poor condition**

79

Who has been invited to attend a city council meeting?
(A) Engineers
(B) Educators
(C) Finance experts
(D) Business owners

시 의회 회의에 초대받은 사람은 누구인가?
(A) 기술자
(B) 교육자
(C) 금융 전문가
(D) 사업주

해설 세부 사항 관련 – 시 의회 회의에 초대받은 사람
화자가 중반부에 시 의회가 다음 회의에 콘크리트 기술자 몇 명을 초청했다(The city council has invited a few concrete engineers to their next meeting)고 말하고 있으므로 정답은 (A)이다.

80-82 공지

> W-Br Thank you for coming to this short meeting for all residents of Atrium Apartment Complex. **80 Our power provider, Crewdson Energy Company, will be updating the electrical equipment in all units starting next week.** This update is to improve the energy efficiency in our buildings. **81 Please be warned that there will be intermittent power failures while work is being done. 82 If you work from home and need alternate space to work during power failures, you're free to use the apartment complex clubhouse.** We'll make sure there's power there at all times.

> 아트리움 아파트 단지 주민 모두를 위한 짧은 회의에 참석해 주셔서 감사합니다. 전력 공급사인 크루슨 에너지 회사에서 다음 주부터 전체 가구의 전기 장비를 개선할 예정입니다. 이번 개선 작업은 건물의 에너지 효율을 높이기 위해서입니다. 작업이 진행되는 동안 간간이 정전이 발생하므로 유의하시기 바랍니다. 집에서 일하는데 정전된 사이 대체 공간이 필요하시면 아파트 단지 클럽하우스를 자유롭게 이용할 수 있습니다. 거기에는 반드시 전기가 항상 들어오게 하겠습니다.

> 어휘 equipment 장비 efficiency 효율 intermittent 간간이 일어나는 alternate 대체하는 power failure 정전

80

What is the purpose of an equipment update?

(A) To promote healthy lifestyles

(B) To protect consumer privacy

(C) To comply with safety standards

(D) To increase energy efficiency

장비 개선의 목적은 무엇인가?

(A) 건강한 생활 방식 조성

(B) 소비자 사생활 보호

(C) 안전 기준 준수

(D) 에너지 효율 증대

어휘 comply with ~을 준수하다

해설 세부 사항 관련 – 장비 개선의 목적

화자가 초반부에 전력 공급사인 크루슨 에너지 회사에서 다음 주부터 전체 가구의 전기 장비를 개선할 예정(Our power provider, ~ equipment in all units starting next week)이라면서 이번 개선 작업은 건물의 에너지 효율을 높이기 위한 것(This update is to improve the energy efficiency in our buildings)이라고 말하고 있으므로 정답은 (D)이다.

>> Paraphrasing 담화의 **improve** → 정답의 **increase**

81

What are the listeners warned about?

(A) Price increases

(B) Service interruptions

(C) Loud noises

(D) Increased traffic

청자들은 무엇에 관해 주의받는가?

(A) 가격 인상

(B) 서비스 중단

(C) 시끄러운 소음

(D) 늘어난 교통량

어휘 interruption 중단

해설 세부 사항 관련 – 청자들이 주의받은 것

화자가 중반부에 작업이 진행되는 동안 간간이 정전이 발생하므로 유의하시기 바란다(Please be warned that there will be intermittent power failures while work is being done)고 말하고 있으므로 정답은 (B)이다.

>> Paraphrasing 담화의 **power failures**
→ 정답의 **Service interruptions**

82

What are some listeners encouraged to do?

(A) Sign up early for a service

(B) Use a community space

(C) Attend an information session

(D) Take public transportation

청자들은 무엇을 하라고 권유받는가?

(A) 서비스 조기 가입

(B) 공동체 공간 사용

(C) 설명회 참석

(D) 대중교통 이용

해설 세부 사항 관련 – 청자들이 권유받은 일

화자가 후반부에 집에서 일하는데 정전된 사이 대체 공간이 필요하면 아파트 단지 클럽하우스를 자유롭게 이용할 수 있다(If you work from home ~ free to use the apartment complex clubhouse)고 말하고 있으므로 정답은 (B)이다.

>> Paraphrasing 담화의 the apartment complex clubhouse
→ 정답의 a community space

83-85 담화

W-Am Hello. **83 As your senior vice president of Product Development, it has been a privilege leading this team over the past several decades.** As you may have heard, **84 I will be ending my time with the company next month.** Now, **85 when I shared this news with a few of you individually, there were some concerns about the future of the team under new leadership. Frankly, that surprised me. I mean, look around the room.** There are a lot of talented people in this group. In fact, I should take this opportunity to thank you all for our collective success.

안녕하세요. 제품 개발부 수석 부사장으로 지난 수십 년 동안 이 팀을 이끌 수 있어 영광이었습니다. 들으셨겠지만, 저는 다음 달에 회사와 함께했던 시간을 끝냅니다. 자, 제가 이 소식을 몇 분과 개인적으로 나누었는데, 새 지도부가 이끄는 팀의 미래를 걱정하시더군요. 솔직히 놀랐어요. 그러니까, 방을 둘러보세요. 여기 모인 분들 중에는 인재가 많습니다. 사실, 저는 이 기회에 우리가 함께 이룬 성공에 대해 여러분 모두에게 감사드립니다.

어휘 privilege 영광 decade 10년 frankly 솔직히 opportunity 기회 collective 공동의

83

Who is the speaker?

(A) A sports coach

(B) A computer programmer

(C) A company executive

(D) A sales representative

화자는 누구인가?

(A) 스포츠 코치

(B) 컴퓨터 프로그래머

(C) 회사 임원

(D) 영업 담당자

해설 전체 내용 관련 - 화자의 직업

화자가 초반부에 제품 개발부 수석 부사장으로 지난 수십 년 동안 이 팀을 이끌 수 있어 영광이었다(As your senior vice president of Product Development, it has been a privilege leading this team over the past several decades)고 말하고 있으므로 정답은 (C)이다.

> Paraphrasing 담화의 your senior vice president
> → 정답의 A company executive

84

What is the speaker mainly discussing?

(A) An upcoming retirement
(B) A corporate fund-raiser
(C) An innovative product
(D) An annual dinner

화자는 주로 무엇을 논의하고 있는가?

(A) 임박한 은퇴
(B) 기업 모금 행사
(C) 혁신적인 제품
(D) 연례 만찬

어휘 retirement 은퇴 fund-raiser 모금 행사

해설 전체 내용 관련 - 담화의 주제

화자가 초반부에 저는 다음 달에 회사와 함께했던 시간을 끝낸다(I will be ending my time with the company next month)고 말하며 자신의 은퇴와 관련된 이야기를 이어 가고 있으므로 정답은 (A)이다.

85

Why does the speaker say, "There are a lot of talented people in this group"?

(A) To question a management policy
(B) To suggest a group size be decreased
(C) To reassure the listeners about a decision
(D) To express appreciation for an award

화자가 "여기 모인 분들 중에는 인재가 많습니다"라고 말하는 이유는 무엇인가?

(A) 경영 방침에 의문을 제기하려고
(B) 단체 규모를 줄이자고 제안하려고
(C) 청자들에게 결정에 대해 안심시키려고
(D) 상에 감사를 표시하려고

어휘 decrease 줄이다 reassure 안심시키다

해설 화자의 의도 파악 - 여기 모인 분들 중에는 인재가 많다는 말의 의도

화자가 앞에서 제가 이 소식을 몇 분과 개인적으로 나누었는데 새 지도부가 이끄는 팀의 미래를 걱정했다(when I shared this news with a few of you ~ future of the team under new leadership)는 말을 전하고 나서 솔직히 놀랐다(Frankly, that surprised me)며 그러니까 방을 둘러보라(I mean, look around the room)고 한 뒤 인용문을 언급한 것으로 보아, 자신이 은퇴하고 나서도 팀에 인재가 많아 걱정할 것 없다는 확신을 주기 위해 한 말임을 알 수 있다. 따라서 정답은 (C)이다.

86-88 전화 메시지

M-Cn Hello, Ms. Schulz. **86 This is Yuri Federov, calling from our downtown store.** I was just going over the checklist that you gave us. **87 We've already done most of the things you've asked us to do in preparation for our outdoor sale, but there's a bit of a problem. 87, 88 You wanted us to rope off the parking spaces in front of the shop after we closed today so we can set up tables there tomorrow morning.** Well, it's eight fifteen, and there are three cars parked there now. Please give me a call back as soon as you can.

안녕하세요, 슐츠 씨. 저는 유리 페데로프이고, 시내 매장에서 전화드립니다. 주신 점검 목록을 검토하고 있었는데요. 옥외 할인 준비로 요청하신 일은 벌써 대부분 다 했어요. 그런데 문제가 좀 있어요. 내일 아침 테이블을 설치할 수 있도록 오늘 마무리한 후에 가게 앞에 있는 주차 공간을 밧줄로 둘러막으라고 하셨잖아요. 음, 8시 15분인데, 지금 거기에 차가 석 대 주차되어 있어요. 가능한 한 빨리 다시 전화 주세요.

어휘 preparation 준비 rope off ~을 밧줄로 둘러막다

86

Who is the man most likely calling?

(A) A police officer
(B) A customer
(C) A mechanic
(D) A supervisor

남자는 누구에게 전화하고 있겠는가?

(A) 경찰관
(B) 고객
(C) 정비사
(D) 상관

해설 전체 내용 관련 - 전화 수신자의 직업

화자가 초반부에 저는 유리 페데로프이고 시내 매장에서 전화드린다(This is Yuri Federov, calling from our downtown store)며 주신 점검 목록을 검토하고 있었다(I was just going over the checklist that you gave us)고 말하는 것으로 보아 남자는 상점에서 일하는 사람으로 자신의 상관에게 전화를 걸고 있음을 알 수 있다. 따라서 정답은 (D)이다.

87

What will take place tomorrow?

(A) A store sale
(B) A road closure
(C) A farmers market
(D) A musical performance

내일 무슨 일이 있을 것인가?

(A) 매장 할인
(B) 도로 폐쇄
(C) 농산물 직판장
(D) 음악 공연

해설 세부 사항 관련 - 내일 일어날 일

화자가 중반부에 옥외 할인 준비로 요청하신 일은 벌써 대부분 다 했는데 문제가 좀 있다(We've already done ~ there's a bit of a problem)며 내일 아침 테이블을 설치할 수 있도록 오늘 마무리한 후에 가게 앞에 있는 주차 공간을 밧줄로 둘러막으라고 하셨다(You wanted us to rope off the parking spaces ~ set up tables there tomorrow morning)고 말하는 것으로 보아 화자는 내일 있을 옥외 할인을 준비 중임을 알 수 있다. 따라서 정답은 (A)이다.

88

What does the speaker mean when he says, "there are three cars parked there now"?

(A) An event is not popular.
(B) A task cannot be completed.
(C) A parking fee has been paid.
(D) A delivery will be delayed.

화자가 "지금 거기에 차가 석 대 주차되어 있어요"라고 말하는 의도는 무엇인가?
(A) 행사는 인기가 없다.
(B) 작업을 완료할 수 없다.
(C) 주차 요금이 지불되었다.
(D) 배송이 지연될 것이다.

해설 화자의 의도 파악 - 지금 거기에 차가 석 대 주차되어 있다는 말의 의도

앞에서 내일 아침 테이블을 설치할 수 있도록 오늘 마무리한 후에 가게 앞에 있는 주차 공간을 밧줄로 둘러막으라고 하셨다(You wanted us to rope off the parking spaces ~ set up tables there tomorrow morning)고 지시 사항을 되짚고 나서 8시 15분(Well, it's eight fifteen)이라고 시간을 알려 주며 인용문을 언급한 것으로 보아, 시간이 늦었는데도 주차 공간에 아직 주차되어 있는 차량들 때문에 지시받은 작업을 완수하지 못하고 있음을 알리려고 한 말임을 알 수 있다. 따라서 정답은 (B)이다.

89-91 담화

W-Br **89,90We'll be rolling out some changes starting next week. When customers call the service number, they'll be prompted to say which department they're trying to reach, and then voice-recognition software will direct their call automatically.** I'm sure most of you have experiences of your own calling customer-service hotlines that utilize this kind of system. Usually, it works, but it can be frustrating when it doesn't. **90,91Some customers might be upset with you if they were unable to reach the right department quickly. If this happens to you, please summarize the exchange in writing.** I'll give the feedback to the programmers so they can make improvements to the program accordingly.

다음 주부터 몇 가지 변화가 시작됩니다. 고객이 서비스 번호로 전화하면 어느 부서에 연락하려고 하는지 말하라는 메시지가 나오고 이후 음성 인식 소프트웨어가 자동으로 전화를 돌립니다. 여러분 대다수가 이런 유형의 시스템을 이용하는 고객 서비스 긴급 전화로 직접 전화해 본 경험이 있을 겁니다. 대체로 되긴 하지만, 안 되면 답답하죠. **일부 고객은 정확한 부서에 빨리 연결 안 되면 여러분에게 화를 내기도 하죠. 만약 이런 일이 생기면, 대화 내용을 요약해서 적으세요.** 프로그래머들이 그에 맞춰 프로그램을 개선할 수 있도록 의견을 전달하겠습니다.

어휘 roll out ~을 시작하다 prompt 촉구하다 recognition 인식 utilize 이용하다 frustrating 답답한 summarize 요약하다 accordingly 그에 맞춰

89

What change does the speaker announce?

(A) Departments will be reorganized.
(B) New technicians will be hired.
(C) An additional warehouse will open.
(D) An automated system will be used.

화자는 어떤 변화를 발표하는가?
(A) 부서들이 개편될 것이다.
(B) 새로 기술자들이 채용될 것이다.
(C) 추가로 창고가 문을 열 것이다.
(D) 자동화 시스템이 사용될 것이다.

어휘 reorganize 개편하다

해설 세부 사항 관련 - 화자가 발표하는 변화

화자가 도입부에 다음 주부터 몇 가지 변화가 시작된다(We'll be rolling out some changes starting next week)며 고객이 서비스 번호로 전화하면 어느 부서에 연락하려고 하는지 말하라는 메시지가 나오고 이후 음성 인식 소프트웨어가 자동으로 전화를 돌린다(When customers call the service number, ~ voice-recognition software will direct their call automatically)고 설명하고 있으므로 정답은 (D)이다.

90

Who most likely are the listeners?

(A) Accountants
(B) Warehouse stockers
(C) Human resources managers
(D) Customer service representatives

청자들은 누구이겠는가?
(A) 회계사
(B) 창고 재고 담당자
(C) 인사부 관리자
(D) 고객 서비스 담당자

해설 전체 내용 관련 - 청자들의 직업

화자가 도입부에 다음 주부터 우리에게 몇 가지 변화가 시작된다(We'll be rolling out some changes starting next week)면서 고객이 서비스 번호로 전화할 때(When customers call the service number)라고 운을 떼며 고객 서비스 업무와 관련된 변화 내용에 대해 설명하고 있고, 중반부에 일부 고객은 정확한 부서에 빨리 연결 안 되면 여러분에게 화를 내기도 한다(Some customers might be upset with you ~ the right department quickly)고 말하는 것으로 보아 청자들은 고객 서비스 담당 직원들임을 알 수 있다. 따라서 정답은 (D)이다.

91

What does the speaker ask the listeners to do?

(A) Update service numbers
(B) Submit salary requirements
(C) Keep a record of complaints
(D) Post some shipping schedules

화자는 청자들에게 무엇을 해 달라고 요청하는가?

(A) 서비스 번호 수정
(B) 급여 요구 사항 제출
(C) 불만 사항 기록
(D) 출하 일정 게시

해설 세부 사항 관련 - 화자의 요청 사항

화자가 중반부에 일부 고객은 정확한 부서에 빨리 연결 안 되면 화를 내기도 한다(Some customers might be upset ~ reach the right department quickly)며 만약 이런 일이 생기면 대화 내용을 요약해서 적으라(If this happens to you, please summarize the exchange in writing)고 요청하고 있으므로 정답은 (C)이다.

▸▸Paraphrasing 담화의 summarize the exchange in writing
→ 정답의 Keep a record of complaints

92-94 담화

M-Cn Welcome to the booth for Pondrew Technologies. I hope you're enjoying today's trade show. ⁹²**Let me tell you about the software we released last month.** ⁹³**It's designed to make your factory's production cycle more efficient.** How? Well, as you know, if a machine in an assembly line malfunctions, it can trigger significant downtime. Pondrew's software continuously gathers and processes data from each machine, so issues can be diagnosed faster. Yes, ⁹⁴**there are other software programs on the market that perform similar tasks, but they're complicated and require hours of training. Consider this about Pondrew's:** the manual's just fifteen pages long.

어서 오세요. 폰드루 테크놀로지스 부스입니다. 오늘 무역 박람회가 즐거우시길 바랍니다. **지난달에 저희가 출시한 소프트웨어에 대해 말씀드**

리겠습니다. **이 제품은 공장의 생산 주기를 더 효율적으로 만들기 위해 제작됐습니다.** 어떻게요? 아시다시피 조립 라인에서 기계가 오작동하면 가동이 한참 중단되기도 합니다. 폰드루의 소프트웨어는 기계 하나하나에서 지속적으로 데이터를 수집하고 처리하므로 문제를 더 빨리 진단할 수 있습니다. 네, **시중에 비슷한 작업을 수행하는 다른 소프트웨어 프로그램들도 있지만, 복잡하고 몇 시간씩 교육을 받아야 합니다. 폰드루에 대해 이 점을 기억하세요.** 설명서가 15페이지밖에 안 됩니다.

어휘 release 출시하다 be designed to ~하기 위해 제작되다 efficient 효율적인 malfunction 오작동하다 trigger 일으키다 downtime 가동 중단 시간 continuously 지속적으로 diagnose 진단하다 complicated 복잡한

92

What is the speaker promoting?

(A) Audio equipment
(B) Cleaning tools
(C) A security device
(D) A software program

화자는 무엇을 홍보하고 있는가?

(A) 오디오 장비
(B) 청소 도구
(C) 보안 장치
(D) 소프트웨어 프로그램

해설 세부 사항 관련 - 화자가 홍보하고 있는 것

화자가 초반부에 지난달에 저희가 출시한 소프트웨어에 대해 말씀드리겠다(Let me tell you about the software we released last month)고 말하고 있으므로 정답은 (D)이다.

93

What industry do the listeners most likely work in?

(A) Transportation
(B) Manufacturing
(C) Banking
(D) Health care

청자들은 어떤 업계에서 일하겠는가?

(A) 운송
(B) 제조
(C) 금융
(D) 의료

해설 전체 내용 관련 - 청자들의 근무 업계

화자가 초반부에 자사 제품을 홍보하며, 이 제품은 여러분 공장의 생산 주기를 더 효율적으로 만들기 위해 제작됐다(It's designed to make your factory's production cycle more efficient)고 말하는 것으로 보아 청자들은 공장에서 생산하는 일을 하고 있음을 알 수 있다. 따라서 정답은 (B)이다.

▸▸Paraphrasing 담화의 production → 정답의 Manufacturing

TEST 8

94

What does the speaker mean when he says, "the manual's just fifteen pages long"?

(A) The listeners should read the manual now.

(B) A manual would be inexpensive to print.

(C) A product is not ready to be released.

(D) A product is easy to use.

화자가 "설명서가 15페이지밖에 안 됩니다"라고 말하는 의도는 무엇인가?

(A) 청자들은 지금 설명서를 읽어야 한다.

(B) 설명서는 인쇄하기에 저렴할 것이다.

(C) 제품이 출시될 준비가 되지 않았다.

(D) 제품이 사용하기 쉽다.

어휘 inexpensive 저렴한

해설 화자의 의도 파악 – 설명서가 15페이지밖에 안 된다는 말의 의도 앞에서 시중에 비슷한 작업을 수행하는 다른 소프트웨어 프로그램들도 있지만 복잡하고 몇 시간씩 교육을 받아야 한다(there are other software programs ~ they're complicated and require hours of training)고 했고 폰드루는 이 점을 기억하라(Consider this about Pondrew's)고 강조하며 인용문을 언급하고 있으므로 타사 제품들에 비해 배우고 사용하기가 훨씬 쉽다는 의도로 한 말임을 알 수 있다. 따라서 정답은 (D)이다.

95-97 공지 + 사무실 배치도

> W-Am I have an announcement for the team. ⁹⁵**We'll be making a big purchase—a top-of-the-line 3-D printer.** ⁹⁶**We've been outsourcing the work to a printing company, but it recently doubled its prices. We think it's time to have our own in-house printer.** The only issue is size—the only space big enough for the new machine is the office next to the reception area, so we'll be rearranging our work space. ⁹⁷**Jerome, I'm sorry, but you'll have to move. We hope you won't mind using the office in the corner across from the conference room.**

> 팀에 전할 소식이 있어요. **거창한 걸 구매할 건데요, 최신식 3D 프린터예요. 작업을 인쇄 회사에 외주로 맡겼지만, 최근에 가격이 두 배로 뛰었어요. 이제 사내 프린터를 마련할 때가 된 것 같아요.** 유일한 문제는 크기인데요. 새 기계가 들어갈 만큼 넓은 공간은 로비 옆 사무실뿐이라서 작업 공간을 재배치할 겁니다. **제롬, 미안하지만 당신이 옮겨야겠어요. 회의실 맞은편 구석에 있는 사무실을 써도 괜찮았으면 해요.**

> 어휘 make a purchase 구매하다 top-of-the-line 최고급의, 최신식의 outsource 외부에 위탁하다 in-house 사내의 rearrange 재배치하다

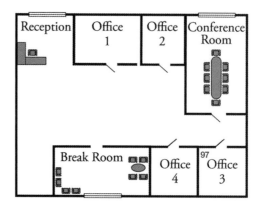

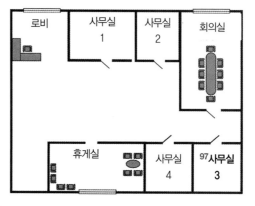

95

What is the speaker's company planning to purchase?

(A) A 3-D printer

(B) A large-screen television

(C) Some new laptops

(D) Some adjustable desks

화자의 회사는 무엇을 구매할 계획인가?

(A) 3-D 프린터

(B) 대형 화면 텔레비전

(C) 새 노트북

(D) 높낮이 조절 책상

어휘 adjustable 조절 가능한

해설 세부 사항 관련 – 화자의 회사가 구매할 계획인 것

화자가 초반부에 거창한 것을 구매할 것(We'll be making a big purchase)이라며 최신식 3D 프린터(a top-of-the-line 3-D printer)라고 말하고 있으므로 정답은 (A)이다.

96

Why has the company decided to make the purchase?

(A) More employees were hired.

(B) A vendor increased its prices.

(C) A store went out of business.

(D) Some software was out-of-date.

회사는 왜 구매를 결정했는가?

(A) 직원이 더 채용되었다.

(B) 업체가 가격을 올렸다.

(C) 매장이 폐업했다

(D) 소프트웨어가 구식이었다.

해설 세부 사항 관련 - 회사가 구매를 결정한 이유

화자가 중반부에 작업을 인쇄 회사에 외주로 맡겼지만 최근에 가격이 두 배로 뛰었다(We've been outsourcing the work ~ doubled its prices)며 이제 사내 프린터를 마련할 때가 된 것 같다(We think it's time to have our own in-house printer)고 말하고 있으므로 정답은 (B)이다.

> ▶▶ Paraphrasing 담화의 **doubled its prices**
> → 정답의 **increased its prices**

97

Look at the graphic. Where will Jerome move to?

(A) Office 1

(B) Office 2

(C) Office 3

(D) Office 4

시각 정보에 의하면 제롬은 어디로 옮기겠는가?

(A) 사무실 1

(B) 사무실 2

(C) 사무실 3

(D) 사무실 4

해설 시각 정보 연계 - 제롬이 옮겨갈 장소

화자가 마지막에 제롬(Jerome)을 부르며 미안하지만 옮겨야 하겠다(I'm sorry, but you'll have to move)면서 회의실 맞은편 구석에 있는 사무실을 써도 괜찮았으면 한다(We hope you won't ~ in the corner across from the conference room)고 말하고 있고, 사무실 배치도에 따르면 회의실 맞은편 구석에 있는 사무실은 사무실 3이므로 정답은 (C)이다.

98-100 전화 메시지 + 주문서

M-Au Hi, Amy! ⁹⁸**This is Paul Baxter from the manufacturing team.** Listen, ⁹⁹**I made a mistake in the order form I left on your desk earlier today. I actually only need ten pairs of safety goggles for my team on the assembly floor.** Hopefully, you get this message before you submit the order. Oh, and by the way—¹⁰⁰**when you place the order, could you add my e-mail address to the notification list,** so I know when everything's scheduled to arrive? It's paul.baxter@allymanufacturing.com. Thanks.

안녕, 에이미! 저는 제조팀 폴 백스터예요. 저기, 오늘 아까 당신 책상 위에 놓고 온 주문서에 실수가 있었어요. 실은 조립장에서 저희 팀이 쓸 안전 고글이 10개만 있으면 돼요. 주문서를 제출하기 전에 이 메시지를 받으면 좋겠네요. 아, 그건 그렇고, 주문하실 때 참조 목록에 제 이메일 주

소를 추가해 주시겠어요? 모두 언제 도착할 예정인지 제가 알 수 있도록요. paul.baxter@allymanufacturing.com입니다. 고마워요.

어휘 manufacturing 제조 assembly 조립 submit 제출하다

Item	Quantity
⁹⁹Safety Goggles	20 pairs
Cloth Rags	12 boxes
Adjustable Stools	8
Hard Hats	15

품목	수량
⁹⁹안전 고글	20개
걸레	12상자
높낮이 조절 의자	8
안전모	15

98

Where does the speaker most likely work?

(A) At a factory

(B) At an architecture firm

(C) At a landscaping service

(D) At a government inspection office

화자는 어디에서 일하겠는가?

(A) 공장

(B) 건축사 사무소

(C) 조경업체

(D) 정부 검사소

해설 전체 내용 관련 - 화자의 근무지

화자가 초반부에 저는 제조팀의 폴 백스터(This is Paul Baxter from the manufacturing team)라고 말하고 있으므로 정답은 (A)이다.

99

Look at the graphic. Which number does the speaker want to change?

(A) 20

(B) 12

(C) 8

(D) 15

시각 정보에 의하면 화자는 어떤 숫자를 바꾸고 싶어 하는가?

(A) 20

(B) 12

(C) 8

(D) 15

해설 시각 정보 연계 - 화자가 바꾸고 싶어 하는 숫자

화자가 초반부에 오늘 아까 당신 책상 위에 놓고 온 주문서에 실수가 있었다(I made a mistake in the order form I left on your desk earlier today)며 실은 조립장에서 저희 팀이 쓸 안전 고글이 10개만 있으면 된다(I actually only need ten pairs of safety goggles for my team on the assembly floor)고 말하는 것으로 보아 화자는 안전 고글의 수량을 수정하고 싶어 하고, 주문서에 따르면 안전 고글의 수량이 20이므로 정답은 (A)이다.

100

What information would the speaker like added to a list?

(A) His home address
(B) His office location
(C) His telephone number
(D) His e-mail address

화자는 어떤 정보를 목록에 추가하려고 하는가?

(A) 자신의 집 주소
(B) 자신의 사무실 위치
(C) 자신의 전화번호
(D) 자신의 이메일 주소

해설 세부 사항 관련 – 화자가 목록에 추가하려는 정보

화자가 후반부에 주문하실 때 참조 목록에 제 이메일 주소를 추가해 줄 수 있는지(when you place the order, could you add my e-mail address to the notification list) 묻고 있으므로 정답은 (D)이다.

ETS TEST 9

1 (C)	**2** (D)	**3** (B)	**4** (A)	**5** (D)
6 (B)	**7** (C)	**8** (C)	**9** (C)	**10** (A)
11 (C)	**12** (B)	**13** (B)	**14** (B)	**15** (A)
16 (B)	**17** (A)	**18** (C)	**19** (A)	**20** (C)
21 (C)	**22** (A)	**23** (B)	**24** (B)	**25** (A)
26 (C)	**27** (B)	**28** (C)	**29** (B)	**30** (B)
31 (A)	**32** (D)	**33** (C)	**34** (B)	**35** (A)
36 (C)	**37** (A)	**38** (C)	**39** (B)	**40** (C)
41 (B)	**42** (D)	**43** (C)	**44** (B)	**45** (D)
46 (C)	**47** (C)	**48** (C)	**49** (A)	**50** (B)
51 (C)	**52** (D)	**53** (B)	**54** (A)	**55** (D)
56 (A)	**57** (B)	**58** (A)	**59** (B)	**60** (A)
61 (C)	**62** (B)	**63** (B)	**64** (D)	**65** (D)
66 (D)	**67** (A)	**68** (C)	**69** (A)	**70** (D)
71 (D)	**72** (A)	**73** (D)	**74** (C)	**75** (D)
76 (A)	**77** (C)	**78** (B)	**79** (D)	**80** (B)
81 (A)	**82** (D)	**83** (A)	**84** (C)	**85** (D)
86 (A)	**87** (C)	**88** (C)	**89** (D)	**90** (C)
91 (D)	**92** (C)	**93** (B)	**94** (D)	**95** (B)
96 (C)	**97** (A)	**98** (B)	**99** (D)	**100** (A)

PART 1

1 M-Au

(A) He's untying a cloth apron.
(B) He's setting a plastic bin on a shelf.
(C) He's using a knife to slice some food.
(D) He's putting some groceries in a drawer.

(A) 남자가 천 앞치마를 풀고 있다.
(B) 남자가 선반에 플라스틱 통을 놓고 있다.
(C) 남자가 칼을 써서 음식을 썰고 있다.
(D) 남자가 식료품을 서랍에 넣고 있다.

어휘 drawer 서랍

해설 1인 등장 사진 – 사람의 동작/상태 묘사

(A) 동사 오답. 남자가 천 앞치마를 풀고 있는(is untying a cloth apron) 모습이 아니므로 오답.
(B) 동사 오답. 남자가 선반에 플라스틱 통을 놓고 있는(is setting a plastic bin on a shelf) 모습이 아니므로 오답.
(C) 정답. 남자가 칼을 써서 음식을 썰고 있는(is using a knife to slice some food) 모습이므로 정답.

(D) 동사 오답. 남자가 식료품을 서랍에 넣고 있는(is putting some groceries in a drawer) 모습이 아니므로 오답.

2 W-Am

(A) She's fixing her sunglasses.
(B) She's resting her hand on a bench.
(C) She's reaching into a handbag.
(D) She's talking on the phone.

(A) 여자가 선글라스를 매만지고 있다.
(B) 여자가 손을 벤치 위에 얹고 있다.
(C) 여자가 핸드백 안에 손을 넣고 있다.
(D) 여자가 통화를 하고 있다.

어휘 fix 매만지다 rest 얹다

해설 1인 등장 사진 – 사람의 동작/상태 묘사

(A) 동사 오답. 여자가 선글라스를 매만지고 있는(is fixing her sunglasses) 모습이 아니므로 오답.
(B) 동사 오답. 여자가 손을 벤치 위에 얹고 있는(is resting her hand on a bench) 모습이 아니므로 오답.
(C) 동사 오답. 여자가 핸드백 안에 손을 넣고 있는(is reaching into a handbag) 모습이 아니므로 오답.
(D) 정답. 여자가 통화를 하고 있는(is talking on the phone) 모습이므로 정답.

3 M-Cn

(A) One of the women is leaning over a trash can.
(B) One of the women is looking at a post on a bulletin board.
(C) One of the women is standing next to an entrance.
(D) One of the women is counting money from a machine.

(A) 여자들 중 한 명이 쓰레기통 위로 몸을 숙이고 있다.
(B) 여자들 중 한 명이 게시판에 붙은 게시물을 보고 있다.
(C) 여자들 중 한 명이 입구 옆에 서 있다.
(D) 여자들 중 한 명이 기계로 돈을 세고 있다.

어휘 lean 숙이다 bulletin board 게시판

TEST **9**

해설 2인 이상 등장 사진 – 사람의 동작/상태 묘사

(A) 사진에 없는 명사를 이용한 오답. 사진에 쓰레기통(a trash can)의 모습이 보이지 않으므로 오답.

(B) 정답. 여자들 중 한 명(one of the women)이 게시판에 붙은 게시물을 보고 있는(is looking at a post on a bulletin board) 모습이므로 정답.

(C) 사진에 없는 명사를 이용한 오답. 사진에 입구(an entrance)의 모습이 보이지 않으므로 오답.

(D) 동사 오답. 기계로 돈을 세고 있는(is counting money from a machine) 여자의 모습이 보이지 않으므로 오답.

---

4 W-Am

(A) A car has been parked beside a building.

(B) A door has been propped open.

(C) There's a sign posted on a fence.

(D) Some plants have been arranged in a row.

(A) 차 한 대가 건물 옆에 주차되어 있다.
(B) 문을 열어 받쳐 놓았다.
(C) 팻말이 울타리에 붙어 있다.
(D) 식물들이 일렬로 배열되어 있다.

어휘 prop 받쳐 놓다   arrange 배열하다   in a row 일렬로

해설 사물/풍경 사진 – 풍경 묘사

(A) 정답. 차 한 대(a car)가 건물 옆에 주차되어 있는(has been parked beside a building) 모습이므로 정답.

(B) 동사 오답. 문(a door)이 받쳐서 열려 있는(has been propped open) 모습이 아니므로 오답.

(C) 사진에 없는 명사를 이용한 오답. 사진에 팻말(a sign)의 모습이 보이지 않으므로 오답.

(D) 동사 오답. 식물들(some plants)이 일렬로 배열되어 있는(have been arranged in a row) 모습이 아니므로 오답.

---

5 W-Br

(A) Some light fixtures are being installed.

(B) A display case is being wiped.

(C) A server is distributing menus.

(D) A server is taking an order.

(A) 조명 설비가 설치되고 있다.
(B) 진열장을 닦고 있다.
(C) 종업원이 메뉴를 나눠주고 있다.
(D) 종업원이 주문을 받고 있다.

어휘 light fixture 조명 설비   install 설치하다   distribute 나눠주다
    take an order 주문을 받다

해설 혼합 사진 – 사람/사물/풍경 혼합 묘사

(A) 동사 오답. 조명 설비(some light fixtures)가 설치되고 있는(are being installed) 모습이 아니므로 오답.

(B) 동사 오답. 진열장(a display case)이 닦이고 있는(is being wiped) 모습이 아니므로 오답.

(C) 동사 오답. 종업원(a server)이 메뉴를 나눠주고 있는(is distributing menus) 모습이 아니므로 오답.

(D) 정답. 종업원(a server)이 주문을 받고 있는(is taking an order) 모습이므로 정답.

---

6 M-Au

(A) A vehicle is covered in snow.

(B) Some equipment is leaning against a truck.

(C) He's driving a vehicle through some snow.

(D) He's closing the back of a truck.

(A) 차량이 눈으로 덮여 있다.
(B) 장비가 트럭에 기대어 있다.
(C) 남자가 눈밭을 뚫고 차를 몰고 있다.
(D) 남자가 트럭 뒷부분을 닫고 있다.

어휘 lean against ~에 기대다

해설 혼합 사진 – 사람/사물/풍경 혼합 묘사

(A) 동사 오답. 차량(a vehicle)이 눈으로 덮여 있는(is covered in snow) 모습이 아니므로 오답.

(B) 정답. 장비(some equipment)가 트럭에 기대어 있는(is leaning against a truck) 모습이므로 정답.

(C) 동사 오답. 남자가 눈밭을 뚫고 차를 몰고 있는(is driving a vehicle through some snow) 모습이 아니므로 오답.

(D) 동사 오답. 남자가 트럭 뒷부분을 닫고 있는(is closing the back of a truck) 모습이 아니므로 오답.

PART 2

7

W-Am   Why is this restaurant so popular?
M-Au   (A) A table for five, please.
       (B) On the corner of Fourth and Main.
       (C) Because they hired a new chef.

이 식당은 왜 이렇게 인기가 많은가요?
(A) 5인용 테이블로 주세요.
(B) 4번 가와 메인 가 모퉁이에 있어요.
(C) 새 요리사를 고용했거든요.

해설 식당이 인기 있는 이유를 묻는 Why 의문문

(A) 연상 단어 오답. 질문의 restaurant에서 연상 가능한 table을 이용한 오답.

(B) 질문과 상관없는 오답. Where 의문문에 대한 응답이므로 오답.

(C) 정답. 식당이 인기가 많은 이유를 묻는 질문에 새 요리사를 고용했기 때문이라고 이유를 제시하고 있으므로 정답.

8

M-Cn　When does the park close?
W-Br　**(A) I parked over there.**
　　　(B) The bank's already closed.
　　　(C) Every night at eight.

공원은 언제 문을 닫나요?
(A) 저는 저쪽에 주차했어요.
(B) 은행은 벌써 닫았어요.
(C) 매일 밤 8시예요.

해설 공원이 문 닫는 시간을 묻는 When 의문문

(A) 유사 발음 오답. 질문의 park와 부분적으로 발음이 유사한 parked를 이용한 오답.

(B) 파생어 오답. 질문의 close와 파생어 관계인 closed를 이용한 오답.

(C) 정답. 공원이 문 닫는 시간을 묻는 질문에 매일 밤 8시라고 구체적으로 응답하고 있으므로 정답.

9

M-Au　Which house did Ms. Lopez move into?
W-Br　**(A) A real estate agent.**
　　　(B) Leave the box at the door, please.
　　　(C) The yellow one down the street.

로페즈 씨는 어느 집으로 이사했나요?
(A) 부동산 중개업자예요.
(B) 상자는 문 앞에 두세요.
(C) 도로 저쪽에 있는 노란색 집이에요.

어휘 real estate 부동산

해설 로페즈 씨가 이사한 집을 묻는 Which 의문문

(A) 연상 단어 오답. 질문의 house에서 연상 가능한 real estate agent를 이용한 오답.

(B) 연상 단어 오답. 질문의 house에서 연상 가능한 door를 이용한 오답.

(C) 정답. 로페즈 씨가 이사한 집을 묻는 질문에 도로 저쪽에 있는 노란색 집이라고 구체적으로 응답하고 있으므로 정답. Which 의문문은 the ~ one을 사용한 응답의 정답률이 높다는 점을 알아 두자.

10

W-Am　Excuse me, how do I get to platform six?

M-Cn　**(A) There's a map over there on the wall.**
　　　(B) Because it's only 50 cents.
　　　(C) An office downtown.

실례합니다, 6번 승강장은 어떻게 가나요?
(A) 저기 벽에 지도가 있어요.
(B) 고작 50센트거든요.
(C) 시내에 있는 사무실이에요.

해설 길을 묻는 How 의문문

(A) 정답. 6번 승강장으로 가는 길을 묻는 질문에 저기 벽에 지도가 있다며 길을 찾을 수 있는 방법을 간접적으로 알려 주고 있으므로 정답.

(B) 질문과 상관없는 오답. Why 의문문에 대한 응답이므로 오답.

(C) 질문과 상관없는 오답. Where 의문문에 대한 응답이므로 오답.

11

M-Cn　Who's responsible for ordering equipment?
W-Br　**(A) A long time ago.**
　　　(B) In the storage closet.
　　　(C) That's Robert's job.

장비 주문은 누가 담당하죠?
(A) 오래 전이에요.
(B) 창고 벽장 안이요.
(C) 그건 로버트 업무예요.

어휘 responsible for ~을 담당하는　storage 창고

해설 장비 주문 담당자를 묻는 Who 의문문

(A) 질문과 상관없는 오답. When 의문문에 대한 응답이므로 오답.

(B) 연상 단어 오답. 질문의 equipment에서 연상 가능한 storage를 이용한 오답.

(C) 정답. 장비 주문을 담당하는 사람이 누구인지 묻는 질문에 그것은 로버트의 업무라고 알려 주고 있으므로 정답.

12

W-Am　What was wrong with the refrigerator?
M-Au　**(A) On the right side of the road.**
　　　(B) The technician left a report.
　　　(C) Yeah, it's a good recipe!

냉장고는 뭐가 문제였나요?
(A) 도로 오른편에 있어요.
(B) 기술자가 보고서를 남겼어요.
(C) 그럼요, 훌륭한 조리법이군요!

어휘 refrigerator 냉장고

해설 냉장고의 문제에 대해 묻는 What 의문문

(A) 연상 단어 오답. 질문의 wrong에서 연상 가능한 right을 이용한 오답.

(B) 정답. 냉장고가 갖고 있는 문제가 무엇인지 묻는 질문에 기술자가 보고서를 남겼다며 문제를 파악할 수 있는 단서를 간접적으로 제시하고 있으므로 정답.

(C) Yes/No 불가 오답. What 의문문에는 Yes/No 응답이 불가능한데, Yeah도 일종의 Yes 응답이라고 볼 수 있으므로 오답.

TEST 9

13

M-Au This document needs a signature before it's sent out.

W-Br (A) A total of fifteen pages.

(B) OK, I'll do that now.

(C) A book of stamps.

이 문서는 발송 전에 서명이 필요합니다.

(A) 총 15페이지예요.

(B) 네, 지금 할게요.

(C) 우표첩이요.

해설 부탁/요청의 평서문

(A) 연상 단어 오답. 평서문의 document에서 연상 가능한 pages를 이용한 오답.

(B) 정답. 이 문서는 발송 전에 서명이 필요하다는 평서문에 네(OK)라고 대답한 뒤, 지금 하겠다고 긍정 답변과 일관된 내용을 덧붙이며 요청에 응하고 있으므로 정답.

(C) 연상 단어 오답. 평서문의 sent out에서 연상 가능한 stamps를 이용한 오답.

14

W-Br Why do you have so much luggage?

M-Cn (A) Here are your tickets.

(B) Because I'll be traveling for six months.

(C) When the taxi gets here.

짐이 왜 이렇게 많죠?

(A) 표 여기 있습니다.

(B) 6개월 동안 여행할 거라서요.

(C) 택시가 여기 오면요.

어휘 luggage 짐

해설 짐이 많은 이유를 묻는 Why 의문문

(A) 연상 단어 오답. 질문의 luggage에서 연상 가능한 tickets를 이용한 오답.

(B) 정답. 짐이 많은 이유를 묻는 질문에 6개월 동안 여행할 것이기 때문이라고 이유를 제시하고 있으므로 정답.

(C) 질문과 상관없는 오답. When 의문문에 대한 응답이므로 오답.

15

W-Am You must be the new sales director, right?

W-Br (A) Yes, it's nice to meet you.

(B) Sorry, I don't have the directions.

(C) It's our year-end sale.

새로 오신 영업부장님이시죠?

(A) 네, 만나서 반가워요.

(B) 죄송하지만, 저한테 설명서가 없어요.

(C) 연말 할인입니다.

해설 새로 온 영업부장을 확인하는 부가 의문문

(A) 정답. 상대가 새로 온 영업부장인지 여부를 확인하는 질문에 네(Yes)라고 대답한 뒤, 만나서 반갑다며 긍정 답변과 일관된 내용을 덧붙였으므로 정답.

(B) 파생어 오답. 질문의 director와 파생어 관계인 directions를 이용한 오답.

(C) 파생어 오답. 질문의 sales와 파생어 관계인 sale을 이용한 오답.

16

W-Br Are you running the workshop in the morning or in the afternoon?

M-Au (A) That was a long race.

(B) Attendees are arriving after lunch.

(C) Yes, I actually enjoy shopping.

공방을 오전에 운영하시나요, 오후에 운영하시나요?

(A) 장거리 경주였어요.

(B) 참석자들이 점심을 먹은 뒤 도착할 거예요.

(C) 네, 사실 쇼핑을 즐겨요.

해설 공방의 운영 시간을 묻는 선택 의문문

(A) 연상 단어 오답. 질문의 running에서 연상 가능한 race를 이용한 오답.

(B) 정답. 오전과 오후 중 공방을 운영하는 시간을 묻는 질문에 참석자들이 점심을 먹은 뒤 도착할 것이라며 오후에 한다는 것을 우회적으로 표현하고 있으므로 정답.

(C) Yes/No 불가 오답. 문장과 문장을 연결하는 경우를 제외하고는 선택 의문문에는 Yes/No 응답이 불가능하므로 오답.

17

M-Cn When should I return your book?

W-Br (A) Actually, I have another copy.

(B) On page 25.

(C) This is a beautiful library.

책은 언제 돌려 드릴까요?

(A) 실은 저한테 한 권 또 있어요.

(B) 25페이지예요.

(C) 멋진 도서관이네요.

해설 책의 반환 시기를 묻는 When 의문문

(A) 정답. 책을 돌려주어야 할 때를 묻는 질문에 실은 저한테 한 권이 또 있다며 책을 돌려주지 않아도 된다는 말을 우회적으로 표현하고 있으므로 정답.

(B) 연상 단어 오답. 질문의 book에서 연상 가능한 page를 이용한 오답.

(C) 연상 단어 오답. 질문의 book에서 연상 가능한 library를 이용한 오답.

18

M-Cn Where can I find the event schedule?

M-Au (A) Yeah, that's right.
　　　(B) Yesterday afternoon.
　　　(C) On the conference Web site.

행사 일정은 어디서 확인할 수 있나요?
(A) 네, 맞아요.
(B) 어제 오후예요.
(C) 회의 웹사이트에서요.

해설 행사 일정 확인 장소를 묻는 Where 의문문
(A) Yes/No 불가 오답. Where 의문문에는 Yes/No 응답이 불가능한데, Yeah도 일종의 Yes 응답이라고 볼 수 있으므로 오답.
(B) 질문과 상관없는 오답. When 의문문에 대한 응답이므로 오답.
(C) 정답. 행사 일정을 확인할 수 있는 장소를 묻는 질문에 회의 웹사이트라고 알려 주고 있으므로 정답.

19

W-Am I'll be late to the luncheon if I take the eleven o'clock bus.
M-Cn (A) I have room in my car.
　　　(B) Sure, Heidi can make some now.
　　　(C) That'll be five dollars, please.

11시 버스를 타면 오찬에 늦을 거예요.
(A) 제 차에 자리가 있어요.
(B) 그럼요, 하이디가 지금 만들 수 있어요.
(C) 5달러입니다.

해설 정보 전달의 평서문
(A) 정답. 11시 버스를 타면 오찬에 늦을 것이라는 평서문에 제 차에 자리가 있다며 자신의 차를 타고 가자고 우회적으로 제안하며 문제에 대한 해결책을 제시하고 있으므로 정답.
(B) 평서문과 상관없는 오답.
(C) 연상 단어 오답. 평서문의 eleven에서 연상 가능한 숫자 five를 이용한 오답.

20

M-Au How many shipments are we sending out every day?
W-Am (A) No, I'll make it on time.
　　　(B) It should arrive tomorrow.
　　　(C) We're up to 50.

매일 발송하는 출하량은 얼마나 되나요?
(A) 아뇨, 제시간에 갈게요.
(B) 내일 도착해요.
(C) 우리는 50까지예요.

어휘 shipment 출하량

해설 매일 발송하는 출하량을 묻는 How many 의문문
(A) Yes/No 불가 오답. How many 의문문에는 Yes/No 응답이 불가능하므로 오답.
(B) 연상 단어 오답. 질문의 shipments에서 연상 가능한 arrive를 이용한 오답.

(C) 정답. 매일 발송하는 출하량이 얼마나 되는지를 묻는 질문에 우리는 50까지라고 개수로 응답하고 있으므로 정답.

21

W-Br Should we replace the insulation in the building?
M-Cn (A) My office is 34C, near the lobby.
　　　(B) Well, I have considered retiring soon.
　　　(C) No, it's too expensive.

건물 안 단열재를 교체해야 할까요?
(A) 제 사무실은 로비 근처 34C예요.
(B) 음, 곧 은퇴할까 고민했어요.
(C) 아뇨, 그건 너무 비싸요.

어휘 replace 교체하다 insulation 단열(재) retire 은퇴하다

해설 제안/권유의 의문문
(A) 연상 단어 오답. 질문의 building에서 연상 가능한 lobby를 이용한 오답.
(B) 연상 단어 오답. 질문의 replace에서 연상 가능한 retiring을 이용한 오답.
(C) 정답. 건물 안 단열재를 교체해야 할지 묻는 질문에 아니요(No)라고 대답한 뒤, 그것은 너무 비싸다며 부정 답변과 일관된 내용을 덧붙였으므로 정답.

22

M-Au Do we have to stop at the post office?
W-Am (A) No, the mail carrier picked up the letter.
　　　(B) Can you call me a taxi, please?
　　　(C) Our office is close by.

우체국에 들러야 하나요?
(A) 아뇨, 집배원이 편지를 가져갔어요.
(B) 택시 좀 불러 주시겠어요?
(C) 우리 사무실이 근처에 있어요.

해설 우체국을 방문할지 여부를 묻는 조동사(Do) 의문문
(A) 정답. 우체국에 들러야 하는지 여부를 묻는 질문에 아니요(No)라고 대답한 뒤, 집배원이 편지를 가져갔다며 우체국에 갈 필요가 없음을 우회적으로 표현하고 있으므로 정답.
(B) 질문과 상관없는 오답.
(C) 단어 반복 오답. 질문의 office를 반복 이용한 오답.

23

W-Am Hasn't Alan seen the doctor yet?
M-Cn (A) It's in the medical building.
　　　(B) He hasn't had any time.
　　　(C) No, we didn't see it.

앨런이 아직 진찰을 안 받았나요?
(A) 병원 건물에 있어요.
(B) 그는 시간이 없었어요.
(C) 아뇨, 우리는 그것을 못 봤어요.

해설 앨런의 수진 여부를 확인하는 부정 의문문

(A) 연상 단어 오답. 질문의 doctor에서 연상 가능한 medical을 이용한 오답.

(B) 정답. 앨런이 진찰을 받았는지 여부를 묻는 질문에 그는 시간이 없었다며 아직 진찰을 받지 않았음을 우회적으로 표현하고 있으므로 정답.

(C) 파생어 오답. 질문의 seen과 파생어 관계인 see를 이용한 오답.

24

M-Cn Did you correct the error in the spreadsheet?

W-Br (A) The bank on Fourteenth Street.

(B) Actually, I fixed a few things.

(C) Everyone should get a copy.

스프레드시트 오류를 수정했나요?

(A) 14번 가에 있는 은행이에요.

(B) 실은 몇 가지 고쳤어요.

(C) 모두 사본을 받아야 해요.

해설 오류 수정 여부를 묻는 조동사(Did) 의문문

(A) 질문과 상관없는 오답. Where 의문에 대한 응답이므로 오답.

(B) 정답. 스프레드시트의 오류를 수정했는지 여부를 묻는 질문에 실은 몇 가지를 고쳤다며 네(Yes)를 생략한 긍정 답변을 하고 있으므로 정답.

(C) 연상 단어 오답. 질문의 spreadsheet에서 연상 가능한 copy를 이용한 오답.

25

W-Am Don't you want to come with us to the art gallery opening tonight?

M-Cn (A) I have a presentation tomorrow morning.

(B) The prices are marked on the frames.

(C) Leave it closed, please.

오늘밤 개관하는 미술관에 우리랑 같이 가지 않으실래요?

(A) 내일 아침에 발표가 있어요.

(B) 가격은 액자에 표시되어 있어요.

(C) 닫아 두세요.

해설 미술관 개관식에 동행할지 여부를 확인하는 부정 의문문

(A) 정답. 미술관에 같이 갈지 여부를 묻는 질문에 내일 아침에 발표가 있다며 거절의 의사를 우회적으로 표현하고 있으므로 정답.

(B) 연상 단어 오답. 질문의 art gallery에서 연상 가능한 frames를 이용한 오답.

(C) 연상 단어 오답. 질문의 opening에서 연상 가능한 closed를 이용한 오답.

26

W-Br Does your restaurant buy vegetables from wholesalers or local farmers?

M-Au (A) The carrots were overcooked.

(B) This table seats five people comfortably.

(C) Only from local farmers.

식당에서 도매상에게 채소를 구입하나요, 아니면 지역 농부들에게 구입하나요?

(A) 당근이 너무 익었더군요.

(B) 이 테이블은 다섯 사람이 편하게 앉을 수 있어요.

(C) 지역 농부들에게서만요.

어휘 wholesaler 도매상 overcook 너무 익히다 comfortably 편하게

해설 식당의 채소 구입처를 묻는 선택 의문문

(A) 연상 단어 오답. 질문의 vegetables에서 연상 가능한 carrots를 이용한 오답.

(B) 연상 단어 오답. 질문의 restaurant에서 연상 가능한 table을 이용한 오답.

(C) 정답. 도매상과 지역 농부들 중 식당에서 채소를 구입하는 곳을 묻는 질문에 지역 농부들한테서만이라며 둘 중 하나를 선택해 응답하고 있으므로 정답.

27

M-Cn Who supplies your copy paper?

W-Br (A) Under the printer.

(B) Check with the office manager.

(C) No, I don't have an extra copy.

복사용지는 누가 납품하나요?

(A) 프린터 밑에요.

(B) 총무 과장에게 확인하세요.

(C) 아뇨, 여분의 사본이 없어요.

어휘 supply 납품하다

해설 복사용지 납품업자를 묻는 Who 의문문

(A) 연상 단어 오답. 질문의 copy에서 연상 가능한 printer를 이용한 오답.

(B) 정답. 복사용지를 납품하는 사람이 누구인지 묻는 질문에 총무 과장에게 확인하라고 답변해 줄 수 있는 사람을 알려 주며 우회적으로 응답하고 있으므로 정답.

(C) Yes/No 불가 오답. Who 의문문에는 Yes/No 응답이 불가능하므로 오답.

28

M-Au Could you take a look at my article before I submit it?

W-Am (A) A magazine subscription.

(B) He submitted a payment online.

(C) I do have some editing experience.

제출하기 전에 제 기사 좀 봐 주실래요?

(A) 잡지 구독이요.

(B) 그는 온라인으로 대금을 냈어요.

(C) 제가 편집 경험이 있어요.

어휘 article 기사 submit 제출하다 subscription 구독

해설 부탁/요청의 의문문

(A) 연상 단어 오답. 질문의 article에서 연상 가능한 magazine을 이용한 오답.

(B) 파생어 오답. 질문의 submit과 파생어 관계인 submitted를 이용한 오답.

(C) 정답. 기사를 제출하기 전에 좀 봐 달라는 요청에 제가 편집 경험이 있다며 요청을 수락한다는 의사를 우회적으로 표현하고 있으므로 정답.

29

W-Am Let me look into renting a storage unit for this furniture.

M-Au (A) Put the leftover soup in the refrigerator.
(B) Thanks, that would be helpful.
(C) A sofa and two chairs.

이 가구를 둘 창고를 대여하는 문제에 대해 알아볼게요.
(A) 남은 수프는 냉장고에 넣으세요.
(B) 고마워요, 도움이 되겠어요.
(C) 소파 하나와 의자 두 개요.

어휘 leftover 먹다 남은

해설 제안/권유의 평서문
(A) 연상 단어 오답. 평서문의 storage에서 연상 가능한 leftover를 이용한 오답.
(B) 정답. 가구를 둘 창고를 대여하는 문제에 대해 알아보겠다는 제안에 고맙다(Thanks)고 대답한 뒤 도움이 되겠다며 제안을 받아들이고 있으므로 정답.
(C) 연상 단어 오답. 평서문의 furniture에서 연상 가능한 sofa와 chairs를 이용한 오답.

30

M-Cn Will the Henderson invoice be ready for review this afternoon?

W-Am (A) At the main post office.
(B) Carol checked it this morning.
(C) Either cash or credit card.

오늘 오후에 검토하게 헨더슨 송장이 준비될까요?
(A) 중앙 우체국에서요.
(B) 캐롤이 오늘 아침에 확인했어요.
(C) 현금이나 신용카드요.

해설 송장의 준비 완료 여부를 확인하는 조동사(Will) 의문문
(A) 질문과 상관없는 오답. Where 의문문에 대한 응답이므로 오답.
(B) 정답. 오늘 오후에 검토할 수 있도록 헨더슨 송장이 준비될지를 묻는 질문에 캐롤이 오늘 아침에 확인했다며 캐롤이 답변해 줄 수 있음을 우회적으로 알려 주고 있으므로 정답.
(C) 연상 단어 오답. 질문의 invoice에서 연상 가능한 지불 수단인 cash와 credit card를 이용한 오답.

31

M-Au Would you like a beverage while you wait for our loan specialist?

W-Br (A) Do you think I'll be waiting very long?
(B) No, we haven't seen her.
(C) Yes, we have a special on shoes.

대출 전문가를 기다리시는 동안 음료수 드시겠어요?
(A) 제가 오래 기다리게 될까요?
(B) 아뇨, 우리는 그녀를 못 봤어요.
(C) 네, 신발 특가 할인이 있습니다.

해설 제안/권유의 의문문
(A) 정답. 대출 전문가를 기다리는 동안 음료수를 마시겠냐고 제안하는 질문에 오래 기다리게 될 것인지를 되물으며 음료수를 마실지를 결정하는 데 필요한 추가 정보를 확인하고 있으므로 정답.
(B) 질문과 상관없는 오답.
(C) 파생어 오답. 질문의 specialist와 파생어 관계인 special을 이용한 오답.

PART 3

32-34

M-Cn 32 **Oakview Apartments. Chan-Ho speaking.**

W-Am Good morning. I'm a resident here, and 33 **I lost my key. It must have fallen off my key chain. I'll need a new one.**

M-Cn I'm sorry to hear that. I have an extra key here in the management office. I'll send one of the maintenance workers over with it.

W-Am Thank you so much. I really appreciate it.

M-Cn No problem. 34 **Can you tell me which unit is yours?**

남 **오크뷰 아파트 찬호입니다.**
여 안녕하세요. 여기 주민인데 **열쇠를 잃어버렸어요. 열쇠고리에서 떨어졌나 봐요. 새것이 필요해요.**
남 안타깝네요. 여기 관리실에 여분의 열쇠가 있어요. 관리 직원 중 한 사람 보낼게요.
여 정말 고마워요. 그렇게 해 주시면 정말 감사하죠.
남 괜찮습니다. **몇 호인지 알려 주시겠어요?**

어휘 maintenance 관리

32

Where does the man work?
(A) At a department store
(B) At a bank
(C) At an electronics store
(D) At an apartment complex

남자는 어디에서 일하는가?
(A) 백화점
(B) 은행
(C) 전자 제품 매장
(D) 아파트 단지

해설 전체 내용 관련 - 남자의 근무지

남자가 첫 대사에서 오크뷰 아파트(Oakview Apartments)의 찬호(Chan-Ho speaking)라고 전화를 받고 있으므로 남자는 아파트 단지에서 근무하고 있음을 알 수 있다. 따라서 정답은 (D)이다.

33

Why is the woman calling?

(A) To confirm a payment amount
(B) To schedule an appointment
(C) To ask for a replacement item
(D) To check on a delayed shipment

여자는 왜 전화하는가?
(A) 납부액을 확인하려고
(B) 예약 일정을 잡으려고
(C) 대체 품목을 요청하려고
(D) 지연된 배송품을 확인하려고

어휘 appointment 예약   replacement 대체

해설 전체 내용 관련 - 여자가 전화한 목적

여자가 첫 대사에서 열쇠를 잃어버렸다(I lost my key)고 했고 열쇠고리에서 떨어진 것 같다(It must have fallen off my key chain)며 새것이 필요하다(I'll need a new one)고 말하며 새 열쇠를 요청하고 있으므로 정답은 (C)이다.

> **Paraphrasing** 대화의 a new one
> → 정답의 a replacement item

34

What does the man ask for?

(A) A confirmation number
(B) A location
(C) An event date
(D) A completed form

남자는 무엇을 요청하는가?
(A) 확인 번호
(B) 위치
(C) 행사 일자
(D) 작성된 양식

해설 세부 사항 관련 - 남자의 요청 사항

남자가 마지막 대사에서 여자의 집이 몇 호인지 알려줄 것(Can you tell me which unit is yours?)을 요청하고 있으므로 정답은 (B)이다.

> **Paraphrasing** 대화의 unit → 정답의 location

35-37

W-Am ³⁵**Here's your admission ticket. It includes access to our seventeenth-century pottery exhibit**—it just opened this weekend.

M-Au Thanks, I came here specifically to see that. ³⁶**I'm writing a book about European pottery, and there's a vase I want to take a closer look at.**

W-Am Then ³⁷**you might also be interested in today's special lecture.** We have an archaeologist here to talk about how pottery is dated. ³⁷**You'll have to hurry though. It starts in just a few minutes.**

여 여기 입장권 받으세요. 입장권으로 17세기 도자기 전시회에도 갈 수 있습니다. 이번 주말에 막 열렸어요.

남 감사합니다. 그걸 보려고 특별히 왔어요. 유럽 도자기에 관한 책을 쓰고 있는데, 자세히 보고 싶은 꽃병이 있어서요.

여 그러면 오늘 특강에도 관심이 있으실 거예요. 고고학자를 여기 모셔서 도자기의 연대를 추정하는 방법에 대해 이야기하거든요. 그런데 서두르셔야 해요. 몇 분 뒤에 시작하거든요.

어휘 admission 입장 access 접근 pottery 도자기 exhibit 전시(회) vase 꽃병 archaeologist 고고학자 date 연대를 추정하다

35

Where does the conversation most likely take place?

(A) At a museum
(B) At a library
(C) At a theater
(D) At an art school

대화는 어디에서 이루어지겠는가?
(A) 박물관
(B) 도서관
(C) 극장
(D) 미술 학교

해설 전체 내용 관련 - 대화의 장소

여자가 첫 대사에서 여기 입장권이 있다(Here's your admission ticket)면서 입장권으로 17세기 도자기 전시회에도 갈 수 있다(It includes access to our seventeenth-century pottery exhibit)고 말하는 것으로 보아 대화 장소는 전시회를 관람하는 곳이므로 정답은 (A)이다.

36

Why is the man visiting?

(A) To meet a friend
(B) To take some photographs
(C) To do research for a book
(D) To deliver a shipment

남자는 왜 방문하는가?
(A) 친구를 만나려고
(B) 사진을 찍으려고
(C) 책을 위해 조사하려고
(D) 배송품을 배달하려고

남1 음, 제대로 찾아오셨네요. 이 공장에는 숙련된 작업자도 많고 실습 기회도 많아요.

남2 시작한다니 신나는데요.

여 저, 우리는 그만 가 볼 테니 다시 일하세요. 저는 교대 근무가 끝나기 전에 크리스에게 몇 사람 더 소개하려고요.

어휘 | apprentice 견습생 welder 용접공 machinist 기계공
plenty of 많은 hands-on practice 실습

해설 세부 사항 관련 – 남자의 방문 이유

남자가 첫 대사에서 유럽 도자기에 관한 책을 쓰고 있는데 자세히 보고 싶은 꽃병이 있다(I'm writing a book about European pottery, and there's a vase I want to take a closer look at)고 말하고 있으므로 정답은 (C)이다.

37

Why does the woman suggest that the man hurry?

(A) An event will begin shortly.
(B) Closing time is approaching.
(C) A wait time is long.
(D) Seating is limited.

여자는 왜 남자에게 서두르라고 권하는가?

(A) 행사가 곧 시작될 것이다.
(B) 폐관 시간이 다가오고 있다.
(C) 대기 시간이 길다.
(D) 좌석이 제한되어 있다.

해설 세부 사항 관련 – 여자가 남자에게 서두르라고 권하는 이유

여자가 마지막 대사에서 오늘 특강에도 관심이 있을 것(you might also be interested in today's special lecture)이라고 한 뒤 그런데 서둘러야 한다(You'll have to hurry though)며 몇 분 뒤에 시작한다(It starts in just a few minutes)고 말하고 있으므로 정답은 (A)이다.

▸▸ Paraphrasing 대화의 starts in just a few minutes
→ 정답의 begin shortly

38-40 3인 대화

W-Br Hey, Pierre. ³⁸**This is Chris Suzuki. He's our new apprentice.**

M-Cn Nice to meet you, Chris. So you're training to become a welder?

M-Au Actually, a machinist. I'll spend part of my apprenticeship studying welding, and I'll also learn to read blueprints and operate machinery.

M-Cn Well, ³⁹**you came to the right place. There's plenty of experienced workers and opportunities for hands-on practice in this factory.**

M-Au I'm excited to get started.

W-Br Well, ⁴⁰**we'll let you get back to work. I want Chris to meet a few more people before the shift ends.**

여 안녕, 피에르. **여기는 크리스 스즈키예요. 새로 온 견습생이죠.**

남1 만나서 반가워요, 크리스. 그러니까 용접공이 되려고 훈련하고 있나요?

남2 실은 기계공입니다. 견습 기간 일부는 용접을 배우고, 또 청사진 읽는 법과 기계 작동법도 배우려고요.

38

Who is Chris Suzuki?

(A) A shift manager
(B) An inspector
(C) An apprentice
(D) A new client

크리스 스즈키는 누구인가?

(A) 교대조 관리자
(B) 검사원
(C) 견습생
(D) 신규 고객

해설 세부 사항 관련 – 크리스 스즈키의 직업

여자가 첫 대사에서 여기는 크리스 스즈키(This is Chris Suzuki)라고 남자를 소개하며 새로 온 견습생(He's our new apprentice)이라고 말하고 있으므로 정답은 (C)이다.

39

Where is the conversation most likely taking place?

(A) In a hardware store
(B) In a factory
(C) In a storage facility
(D) In a product showroom

대화는 어디에서 이루어지겠는가?

(A) 철물점
(B) 공장
(C) 보관 시설
(D) 제품 전시장

해설 전체 내용 관련 – 대화의 장소

첫 번째 남자가 두 번째 대사에서 제대로 찾아오셨다(you came to the right place)며 이 공장에는 숙련된 작업자도 많고 실습 기회도 많다(There're plenty of experienced workers ~ in this factory)고 말하고 있으므로 화자들이 공장에서 대화하고 있다는 것을 알 수 있다. 따라서 정답은 (B)이다.

40

What will the woman probably do next?

(A) Negotiate a contract with Chris
(B) Review scheduling procedures with Chris
(C) Introduce Chris to some colleagues
(D) Show Chris the cafeteria

TEST 9

여자는 다음에 무엇을 하겠는가?

(A) 크리스와 계약 협상

(B) 크리스와 일정 관리 절차 검토

(C) 크리스를 동료들에게 소개

(D) 크리스에게 구내식당 안내

어휘 contract 계약(서) procedure 절차 colleague 동료

해설 세부 사항 관련 - 여자가 다음에 할 일

여자가 마지막 대사에서 우리는 그만 가 볼 테니 다시 일하라(we'll let you get back to work)며 교대 근무가 끝나기 전에 크리스에게 몇 사람 더 소개하려고 한다(I want Chris to meet a few more people before the shift ends)고 말하고 있으므로 정답은 (C)이다.

> ▸▸ Paraphrasing 대화의 want Chris to meet a few more people → 정답의 Introduce Chris to some colleagues

41-43

M-Cn	Hi, Marisol. **41 I got the invitation from Sunita about your party on Friday. I can't believe this is your last week here.** You've had quite a career.
W-Am	Thank you. It's been great.
M-Cn	I'll definitely be at the party. **42 What's your favorite dessert?**
W-Am	Oh, **42 I love cheesecake.**
M-Cn	OK, **42 I have the perfect recipe.** Well, this is exciting. So, what's next for you?
W-Am	**43 I'm going overseas to Europe for a couple of weeks. I can't wait.**
M-Cn	Sounds amazing.

남	안녕, 마리솔. **금요일에 당신을 위한 파티가 있다고 수니타에게 초대받았어요. 이번 주가 여기서 근무하시는 마지막 주라니 믿기지가 않네요.** 경력이 상당하시니까요.
여	감사합니다. 정말 좋았어요.
남	파티에 꼭 갈게요. **어떤 디저트를 제일 좋아하시죠?**
여	아, **치즈케이크를 좋아해요.**
남	그렇군요, **저한테 완벽한 조리법이 있어요.** 음, 설레는데요. 그래서 이제 뭘 하실 건가요?
여	**2주 동안 유럽으로 해외여행을 가려고요. 얼른 가고 싶어요.**
남	멋지네요.

어휘 definitely 꼭 overseas 해외로

41

What will most likely be celebrated on Friday?

(A) A promotion

(B) A retirement

(C) A graduation

(D) A business deal

금요일에 무엇을 축하하겠는가?

(A) 승진

(B) 은퇴

(C) 졸업

(D) 사업 계약

해설 세부 사항 관련 - 금요일에 축하할 일

남자가 첫 대사에서 금요일에 당신을 위한 파티가 있다고 수니타에게 초대받았다(I got the invitation from Sunita about your party on Friday)며 이번 주가 여기서 근무하시는 마지막 주라니 믿기지가 않는다(I can't believe this is your last week here)고 말하고 있으므로 금요일에 여자의 은퇴 기념 파티가 있다는 것을 알 수 있다. 따라서 정답은 (B)이다.

> ▸▸ Paraphrasing 대화의 last week here → 정답의 retirement

42

What does the man offer to do?

(A) Look for a receipt

(B) Send invitations

(C) Reserve a room

(D) Prepare a dessert

남자는 무엇을 하겠다고 제안하는가?

(A) 영수증 찾기

(B) 초대장 발송하기

(C) 방 예약하기

(D) 디저트 준비하기

어휘 receipt 영수증

해설 세부 사항 관련 - 남자의 제안 사항

남자가 두 번째 대사에서 여자에게 어떤 디저트를 제일 좋아하는지(What's your favorite dessert?) 물었고 여자가 치즈케이크를 좋아한다(I love cheesecake)고 대답하자 저한테 완벽한 조리법이 있다(I have the perfect recipe)고 말하는 것으로 보아, 남자는 여자를 위해 치즈케이크를 만들겠다고 제안하고 있음을 알 수 있다. 따라서 정답은 (D)이다.

43

What does the woman say she is looking forward to?

(A) Visiting her family

(B) Moving to a different city

(C) Traveling internationally

(D) Organizing a team

여자는 무엇을 고대하고 있다고 말하는가?

(A) 가족 방문
(B) 다른 도시로 이사
(C) 해외여행
(D) 팀 구성

어휘 organize 구성하다

해설 세부 사항 관련 – 여자가 고대하고 있다고 말하는 일

여자가 세 번째 대사에서 2주 동안 유럽으로 해외여행을 갈 것(I'm going overseas to Europe for a couple of weeks)이라며 얼른 가고 싶다(I can't wait)고 말하고 있으므로 정답은 (C)이다.

> ▶▶ Paraphrasing 대화의 going overseas
> → 정답의 Traveling internationally

44-46

M-Au	Excuse me. I'm looking at these floor mats. My office chair scratches my hardwood floor, so I need something to protect it. ⁴⁴**I bought a mat somewhere else, but it had a strong plastic smell.**
W-Am	That shouldn't be a problem with our floor mats. ⁴⁵**You're welcome to take one out of the box to see for yourself.**
M-Au	Thanks. Is there a chair I can try it with? I want to make sure the wheels won't sink into it.
W-Am	Sure. ⁴⁶**These mats have a patented easy-glide surface, meaning they're firm enough to let you freely maneuver around your work space in a rolling chair. It's something the manufacturer's particularly proud of.**
남	실례합니다. 이 바닥 매트를 보고 있는데요. 제 사무실 의자가 원목 바닥을 긁어서, 바닥을 보호할 게 필요하거든요. **다른 곳에서 매트를 샀는데, 플라스틱 냄새가 심했어요.**
여	저희 바닥 매트라면 그런 문제는 없어요. **상자에서 꺼내서 직접 보셔도 돼요.**
남	고마워요. 매트를 시험해 볼 만한 의자가 있나요? 바퀴가 빠지지 않는지 확인하고 싶어서요.
여	물론이죠. 이 매트들은 쉽게 미끄러지는 특허 받은 표면으로 돼 있어요. 그러니까 회전의자로 작업 공간에서 자유롭게 움직일 수 있을 만큼 견고합니다. 제조업체가 특히 자부하는 **부분이죠.**
어휘	protect 보호하다 patented 특허 받은 easy-glide 쉽게 미끄러지는 maneuver 움직이다 manufacturer 제조업체

44

What was the problem with the man's previous floor mat?

(A) It was not durable.
(B) It had a strong odor.
(C) It damaged the floor.
(D) It was too small.

남자의 이전 바닥 매트에 어떤 문제가 있었는가?

(A) 튼튼하지 않았다.
(B) 냄새가 심했다.
(C) 바닥을 훼손했다.
(D) 너무 작았다.

어휘 durable 튼튼한 odor 냄새

해설 세부 사항 관련 – 남자의 이전 바닥 매트의 문제

남자가 첫 대사에서 다른 곳에서 매트를 샀는데 플라스틱 냄새가 심했다(I bought a mat somewhere else, but it had a strong plastic smell)고 말하고 있으므로 정답은 (B)이다.

> ▶▶ Paraphrasing 대화의 smell → 정답의 odor

45

What does the woman invite the man to do?

(A) View images in a catalog
(B) Read about special features
(C) Watch a demonstration
(D) Open a package

여자는 남자에게 무엇을 하라고 권유하는가?

(A) 카탈로그에서 사진 보기
(B) 특별한 기능에 관해 읽기
(C) 시연 보기
(D) 포장 풀기

어휘 feature 기능

해설 세부 사항 관련 – 여자의 권유 사항

여자가 첫 대사에서 상자에서 물건을 꺼내어 직접 봐도 된다(You're welcome to take one out of the box to see for yourself)고 말하고 있으므로 정답은 (D)이다.

> ▶▶ Paraphrasing 대화의 take one out of the box
> → 정답의 Open a package

46

According to the woman, why is a manufacturer proud of its floor mats?

(A) They are easy to clean.
(B) They can be used on a variety of surfaces.
(C) They allow for free movement.
(D) They can be rolled or folded.

TEST 9

여자의 말에 따르면, 제조업체는 왜 바닥 매트에 자부심을 갖는가?

(A) 청소하기 쉽다.

(B) 다양한 표면에 사용할 수 있다.

(C) 자유롭게 움직일 수 있다.

(D) 말거나 접을 수 있다.

해설 세부 사항 관련 - 여자가 제조업체가 바닥 매트에 자부심을 갖는 이유라고 말하는 것

여자가 마지막 대사에서 이 매트들은 쉽게 미끄러지는 특허 받은 표면으로 되어 있어 회전의자로 작업 공간에서 자유롭게 움직일 수 있을 만큼 견고하다(These mats have a patented easy-glide ~ work space in a rolling chair)며 제조업체가 특히 자부하는 부분(It's something the manufacturer's particularly proud of)이라고 말하고 있으므로 정답은 (C)이다.

> ▸▸ **Paraphrasing** 대화의 let you freely maneuver around your work space
> → 정답의 allow for free movement

47-49

W-Am	Abdullah, ⁴⁷**have you edited the film footage for that frozen food commercial yet?**
M-Cn	⁴⁷**The video and music are done, but I'm still working on the dubbing to add the actors' voices in.**
W-Am	⁴⁸**Can you have it finished by the end of the week? The client hoped to have it air on television next Monday.**
M-Cn	Well, we just switched to a new software program.
W-Am	Hmm... OK. I'll ask the client if they'd be willing to move the deadline for us. By the way, ⁴⁹**congratulations. I heard that you recently won a best effects award in an industry competition.**
M-Cn	Oh, thanks. Yes, I worked hard on the entry I submitted, so I was happy to be selected.

여 압둘라, 냉동식품 광고 영상 편집하셨어요?

남 영상과 음악은 끝났지만, 배우들 목소리를 입히려고 아직 더빙 작업을 하고 있어요.

여 이번 주말까지 끝낼 수 있을까요? 고객이 다음 주 월요일에 TV로 방송하고 싶다고 했어요.

남 음, 얼마 전에 새 소프트웨어 프로그램으로 교체했어요.

여 음… 알겠어요. 우리한테 맞춰 마감일을 옮길 생각이 있는지 고객에게 물어볼게요. 그나저나, **축하해요**. 최근에 업계 대회에서 최우수 효과상을 수상했다고 들었어요.

남 아, 고마워요. 네, 제출한 응모작을 열심히 준비했던 터라 뽑혀서 기뻤어요.

어휘   footage 영상 commercial 광고 air 방송하다, 방송되다 effect 효과 competition 대회 entry 응모작

47

What industry do the speakers most likely work in?

(A) Music

(B) Restaurant

(C) Film production

(D) Book publishing

화자들은 어떤 업계에서 일하겠는가?

(A) 음악

(B) 식당

(C) 영상 제작

(D) 도서 출판

해설 전체 내용 관련 - 화자들의 근무 업계

여자가 첫 대사에서 냉동식품 광고 영상을 편집했는지(have you edited the film ~ commercial yet?) 묻고 있고, 뒤이어 남자가 영상과 음악은 끝났지만 배우들 목소리를 입히려고 아직 더빙 작업을 하고 있다(The video and music are done ~ add the actors' voices in)고 말하는 것으로 보아 정답은 (C)이다.

48

What does the man mean when he says, "we just switched to a new software program"?

(A) He needs to consult a user's manual.

(B) The quality of his work will improve.

(C) A task may take longer than expected.

(D) A training session should be organized.

남자가 "얼마 전에 새 소프트웨어 프로그램으로 교체했어요"라고 말하는 의도는 무엇인가?

(A) 사용 설명서를 참고해야 한다.

(B) 작품의 질이 향상될 것이다.

(C) 작업이 예상보다 오래 걸릴 수 있다.

(D) 교육 세션을 준비해야 한다.

해설 화자의 의도 파악 - 얼마 전에 새 소프트웨어 프로그램으로 교체했다는 말의 의도

앞에서 여자가 이번 주말까지 일을 끝낼 수 있을지(Can you have it finished by the end of the week?)를 물으며 고객이 다음 주 월요일에 TV로 방송하고 싶다고 했다(The client hoped to have it air on television next Monday)고 재촉하자 인용문을 언급한 것이므로, 새 소프트웨어 프로그램이 아직 익숙하지 않아 평소보다 작업 시간이 더 걸릴 수 있다는 의도로 한 말임을 알 수 있다. 따라서 정답은 (C)이다.

49

Why does the woman congratulate the man?

(A) He won an award.

(B) He received a promotion.

(C) He will be leading a team.

(D) He developed some new software.

여자는 남자를 왜 축하하는가?

(A) 상을 받았다.
(B) 승진했다.
(C) 팀을 이끌 것이다.
(D) 새로운 소프트웨어를 개발했다.

해설 세부 사항 관련 - 여자가 남자를 축하하는 이유

여자가 세 번째 대사에서 남자에게 축하한다(congratulations)며 최근에 업계 대회에서 최우수 효과상을 수상했다고 들었다(I heard that you recently won a best effects award in an industry competition)고 이유를 말하고 있으므로 정답은 (A)이다.

50-52 3인 대화

M-Au	Hello. Welcome to New York Ferry Service. ⁵⁰**How can I help you two?**
W-Br	Hi. ⁵⁰**We're trying to catch the next ferry to the city.**
W-Am	⁵⁰**Yeah, how much are one-way commuter tickets?**
M-Au	OK. It's ten dollars per person. Have you heard of our new payment option?
W-Br	No. What is it?
M-Au	Well, ⁵¹**we just introduced a payment system that allows you to pay for your tickets right from your smartphone. No cash is needed.**
W-Am	That sounds great.
M-Au	It definitely is! ⁵²**I suggest you both download our app** so you can use this method in the future.

남	안녕하세요. 어서 오세요. 뉴욕 페리 서비스입니다. **두 분, 어떻게 도와 드릴까요?**
여1	안녕하세요. **시로 가는 다음 페리를 타려고요.**
여2	**맞아요, 편도 정기권이 얼마죠?**
남	네. 1인당 10달러입니다. 새로운 결제 옵션에 대해 들어 보셨어요?
여1	아뇨. 뭔데요?
남	어, 스마트폰에서 바로 티켓값을 결제할 수 있는 결제 시스템을 얼마 전에 도입했습니다. 현금이 필요 없죠.
여2	좋네요.
남	그렇고 말고요! 앞으로는 이 방법을 사용할 수 있도록 **두 분 다 앱을 다운로드하시길 권합니다.**

어휘 commuter ticket 정기권 payment 결제

50

What do the women want to do?

(A) Rent a car
(B) Buy ferry tickets
(C) Take a city tour
(D) Book a hotel

여자들은 무엇을 하고 싶어 하는가?

(A) 차 임대
(B) 페리 티켓 구매
(C) 시내 관광
(D) 호텔 예약

해설 세부 사항 관련 - 여자들이 하고 싶어 하는 일

남자가 첫 대사에서 두 분을 어떻게 도와 드릴지(How can I help you two?) 묻자 첫 번째 여자는 시로 가는 다음 페리를 타려고 한다(We're trying to catch the next ferry to the city)고 했고 뒤어어 두 번째 여자는 맞다(Yeah)며 편도 정기권이 얼마인지(how much are one-way commuter tickets?)를 묻고 있으므로 여자들이 페리 티켓을 사려는 것임을 알 수 있다. 따라서 정답은 (B)이다.

51

What does the man say was recently introduced?

(A) A customer loyalty program
(B) An online feedback form
(C) A cashless payment system
(D) A renovated waiting area

남자는 최근에 무엇이 도입됐다고 말하는가?

(A) 고객 보상 프로그램
(B) 온라인 의견 제시 양식
(C) 현금이 필요 없는 결제 시스템
(D) 개조한 대합실

어휘 renovate 개조하다

해설 세부 사항 관련 - 남자가 최근에 도입되었다고 말하는 것

남자가 세 번째 대사에서 스마트폰에서 바로 티켓값을 결제할 수 있는 결제 시스템을 얼마 전에 도입했다(we just introduced a payment system ~ from your smartphone)며 현금이 필요 없다(No cash is needed)고 말하고 있으므로 정답은 (C)이다.

▸▸ Paraphrasing 대화의 No cash is needed → 정답의 cashless

52

What does the man suggest the women do?

(A) Purchase some postcards
(B) Visit a historic site
(C) Call a taxi service
(D) Download a mobile application

남자는 여자들에게 무엇을 하라고 권하는가?

(A) 엽서 구입
(B) 유적지 방문
(C) 택시 회사에 전화
(D) 모바일 애플리케이션 다운로드

어휘 purchase 구입하다 historic site 유적지

해설 세부 사항 관련 - 남자의 권유 사항

남자가 마지막 대사에서 두 분 다 앱을 다운로드하기를 권한다(I suggest you both download our app)고 말하고 있으므로 정답은 (D)이다.

> ▸▸ Paraphrasing   대화의 app → 정답의 application

53-55

W-Br	Hans Jones Jewelry? Hmm, [53]**I don't remember seeing your booth at this trade show before.** Can you tell me about your company?
M-Cn	Sure. We're a relatively new company, and we're just starting to visit trade shows. [54]**We specialize in creating affordable jewelry made with high-quality materials.**
W-Br	Your necklaces are beautiful. I'd love to sell them at my fashion boutiques. Do you make any earrings or bracelets?
M-Cn	Yes, I just didn't have room to display them here. But [55]**take one of our catalogs.** It has pictures of our entire collection.

여	한스 존스 주얼리? 흠, **이 무역 박람회에선 귀사의 부스를 본 기억이 없네요.** 회사에 대해 얘기해 주시겠어요?
남	물론이죠. 비교적 신생 회사라서 이제 막 무역 박람회를 다니기 시작했어요. **저희는 고급 재료로 만드는 저렴한 보석을 전문으로 제작하고 있어요.**
여	목걸이 예쁘네요. 제 패션 부티크에서 판매하고 싶어요. 귀걸이나 팔찌를 만드나요?
남	네, 여기에 전시할 공간이 없었을 뿐이에요. 그래도 **카탈로그 하나를 가져가세요.** 전체 상품 사진이 있어요.

어휘	relatively 비교적 affordable 저렴한 bracelet 팔찌

53

Where are the speakers?

(A) At a fund-raiser
(B) At a trade show
(C) At a job fair
(D) At a store opening

화자들은 어디에 있는가?

(A) 모금 행사
(B) **무역 박람회**
(C) 취업 박람회
(D) 매장 개업식

해설 전체 내용 관련 - 대화의 장소

여자가 첫 대사에서 이 무역 박람회에서는 귀사의 부스를 본 기억이 없다(I don't remember seeing your booth at this trade show before)고

말하고 있으므로 화자들은 지금 무역 박람회에 참석하고 있다는 것을 알 수 있다. 따라서 정답은 (B)이다.

54

What kind of products does the man's company make?

(A) Jewelry
(B) Handbags
(C) Floor rugs
(D) Picture frames

남자의 회사는 어떤 종류의 제품을 만드는가?

(A) **보석**
(B) 핸드백
(C) 바닥 깔개
(D) 액자

해설 세부 사항 관련 - 남자의 회사가 만드는 제품

남자가 첫 대사에서 저희는 고급 재료로 만드는 저렴한 보석을 전문으로 제작하고 있다(We specialize in creating affordable jewelry made with high-quality materials)고 말하고 있으므로 정답은 (A)이다.

55

What does the man suggest doing?

(A) Leaving a business card
(B) Registering online
(C) Placing an order
(D) Taking a catalog

남자는 무엇을 하라고 권하는가?

(A) 명함 남기기
(B) 온라인으로 등록하기
(C) 주문하기
(D) **카탈로그 가져가기**

해설 세부 사항 관련 - 남자의 권유 사항

남자가 마지막 대사에서 여자에게 카탈로그 하나를 가져가라(take one of our catalogs)고 권하고 있으므로 정답은 (D)이다.

56-58

W-Br	Hi, Carlos. [56]**I have a question about the news story you're working on**—the one about the local bus system. [58]**Did you get a quote from someone at the transit agency?**
M-Au	[58]**No, I haven't been able to contact anyone there yet.** And [56,57]**our deadline to get this story on tonight's news is five** P.M. [58]**I'm concerned we'll miss it if they don't respond soon.**

W-Br	Well, I just heard **they're hosting a big press conference at noon.**
M-Au	What a great idea—I'll leave now.

여	안녕하세요, 카를로스. 작성 중인 뉴스 기사에 관해 물어볼게 있어요. 시내버스 시스템에 대한 기사 말이에요. **교통부 사람한테 인터뷰를 따셨나요?**
남	아뇨, 거긴 아직 아무도 연락이 안 닿았어요. 오늘 저녁 뉴스에 기사를 내보내려면 마감 시간이 오후 5시예요. 그쪽에서 빨리 응하지 않으면 마감 시간을 놓칠까 봐 걱정이에요.
여	아, 좀 전에 들었는데 **정오에 대규모 기자 회견을 연다**고 하던데요.
남	정말 기발한 생각이에요. 지금 갈게요.

어휘	quote 인용 transit agency 교통부 press conference 기자 회견

56

Who most likely are the speakers?

(A) News reporters
(B) Travel agents
(C) Bus drivers
(D) City officials

화자들은 누구이겠는가?

(A) 기자
(B) 여행사 직원
(C) 버스 기사
(D) 시 공무원

해설 전체 내용 관련 - 화자들의 직업

여자가 첫 대사에서 작성 중인 뉴스 기사에 관해 물어볼 게 있다(I have a question about the news story you're working on)고 했고, 뒤이어 남자도 오늘 저녁 뉴스에 기사를 내보내려면 마감 시간이 오후 5시(our deadline to get this story on tonight's news is five P.M.)라고 말하는 것으로 보아 화자들은 기자들임을 알 수 있다. 따라서 정답은 (A)이다.

57

Why is the man concerned?

(A) He forgot to make a phone call.
(B) He might miss a deadline.
(C) A contract requires a signature.
(D) A colleague is late for work.

남자는 왜 걱정하는가?

(A) 깜박하고 전화를 안 했다.
(B) 마감 시간을 놓칠 수도 있다.
(C) 계약서에 서명이 필요하다.
(D) 동료가 직장에 지각한다.

해설 세부 사항 관련 - 남자가 걱정하는 이유

남자가 첫 대사에서 오늘 저녁 뉴스에 기사를 내보내려면 마감 시간이 오후 5시(our deadline to get this story on tonight's news is five P.M.)라면서 그쪽에서 빨리 응하지 않으면 마감 시간을 놓칠까 봐 걱정된다

(I'm concerned we'll miss it if they don't respond soon)고 말하고 있으므로 정답은 (B)이다.

58

Why does the woman say, "they're hosting a big press conference at noon"?

(A) To suggest attending an event
(B) To inform the man about a schedule change
(C) To complain about a decision
(D) To ask the man for a ride

여자는 왜 "정오에 대규모 기자 회견을 연다"라고 말하는가?

(A) 행사 참석을 제안하려고
(B) 남자에게 일정 변경을 알리려고
(C) 결정에 불만을 제기하려고
(D) 남자에게 차를 태워다 달라고 부탁하려고

해설 화자의 의도 파악 - 정오에 대규모 기자 회견을 연다는 말의 의도

앞에서 여자가 교통부 사람한테 인터뷰를 땄는지(Did you get a quote from someone at the transit agency?)를 물었고 남자가 거기는 아직 아무도 연락이 안 닿았다(No, I haven't been able to contact anyone there yet)고 대답하며 그쪽에서 빨리 응하지 않으면 마감 시간을 놓칠까 봐 걱정된다(I'm concerned we'll miss it if they don't respond soon)고 하자 여자가 인용문을 언급한 것이므로, 교통부에서 여는 기자 회견에 직접 가서 인터뷰할 것을 제안하려고 한 말임을 알 수 있다. 따라서 정답은 (A)이다.

59-61

M-Au	Tomoko, [59] **our sales of fresh flowers have always been strong, but to increase business, I think we should try to sell more indoor potted plants.** I'm sure we could find customers in local office buildings.
W-Br	Not just offices. People working from home would be interested, too. [60] **Why don't we start promoting the idea by featuring some plants on our Web site?**
M-Au	[60] **OK, let's do that.** [61] **I know a photographer who specializes in product pictures. I'll get in touch and see when she's available.**

남	토모코, 생화 판매는 항상 잘됐지만, 사업을 키우려면 실내 화분을 더 많이 팔도록 애써야 할 것 같아요. 틀림없이 지역 사무용 건물들에서 고객을 찾을 수 있을 거예요.
여	사무실뿐만 아니죠. 집에서 일하는 사람들도 관심 있을 거예요. 우리 웹사이트에 식물 몇 개를 선보이면서 이런 아이디어를 홍보하는 게 어때요?
남	좋아요, 그렇게 하죠. 제품 사진을 전문으로 하는 사진작가를 알고 있어요. 제가 연락해서 언제 시간이 되는지 알아볼게요.

59

Where do the speakers most likely work?

(A) At a real estate agency

(B) At a florist shop

(C) At a construction company

(D) At an interior design firm

화자들은 어디에서 일하겠는가?

(A) 부동산 중개업소

(B) 꽃집

(C) 건설 회사

(D) 인테리어 디자인 업체

해설 전체 내용 관련 - 화자들의 근무지

남자가 첫 대사에서 생화 판매는 항상 잘됐지만 사업을 키우려면 실내 화분을 더 많이 팔도록 애써야 할 것 같다(our sales of fresh flowers ~ to sell more indoor potted plants)고 말하는 것으로 보아 화자들은 꽃을 판매하는 일을 하고 있음을 알 수 있다. 따라서 정답은 (B)이다.

60

What do the speakers agree to do?

(A) Promote some products on a Web site

(B) Send e-mails to previous customers

(C) Leave brochures in a building lobby

(D) Put up signs near a highway

화자들은 무엇을 하는 데 동의하는가?

(A) 웹사이트에서 제품 홍보

(B) 이전 고객들에게 이메일 발송

(C) 건물 로비에 소책자 비치

(D) 고속도로 주변에 팻말 설치

해설 세부 사항 관련 - 화자들이 동의한 일

여자가 첫 대사에서 우리 웹사이트에 식물 몇 개를 선보이면서 이런 아이디어를 홍보하는 게 어떨지(Why don't we start promoting the idea by featuring some plants on our Web site?)를 묻자 남자도 좋다 (OK)며 그렇게 하자(let's do that)고 동의하고 있으므로 정답은 (A)이다.

61

Who does the man say he will contact?

(A) An administrative assistant

(B) An Internet provider

(C) A photographer

(D) An accountant

남자는 누구에게 연락하겠다고 말하는가?

(A) 행정 보조

(B) 인터넷 공급업체

(C) 사진작가

(D) 회계사

해설 세부 사항 관련 - 남자가 연락하겠다고 말하는 사람

남자가 마지막 대사에서 제품 사진을 전문으로 하는 사진작가를 알고 있다 (I know a photographer who specializes in product pictures)며 제가 연락해서 언제 시간이 되는지 알아보겠다(I'll get in touch and see when she's available)고 말하고 있으므로 정답은 (C)이다.

62-64 대화 + 표

M-Cn	Hello, this is the Vega Event Center. How can I help you?
W-Br	Hi. **62I work for Thomson Manufacturing Company, and we're planning a charity auction.**
M-Cn	Great, we've definitely hosted those before. How many guests do you anticipate?
W-Br	Well, **63we want to invite 250 guests. Do you have an event space that would accommodate us?**
M-Cn	Oh, yes. **63One of our banquet rooms fits between 200 and 300 people.**
W-Br	Excellent. **64We'd also like to have a musical act perform during the auction. Can you recommend some bands?**
M-Cn	Absolutely. **64I'll send you a list of groups that we regularly hire.**

남	안녕하세요, 베가 이벤트 센터입니다. 어떻게 도와 드릴까요?
여	안녕하세요. **저는 톰슨 제조 회사에서 일하는데 자선 경매를 계획하고 있어요.**
남	잘됐네요, 저희가 전에 분명 그런 행사를 주최한 적이 있습니다. 손님은 몇 명으로 예상하시나요?
여	음, 손님 250명을 초대하고 싶어요. 수용할 수 있는 행사 공간이 있나요?
남	아, 네. 연회실 중 한 곳이 200명에서 300명까지 들어갑니다.
여	좋아요. 경매가 진행되는 동안 음악 그룹에게 공연을 맡기고 싶어요. 밴드 좀 추천해 주시겠어요?
남	물론이죠. 저희가 자주 고용하는 그룹 목록을 보내 드릴게요.

Vega Event Center	
Arroyo Room	100–200 people
Salinas Room	63200–300 people
Reyes Room	300–400 people
Miramar Room	400–500 people

베가 이벤트 센터	
아로요 룸	100-200명
살리나스 룸	[63]**200-300명**
레이예스 룸	300-400명
미라마 룸	400-500명

62

What is the woman planning?

(A) A product launch
(B) A charity event
(C) A retirement party
(D) A factory inspection

여자는 무엇을 계획하고 있는가?

(A) 제품 출시
(B) 자선 행사
(C) 은퇴 파티
(D) 공장 점검

어휘 retirement 은퇴 inspection 점검

해설 세부 사항 관련 - 여자가 계획하는 일

여자가 첫 대사에서 저는 톰슨 제조 회사에서 일하는데 자선 경매를 계획하고 있다(I work for Thomson Manufacturing Company, and we're planning a charity auction)고 말하고 있으므로 정답은 (B)이다.

> ▸▸ Paraphrasing 대화의 a charity auction
> → 정답의 A charity event

63

Look at the graphic. Which room will the woman most likely reserve?

(A) The Arroyo Room
(B) The Salinas Room
(C) The Reyes Room
(D) The Miramar Room

시각 정보에 의하면 여자는 어떤 방을 예약하겠는가?

(A) 아로요 룸
(B) 살리나스 룸
(C) 레이예스 룸
(D) 미라마 룸

해설 시각 정보 연계 - 여자가 예약할 것 같은 방

여자가 두 번째 대사에서 손님 250명을 초대하고 싶다(we want to invite 250 guests)며 수용할 수 있는 행사 공간이 있는지(Do you have an event space that would accommodate us?) 묻자 남자가 연회실 중 한 곳이 200명에서 300명까지 들어간다(One of our banquet rooms fits between 200 and 300 people)고 안내하고 있고, 표에 따르면 200~300명을 수용할 수 있는 방은 살리나스 룸이므로 정답은 (B)이다.

64

What does the man say he will provide?

(A) Some measurements
(B) Some menu options
(C) Proof of insurance
(D) A list of musicians

남자는 무엇을 제공하겠다고 말하는가?

(A) 치수
(B) 메뉴 옵션
(C) 보험 증빙 서류
(D) 음악가 목록

어휘 measurement 치수 insurance 보험

해설 세부 사항 관련 - 남자가 제공하겠다고 말하는 것

여자가 세 번째 대사에서 경매가 진행되는 동안 음악 그룹에게 공연을 맡기고 싶다(We'd also like to have a musical act perform during the auction)며 밴드를 추천해 줄 수 있는지(Can you recommend some bands?) 묻자 남자가 저희가 자주 고용하는 그룹 목록을 보내 드리겠다(I'll send you a list of groups that we regularly hire)고 말하고 있으므로 정답은 (D)이다.

65-67 대화 + 그래프

W-Br	[65]**Joining me for tonight's news broadcast is aviation expert Dmitry Petrov.**
M-Au	Thanks for having me.
W-Br	Airports around the country are seeing more and more flight delays. What might be causing this trend?
M-Au	Air travel has been steadily increasing. More travelers and flights cause airport congestion—and delays.
W-Br	Is this trend consistent across airports?
M-Au	Actually, no. [66]**Look at this graph. Some see average delays of around twenty minutes, but some like this airport here, can be over forty.**
W-Br	What would you tell travelers to do?
M-Au	[67]**If possible, try changing your plans to avoid cities known for delays, and if you can, shift your travel to off-peak times.**

여	**오늘밤 뉴스 방송에 저와 함께하실 항공 전문가 드미트리 페트로프 씨입니다.**
남	초대해 주셔서 감사합니다.
여	전국에 있는 공항들에서 비행편 지연이 점점 더 많아지고 있습니다. 이런 추세의 원인이 뭘까요?
남	항공 여행이 꾸준히 늘고 있어요. 여행객과 비행편이 많아지면서 공항 혼잡과 지연이 일어나고 있죠.

여	이런 추세가 전체 공항에 일관되게 나타나나요?
남	사실 그렇지 않습니다. 이 그래프를 보세요. 어떤 공항은 평균 20분 정도 지연되지만, 여기 이 공항처럼 일부는 40분 이상 지연되기도 합니다.
여	여행자들에게 권고하실 말씀은요?
남	가능하면 지연이 잦은 것으로 알려진 도시는 피하도록 계획을 변경하고, 할 수 있다면 여행 시기를 비수기로 바꾸세요.
어휘	aviation 항공 expert 전문가 steadily 꾸준히 congestion 혼잡 consistent 일관된 off-peak 비수기의

Flight Delays by Airport, in Minutes

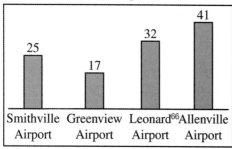

공항별 비행편 지연, 분 단위

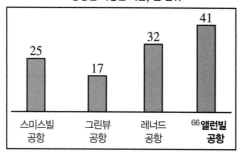

65

Who most likely is the woman?

(A) A commercial pilot
(B) A regional manager
(C) A travel agent
(D) A news reporter

여자는 누구이겠는가?
(A) 민간 항공기 조종사
(B) 지역 관리자
(C) 여행사 직원
(D) **뉴스 기자**

해설 전체 내용 관련 - 여자의 직업

여자가 첫 대사에서 오늘밤 뉴스 방송에 저와 함께하실 항공 전문가 드미트리 페트로프 씨(Joining me for tonight's news broadcast is aviation expert Dmitry Petrov)라고 말하는 것으로 보아 여자는 뉴스 방송에서 인터뷰를 진행 중인 기자임을 알 수 있다. 따라서 정답은 (D)이다.

66

Look at the graphic. Which airport does the man point out?

(A) Smithville Airport
(B) Greenview Airport
(C) Leonard Airport
(D) **Allenville Airport**

시각 정보에 의하면 남자는 어느 공항을 가리키는가?
(A) 스미스빌 공항
(B) 그린뷰 공항
(C) 레너드 공항
(D) **앨런빌 공항**

해설 시각 정보 연계 - 남자가 가리키는 공항

남자가 세 번째 대사에서 이 그래프를 보라(Look at this graph)고 했고 어떤 공항은 평균 20분 정도 지연되지만 여기 이 공항처럼 일부는 40분 이상 지연되기도 한다(Some see average delays of ~ here, can be over forty)며 40분 이상 지연되는 공항을 지적하는데, 그래프에 따르면 40분 이상 지연된다고 표시된 공항은 앨런빌 공항이 유일하므로 정답은 (D)이다.

67

What does the man recommend?

(A) Adjusting travel plans
(B) Changing a delivery time
(C) Finding discounted tickets
(D) Hiring additional agents

남자는 무엇을 추천하는가?
(A) **여행 계획 조정**
(B) 배송 시간 변경
(C) 할인 티켓 찾기
(D) 대행업자 추가 채용

해설 세부 사항 관련 - 남자의 추천 사항

남자가 마지막 대사에서 가능하면 지연이 잦은 도시는 피하도록 계획을 변경하고 할 수 있다면 여행 시기를 비수기로 바꾸라(If possible, try changing your plans ~ shift your travel to off-peak times)고 권하고 있으므로 정답은 (A)이다.

> ▸▸ Paraphrasing   대화의 **changing your plans**
> → 정답의 **Adjusting travel plans**

68-70 대화 + 기념품

M-Cn	Helen, [68]**remember we discussed doing something special for our bakery's anniversary next month?**
W-Am	Yes, we talked about having a souvenir item with our logo on it.
M-Cn	Right. [69]**Here are four options I came up with.**

W-Am Let's see... **⁶⁹I think the short-sleeved shirt with our business logo on the front will have the widest appeal, since it'll be hot in the summer.** It will really help advertise our store too.

M-Cn **⁶⁹OK. ⁷⁰I'll go ahead and order those now.**

남 **헬렌, 다음 달 제과점 기념일에 뭔가 특별한 걸 하자고 얘기했던 거 기억나요?**

여 네, 로고가 찍힌 기념품을 하자고 얘기했죠.

남 **맞아요. 여기 제가 생각해 낸 네 가지 옵션이에요.**

여 어디 보자… **여름에 더울 테니까 앞면에 회사 로고가 있는 반팔 셔츠를 두루두루 좋아할 것 같아요.** 매장 광고에도 정말 도움이 될 거예요.

남 **알겠어요. 지금 바로 주문할게요.**

어휘 anniversary 기념일 souvenir 기념품 come up with ~을 생각해 내다

⁶⁹**$5.00** $6.00

$7.00 $8.00

⁶⁹**5달러**   6달러

7달러   8달러

68
What event is taking place next month?

(A) A concert
(B) A fund-raiser
(C) An anniversary celebration
(D) A community festival

다음 달에 무슨 행사가 열리는가?

(A) 음악회
(B) 모금 행사
(C) 기념일 축하 행사
(D) 지역 축제

해설 세부 사항 관련 – 다음 달에 열릴 행사

남자가 첫 대사에서 다음 달 제과점 기념일에 뭔가 특별한 걸 하자고 얘기했던 것을 기억나는지(remember we discussed doing something special for our bakery's anniversary next month?) 물으며 다음 달에 있을 기념일에 대해 언급하고 있으므로 정답은 (C)이다.

69
Look at the graphic. How much will the selected item cost?

(A) $5.00
(B) $6.00
(C) $7.00
(D) $8.00

시각 정보에 의하면 선택된 품목의 가격은 얼마인가?

(A) 5달러
(B) 6달러
(C) 7달러
(D) 8달러

해설 시각 정보 연계 – 선택된 품목의 가격

남자가 두 번째 대사에서 여기 제가 생각해낸 네 가지 옵션이 있다(Here are four options I came up with)고 보여 주자 여자가 여름에 더울 테니까 앞면에 회사 로고가 있는 반팔 셔츠를 두루두루 좋아할 것 같다(I think the short-sleeved shirt ~ be hot in the summer)고 했고 남자가 알겠다(OK)고 대답하고 있으므로 화자들은 반팔 셔츠를 선택했음을 알 수 있고, 기념품을 보면 반팔 셔츠는 5달러이므로 정답은 (A)이다.

70
What will the man do next?

(A) Revise a design
(B) Search a Web site
(C) Book a venue
(D) Place an order

남자는 다음에 무엇을 하겠는가?

(A) 디자인 수정
(B) 웹사이트 검색
(C) 장소 예약
(D) 주문

어휘 venue 장소

해설 세부 사항 관련 – 남자가 다음에 할 일

남자가 마지막 대사에서 지금 바로 주문하겠다(I'll go ahead and order those now)고 말하고 있으므로 정답은 (D)이다.

▸▸ Paraphrasing 대화의 order those
                → 정답의 Place an order

TEST 9

PART 4

71-73 광고

W-Br Are you looking to buy a new car, but you're also concerned about the environment? Then there's no better place to shop than at Henry's Car Dealership! Unlike other dealerships, ⁷¹**we only sell electric cars.** That means ⁷²**our vehicles produce zero direct emissions, which specifically helps improve air quality.** And ⁷³**we have a limited-time offer for you. If you buy a car by Sunday, you will get a year of free car washes!**

새 차를 사려고 하는데 환경도 걱정되시나요? 그렇다면 헨리 자동차 영업소만큼 쇼핑하기 좋은 곳은 없습니다! 다른 대리점과 달리 **저희는 전기차만 판매합니다.** 그러니까 **저희 차량은 직접 배출하는 가스가 없습니다. 공기 질을 개선하는 데 특별히 도움이 된다는 의미죠.** 그리고 **여러분을 위해 한정된 기간에 드리는 특별 혜택이 있습니다. 일요일까지 차를 구입하시면 1년 동안 무료로 세차하실 수 있습니다!**

어휘 environment 환경 emission 배출 limited-time offer 한정된 기간에만 제공하는 특별 할인[혜택]

71

What does the company sell?

(A) Racing bicycles
(B) Motorcycle parts
(C) Camping equipment
(D) Electric cars

회사는 무엇을 판매하는가?

(A) 경주용 자전거
(B) 오토바이 부품
(C) 캠핑 장비
(D) 전기차

해설 세부 사항 관련 – 회사가 판매하는 것

화자가 중반부에 저희는 전기차만 판매한다(we only sell electric cars)고 말하고 있으므로 정답은 (D)이다.

72

What does the speaker emphasize about the products?

(A) They are safe for the environment.
(B) They come with an extended warranty.
(C) They can be used with a mobile application.
(D) They are designed for all weather conditions.

화자는 제품에 대해 무엇을 강조하는가?

(A) 환경에 안전하다.
(B) 연장된 보증 기간이 주어진다.
(C) 모바일 애플리케이션으로 사용할 수 있다.
(D) 모든 기상 조건에 맞도록 설계되었다.

해설 세부 사항 관련 – 화자가 제품에 대해 강조하는 것

화자가 중반부에 저희 차량은 직접 배출하는 가스가 없어 공기 질을 개선하는 데 특별히 도움이 된다(our vehicles produce zero direct emissions, which specifically helps improve air quality)며 자사 제품이 환경에 미치는 긍정적인 영향에 대해 강조하고 있으므로 정답은 (A)이다.

73

What ends on Sunday?

(A) A contest
(B) A festival
(C) A factory tour
(D) A special offer

일요일에 무엇이 끝나는가?

(A) 대회
(B) 축제
(C) 공장 견학
(D) 특별 혜택

해설 세부 사항 관련 – 일요일에 끝나는 것

화자가 후반부에 여러분을 위해 한정된 기간에 드리는 특별 혜택이 있다(we have a limited-time offer for you)며 일요일까지 차를 구입하시면 1년 동안 무료로 세차하실 수 있다(If you buy a car by Sunday, you will get a year of free car washes!)고 말하고 있으므로 특별 혜택 행사는 일요일에 종료된다는 것을 알 수 있다. 따라서 정답은 (D)이다.

▶▶ **Paraphrasing**   담화의 a limited-time offer
→ 정답의 A special offer

74-76 견학 정보

M-Cn Welcome to Soo-Min's Factory. I'm delighted to give you a tour of our facility. Today, ⁷⁴**you'll see how we manufacture some of the world's favorite candies.** Unlike many candy factories, ⁷⁵**we still make our products by hand, just like we've been doing since the factory opened over 50 years ago. It's what we're known for.** Now before we go in, ⁷⁶**you'll need to leave your belongings in the lockers behind me.** We need to maintain a clean environment inside the factory, so it's very important that you don't take anything in with you.

수민의 공장에 오신 것을 환영합니다. 저희 시설을 둘러보시도록 안내하게 되어 기쁩니다. 오늘 여러분은 **저희가 세계에서 가장 사랑받는 사탕을 만드는 과정을 보시겠습니다.** 다른 많은 사탕 공장들과 달리, **저희는 아직도 손으로 제품을 만듭니다. 50여 년 전에 공장이 문을 연 이후로 쭉 해왔던 것처럼 말이죠. 저희는 그걸로 유명합니다.** 이제 들어가기 전에 제 **뒤에 있는 사물함에 소지품을 두세요.** 공장 내부는 깨끗한 환경을 유지해야 하므로, 아무것도 가지고 들어가지 않는 것이 매우 중요합니다.

어휘 manufacture 만들다 belongings 소지품 maintain 유지하다

254

74

What does the business make?

(A) Ice cream

(B) Beverages

(C) Candy

(D) Pretzels

업체는 무엇을 만드는가?

(A) 아이스크림

(B) 음료

(C) 사탕

(D) 프레첼

해설 세부 사항 관련 - 업체가 만드는 제품

화자가 초반부에 여러분은 저희가 세계에서 가장 사랑받는 사탕을 만드는 과정을 보게 될 것(you'll see how we manufacture some of the world's favorite candies)이라고 말하고 있으므로 정답은 (C)이다.

75

What does the speaker say the business is known for?

(A) Its high-quality ingredients

(B) Its clever packaging

(C) Its unique flavors

(D) Its handmade products

화자는 업체가 무엇으로 유명하다고 말하는가?

(A) 고급 재료

(B) 기발한 포장

(C) 독특한 맛

(D) 수제품

해설 세부 사항 관련 - 화자가 업체가 유명하다고 말하는 것

화자가 중반부에 50여 년 전에 공장이 문을 연 이후로 쭉 해 왔던 것처럼 저희는 아직도 손으로 제품을 만든다(we still make our products by hand, just like we've been doing since the factory opened over 50 years ago)며 저희가 그것으로 유명하다(It's what we're known for)고 말하고 있으므로 정답은 (D)이다.

> ▸▸ **Paraphrasing** 담화의 **make our products by hand**
> → 정답의 **handmade products**

76

What does the speaker ask the listeners to do?

(A) Leave their personal items in a locker

(B) Turn in their tickets

(C) Divide into smaller groups

(D) Put on some protective clothing

화자는 청자들에게 무엇을 해 달라고 요청하는가?

(A) 사물함에 개인 물품 두기

(B) 표 제출하기

(C) 소집단으로 나누기

(D) 보호복 착용하기

해설 세부 사항 관련 - 화자의 요청 사항

화자가 후반부에 자신의 뒤에 있는 사물함에 소지품을 두어야 한다(you'll need to leave your belongings in the lockers behind me)고 말하고 있으므로 정답은 (A)이다.

> ▸▸ **Paraphrasing** 담화의 **belongings**
> → 정답의 **personal items**

77-79 회의 발췌

> W-Br ⁷⁷**First on the staff meeting agenda is the new time-tracking software we're implementing.** All employees will start using it to record their hours beginning next month. Because it's very different from our previous software, everyone will receive access to an online training session. ⁷⁸**Note that you'll use the same log-on name and password as you used on the old system.** OK, next. ⁷⁹**Remember that a photographer will be here tomorrow to take pictures for the company Web site. Please wear professional attire.**

> **직원 회의 첫 번째 안건은 우리가 시행하게 될 새로운 시간 기록 소프트웨어입니다.** 다음 달부터 전 직원이 이 프로그램을 사용해 근무 시간을 기록하기 시작합니다. 이전 소프트웨어와 아주 다르기 때문에 모두 온라인 교육 세션에 접근할 권한을 받을 겁니다. **이전 시스템에서 사용한 것과 동일한 로그온 이름과 암호를 사용한다는 점 유념하세요.** 자, 다음 안건입니다. **내일 사진작가가 회사 웹사이트용 사진을 찍으러 온다는 것, 기억하세요. 근무에 적합한 복장을 착용해 주세요.**

> 어휘 agenda 안건 implement 시행하다 previous 이전의 access 접근 권한 attire 복장

77

What is the speaker mainly discussing?

(A) An upcoming conference

(B) A vacation policy

(C) Some new software

(D) Some new equipment

화자는 주로 무엇을 논의하고 있는가?

(A) 곧 있을 회의

(B) 휴가 규정

(C) 새로운 소프트웨어

(D) 새로운 장비

해설 전체 내용 관련 - 담화의 주제

화자가 도입부에 직원 회의 첫 번째 안건은 우리가 시행하게 될 새로운 시간 기록 소프트웨어(First on the staff meeting agenda is the new time-tracking software we're implementing)라고 회의 안건을 밝히고 있으므로 정답은 (C)이다.

TEST 9

78

What does the speaker tell the listeners to take note of?

(A) Some travel arrangements will be made online.

(B) Some log-on information will remain the same.

(C) A training session will be rescheduled.

(D) A security policy will be enforced.

화자는 청자들에게 무엇을 주의하라고 말하는가?

(A) 출장 준비는 온라인으로 이루어진다.

(B) 로그온 정보는 동일하게 유지된다.

(C) 교육 일정이 변경된다.

(D) 보안 규정이 시행된다.

어휘 arrangement 준비 enforce 시행하다

해설 세부 사항 관련 - 화자가 청자들에게 주의하라고 말하는 것

화자가 중반부에 이전 시스템에서 사용한 것과 동일한 로그온 이름과 암호를 사용한다는 점을 유념하라(Note that you'll use the same log-on name and password as you used on the old system)고 주의를 주고 있으므로 정답은 (B)이다.

> ▸▸ Paraphrasing   담화의 name and password
> → 정답의 information

79

What should the listeners do tomorrow?

(A) Confirm their work schedules

(B) Prepare a presentation

(C) Park in a different location

(D) Dress professionally

청자들은 내일 무엇을 해야 하는가?

(A) 근무 일정 확인하기

(B) 발표 준비하기

(C) 다른 장소에 주차하기

(D) 근무에 적합하게 입기

해설 세부 사항 관련 - 청자들이 내일 할 일

화자가 후반부에 내일 사진작가가 회사 웹사이트용 사진을 찍으러 온다는 것을 기억하라(Remember that a photographer will be here tomorrow to take pictures for the company Web site)면서 근무에 적합한 복장을 착용해 줄 것(Please wear professional attire)을 요청하고 있으므로 정답은 (D)이다.

> ▸▸ Paraphrasing   담화의 **wear professional attire**
> → 정답의 **Dress professionally**

80-82 방송

> M-Au   Welcome back to *Artist Hour* on Freetown Public Radio. ⁸⁰**With me here in the studio is Carol Thompson, the longtime director of the Freetown Art Museum.** Ms. Thompson has just announced that she'll be retiring at the end of the year, so she joins us today to talk about her career and future plans. As we'll discuss later, ⁸¹**she has always had a particular talent for fund-raising.** Over her 30-year career, she has raised a total of five million dollars for art restoration projects across the country. ⁸²**Ms. Thompson plans to write children's books about well-known artists when she retires.** The first will be based on the life of French painter Claude Monet.

다시 프리타운 공영 라디오, 〈아티스트 아워〉입니다. **여기 스튜디오에 저와 함께하신 분은 프리타운 미술관에서 오랫동안 관장을 지내신 캐롤 톰슨입니다.** 톰슨 씨는 얼마 전 올 연말에 은퇴한다고 발표하셨는데요, 오늘 진로와 앞으로의 계획에 대해 이야기하시고자 함께하셨습니다. 나중에 얘기하겠지만, **톰슨 씨는 항상 기금 모금에 특별한 수완을 보이셨죠.** 30년 경력에 걸쳐 미술품 복원 사업을 위해 전국에서 총 5백만 달러를 모금했습니다. **톰슨 씨는 은퇴하면 유명한 미술가들에 관한 아동 도서를 쓸 계획입니다.** 첫 번째는 프랑스 화가 클로드 모네의 인생을 토대로 합니다.

어휘 retire 은퇴하다 fund-raising 기금 모금 restoration 복원 well-known 유명한

80

Where does Ms. Thompson work?

(A) At an art supply store

(B) At a museum

(C) At a photography studio

(D) At a library

톰슨 씨는 어디에서 일하는가?

(A) 미술용품 매장

(B) 미술관

(C) 사진관

(D) 도서관

해설 세부 사항 관련 - 톰슨 씨의 근무지

화자가 초반부에 여기 스튜디오에 저와 함께하신 분은 프리타운 미술관에서 오랫동안 관장을 지내신 캐롤 톰슨(With me here in the studio is Carol Thompson, the longtime director of the Freetown Art Museum)이라고 말하고 있으므로 정답은 (B)이다.

81

According to the speaker, what special talent does Ms. Thompson have?

(A) Raising money

(B) Painting landscapes

(C) Negotiating contracts

(D) Taking photographs

256

화자의 말에 따르면, 톰슨 씨는 어떤 특별한 수완이 있는가?

(A) 모금
(B) 풍경 그리기
(C) 계약 협상
(D) 사진 촬영

해설 세부 사항 관련 - 톰슨 씨가 가진 특별한 수완
화자가 중반부에 톰슨 씨는 항상 기금 모금에 특별한 수완을 보였다(she has always had a particular talent for fund-raising)고 말하고 있으므로 정답은 (A)이다.

> ▸▸ Paraphrasing 담화의 **fund-raising**
> → 정답의 **Raising money**

82

What does Ms. Thompson plan to do after she retires?

(A) Restore paintings
(B) Volunteer as a consultant
(C) Relocate to France
(D) Become an author

톰슨 씨는 은퇴 후 무엇을 할 계획인가?
(A) 그림 복원하기
(B) 고문으로 자원봉사하기
(C) 프랑스로 이주하기
(D) 작가 되기

해설 세부 사항 관련 - 톰슨 씨가 은퇴 후 계획한 일
화자가 후반부에 톰슨 씨는 은퇴하면 유명한 미술가들에 관한 아동 도서를 쓸 계획(Ms. Thompson plans to write children's books about well-known artists when she retires)이라고 말하고 있으므로 정답은 (D)이다.

> ▸▸ Paraphrasing 담화의 **write children's books**
> → 정답의 **Become an author**

83-85 회의 발췌

> **W-Am** OK, everyone. [83]**I want to talk about your new writing assignments. As you know, the special restaurant issue of our magazine is coming out in May.** But we still have quite a few restaurants we haven't reviewed yet. So, [84]**I've assigned a different restaurant to each reporter— you can check your e-mail to find out which one you'll be reviewing.** [85]**This might seem like a fun assignment, but remember, thousands of people will buy this issue.**

좋습니다, 여러분. 새로운 집필 업무에 대해 얘기하고 싶습니다. 아시다시피 우리 잡지의 식당 특집호가 5월에 나오죠. 그런데 아직 평가하지 않은 식당들이 꽤 있어요. 그래서 제가 기자 한 명 한 명에게 다른 식당을 지정해 놓았습니다. 이메일을 확인하면 자신이 어떤 식당을 평가할지 알 수 있

어요. 재미있는 과제처럼 보이겠지만, 명심하세요. 수천 명이 이번 호를 살 겁니다.

> 어휘 assignment 업무, 과제 assign 지정하다

83

Who most likely are the listeners?

(A) Journalists
(B) Editors
(C) Photographers
(D) Salespeople

청자들은 누구이겠는가?
(A) 기자
(B) 편집자
(C) 사진작가
(D) 영업 사원

해설 전체 내용 관련 - 청자들의 직업
화자가 초반부에 새로운 집필 업무에 대해 얘기하고 싶다(I want to talk about your new writing assignments)며 아시다시피 우리 잡지의 식당 특집호가 5월에 나온다(As you know, the special restaurant issue of our magazine is coming out in May)고 말하고 있으므로 청자들은 잡지사 기자임을 알 수 있다. 따라서 정답은 (A)이다.

84

According to the speaker, what will the listeners receive in an e-mail?

(A) A book title
(B) A concert ticket
(C) A restaurant name
(D) An account number

화자의 말에 따르면, 청자들은 이메일로 무엇을 받을 것인가?
(A) 책 제목
(B) 콘서트 티켓
(C) 식당 이름
(D) 계정 번호

해설 세부 사항 관련 - 화자가 청자들이 이메일로 받을 것이라고 말하는 것
화자가 중반부에 제가 기자 한 명 한 명에게 다른 식당을 지정해 놓았다 (I've assigned a different restaurant to each reporter)며 이메일을 확인하면 자신이 어떤 식당을 평가할지 알 수 있다(you can check your e-mail to find out which one you'll be reviewing)고 설명하고 있으므로 정답은 (C)이다.

85

Why does the speaker say, "thousands of people will buy this issue"?

(A) To reassure the listeners
(B) To correct a misunderstanding
(C) To express surprise about a decision
(D) To emphasize the importance of a task

화자가 "수천 명이 이번 호를 살 겁니다"라고 말하는 이유는 무엇인가?

(A) 청자들을 안심시키려고
(B) 오해를 바로잡으려고
(C) 결정에 대해 놀라움을 나타내려고
(D) 과제의 중요성을 강조하려고

어휘 reassure 안심시키다 emphasize 강조하다 importance 중요성

해설 화자의 의도 파악 – 수천 명이 이번 호를 살 것이라는 말의 의도
앞에서 재미있는 과제처럼 보이겠지만 명심하라(This might seem like a fun assignment, but remember)고 당부한 뒤 인용문을 언급하고 있으므로, 많은 독자들이 잡지를 읽는다는 것을 새기며 신중하게 업무에 임하라고 강조하려고 한 말임을 알 수 있다. 따라서 정답은 (D)이다.

86-88 공지

W-Br ⁸⁶**Welcome, everyone, to the Pine City Community Center.** I'm Dr. Garcia, and I'm here at the community center today for the annual wellness fair. ⁸⁷**We'll be doing free vision exams all day. If you don't have time today, we'll be offering the exams at our clinic for the rest of the month.** Just remember, many eye problems are easily treated. OK, so ⁸⁸**first on our agenda at nine o'clock A.M., eye specialist Dr. Yan Zhou will give a presentation in the auditorium about maintaining good eye health. Let's head over there now.**

어서 오세요, 여러분. 파인 시티 주민 센터입니다. 저는 가르시아 박사고요. 오늘 저는 해마다 열리는 건강 박람회를 위해 이곳 주민 센터에 왔습니다. **저희가 하루 종일 무료로 시력 검사를 실시할 예정입니다. 오늘 시간이 안 되시면 이번 달 남은 기간 동안 저희 병원에서 검사해 드립니다.** 이것만 기억하세요. 많은 안과 질환은 쉽게 치료됩니다. 자, **첫 번째 일정으로 오전 9시에 안과 전문의 옌 저우 박사님이 강당에서 눈 건강 유지에 관해 발표하시겠습니다. 지금 그쪽으로 가시죠.**

어휘 annual 해마다 열리는 wellness 건강 vision exam 시력 검사 treat 치료하다 auditorium 강당 maintain 유지하다

86

Where are the listeners?

(A) In a community center
(B) In a medical clinic
(C) In a university classroom
(D) In a government office

청자들은 어디에 있는가?

(A) 주민 센터
(B) 병원
(C) 대학 강의실
(D) 관공서

해설 전체 내용 관련 – 공지의 장소
화자가 도입부에 파인 시티 주민 센터에 오신 것을 환영한다(Welcome, everyone, to the Pine City Community Center)고 말하고 있으므로 주민 센터를 방문한 청자들을 향해 공지 중임을 알 수 있다. 따라서 정답은 (A)이다.

87

Why does the speaker say, "many eye problems are easily treated"?

(A) To indicate that a health fair is unnecessary
(B) To suggest hiring additional staff
(C) To encourage the listeners to get tested
(D) To correct a statistical error

화자가 "많은 안과 질환이 쉽게 치료된다"라고 말하는 이유는 무엇인가?

(A) 건강 박람회가 필요 없다고 지적하려고
(B) 추가 인력 채용을 제안하려고
(C) 청자들에게 검사를 받으라고 권장하려고
(D) 통계 오류를 바로잡으려고

어휘 unnecessary 필요 없는 statistical 통계의

해설 화자의 의도 파악 – 많은 안과 질환이 쉽게 치료된다는 말의 의도
앞에서 저희가 하루 종일 무료로 시력 검사를 실시할 예정(We'll be doing free vision exams all day)이라고 했고 오늘 시간이 안 되시면 이번 달 남은 기간 동안 저희 병원에서 검사해 드린다(If you don't have time today, ~ for the rest of the month)며 오늘 시력 검사를 받지 못할 경우를 위한 차선책까지 알려 주고 난 뒤 인용문에서 시력 검사의 당위성을 언급한 것으로 보아, 청자들이 무료 시력 검사를 받도록 권유하려고 한 말임을 알 수 있다. 따라서 정답은 (C)이다.

88

What will the listeners do next?

(A) Pick up some nutritional information
(B) Sign up for an appointment
(C) Listen to a presentation
(D) Watch a product demonstration

청자들은 다음에 무엇을 할 것인가?

(A) 영양 정보 얻기
(B) 예약 신청하기
(C) 발표 듣기
(D) 제품 시연 보기

어휘 nutritional 영양의 appointment 예약 demonstration 시연

해설 세부 사항 관련 – 청자들이 다음에 할 일
화자가 후반부에 첫 번째 일정으로 오전 9시에 안과 전문의 옌 저우 박사님이 강당에서 눈 건강 유지에 관해 발표할 것(first on our agenda ~ about maintaining good eye health)이라며 지금 그쪽으로 가자(Let's head over there now)고 말하고 있으므로 정답은 (C)이다.

89-91 담화

M-Cn Hi, I'm Takumi from Logan's Flooring. Thanks for watching this video. **89Carpets come in various designs and materials, and selecting one can be overwhelming. Today, I'll be sharing a few tips that'll make that process easier.** First, consider where you're going to put the carpet. For example, **90if you're carpeting a children's playroom, you probably don't want to select a wool carpet, since they're difficult to clean.** Second, we recommend making sure your carpet is protected under our warranty in case of damage. **91At Logan's Flooring, we provide one-year warranties on all our carpets!** Be sure to subscribe to this video channel for free weekly tips and ideas.

안녕하세요, 로건스 플로어링의 타쿠미입니다. 이 영상을 시청해 주셔서 감사합니다. 카펫은 다양한 디자인과 소재로 나오므로 하나를 고르기가 매우 부담될 수도 있습니다. 오늘은 이 과정을 더 쉽게 만들어 줄 몇 가지 팁을 공유하려고 합니다. 우선 카펫을 어디에 깔지 생각하세요. 예를 들어 어린이 놀이방에 카펫을 깔려고 한다면, 청소가 까다로운 양모 카펫은 고르지 않는 것이 좋습니다. 둘째, 손상될 경우 당사 보증으로 보장되는지 확인하실 것을 권합니다. 로건스 플로어링에서는 모든 카펫에 대해 1년 보증을 제공합니다! 꼭 이 영상 채널을 구독하시고 매주 무료 팁과 아이디어를 얻으세요.

어휘 overwhelming 매우 부담스러운 carpet 카펫을 깔다
protect 보장하다 warranty 보증 subscribe to ~을 구독하다

89

What is the talk mainly about?
(A) Cleaning a carpet
(B) Installing a carpet
(C) Designing a carpet
(D) Choosing a carpet

주로 무엇에 관한 담화인가?
(A) 카펫 청소
(B) 카펫 설치
(C) 카펫 디자인
(D) 카펫 선택

해설 전체 내용 관련 - 담화의 주제
화자가 초반부에 카펫은 다양한 디자인과 소재로 나오므로 하나를 고르기가 매우 부담될 수도 있다(Carpets come ~ can be overwhelming)면서 오늘은 이 과정을 더 쉽게 만들어 줄 몇 가지 팁을 공유하려고 한다(Today, I'll be sharing a few tips that'll make that process easier)고 말하고 있으므로 정답은 (D)이다.

90

What does the speaker say about wool carpets?
(A) They are difficult to find.
(B) They are expensive.
(C) They are hard to clean.
(D) They are durable.

화자는 양모 카펫에 대해 무엇이라고 말하는가?
(A) 구하기 어렵다.
(B) 비싸다.
(C) 청소하기 힘들다.
(D) 내구성이 좋다.

어휘 durable 내구성이 좋은

해설 세부 사항 관련 - 화자가 양모 카펫에 대해 말하는 것
화자가 중반부에 어린이 놀이방에 카펫을 깔려고 한다면 청소가 까다로운 양모 카펫은 고르지 않는 것이 좋다(if you're carpeting a children's playroom, you probably don't want to select a wool carpet, since they're difficult to clean)고 말하고 있으므로 정답은 (C)이다.

▶▶ Paraphrasing 담화의 difficult → 정답의 hard

91

What does the speaker say his company provides?
(A) A free in-store consultation
(B) A children's play area
(C) Flooring design samples
(D) One-year warranties

화자는 자신의 회사가 무엇을 제공한다고 말하는가?
(A) 매장 내 무료 상담
(B) 어린이 놀이 공간
(C) 바닥재 디자인 견본
(D) 1년 보증

어휘 consultation 상담

해설 세부 사항 관련 - 화자가 자신의 회사에서 제공한다고 말하는 것
화자가 후반부에 로건스 플로어링에서는 모든 카펫에 대해 1년 보증을 제공한다(At Logan's Flooring, we provide one-year warranties on all our carpets!)고 말하고 있으므로 정답은 (D)이다.

92-94 전화 메시지

W-Br Hi. This is Barbara Chen, head of public relations at Springfield Solutions. **92I'm calling to thank you for your magazine article about our company.** In it, you praised our newest software, Ubex, writing that it helps factories run more efficiently. But **93you also emphasized how expensive the software is. While Ubex is costly, let me point out that** this is just one of our many products. **94I'd appreciate the chance to discuss the full range of our software choices, to give you a balanced view of the company. Please call me back and let me know if you'd be available to meet.**

안녕하세요. 스프링필드 솔루션즈 홍보부장 바바라 첸입니다. **당사에 관한 잡지 기사에 감사드리고 싶어 전화합니다.** 공장이 더 효율적으로 운영되는 데 도움이 된다고 적으시면서 당사의 최신 소프트웨어인 유벡스를 칭찬하셨죠. 그런데 **그 소프트웨어 가격이 얼마나 비싼지도 강조하셨습니다.** 유벡스는 값이 비싸지만, 수많은 당사 제품들 중 하나일 뿐입니다. 당사에 대한 균형 잡힌 시각을 기자님께 제공할 수 있도록 당사의 소프트웨어 종류 전반에 대해 논의할 기회가 있으면 감사하겠습니다. 만날 수 있는지 다시 전화해서 알려 주세요.

어휘 public relations 홍보 praise 칭찬하다 efficiently 효율적으로 emphasize 강조하다 expensive 비싼 costly 값이 비싼

92

Why does the speaker thank the listener?

(A) For renewing a magazine subscription

(B) For inspecting a medical facility

(C) For writing an article

(D) For giving a demonstration

화자는 왜 청자에게 고마워하는가?
(A) 잡지 구독을 갱신해서
(B) 의료 시설을 점검해서
(C) 기사를 작성해서
(D) 시연해서

어휘 renew 갱신하다 subscription 구독 inspect 점검하다 demonstration 시연

해설 세부 사항 관련 – 화자가 청자에게 고마워하는 이유
화자가 초반부에 당사에 관한 잡지 기사에 감사드리고 싶어 전화한다 (I'm calling to thank you for your magazine article about our company)고 말하고 있으므로 정답은 (C)이다.

93

What does the speaker imply when she says, "this is just one of our many products"?

(A) A company is prepared for more competition.

(B) A company also sells less expensive products.

(C) A team will need to work more quickly.

(D) A supervisor will be impressed by some work.

화자가 "수많은 당사 제품 중 하나일 뿐입니다"라고 말하는 의도는 무엇인가?
(A) 회사는 더 치열한 경쟁에 대비한다.
(B) 회사는 덜 비싼 제품도 판매한다.
(C) 팀은 더 빨리 일해야 할 것이다.
(D) 상사가 작업에 감탄할 것이다.

어휘 competition 경쟁 impressed 감탄하는

해설 화자의 의도 파악 – 수많은 당사 제품들 중 하나일 뿐이라는 말의 의도

앞에서 화자가 잡지에서 유벡스가 얼마나 비싼지를 강조했다(you also emphasized how expensive the software is)며 유벡스가 값은 비싸지만 말씀드릴 점이 있다(While Ubex is costly, let me point out that)고 말한 뒤 인용문을 언급한 것이므로, 자사 제품 중에는 비싼 유벡스 외에 더 저렴한 제품들이 많이 있음을 지적하려고 한 말임을 알 수 있다. 따라서 정답은 (B)이다.

94

Why does the speaker ask the listener to call back?

(A) To provide an address

(B) To confirm a deadline

(C) To place an order

(D) To arrange a meeting

화자는 왜 청자에게 다시 전화하라고 요청하는가?
(A) 주소를 제공하려고
(B) 마감일을 확인하려고
(C) 주문하려고
(D) 면담을 준비하려고

해설 세부 사항 관련 – 화자가 청자에게 다시 전화하라고 요청하는 이유
화자가 후반부에 당사에 대한 균형 잡힌 시각을 기자님께 제공할 수 있도록 당사의 소프트웨어 종류 전반에 대해 논의할 기회가 있으면 감사하겠다 (I'd appreciate the chance to discuss ~ to give you a balanced view of the company)고 말한 뒤 만날 수 있는지 다시 전화해서 알려 달라(Please call me back and let me know if you'd be available to meet)고 요청하고 있으므로 정답은 (D)이다.

95-97 담화 + 지도

W-Am Welcome to the grand opening of Oakfield Public Park! **95My fellow city council members and I are glad that everyone could join us.** There are many fun activities for residents to enjoy here. See the beautiful Elm Fountain, which has a special fountain show every hour. There are also several picnic areas throughout the park. But **96I suggest the one between Dogwood Pond and the children's playground.** It offers fantastic views of our city's skyline. Finally, **97for any gardeners among us, the Oakfield Parks Department needs volunteers to help care for the community garden.** If you're interested, please visit the city government Web site.

오크필드 공원 개장식에 오신 것을 환영합니다! **동료 시 의원들과 저는 모두가 함께할 수 있어서 기쁩니다.** 이곳에는 주민들이 즐길 수 있는 재미있는 활동들이 많습니다. 아름다운 엘름 분수를 보세요. 매시간 특별

한 분수 쇼를 펼칩니다. 공원 전역에 피크닉장도 여러 군데 있습니다. 하지만 **도그우드 연못과 어린이 놀이터 사이에 있는 피크닉장을 추천합니다.** 거기서 보이는 도시 스카이라인 경관이 기가 막히거든요. 마지막으로 **우리 중 혹시 원예사가 있으시면, 오크필드 공원부에서 공유 정원 가꾸는 일을 도울 자원봉사자가 필요합니다.** 관심 있으시면 시 정부 웹사이트를 방문하세요.

어휘 gardener 원예사

Oakfield Public Park

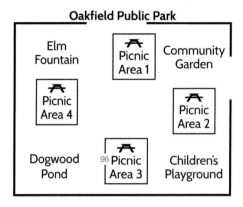

오크필드 공원

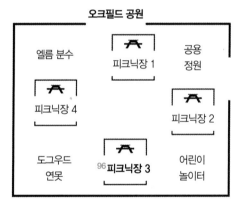

95

Who most likely is the speaker?

(A) A tour guide

(B) A city official

(C) A photographer

(D) A landscape artist

화자는 누구이겠는가?

(A) 관광 안내원

(B) 시 관계자

(C) 사진작가

(D) 조경 예술가

해설 전체 내용 관련 – 화자의 직업

화자가 초반부에 동료 시 의원들과 저는 모두가 함께할 수 있어서 기쁘다(My fellow city council members and I are glad that everyone could join us)라고 말하고 있으므로 화자는 시 의원임을 알 수 있다. 따라서 정답은 (B)이다.

96

Look at the graphic. Which picnic area does the speaker recommend?

(A) Picnic Area 1

(B) Picnic Area 2

(C) Picnic Area 3

(D) Picnic Area 4

시각 정보에 의하면 화자는 어떤 피크닉장을 추천하는가?

(A) 피크닉장 1

(B) 피크닉장 2

(C) 피크닉장 3

(D) 피크닉장 4

해설 시각 정보 연계 – 화자가 추천하는 피크닉장

화자가 중반부에 도그우드 연못과 어린이 놀이터 사이에 있는 피크닉장을 추천한다(I suggest the one between Dogwood Pond and the children's playground)고 말하고 있고, 지도에 따르면 도그우드 연못과 어린이 놀이터 사이에 있는 피크닉장은 3번 피크닉장이므로 정답은 (C)이다.

97

Why are some volunteers needed?

(A) To maintain a garden

(B) To hand out water bottles

(C) To organize park events

(D) To provide free tours

자원봉사자들은 왜 필요한가?

(A) 정원을 관리하려고

(B) 물병을 나눠주려고

(C) 공원 행사를 준비하려고

(D) 무료 관광을 제공하려고

해설 세부 사항 관련 – 자원봉사자들이 필요한 이유

화자가 후반부에 우리 중 혹시 원예사가 있으시면 오크필드 공원부에서 공유 정원 가꾸는 일을 도울 자원봉사자가 필요하다(for any gardeners among us, ~ to help care for the community garden)고 말하고 있으므로 정답은 (A)이다.

▸▸ Paraphrasing 담화의 care for the ~ garden
→ 정답의 maintain a garden

98-100 회의 발췌 + 설문 조사서

M-Cn **⁹⁸Since the hospital hired me, I've been working on making the meals we serve our patients more nutritious.** But **⁹⁹I want to promote healthy eating habits among our staff** as well, because health-care professionals with healthy diets are more likely to teach their patients to make similar choices. With that goal, I'd like to schedule our first nutrition class at a time that's available to as many people as possible, so I'm asking that you complete this short survey. **100 I do have some flexibility in the afternoons so I could move the afternoon session during the week to a later time if necessary.** The weekend session cannot be moved.

병원에서 저를 채용한 이후, 저는 환자식을 더 영양가 있게 만들기 위해 노력해 왔습니다. 하지만 **직원들에게도 건강한 식습관을 장려하고 싶습니다.** 건강한 식사를 하는 의료 서비스 전문가는 환자들에게 비슷한 선택을 하도록 가르쳐 줄 가능성이 더 높기 때문입니다. 이 목표를 위해 첫 번째 영양 수업 일정을 가능한 한 많은 사람이 올 수 있는 시간에 잡고 싶습니다. 그러므로 이 짧은 설문 조사서를 작성해 주시기 바랍니다. **제가 오후 일정은 바꿀 수 있어서 필요하다면 주중 오후 세션을 뒤로 옮길 수 있습니다.** 주말 세션은 옮길 수 없습니다.

어휘 patient 환자　nutritious 영양가 있는　promote 장려하다 similar 비슷한　flexibility 바꿀 수 있음

Please check the box to indicate your availability:

☐ Mondays **100** @ 2:30 P.M.

☐ Wednesdays @ 8:30 A.M.

☐ Thursdays @ 11:00 A.M.

☐ Saturdays @ 12:00 P.M.

공란에 체크해 가능한 시간을 표시하세요:

☐ 월요일 @**100**오후 2:30

☐ 수요일 @ 오전 8:30

☐ 목요일 @ 오전 11:00

☐ 토요일 @ 오후 12:00

98

Where do the listeners most likely work?

(A) At a supermarket

(B) At a hospital

(C) At a community center

(D) At a fitness club

청자들은 어디에서 일하겠는가?

(A) 슈퍼마켓

(B) 병원

(C) 주민 센터

(D) 헬스장

해설 전체 내용 관련 - 화자들의 근무지

화자가 도입부에 병원에서 저를 채용한 이후 저는 환자식을 더 영양가 있게 만들기 위해 노력해 왔다(Since the hospital hired me, ~ serve our patients more nutritious)고 말하고 있으므로 정답은 (B)이다.

99

What does the speaker say is his goal?

(A) To attract qualified job candidates

(B) To reduce costs

(C) To boost membership sales

(D) To encourage healthy eating habits

화자는 자신의 목표가 무엇이라고 말하는가?

(A) 자격 있는 구직자 모집

(B) 비용 절감

(C) 회원 매출 증대

(D) 건강한 식습관 장려

어휘 reduce 줄이다　boost 늘리다

해설 세부 사항 관련 - 화자가 자신의 목표라고 말하는 것

화자가 초반부에 직원들에게 건강한 식습관을 장려하고 싶다(I want to promote healthy eating habits among our staff)고 말하고 있으므로 정답은 (D)이다.

▸▸ Paraphrasing　담화의 **promote** → 정답의 **encourage**

100

Look at the graphic. On which days can the speaker change his schedule?

(A) Mondays

(B) Wednesdays

(C) Thursdays

(D) Saturdays

시각 정보에 의하면 화자는 어느 요일에 자신의 일정을 변경할 수 있는가?

(A) 월요일

(B) 수요일

(C) 목요일

(D) 토요일

해설 시각 정보 연계 - 화자가 자신의 일정을 변경할 수 있는 요일

화자가 후반부에 제가 오후 일정은 바꿀 수 있어서 필요하다면 주중 오후 세션을 뒤로 옮길 수 있다(I do have some flexibility in the afternoons ~ to a later time if necessary)고 말하고 있고, 설문 조사서에 따르면 주중 오후에 세션이 있는 날은 월요일뿐이므로 정답은 (A)이다.

ETS TEST 10

1 (B)	**2** (A)	**3** (C)	**4** (B)	**5** (A)
6 (D)	**7** (C)	**8** (A)	**9** (B)	**10** (C)
11 (C)	**12** (B)	**13** (A)	**14** (A)	**15** (A)
16 (B)	**17** (A)	**18** (C)	**19** (B)	**20** (B)
21 (C)	**22** (A)	**23** (A)	**24** (A)	**25** (C)
26 (C)	**27** (B)	**28** (A)	**29** (C)	**30** (A)
31 (C)	**32** (D)	**33** (A)	**34** (A)	**35** (A)
36 (D)	**37** (B)	**38** (A)	**39** (B)	**40** (C)
41 (D)	**42** (A)	**43** (B)	**44** (C)	**45** (A)
46 (C)	**47** (B)	**48** (C)	**49** (C)	**50** (A)
51 (D)	**52** (C)	**53** (B)	**54** (A)	**55** (C)
56 (A)	**57** (D)	**58** (C)	**59** (B)	**60** (D)
61 (C)	**62** (C)	**63** (D)	**64** (B)	**65** (D)
66 (B)	**67** (A)	**68** (B)	**69** (B)	**70** (A)
71 (B)	**72** (C)	**73** (C)	**74** (C)	**75** (B)
76 (A)	**77** (A)	**78** (D)	**79** (C)	**80** (B)
81 (D)	**82** (A)	**83** (B)	**84** (D)	**85** (C)
86 (A)	**87** (B)	**88** (C)	**89** (D)	**90** (B)
91 (C)	**92** (B)	**93** (A)	**94** (B)	**95** (C)
96 (C)	**97** (B)	**98** (A)	**99** (B)	**100** (B)

PART 1

1 M-Au

(A) A man is organizing a display of fruit.
(B) A man is getting some food from a cafeteria.
(C) A man is cooking a meal in a kitchen.
(D) A man is standing behind a cash register.

(A) 남자가 진열대 과일을 정리하고 있다.
(B) **남자가 구내식당에서 음식을 가져가고 있다.**
(C) 남자가 주방에서 음식을 요리하고 있다.
(D) 남자가 금전 등록기 뒤에 서 있다.

어휘 organize 정리하다   cash register 금전 등록기

해설 1인 등장 사진 – 사람의 동작/상태 묘사
(A) 동사 오답. 남자가 진열대 과일을 정리하고 있는(is organizing a display of fruit) 모습이 아니므로 오답.
(B) 정답. 남자가 구내식당에서 음식을 가져가고 있는(is getting some food from a cafeteria) 모습이므로 정답.

(C) 동사 오답. 남자가 주방에서 음식을 요리하고 있는(is cooking a meal in a kitchen) 모습이 아니므로 오답.
(D) 사진에 없는 명사를 이용한 오답. 사진에 금전 등록기(a cash register)의 모습이 보이지 않으므로 오답.

2 W-Am

(A) The man is pointing at a location on a map.
(B) The man is talking on a mobile phone.
(C) The woman is taping a sign to the wall.
(D) The woman is taking a pen from a drawer.

(A) **남자가 지도 위의 지점을 가리키고 있다.**
(B) 남자가 핸드폰으로 통화하고 있다.
(C) 여자가 벽에 표지판을 붙이고 있다.
(D) 여자가 서랍에서 펜을 꺼내고 있다.

어휘 drawer 서랍

해설 2인 이상 등장 사진 – 사람의 동작/상태 묘사
(A) 정답. 남자가 지도 위의 지점을 가리키고 있는(is pointing at a location on a map) 모습이므로 정답.
(B) 동사 오답. 남자가 핸드폰으로 통화하고 있는(is talking on a mobile phone) 모습이 아니므로 오답.
(C) 동사 오답. 여자가 벽에 표지판을 붙이고 있는(is taping a sign to the wall) 모습이 아니므로 오답.
(D) 동사 오답. 여자가 서랍에서 펜을 꺼내고 있는(is taking a pen from a drawer) 모습이 아니므로 오답.

3 M-Cn

(A) She's walking toward a trash bin.
(B) She has set a basket on a lawn.
(C) She has a rolled mat under her arm.
(D) She's unpacking a picnic lunch near a tree.

(A) 여자가 쓰레기통 쪽으로 걸어가고 있다.
(B) 여자가 잔디밭에 바구니를 놓았다.
(C) **여자가 겨드랑이에 돌돌 만 매트를 끼고 있다.**
(D) 여자가 나무 근처에서 소풍 도시락을 풀고 있다.

어휘 trash bin 쓰레기통   unpack 풀다

해설 1인 등장 사진 - 사람의 동작/상태 묘사

(A) 동사 오답. 여자가 쓰레기통 쪽으로 걸어가고 있는(is walking toward a trash bin) 모습이 아니므로 오답.

(B) 동사 오답. 여자가 잔디밭에 바구니를 놓은(has set a basket on a lawn) 모습이 아니라 바구니를 들고 있는(is holding a basket) 모습이므로 오답.

(C) 정답. 여자가 겨드랑이에 돌돌 만 매트를 끼고 있는(has a rolled mat under her arm) 모습이므로 정답.

(D) 동사 오답. 여자가 나무 근처에서 소풍 도시락을 풀고 있는(is unpacking a picnic lunch near a tree) 모습이 아니므로 오답.

4 M-Au

(A) A man is staring out a window.

(B) A woman is reaching into her bag.

(C) Some people are holding coffee cups.

(D) Some people are waiting in line.

(A) 남자가 창밖을 응시하고 있다.

(B) 여자가 가방 안에 손을 넣고 있다.

(C) 사람들이 커피잔을 들고 있다.

(D) 사람들이 줄을 서서 기다리고 있다.

어휘 stare 응시하다

해설 2인 이상 등장 사진 - 사람의 동작/상태 묘사

(A) 동사 오답. 남자가 창밖을 응시하고 있는(is staring out a window) 모습이 아니므로 오답.

(B) 정답. 여자가 가방 안에 손을 넣고 있는(is reaching into her bag) 모습이므로 정답.

(C) 동사 오답. 사람들이 커피잔을 들고 있는(are holding coffee cups) 모습이 아니므로 오답.

(D) 동사 오답. 사람들이 줄을 서서 기다리고 있는(are waiting in line) 모습이 아니므로 오답.

5 W-Am

(A) Sets of utensils have been arranged on napkins.

(B) Containers have been placed on chairs.

(C) A tablecloth is being removed.

(D) There is a stack of books next to some plates.

(A) 식탁용 집기 세트들이 냅킨 위에 정리되어 있다.

(B) 용기들이 의자 위에 놓여 있다.

(C) 식탁보를 치우고 있다.

(D) 책 무더기가 접시들 옆에 있다.

어휘 utensil 식탁용 집기 arrange 정리하다 container 용기
     remove 치우다 a stack of 쌓아 올린 무더기

해설 사물/풍경 사진 - 사물 묘사

(A) 정답. 식탁용 집기 세트들(sets of utensils)이 냅킨 위에 정리되어 있는(have been arranged on napkins) 모습이므로 정답.

(B) 사진에 없는 명사를 이용한 오답. 사진에 용기들(containers)의 모습이 보이지 않으므로 오답.

(C) 동사 오답. 식탁보(a tablecloth)가 치워지고 있는(is being removed) 모습이 아니므로 오답.

(D) 위치 오답. 책 무더기(a stack of books)가 접시들 옆(next to some plates)에 있는 모습이 아니라 테이블 한가운데(in the middle of the table)에 있는 모습이므로 오답.

6 W-Br

(A) A box is being loaded onto a truck.

(B) Some people are inspecting the contents of a box.

(C) Some boxes have been piled on a desk.

(D) One of the people is lifting a box.

(A) 상자가 트럭에 실리고 있다.

(B) 사람들이 상자의 내용물을 검사하고 있다.

(C) 상자들이 책상 위에 쌓여 있다.

(D) 사람들 중 한 명이 상자를 들어올리고 있다.

어휘 load 싣다 inspect 검사하다 pile 쌓다

해설 혼합 사진 - 사람/사물/풍경 혼합 묘사

(A) 사진에 없는 명사를 이용한 오답. 사진에 트럭(a truck)의 모습이 보이지 않으므로 오답.

(B) 동사 오답. 사람들이 상자의 내용물을 검사하고 있는(are inspecting the contents of a box) 모습이 아니므로 오답.

(C) 위치 오답. 상자들(some boxes)이 책상 위에 쌓여 있는(have been piled on a desk) 모습이 아니므로 오답.

(D) 정답. 사람들 중 한 명(one of the people)이 상자를 들어올리고 있는(is lifting a box) 모습이므로 정답.

PART 2

7

M-Cn Where's the marketing department?

W-Br (A) Are the shoes on sale?

(B) I've been to the farmers market.

(C) On the third floor.

마케팅 부서는 어디인가요?

(A) 신발 할인되나요?

(B) 저는 농산물 직판장에 가봤어요.

(C) 3층이에요.

어휘 farmers market 농산물 직판장

해설 마케팅 부서의 위치를 묻는 Where 의문문

(A) 연상 단어 오답. 질문의 marketing에서 연상 가능한 sale을 이용한 오답.

(B) 파생어 오답. 질문의 marketing과 파생어 관계인 market을 이용한 오답.

(C) 정답. 마케팅 부서의 위치를 묻는 질문에 3층이라고 위치를 알려 주고 있으므로 정답.

8

W-Br What time does your flight leave?

M-Cn **(A) At nine in the morning.**

(B) Only one suitcase.

(C) That's a great destination.

몇 시 비행기로 떠나세요?

(A) 오전 9시예요.

(B) 여행 가방 하나뿐이에요.

(C) 아주 좋은 곳이죠.

어휘 destination (여행 등의) 목적지, 장소

해설 비행기의 출발 시간을 묻는 What time 의문문

(A) 정답. 비행기가 떠나는 시간을 묻는 질문에 오전 9시라고 알려 주고 있으므로 정답.

(B) 연상 단어 오답. 질문의 flight에서 연상 가능한 suitcase를 이용한 오답.

(C) 연상 단어 오답. 질문의 flight에서 연상 가능한 destination을 이용한 오답.

9

W-Am Who reviewed the order forms?

M-Au (A) Today at noon.

(B) The manager did.

(C) Sure, I'll sign for the delivery.

누가 주문서를 검토했죠?

(A) 오늘 정오예요.

(B) 매니저가 했어요.

(C) 그럼요, 제가 배송받았다고 서명할게요.

해설 주문서를 검토한 사람을 묻는 Who 의문문

(A) 질문과 상관없는 오답. When 의문문에 대한 응답이므로 오답.

(B) 정답. 주문서를 검토한 사람이 누구인지 묻는 질문에 매니저가 했다고 알려 주고 있으므로 정답.

(C) Yes/No 불가 오답. Who 의문문에는 Yes/No 응답이 불가능한데, Sure도 일종의 Yes 응답이라고 볼 수 있으므로 오답.

10

M-Au How much do the tickets cost?

W-Br (A) It's on the coast.

(B) The concert was great!

(C) Twenty dollars, I think.

표는 얼마인가요?

(A) 해안가에 있어요.

(B) 콘서트는 정말 좋았어요!

(C) 20달러일 거예요.

해설 표의 가격을 묻는 How much 의문문

(A) 유사 발음 오답. 질문의 cost와 부분적으로 발음이 유사한 coast를 이용한 오답.

(B) 연상 단어 오답. 질문의 tickets에서 연상 가능한 concert를 이용한 오답.

(C) 정답. 표가 얼마인지를 묻는 질문에 20달러일 것이라고 가격을 알려 주고 있으므로 정답.

11

M-Cn Would you like to have lunch with us?

W-Am (A) They don't work together.

(B) She called yesterday.

(C) No, thanks—I already ate.

우리랑 같이 점심 먹을래요?

(A) 그들은 함께 일하지 않아요.

(B) 그녀가 어제 전화했어요.

(C) 괜찮아요. 저는 벌써 먹었어요.

해설 제안/권유의 의문문

(A) 질문과 상관없는 오답.

(B) 질문과 상관없는 오답. 질문에 3인칭 대명사 she로 지칭할 인물이 언급된 적이 없으므로 오답.

(C) 정답. 같이 점심을 먹을지 제안하는 질문에 괜찮다(No thanks)고 거절한 뒤, 벌써 먹었다고 거절의 이유를 밝히며 부정 답변과 일관된 내용을 덧붙였으므로 정답.

12

M-Cn Should we discuss the merger tomorrow or Friday?

W-Br (A) He's a vegetarian.

(B) Tomorrow is better.

(C) A few weeks ago.

합병 건은 내일 이야기할까요, 아니면 금요일에 이야기할까요?
(A) 그는 채식주의자예요.
(B) 내일이 나아요.
(C) 몇 주 전에요.

어휘 merger 합병

해설 합병 논의 시기를 묻는 선택 의문문
(A) 질문과 상관없는 오답. 질문에 3인칭 대명사 he로 지칭할 인물이 언급된 적이 없으므로 오답.
(B) 정답. 내일과 금요일 중 합병을 논의할 시기를 묻는 질문에 내일이 낫다며 둘 중 하나를 선택해 응답하고 있으므로 정답.
(C) 연상 단어 오답. 질문의 Friday에서 연상 가능한 weeks를 이용한 오답.

13

W-Am Why are you still at the office?
M-Au (A) Because my meeting ran late.
      (B) Please leave it with my assistant.
      (C) The room at the end of the hall.

왜 아직 사무실에 계세요?
(A) 회의가 늦어져서요.
(B) 제 비서에게 맡겨 주세요.
(C) 복도 끝에 있는 방이에요.

어휘 run (어떤 상태로) 되다

해설 아직 사무실에 있는 이유를 묻는 Why 의문문
(A) 정답. 아직 사무실에 있는 이유를 묻는 질문에 회의가 늦어졌기 때문이라고 이유를 제시하고 있으므로 정답.
(B) 연상 단어 오답. 질문의 office에서 연상 가능한 assistant를 이용한 오답.
(C) 질문과 상관없는 오답. Where 의문문에 대한 응답이므로 오답.

14

W-Br Doesn't the art exhibit open today?
M-Au (A) No, not until next week.
      (B) Sure, you can leave it open.
      (C) Many local artists.

오늘 미술 전시회가 열리지 않나요?
(A) 아뇨, 다음 주나 되어야 해요.
(B) 네, 열어 두셔도 돼요.
(C) 많은 지역 화가들이요.

어휘 exhibit 전시(회)

해설 오늘 전시회가 열리는지 여부를 확인하는 부정 의문문
(A) 정답. 오늘 미술 전시회가 열리는지 확인하는 질문에 아니요(No)라고 대답한 뒤, 다음 주나 되어야 한다며 부정 답변과 일관된 내용을 덧붙였으므로 정답.
(B) 단어 반복 오답. 질문의 open을 반복 이용한 오답.
(C) 파생어 오답. 질문의 art와 파생어 관계인 artists를 이용한 오답.

15

W-Am When did Takumi start working here?
M-Cn (A) I think it was a year ago.
      (B) Since my computer isn't working.
      (C) No, he retired last month.

타쿠미는 언제부터 여기서 일을 시작했나요?
(A) 1년 전인 것 같아요.
(B) 제 컴퓨터가 고장 나서요.
(C) 아뇨, 그는 지난달에 은퇴했어요.

어휘 retire 은퇴하다

해설 타쿠미의 근무 시작 시기를 묻는 When 의문문
(A) 정답. 타쿠미가 일을 시작한 시기를 묻는 질문에 1년 전인 것 같다고 알려 주고 있으므로 정답.
(B) 단어 반복 오답. 질문의 working을 반복 이용한 오답.
(C) Yes/No 불가 오답. When 의문문에는 Yes/No 응답이 불가능하므로 오답.

16

M-Au We still sell this brand of washing machine, don't we?
W-Br (A) I appreciate the help.
      (B) Yes, there are some in stock.
      (C) Adjust the temperature setting.

아직도 이 브랜드 세탁기 팔고 있죠?
(A) 도와주셔서 감사합니다.
(B) 네, 재고가 좀 있어요.
(C) 온도 설정을 조절하세요.

어휘 adjust 조절하다 temperature 온도

해설 해당 브랜드 세탁기의 판매 여부를 확인하는 부가 의문문
(A) 질문과 상관없는 오답.
(B) 정답. 해당 브랜드의 세탁기를 아직 판매하는지 여부를 확인하는 질문에 네(Yes)라고 대답한 뒤, 재고가 좀 있다며 긍정 답변과 일관된 내용을 덧붙였으므로 정답.
(C) 연상 단어 오답. 질문의 washing machine에서 연상 가능한 temperature setting을 이용한 오답.

17

W-Am Haven't you finished the report yet?
M-Cn (A) The deadline's been extended.
      (B) Usually once a week.
      (C) That would help, thanks.

아직 보고서를 못 끝냈나요?
(A) 마감 기한이 연장됐어요.
(B) 보통 일주일에 한 번이에요.
(C) 도움이 되겠어요, 고마워요.

어휘 extend 연장하다

해설 보고서의 작성 완료 여부를 확인하는 부정 의문문

(A) 정답. 보고서를 끝냈는지 여부를 묻는 질문에 마감 기한이 연장되었다는 이유를 제시하며 아직 마무리하지 않았음을 우회적으로 알리고 있으므로 정답.

(B) 질문과 상관없는 오답. How often 의문문에 대한 응답이므로 오답.

(C) 질문과 상관없는 오답.

18

W-Br Do you want to fly or drive to the trade show?

M-Cn (A) The new French film is showing tonight.
(B) That's a positive trend.
(C) Where is it this year?

무역 박람회에 비행기로 가실래요, 아니면 자동차로 가실래요?
(A) 오늘 저녁에 신작 프랑스 영화가 상영돼요.
(B) 긍정적인 추세네요.
(C) 올해는 어디죠?

어휘 positive 긍정적인

해설 원하는 이동 수단을 묻는 선택 의문문

(A) 파생어 오답. 질문의 show와 파생어 관계인 showing을 이용한 오답.

(B) 연상 단어 오답. 질문의 trade show에서 연상 가능한 trend를 이용한 오답.

(C) 정답. 비행기와 자동차 중 무역 박람회에 갈 때 원하는 이동 수단을 묻는 질문에 올해는 박람회가 어디냐며 결정을 내리는 데 필요한 추가 정보를 묻고 있으므로 정답.

19

W-Am Who's leading the focus group meeting on Friday?

M-Au (A) In the second-floor conference room.
(B) John is making those assignments.
(C) At the management seminar.

금요일 포커스 그룹 회의는 누가 진행하나요?
(A) 2층 회의실이에요.
(B) 존이 업무를 준비하고 있어요.
(C) 경영 세미나에서요.

어휘 focus group 포커스 그룹(시장 조사를 위해 각계각층에서 선별된 소수 집단) assignment 업무 분장

해설 회의 진행자를 묻는 Who 의문문

(A) 질문과 상관없는 오답. Where 의문문에 대한 응답이므로 오답.

(B) 정답. 금요일에 포커스 그룹 회의를 진행할 사람을 묻는 질문에 존이 준비 중이라고 알려 주고 있으므로 정답.

(C) 연상 단어 오답. 질문의 meeting에서 연상 가능한 seminar를 이용한 오답.

20

W-Am Why don't we create some videos for the interns?

M-Cn (A) It was very creative.
(B) Sure, let's work on that.
(C) A review of our television show.

인턴들을 위한 영상을 만드는 게 어떨까요?
(A) 매우 창의적이었어요.
(B) 좋아요, 만들어 보죠.
(C) 우리 텔레비전 쇼에 관한 평가예요.

해설 제안/권유의 의문문

(A) 파생어 오답. 질문의 create와 파생어 관계인 creative를 이용한 오답.

(B) 정답. 인턴들을 위한 영상을 만들자고 제안하는 질문에 좋아요(Sure)라고 제안을 받아들인 뒤, 만들어 보자며 긍정 답변과 일관된 내용을 덧붙였으므로 정답.

(C) 연상 단어 오답. 질문의 videos에서 연상 가능한 television show를 이용한 오답.

21

M-Au Prackwood Bank has extended business hours today, doesn't it?

W-Br (A) My extension is 204.
(B) Small business loans.
(C) Only at the Main Street location.

프랙우드 은행이 오늘 영업 시간을 연장했죠?
(A) 제 내선 번호는 204예요.
(B) 중소기업 대출이에요.
(C) 메인 가 지점만요.

어휘 extend 연장하다 extension 내선 번호 location 지점

해설 은행의 영업 시간 연장 여부를 확인하는 부가 의문문

(A) 파생어 오답. 질문의 extended와 파생어 관계인 extension을 이용한 오답.

(B) 연상 단어 오답. 질문의 bank에서 연상 가능한 loans를 이용한 오답.

(C) 정답. 프랙우드 은행이 오늘 영업 시간을 연장했는지 여부를 확인하는 질문에 메인 가 지점만이라고 알려 주고 있으므로 정답.

22

M-Au When do concert tickets go on sale?

W-Am (A) They're already sold out.
(B) At the ticket office.
(C) That's a good price!

콘서트 티켓은 언제 판매하나요?
(A) 벌써 매진됐어요.
(B) 매표소에서요.
(C) 괜찮은 가격이네요!

해설 콘서트 티켓의 판매 시점을 묻는 When 의문문
(A) 정답. 콘서트 티켓을 판매하는 시점을 묻는 질문에 벌써 매진되었다며
　　 이미 판매가 완료되었음을 간접적으로 알려 주고 있으므로 정답.
(B) 파생어 오답. 질문의 tickets와 파생어 관계인 ticket을 이용한 오답.
(C) 연상 단어 오답. 질문의 sale에서 연상 가능한 price를 이용한 오답.

23

W-Am　Has anyone volunteered to organize the
　　　 reception?
M-Cn　(A) The event's been canceled.
　　　 (B) Sorry, I don't have a receipt.
　　　 (C) It is a well-known organization.

　　　 환영회 준비에 자원한 사람 있나요?
　　　 (A) 행사가 취소됐어요.
　　　 (B) 죄송하지만, 영수증이 없어요.
　　　 (C) 유명한 단체예요.

어휘 organize 준비하다　well-known 유명한　organization 단체

해설 환영회 준비에 자원한 사람이 있는지 여부를 묻는 조동사(Has) 의
　　　 문문
(A) 정답. 환영회 준비에 자원한 사람이 있는지 묻는 질문에 행사가 취소
　　 되었다고 알려 주고 있으므로 정답.
(B) 유사 발음 오답. 질문의 reception과 부분적으로 발음이 유사한
　　 receipt를 이용한 오답.
(C) 파생어 오답. 질문의 organize와 파생어 관계인 organization을 이
　　 용한 오답.

24

M-Au　How do I turn off the copy machine?
W-Br　(A) I still need to make a few copies.
　　　 (B) At the traffic light.
　　　 (C) Yes, the machine is new.

　　　 복사기는 어떻게 끄나요?
　　　 (A) 저는 아직 몇 장 더 복사해야 해요.
　　　 (B) 신호등에서요.
　　　 (C) 네, 새 기계예요.

해설 복사기를 끄는 방법을 묻는 How 의문문
(A) 정답. 복사기를 끄는 방법을 묻는 질문에 몇 장 더 복사해야 한다며 복
　　 사기를 사용 중이니 아직 끌 필요가 없다는 것을 우회적으로 표현하고
　　 있으므로 정답.
(B) 연상 단어 오답. 질문의 turn off에서 연상 가능한 light를 이용한
　　 오답.
(C) Yes/No 불가 오답. How 의문문에는 Yes/No 응답이 불가능하므로
　　 오답.

25

W-Br　I'm calling to make an appointment with a
　　　 physical therapist.

M-Au　(A) Yes, that is my home address.
　　　 (B) A lot of exercise.
　　　 (C) OK—your options are next Monday or
　　　　　 Tuesday.

　　　 물리 치료 예약하려고 전화드렸어요.
　　　 (A) 네, 제 집 주소예요.
　　　 (B) 운동을 많이 해요.
　　　 (C) 알겠습니다. 다음 주 월요일이나 화요일을 선택하실 수 있어요.

어휘 make an appointment 예약하다　physical therapist 물리
　　　 치료사

해설 정보 전달의 평서문
(A) 평서문과 상관없는 오답.
(B) 연상 단어 오답. 평서문의 physical에서 연상 가능한 exercise를 이
　　 용한 오답.
(C) 정답. 물리 치료를 예약하려고 전화했다는 평서문에 알겠다(OK)고 대
　　 답한 뒤, 다음 주 월요일이나 화요일을 선택할 수 있다며 예약 가능한
　　 시간을 제시하고 있으므로 정답.

26

M-Cn　Our fabric shipment hasn't arrived yet, has
　　　 it?
W-Br　(A) A large number of orders.
　　　 (B) There's a printer on my desk.
　　　 (C) I'll call our supplier now.

　　　 원단 배송품이 아직 도착 안 했죠?
　　　 (A) 주문 건수가 많아요.
　　　 (B) 제 책상 위에 프린터가 있어요.
　　　 (C) 지금 납품업체에 전화할게요.

어휘 supplier 납품업체

해설 배송품의 도착 여부를 확인하는 부가 의문문
(A) 연상 단어 오답. 질문의 shipment에서 연상 가능한 orders를 이용
　　 한 오답.
(B) 질문과 상관없는 오답.
(C) 정답. 원단 배송품이 도착했는지 여부를 확인하는 질문에 지금 납품업
　　 체에 전화하겠다며 자신도 알지 못한다는 것을 우회적으로 표현하고
　　 있으므로 정답.

27

W-Br　Did you send all staff the revised vacation
　　　 policy?
M-Au　(A) You'll need a visitor badge to enter the
　　　　　 building.
　　　 (B) Our computer system has been down all
　　　　　 morning.
　　　 (C) A two-week trip to Boston.

　　　 수정된 휴가 규정을 전 직원에게 보냈나요?
　　　 (A) 건물에 들어가려면 방문증이 필요할 겁니다.
　　　 (B) 컴퓨터 시스템이 오전 내내 작동이 안 됐어요.
　　　 (C) 2주 동안 보스턴으로 여행 가요.

어휘 revise 수정하다 policy 규정

해설 수정된 휴가 규정의 직원 발송 여부를 묻는 조동사(Did) 의문문

(A) 연상 단어 오답. 질문의 policy에서 연상 가능한 a visitor badge를 이용한 오답.

(B) 정답. 수정된 휴가 규정을 전 직원에게 보냈는지 여부를 묻는 질문에 컴퓨터 시스템이 오전 내내 작동이 안 됐다고 이유를 제시하며 아직 보내지 못했음을 우회적으로 알리고 있으므로 정답.

(C) 연상 단어 오답. 질문의 vacation에서 연상 가능한 trip을 이용한 오답.

28

M-Au What's the telephone number for Primavera restaurant?

W-Am (A) It's closed for renovations.

(B) Chicken or pasta?

(C) Our supervisor is expecting his call.

프리마베라 식당 전화번호가 어떻게 되죠?

(A) 수리 때문에 문을 닫았어요.

(B) 치킨, 파스타 어느 걸로 하실래요?

(C) 상사가 그 사람 전화를 기다리고 있어요.

어휘 renovation 수리

해설 식당의 전화번호를 묻는 What 의문문

(A) 정답. 프리마베라 식당의 전화번호를 묻는 질문에 수리 때문에 문을 닫았다며 전화번호를 알 필요가 없음을 우회적으로 알려 주고 있으므로 정답.

(B) 연상 단어 오답. 질문의 restaurant에서 연상 가능한 chicken과 pasta를 이용한 오답.

(C) 연상 단어 오답. 질문의 telephone number에서 연상 가능한 call을 이용한 오답.

29

M-Cn Could you represent our company at the recruitment fair this week?

W-Br (A) Five new interns.

(B) Thomas said not to get him any presents.

(C) I always enjoy meeting new people.

이번 주 채용 박람회에 회사 대표로 나가실 수 있나요?

(A) 새로 온 인턴 다섯 명이에요.

(B) 토마스가 선물 사 오지 말라고 했어요.

(C) 저는 새로운 사람들을 만나는 게 늘 즐거워요.

어휘 represent 대표하다 recruitment fair 채용 박람회 present 선물

해설 부탁/요청의 의문문

(A) 연상 단어 오답. 질문의 recruitment에서 연상 가능한 interns를 이용한 오답.

(B) 유사 발음 오답. 질문의 represent와 부분적으로 발음이 유사한 presents를 이용한 오답.

(C) 정답. 이번 주 채용 박람회에 회사 대표로 나가 달라는 요청에 자신은 새로운 사람들을 만나는 것이 늘 즐겁다며 요청에 응하겠다는 의사를 우회적으로 표현하고 있으므로 정답.

30

M-Au The engine's been making a strange noise for the past hour.

W-Br (A) We'd better go find some oil.

(B) No, I'm not going to make anything for the party.

(C) Let's turn down the volume on the TV.

지난 한 시간 동안 엔진에서 이상한 소리가 나요.

(A) 가서 오일을 좀 찾아야겠어요.

(B) 아뇨, 저는 파티를 위해 아무것도 안 만들 거예요.

(C) TV 음량을 낮춥시다.

해설 정보 전달의 평서문

(A) 정답. 지난 한 시간 동안 엔진에서 이상한 소리가 난다는 평서문에 가서 오일을 좀 찾아야겠다며 문제에 대한 해결 방법을 제시하고 있으므로 정답.

(B) 파생어 오답. 평서문의 making과 파생어 관계인 make를 이용한 오답.

(C) 연상 단어 오답. 평서문의 noise에서 연상 가능한 volume을 이용한 오답.

31

M-Cn Where can we buy a microwave oven for the office kitchen?

W-Am (A) Yes, I really like cooking.

(B) My office is located near the kitchen.

(C) There's one in the storage area.

사무실 주방에 쓸 전자레인지는 어디서 살 수 있나요?

(A) 네, 저는 요리하는 걸 정말 좋아해요.

(B) 제 사무실은 주방 근처에 있어요.

(C) 창고에 하나 있어요.

어휘 microwave oven 전자레인지 storage 창고

해설 전자레인지를 살 수 있는 장소를 묻는 Where 의문문

(A) Yes/No 불가 오답. Where 의문문에는 Yes/No 응답이 불가능하므로 오답.

(B) 단어 반복 오답. 질문의 office를 반복 이용한 오답.

(C) 정답. 사무실 주방에 쓸 전자레인지를 살 수 있는 장소를 묻는 질문에 창고에 하나 있다며 전자레인지를 구입할 필요가 없음을 우회적으로 알려 주고 있으므로 정답.

PART 3

32-34

> W-Am Jung-Soo, ³²**are you ready for your conference in Greenville Shores?**
>
> M-Cn Yes, I'm leaving tomorrow morning.
>
> W-Am That's a great city. ³²**Are you doing any sightseeing before the conference?**
>
> M-Cn Actually, ³³**I've been so busy finishing my presentation** that I haven't looked at what there is to do.
>
> W-Am Last time, I did a walking tour of the historic district.
>
> M-Cn That sounds interesting.
>
> W-Am It was! I used Greenville Guides—I can pass on their Web site. ³⁴**Just don't wait too long before booking—slots fill up quickly.**

> 여 정수 씨, 그린빌 쇼어즈에서 열리는 회의에 가실 준비는 됐나요?
>
> 남 네, 내일 아침에 떠나요.
>
> 여 정말 멋진 도시예요. 회의 전에 관광을 좀 하시나요?
>
> 남 실은 발표 자료를 마무리하느라 너무 바빠서 거기 뭐가 있는지 알아보지도 못했어요.
>
> 여 지난번에 저는 역사 지구를 걸어서 둘러봤어요.
>
> 남 흥미롭군요.
>
> 여 그럼요! 그린빌 가이즈를 이용했는데 거기 웹사이트를 전달해 드릴게요. 너무 오래 기다리지 말고 예약하세요. 자리가 금방 차거든요.

> 어휘 sightseeing 관광 pass on 전달하다, 건네주다 slot 자리 fill up 차다

32

What is the conversation mainly about?

(A) A product launch
(B) A grand opening
(C) Some investment options
(D) Some travel plans

주로 무엇에 관한 대화인가?
(A) 제품 출시
(B) 개업식
(C) 투자 옵션
(D) 여행 계획

어휘 investment 투자

해설 전체 내용 관련 - 대화의 주제

여자가 첫 대사에서 그린빌 쇼어즈에서 열리는 회의에 갈 준비가 되었는지(are you ready for your conference in Greenville Shores?) 묻는 것으로 대화를 시작했고, 두 번째 대사에서도 회의 전에 관광을 좀 하는지(Are you doing any sightseeing before the conference?) 물으며 여행 계획에 대한 대화를 이어 가고 있으므로 정답은 (D)이다.

33

Why has the man been busy?

(A) He has been working on a presentation.
(B) He has just returned from a family vacation.
(C) He is organizing a conference.
(D) He has been assigned a new client account.

남자는 왜 바빴는가?
(A) 발표 준비를 하고 있었다.
(B) 가족과 휴가를 보내고 막 돌아왔다.
(C) 회의를 준비하고 있다.
(D) 새 고객 계정을 배정받았다.

어휘 organize 준비하다 assign 배정하다

해설 세부 사항 관련 - 남자가 바빴던 이유

남자가 두 번째 대사에서 발표 자료를 마무리하느라 너무 바빴다(I've been so busy finishing my presentation)고 말하고 있으므로 정답은 (A)이다.

34

What does the woman suggest that the man do soon?

(A) Make a reservation
(B) Review some sales data
(C) Use a voucher before it expires
(D) Speak with an adviser

여자는 남자에게 무엇을 빨리 하라고 권하는가?
(A) 예약
(B) 매출 자료 검토
(C) 유효 기간 만료 전에 쿠폰 사용
(D) 조언자와 대화

어휘 make a reservation 예약하다 expire 유효 기간이 만료되다

해설 세부 사항 관련 - 여자가 남자에게 빨리 하라고 권하는 일

여자가 마지막 대사에서 너무 오래 기다리지 말고 예약하라(Just don't wait too long before booking)며 자리가 금방 찬다(slots fill up quickly)고 말하고 있으므로 정답은 (A)이다.

> ▸▸ Paraphrasing 대화의 booking
> → 정답의 Make a reservation

35-37

M-Au ³⁵**Welcome to Patterson Bakery. How can I help you?**

W-Am Actually, ³⁶**I noticed the sign in your window advertising a temporary job for a baker.**

M-Au Right—we always need extra help during the summer months because many employees go on vacation.

W-Am I see. ³⁶**How can I apply?**

M-Au Let me get you an application form. You can fill out the form here if you'd like. ³⁷**Just remember to e-mail us your résumé later.**

W-Am All right, thanks!

남 어서 오세요. 패터슨 베이커리입니다. 어떻게 도와 드릴까요?

여 실은 창문에 임시직 제빵사를 구하는 광고가 붙어 있는 걸 봤어요.

남 맞아요. 여름 몇 달 동안에는 휴가를 떠나는 직원이 많아서 항상 도움이 더 필요해요.

여 그렇군요. 어떻게 지원하나요?

남 지원서를 갖다 드릴게요. 원하시면 여기서 양식을 작성하셔도 됩니다. 나중에 잊지 말고 이력서만 이메일로 보내 주세요.

여 알겠습니다, 감사합니다!

어휘 temporary 임시의 application 지원 fill out ~을 작성하다 résumé 이력서

35

Where is the conversation taking place?

(A) At a bakery
(B) At an employment agency
(C) At a farmers market
(D) At a restaurant

대화는 어디에서 이루어지는가?

(A) 제과점
(B) 직업 소개소
(C) 농산물 직판장
(D) 식당

해설 전체 내용 관련 - 대화의 장소

남자가 첫 대사에서 패터슨 베이커리에 오신 것을 환영한다(Welcome to Patterson Bakery)면서 어떻게 도와 드릴지(How can I help you?)를 묻고 있으므로 정답은 (A)이다.

36

What does the woman ask about?

(A) An upcoming event
(B) A project deadline
(C) A delivery service
(D) A job opening

여자는 무엇에 관해 문의하는가?

(A) 곧 있을 행사
(B) 프로젝트 마감 기한
(C) 배송 서비스
(D) 일자리

해설 세부 사항 관련 - 여자가 질문하는 것

여자가 첫 대사에서 창문에 임시직 제빵사를 구하는 광고가 붙어 있는 것을 봤다(I noticed the sign in your window advertising a temporary job for a baker)고 했고, 두 번째 대사에서 어떻게 지원하는지(How can I apply?)를 묻고 있으므로 정답은 (D)이다.

37

What does the man remind the woman to do?

(A) Register on a Web site
(B) Send a document
(C) Update a budget
(D) Change an address

남자는 여자에게 무엇을 하라고 알려 주는가?

(A) 웹사이트에 등록하기
(B) 문서 보내기
(C) 예산 수정하기
(D) 주소 변경하기

어휘 register 등록하다 budget 예산

해설 세부 사항 관련 - 남자가 여자에게 하라고 알려 주는 일

남자가 세 번째 대사에서 나중에 잊지 말고 이력서만 이메일로 보내 달라(Just remember to e-mail us your résumé later)고 말하고 있으므로 정답은 (B)이다.

▸▸ Paraphrasing 대화의 e-mail us your résumé
→ 정답의 Send a document

38-40 3인 대화

M-Cn Thank you for hiring me as a business consultant. What sort of advice are you looking for? ³⁸**I know your bookstore is already well-known in the community.**

W-Am But ³⁹**a lot of people are shopping online these days, and we're worried about our ability to compete.**

W-Br ³⁹**Yes, we think that's why fewer people are coming into the bookstore these days.**

M-Cn I see. **⁴⁰Have you considered making a significant change to the store—like adding a café?**

W-Am Interesting. We probably have enough space in the back of the store for that.

M-Cn That way customers could come in to browse and have a cup of coffee.

남 저를 기업 컨설턴트로 채용해 주셔서 감사합니다. 어떤 조언을 구하시나요? 서점이 동네에서 이미 유명하던데요.

여1 하지만 요즘에는 많은 사람이 온라인으로 구매하고 있어서 우리한테 경쟁할 역량이 있는지 걱정이 되어서요.

여2 맞아요, 요즘 서점에 오는 사람이 줄어든 것도 그 때문인 것 같아요.

남 그렇군요. 매장에 특별한 변화를 주는 건 고려해 보셨나요, 가령 카페를 추가한다든가?

여1 흥미롭군요. 아마 매장 뒤쪽에 공간이 충분할 거예요.

남 그러면 손님들이 둘러보러 와서 커피도 마실 겁니다.

어휘 ability 역량 compete 경쟁하다 significant 중요한

38

Where do the women work?

(A) At a bookstore
(B) At a computer store
(C) At a food market
(D) At a publishing company

여자들은 어디에서 일하는가?

(A) 서점
(B) 컴퓨터 매장
(C) 식료품점
(D) 출판사

해설 전체 내용 관련 – 여자들의 근무지

남자가 첫 대사에서 당신들의 서점이 동네에서 이미 유명하더라(I know your bookstore is already well-known in the community)고 말하고 있으므로 여자들이 서점에서 일하고 있다는 것을 알 수 있다. 따라서 정답은 (A)이다.

39

What are the women worried about?

(A) Opening a branch office
(B) Competing with online stores
(C) Finding a new supplier
(D) Hiring enough delivery drivers

여자들은 무엇을 걱정하는가?

(A) 지점 개설하기
(B) 온라인 매장과 경쟁하기
(C) 새 납품업체 찾기
(D) 배송 기사 충분히 채용하기

어휘 supplier 납품업체

해설 세부 사항 관련 – 여자들의 우려 사항

첫 번째 여자가 첫 대사에서 요즘에는 많은 사람이 온라인으로 구매하고 있어서 우리한테 경쟁할 역량이 있는지 걱정된다(a lot of people are shopping online ~ our ability to compete)고 했고, 뒤이어 두 번째 여자도 맞다(Yes)고 동의하며 요즘 서점에 오는 사람이 줄어든 것도 그 때문인 것 같다(we think that's why fewer people are coming into the bookstore these days)고 말하고 있으므로 정답은 (B)이다.

40

What does the man recommend?

(A) Advertising online
(B) Attending a trade show
(C) Adding food service
(D) Offering a home repair service

남자는 무엇을 권하는가?

(A) 온라인 광고
(B) 무역 박람회 참석
(C) 식품 서비스 추가
(D) 집수리 서비스 제공

어휘 repair 수리

해설 세부 사항 관련 – 남자의 권장 사항

남자가 두 번째 대사에서 카페를 추가하는 것처럼 매장에 특별한 변화를 주는 것을 고려해 보았는지(Have you considered making a significant change to the store—like adding a café?) 묻고 있으므로 정답은 (C)이다.

▶▶ Paraphrasing 대화의 a café → 정답의 food service

41-43

W-Am Hey, Taro. **⁴¹A customer just bought five bags of our Super Boost potting soil. ⁴²Could you carry them to his car for him?**

M-Cn **⁴²Can I finish organizing the flower seeds on this display first? I'll be done in a minute.**

W-Am He's probably waiting outside. I told him to pull his car up by the entrance.

M-Cn Oh, OK. And he already paid, right?

W-Am Yes. **⁴³Just be sure to sign your initials on his receipt once you're done. It's something we keep forgetting to do.**

여 안녕, 타로. 방금 고객이 슈퍼 부스트 화분용 흙 다섯 봉지를 구입했어요. 고객을 위해 고객 차까지 운반해 주실래요?

남 이 진열대에 있는 꽃씨 정리하는 일부터 마칠 수 있을까요? 금방 끝날 거예요.

여	밖에서 기다리고 있을 거예요. 제가 입구 옆에 차를 세우라고 했거든요.
남	아, 알겠어요. 돈은 벌써 냈죠?
여	네. **마치면 꼭 영수증에 첫 글자로 서명하세요. 우리가 계속 그걸 깜박하잖아요.**

어휘	potting soil 화분용 흙 seed 씨앗 pull up 차를 세우다
	entrance 입구 receipt 영수증

41

What kind of products do the speakers sell?

(A) Cleaning products
(B) Car accessories
(C) Kitchen tools
(D) Garden supplies

화자들은 어떤 종류의 제품을 판매하는가?

(A) 청소용품
(B) 자동차 부속품
(C) 주방 도구
(D) 원예용품

해설 세부 사항 관련 – 화자들이 판매하는 제품

여자가 첫 대사에서 방금 고객이 우리 슈퍼 부스트 화분용 흙 다섯 봉지를 구입했다(A customer just bought five bags of our Super Boost potting soil)고 말하고 있으므로 정답은 (D)이다.

▸▸ Paraphrasing	대화의 **potting soil**
	→ 정답의 **Garden supplies**

42

What does the woman mean when she says, "He's probably waiting outside"?

(A) A customer needs help immediately.
(B) A manager wants to discuss a complaint.
(C) A store is unusually crowded.
(D) Some instructions were confusing.

여자가 "밖에서 기다리고 있을 거예요"라고 말하는 의도는 무엇인가?

(A) 고객은 즉시 도움이 필요하다.
(B) 관리자가 불만 사항에 대해 논의하려고 한다.
(C) 매장이 유난히 붐빈다
(D) 일부 지시가 혼란스러웠다.

어휘	immediately 즉시 unusually 유난히 crowded 붐비는
	instruction 지시 confusing 혼란스러운

해설 화자의 의도 파악 – 밖에서 기다리고 있을 것이라는 말의 의도

앞에서 여자가 고객을 위해 물건을 고객의 차까지 운반해 줄 것(Could you carry them to his car for him?)을 요청하는 말에 남자가 진열대에 있는 꽃씨를 정리하는 일부터 마쳐도 될지(Can I finish organizing the flower seeds on this display first?)를 물으며 금방 끝날 것(I'll be done in a minute)이라고 하자 여자가 인용문을 언급한 것으로 보아, 고객이 기다리지 않도록 물건부터 먼저 옮겨 주라는 의도로 한 말임을 알 수 있다. 따라서 정답은 (A)이다.

43

What do the staff sometimes forget to do?

(A) Restock inventory
(B) Sign receipts
(C) Hand out flyers
(D) Mention an upcoming sale

직원들은 가끔 무엇을 잊는가?

(A) 재고 보충
(B) 영수증에 서명
(C) 전단 배포
(D) 곧 있을 할인 언급

어휘 restock 보충하다 inventory 재고 receipt 영수증 flyer 전단

해설 세부 사항 관련 – 직원들이 가끔 잊는 일

여자가 마지막 대사에서 마치면 꼭 영수증에 첫 글자로 서명하라(Just be sure to sign your initials on his receipt once you're done)면서 우리가 계속 깜박하는 부분(It's something we keep forgetting to do)이라고 말하고 있으므로 정답은 (B)이다.

44-46 3인 대화

W-Am	**44 Hi, Paul and Mark. Uh, you've already installed the electrical wiring in the new classrooms on the west end of the building, right?**
M-Cn	Yes, we're almost finished. Is there a problem?
W-Am	Well... there's just a last-minute change. The school district has decided that each classroom should have a projector mounted on the ceiling.
M-Au	**45 That's really frustrating. We'll have to redo some of the connections so that we can run wiring through the ceilings.**
M-Cn	That's going to take more time. Maybe another week or so.
W-Am	That's OK. **46 Here are the new blueprints for the classroom design. I'd like you to look them over and let me know if you have any questions.**

여	안녕, 폴, 마크. 어, 건물 서쪽 끝에 있는 새 교실들에 전기 배선 벌써 설치하셨죠?
남1	네, 거의 다 됐어요. 문제가 있나요?
여	음… 그냥 막바지에 바뀌었어요. 교육청에서 결정하기를 교실마다 천장에 프로젝터를 설치해야 한다네요.
남2	정말 맥 빠지네요. 전선이 천장을 통과하려면 연결 일부를 다시 해야 합니다.
남1	시간이 더 걸릴 겁니다. 아마 일주일 정도 더 걸릴 거예요.

TEST 10

여	괜찮아요. **여기 교실 설계용 새 청사진들이 있어요. 검토하시고 궁금한 점이 있으면 알려 주세요.**
어휘	install 설치하다 electrical wiring 전기 배선 last-minute 막바지의 mount 설치하다 ceiling 천장 frustrating 맥 빠지는 redo 다시 하다

44

Who most likely are the men?

(A) Teachers

(B) Bakers

(C) Electricians

(D) Doctors

남자들은 누구이겠는가?

(A) 교사

(B) 제빵사

(C) 전기 기사

(D) 의사

해설 전체 내용 관련 – 남자들의 직업

여자가 첫 대사에서 폴과 마크에게 인사(Hi, Paul and Mark)를 건네며 건물 서쪽 끝에 있는 새 교실들에 전기 배선을 벌써 설치했는지(you've already installed the electrical wiring ~ of the building, right?)를 묻고 있는 것으로 보아 남자들은 전기 기사임을 알 수 있다. 따라서 정답은 (C)이다.

45

Why are the men frustrated?

(A) Some work will have to be redone.

(B) Some tools have been misplaced.

(C) Some staff members are unavailable.

(D) Some supplies have run out.

남자들은 왜 맥이 빠졌는가?

(A) 작업을 다시 해야 한다.

(B) 공구를 잘못 둬서 못 찾는다.

(C) 직원이 시간이 없다.

(D) 비품이 다 떨어졌다.

어휘 unavailable 시간이 없는 supplies 비품 run out 다 떨어지다

해설 세부 사항 관련 – 남자들이 맥 빠진 이유

두 번째 남자가 첫 대사에서 정말 맥 빠진다(That's really frustrating)면서 전선이 천장을 통과하려면 연결 일부를 다시 해야 한다(We'll have to redo some of the connections so that we can run wiring through the ceilings)고 그 이유를 말하고 있으므로 정답은 (A)이다.

46

What does the woman want the men to review?

(A) A revised budget

(B) A meeting agenda

(C) Some design plans

(D) Some contract terms

여자는 남자들이 무엇을 검토하기를 바라는가?

(A) 수정된 예산

(B) 회의 안건

(C) 설계 계획

(D) 계약 조건

어휘 revised 수정된 budget 예산 contract 계약 terms (계약) 조건

해설 세부 사항 관련 – 여자가 남자들이 검토하기를 바라는 것

여자가 마지막 대사에서 여기 교실 설계용 새 청사진들이 있다(Here are the new blueprints for the classroom design)며 검토하고 궁금한 점이 있으면 알려 달라(I'd like you to look them over and let me know if you have any questions)고 말하고 있으므로 정답은 (C)이다.

> ▸▸ Paraphrasing 대화의 **blueprints for the classroom design** → 정답의 **Some design plans**

47-49

M-Cn	Thanks for agreeing to meet with me, Mayor Jackson. **⁴⁷I wanted to discuss the possibility of creating a community garden in my neighborhood.** It would be a space where we could grow flowers and vegetables.
W-Br	Great idea. But **⁴⁸finding a place for it could be a problem.**
M-Cn	Not necessarily. There's a vacant lot on the corner of Main Street and Linwood Avenue. It's city property, and it's been empty for years.
W-Br	Well, you'll need to have the city council approve a request like that. **⁴⁹I suggest you start a neighborhood petition. If you get enough signatures, you can bring it to the city council.**

남	잭슨 시장님, 만나 주셔서 감사합니다. **저는 저희 동네에 공동 텃밭을 조성할 수 있는 가능성에 대해 논의하고 싶었습니다.** 공동 텃밭은 우리가 꽃과 채소를 기를 수 있는 공간이 되죠.
여	좋은 생각입니다. 하지만 **장소를 찾는 일이 문제가 될 수 있습니다.**
남	꼭 그렇지는 않습니다. 메인 가와 린우드 대로 모퉁이에 공터가 있거든요. 시 소유고, 몇 년째 비어 있어요.
여	글쎄요, 그런 요청은 시 의회 승인을 받으셔야 할 겁니다. **주민 청원을 시작하시라고 권합니다. 서명을 충분히 받으면 시 의회에 제출할 수 있어요.**

어휘	possibility 가능성 not necessarily 반드시 ~은 아니다 vacant 비어 있는 lot 부지 property 소유물 approve 승인하다 petition 청원 signature 서명

47

What does the man want to do?

(A) Renovate a building
(B) Create a community garden
(C) Install some new road signs
(D) Move a business to a new location

남자는 무엇을 하고 싶어 하는가?

(A) 건물 개조
(B) 공동 텃밭 조성
(C) 새로운 도로 표지판 설치
(D) 새로운 장소로 업체 이전

해설 세부 사항 관련 – 남자가 하고 싶어 하는 일

남자가 첫 대사에서 우리 동네에 공동 텃밭을 조성할 수 있는 가능성에 대해 논의하고 싶었다(I wanted to discuss the possibility of creating a community garden in my neighborhood)고 말하는 것으로 보아 정답은 (B)이다.

48

What problem does the woman mention about a project?

(A) It will be noisy.
(B) It will be expensive.
(C) Finding available space may be difficult.
(D) The approval process may take a long time.

여자는 프로젝트에 관해 어떤 문제를 언급하는가?

(A) 시끄러울 것이다.
(B) 비쌀 것이다.
(C) 이용할 수 있는 공간을 찾기가 어려울 수 있다.
(D) 승인 절차가 오래 걸릴 수 있다.

해설 세부 사항 관련 – 여자가 프로젝트에 관해 언급한 문제

여자가 첫 대사에서 장소를 찾는 일이 문제가 될 수 있다(finding a place for it could be a problem)고 말하고 있으므로 정답은 (C)이다.

▸▸ Paraphrasing 대화의 **a place** → 정답의 **space**
대화의 **could be a problem**
→ 정답의 **may be difficult**

49

What does the woman suggest the man do?

(A) Apply for a loan
(B) Check a city map
(C) Collect some signatures
(D) Post an announcement online

여자는 남자에게 무엇을 하라고 권하는가?

(A) 대출 신청하기
(B) 시 지도 확인하기
(C) 서명 모으기
(D) 온라인에 공고 게시하기

해설 세부 사항 관련 – 여자의 권장 사항

여자가 마지막 대사에서 주민 청원을 시작할 것을 권한다(I suggest you start a neighborhood petition)며 서명을 충분히 받으면 시 의회에 제출할 수 있다(If you get enough signatures, you can bring it to the city council)고 제안하고 있으므로 정답은 (C)이다.

▸▸ Paraphrasing 대화의 **get enough signatures**
→ 정답의 **Collect some signatures**

50-52

M-Au	It's been great speaking with you on our radio program today. **50 I'm sure our listeners enjoyed hearing about your career in finance.**
W-Br	Thanks for having me! **51 I especially enjoyed sharing passages from the book I recently published,** *Choosing the Right Finance Career*.
M-Au	I'm glad you did. Actually, a listener just sent in one more question for you. Let's see… **52 Isabel from Rhode Island would like to know your tips for choosing the right finance degree program. Any advice?**

남	오늘 저희 라디오 프로그램에서 함께 이야기를 나눠서 정말 좋았어요. 청취자들도 틀림없이 선생님의 재무 분야 경력에 대해 재미있게 들었을 거예요.
여	초대해 줘서 감사해요! 특히 제가 최근에 출판한 책 〈재무 분야 경력 제대로 선택하기〉에 나오는 구절들을 공유해서 좋았어요.
남	좋으셨다니 다행입니다. 실은 청취자 한 분이 방금 질문을 또 보내셨는데요. 어디 보자… 로드 아일랜드에 사는 이사벨 씨가 재무학 학위 과정을 선택하는 문제에 관해 조언을 구하시네요. 조언 좀 해 주시겠어요?

어휘	recently 최근 publish 출판하다 degree 학위

50

What industry does the woman work in?

(A) Finance
(B) Farming
(C) Advertising
(D) Hospitality

여자는 어떤 업계에서 일하는가?

(A) 재무
(B) 농업
(C) 광고
(D) 접객

어휘 hospitality (주로 숙박업) 접객

남자가 첫 대사에서 여자에게 청취자들도 틀림없이 당신의 재무 분야 경력에 대해 재미있게 들었을 것(I'm sure our listeners enjoyed hearing about your career in finance)이라고 말하고 있으므로 정답은 (A)이다.

51

What did the woman do recently?

(A) She received an award.

(B) She opened a new business.

(C) She invented a new product.

(D) **She published a book.**

여자는 최근에 무엇을 했는가?

(A) 상을 받았다.

(B) 새로 개업했다.

(C) 신제품을 발명했다.

(D) **책을 발간했다.**

해설 세부 사항 관련 - 여자가 최근에 한 일

여자가 첫 대사에서 특히 제가 최근에 출판한 책인 〈재무 분야 경력 제대로 선택하기〉에 나오는 구절들을 공유해서 좋았다(I especially enjoyed sharing passages ~ *Choosing the Right Finance Career*)고 말하고 있으므로 여자가 최근에 책을 발간했음을 알 수 있다. 따라서 정답은 (D)이다.

52

What will the woman most likely discuss next?

(A) Choosing an appropriate software program

(B) Preparing for a job interview

(C) **Deciding on a program of study**

(D) Improving networking skills

여자는 다음에 무슨 이야기를 하겠는가?

(A) 적절한 소프트웨어 프로그램 선택

(B) 취업 면접 준비

(C) **학습 프로그램 결정**

(D) 인맥 형성 역량 강화

어휘 appropriate 적절한 decide 결정하다

해설 세부 사항 관련 - 여자가 다음에 할 이야기

남자가 마지막 대사에서 로드 아일랜드에 사는 이사벨 씨가 재무학 학위 프로그램을 선택하는 문제에 관해 조언을 구한다(Isabel from Rhode Island would like ~ right finance degree program)며 여자에게 조언을 해 줄 수 있는지(Any advice?)를 묻고 있으므로 정답은 (C)이다.

> ▶ Paraphrasing 대화의 choosing the right ~ degree program → 정답의 Deciding on a program of study

53-55

M-Cn Priyanka, 53**are you looking forward to the new restaurant opening next month?**

W-Br Definitely. 53**It's about time we opened a second location.**

M-Cn Yes! I was looking at the layout again, and 54**I think we should order three more sets of tables and benches for the outdoor patio.**

W-Br Good idea.

M-Cn But 55**I'm worried about placing the order right away. I know our bank account was used for payroll earlier today, so we may not have enough funds in that account to cover the costs.**

W-Br I just checked the account balance an hour ago.

M-Cn OK, I'll go ahead and place the order.

남 프리안카, 다음 달 새로 식당을 개업하는데 기대되죠?

여 물론이죠. 이제 두 번째 지점을 열 때가 됐죠.

남 그럼요! 배치도를 다시 보고 있는데 야외 테라스에 사용할 탁자와 벤치를 세 세트 더 주문해야 할 것 같아요.

여 좋은 생각이에요.

남 그런데 지금 당장 주문할 수 있을지 걱정이에요. 오늘 좀 전에 은행 계좌에서 급여가 나갔으니, 비용을 충당하기에 계좌에 자금이 부족할 수도 있어요.

여 제가 한 시간 전에 계좌 잔고를 확인했어요.

남 좋아요, 얼른 주문할게요.

어휘 Definitely 물론이죠 patio 테라스 payroll 급여 지급액 account balance 계좌 잔고

53

What kind of business do the speakers most likely own?

(A) An architecture studio

(B) **A restaurant**

(C) A real estate agency

(D) An accounting firm

화자들은 어떤 업체를 소유하고 있겠는가?

(A) 건축 스튜디오

(B) **식당**

(C) 부동산 중개업소

(D) 회계 법인

해설 세부 사항 관련 - 화자들이 소유하고 있는 업체

남자가 첫 대사에서 다음 달 새로 식당을 개업하는데 기대되는지(are you looking forward to the new restaurant opening next month?)를 묻고 있고, 여자도 이제 두 번째 지점을 열 때가 됐다(It's about time we opened a second location)고 말하고 있는 것으로 보아 정답은 (B)이다.

54

What does the man want to order?

(A) Furniture
(B) Office supplies
(C) Food
(D) Lighting fixtures

남자는 무엇을 주문하고 싶어 하는가?

(A) 가구
(B) 사무용품
(C) 식품
(D) 조명 설비

해설 세부 사항 관련 – 남자가 주문하고 싶어 하는 것

남자가 두 번째 대사에서 야외 테라스에 사용할 탁자와 벤치 세 세트를 더 주문해야 할 것 같다(I think we should order three more sets of tables and benches for the outdoor patio)고 말하고 있으므로 정답은 (A)이다.

> ▶▶ Paraphrasing   대화의 **tables and benches**
> → 정답의 **Furniture**

55

Why does the woman say, "I just checked the account balance an hour ago"?

(A) To offer an excuse
(B) To make a complaint
(C) To provide reassurance
(D) To express surprise

여자가 "제가 한 시간 전에 계좌 잔고를 확인했어요"라고 말하는 이유는 무엇인가?

(A) 변명하려고
(B) 불평하려고
(C) 안심시키려고
(D) 놀라움을 나타내려고

어휘 reassurance 안심시키는 말

해설 화자의 의도 파악 – 제가 한 시간 전에 계좌 잔고를 확인했다는 말의 의도

앞에서 남자가 지금 당장 주문을 할 수 있을지 걱정(I'm worried about placing the order right away)이라며 오늘 좀 전에 은행 계좌에서 급여가 나갔으니 비용을 충당하기에 계좌에 자금이 부족할 수도 있다(I know our bank account was used ~ in that account to cover the costs)고 말하자 여자가 인용문을 언급한 것이므로, 자신이 이미 잔고를 확인했으니 걱정하지 않아도 된다고 남자를 안심시키려고 한 말임을 알 수 있다. 따라서 정답은 (C)이다.

56-58

W-Br	Hello, Gerard. This is Patricia Santos calling.
M-Au	Patricia! ⁵⁶**I haven't talked to you since your lease ended last year.** How are you?

W-Br	I'm doing well, thanks. I've been staying with my parents in London, but ⁵⁷**I'm about to start trade school in Glasgow.**
M-Au	Oh, congratulations!
W-Br	Actually, that's why I'm calling—⁵⁸**I found a new apartment that I'd like, and the rental application requires a letter from a previous landlord. Could you write that for me?**
M-Au	Yes, of course. What should I say?
W-Br	⁵⁸**It can be short—just say that I'm a quiet, clean tenant who paid rent on time.**
M-Au	No problem. Just text me the contact information.

여	안녕, 제라드. 패트리샤 산토스예요.
남	패트리샤! **작년에 임대 기간이 끝난 뒤로는 통 얘기를 못했네요.** 어떻게 지내세요?
여	잘 지내요, 고마워요. 런던에서 부모님과 함께 지냈지만, **곧 글래스고에 있는 직업 학교에 다니려고 해요.**
남	오, 축하해요!
여	실은 그래서 전화드렸는데요. **제가 원하는 새 아파트를 구했는데, 임대 신청서에 이전 집주인의 편지가 필요해서요. 써 주시겠어요?**
남	네, 물론이죠. 뭐라고 해야 하죠?
여	**짧아도 돼요. 그냥 조용하고 깨끗한 세입자고 집세를 제때 냈다고 얘기해 주세요.**
남	문제없죠. 연락처만 문자로 보내 주세요.

어휘 trade school 직업 학교   previous 이전의   landlord 집주인   tenant 세입자

56

Who most likely is the man?

(A) The woman's former landlord
(B) The woman's professor
(C) The woman's relative
(D) The woman's previous employer

남자는 누구이겠는가?

(A) 여자의 이전 집주인
(B) 여자의 교수
(C) 여자의 친척
(D) 여자의 이전 고용주

어휘 relative 친척   employer 고용주

해설 전체 내용 관련 – 남자의 신분

남자가 첫 대사에서 여자에게 작년에 당신의 임대 기간이 끝난 뒤로는 통 얘기를 못했다(I haven't talked to you since your lease ended last year)고 말하고 있으므로 정답은 (A)이다.

57

What does the woman say she will do soon?

(A) Return to her parents' house

(B) Apply for a job

(C) Pick up her belongings

(D) Begin coursework at school

여자는 곧 무엇을 할 것이라고 말하는가?

(A) 부모님 댁으로 돌아가기

(B) 일자리에 지원하기

(C) 소지품 찾아가기

(D) 학교에서 학업 시작하기

해설 세부 사항 관련 - 여자가 곧 할 것이라고 말하는 일

여자가 두 번째 대사에서 곧 글래스고에 있는 직업 학교에 다니려고 한다(I'm about to start trade school in Glasgow)고 말하고 있으므로 정답은 (D)이다.

> ▸▸ Paraphrasing 대화의 **start trade school**
> → 정답의 **Begin coursework at school**

58

What does the woman ask for?

(A) A house key

(B) A copy of a certificate

(C) A reference letter

(D) A colleague's e-mail address

여자는 무엇을 요청하는가?

(A) 집 열쇠

(B) 자격증 사본

(C) 추천서

(D) 동료의 이메일 주소

어휘 certificate 자격증 reference letter 추천서

해설 세부 사항 관련 - 여자의 요청 사항

여자가 세 번째 대사에서 원하는 새 아파트를 구했는데 임대 신청서에 이전 집주인의 편지가 필요하다(I found a new apartment ~ requires a letter from a previous landlord)며 써 줄 수 있는지(Could you write that for me?)를 묻고 있고, 네 번째 대사에서 짧아도 되며 그냥 조용하고 깨끗한 세입자로 집세를 제때 냈다고 얘기해 달라(It can be short ~ paid rent on time)며 긍정적인 내용을 언급한 편지를 써 줄 것을 요청하고 있으므로 정답은 (C)이다.

59-61

> W-Am **59 Thank you for listening to Channel Three news this morning. It's time to go to Hao Nan with our traffic report.**
>
> M-Au Thanks, Sameera. While most commuters are seeing a fairly smooth ride this morning, **60 crews have begun repairs to the Lansing Bridge, and it's closed to all traffic.** Drivers can take a detour on Canal Road.
>
> W-Am And when is construction expected to be completed?
>
> M-Au It's scheduled to wrap up by November seventh. **61 Head to our Web site at NewsThree.com to learn more about the progress of the repairs.**

여	오늘 아침 채널 3 뉴스를 청취해 주셔서 감사합니다. 하오난 교통 정보를 확인할 시간입니다.
남	고마워요, 사미라. 대다수 통근자들에게 오늘 아침은 교통 흐름이 상당히 원활합니다만, **작업반이 랜싱 다리 보수 공사를 시작했고, 다리에는 모든 교통이 통제되고 있습니다.** 운전자들은 커넬 로에서 우회하시면 됩니다.
여	그러면 공사는 언제 끝날 예정입니까?
남	11월 7일에 마무리될 예정입니다. 보수 공사 진행 상황에 대한 자세한 정보는 웹사이트 NewsThree.com을 방문하세요.

어휘	commuter 통근자 fairly 상당히 detour 우회로 construction 공사 wrap up 마무리되다 head to ~로 향하다 progress 진행

59

Where most likely are the speakers?

(A) In a government office

(B) In a television studio

(C) At a bus terminal

(D) At a construction site

화자들은 어디에 있겠는가?

(A) 관공서

(B) 텔레비전 스튜디오

(C) 버스 터미널

(D) 건설 현장

해설 전체 내용 관련 - 대화의 장소

여자가 첫 대사에서 오늘 아침 채널 3 뉴스를 청취해 주셔서 감사하다(Thank you for listening to Channel Three news this morning)고 말하는 것으로 보아 현재 뉴스를 진행 중임을 알 수 있다. 따라서 정답은 (B)이다.

60

What does the man mention about the Lansing Bridge?

(A) There is a lot of traffic on it today.

(B) There is a beautiful view from it.

(C) It now has a walkway.

(D) It is temporarily closed.

남자는 랜싱 다리에 관해 무엇을 언급하는가?

(A) 오늘 다리에 차가 막힌다.
(B) 다리에서 멋진 경치가 보인다.
(C) 지금은 보도가 있다.
(D) 임시로 폐쇄됐다.

어휘 temporarily 임시로

해설 세부 사항 관련 - 남자가 랜싱 다리에 관해 언급한 사항

남자가 첫 대사에서 작업반이 랜싱 다리 보수 공사를 시작했고 다리에는 모든 교통이 통제되고 있다(crews have begun repairs to the Lansing Bridge, and it's closed to all traffic)고 말하고 있으므로 정답은 (D)이다.

61

How can the listeners find out more information?

(A) By visiting an information desk
(B) By requesting a brochure
(C) By checking a Web site
(D) By calling a help line

청자들은 어떻게 더 많은 정보를 찾을 수 있는가?

(A) 안내 데스크를 방문해서
(B) 소책자를 요청해서
(C) 웹사이트를 확인해서
(D) 전화 상담 서비스에 전화해서

어휘 help line 전화 상담 서비스

해설 세부 사항 관련 - 청자들이 추가 정보를 찾을 수 있는 방법

남자가 마지막 대사에서 보수 공사 진행 상황에 대한 자세한 정보는 웹사이트 NewsThree.com을 방문하라(Head to our Web site at NewsThree.com to learn more about the progress of the repairs)고 말하고 있으므로 정답은 (C)이다.

> ▶ Paraphrasing   대화의 Head to our Web site
> → 정답의 checking a Web site

62-64 대화 + 일정표

W-Am Hello, Elmbrook Community Center.

M-Cn Hi, 62,63 **I'll be attending the class that starts on Friday this week, and I'm wondering what to bring.** Details weren't listed in the class description.

W-Am Oh, the materials are always provided. But please note that classes don't start until next week.

M-Cn Really? 64 **I'll be in Chicago next week—my son's getting married.** I'm afraid I'm going to have to miss the first class, then.

여   안녕하세요, 엘름브룩 주민 센터입니다.

남   안녕하세요, **이번 주 금요일에 시작하는 수업에 참석하려고 하는데, 뭘 가져가야 하는지 궁금해서요.** 수업 설명에 세부 정보가 없었어요.

여   아, 자료는 항상 제공됩니다. 하지만 수업은 다음 주가 돼야 시작된다는 점 유념하세요.

남   그래요? 다음 주에는 시카고에 가는데, 아들이 결혼하거든요. 그럼 안타깝지만 첫 수업은 빠져야겠네요.

어휘 community center 주민 센터 description 설명

Community Center Class Schedule

Monday	Tuesday	Wednesday	Thursday	Friday
Ceramics	Knitting	Painting	Sculpture	Drawing

주민 센터 강좌 일정

월	화	수	목	금
도자기	뜨개질	회화	조각	**소묘**

62

Why is the man calling?

(A) To confirm he will teach a class
(B) To complain about a recent class
(C) To inquire about class supplies
(D) To request directions to a community center

남자는 왜 전화하는가?

(A) 자신이 강의한다고 확정하려고
(B) 최근 강좌에 대해 불만을 제기하려고
(C) 수업 물품에 대해 문의하려고
(D) 주민 센터로 가는 길을 물어보려고

해설 전체 내용 관련 - 남자가 전화하는 이유

남자가 첫 대사에서 이번 주 금요일에 시작하는 수업에 참석하려고 하는데 무엇을 가져가야 하는지 궁금하다(I'll be attending the class ~ wondering what to bring)고 말하고 있으므로 정답은 (C)이다.

63

Look at the graphic. Which class are the speakers discussing?

(A) Knitting
(B) Painting
(C) Sculpture
(D) Drawing

TEST 10

시각 정보에 의하면 화자들은 어떤 수업에 관해 논의하고 있는가?

(A) 뜨개질
(B) 회화
(C) 조각
(D) 소묘

해설 시각 정보 연계 - 화자들이 대화 중인 수업

남자가 첫 대사에서 이번 주 금요일에 시작하는 수업에 참석하려고 하는데 무엇을 가져가야 하는지 궁금하다(I'll be attending the class ~ wondering what to bring)며 금요일 수업에 관해 문의하고 있고, 일정표에 따르면 금요일 수업은 소묘라고 나와 있으므로 정답은 (D)이다.

64

What does the man plan to do in Chicago?

(A) Go to a graduation ceremony
(B) Attend a wedding
(C) Complete a certification
(D) See an art exhibit

남자는 시카고에서 무엇을 할 계획인가?

(A) 졸업식 참석
(B) 결혼식 참석
(C) 자격증 따기
(D) 미술 전시회 관람

어휘 certification 자격증

해설 세부 사항 관련 - 남자가 시카고에서 하려고 계획한 일

남자가 마지막 대사에서 다음 주에는 시카고에 간다(I'll be in Chicago next week)며 아들이 결혼한다(my son's getting married)고 말하고 있으므로 시카고에서 아들의 결혼식에 참석할 것임을 알 수 있다. 따라서 정답은 (B)이다.

65-67 대화 + 그래프

M-Au Thanks for attending this planning meeting. As I explained in my e-mail, [65]**since the company's expanding its fleet of trucks, we need to figure out how to recruit more truck drivers**. Any ideas?

W-Am I did some research. This graph shows where people most frequently search for jobs online.

M-Au Hmm, [66]**eighty-four percent use job search engines, so it's good we already post our job openings on those. But, look at the next-highest category. At sixty-six percent, it'd be worth investing in.**

W-Am [66]**I thought so, too.** We'd need to increase our recruitment budget, though.

M-Au [67]**I'm meeting with the rest of the management team later today. I'll mention our need for extra funds.**

남 이번 기획 회의에 참석해 주셔서 감사합니다. 제가 이메일에서 설명했듯이, 회사가 보유 트럭을 늘리고 있으므로 트럭 운전기사를 더 고용할 방안을 알아봐야 합니다. 좋은 생각 있나요?

여 조사를 좀 해 봤어요. 이 그래프는 사람들이 온라인으로 일자리를 가장 자주 검색하는 곳을 보여 줍니다.

남 음, 84퍼센트가 구직 검색 엔진을 사용하니까 우리가 이미 채용 공고를 거기에 올려서 다행이네요. 하지만 다음으로 가장 높은 범주를 보세요. 66퍼센트라면 돈을 쓸 가치가 있을 겁니다.

여 저도 그렇게 생각했어요. 하지만 채용 예산을 늘려야 해요.

남 오늘 이따가 나머지 경영진과 만나기로 했어요. 추가 자금이 필요하다고 이야기하겠습니다.

어휘 expand 확장하다 fleet 보유한 전체 차량 figure out ~을 알아보다 frequently 자주 increase 늘리다 budget 예산

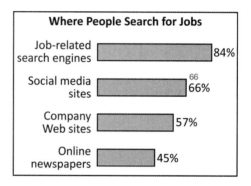

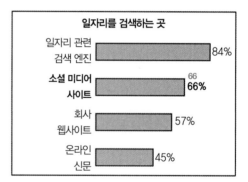

65

Where do the speakers most likely work?

(A) At a car rental service
(B) At a market research firm
(C) At an electronics store
(D) At a trucking company

화자들은 어디에서 일하겠는가?

(A) 렌터카 서비스 업체
(B) 시장 조사 업체
(C) 전자 제품 매장
(D) 트럭 운송업체

해설 전체 내용 관련 – 화자들의 근무지
남자가 첫 대사에서 회사가 보유 트럭을 늘리고 있으므로 트럭 운전기사를 더 고용할 방안을 알아봐야 한다(since the company's expanding its fleet of trucks, ~ recruit more truck drivers)고 말하고 있으므로 정답은 (D)이다.

66

Look at the graphic. Where do the speakers plan to start advertising job openings?

(A) On job-related search engines
(B) On social media sites
(C) On company Web sites
(D) In online newspapers

시각 정보에 의하면 화자들은 어디에 구인 광고를 시작할 계획인가?
(A) 일자리 관련 검색 엔진
(B) 소셜 미디어 사이트
(C) 회사 웹사이트
(D) 온라인 신문

해설 시각 정보 연계 – 화자들이 구인 광고를 시작하려는 곳
남자가 두 번째 대사에서 84퍼센트가 구직 검색 엔진을 사용하니까 우리가 이미 채용 공고를 거기에 올려서 다행이다(eighty-four percent use ~ our job openings on those)라고 말한 뒤, 하지만 다음으로 가장 높은 범주를 보라(But, look at the next-highest category)며 66퍼센트라면 돈을 쓸 가치가 있을 것(At sixty-six percent, it'd be worth investing in)이라고 제안하자 여자가 저도 그렇게 생각했다(I thought so, too)며 동의한 것으로 보아, 화자들은 66퍼센트를 기록한 카테고리에서도 채용 공고를 시작할 계획임을 알 수 있다. 그래프에 따르면 두 번째로 높은 66퍼센트를 기록한 카테고리는 소셜 미디어 사이트이므로 정답은 (B)이다.

67

What does the man say he will do later today?

(A) Propose a budget adjustment
(B) Attend a training session
(C) Write a letter of recommendation
(D) Approve a timeline

남자는 오늘 나중에 무엇을 할 것이라고 말하는가?
(A) 예산 조정 제안
(B) 교육 세션 참석
(C) 추천서 작성
(D) 일정 승인

어휘 adjustment 조정 recommendation 추천

해설 세부 사항 관련 – 남자가 오늘 나중에 할 것이라고 말하는 일
남자가 마지막 대사에서 오늘 이따가 나머지 경영진과 만나기로 했다(I'm meeting with the rest of the management team later today)며 추가 자금이 필요하다고 이야기하겠다(I'll mention our need for extra funds)고 말하고 있으므로 정답은 (A)이다.

▸▸ **Paraphrasing** 대화의 **mention our need for extra funds**
→ 정답의 **Propose a budget adjustment**

68-70 대화 + 디자인 이미지

M-Au The design for next season's backpack looks nice! [68]**What materials will you use?**

W-Br Well, [68]**polyester for the body of the bag, but it's hard to decide what to use for the straps.** Any suggestions?

M-Au How about cotton canvas?

W-Br Hmm. Yes, OK. That would create an interesting texture contrast. Perfect!

M-Au By the way, [69]**remember how we commissioned an artist to redesign our logo in honor of our company's fifty years in business?** Well, [70]**the new logo is ready. Where would you like it to go?**

W-Br Last year the logo went on the left side pocket. But [70]**for this model I'd like to do something different, so put it on the top flap.**

M-Au No problem.

남 다음 시즌 백팩 디자인이 멋지네요! **어떤 소재를 쓰실 건가요?**

여 글쎄요, **가방 본체는 폴리에스테르로 하는데, 끈에 어떤 걸 사용할지 결정하기 어렵네요.** 좋은 의견 있으세요?

남 면 캔버스 어때요?

여 음, 네, 좋아요. 질감 대비가 흥미롭겠는데요. 완벽해요!

남 그런데 회사 창립 50주년을 기념하려고 아티스트에게 로고를 다시 디자인해 달라고 의뢰했던 거 기억하세요? 어, 새 로고가 준비됐어요. 로고가 어디에 들어가면 좋을까요?

여 지난해에는 로고가 왼쪽 주머니에 들어갔어요. 하지만 이 모델은 좀 색다른 걸 해 보고 싶으니까 상단 덮개에 넣죠.

남 문제없어요.

어휘 texture 질감 contrast 대비 flap 덮개

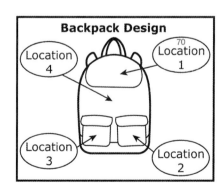

Backpack Design

Location 4
Location 1 (70)
Location 3
Location 2

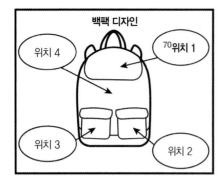

백팩 디자인

위치 4
70위치 1
위치 3
위치 2

68

What is the woman having difficulty deciding on?

(A) A color

(B) A fabric

(C) Storage capacity

(D) Strap placement

여자는 무엇을 결정하는 데 어려움을 겪고 있는가?

(A) 색상

(B) 직물

(C) 보관 용량

(D) 끈 배치

해설 세부 사항 관련 – 여자가 결정하는 데 어려움을 겪는 것

남자가 첫 대사에서 어떤 소재를 쓸 것인지(What materials will you use?) 묻자 여자가 가방 본체는 폴리에스테르로 하는데 끈에는 어떤 것을 사용할지 결정하기 어렵다(polyester for the body ~ what to use for the straps)고 말하고 있으므로 정답은 (B)이다.

> ▸▸ **Paraphrasing** 대화의 **materials** → 정답의 **A fabric**

69

Why was the company's logo redesigned?

(A) To reflect design trends

(B) To celebrate an anniversary

(C) To appeal to a wider audience

(D) To avoid a copyright problem

회사 로고는 왜 다시 디자인되었는가?

(A) 디자인 추세를 반영하려고

(B) 기념일을 축하하려고

(C) 더 많은 관객의 마음을 끌려고

(D) 저작권 문제를 피하려고

어휘 reflect 반영하다 copyright 저작권

해설 세부 사항 관련 – 회사 로고가 다시 디자인된 이유

남자가 세 번째 대사에서 회사 창립 50주년을 기념하려고 아티스트에게 로고를 다시 디자인해 달라고 의뢰했던 것을 기억하는지(remember how we ~ in honor of our company's fifty years in business?) 묻고 있는 것으로 보아 정답은 (B)이다.

> ▸▸ **Paraphrasing** 대화의 **in honor of our company's fifty years** → 정답의 **celebrate an anniversary**

70

Look at the graphic. Where will the company's logo be placed?

(A) Location 1

(B) Location 2

(C) Location 3

(D) Location 4

시각 정보에 의하면 회사 로고는 어디에 배치될 것인가?

(A) 위치 1

(B) 위치 2

(C) 위치 3

(D) 위치 4

해설 시각 정보 연계 – 회사 로고가 배치될 위치

남자가 세 번째 대사에서 새 로고가 준비됐다(the new logo is ready)며 로고가 어디에 들어가면 좋을지(Where would you like it to go?) 묻자 여자가 이 모델은 좀 색다른 걸 해 보고 싶으니 상단 덮개에 넣자(for this model I'd like to do something different, so put it on the top flap)고 말하고 있고, 디자인 이미지에 따르면 상단 덮개 위치는 위치 1이므로 정답은 (A)이다.

PART 4

71-73 전화 메시지

M-Au Hello, [71]**I recently ordered a pair of reading glasses from your Web site.** [72]**I chose blue frames, but when the package arrived, the glasses had black frames instead.** I'm going to send these back to you now to be exchanged for the correct color. But [73]**I wanted to ask how long it'll take for the blue pair to arrive.** The original shipment took about three weeks, and I'd like to get the replacement sooner. My number's 555-0156. Thanks.

안녕하세요, **최근에 웹사이트에서 독서용 안경을 주문했어요. 파란색 안경테를 골랐는데, 택배가 도착해서 보니 안경이 검은색 테였어요.** 그쪽으로 반품할 테니 정확한 색으로 교환해 주세요. 그런데 **파란색 안경이 도착하는 데 얼마나 걸릴지 궁금해요.** 원래 배송은 3주 정도 걸렸는데, 빨리 대체품을 받고 싶어요. 제 번호는 555-0156입니다. 고마워요.

어휘 recently 최근에 replacement 대체품

71

What kind of product did the speaker order?

(A) Printer ink

(B) Eyeglasses

(C) Picture frames

(D) Furniture

화자는 어떤 종류의 제품을 주문했는가?

(A) 프린터 잉크
(B) 안경
(C) 액자
(D) 가구

해설 세부 사항 관련 – 화자가 주문한 제품

화자가 초반부에 최근에 웹사이트에서 독서용 안경을 주문했다(I recently ordered a pair of reading glasses from your Web site)고 말하고 있으므로 정답은 (B)이다.

72

What problem does the speaker mention?

(A) A package was not received.
(B) An invoice is missing.
(C) A product is the wrong color.
(D) A Web site is down.

화자는 어떤 문제를 언급하는가?

(A) 소포를 받지 못했다.
(B) 송장이 누락되었다.
(C) 제품이 엉뚱한 색깔이다.
(D) 웹사이트가 작동하지 않는다.

어휘 receive 받다 invoice 송장

해설 세부 사항 관련 – 화자가 언급하는 문제

화자가 초반부에 파란색 안경테를 골랐는데 택배가 도착해서 보니 안경이 검은색 테였다(I chose blue frames, ~ the glasses had black frames instead)고 말하고 있으므로 주문한 제품과 다른 색상의 제품이 배송되었음을 알 수 있다. 따라서 정답은 (C)이다.

73

What does the speaker ask about?

(A) A refund policy
(B) A delivery fee
(C) A shipping time
(D) A mailing address

화자는 무엇에 관해 문의하는가?

(A) 환불 규정
(B) 배송비
(C) 배송 시간
(D) 우편 주소

해설 세부 사항 관련 – 화자가 질문하는 것

화자가 후반부에 파란색 안경이 도착하는 데 얼마나 걸릴지 궁금하다(I wanted to ask how long it'll take for the blue pair to arrive)고 말하고 있으므로 정답은 (C)이다.

▸▸ Paraphrasing 담화의 how long it'll take ~ to arrive
→ 정답의 A shipping time

74-76 발표

W-Am Good afternoon, everyone. As you know, **74 it's time to announce our newest employee of the month, and it goes to Haru Watanabe.** Congratulations! Haru did outstanding work this month securing the Thompson Limited account. He also volunteers in the community. **75 As our winner, Haru will receive a preferred parking space right outside the building for the next 30 days.** Haru, please come up here to have your picture taken. **76 Like all our employees of the month, your photo will be featured on the company Web site.**

안녕하세요, 여러분. 아시겠지만 **이달의 사원을 새로 발표할 때가 됐군요. 상은 와타나베 하루 씨에게 돌아갑니다.** 축하합니다! 하루 씨는 이번 달에 톰슨 사를 거래처로 확보하는 데 혁혁한 공을 세웠죠. 지역 사회에서 자원봉사도 하고요. **수상자로서 하루 씨는 앞으로 30일 동안 건물 바로 바깥에 선호하는 주차 공간을 받게 됩니다.** 하루 씨, 여기 와서 사진 찍으세요. **다른 이달의 직원들과 마찬가지로, 하루 씨 사진도 회사 웹사이트에 실립니다.**

어휘 outstanding 혁혁한 secure 확보하다 account 거래처 preferred 선호하는 feature 특별히 포함하다, 싣다

74

What award is being announced?

(A) Best design
(B) Top salesperson
(C) Employee of the month
(D) Excellence in research

어떤 상이 발표되고 있는가?

(A) 최고 디자인
(B) 최우수 영업 사원
(C) 이달의 사원
(D) 우수 연구

해설 세부 사항 관련 – 발표되고 있는 상

화자가 초반부에 이달의 사원을 새로 발표할 때가 되었는데 상은 와타나베 하루 씨에게 돌아간다(it's time to announce our newest employee of the month, and it goes to Haru Watanabe)고 발표하고 있으므로 정답은 (C)이다.

75

According to the speaker, what will the winner receive?

(A) A commemorative plaque
(B) A parking space
(C) A gift certificate
(D) A recognition dinner

화자의 말에 따르면, 수상자는 무엇을 받을 것인가?

(A) 기념패
(B) 주차 공간
(C) 상품권
(D) 포상 만찬

어휘 commemorative 기념하는 plaque 패 recognition 포상

해설 세부 사항 관련 - 화자가 수상자가 받을 것이라고 말하는 것

화자가 중반부에 수상자로서 하루 씨는 앞으로 30일 동안 건물 바로 바깥에 선호하는 주차 공간을 받게 된다(As our winner, Haru will receive a preferred parking space right outside the building for the next 30 days)고 말하고 있으므로 정답은 (B)이다.

76

What does the speaker say will be published on a Web site?

(A) A photograph
(B) A biography
(C) Professional accomplishments
(D) Company event details

화자는 웹사이트에 무엇이 실린다고 말하는가?

(A) 사진
(B) 약력
(C) 직무 성과
(D) 회사 행사 세부 내용

어휘 biography 약력 accomplishment 성과

해설 세부 사항 관련 - 화자가 웹사이트에 실린다고 말하는 것

화자가 마지막에 다른 이달의 직원들과 마찬가지로 하루 씨 사진도 회사 웹사이트에 실린다(Like all our employees of the month, your photo will be featured on the company Web site)고 말하고 있으므로 정답은 (A)이다.

▸▸ Paraphrasing 담화의 **photo** → 정답의 **photograph**

77-79 안내

M-Cn Hi, everyone! My name is Sanjeep Gupta. ⁷⁷**We're excited to have so many new people working at our bicycle stores.** During the week, you will learn how to repair bicycles and scooters for our customers. ⁷⁸**Before we begin your training, I'm going to show you around this model facility,** which has been built to simulate the repair shop in the back of every one of our stores. Oh—⁷⁹**a couple of you asked about your schedule this week. I'll be overseeing your work,** and I come in at eight.

안녕하세요, 여러분! 제 이름은 산지프 굽타입니다. **우리 자전거 가게에서 새로운 분들이 많이 일하게 돼서 기쁩니다.** 주중에는 고객을 위한 자전거와 스쿠터 수리법을 배우게 됩니다. **교육을 시작하기 전에 이 견본**

시설을 보여 드릴게요. 우리 매장마다 뒤쪽에 수리점이 있는데 그걸 본떠 만든 시설이죠. 아, **두 분이 이번 주 일정에 대해 물어보셨는데요. 제가 여러분 작업을 감독하는데** 8시에 들어옵니다.

어휘 repair 수리하다 facility 시설 simulate 본뜨다 oversee 감독하다

77

What kind of product does the speaker's company sell?

(A) Bicycles
(B) Tools
(C) Cars
(D) Toys

화자의 회사는 어떤 종류의 제품을 판매하는가?

(A) 자전거
(B) 공구
(C) 자동차
(D) 장난감

해설 세부 사항 관련 - 화자의 회사가 판매하는 제품

화자가 초반부에 우리 자전거 가게에서 새로운 분들이 많이 일하게 돼서 기쁘다(We're excited to have so many new people working at our bicycle stores)고 말하고 있으므로 정답은 (A)이다.

78

What will the listeners do next?

(A) Watch a video
(B) Vote on a policy
(C) Inspect a brochure
(D) Tour a facility

청자들은 다음에 무엇을 할 것인가?

(A) 영상 보기
(B) 규정을 놓고 투표하기
(C) 소책자 점검하기
(D) 시설 견학하기

해설 세부 사항 관련 - 청자들이 다음에 할 일

화자가 중반부에 교육을 시작하기 전에 이 견본 시설을 보여 주겠다(Before we begin your training, I'm going to show you around this model facility)고 말하고 있으므로 정답은 (D)이다.

79

What does the speaker mean when he says, "I come in at eight"?

(A) He is very busy this week.
(B) A store usually opens early.
(C) The listeners should arrive at that time.
(D) The listeners should prepare a shipment.

화자가 "8시에 들어옵니다"라고 말하는 의도는 무엇인가?

(A) 그는 이번 주에 매우 바쁘다.

(B) 매장은 대개 일찍 문을 연다.

(C) **청자들은 그 시간에 도착해야 한다.**

(D) 청자들은 출하를 준비해야 한다.

해설 화자의 의도 파악 – 8시에 들어온다는 말의 의도

앞에서 두 분이 이번 주 일정에 대해 물어보았다(a couple of you asked about your schedule this week)면서 제가 여러분 작업을 감독할 것 (I'll be overseeing your work)이라고 말한 뒤 인용문을 언급하고 있으므로, 감독관인 자신이 8시에 올 테니 청자들도 그때까지 자리에 있어야 한다는 것을 알려 주려는 의도로 한 말임을 알 수 있다. 따라서 정답은 (C) 이다.

80-82 회의 발췌

> M-Au ⁸⁰**A new report shows that customers prefer sustainable packaging in the products they buy. In order to expand our customer base, we've decided to look into using biodegradable packaging for the personal care products we make.** ⁸¹**Just last month, we hired a packaging consultant** to develop environmentally friendly packaging for our products. Now we need to set up a committee to oversee the project. ⁸²**If you're interested in participating, contact your manager by the end of the week.**

> 새로운 보고서를 보면 고객들은 구매하는 제품에서 지속 가능한 포장을 선호합니다. 고객층을 넓히기 위해 우리가 만드는 개인 생활용품에 생분해성 포장을 사용하는 방안을 검토하기로 했습니다. 바로 지난달, 우리 제품에 쓸 환경친화적 포장을 개발하기 위해 포장 컨설턴트를 고용했습니다. 이제 프로젝트를 감독할 위원회를 설치해야 하는데요. **참여에 관심이 있으면 주말까지 여러분의 관리자에게 연락하세요.**

> 어휘 sustainable 지속 가능한 expand 넓히다
> biodegradable 생분해성이 있는 environmentally friendly
> 환경친화적인 participate 참석하다

80

What does the speaker mainly discuss?

(A) Offering training opportunities

(B) **Changing product packaging**

(C) Updating safety regulations

(D) Revising an advertising strategy

화자는 주로 무엇을 논의하는가?

(A) 교육 기회 제공

(B) **제품 포장 변경**

(C) 안전 규정 개선

(D) 광고 전략 수정

어휘 opportunity 기회 regulation 규정 revise 수정하다

해설 전체 내용 관련 – 담화의 주제

화자가 도입부에 새로운 보고서를 보면 고객들은 구매하는 제품에서 지속 가능한 포장을 선호한다(A new report shows ~ in the products they buy)면서 고객층을 넓히기 위해 우리가 만드는 개인 생활용품에 생분해성 포장을 사용하는 방안을 검토하기로 했다(In order to expand our customer base, ~ for the personal care products we make)고 말하고 있으므로 제품의 포장재를 바꾸는 것에 대해 주로 말하고 있음을 알 수 있다. 따라서 정답은 (B)이다.

81

What did the company do last month?

(A) It expanded its social media presence.

(B) It agreed to organize a conference.

(C) It published a training manual.

(D) **It hired an outside consultant.**

회사는 지난달에 무엇을 했는가?

(A) 소셜 미디어에서 입지를 넓혔다.

(B) 회의를 개최하기로 합의했다.

(C) 훈련 교본을 발간했다.

(D) **외부 컨설턴트를 고용했다.**

어휘 expand one's presence 입지를 넓히다 organize 개최하다

해설 세부 사항 관련 – 회사가 지난달에 한 일

화자가 중반부에 바로 지난달에 우리 제품에 쓸 환경친화적 포장을 개발하기 위해 포장 컨설턴트를 고용했다(Just last month, we hired a packaging consultant)고 말하고 있으므로 정답은 (D)이다.

82

What should interested listeners do?

(A) **Contact their managers**

(B) Recruit some volunteers

(C) Answer a survey

(D) Watch a video

관심 있는 청자들은 무엇을 해야 하는가?

(A) **자신들의 관리자에게 문의하기**

(B) 자원봉사자 모집하기

(C) 설문 조사 응답하기

(D) 영상 보기

해설 세부 사항 관련 – 관심 있는 청자들이 할 일

화자가 마지막에 참여에 관심이 있으면 주말까지 여러분의 관리자에게 연락하라(If you're interested in participating, contact your manager by the end of the week)고 권하고 있으므로 정답은 (A) 이다.

83-85 담화

> W-Br ⁸³**Thank you all for attending the thirtieth annual Dental Healthcare Conference. We have**

six sessions planned on the latest advances in tooth restoration. As a reminder, **⁸⁴if you'd like to receive continuing education credit for attending the conference, you'll have to complete additional paperwork. Some of you may want to hear more details about that. I'll be at the booth in the lobby until noon.** And finally, just a reminder that **⁸⁵you are all invited to attend a dinner reception tonight** starting right after the last presentation session.

제 30회 연례 구강 보건 회의에 참석해 주셔서 감사합니다. 치아 복원의 최근 발전에 대해 6개의 세션을 계획했습니다. 다시 일러 드리지만 회의 참석으로 평생 교육 이수 학점을 받으려면 추가 서류 작업을 완료해야 합니다. 여러분 중 몇 분은 더 자세히 듣고 싶으실 텐데요. 제가 정오까지 로비에 있는 부스에 있을 겁니다. 마지막으로 알려 드립니다. 마지막 발표회 직후에 시작되는 오늘 저녁 만찬 환영회에 모두 참석해 주세요.

어휘 advance 발전 restoration 복원 continuing education 평생 교육 credit 이수 학점

83

Who most likely are the listeners?

(A) Engineers
(B) Dentists
(C) Educators
(D) Architects

청자들은 누구이겠는가?
(A) 엔지니어
(B) 치과 의사
(C) 교육자
(D) 건축가

해설 전체 내용 관련 - 청자들의 직업
화자가 도입부에 청자들에게 제 30회 연례 구강 보건 회의에 참석해 줘서 감사하다(Thank you all for attending the thirtieth annual Dental Healthcare Conference)며 치아 복원의 최근 발전에 대해 6개의 세션을 계획했다(We have six sessions planned on the latest advances in tooth restoration)고 안내하고 있는 것으로 보아 정답은 (B)이다.

84

Why does the speaker say, "I'll be at the booth in the lobby until noon"?

(A) To request volunteers for the afternoon
(B) To explain that a booth location has changed
(C) To apologize for a scheduling conflict
(D) To indicate availability to answer questions

화자가 "제가 정오까지 로비에 있는 부스에 있을 겁니다"라고 말하는 이유는 무엇인가?
(A) 오후 자원봉사자를 요청하려고
(B) 부스 위치가 바뀌었다고 설명하려고
(C) 일정이 겹쳐서 사과하려고
(D) 질문에 답변할 수 있다고 알리려고

어휘 scheduling conflict 일정 겹침

해설 화자의 의도 파악 - 제가 정오까지 로비에 있는 부스에 있겠다는 말의 의도

앞에서 화자가 회의 참석으로 평생 교육 이수 학점을 받으려면 추가 서류 작업을 완료해야 한다(if you'd like to receive continuing education credit ~ complete additional paperwork)고 안내하며 여러분 중 몇 분은 더 자세히 듣기를 원할 수도 있다(Some of you may want to hear more details about that)고 말한 뒤 인용문을 언급하고 있으므로, 평생 교육 이수 학점을 받는 것에 대해 질문이 있는 청자들은 자신을 찾아오면 추가 정보를 줄 수 있다고 말하려는 의도임을 알 수 있다. 따라서 정답은 (D)이다.

85

What does the speaker say will happen tonight?

(A) A book signing
(B) A photo shoot
(C) A dinner reception
(D) An award ceremony

화자는 오늘밤에 무슨 일이 있다고 말하는가?
(A) 도서 사인회
(B) 사진 촬영
(C) 만찬 환영회
(D) 시상식

해설 세부 사항 관련 - 화자가 오늘밤에 있을 것이라고 말하는 일
화자가 마지막에 오늘 저녁 만찬 환영회에 모두 참석해 달라(you are all invited to attend a dinner reception tonight)고 말하고 있으므로 정답은 (C)이다.

86-88 방송

W-Am Welcome to this episode of our radio show, *Research Now*. On every show we talk to a different scientist about their work. **⁸⁶Today's guest is Geeta Prasad. She's a scientist at McMillan Shoe Manufacturers. Her job is to research how people move their feet when they exercise. ⁸⁷She then provides that data to the design team, who use it to design new shoes.** In fact, **⁸⁸her team is looking for participants to take part in their next study. To sign up, visit McMillan Shoe Manufacturers' Web site.**

라디오 쇼 〈리서치 나우〉 이번 회차에 오신 것을 환영합니다. 매 회마다 다른 과학자와 함께 그분들의 연구에 관해 이야기하고 있는데요. 오늘 초대 손님은 지타 프라사드 씨로, 맥밀런 신발 제조사의 과학자입니다. 프라사드 씨가 하는 일은 사람들이 운동할 때 발을 어떻게 움직이는지 연구하는 것입니다. 그런 다음 데이터를 디자인팀에 제공하면 디자인팀이 이 데이터를 활용해 새로운 신발을 디자인합니다. 실은 프라사드 팀에서 다음 연구에 참여할 참가자를 찾고 있습니다. 신청하시려면 맥밀런 신발 제조사 웹사이트를 방문하세요.

86

What is Geeta Prasad's profession?

(A) Research scientist

(B) Medical doctor

(C) University professor

(D) Government official

지타 프라사드의 직업은 무엇인가?

(A) 연구원

(B) 의사

(C) 대학교수

(D) 공무원

해설 세부 사항 관련 - 지타 프라사드의 직업

화자가 초반부에 오늘 초대 손님은 지타 프라사드 씨(Today's guest is Geeta Prasad)로 맥밀런 신발 제조사의 과학자(She's a scientist at McMillan Shoe Manufacturers)라고 소개하며, 프라사드 씨가 하는 일은 사람들이 운동할 때 발을 어떻게 움직이는지 연구하는 것(Her job is to research how people move their feet when they exercise)이라고 설명하고 있으므로 지타 프라사드는 연구원임을 알 수 있다. 따라서 정답은 (A)이다.

87

According to the speaker, what are some data used for?

(A) To evaluate a budget

(B) To design new products

(C) To make hiring decisions

(D) To develop an exercise program

화자의 말에 따르면, 데이터는 어떤 용도로 사용되는가?

(A) 예산 평가

(B) 신제품 디자인

(C) 채용 결정

(D) 운동 프로그램 개발

어휘 evaluate 평가하다 budget 예산

해설 세부 사항 관련 - 화자가 데이터의 용도라고 말하는 것

화자가 중반부에 지타 프라사드 씨가 데이터를 디자인팀에 제공하면 디자인팀이 이 데이터를 활용해 새로운 신발을 디자인한다(She then provides that data to the design team, who use it to design new shoes)고 말하고 있으므로 정답은 (B)이다.

88

Why should the listeners visit a Web site?

(A) To download a manual

(B) To read a report

(C) To register for a study

(D) To provide some feedback

청자들은 왜 웹사이트를 방문해야 하는가?

(A) 설명서를 다운로드하려고

(B) 보고서를 읽으려고

(C) 연구에 참여하려고

(D) 의견을 제공하려고

해설 세부 사항 관련 - 청자들이 웹사이트를 방문해야 하는 이유

화자가 후반부에 프라사드 팀에서 다음 연구에 참여할 참가자를 찾고 있다(her team is looking for participants to take part in their next study)며 신청하려면 맥밀런 신발 제조사 웹사이트를 방문하라(To sign up, visit McMillan Shoe Manufacturers' Web site)고 안내하고 있으므로 정답은 (C)이다.

> ▸▸ **Paraphrasing** 담화의 **sign up** → 정답의 **register**

89-91 회의 발췌

M-Cn Thanks for attending this management meeting. As you know, **89 despite our strategy of positioning ourselves as a seller of high-quality furniture, 90 we've been losing business to several secondhand stores selling used furniture in the area.** There's one thing that we can start doing that many other furniture stores aren't: offering free assembly. By developing cross-functional delivery teams, we'll be able to gain a competitive edge. So **91 next month, all of our delivery teams will attend sessions where they'll learn how to assemble our products in customers' homes.**

이번 경영진 회의에 참석해 주셔서 감사합니다. 아시다시피, **고급 가구 판매업체로 입지를 다진다는 전략에도 불구하고, 지역에서 중고 가구를 파는 몇몇 중고품 매장에 밀려 거래를 놓치고 있습니다.** 우리가 시작할 수 있는 일이 한 가지 있습니다. 다른 다수 가구점은 하지 않고 있는데요, 바로 무료 조립을 제공하는 겁니다. 다기능 배송 팀을 만들면 경쟁 우위를 점할 수 있습니다. 따라서 **다음 달에는 모든 배송 팀이 고객의 집에서 제품을 조립하는 방법에 대해 배우는 세션에 참석하게 됩니다.**

어휘 despite ~에도 불구하고 secondhand 중고의 assembly 조립 cross-functional 여러 가지 기능을 하는 competitive edge 경쟁 우위

89

Where do the listeners most likely work?

(A) At a home appliance store

(B) At a hardware store

(C) At a shipping company

(D) At a furniture store

청자들은 어디에서 일하겠는가?

(A) 가전제품 매장

(B) 철물점

(C) 운송 회사

(D) 가구 판매점

화자가 초반부에 고급 가구 판매업체로 입지를 다진다는 우리의 전략 (despite our strategy of positioning ourselves as a seller of high-quality furniture)에 대해 말하고 있는 것으로 보아 청자들은 가구 판매점에서 일하고 있음을 알 수 있다. 따라서 정답은 (D)이다.

90

According to the speaker, what has caused a problem?

(A) Low-quality merchandise
(B) Competition from other businesses
(C) Increased rental costs
(D) Poor customer service

화자의 말에 따르면, 무엇이 문제를 일으켰는가?

(A) 품질이 낮은 상품
(B) 타사와 경쟁
(C) 인상된 임대료
(D) 형편없는 고객 서비스

해설 세부 사항 관련 - 화자가 문제의 원인이라고 말하는 것

화자가 초반부에 지역에서 중고 가구를 파는 몇몇 중고품 매장에 밀려 거래를 놓치고 있다(we've been losing business to several secondhand stores selling used furniture in the area)고 말하고 있으므로 중고 가구 판매점과의 경쟁이 판매가 감소하고 있는 원인임을 알수 있다. 따라서 정답은 (B)이다.

91

What will happen next month?

(A) A focus group will be assembled.
(B) A customer loyalty program will be introduced.
(C) Some employees will receive training.
(D) New advertisements will be designed.

다음 달에 무슨 일이 있을 것인가?

(A) 포커스 그룹이 소집된다.
(B) 고객 보상 프로그램이 도입된다.
(C) 직원들이 교육을 받을 것이다.
(D) 새로운 광고가 입안될 것이다.

어휘 assemble 소집하다 customer loyalty program (단골 고객에게 포인트를 적립해 주는) 고객 보상 프로그램

해설 세부 사항 관련 - 다음 달에 일어날 일

화자가 마지막에 다음 달에는 모든 배송 팀이 고객의 집에서 제품을 조립하는 방법에 대해 배우는 세션에 참석하게 된다(next month, all of our delivery ~ assemble our products in customers' homes)고 말하고 있으므로 정답은 (C)이다.

> ▶▶Paraphrasing 담화의 attend sessions where they'll learn → 정답의 receive training

---

92-94 담화

W-Br Hello everyone. ⁹²**Thanks for coming to this press conference.** On behalf of the City of Sommerville, ⁹³**I want to sincerely apologize to all community members affected by this week's train delays.** My department has received reports of delays averaging an hour at peak periods. ⁹³**It has become clear that the ongoing track and wire repair work has become far too disruptive for city commuters.** ⁹⁴**With this week's unacceptable delays in mind, my department, the city transportation office, is negotiating with the contractor, National Rail.** That's the company that owns the tracks and runs the trains for Sommerville. To be clear, the tracks and trains are not city property. OK, now I can take some questions.

안녕하세요, 여러분. 이번 기자 회견에 와 주셔서 감사합니다. 서머빌 시를 대표해 이번 주 기차 연착으로 피해를 입은 모든 지역 주민께 진심으로 사과드립니다. 우리 부서는 가장 혼잡한 기간에 평균 한 시간씩 지연된다는 보고를 받았습니다. 현재 진행 중인 선로와 전선 보수 공사가 시 통근자들에게 너무 지장을 많이 준다는 게 분명해졌습니다. 이번 주에 발생한 용납할 수 없는 지연을 염두에 두고, 제 담당 부서인 시 교통국이 계약사인 내셔널 레일과 협상하고 있습니다. 선로를 소유하고 서머빌행 기차를 운영하는 회사입니다. 분명히 말하지만 선로와 기차는 시 소유가 아닙니다. 자, 이제 몇 가지 질문을 받겠습니다.

어휘 press conference 기자 회견 on behalf of ~을 대표해 affect 피해를 주다 ongoing 진행 중인 disruptive 지장을 주는 unacceptable 용납할 수 없는 negotiate 협상하다 contractor 계약사 property 소유물

92

Where is the speech being given?

(A) At a training session
(B) At a press conference
(C) At a job fair
(D) At a store grand opening

연설은 어디에서 이루어지는가?

(A) 교육 세션
(B) 기자 회견
(C) 취업 박람회
(D) 매장 개업식

해설 전체 내용 관련 - 담화의 장소

화자가 초반부에 이번 기자 회견에 와 주셔서 감사하다(Thanks for coming to this press conference)고 말하고 있으므로 정답은 (B)이다.

93

Why does the speaker apologize?

(A) Some repair work has caused delays.

(B) Some employees have been transferred.

(C) Some materials have not arrived.

(D) Some businesses have been temporarily closed.

화자는 왜 사과하는가?

(A) 수리 작업으로 지연이 발생했다.

(B) 직원들이 전근 조치를 받았다.

(C) 자재가 도착하지 않았다.

(D) 업체들이 임시로 문을 닫았다.

어휘 transfer 전근 조치를 하다 temporarily 임시로

해설 세부 사항 관련 - 화자가 사과하는 이유

화자가 초반부에 이번 주 기차 연착으로 피해를 입은 모든 지역 주민께 진심으로 사과드린다(I want to sincerely apologize ~ by this week's train delays)고 했고, 중반부에 현재 진행 중인 선로와 전선 보수 공사가 시 통근자들에게 너무 지장을 많이 준다는 것이 분명해졌다(It has become clear that ~ far too disruptive for city commuters)며 보수 공사로 인한 기차 연착에 대해 사과하고 있으므로 정답은 (A)이다.

94

What does the speaker mean when she says, "the tracks and trains are not city property"?

(A) She did not follow a recommendation.

(B) She is not responsible for a problem.

(C) Some directions were misleading.

(D) A contract contained errors.

화자가 "선로와 기차는 시 소유가 아닙니다"라고 말하는 의도는 무엇인가?

(A) 그녀는 권고를 따르지 않았다.

(B) 그녀는 문제에 대해 책임이 없다.

(C) 지시에 오해의 소지가 있었다.

(D) 계약서에 오류가 있었다.

어휘 recommendation 권고 responsible for ~에 책임이 있는
 misleading 오해의 소지가 있는

해설 화자의 의도 파악 - 선로와 기차는 시 소유가 아니라는 말의 의도

앞에서 이번 주에 발생한 용납할 수 없는 지연을 염두에 두고, 제 담당 부서인 시 교통국이 계약사인 내셔널 레일과 협상하고 있다(With this week's unacceptable delays ~ negotiating with the contractor, National Rail)면서 선로를 소유하고 서머빌행 기차를 운영하는 회사(That's the company that owns the tracks and runs the trains for Sommerville)라고 내셔널 레일 사에 대해 소개한 뒤 인용문을 언급하고 있는 것으로 보아, 기차 연착에 대한 책임은 시가 아니라 내셔널 레일 사에 있다는 것을 강조하려고 한 말임을 알 수 있다. 따라서 정답은 (B)이다.

95-97 전화 메시지 + 헤어스타일

W-Am Hi, Susan. It's Maria. You asked me to suggest a new hairstyle for your appointment tomorrow. **95 I'd recommend something cut all the way up to your chin.** I think that a style like this would give you a very professional look. I'll show you the picture from my hairstyle catalog when you come in. **96 If you'd like me to blow-dry your hair during your appointment, that's included in the price.** Oh, and by the way, **97 yesterday we got a shipment in of the Hydro Five hair moisturizer that always sells out.** I know you like to use it, so I thought you might want to know.

안녕하세요, 수잔. 마리아예요. 내일 약속을 위해 새로운 헤어스타일을 제안해 달라고 요청하셨죠. **턱선까지 자른 머리를 추천해 드리고 싶어요.** 이런 스타일은 아주 전문가다운 느낌을 줄 거라고 생각해요. 오시면 제 헤어스타일 카탈로그에 있는 사진을 보여 드릴게요. **예약 시간에 드라이를 받고 싶으시면 요금에 포함돼 있어요.** 아, 그런데 어제 모발 보습제인 하이드로 파이브가 입고됐는데 늘 품절되는 제품이죠. 이 제품을 잘 쓰시니까 알고 싶으실 것 같아서요.

어휘 chin 턱 blow-dry (머리를) 드라이하다 moisturizer 보습제

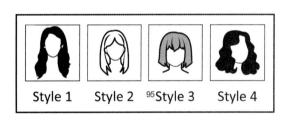

Style 1   Style 2   95 Style 3   Style 4

스타일 1   스타일 2   95 스타일 3   스타일 4

95

Look at the graphic. Which hairstyle does the speaker recommend?

(A) Style 1

(B) Style 2

(C) Style 3

(D) Style 4

시각 정보에 의하면 화자는 어떤 헤어스타일을 추천하는가?

(A) 스타일 1

(B) 스타일 2

(C) 스타일 3

(D) 스타일 4

화자가 초반부에 턱선까지 자른 머리를 추천해 드리고 싶다(I'd recommend something cut all the way up to your chin)고 말하고 있고, 헤어스타일 카탈로그에 따르면 턱선까지 자른 헤어스타일은 스타일 3이므로 정답은 (C)이다.

96

What does the speaker say is included in the price?

(A) A comb
(B) A beverage
(C) Blow-drying
(D) Hair care instructions

화자는 요금에 무엇이 포함되어 있다고 말하는가?

(A) 빗
(B) 음료수
(C) 드라이
(D) 모발 관리 지침

해설 세부 사항 관련 – 화자가 요금에 포함되어 있다고 말하는 것

화자가 중반부에 예약 시간에 드라이를 받고 싶으시면 요금에 포함되어 있다(If you'd like me to blow-dry your hair during your appointment, that's included in the price)고 안내하고 있으므로 정답은 (C)이다.

97

What does the speaker say happened yesterday?

(A) A photo shoot was held.
(B) A popular product arrived.
(C) A new hairstylist was hired.
(D) A product demonstration was conducted.

화자는 어제 무슨 일이 있었다고 말하는가?

(A) 사진 촬영이 있었다.
(B) 인기 많은 제품이 도착했다.
(C) 헤어 스타일리스트가 새로 채용됐다.
(D) 제품 시연을 실시했다.

어휘 demonstration 시연

해설 세부 사항 관련 – 화자가 어제 일어난 일이라고 말하는 것

화자가 후반부에 어제 늘 품절되는 모발 보습제인 하이드로 파이브가 입고됐다(yesterday we got a shipment in of the Hydro Five hair moisturizer that always sells out)고 말하고 있으므로 정답은 (B)이다.

▸▸ Paraphrasing 담화의 hair moisturizer that always sells out → 정답의 A popular product

---

98-100 회의 발췌 + 도표

M-Cn **98 Our first topic is an update on the data analytic software we installed last week to identify problems with our plastic molding machines.** As I'm sure you're aware, **100 we've missed our production targets for the last two quarters.** That means we're spending too much time assembling our products. As you can see on this chart, **99 the data show that one of our machines is running a very slow production cycle at an average of six minutes, twenty-two seconds per cycle.** We've already flagged it for repair by a technician. By next week, that machine should be at normal output. **100 We're very optimistic about the impact the new analytic software will have on next quarter's targets.**

첫 번째 주제는 우리 플라스틱 성형 기계의 문제를 파악하기 위해 지난주에 설치한 데이터 분석 소프트웨어에 관한 소식입니다. 아시겠지만, 지난 2분기 동안 생산 목표를 달성하지 못했는데요. 그러니까 제품을 조립하는 데 너무 시간을 많이 소비하고 있다는 말이죠. 이 도표에서 알 수 있듯, 데이터를 보면 기계 한 대가 주기당 평균 6분 22초로 생산 주기가 매우 느리게 돌아가고 있습니다. 기술자가 수리할 수 있도록 벌써 표시해 두었습니다. 다음 주면 기계는 정상 생산 상태가 될 겁니다. 새로운 분석 소프트웨어가 다음 분기 목표에 미칠 영향에 대해 아주 낙관하고 있습니다.

어휘 analytic 분석하는 assemble 조립하다 flag 표시해 두다 normal 정상인 output 생산 optimistic 낙관하는 impact 영향

Plastic Molding Output	
Machine Number	**Cycle Duration**
1	5:30
2	99 6:22
3	4:15
4	5:02

플라스틱 성형 생산	
기계 번호	주기
1	5:30
2	99 6:22
3	4:15
4	5:02

98

According to the speaker, what did the company do last week?

(A) It installed software to monitor machines.
(B) It added a new machine to an assembly line.
(C) It hired some expert technicians.
(D) It reorganized a production team.

화자의 말에 따르면, 회사는 지난주에 무엇을 했는가?

(A) 기계를 점검하기 위해 소프트웨어를 설치했다.
(B) 조립 라인에 새 기계를 추가했다.
(C) 노련한 기술자 몇 명을 채용했다.
(D) 생산 팀을 개편했다.

어휘 expert 노련한 reorganize 개편하다

해설 세부 사항 관련 - 화자가 지난주에 회사가 했다고 말하는 일

화자가 도입부에 첫 번째 주제는 플라스틱 성형 기계의 문제를 파악하기 위해 지난주에 설치한 데이터 분석 소프트웨어에 관한 소식(Our first topic is an update on the data analytic software we installed last week to identify problems with our plastic molding machines)이라고 말하고 있으므로 정답은 (A)이다.

> ▸▸ Paraphrasing 담화의 **identify problems with ~ machines**
> → 정답의 **monitor machines**

99

Look at the graphic. Which machine will a technician look at?

(A) Machine 1
(B) Machine 2
(C) Machine 3
(D) Machine 4

시각 정보에 의하면 기술자는 어떤 기계를 살펴볼 것인가?

(A) 기계 1
(B) 기계 2
(C) 기계 3
(D) 기계 4

해설 시각 정보 연계 - 기술자가 살펴볼 기계

화자가 중반부에 데이터를 보면 기계 한 대가 주기당 평균 6분 22초로 생산 주기가 매우 느리게 돌아가고 있다(the data show that ~ twenty-two seconds per cycle)며 기술자가 수리할 수 있도록 벌써 표시해 두었다(We've already flagged it for repair by a technician)고 말하고 있고, 도표에 따르면 주기가 6분 22초인 기계는 2번 기계이므로 기술자는 기계 2를 살펴볼 것임을 알 수 있다. 따라서 정답은 (B)이다.

100

What does the company hope to do next quarter?

(A) Update their logo
(B) Meet their production targets
(C) Purchase similar technologies
(D) Begin replacing outdated computers

회사는 다음 분기에 무엇을 하고자 하는가?

(A) 로고 개선
(B) 생산 목표 달성
(C) 비슷한 기계 구매
(D) 구형 컴퓨터 교체 시작

어휘 technology 기계 (장비) outdated 구식인, 구형의

해설 세부 사항 관련 - 회사가 다음 분기에 하고자 하는 일

화자가 초반부에 지난 2분기 동안 생산 목표를 달성하지 못했다(we've missed our production targets for the last two quarters)며 생산 목표에 미달한 일에 대해 언급하고 있고, 마지막에 새로운 분석 소프트웨어가 다음 분기 목표에 미칠 영향에 대해 아주 낙관하고 있다(We're very optimistic about the impact ~ have on next quarter's targets)고 말하고 있으므로 회사가 다음 분기에는 생산 목표를 달성할 것이라고 기대하고 있음을 알 수 있다. 따라서 정답은 (B)이다.